Recommended by **Teachers**
Trusted by **Toppers**

All in One

COMPUTER SCIENCE
WITH PYTHON
Class 12

EVERYTHING YOU NEED TO SCORE

- Simplified Theory
- Topic & Chapter Exercises
- Solved NCERT Exercise
- All Types of Exam Pattern Questions
- CBQs; MCQs, A-R, Case Based
- Board Questions Upto 2025
- Sample Question Papers

CBSE Exams 2026

Authors
Sanjib Pal, Lalita Kaler,
Abhishek

arihant
SUCCESS AND NOTHING LESS

ARIHANT PRAKASHAN
(School Division Series)

卐 ADMINISTRATIVE & PRODUCTION OFFICES

Regd. Office
'Ramchhaya' 4577/15, Agarwal Road, Darya Ganj, New Delhi -110002
Tele: 011- 47630600, 43518550; Fax: 011- 23280316

卐 *Head Office*
Kalindi, TP Nagar, Meerut (UP) - 250002, Tel: 0121-7156203, 7156204

卐 SALES & SUPPORT OFFICES
Agra, Ahmedabad, Bengaluru, Bareilly, Chennai, Delhi, Guwahati, Hyderabad, Jaipur, Jhansi, Kolkata, Lucknow, Nagpur & Pune.

PO No : TXT-XX-XXXXXXX-X-XX

Published By Arihant Publications (India) Ltd.

For further information about the books published by Arihant, log on to www.arihantbooks.com or e-mail at info@arihantbooks.com

Follow us on

卐 PRICE ₹350.00

PRODUCTION TEAM

Publishing Managers
Mahendra Singh Rawat & Keshav Mohan

Cover Designer
Rakesh Rawat

Inner Designer
Ankit Tyagi

Project Head
Shruti Aggarwal

Page Layouting
Ravinder Kumar

Index *cum* Study Planner

			Studied	Revised	Exam ready
1.	**Python Revision Tour I**	**1-27**			
	Python Character Set		☐	☐	☐
	Python Tokens		☐	☐	☐
	Basic Structure of Python Program		☐	☐	☐
	Input and Output in Python		☐	☐	☐
	Data Types in Python		☐	☐	☐
	Expressions		☐	☐	☐
	Type Conversion		☐	☐	☐
	Statements		☐	☐	☐
	Program Designing Tools		☐	☐	☐
	Control Structure		☐	☐	☐
	Jump Statement		☐	☐	☐
	Exam Pattern Questions		☐	☐	☐
	Self Assessment Test		☐	☐	☐
2.	**Python Revision Tour-II**	**28-64**			
	Strings		☐	☐	☐
	String Traversal		☐	☐	☐
	String Operators		☐	☐	☐
	Built-in String Methods		☐	☐	☐
	Lists		☐	☐	☐
	Operations on Lists		☐	☐	☐
	List Slicing		☐	☐	☐
	Built-in Methods in Lists		☐	☐	☐
	Tuples		☐	☐	☐
	Operations on Tuples		☐	☐	☐
	Tuple Slicing		☐	☐	☐
	Built-in Methods in Tuples		☐	☐	☐
	Dictionary		☐	☐	☐
	Built-in Methods in Dictionary		☐	☐	☐
	Module		☐	☐	☐
	Errors		☐	☐	☐
	Exceptions		☐	☐	☐
	Exam Pattern Questions		☐	☐	☐
	Self Assessment Test		☐	☐	☐
3.	**Functions**	**65-85**			
	Types of Python Function		☐	☐	☐
	Parameters and Arguments		☐	☐	☐
	Passing Parameters		☐	☐	☐

			Studied	Revised	Exam ready
	Scope of Variables		☐	☐	☐
	Namespace		☐	☐	☐
	Exam Pattern Questions		☐	☐	☐
	Self Assessment Test		☐	☐	☐
4.	**File Handling**	**86-129**			
	Data File		☐	☐	☐
	Working with Text Files		☐	☐	☐
	Working with Binary Files		☐	☐	☐
	Working with CSV Files		☐	☐	☐
	NCERT Folder		☐	☐	☐
	Exam Pattern Questions		☐	☐	☐
	Self Assessment Test		☐	☐	☐
5.	**Data Structures**	**130-155**			
	Need of Data Structure		☐	☐	☐
	Types of Data Structure		☐	☐	☐
	Common Data Structures		☐	☐	☐
	Stack		☐	☐	☐
	NCERT Folder		☐	☐	☐
	Exam Pattern Questions		☐	☐	☐
	Self Assessment Test		☐	☐	☐
6.	**Computer Network**	**156-187**			
	Evolution of Networking		☐	☐	☐
	Type of Networks		☐	☐	☐
	Network Devices		☐	☐	☐
	Network Topology		☐	☐	☐
	WWW or World Wide Web		☐	☐	☐
	XML Domain Names System		☐	☐	☐
	Web Server		☐	☐	☐
	Web Hosting		☐	☐	☐
	Web Browser		☐	☐	☐
	Website		☐	☐	☐
	Web Page		☐	☐	☐
	NCERT Folder		☐	☐	☐
	Exam Pattern Questions		☐	☐	☐
	Self Assessment Test		☐	☐	☐
7.	**Data Communication**	**188-205**			
	Concept of Data Communication		☐	☐	☐
	Measuring Capacity of Communication Media		☐	☐	☐
	Switching Techniques		☐	☐	☐
	Transmission Media		☐	☐	☐
	Identifying Nodes in a Networked Communication		☐	☐	☐
	Network Protocols		☐	☐	☐

		Studied	Revised	Exam ready
	NCERT Folder	☐	☐	☐
	Exam Pattern Questions	☐	☐	☐
	Self Assessment Test	☐	☐	☐
8.	**Database Concept** **206-223**			
	Database Management System (DBMS)	☐	☐	☐
	File Sytem	☐	☐	☐
	Data Abstraction	☐	☐	☐
	Data Independence	☐	☐	☐
	Data Models	☐	☐	☐
	NCERT Folder	☐	☐	☐
	Exam Pattern Questions	☐	☐	☐
	Self Assessment Test	☐	☐	☐
9.	**Structured Query Language** **224-273**			
	SQL Statements	☐	☐	☐
	SQL Data Types	☐	☐	☐
	DDL Statements/Commands	☐	☐	☐
	DML Statements/Commands	☐	☐	☐
	Working with NULL Values	☐	☐	☐
	SQL Functions	☐	☐	☐
	GROUP BY Statement	☐	☐	☐
	HAVING Clause	☐	☐	☐
	Cartesian Product on Two Tables	☐	☐	☐
	Join	☐	☐	☐
	NCERT Folder	☐	☐	☐
	Exam Pattern Questions	☐	☐	☐
	Self Assessment Test	☐	☐	☐
10.	**Interface Python with MySQL** **274-296**			
	Connecting to MySQL from Python	☐	☐	☐
	To Show the List of Existing Database	☐	☐	☐
	Create the New Database	☐	☐	☐
	Creating Table	☐	☐	☐
	ALTER Table	☐	☐	☐
	INSERT Operation	☐	☐	☐
	Exam Pattern Questions	☐	☐	☐
	Self Assessment Test	☐	☐	☐
	Practical Work **297-307**			
	CBSE Examination Paper 2025 **308-313**			
	Sample Question Papers **314-328**			

Latest Course *Structure*

Prerequisites

Computer Science-Class XI

LEARNING OUTCOMES

Student should be able to

- Apply the concept of function.
- Explain and use the concept of file handling.
- Use basic data structure: Stacks
- Explain basics of computer networks.
- Use Database concepts, SQL along with connectivity between Python and SQL.

DISTRIBUTION OF MARKS

Unit No.	Unit Name	Marks
I	Computational Thinking and Programming - 2	40
II	Computer Networks	10
III	Database Management	20
	TOTAL	**70**

UNIT WISE SYLLABUS

UNIT I Computational Thinking and Programming – 2

- Revision of Python topics covered in Class XI.
- Functions: types of function (built-in functions, functions defined in module, user defined functions), creating user defined function, arguments and parameters, default parameters, positional parameters, function returning value(s), flow of execution, scope of a variable (global scope, local scope)
- Exception Handling : Introduction, Handling Exception using try-except-finally blocks.
- Introduction to files, types of files (Text file, Binary file, CSV file), relative and absolute paths
- Text file: opening a text file, text file open modes (r, r+, w, w+, a, a+), closing a text file, opening a file using with clause, writing/appending data to a text file using write() and writelines(), reading from a text file using read(), readline() and readlines(), seek and tell methods, manipulation of data in a text file
- Binary file: basic operations on a binary file: open using file open modes (rb, rb+, wb, wb+, ab, ab+), close a binary file, import pickle module, dump() and load() method, read, write/create, search, append and update operations in a binary file
- CSV file: import csv module, open / close csv file, write into a csv file using writer(), writerow(), writerows() and read from a csv file using reader( )
- Data Structure: Stack, operations on stack (push and pop), implementation of stack using list.

UNIT II Computer Networks

- Evolution of networking: introduction to computer networks, evolution of networking (ARPANET, NSFNET, INTERNET)
- Data communication terminologies: concept of communication, components of data communication (sender, receiver, message, communication media, protocols), measuring capacity of communication media (bandwidth, data transfer rate), IP address, switching techniques (Circuit switching, Packet switching)
- Transmission media: Wired communication media (Twisted pair cable, Co-axial cable, Fiber-optic cable), Wireless media (Radio waves, Micro waves, Infrared waves)
- Network devices (Modem, Ethernet card, RJ45, Repeater, Hub, Switch, Router, Gateway, Wi-Fi card)
- Network topologies and Network types: types of networks (PAN, LAN, MAN, WAN), networking topologies (Bus, Star, Tree)
- Network protocols: HTTP, FTP, PPP, SMTP, TCP/IP, POP3, HTTPS, TELNET, VoIP,
- Introduction to web services: WWW, HyperText Markup Language (HTML), Extensible Markup Language (XML), domain names, URL, website, web browser, web servers, web hosting

UNIT III Database Management

- Database concepts: introduction to database concepts and its need
- Relational data model: relation, attribute, tuple, domain, degree, cardinality, keys (candidate key, primary key, alternate key, foreign key)
- Structured Query Language: introduction, Data Definition Language and Data Manipulation Language, data type (char(n), varchar(n), int, float, date), constraints (not null, unique, primary key), create database, use database, show databases, drop database, show tables, create table, describe table, alter table (add and remove an attribute, add and remove primary key), drop table, insert, delete, select, operators (mathematical, relational and logical), aliasing, distinct clause, where clause, in, between, order by, meaning of null, is null, is not null, like, update command, delete command, aggregate functions (max, min, avg, sum, count), group by, having clause, joins: cartesian product on two tables, equi-join and natural join
- Interface of Python with an SQL database: connecting SQL with Python, performing insert, update, delete queries using cursor, display data by using connect(), cursor(), execute(), commit(), fetchone(), fetchall(), rowcount, creating database connectivity applications, use of %s format specifier or format() to perform queries

PRACTICAL MARKS DISTRIBUTION :

S. No	Unit Name	Marks (Total=30)
1	Lab Test: 1. Python program (60% logic + 20% documentation + 20% code quality) 2. SQL queries (4 queries based on one or two tables)	 8 4
2	Report file: Minimum 15 Python programs. • SQL Queries - Minimum 5 Sets using one table/two tables. • Minimum 4 programs based on Phython-SQL connectivity.	7
3	Project (using concepts learnt in Classes 11 and 12)	8
4	Viva Voce	3

Suggested Practical List

Python Programming

- Read a text file line by line and display each word separated by a #.
- Read a text file and display the number of vowels/consonants/upper case/lower case characters in the file.
- Remove all the lines that contain the character 'a' in a file and write it to another file.
- Create a binary file with name and roll number. Search for a given roll number and display the name, if not found display appropriate message.
- Create a binary file with roll number, name and marks. Input a roll number and update the marks.
- Write a random number generator that generates random numbers between 1 and 6 (simulates a dice).
- Write a Python program to implement a stack using list.
- Create a CSV file by entering user-id and password, read and search the password for given user-id.

Database Management

- Create a student table and insert data. Implement the following SQL commands on the student table
  - ALTER table to add new attributes / modify data type / drop attribute
  - UPDATE table to modify data
  - ORDER By to display data in ascending / descending order
  - DELETE to remove tuple(s)
  - GROUP BY and find the min, max, sum, count and average
- Similar exercise may be framed for other cases.
- Integrate SQL with Python by importing suitable module.

PROJECT

- The aim of the class project is to create something that is tangible and useful using Python file handling/ Python-SQL connectivity. This should be done in groups of two to three students and should be started by students at least 6 months before the submission deadline. The aim here is to find a real world problem that is worthwhile to solve.
- Students are encouraged to visit local businesses and ask them about the problems that they are facing. For example, if a business is finding it hard to create invoices for filling GST claims, then students can do a project that takes the raw data (list of transactions), groups the transactions by category, accounts for the GST tax rates, and creates invoices in the appropriate format. Students can be extremely creative here. They can use a wide variety of Python libraries to create user friendly applications such as games, software for their school, software for their disabled fellow students, and mobile applications, of course to do some of these projects, some additional learning is required, this should be encouraged. Students should know how to teach themselves.
- The students should be sensitised to avoid plagiarism and violations of copyright issues while working on projects. Teachers should take necessary measures for this.

01

CHAPTER

Python is a simple and powerful programming language. It uses a character set to form tokens like keywords, identifiers, and operators. Programs interact using input and output functions. Python supports various data types and allows writing expressions with automatic type conversions.

YOUR STUDY GOALS

1.1 Python Character Set
1.2 Python Tokens
1.3 Basic Structure of Python Program
1.4 Input and Output in Python
1.5 Data Types in Python
1.6 Expressions
1.7 Type Conversion
1.8 Statements
1.9 Program Designing Tools
1.10 Control Structure
1.11 Jump Statement

YOUR PRACTICE GOAL

- Objective Type Questions (64 Qs ; MCQs, True or False, Fill in the Blanks, Assertion and Reason)
- Subjective Type Questions (52 Qs ; VSA, SA, LA)
- Case Based Questions (Subjective Case Studies-2, Objective Case Study-1)

Python Revision Tour I

Python was designed by Guido Van Rossum in 1991 and developed by Python Software Foundation.

Python is used in various fields like **web development, data science, artificial intelligence, and automation**, making it a versatile tool for professionals and learners alike.

Let's us discuss all the basic concepts of Python that were learned in class XI.

1.1 Python Character Set

Character set is a set of valid characters that represents any digit, alphabet and special symbol. The character used in a Python source program belongs to Unicode standard.

- **Alphabets** All capital (A-Z) and small (a-z) alphabets.
- **Digits** All digits 0-9.
- **Special Symbols** Python supports all kind of special symbols like, " ' | ; : ! ~ @ # $ % ^ ` & * ( ) _ + − = { } [ ] \ .
- **White Spaces** White spaces like tab space, blank space, newline, and carriage return.
- **Other** All ASCII and UNICODE characters are supported by Python that constitutes the Python character set.

1.2 Python Tokens

Token is the smallest unit of any programming language. It is also known as **Lexical unit**. Types of token are

- Identifiers
- Keywords
- Literals
- Operators
- Punctuators

1. Identifiers

Identifiers are names used to identify a variable, function, or other entities in a program. The rules for naming an identifier in Python are as follows :

- The name should begin with an uppercase or a lowercase alphabet or an underscore sign (_). This may be followed by any combination of characters a-z, A-Z,0-9 or underscore (_). Thus, an identifier cannot start with a digit.
- It can be of any length.
- It should not be a keyword or reserved word.
- We cannot use special symbols like !, @, #, $, %, etc. in identifiers.

There are some valid identifiers are given below

Name	capital letters with small letters are allowed
name_1	digits and underscore are allowed with alphabet
_SUM	underscore at the first position is allowed

There are some invalid identifiers are given below

global	keywords are not allowed
num^2	special symbols are not allowed
2num	digits are allowed but not as first character

2. Keywords

Keywords are predefined reserved words that have some special or predefined meanings. These are reserved for special purpose and must not be used as identifier names. Some commonly used keywords in Python, are listed below.

False	assert	del	for	in	or	while
None	break	elif	from	is	pass	with
True	class	else	global	lambda	raise	yield
and	continue	except	if	nonlocal	return	
as	def	finally	import	not	try	

3. Constants or Literals

Literals refer to fixed values that the program may not alter(change) during the program execution.

Python allows several types of literals as follows

(i) Numeric Literals

A numeric literal is a character string whose characters are selected from the digits 0-9, a sign character (+ or -) and the decimal point.

Numeric literals are immutable(unchangeable). Numeric literals can belong to three different numerical types as **Integer, Float** and **Complex.**

- **Integer Literal** It includes both positive and negative numbers along with 0. It doesn't include fractional parts. It can also include binary, decimal, octal, hexadecimal literal.
- **Float Literal** It includes both positive and negative real numbers. It also includes fractional parts.
- **Complex Literal** It includes a+bi numeral, here a represents the real part and b represents the complex part.

(ii) String Literals

The literal which is stored in a variable within single quotation mark or double quotation marks is called string literal. These represent a sequence of zero or more characters enclosed by double quotes. It can also include blank spaces.

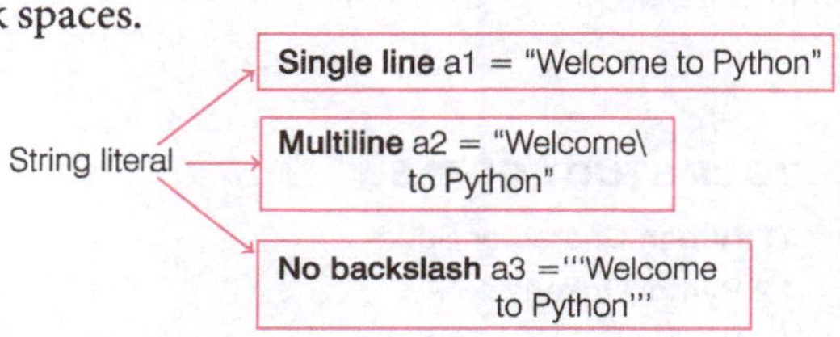

Some valid string constants are

"j"	" ₹ 56,234.50 "	"computer"	'math'
"T"	"The result is: "	"Intel"	'2456'

Some invalid string constants are

No	Not enclosed in double quotes
'Python"	Both quotes must be double or single quotes
"She said, "OK"	Number of double quotes must be even

To insert characters that are illegal in a string, use an escape character.

Escape Sequence	Meaning
\'	Single quote
\\'	Double quote
\\	Backslash
\n	Newline
\r	Carriage Return
\t	Horizontal Tab
\b	Backspace
\f	Form feed
\v	Vertical Tab
\0	Null Character

(iii) Boolean Literals

A Boolean literals is used to represent one of the two Boolean values **True** and **False**.

True represents a true value and False represents a false value. Literals True or False should not be represented by the quotation marks around it. Python interpreter will take it as a string of characters, if it is represented in quotation marks.

e.g.
```
>>>a=7
>>>b=5
>>>a>b
```
Output True

(iv) Special Literal-None

In Python, you have one special literal None. None is used to define a field that is not created. It is also used to indicate the end of lists in Python.

e.g.
```
>>>a=None
>>>if a== None
  Print('This is none')
```
In the above program, we assigned None to a variable. You can use it anywhere in the program for conditions, loops, structures etc.

(v) Literal Collections

In Python, you have literal collections like list, tuple, dictionary and set.

We will discuss list, tuple and dictionary in forward chapters.

4. Operators

An operator is used to perform specific mathematical or logical operation on values. The values that the operators work on are called **operands**.

e.g. In the expression 10+num, the value 10 , and the variable num are operands and the + (plus) sign is an operator. Python supports two types of operators as follows

(i) Unary Operators

The operators that work on single operand to form an expression are known as unary operators.

These operators are

+	unary plus
–	unary minus
~	Bitwise complement
not	logical negation

(ii) Binary Operators

The operators that work upon two operands are known as binary operators. There are various types of binary operators in Python as follows :

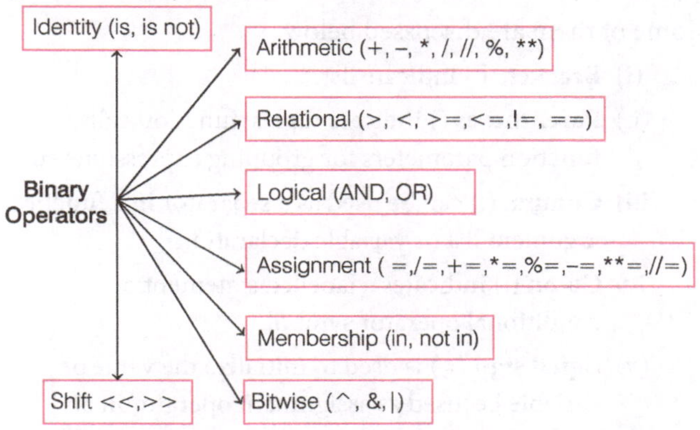

Operator Precedence and Associativity in Python

This table lists all operators from the highest precedence to the lowest precedence.

Priority	Operator	Description	Associativity
1. (Highest)	( )	Parentheses	left-to-right
2.	++, – –	Pre-increment/ pre-decrement	right-to-left
3.	sizeof	Determine size in bytes	right-to-left
4.	*, /, %	Multiplication, Division, Modulus	left-to-right
5.	+, –	Addition, Subtraction	left-to-right
6.	<, < =, >, > =	Relational less than, less than or equals to, greater than, greater than or equals to	left-to-right
7.	= =, ! =	Relational is equal to/is not equal to	left-to-right
8.	++, --	Post-increment/Post-decrement	right-to-left
9.	&&	Logical AND	left-to-right
10.	||	Logical OR	left-to-right
11	?:	Ternary conditional	right-to-left
12. (Lowest)	=, – =, + =, > =, =, < =	Assignment	right-to-left

5. Punctuators

A punctuator is a token that has syntactic and semantic meaning to the compiler, but the exact significance depends on the context. Punctuators (separators) are used to separate line of codes, variables etc.

The following characters are used as punctuators in Python: ' " # \ ( ) [ ] { } @ , : . = ;

Some of them are discussed below

(i) **Brackets** [ ] indicate list.

(ii) **Parentheses** () indicate tuples, function calls, function parameters for grouping expressions etc.

(iii) **Comma** (,) can be used as a separator in a function argument list or variable declaration.

(iv) **Colon** (:) indicates a labelled statement or conditional operator symbol.

(v) **Equal sign** (=) is used to initialize the value of variable i.e. used as assignment operator in an expression.

Quick Test 1

1. Name any two character sets.
2. Mark a cross(×) for the invalid identifiers.

   Abc123 ☐   123_tye ☐   break123 ☐

3. Which characters are not allowed in variable names ?
4. What is the use of punctuators?
5. What are the different types of operators? Give examples.
6. Which operator is used for shifting value?

1.3 Basic Structure of Python Program

Here, is a sample program of Python which will describe the basic structure or components of program

```
# This is the basic structure of Python program
def Add ( ) :  ← function
  print (" Let us do some addition")
  # Main program code
  x = 50
  y = 35
  z = x - y + 10
  print (z - 5)
  if z < 30:
     print ("value of z is less than 30.")
  else:
     print ("value of z is more than 30.")
Add() #Above defined function is calling
```

Comments — Statements — Indentation — Colon (:) represents block — Expressions — Inline comment

1. Expressions

An expression is a combination of operators, constants and variables. Any part in a program which can have a value, is an expression.

It will have operands and operators together to produce a value.

From the above program, we have 4 expressions

50, 35, x − y + 10, z < 30

2. Statements

A statement in Python is a logical instruction which Python interpreter can read and execute. It could be an expression or assignment statement.

e.g.
```
if x = = y:
   print ("x is equal to y")
```

when expression will be evaluated, statement or group of statements executed.

From the above program, we have 5 statements as

```
x = 50
y = 35
z = x - y + 10
print (z - 5)
if z < 30:
```

3. Comments

Comments are used to add a remark or a note in the source code that are ignored by the interpreter or compiler and are not executed by the computer.

Comments are written to explain 'what each block of the program is doing.'

In above program, we have 3 comments

This is the basic structure of Python program

Main program code

Above defined function is calling here

- Which comments start with the beginning of line are called **full line comments**. First two comments are full line comments in given program.
- Which comments start with the middle of line are called **inline comments**. Last comment is inline comment in given program.

Types of Comment

- **Single line** : Start with #symbol and have a single line of description.
- **Multiline** : Start and end with''' (Triple quotes) and can describe in multiple line.

4. Function

A function is a self contained block of statements which are kept together to perform a specific task in related manner.

In above program, we have one function Add ( ). All the statements which indented below Add ( ) function are the part of Add ( ). All statements below Add ( ) are executed by calling this function by following statement:

Add ( )

5. Blocks and Indentation

It indicate the relationship between various statements and thus allow us to get a better picture of the overall organization and structure of the solution given in the program. It improves the readability of the program.

```
if a==b :
    print("Value of a is equal to b")
    print("Finished")
```

Statements inside if block

This block with all its statements have same indentation. Python uses indentation while other programming languages such as C / C ++, Java use curly braces { } .

In above program, we have two blocks

```
if z<30:
   :
else :
   :
```

Variables and Assignments

In a program, a variable is uniquely identified by a name (identifier). Variable refers to an object, an item or element that is stored in the memory. Value of a variable can be a string, numeric or any combination of alphanumeric characters.

In Python, we can use an assignment statement to create new variables and assign specific values to them.

To Create a Variable

Creating of variables means providing an initial value when it is declared. A variable can be created any where in Python program.

e.g.
```
Name = 'Neha'
Subject = 'Computer'
Marks = 80
```

Above are assignment statements which used to assign values to the variables. The equal (=) sign causes the value on the right hand side of the variables to be assigned to the variable on the left.

Multiple Assignments

Python allows us to assign a value to multiple variables in a single statement which is also known as multiple assignment.

We can apply multiple assignments in two ways as follows

(i) Assigning Single Value to Multiple Variables

You can assign single value to multiple variables in a single statement.

e.g. `x = y=z= 1`

Here, an integer object is created with the value 1 and all three variables a, b and c are assigned to the same memory location.

(ii) Assigning Multiple Values to Multiple Variables

You can even assign multiple values to multiple variables in a single statement.

e.g. `a, b, c =5, 8, "Rahul"`

It will assign the values order wise, i.e. two integer objects with values 5 and 8 are assigned to variables a and b, respectively. One string object with the value "Rahul" is assigned to the variable c.

Dynamic Typing in Python

Python is a dynamically typed language. It does not know about the type of the variable until the code is run, so declaration is of no use. It stores that value at some memory location and then binds that variable name to that memory container.

We have assigned three values to three variables

```
>>> a = 10
>>> name = "Neha"
>>> x = 34.6
```

But what types are these variables ? Let's use the type( ) module to find out:

Syntax `type (variable_name)`

To find the type of above variables, we use

```
>>> a = 10
>>> type (a)
<class 'int'>
>>> name = "Neha"
>>> type (name)
<class 'str'>
>>>x = 34.6
>>> type (x)
<class 'float'>
```

1.4 Input and Output in Python

In almost every computer program, the user has to input some data that will be stored in computer's memory and then subsequently processed.

Input from User

Sometimes, a program needs to interact with the users to get some input data or information from the end user and process it to give desired output.

Python provides the built-in function input( ) to read a line of text from standard input, which by default comes from the keyboard.

These functions are as follows

input( )

This function first takes the input from the user and then evaluates the expression. If the provided input is not correct, then either syntax error or exception is raised by Python.

In Python 3, input() is capable of handing anything other than numbers like string.

Syntax

```
variable_name = input (< Message to be
displayed >)
```

eval() The eval() function can be used with input( ) function to take numeric or data of other types into appropriate data types.

```
x=eval(input("Enter age:"))
L=eval(input("Enter list of elements :"))
Varname=input("Message for input")
print(Varname)
```

Output through print() Statement

To output your data to the screen, use print( ) function.

print() evaluates the expression before printing it on the monitor.

print() statement gives output an entire (complete) line and then goes to next line for subsequent output. To print more than one item on a single line, comma (,) may be used.

Syntax

```
print(object(s), sep=separator, end=end,
file=file, flush=flush)
```

Quick Test 2

1. What are comments? What are single line and multiline comments.
2. What is dynamic typing in python.
3. How many functions are there to take input by user in Python?
4. Write the use of type() function in python.
5. How are blocks made in python?
6. What do you mean by inline comment?
7. Write the output
   ```
   >>>print('2' +'3')
   ```
8. Give an example to assign multiple values to multiple variables in single line.

1.5 Data Types in Python

Data type is a term that is used to show the kind of data values or the type of data that is expected to be handled.

i.e. Data types are used to identify the type of data and associated operations to handle it.

There are different data types available in Python

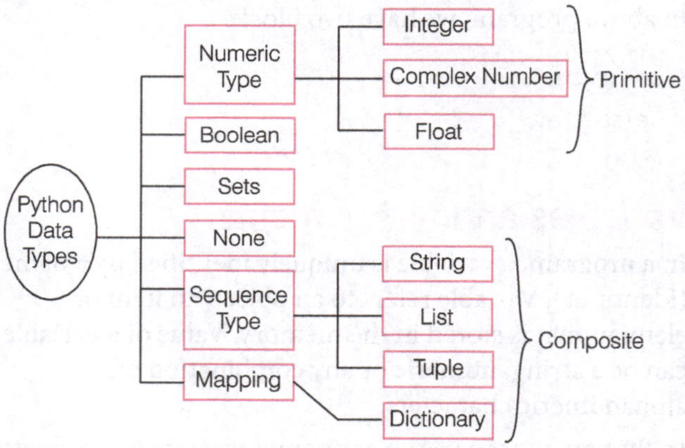

1. Numeric

This data type stores only numeric value in Python. It is further classified into three different types:

(i) Integers

Integers are the whole numbers having different storage range supported by particular machine.

Integers have no fractional parts. They can be positive or negative.

e.g. `8, 17, -195` etc.

(ii) Complex Numbers

A complex number is a number expressed in the form a+ib, where, a (real part) and b (imaginary part) are real numbers and i is the imaginary part.

So, we can say that complex number is made up of both real numbers and imaginary numbers.

e.g. `2 +3i, 1 + 4i, 2 - 5i etc.`

(iii) Floating Point Numbers

The float data type in Python designates a floating point number. Float values are specified with a decimal point. The decimal point signals that it is a floating point number not an integer.

e.g. `159.12, 734.30 etc.`

2. Boolean

Boolean data type is a unique data type, consisting of two values - True and False.

3. Sets

A Set is an unordered collections of items separated by commas and the items are enclosed in curly brackets { }. A set is similar to list, except that it cannot have duplicated entries. Once created , elements of a set cannot be changed.

e.g.
```
>>> set1 = {10, 20, 3.14, "Delhi"}
>>> print (type (set1))
<class 'set'>
>>> print (set1)
{10, 20, 3.14, "Delhi"}
>>> set2 = {1, 2, 1, 3}
>>> print (set2)
{1, 2, 3}
```

4. None

None is a special data type with a single value. It is used to signify the absence of value in a situation. None supports no special operations and it is neither False nor 0 (zero).

e.g.
```
>>> myFav = None
>>> print (type (myfav))
<class 'NoneType'>
>>> print (myfav)
None
```

5. Sequence

A Python sequence is an ordered collection of items, where each item is indexed by an integer. Three types of sequence data types are available in Python

(i) Strings

Strings are group of characters. These characters may be alphabets, digit or special character including spaces. String values may be delimited using either single quotes or double quotes, such as "Rahul", 'ABC', '$ABC' etc.

e.g.
```
>>>print('Arihant Publication')
Arihant Publication
>>>type('Arihant Publication')
class <'str'>
```

A string in Python can contain as many characters as you want. The string limit is dependent on your machine's memory resources. A string can also be empty. In Python, the string type is called str.

(ii) List

List is a sequence of items separated by commas and the items are enclosed in the square brackets [ ]. Lists are mutable that means they can be changed after creation.

e.g.
```
x = []
y = [1,2,'Neha']
z = [ 23, 46, 52, 98]
```

All lists in Python are zero base indexed. The length of the list is always one more than the last index.

(iii) Tuples

Tuple is an ordered sequence of items same as list. The only difference is that tuples are immutable and lists are mutable.

Tuples once created cannot be modified. Tuples are used to write-protect data and are usually faster than list as it cannot change dynamically. Tuples are defined by parentheses ( ).

e.g. `sub = ('Maths','English','Hindi','Computer')`

6. Mapping

Mapping is an unordered data type in Python. In Python, there is only one standard mapping data type called dictionary.

Dictionary

Dictionaries in Python are lists of key: value pairs.

Dictionaries are created by using braces { } with pairs separated by a comma (,) and the key values associated with a colon (:).

In dictionaries, the key must be unique. Dictionaries can also be used to sort, iterate and compare data.

e.g.
```
dict = {'Name':'Neha','Salary':25000,
'Post':'Coordinator'}
```

Mutable and Immutable Types

Every variable in Python holds an instance of an object. There are two types of objects in Python as follow

1. Mutable Types

The word Mutable means "Changeable" .The values of mutable types can be changed after it is created. These are list, dictionary and sets.

2. Immutable Types

The word Immutable means "Unchangeable". The values of immutable data types cannot be changed after they are created. These are integer, float, boolean, string and tuple.

1.6 Expressions

An expression is a combination of operators and operands that is interpreted to produce some other value. In any programming language, an expression is evaluated as per the precedence of its operators. So that if there is more than one operator in an expression, their precedence decides which operation will be performed first.

We have many different types of expressions in Python

1. Constant Expressions

These are the expressions that have constant values only.

e. g. `x=1.6 +76`

2. Arithmetic Expressions

An arithmetic expression is a combination of numeric values, operators, and sometimes parenthesis. The result of this type of expression is also a numeric value. The operators used in these expressions are arithmetic operators like addition, subtraction, etc.

e.g.
```
x =40, y =12
add =x +y
sub =x -y
pro =x *y
div =x /y
```

3. Logical Expressions

Logical expressions are those that work on Boolean values and logical operators.

e.g. `(90>34) and (45%7>5)   or (20//7>8%5)`

4.Relational Expression

The expressions that make use of relational operators and usually give output in True or False are relational expressions

e.g.
```
67>82
56!=90
85==87
```

5. String Expression

This type of expression includes string operators with string operands and integers.

e.g. `"AISSCE"+ "2025"`

Output 'AISSCE2025'

e.g. `"ComputerSc" * 3`

Output 'ComputerScComputerScComputerSc'

Expression Evaluation

Evaluation means simplifying an expression down to a single numerical value. When a mixed expression evaluates, it is divided in sub-expressions. Expression evaluation is done from left-to-right and based on operators precedence.

Let us take an example :

$a = b = 10, c = 5$

$a = b * 3//4 + c//4 + 4 - b + 5//6$

$= 10 * 3//4+5//4+4-10+5//6$

$= 30//4+5//4+4-10+5//6$

$= 7+5//4+4-10+5//6$

$= 7+1+4-10+5//6 = 7+1+4-10+0$

$= 8+4-10+0 = 12-10+0$

$a = 2+0 = 2$

Quick Test 3

1. Give an example of complex number.
2. Tuples are defined by which type of bracket?
3. What are the possible values for Boolean data types in python?
4. Write examples of two mutable and two immutable data types.
5. Find the output of `type(18.6 + 15)`

1.7 Type Conversion

Type conversion is the process of converting a data type into another data type.

Implicit Type Conversion

In implicit type conversion, Python automatically converts one data type to another data type. This process does not need user involvement. This conversion takes place during compilation or run time.

Explicit Type Conversion

In explicit type conversion, user converts the data type of an object to required data type. This type conversion is also called typecasting because the user casts (change) the data type of the object.

1.8 Statements

A computer program is a set of instructions and are also known as **statements.** These instructions are given to the computer to carry out an action.

Different types of statements used in computer program are listed below

- The **empty** or **null statement** is a statement which does not carry out any action.
- A **compound statement** is a sequence of more than one statements. These statements are executed sequentially one after other as they appear in a program.
- **Control statement** specify the order in which actions are executed.
- **Simple statement** is the statement which carries only single executable statement.

1.9 Program Designing Tools

There are certain tools that can be used to design the flow of a program code.

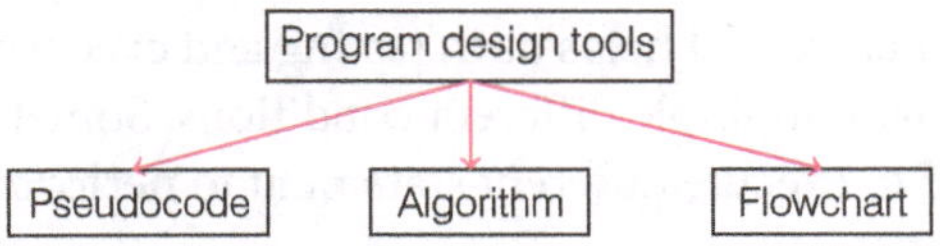

1. Pseudocode

Pseudocode is a simple way of writing a program design in English. It is not actual programming language.

It uses short phrases to write program's code before they are actually created in a specific language.

2. Algorithm

An algorithm is a set of instructions, sometimes called a procedure or a function that is used to perform a certain task.

3. Flowchart

A flowchart is a graphical representation of the design or steps to solve a computational problem.

It not only shows the flow of the process but also uses special symbols for the purpose , so that they are easily understandable by the programmers.

Symbol are used for making flowchart are as follows:

Symbols	Names
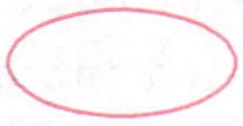	Start/Stop Box
	Input/Output Box
	Processing Box
	Decision Box
	Connectors
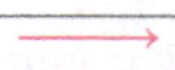	Flow lines

Quick Test 4

1. Which statement specifies the order in which actions are executed?
2. Name different program development tools.
3. What is an algorithm?
4. Name the given flowchart's box

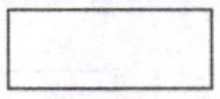

5. Which of the following uses drawing symbols showing programming steps :
   (a) Flowchart
   (b)Pseudocode
   (c) Algorithm
   (d) None
6. Which symbol is used for decision making in a flowchart.

1.10 Control Structure

A control structure is a programming language construct which affects the flow of the execution of program.

Various types of control structure are described below

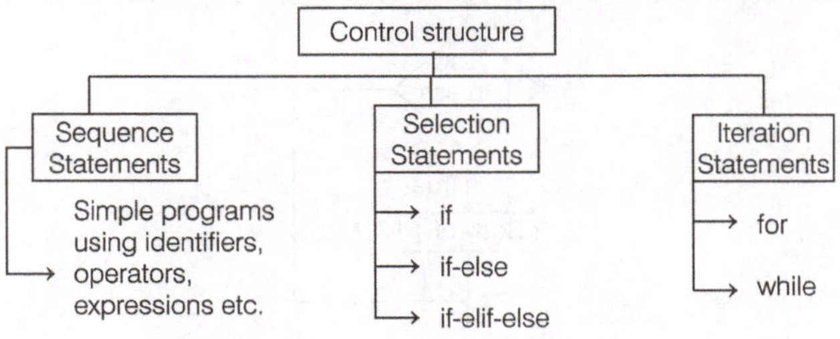

Sequence Statements

In these kind of programs, instructions are executed in the sequence in which they are written in the program.

e.g.
```
print("A program which adds two integers\n")
x=int(input("Enter first integer :"))
y=int(input("Enter second integer :"))
sum=x+y
print("Sum is :",sum)
```

Output

A program which adds two integers

Enter first integer : 5

Enter second integer : 11

Sum is : 16

Selection Statements

A selection statement / decision making statement is a control statement that allows the program to branch between two or more execution paths in a program. These statements allow a program to execute a statement or a set of statements depending upon a given condition.

These statements are also called conditional statements or decision making statements.

Python provides three types of decision making structures :

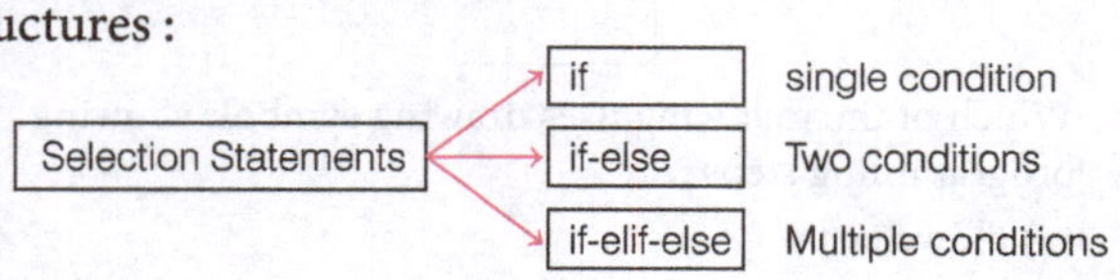

1. if Statement

It is the simplest form of decision making. if statement is used to decide whether a certain statement or block of statements will be executed or not, i.e. if a certain condition is True, then a block of statement is executed, otherwise not.

Syntax
```
if(conditional expression):
    statement(s)
```

Flowchart - if statement

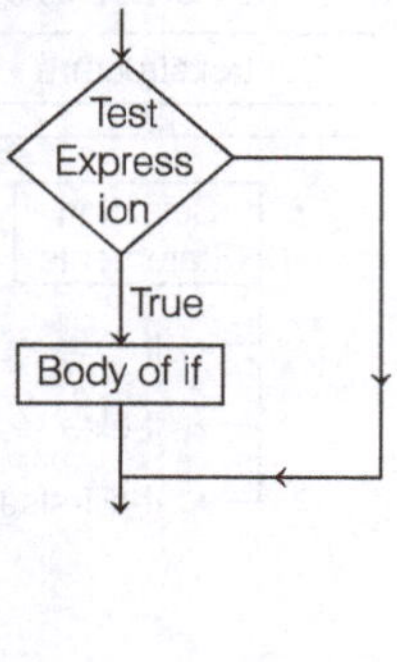

2. if-else Statement

This statement also tests a conditional expression, but it allows to take another branch if the test condition is not true.

If the condition is True, the entire block of statements following the if will be executed.

Otherwise, the entire block of statements following the else will be executed.

Syntax
```
if<condition> :
    Statement(s)
else:
    Statements(s)
```

Flowchart - if-else statement

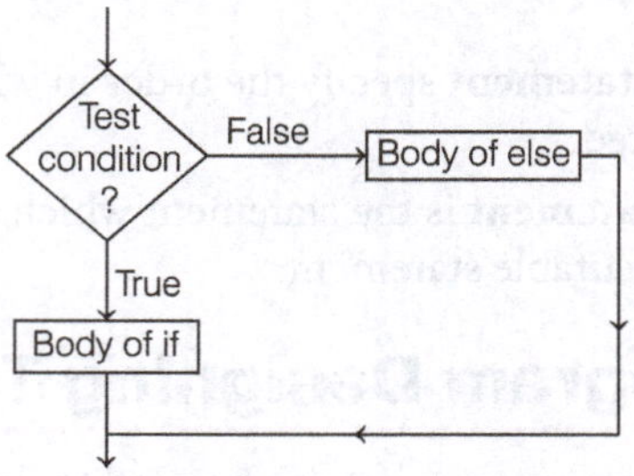

3. if-elif-else Statement

This structure of if helps us in testing and executing results, with multiple different conditions. Sometimes, we need to execute different statement to perform in different conditions.

It requires the evaluation of several conditions. First of all, the first condition is evaluated, if it is true then respective statements are processed. Otherwise, the next condition is evaluated to process another statements. This process continues for as many conditions are available in the situation.

Syntax
```
if (condition 1):
    statement 1
elif(condition 2):
    statement 2
else:
    statement 3
```

Or

```
if(condition 1):
    statement 1
elif(condition 2):
    statement 2
```

Flowchart - if-elif-else statement

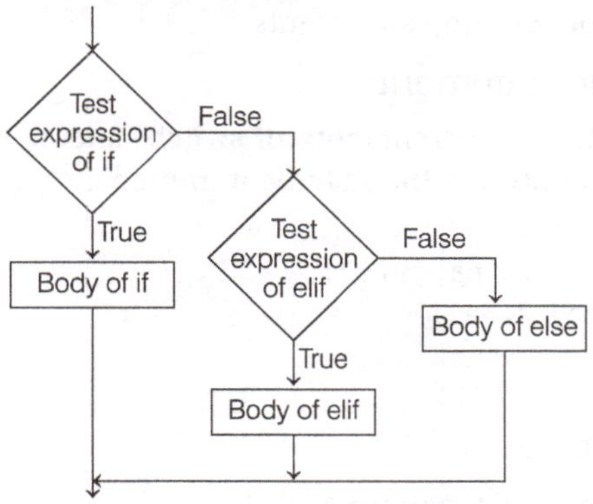

Expression is tested from the top towards the downside. As soon as the true condition is found, the associated set of statements are executed.

4. nested if Statement

Nested if means if inside if , that is a condition inside a condition. A situation where a condition needs to be checked if a parent condition is valid, nested ifs help us in such situations.

Syntax

```
if(condition 1):
   if(condition 2):
      statement 1
   else:
      statement 2
else:
   statement 3
```

Important Points

- A logical statement always evaluates True/False.
- Any value in Python other than zero is considered to be True whereas a zero(0) is considered to be False.
- (= =) must be used for comparison in the expression of if condition, if you use (=) the expression will always return True, because it performs assignment not comparison.

range( ) Function

The range( ) function is used to generate a sequence of numbers from a specified start to end.

The range( ) function has three parameters, as follows range ([start,] stop [,step])

- **Start** starting number of the sequence.
- **Stop** generate numbers upto, but not including this number.
- **Step** The progression of the sequence.

Quick Test 5

1. Name two selection statements used in Python.
2. What is the use of range function?
3. Fill up the blank : range(12 , 5 , -3) gives : 12 , 9 , ____
4. What are nested if structures?
5. Write the value of range(6) ?
6. What values will the statement range(10,2,-2) generate?

Iterative Statements

Iteration is the repetition of a process in order to generate an outcome. Iterative statements or loops enable a program with a cyclic flow of logic.

Each statement which is written under the scope of a looping statement gets executed the number of times the iteration/looping continues for.

There are basic types of looping statements available in Python, they are as follows

while loop

A while() loop tests for its ending condition before executing the statements enclosed in the loop body even the first time.

Syntax

```
while(loop-condition):
    statement(s)
```

Flowchart - while loop

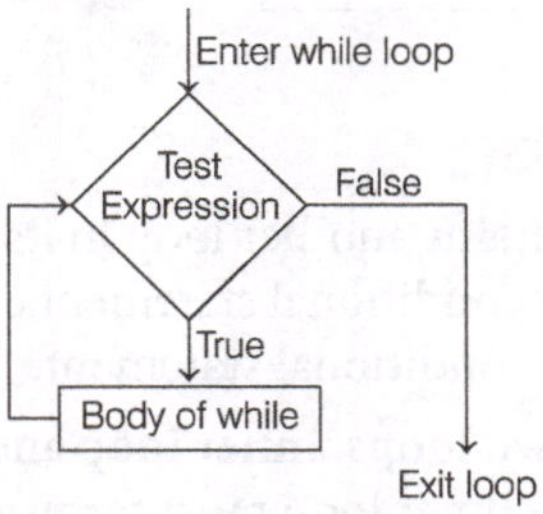

A while loop continues iteration cycle till its loop condition is evaluated as true.

If the loop-condition is false, then loop will not execute even once.

In while( ) loop, the looping condition is evaluated at the beginning of the loop's scope, i.e. prior to entering into the scope of loop.

This type of checking is called "Entry controlled checking", if the condition fails this checking, then the entry into the scope of loop will not be allowed.

So, while( ) loops are often called as Entry Controlled Loop.

The while( ) loop can accept expression and not just conditions, the following are all illegal expressions:

(i) while(x = x + 1)
(ii) while (n- -)
(iii) while(count + =i)

for loop

The for statement encloses one or more statements that form the body of the loop, the statements in the loop repeat continuously a certain number of times.

This loop is also known as entry controlled loop, as the condition is checked before entering into the scope of the loop.

Syntax

```
for(variable) in <sequence>:
    statement(s)
```

or

```
for(variable) in range (start, stop, step):
    statement(s)
```

Flowchart - for loop

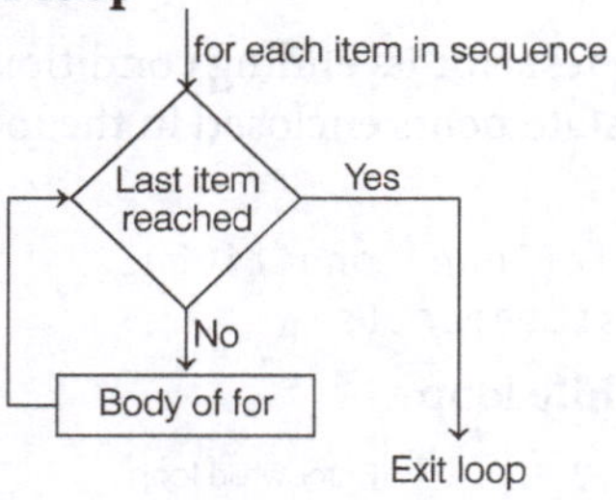

Nested Loop

When a loop contains another loop in its body, it is called nested loop. Any conditional statement can be nested within any other conditional statement.

In nested loop, **two loops; inner loop** and **outer loop** are executed. But the inner loop must terminate before the outer loop.

Syntax

```
for<variable> in <sequence>:
      for<variable>in <sequence>:
           statements
```

1.11 Jump Statement

Jump statements allow us to change the normal flow of program execution by transferring control to another part of the code. These statements are essential in scenarios where you want to terminate loops early, skip iterations, or exit functions. They make programs more flexible but should be used judiciously to avoid confusing logic. Types of jump statements

1. break Statement

Terminates the current loop (or switch statement) and transfers control to the statement immediately following the loop.

e.g.

```
for i in range(5):
    if i == 3:
        break
    print(i)
```

Output 0, 1, 2

2. continue Statement

Skips the remaining code in the current iteration and moves control to the next iteration of the loop.

e.g.

```
for i in range(5):
    if i == 3:
        continue
    print(i)
```

Output 0, 1, 2, 4

3. pass Statement

A placeholder statement that does nothing when executed. It is often used where a statement is syntactically required but no action is needed.

e.g.

```
for i in range(5):
    if i == 3:
        pass   # No operation
    print(i)
```

Output 0, 1, 2, 3, 4

4. return Statement

Exits a function and optionally returns a value to the caller.

e.g.

```
def add(a, b):
    return a + b
result = add(3, 4)
print(result)
```

Output 7

Quick Test 6

1. How many types of loop statements are there in Python?
2. Give the another name of entry control loop.
3. Write the syntax of for() loop?
4. When is break statement used?
5. What do you mean by jump statement.
6. Write a point of difference between break and continue statements.

Mind Map

PYTHON REVISION TOUR I

A program consist of various components
- **Expression** Combination of operators, constants and variables.
- **Statement** Logical instruction which Python interpreter can read and execute.
- **Comments** Used to add a remark or a note in the source code that are ignored by the interpreter or compiler and are not executed by the computer.
- **Function** Self contained block of statements which are kept together to perform a specific task.
- **Blocks and Indentation** Indicate the relationship between various statements.
- **Variables and Assignments** Refers to an object, an item or element that is stored in the memory.

Basic Structure of Python Program

Python Character Set
Set of valid characters that represents any digit (0-9), alphabet (A-Z, a-z), special symbol (, " '| ; : ! ~ @ # $ % ^ ` & * ( ) _ + − = { } [ ] \) and other.

Python Tokens
Smallest unit of any programming language.

- **Identifiers** Used to identify a variable, function, or other entities in a program. **Valid identifiers** Name, name_1, _SUM **Invalid identifiers** global, num^2, 2num.
- **Keywords** Pre-defined reserved words that have some special or predefined meanings.
- **Constants/Literals** Refer to fixed values that the program may not alter (change) during the program execution.
  Types Numeric Literals, String Literals, Boolean Literals, Special Literal-None and Literal Collections (list, tuple and dictionary).
- **Operators** Perform specific mathematical or logical operation on values.
  Types
  - **Unary Operators** (+, −, ~, not)
  - **Binary Operators** Identity, Arithmetic, Relational, Logical, Assignment, Membership, Bitwise, Shift
- **Punctuators** Used to separate line of codes, variables etc. e.g. Brackets, Parentheses, Comma, Colon, Equal sign

Input and Output in Python

input( ) First takes the input from the user and then evaluates the expression.
eval() Used with input( ) function to take numeric or data of other types into appropriate data types.
print() It evaluates the expression before printing it on the monitor.

Expressions
It combine operators, variables, literals and function calls to produce a value.

Types of Expressions
- **Constant Expressions** These are the expressions that have constant values only.
- **Arithmetic Expressions** Combination of numeric values, operators, and sometimes parenthesis.
- **Logical Expressions** Work on Boolean values and logical operators.
- **Relational Expression** The expressions that make use of relational operators and usually give output in True or False are relational expressions
- **String Expression** Includes string operators with string operands and integers.

Data Types in Python
Identify the type of data being used, its size and the functions associated it.

There are different data types available in Python

Data Types	Classes	Description
Numeric	int, float, complex	numeric values
Boolean	bool	either True of False
Set	set	collection of unique items
None	none	to signify the absence of value
Sequence	list, tuple, string	collection of items
Mapping	dictionary	data in key-value pair form

Note
- *In **mutable data types**, values can be changed after it is created. These are list, dictionary and sets.*
- *In **immutable data types**, values cannot be changed after they are created. These are integer, float, boolean, string and tuple.*

Type Conversion
It is the process of converting a data type into another data type.

Implicit Type Conversion Python automatically converts one data type to another data type.
Explicit Type Conversion Python needs user involvement to convert the variable data type into the required data type.

Statements
Any instruction written in the source code and executed by the Python interpreter is called a statement. The Python language has many different types of statements like empty or null statement, compound statement, control statement, simple statement.

Program Designing Tools

Pseudocode It uses short phrases to write program's code before they are actually created in a specific language.
Algorithm It is a set of instructions, sometimes called a procedure or a function that is used to perform a certain task.
Flowchart Graphical representation of the design or steps to solve a computational problem.

Control Structure
A control structure is a programming language construct which affects the flow of the execution of program.

Sequence Statements
Simple programs using identifiers, operators, expressions etc.

Selection Statements

if Statement
Syntax
```
if(conditional
expression): statement(s)
```

if-else Statement
Syntax
```
if<condition> :
      Statement(s)
else:
      Statements(s)
```

if-elif-else Statement
Syntax
```
if (condition 1):
 statement 1
elif(condition 2):
 statement 2
else:
 statement 3
```

nested if Statement
Syntax
```
if(condition 1):
if(condition 2):
statement 1
else:
statement 2
else:
statement 3
```

Iterative Statements

while loop
Syntax
```
while(loop-condition):
statement(s)
```

for loop
Syntax
```
for(variable)in
<sequence>:
statement(s)
```

Nested Loop
Syntax
```
for<variable> in <sequence>:
    for<variable>in <sequence>:
        statements
```

Jump Statement Used to alter the normal flow of a program by skipping or repeating parts of the code.
Types – break, continue, pass, return.

EXAM PATTERN QUESTIONS

Objective Type Questions

Multiple Choice Questions

1. The process of converting a data type into another data type is known as ....

(a) expression (b) operator
(c) type conversion (d) comparison

2. Find the invalid identifier from the following. CBSE SQP 2021-22 Term I

(a) none (b) address
(c) Name (d) pass

3. Find the invalid identifier from the following. CBSE 2021-22 Term I

(a) name (b) class (c) section (d) break

4. What will be the output of the following statement?

```
print (14%3**2*4)
```

(a) 16 (b) 64
(c) 20 (d) 256

5. Which of the following is a valid keyword in Python ? CBSE 2023

(a) false (b) return (c) non_local (d) none

6. Identify the correct output of the following code snippet:

```
game="Olympic2024"
print(game.index("C"))
```

(a) 0 (b) 6
(c) -1 (d) ValueError

7. In complex number a + ib, b represents as

(a) real part (b) imaginary part
(c) special part (d) None of these

8. Which of the following is the correct identifier?

(a) global (b) Break
(c) def (d) with

9. Identify the invalid Python statement out of the following options:

(a) print ("A",10, end="*") (b) print ("A",sep="*",10)
(c) print ("A",10, sep="*") (d) print("A"*10)

10. Which of the following operators will return either True or False? CBSE 2023

(a) += (b) != (c) = (d) *=

11. These operators are used to make a decision on two conditions.

(a) Logical (b) Arithmetic
(c) Relational (d) Assignment

12. Which of the following is an incorrect logical operator in Python? CBSE 2021-22 Term I

(a) NOT (b) IN
(c) OR (d) AND

13. Which of the following operator evaluates to True if the variable on either side of the operator points towards the same memory location and False otherwise?

(a) is (b) is not
(c) and (d) or

14. Which comments start with # symbol?

(a) Double line (b) Multi-line
(c) Single line (d) All of these

15. Which of the following symbol is used in Python for comments? CBSE SQP 2021-22 Term I

(a) $ (b) @ (c) // (d) #

16. The return type of the input() function is CBSE SQP 2021-22 Term I

(a) string (b) integer
(c) list (d) tuple

17. Which one of the following is the default extension of a Python file? CBSE SQP 2021-22 Term I

(a) .exe (b) .p++ (c) .py (d) .p

18. Which data type contains only numeric value in Python?

(a) Numbers (b) Strings
(c) Lists (d) Tuples

19. Which of the following is an invalid datatype in Python? CBSE SQP 2022-23

(a) Set (b) None
(c) Integer (d) Real

20. Which of the following operator cannot be used with string data type? CBSE SQP 2021-22 Term I

(a) + (b) in (c) * (d) /

21. Which of the following are sequence of character data?

(a) Lists (b) Tuples
(c) Strings (d) Dictionaries

22. List, dictionary and sets are

(a) mutable (b) immutable
(c) Both (a) and (b) (d) None of these

23. What is the output of the following code? CBSE SQP 2021-22 Term I

```
T=(100)
print(T*2)
```

(a) Syntax error (b) (200,)
(c) 200 (d) (100,100)

24. What will be the output of the following code :

```
2**3**2 + 625**0.5 + 7//2
```

(a) 542.50 (b) 540.0
(c) 539 (d) 541.0

25. Which of the following expressions evaluates to False? CBSE SQP 2024-25

(a) not(True) and False (b) True or False
(c) not(False and True) (d) True and not(False)

26. What will be the output of the following statement? CBSE 2024

```
print(16*5/4*2/5 - 8)
```

(a) -3.33 (b) 6.0
(c) 0.0 (d) -13.33

27. What will be the output of the following statement? CBSE SQP 2023-24

```
print(3-2**2**3+99/11)
```

(a) 244 (b) 244.0
(c) - 244.0 (d) Error

28. Consider the given expression CBSE 2023

```
5<10 and 12>7 or not 7>4
```

Which of the following will be the correct output, if the given expression is evaluated ?

(a) True (b) False
(c) NONE (d) NULL

29. What will the following expression be evaluated to in Python? CBSE 2023

```
print(4+3*5/3-5%2)
```

(a) 8.5 (b) 8.0 (c) 10.2 (d) 10.0

30. Consider the given expression: CBSE SQP 2022-23

```
not True and False or True
```

Which of the following will be correct output if the given expression is evaluated?

(a) True (b) False
(c) NONE (d) NULL

31. What will the following expression be evaluated to in Python? CBSE SQP 2022-23

```
print(15.0/4 + (8+3.0))
```

(a) 14.75 (b) 14.0
(c) 15 (d) 15.5

32. Evaluate the following expression and identify the correct answer. CBSE SQP 2021-22 Term I

```
16 - (4 + 2)* 5 + 2**3 * 4
```

(a) 54 (b) 46 (c) 18 (d) 32

33. Which of the following is the correct output for the execution of the following Python statement? CBSE 2021-22 Term I

```
print(5 + 3 ** 2 /2)
```

(a) 32 (b) 8.0
(c) 9.5 (d) 32.0

34. These statements enable a program with a cyclicflow of logic.

(a) Sequence (b) Compound
(c) Single (d) Iterative

35. Which function is used to generate a sequence of numbers overtime?

(a) range() (b) len()
(c) limit() (d) lim()

36. Identify the output of the following Python statement. CBSE SQP 2021-22 Term I

```
x = 2
while x < 9:
        print(x, end=' ')
        x = x + 1
```

(a) 12345678 (b) 3456789
(c) 2345678 (d) 23456789

37. Identify the output of the following Python statement. CBSE SQP 2021-22 Term I

```
b = 1
for a in range(1, 10, 2):
        b += a + 2
print(b)
```

(a) 31 (b) 33 (c) 36 (d) 39

Fill in the Blanks

38. .... operators work upon two operands.

39. A logical statement always evaluates ....

40. A/An .... in Python is a legal combination of tokens.

41. Every variable in Python holds an instance of a/an ....

42. .... are used to identify the type of data and associated operations to handle it.

43. Explicit type conversion is also called ....

44. .... structure is also known as straight line path.

45. .... statement allows branch depending upon the value or state of variables.

46. while() loops are called as ....

47. Jump statements defined in Python are .... and ....

State Whether True or False

48. "Identifiers are names used to identify a variable, function in a program". **CBSE 2023**

49. "Variable declaration is implicit in Python." **CBSE SQP 2022-23**

50. In a python if…elif block the else block is compulsory to write.

51. range(-1,-5) returns values -1,-2,-3,-4.

52. "In a Python program, if a break statement is given in a nested loop, it terminates the execution of all loops in one go." **CBSE SQP 2023-24**

Assertion and Reason Based Questions

Directions: In the following questions, A statement of Assertion (A) is followed by a statement of Reason (R). Mark the correct choice as.

(a) Both A and R are true and R is the correct explanation for A.
(b) Both A and R are true and R is not correct explanation for A.
(c) A is true but R is false.
(d) A is false but R is true.

53. **Assertion (A)** Python is portable and platform independent.
Reason (R) Portable and platform independent, means it can run on various operating systems and hardware platforms.

54. **Assertion (A)** Value and value are two different identifiers in Python.
Reason (R) Python is a case sensitive programming language.

55. **Assertion (A)** Assignment operator assigns or changes the value of the variable on its right.
Reason (R) The logical operator evaluates to either True or False based on the logical operands on either side.

56. **Assertion (A)** Higher precedence operator is evaluated before the lower precedence operator.
Reason (R) For operators with equal precedence, the expression is evaluated from right to left.

57. **Assertion (A)** A Python sequence is an ordered collection of items, where each item is indexed by an integer.
Reason (R) Variables whose values can be changed after they are created and assigned are called mutable.

58. **Assertion (A)** Data types are used to identify the type of data.
Reason (R) Data types are two types as numbers and strings.

59. **Assertion (A)** The order of execution of the statements in a program is known as flow of control.
Reason (R) The flow of control can be implemented using control structures.

60. **Assertion (A)** If one of the conditions is true, then the corresponding indented block executes, and the if statement terminates in elif statement.
Reason (R) Number of elif is dependent on the number of conditions to be checked.

61. **Assertion (A)** range() is used to create a list containing a sequence of integers from the given start value upto stop value (excluding stop value), with a difference of the given step value.
Reason (R) The range() is a User-defined function in Python.

62. **Assertion (A)** Looping constructs provide the facility to execute a set of statements in a program repetitively, based on a condition.
Reason (R) When the condition becomes true, the loop terminates.

63. **Assertion (A)** The while statement is used to iterate over a range of values or a sequence.
Reason (R) These values can be either numeric, or, as we shall see in later chapters, they can be elements of a data type like a string, list, or tuple.

64. **Assertion (A)** The while statement executes a block of code repeatedly as long as the control condition of the loop is false.
Reason (R) If the condition of the while loop is initially false, the body is not executed even once.

Answers

1. (c) type conversion
2. (d) pass
3. (d) break
4. (c) 20
5. (b) return
6. (d) ValueError
7. (b) imaginary part
8. (b) Break
9. (b) print ("A",sep="*",10)
10. (b) !=
11. (a) Logical
12. (b) IN
13. (a) is
14. (c) Single line
15. (d) #
16. (a) string
17. (c) .py
18. (a) Numbers
19. (d) Real
20. (d) /
21. (c) Strings
22. (a) mutable
23. (c) 200
24. (b) 540.0
25. (a) not(True) and False
26. (c) 0.0
27. (c) - 244.0
28. (a) True
29. (b) 8.0
30. (a) True
31. (a) 14.75
32. (c) 18
33. (c) 9.5
34. (d) Iterative
35. (a) range()
36. (c) 2345678
37. (c) 36
38. Binary
39. True/False
40. Expression
41. Object
42. Data types
43. Typecasting
44. Sequence
45. if
46. Entry control loops
47. break, continue
48. True
49. True
50. False
51. False
52. False
53. (a) Both A and R are true and R is the correct explanation for A.
54. (a) Both A and R are true and R is the correct explanation for A.
55. (d) A is false but R is true.
56. (c) A is true but R is false.
57. (b) Both A and R are true and R is not correct explanation for A.
58. (c) A is true but R is false.
59. (b) Both A and R are true and R is not correct explanation for A.
60. (a) Both A and R are true and R is the correct explanation for A.
61. (c) A is true but R is false.
62. (c) A is true but R is false.
63. (d) A is false but R is true.
64. (d) A is false but R is true.

Subjective Type Questions

Very Short Answer Type Questions

1. Write the type of the tokens from the following:

(i) ; (ii) while

Ans. (i) Punctuator (ii) Keyword

2. Name the tokens that are available in Python.

Ans. Python has the following tokens

- Identifiers
- Keywords
- Punctuators
- Literals
- Operators

3. Write the one example of following terms.

(i) Identifier
(ii) Punctuator
(iii) Keyword
(iv) Constant

Ans. (i) Identifier → Sum_1

(ii) Punctuator → Bracket ( )

(iii) Keyword → for

(iv) Constant → 'Neha'

4. Identify the types of following literals.

False 'True' "False"

45345 0O434 435.3

Ans. False	Boolean
'True'	String
"False"	String
45345	Integer
0O434	Integer (octal)
435.3	Floating point

5. How / operator is different from % operator?

Ans. / operator is used to find the quotient while % operator is used to find the remainder.

6. Name the following operators:

(i) ∧ (ii) – =

Ans. (i) Bitwise XOR (ii) Assignment

7. Give two examples of each of the following:

(i) Arithmetic operators
(ii) Relational operators CBSE SQP 2024-25

Ans. (i) ** Exponentiation, % Modulus or Remainder

(ii) > Greater than, == Equality

8. Which of the following are invalid names and why ?

(i) PaidInterest
(ii) S-num
(iii) Percent
(iv) 123
(v) abc km
(vi) elif

Ans. (i) Valid
(ii) Invalid, - is not allowed in the variable name.
(iii) Valid
(iv) Invalid, first character must be alphabet.
(v) Invalid, space is not allowed
(vi) Invalid, elif is a keyword.

9. How is a mutable object different from an immutable object in Python?
Identify one mutable object and one immutable object from the following:
(1,2), [1,2], {1:1,2:2}, '123'

Ans. An object that can be changed is mutable.While,an object that cannot be changed after its creation is immutable.
Mutable object: [1,2] or {1:1,2:2} (Any one)
Immutable object: (1,2) or '123' (Any one)

10. Convert the equation into corresponding Python statement $y = a^3 + b^2 + c + 2bc$.

Ans. y = (a * *3 + b * *2 + c + 2 * b * c)

11. Write the corresponding Python expression for the following mathematical expression.

(i) $z = a/a + b - d^2$
(ii) $z = x^2 + y^3$

Ans. (i) z = a / (a + b) − (d * d)
(ii) z = (x * *2) + (y * *3)

12. Determine which of the arithmetic expressions are valid. If invalid, explain the reason. [(a, b, c) are integers, (p, q, r) are float and (x, y, z) are float].

(i) p/q + a − c
(ii) q (a + b − z/4)
(iii) p/q + a − c
(iv) x/y + p * a/b
(v) a * + b
(vi) a+b*c*2

Ans. (i) p/q + a − c valid
(ii) q (a + b − z/4) invalid because operator missing between q and a
(iii) p/q + a − c valid
(iv) x/y + p * a/b valid
(v) a * + b invalid because use of two operators together
(vi) a+b*c*2 valid

13. What do you mean by type conversion?

Ans. When constant and variables of different types are mixed in an expression, they are converted to same type. This process is called type conversion.

14. Correct the error if any in the following statement.

(i) `a + 5 = b`
(ii) `1 = 2b + c * d`
(iii) `name = Aryan`
(iv)
```
a = 20
print a;
```

Ans. (i) `b = a + 5`
(ii) `1 = 2 * b + c *d`
(iii) `name = "Aryan"`
(iv) `a = 20 print (a)`

15. Predict the output of the code given below: CBSE SQP 2022-23

```
s="welcome2cs"
n = len(s)
m = "  "
for i in range (0, n):
  if (s[i] > = 'a' and s[i] < = 'm'):
     m = m + s[i].upper()
  elif (s[i] >= 'n' and s[i] <= 'z'):
     m = m + s[i - 1]
  elif (s[i].isupper()):
     m = m + s[i].lower()
  else:
     m = m + '&'
  print(m)
```

Ans. sELCcME&Cc

16. Write a program to print numbers from 1 to 10 (use both for and while loop) .

Ans.
```
#WHILE
num = 0
while num < 10:
num = num + 1 #or num+=1
 print(num)
#FOR
for i in range(1,11):
print(i)
```

17. Find the syntax error in the following program and underline after correct them.

```
W = 90 ;
while(w > 60)
  print(w)
  w = w - 50
```

Ans. Correct code is

```
W = 90
while(w>60):
  print(w)
  w = w - 50
```

18. Rewrite the following program after removing the syntactical error(s), if any. Underline each correction

```
mul=3
value=10
for i in range (1, 6, 1):
    if (value % mul = 0):
        print (value * multiply)
    else
        print (value + multiply)
```

Ans. Rewrite correct code is

```
mul=3
value=10
for i in range (1, 6, 1):
    if (value % mul = = 0):
        print (value * mul)
    else:
        print (value + mul)
```

Short Answer Type I Questions

19. Differentiate between identifier and keyword.

Ans. Differences between identifier and keyword are

Identifier	Keyword
Identifier consists any combination of letters, numbers and underscores.	Keyword must consist only letters.
It allows both uppercase and lowercase.	It allows only lowercase except True, False and None.
e.g. x, sum_5, _mul etc.	e.g. finally, continue, yield etc.

20. Write the value stored in the variable Num byeach of the following statements.

(i) Num = 2 * 3 – 4
(ii) Num = 2+3-1*3
(iii) Num = (2+3)*2

Ans. (i) Num = 2
(ii) Num = 2
(iii) Num = 10

21. Determine the hierarchy of operations and evaluate following expression.

A = 3*4//5 + 5//7 + 8 – 2 + 4//2

Ans. The * operator will be performed before //. Though both have same priority but in this expression * is prior to //.

A = 12 //5 + 5//7 + 8 – 2 + 4//2
= 2 + 5//7 + 8 – 2 + 4//2 operation : //
= 2 + 0 + 8 – 2 + 4//2 operation : //
= 2 + 0 + 8 – 2 + 2 operation : //
= 2 + 0 + 6 + 2 operation : –
= 10 operation : +

22. Determine the hierarchy of operations and evaluate the following expresssion.

a = 2*3//4 + 4//4 + 8 – 2 + 5//8

Ans. a = 2* 3//4 + 4//4 + 8 – 2 + 5//8
= 6//4 + 4 //4 + 8 – 2 + 5//8 operation : *
= 1 + 4//4 + 8 – 2 + 5//8 operation : //
= 1 + 1 + 8 – 2 + 5//8 operation : //
= 1 + 1 + 8 – 2 + 0 operation : //
= 2 + 8 – 2 + 0 operation : +
a = 10 – 2 + 0 operation : +
a = 8 + 0 operation : –
a = 8 operation : +

23. What value will be stored in different variables when the following Python statements are executed?

```
i = 10
j = i + 5
k = i + j/5
l = k + 1 + 4
m= l+ l- i
n = k + m*l
print("i: ", i)
print("j: ", j)
print("k: ", k)
print("l: ", l)
print("m: ", m)
print("n: ", n)
```

Ans. i : 10 j : 15
k : 13.0 l : 18.0
m : 9.0 n : 175.0

24. Predict the output of the following program.

```
a = 5
b = a = 15
c = (a < 15)
print ("a = ", a)
print ("b = ", b)
print ("c = ", c)
```

Ans. a = 15
b = 15
c = False

25. What is the output of the following code ?

```
num=4+float(7)/int(2.0)
print("num=",num)
```

Ans. num=7.5

26. **What will be the output of the following code?**

```
a, b = 10, 5
x, y = a + b, b - 2
z = x - y
print ("x:", x, "y:", y, "z:", z)
```

Ans. **Output**

x:15   y:3   z:12

27. **What is the output of the following code:**

```
>>> a = 10
>>> b = 2
>>> print(" Output is ", (a + 10 * 2 + b))
```

Ans. Output is 32

28. **Predict the output.**

```
a,b=10,15
x=20
y=25
a=x+y-b
x=a+b-y+10
z=y+b*3+a
x=50
a=x+y+z
print("a:",a)
print("b:",b)
print("x:",x)
print("y:",y)
print("z:",z)
```

Ans. **Output**

a : 175
b : 15
x : 50
y : 25
z : 100

29. **Construct logical expressions to represent the following conditions.**

(i) **Weight is greater than or equal to 115 but less than 125.**

(ii) **Donation is in the range of 4000-5000 or Guest is 1.**

Ans. (i) (weight >=115 and weight < 125)

(ii) ((Donation > = 4000 and Donation <= 5000) or Guest = =1)

30. **Write an algorithm to find out whether the given number is divisible by 3 or not.**

Ans. The algorithm is

Step 1 Input " Enter a Number" N

Step 2 Let R = N % 3

Step 3 If R = 0, then "N is divisible by 3"

Step 4 If R!= 0, then "N is not divisible by 3"

Step 5 Stop

31. **Draw a flow chart to find the factorial of any number.**

Ans.

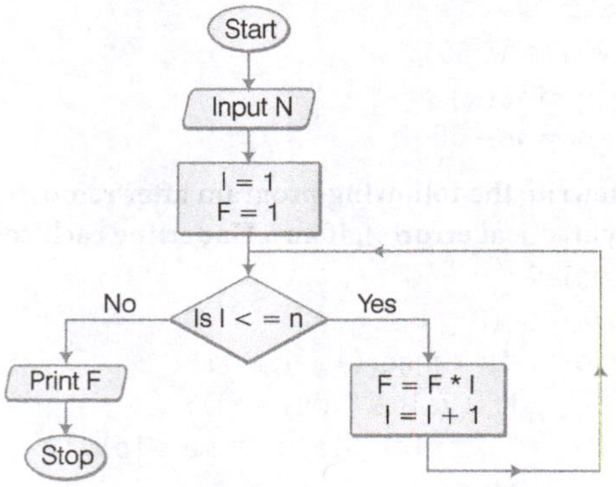

32. **What will be printed on the console by the below code:**

```
x, y, z, k, j = 9, 7, 2, 2, 1
m = 5
if (x > y):
    if (y > z and y > k):
        m = m - 1
    else:
        k = k + 1
else:
    j = j + 1
print ('m =', m)
print ('k =', k)
print ('j =', j)
```

Ans. **Output**

m = 4
k = 2
j = 1

33. **Rewrite the following code into for loop:**

```
i = 3
while (i < 5):
    if (i = = 4):
    print ("Welcome")
    else:
    print ("No entry")
    i = i + 1
print ("value of i", i)
```

Ans.

```
for i in range (3, 5)
    if (i = = 4):
        print ("Welcome")
    else:
        print ("No entry")
print ("value of i", i)
```

34. **Predict the output of the Python code given below**

```
Text1 = "IND-23"
Text2=""
I=0
while I<len(Text1):
    if Text1[I]>="0" and Text1[I]<="9":
```

```
            Val=int(Text1[I])
            Val=Val+1
            Text2=Text2 + str(Val)
        elif Text1[I]>="A" and Text1[I]<="Z":
            Text2=Text2+(Text1[I+1])
        else:
            Text2=Text2 + "*"
        I+=1
    print(Text2)
```

Ans. ND-*34

35. Find the output of the following code:

```
num=123
f=0
s=0
while(num > 3):
  rem = num % 100
  if(rem % 2 ! = 0):
      f + = rem
  else:
      s + = rem
  num / =100
print(f-s)
```

Ans. Output

23

36. Write the output of the following code snippet :

```
tup=('rains',)
n=5
for i in range(int(n)):
    tup=(tup,)
print(tup)
```

Ans.

```
('rains',)
(('rains',),)
((('rains',),),)
(((('rains',),),),)
((((('rains',),),),),)
```

37. Asish has written the following code , but he is getting some errors while executing it. Rewrite the correct code removing all the errors.

```
value=30
for val in range (0, value)
  if valu == 0
      print (val+4)
  else if vals == 0;
      print (val+3)
  else
      print (val+10)
```

Ans.

```
Value = 30
for val in range (0, Value) :  # Error 1
  if val%4 ==0:                # Error 2
      print (val*4)
  elif val%5==0 :              # Error 3
      print (val + 3)
  else :                       # Error 4
      print (val + 10)
```

38. Give the output for the following program segment given below.

```
for i in range(-5,-7,-1):
    print(i+1)
```

Ans. The program segment does not produce any output.

Short Answer Type II Questions

39. Define the following terms

(i) Comments

(ii) Variables

(iii) Data Types

Ans. (i) **Comments** A hash sign (#) that is not inside a string literal begins a single line comment. We can use triple quoted string for giving multi-line comments.

(ii) **Variables** A variable in Python is defined through assignment. There is no concept of declaring a variable outside of that assignment.

(iii) **Data type** It is a set of values and the allowable operations on those values. Python has a great set of useful datatypes.

40. Determine which of the arithmetic expressions are valid. If invalid, explain the reason. [(a, b, c) are integers, (p, q, r) are float and (x, y, z) are float].

(i) p/q + a – c

(ii) q (a + b – z/4)

(iii) p/q + a – c

(iv) x/y + p * a/b

(v) a * + b

(vi) a+b*c*2

Ans. (i) p/q + a – c valid

(ii) q (a + b - z/4) invalid because operator missing between q and a

(iii) p/q + a – c valid

(iv) x/y + p * a/b valid

(v) a * + b invalid because use of two operators together

(vi) a+b*c*2 valid

41. Evaluate the following expressions..

(i) A = 10*4//2 + 4 – 2//2 + 4 – 3 + 5//8

(ii) A = 5 + 6//3 + 10*3//4 + 2 + 3//4

(iii) A = 5*5 + 4//5 + 15 – 9//2 + 10

Ans. (i) A = 10*4//2 + 4 – 2//2 + 4 – 3 + 5//8

= 40//2 + 4 – 2//2 + 4 – 3 + 5//8 operation : *

= 20 + 4 – 2//2 + 4 – 3 + 5//8 operation : //

= 20 + 4 – 1 + 4 – 3 + 5//8 operation : //

= 20 + 4 – 1 + 4 – 3 + 0 operation : //

= 24 – 1 + 4 – 3 + 0 operation : +

$= 23 + 4 - 3$ operation : −
$= 27 - 3 = 24$ operation : +

(ii) $A = 5 + 6//3 + 10*3//4 + 2 + 3//4$
$= 5 + 2 + 10*3//4 + 2 + 3//4$ operation : //
$= 5 + 2 + 30//4 + 2 + 3//4$ operation : *
$= 5 + 2 + 7 + 2 + 3//4$ operation : //
$= 5 + 2 + 7 + 2 + 0$ operation : +
$= 7 + 7 + 2 = 16$ operation : +

(iii) $A = 5*5 + 4//5 + 15 - 9//2 + 10$
$= 25 + 4//5 + 15 - 9//2 + 10$ operation : *
$= 25 + 0 + 15 - 9//12 + 10$ operation : //
$= 25 + 0 + 15 - 4 + 10$ operation : +
$= 40 - 4 + 10$ operation : −
$= 36 + 10 = 46$

42. Predict the output:

(i)
```
a = 3
b = a *2
print(a*3+6+b)
```
(ii)
```
a, b = 12, 10
c = a//b + 4 * 2
d = c - 10
print(d)
```
(iii)
```
a = 5
b = 6
print((a and b)
or (a > b))
```
(iv)
```
a = 4
b = 6
c = 10
print(a >= b)
or ((c = = b)
and (not(c < a))))
```
(v)
```
a = 4
b = 6
c = 10
print ((a <= b)
and print(c)
((c == a)and
(not(c < b))))
```
(vi)
```
a = 60
b = 10
c = 85/b + a
```
(vii)
```
a = 3
b = 4
c = a ** b + 5
print(c)
```
(viii)
```
b = 89
a = 78
c = (a <= b)
print(c)
```

Ans. (i) 21 (ii) −1
(iii) 6 (iv) False
(v) False (vi) 68
(vii) 86 (viii) True

43. Python is dynamic typed. Explain it.

Ans. A language is dynamically typed if the type is associated with run-time values and not named variables/fields etc. This means that you as a programmer can write a little quicker because you do not have to specify types every time. Python is a dynamically type language. It does not know about the type of the variable until the code is run, so declaration is no use. It stores that value at some memory location and then binds that variable name to that memory container.

We have assigned three values to three variables:
```
>>> a = 10
>>> name = "Neha"
>>> x = 34.6
```
But what types are these variables ? Let's use the type ( ) module to find out:

Syntax
```
type (variable_name)
```

44. Write a program to read a number. If the number is even print half the number otherwise print the next number. End your program by printing "Thank You".

Ans.
```
num = int(input("Enter a number: "))
if num %2==0:
    print("The half number is: ",num/2)
else:
    print("The next number is: ", num+1)
print("Thank You!")
```

45. Write a program to print negative, zero or positive according to whether variable x is less than zero, zero or greater than zero respectively.

Ans.
```
x = int(input("Enter a number:"))
if (x>0):
    print("Positive")
elif (x<0):
    print("Negative")
else:
    print("Zero")
```

46. Differentiate between break and continue statement with the help of an example.

Ans. break statement is used to terminate the execution of the loop.

For example:
```
for i in range(6):
if i==3:
    break
print i
```
The output of the above code will be:

0

1

2

The loop terminates when i becomes 3 due to break statement.

Whereas, continue statement is used to force the next iteration while skipping the statements in the present iteration.

Long Answer Type Questions

47. Write a Python program to print the Fibonacci series.

Ans.
```
n = int(input("How many terms?"))
# first two terms
n1, n2 = 0, 1
count = 0
# check if the number of terms is valid
if n < = 0:
 print("please enter a positive integer")
elif n = = 1:
 print ("Fibonacci sequence upto", n, ":")
 print(n1)
else:
 print("Fibonacci sequence:")
 while count < n:
     print(n1)
     nth = n1 + n2
     # update values
     n1 = n2
     n2 = nth
     count + = 1
```

48. Write a program to check whether a number is prime or composite .

Ans.
```
num = int(input("enter a number: "))
flag = False
if num > 1:
for i in range(2, num):
    if (num % i) == 0:
        flag = True
        break
if flag:
      print(num, "is not a prime number")
else:
      print(num, "is a prime number")
```

49. Write a program to print the following pattern:

```
A
B  C  D
E  F  G  H  I
J  K  L  M  N  O  P
Q  R  S  T  U  V  W  X  Y
```

Ans.
```
incr = 1
val = 65
for i in range(0, 5):
  for j in range(0, incr):
     ch = chr(val)
     print(ch, end = "")
     val = val + 1
  incr = incr + 2
  print()
```

50. Write a Python program to generate and display all the armstrong numbers between 1 and 200.

Ans.
```
print("The Armstrong numbers in between 1 and
200 are")
for i in range(1, 201, 1):
    k = 0
    j = i
    while (j > 0):
        I = j%10
        k = k + I * I * I
        j = j//10
    if (k = = i):
        print(i)
```

51. Write a program to print the following pattern.

```
    *
   * *
  * * *
 * * * *
* * * * *
```

Ans.
```
n = 5
    k=k-1
for i in range(0, n):
    for j in range(0, k):
        print(end=" ")
        k = k - 1
    for j in range(0, i+1):
        print("* ", end="")
    print("\r")
```

52. Write a program to check whether a number is palindrome number or not.
(A palindrome number is one which is same as its reverse)

Ans.
```
num = int(input("Enter a number: "))
temp = num
reverse = 0
while temp > 0:
remainder = temp % 10
reverse = (reverse * 10) + remainder
temp = temp // 10
if num == reverse:
     print('Palindrome')
else:
     print("Not Palindrome")
```

Case Study Based Questions

Case Study 1

Data types are the classification or categorisation of data items. It represents the kind of value that tells what operations can be performed on a particular data. Since everything is an object in Python programming, data types are actually classes and variables are instance (object) of these classes.

Following are the standard or built-in data type of Python:

Numeric In Python, numeric data type represents the data which has numeric value. Numeric value can be integer, floating number or even complex numbers.

Sequence Type In Python, sequence is the ordered collection of similar or different data types. Sequences allow storing multiple values in an organised and efficient fashion.

Boolean Data type with one of the two built-in values, True and False. But non-Boolean objects can be evaluated in Boolean context as well and determined to be True and False. It is denoted by the class Bool.

Set In Python, set is an unordered collection of data type that is iterable, mutable and has no duplicate elements. The order of elements in a set is undefined though it may consist of various elements.

Mapping Mapping is an unordered data type in Python. Currently, there is only one standard mapping data type in Python called dictionary.

(i) How many values are there in Boolean data type?

(ii) What do you mean by sequence data type?

(iii) List the types of numeric data type.

(iv) What is the use of None?

(v) Write the output of

```
>>>type("Arihant")
```

Ans. (i) True and False

(ii) A Python sequence is an ordered collection of items, where each item is indexed by an integer.

(iii)
- Integer
- Complex number
- Float

(iv) None is used to signify the absence of value in a situation.

(v) <class 'str'>

Case Study 2

Riya wrote a program to print the Fibonacci series. But some words or lines had missing. Help her to execute the given program.

```
n = int.(input ("How many terms?))
n1, n2 = 0,1
count = 0
if n < = 0
    print ("Please enter a positive number")
elif
    print("fibonacci sequence upto", n, ":")
    print(____)
else :
    print ("Fibonacci sequence :")
    while count <n :
          print (n1)
          n3 = ____
          n1 = n2
          n2 = ____
          count = count +1
```

(i) Write the symbol which will terminate the line 4.

(ii) Fill the blank in line 6 to satify the condition.

(iii) Write the variable which print in line 8

(iv) Write the value which will be assign to variable n3.

(v) Fill the blank in line 15.

Ans. (i) (colon)

(ii) n==1:

(iii) n1

(iv) n1 + n2

(v) n3

Case Study 3

Krrishnav is looking for his dream job but has some restrictions. He loves Delhi and would take a job there, if he is paid over ₹ 40000 a month. He hates Chennai and demands at least ₹ 100000 to work there. In any another location, he is willing to work for ₹ 60000 a month. The following code shows his basic strategy for evaluating a job offer. **[CBSE Question Bank]**

```
pay= ________
location= ________
if location == "Mumbai":
   print ("I'll take it!")                #Statement 1
elif location == "Chennai":
   if pay < 100000:
      print ("No way")                    #Statement 2
```

```
        else:
            print("I am willing!")              #Statement 3
    elif location == "Delhi" and pay > 40000:
        print("I am happy to join")             #Statement 4
    elif pay > 60000:
        print("I accept the offer")             #Statement 5
    else:
        print("No thanks, I can find something better")
                                                #Statement 6
```

On the basis of the above code, choose the right statement which will be executed when different inputs for pay and location are given.

(i) Input: location = "Chennai", pay = 50000

(a) Statement 1 (b) Statement 2
(c) Statement 3 (d) Statement 4

(ii) Input: location = "Surat" ,pay = 50000

(a) Statement 2 (b) Statement 4
(c) Statement 5 (d) Statement 6

(iii) Input : location = "Any Other City", pay = 1

(a) Statement 1 (b) Statement 2
(c) Statement 4 (d) Statement 6

(iv) Input : location = "Delhi", pay = 50000

(a) Statement 6 (b) Statement 5
(c) Statement 4 (d) Statement 3

(v) Input : location = "Lucknow", pay = 65000

(a) Statement 2 (b) Statement 3
(c) Statement 4 (d) Statement 5

Ans. (i) (b) When user enters input as location = Chennai and pay =50000, then location == "Chennai" condition will be true. After that, pay < 100000 : will be check it also true, so print ("No way") statement 2 will be execute.

(ii) (d) When location = "Surat", pay =50000 entered by user then statement 6 will be execute.

(iii) (d) When location = "Any Other City", pay =1 entered by user then statement 6 will be execute because it does not satisfied any given condition.

(iv) (c) When location = "Delhi", pay =50000 entered by user then statement 4 will be execute.

(v) (d) When location = "Lucknow", pay =65000 entered by user then statement 5 will be execute.

SELF ASSESSMENT TEST

Multiple Choice Questions

1. The ______ operator checks presence of a value in another.

(a) in (b) is

(c) and (d) type

2. Which of the following has the highest priority

(a) * (b) **

(c) / (d)//

3. Which of the following is not a composite data type :

(a) Integer (b) List

(c) Tuple (d) None of the above

4. These operators work on single operand.

(a) Binary (b) Unary

(c) Ternary (d) None of these

5. This statement terminates the current iterations of the loop by skipping over the rest statements.

(a) continue (b) break

(c) goto (d) nest

Fill in the Blanks

6. A smallest individual unit in a program is known as ....

7. Float values are specified with a ....

8. The tree like presentation of conditions and actions are called ....

9. .... means repetition of a set of statements depending upon a test condition.

10. .... are used to alter the flow of control unconditionally.

State Whether True or False

11. Identifiers are names used to identify a variable, function in a program.

12. The # symbol used for inserting comments in python is a token.

Assertion and Reason Based Questions

Assertion (A) and Reason (R) Type questions. Choose the correct option as

(a) Both Assertion (A) and Reason (R) are true, and Reason (R) is the correct explanation of Assertion (A)

(b) Both Assertion (A) and Reason (R) are true, but Reason (R) is not the correct explanation of Assertion (A)

(c) Assertion (A) is True, but Reason (R) is False

(d) Assertion (A) is False, but Reason (R) is True

13. **Assertion (A)** Strings are group of characters.

Reason (R) Characters of string may be alphabets, digit or special character including spaces.

14. **Assertion (A)** A flowchart is a graphical representation of the steps taken to reach a certain result.

Reason (R) Flowcharts are drawn using certain special purpose symbols.

Very Short Answer Type Questions

15. What are tokens? Write about any two tokens with examples of each.

16. Identify the type of following literals.

4534 'False' True

17. Differentiate

(a) / and // (b) * and **

18. Evaluate :

True and not (90>70) or not(-9) and 78%6>2

19. What will be the result of following expression?

– x < = 5

(i) if x = 5 (ii) if x = – 5

Short Answer Type Questions

20. Determine the output

(i)
```
a = 2
b = a + 1
print (a, b, a + 1, b - 1)
```

(ii)
```
a = 3
b = a - 2
c = 4 + 2 * b + 4 - a
print ("b = ", b, "c = ", c)
```

21. Find the errors, if any, in the following code:

```
x=55
p=20
while (x>=10)
{
      if p%5=0
         x= -4
      else
         x-=10
      p=p+1
}
```

22. Write a program to generate the first 20 terms of the fibonacci series and then print out those, which are prime numbers.

23. Write a program to input start and end and display all perfect numbers in the range.

(Perfect Number : Is a number whose sum of factors other than itself is equal to the number. Example 6 =3+2+1)

24. Write a program to input a number and check whether it is a Unique number or not.

(Unique Number : A number whose all the digits are distinct . Example 123/672)

Long Answer Type Questions

25. Define data types in python . Write about each category and their subtypes .

26. What ae operators in python . Explain each type with examples.

27. Write a program to input number of lines and print the following pattern.

```
1
0   1
0   1   0
1   0   1   0
1   0   1   0   1
```

Upto n lines.

Case Study Based Question

28. Riya is learning Python programming as part of her school curriculum. One day, her teacher gave her a problem to write a simple Python program that accepts two numbers from the user, checks if the first number is greater than the second number, and prints the difference.

If the first number is not greater, the program should skip the subtraction and display a message. She is also asked to draw a flow diagram, write pseudocode, and explain the control structure and data types used.

She wrote the following Python code:

```
# Program to find the difference
num1 = int(input("Enter first number: "))
num2 = int(input("Enter second number: "))
if num1 > num2:
    diff = num1 - num2
    print("Difference is", diff)
else:
    pass
```

Answer the following Questions:

(i) Which of the following is a valid token used in the given program?

(a) int (b) input()
(c) > (d) All of these

(ii) What type of data type is used to store the variables num1 and num2?

(a) float (b) str
(c) int (d) bool

(iii) Which of the following is an example of type conversion in the given code?

(a) num1 - num2 (b) int(input(...))
(c) print(...) (d) if num1 > num2:

(iv) Which control structure is used in the given program?

(a) Looping (b) Jumping
(c) Selection (d) Sequence

(v) What is the purpose of the pass statement in this program?

(a) It performs a calculation.
(b) It skips the current block without doing anything.
(c) It ends the program.
(d) It prints a message.

Answers

1. (a) 2. (a) 3. (a) 4. (b) 5. (b)
6. Token 7. decimal point 8. Flowcharts
9. Looping 10. Jump statements
11. True 12. False 13. (a) 14. (a)
28. (i) → (d), (ii) → (c), (iii) → (b), (iv) → (c), (v) → (b)

02 CHAPTER

In this chapter, we are going to understand following concept
- Strings
- Lists
- Tuples
- Dictionaries

YOUR STUDY GOALS

2.1 Strings
2.2 String Traversal
2.3 String Operators
2.4 Built-in String Methods
2.5 Lists
2.6 Operations on Lists
2.7 List Slicing
2.8 Built-in Methods in Lists
2.9 Tuples
2.10 Operations on Tuples
2.11 Tuple Slicing
2.12 Built-in Methods in Tuples
2.13 Dictionary
2.14 Built-in Methods in Dictionary
2.15 Module
2.16 Errors
2.17 Exceptions

YOUR PRACTICE GOAL

- Objective Type Questions (100 Qs ; MCQs, True or False, Fill in the Blanks, Assertion and Reason)
- Subjective Type Questions (77 Qs ; VSA, SA, LA)
- Case Based Questions (Objective Case Studies-4 Subjective Case Studies-2)

Python Revision Tour-II

2.1 Strings

A **sequence** of **characters** is called **string**. Strings are used by programming languages to manipulate text such as words and sentences.

Strings literal in Python are enclosed by double quotes or single quotes. String literals can be span multiple lines, to write these strings triple quotes """ or ''' are used.

A String in python is created using single or double quotes

e.g.
```
S= "aissce 2025"
S1= 'Welcome to India'
S2= " "                 # Empty String
```

Accessing Values in Strings

Each individual character in a string can be assessed using a technique called **indexing.**

The index specifies the character to be accessed in the string and is written in square brackets [].

The first character of string is represented by index 0, second character is represented by index 1 and so on. While the index number -1 represents last character of string and so on.

Python allows both positive and negative indexing.

e.g.
```
s = "Python Language"
```

It is called positive index

0	1	2	3	4	5	6	7	8	9	10	11	12	13	14
P	y	t	h	o	n		L	a	n	g	u	a	g	e
–15	–14	–13	–12	–11	–10	–9	–8	–7	–6	–5	–4	–3	–2	–1

It is called negative index

```
>>>s[6]
' '
>>>s[5]
'n'
>>>s[-6]
'n'
```

Accessing outside index gives an IndexError

```
s="Python"
>>>s[22]
```

Traceback (most recent call last):

```
File "<pyshell#1>", line 1, in <module>
s[22]
```

IndexError: string index out of range

Deleting a String

As we know, strings are immutable, so we cannot delete or remove the characters from the string but we can delete entire string using del keyword.

```
>>> str = "HELLOPYTHON"
>>> del str[1]
TypeError:'str' object does not support
item deletion.
```

Deleting entire string

```
>>> S= "California"
>>>del S
>>>print(S)
Traceback (most recent call last):
File "<pyshell#4>", line 1, in <module>
S
NameError: name 'S' is not defined
```

String Slicing

Slicing means Extracting a slice or part from a string. To access some part of a string or substring, we use a method called slicing.

This can be done by specifying an index range. Slice operation is performed on string with the use of colon (:).

Syntax `String[Start : Stop : Step]`

e.g.
```
>>> str1 = "Python Program"
>>> print (str1 [3 : 7])
hon
>>>print(str1[2:10:2])
```

Output to r

Special ways

To display characters from the beginning to a range use [: index], to display characters from end use [:- index] and to display characters from specific index till the end use [index :]

```
>>> print (str1 [: 4])
Pyth
>>> print (str1 [:- 4])
Python Pro
>>> print (str1 [5:])
n Program
```

Printing reverse

e.g.
```
>>> print (str1 [::-1])
margorP nohtyP
```

2.2 String Traversal

Traversing is a technique to iterate the character of string, one character at a time.

It just means to process every character in a string, usually from left end to right end.

Python allows two ways to traverse a string are as follows

The 'for' loop

(a) **'for' loop** can iterate over the elements of a sequence or string. It is used when you want to traverse all characters of a string.

```
D = "Amsterdam"
for i in D:
  print(i, sep= " ")
```

Output A m s t e r d a m

(b) **'for' loop with range** can iterate over the elements of a sequence or string till the particular index.

```
S = "Winter"
for a in range(len(S)) :
  print(a, end = " ")
```

Output W i n t e r

2.3 String Operators

We can manipulate a string in different ways to use various operators. Here, we will discuss various operators:

Operator Name	Explanation	Example
Concatenation (+)	Combines two strings into one.	`print("Hello" + " World") → "Hello World"`
Replication (*)	Repeats a string a specified number of times.	`print("Hi" * 3) → "HiHiHi"`
Comparison (==, !=, <, >, <=, >=)	Compares two strings lexicographically (based on Unicode values).	`print("abc" == "abc") → True;` `print ("abc" < "xyz") → True`
Membership (in, not in)	Checks whether a substring exists within another string.	`print("cat" in "concatenation") → True;` `print("dog" not in "concatenation") → True`
Identity (is, is not)	Checks whether two string objects are the same (have the same memory address).	`str1 = "Hello"; str2 = "Hello"; print(str1 is str2) → True`

2.4 Built-in String Methods

Python includes the following built-in methods to manipulate strings

Method	Description	Example

capitalize( )	This method is used to capitalize first character of a string.
	Syntax `string.capitalize()`
		`>>> s = 'arihant'`
		`>>>s.capitalize()`
		`'Arihant'`

center( )	This method creates and returns a new string which is padded with the specified character.
	Syntax `string.center (length [,fillchar])`
		`>>>s = "This is wow"`
		`>>>s.center (15)`
		`'  This is wow  '`

count( )	This method returns the number of occurrences of a substring in the given string.
	Syntax `string.count(substring, start, end)`
		`>>>s = 'He loves his books and his toys)`
		`>>>s.count ("his")`
		`2`

endswith( )	Determines if a string or a substring endswith suffix; returns True, if so and False otherwise.
	Syntax `string.endswith(suffix, start, end)`
		`>>>s = 'This is wow world.'`
		`>>>s.endswith ('world.')`
		`True`

find( )	It returns the lower index of the substring if it is found in the given string. If it is not found, then it returns –1.
	Syntax `string.find(substring, start, end)`
		`>>>s = 'This is wow world'`
		`>>>s.find ('wow')`
		`8`

index( )	This is same as find() method, but raises an exception if substring is not found.
	Syntax `string.index(substring, start, end)`
		`>>>s = 'This is world'`
		`>>>s.index ('is')`
		`2`

isalnum( )	Returns True if string has atleast 1 character and False otherwise.
	Syntax `string.isalnum()`
		`>>>s = 'python'`
		`>>>s.isalnum ()`
		`True`

isalpha( )	Returns True if string has atleast 1 character and all characters are alphabetic and False otherwise.
	Syntax `string.isalpha()`
		`>>>str = 'arihant'`
		`>>> str.isalpha()`
		`True`

isdigit( )	Returns True if string contains only digits and False otherwise.
	Syntax `string.isdigit()`
		`>>>s = 'abc123'`
		`>>>s.isdigit()`
		`False`

islower( )	Returns True if string has at least one case character and all case characters are in lowercase and False otherwise.
	Syntax `string.islower()`
		`>>>s = 'python'`
		`>>>s.islower()`
		`True`

Method	Description	Example

isupper( )	Returns True if string has atleast one case character and all case characters are in uppercase and False otherwise.
	Syntax `string.isupper()`
		`>>>s = 'Hello'`
		`>>>s.isupper()`
		`False`

isspace( )	Returns True if string contains only whitespace characters and False otherwise.
	Syntax `string.isspace()`
		`>>>s = ' '`
		`>>>s.isspace()`
		`True`

len( )	Returns the length of the string.
	Syntax `len(string)`
		`>>>s = 'Python Program'`
		`>>> l = len(s)`
		`>>> print(l)`
		`14`

lower( )	Converts all uppercase letters in string to lowercase.
	Syntax `string.lower()`
		`>>>s = 'Python'`
		`>>>s.lower()`
		`'python'`

upper( )	This method is used to convert lowercase letters in string to uppercase.
	Syntax `string.upper()`
		`>>>s = 'Hello'`
		`>>>s.upper()`
		`HELLO`

max( )	Returns the maximum alphabetical character from the string.
	Syntax `max(string)`
		`>>>s = 'This is wow world'`
		`>>>max(s)`
		`'w'`

min( )	Returns the minimum alphabetical character from the string.
	Syntax `min(string)`
		`>>>s = 'wonders of world'`
		`>>>min(s)`
		`' '`

Quick Test 1

1. Can we delete a slice from a string ? If yes, how?
2. Given S= "Aeroplane" .
   `print (S[ :: - 1]` gives :_______
3. Write the different parameters used in slicing, explaining each.
4. Write function names in the boxes to perform the following with the string given:
   S=akash123@gmail.com

To convert to uppercase	To count number of 'a' in S

5. Given a string `s="CBSE class XII examination 2025"` Write a statement to check whether the string has the word "cbse" in it.
6. What will the following code produce?
```
a="my school"
b="is best"
print(a+(b*3))
```
7. Explain the following string functions :
   (a) index()
   (b) isalnum()

2.5 Lists

In Python, list is an ordered sequence, which is used to store multiple data at the same time. List contains a sequence of heterogeneous elements which store integer, string as well as object.

It is also useful for implementing stacks and queues. Each element of a list is assigned a number to its position or index. The first index is 0 (zero), the second index is 1, the third index is 2 and so on.

Creating a List

In Python, lists can be created to put the elements separated by the comma (,) in square brackets [ ].

e.g. a =[34, 76, 11, 98]
b = ['s', 3, 6, 't']
c =[34, 0.5, 75]
d =[ ]

Creating List from an Existing Sequence

In Python, list ( ) method is used to create list from an existing sequence.

Syntax `new_list_name = list(sequence/string)`

You can also create an empty list.

e.g. `L=list( )`

Inputting Lists in a Program

By using eval() function

```
L=eval(input("Enter lis elements :"))
```

By using the append( ) function

```
list.append(element)
```

Accessing Lists

To access the list's elements, index number is used. Use the index operator [ ] to access the elements of a list. The index should be an integer.

Index 0 refers to first element, 1 refers to second element and so on. While the index of -1 refers to the last element, -2 refers to the second last element and so on.

e.g. `l1 = [5, 7, 3, 4, 5, 6, 9, 0, 8]`

It is called positive index

0	1	2	3	4	5	6	7	8
5	7	3	4	5	6	9	0	8
−9	−8	−7	−6	−5	−4	−3	−2	−1

It is called negative index

```
>>>l1 = [34, 87, 'Computer', 12, 'Python',
                        11, 76, 'Option']
>>>l1[0]
34
>>>l1[6]
76
>>>l1[-4]
'Python'
```

Traversing a List

Traversing a list is a technique to access an individual element of that list. It is also called iterate over a list. There are multiple ways to iterate over a list in Python. These are as follows

1. Using for loop

for loop is used when you want to traverse each element of a list.

Syntax

```
for variable in list_name:
    process each item
```

e.g.

```
a= ["S","C","I","E","N","C","E"]
for i in a :
print(i, end=" ")
```

Output S C I E N C E

2. Using 'for' loop with range ( )

There is another method to traverse a list using 'for' loop with range( ).

This is also used len( ) function with range. This method is used when you want to traverse particular characters in a list.

Syntax

```
for variable in range (len(list_name)):
    process each item
```

e.g.

```
a= ["S","C","I","E","N","C","E"]
for i in range(len(a)) :
print(a[i],end=" ")
```

Output S C I E N C E

2.6 Operations on Lists

We can perform various operations on list, some common list operations are described below:

Operator Name	Explanation	Example
Concatenation (+)	Combines two or more lists into a single list.	`list1 = [1, 2]; list2 = [3, 4]; print(list1 + list2)` → `[1, 2, 3, 4]`
Replication (*)	Repeats the elements of a list a specified number of times.	`list1 = [1, 2]; print(list1 * 3)` → `[1, 2, 1, 2, 1, 2]`

Comparison (==, !=, >, <, >=, <=)	Checks if two lists are equal by comparing elements at corresponding positions.	`list1 = [2, 4, 6]`
		`list2 = [1, 3, [2,3], 5]`
		`result = list1 <= list2`
		`print (result)` → `False`
		`list1 = [2, 4, 6]`
		`list2 = [1, 3, 6, 5]`
		`result = list1 != list2`
		`print (result)` → `True`

Membership (in)	Checks if an element exists within the list.	`list1 = [1, 2, 3]; print(2 in list1)` → `True`
Identity (is)	Checks if two lists refer to the same memory location.	`list1 = [1, 2]; list2 = list1; print(list1 is list2)` → `True`

2.7 List Slicing

List slicing refers to access a specific portion or a subset of the list for some operation while the original list remains unaffected.

To print a specific range of elements from the list, we use slice operation. Slice operation is performed on lists with the use of colon (:).

Syntax

```
s = list_name [start : end]
```

e.g.
```
>>>list1 = [4, 3, 7, 6, 4, 9, 5, 0, 3, 2]
>>>s = list1 [2 : 5]
>>>s
[7, 6, 4]
```

Lists are also provide slice steps which used to extract elements from list that are not consecutive.

Syntax

```
s = list_name  [start : stop : step]
```

It takes three parameters which are as follows

- **start** starting integer where slicing of the object starts.
- **stop** integer until which the slicing takes place. The slicing stops at index stop -1.
- **step** integer value which determines the increment between each index for slicing.

e.g.
```
>>>list1 = [4, 3, 7, 6, 4, 9, 5, 0, 3, 2]
>>>l1 = list1 [1 : 10 : 3]
>>>l1
[3, 4, 0]
```

List Manipulation

Updating Elements in a List

List can be modified after it created using slicing.

e.g.
```
>>>l1 = [2, 4, "Try", 54, "Again"]
>>>l1 [0 : 1] = [34, "Hello"]
>>>l1
[34, 'Hello', 4, 'Try', 54, 'Again']
>>>l1 [4] = ["World"]
>>>l1
[34, 'Hello', 4, 'Try', ['World'], 'Again']
>>>l1 [2] = "Hiiii"
>>>l1
[34, 'Hello', 'Hiiii', 'Try',
                        ['World'], 'Again']
```

Deleting Elements from a List

del keyword is used to delete the elements from the list.

Syntax

```
del list_name [index]  # to delete individual element
del list_name [start : stop]
                       # to delete elements in list slice
```

e.g.
```
>>> list1 = [2, 5, 4, 7, 7, 7, 8, 90]
>>> print (list1)
[2, 5, 4, 7, 7, 7, 8, 90]
>>> del list1 [3]
>>> list1
[2, 5, 4, 7, 7, 8, 90]
>>> del list1 [2 : 4]
>>> list1
[2, 5, 7, 8, 90]
```

2.8 Built-in Methods in Lists

Python includes the following built-in methods to manipulate lists

Function	Description	Example

append( )	Used for appending and adding elements to a list. It adds the elements to the last position of a list.
	Syntax `list_name.append (element)`
		`>>> l1 = [34, 56, 2]`
		`>>> l1.append(23)`
		`>>> l1`
		`[34, 56, 2, 23]`

insert( )	Used to insert an element at specified position in the list.
	Syntax `list_name.insert(index, element)`
		`>>>l1 = [34, 65, 23]`
		`>>>l1.insert (2, 'Hello')`
		`>>>l1`
		`[34, 65, 'Hello', 23]`

extend( )	Used to add contents of list 2 to the end of list 1.
	Syntax `list1_name.extend(list2_name)`
		`>>>l1 = [43, 'Hello']`
		`>>>l2 = ['Try', 22, 'W']`
		`>>>l1.extend(l2)`
		`>>>l1`
		`[43, 'Hello', 'Try', 22, 'W']`

Function	Description	Example

sum( )	Used to calculate the sum of all the elements in the list.
	Syntax `sum(list_name)`
		`>>>l = [45, 23, 87, 5, 9]`
		`>>> sum(l)`
		`169`

count( )	Used to calculate total occurrence of given elements of list.
	Syntax `list_name.count(element)`
		`>>>list1 = [4, 3, 2, 1, 1, 5]`
		`>>>list1.count(2)`
		`1`

len( )	Used to calculate the total length of list.
	Syntax `len(list_name)`
		`>>>list1 = [4, 3, 2, 1, 1, 5]`
		`>>>len(list1)`
		`6`

index( )	Returns the index of first occurrence
	Syntax `list_name.index(element)`
		`>>>list1 = [3, 'New', 2, 6]`
		`>>>list1.index ('New')`
		`1`

min( )	Used to return the minimum element out of elements of list.
	Syntax `min(list_name)`
		`>>>l1 = [45, 87, 23, 90, 12]`
		`>>>min(l1)`
		`12`

max( )	Used to return the maximum element out of elements of list.
	Syntax `max(list_name)`
		`>>>l1 = [34, 76, 89, 33, 54, 65]`
		`>>>max(l1)`
		`89`

pop( )	Used to remove the element and return last value fromt the list or the given index value.
	Syntax `list_name.pop(index)`
		`>>>l1 = [34, 65, 22, 90, 87, 61]`
		`>>>l1.pop(3)`
		`90`

remove( )	Searches for the given element in the list and removes the first matching element.
	Syntax `list_name.remove(element)`
		`>>>l1 =[34, 61, 'Hindi', 76]`
		`>>>l1.remove ('Hindi')`
		`>>>l1`
		`[34, 61, 76]`

clear( )	Used to remove all the items of a list. This method will empty the entire list.
	Syntax `list_name.clear()`
		`>>>l1 = [23, 45, 87, 12]`
		`>>>l1.clear()`
		`>>>l1`
		`[]`

sort( )	Used to sort the given list in ascending order.
	Syntax `list_name.sort()`
		`>>>l1 = [23, 65, 77, 23, 90, 99, 12]`
		`>>>l1.sort()`
		`>>>print(l1)`
		`[12, 23, 23, 65, 77, 90, 99]`

Quick Test 2

1. Create a list to store two strings, two marks and two Boolean values.
2. Which symbol is used to separate the elements in the list?
3. Write statements to display :
   (a) [50,45,60] (b) [75,60,20,45,30,50]
   (c) [75,20,30]
4. Write the differences between list and strings
5. Write a statement to input a list.
6. Write a code to input elements into a list and display each of its element and its square.
7. Can we delete a element from list?
8. Which parameter is used to increment the integer value in slicing?

2.9 Tuples

A tuple is an ordered sequence of elements of different data types, such as integer, float, string, list or even a tuple.

Tuple holds a sequence of heterogeneous elements, it store a fixed set of elements and do not allow changes.

Tuple *versus* List

- Elements of a tuple are immutable whereas elements of a list are mutable.
- Tuples are declared in parentheses ( ) while lists are declared in square brackets [ ].
- Iterating over the elements of a tuple is faster compared to iterating over a list.

Creating a Tuple

To create a tuple in Python, put all the elements in a parentheses ( ), separated by commas. We can have tuple of same type of data items as well as mixed type of data items.

e.g.
```
a = (34, 76, 12, 90)
b = ('s', 3, 6, 'a')
c = (34, 0.5, 75)
d = ()
```

Creating Tuple from an Existing Sequence

In Python, tuple( ) method is used to create a tuple from an existing sequence or string.

Syntax `new_tuple_name = tuple(sequence/string)`

Here, sequence includes list, string, tuple etc.

e.g.
```
>>>t="PROGRAM"
>>>t1=tuple(t)
>>>t1
('P', 'R', 'O', 'G', 'R', 'A', 'M')
```

or
```
>>>t=tuple("PROGRAM")
>>>t
('P', 'R', 'O', 'G', 'R', 'A', 'M')
>>>t1 = ['P', 'R', 'O', 'G', 'R', 'A', 'M']
>>>t2 = tuple(t1)
>>>t2
('P', 'R', 'O', 'G', 'R', 'A', 'M')
```

Nested Tuple

A tuple can contain sub-tuple which in turn can contain sub-tuples themselves and so on. This is known as nested tuple.

e.g.
```
>>>t=('Neha', 6, 9, (1, 4, 8), 'Rahul')
>>>print(t)
('Neha', 6, 9, (1, 4, 8), 'Rahul')
```

Mixed Data Types Tuple

It can be created to place different data types such as integers, strings, double etc, into one tuple.

e.g.
```
>>>t1=('Maths', 90, 89, 'English', 78.5)
>>>t1
('Maths', 90, 89, 'English', 78.5)
```

Accessing Tuples

To access the tuple's elements, index number is used. Use the index operator [ ], elements of a tuple can be accessed. The index should be an integer. Index of 0 refers to first element, 1 refers to second element and so on. While the index of -1 refers to the last element, -2 refers to the second last element and so on.

e.g.
```
t1 = (87, 90, 'Maths', 'English', 56, 44,
      99, 'Science', 23)
```

It is called positive index ↑

0	1	2	3	4	5	6	7	8
87	90	'Maths'	'English'	56	44	99	'Science'	23
−9	−8	−7	−6	−5	−4	−3	−2	−1

↓ It is called negative index

```
>>>t1[1]
90
>>>t1[- 2]
'Science'
>>>t1[7]
'Science'
>>>t1[4]
56
>>>t1[-3]
99
```

Traversing a Tuple

Traversing a tuple is a technique to access an individual element of that tuple. It is also called iterate over a tuple. There are multiple ways to iterate over a tuple in Python. These are as follows:

1. Using 'for' loop

This method is used when you want to iterate all elements of a tuple.

Syntax
```
for variable in tuple_name :
    process each item
```

e.g.
```
t="Monalisa"
for i  in  t:
    print(i,end=" ")
```

Output

M o n a l i s a

2. Using 'for' loop with range ( )

This method is used when you want to iterate specified elements of a tuple. This is also used len() function with range.

Syntax
```
for variable in range(len(tuple_name)):
    process each item
```

e.g.
```
t="Christmas"
for i in range(len(t)):
    print(i,end=" ")
```

Output

C h r i s t m a s

2.10 Operations on Tuples

We can perform various operations on tuple. Some common tuple operations are described below:

Operator Name	Explanation	Example
Concatenation (+)	Combines two tuples into one.	`tuple1 = (1, 2); tuple2 = (3, 4);` `print( tuple1 + tuple2) → (1, 2, 3, 4)`
Replication (*)	Repeats the elements of a tuple a specified number of times.	`tuple1 = (1, 2);` `print(tuple1 * 2) → (1, 2, 1, 2)`

Comparison (==, !=, >, <, >=, <=)	Compares two tuples element by element. Returns True or False.	`tuple1 = (2, 4, 6)`
		`tuple2 = (1, 3, 5)`
		`result = tuple1!= tuple2`
		`print (result) → True`
		`tuple1 = (2, 4, 6)`
		`tuple2 = (4, 2, 6)`
		`result = tuple1 >= tuple2`
		`print (result) → False`

Membership (in, not in)	Checks if an element exists within a tuple.	`tuple1 = (1, 2, 3);` `print(2 in tuple1) → True`
Identity (is, is not)	Checks if two variables refer to the same object in memory.	`tuple1 = (1, 2); tuple2 = tuple1; print( tuple1 is tuple2 )` `→ True`

Note *Comparison Operator can not compare nested tuples, it gives TypeError [TypeError: '<=' not supported between instances of 'tuple' and 'int']*

2.11 Tuple Slicing

Tuple slicing refers to access a specific portion or a subset of the tuple for some operation, while the original tuple remains unaffected. To display a specific range of elements from the tuple, we use slicing operation. This operation is performed on tuples with the use of colon (:).

Syntax `tuple_name[start : end]`

e.g.
```
>>>tuple1=(4, 7, 3, "This", 6, "That",
"These", 8, 9, "Those")
>>>t1=tuple1 [3:6]
>>>t1
('This', 6, 'That')
```

To display elements from beginning to a range use [: index], to display elements from end use [:-index] and to display elements from specific index till the end use [index :]

e.g.
```
>>>tuple1=(4, 7, 3, "This", 6,
            "That","These", 8,9,"Those")
>>>t2=tuple1[:6]
>>>t2
(4, 7, 3, 'This', 6, 'That')
>>>t3=tuple1[:-4]
>>>t3
(4, 7, 3, 'This', 6, 'That')
```

We can also print all elements of tuple in reverse order using [::-1]

```
>>>t=tuple1[::-1]
>>>t
('Those', 9, 8, 'These', 'That', 6,
                          'This', 3, 7, 4)
>>>t=tuple1[2:-4]
>>>t
(3, 'This', 6, 'That')
```

Tuples are also provide slice steps which used to extract elements from tuple that are not consecutive.

Syntax `t=tuple_name [start : end : step ]`

Here,

- **start** integer where the slicing of the object starts.
- **stop** integer until which the slicing takes place. The slicing stops at index stop-1.
- **step** integer value which determines the increment between each index for slicing.

e.g.
```
>>>t=(5, 3, "He","She", (4, 3, "It"), 3,
                          "They", 8,9 "We")
>>>t1=t[2:8:2]
>>>t1
('He', (4, 3, 'It'), 'They')
```

Packing and Unpacking Tuples

In Python, tuples are collection of elements which are separated by commas. It packs elements or value together so, this is called **packing**. In other way, it is called **unpacking** of a tuple of values into a variable. In packing, we put values together into a new tuple while in unpacking we extract those values into a single variables.

Syntax `variable1, variable 2, ....., variable N = tuple_name`

e.g. `>>>tuple1=(34, "Hello", 54, 89, "world")`

To unpack the tuple, take variables equivalent to number of elements in that tuple and write this

```
>>>a, b, c, d, e = tuple1
```

Now, print individual variable which displays the element of tuple.

```
>>>print(a)
34
>>> print(d)
89
```

2.12 Built-in Methods in Tuples

Python includes the following built in methods of tuple:

Function	Description	Example

len( )	Used to count the number of elements that present in the tuple.
	Syntax `len(tuple_name)`
		`>>>t1 = (45, 'Hello', 67, 45, 2)`
		`>>>len(t1)`
		`5`

count( )	Used to calculate total occurrence of given element of tuple.
	Syntax `tuple_name.count(element)`
		`>>>t1 = (10, 20, 30, 40, 50, 60)`
		`>>>t1.count(20)`
		`1`

any( )	Returns True if atleast one element is present in the tuple, otherwise returns False.
	Syntax `any(tuple_name)`
		`>>>t1 = (3, 5, 4)`
		`>>>any(t1)`
		`True`

max( )	Used to return the element with maximum value out of elements in tuple.
	Syntax `max(tuple_name)`
		`>>>t1 = (34, 65, 89, 17, 70)`
		`>>>max(t1)`
		`89`

min( )	Used to return the element with minimum value out of elements in tuple.
	Syntax `min(tuple_name)`
		`>>>t1 = (34, 65, 89, 17, 70)`
		`>>>min(t1)`
		`17`

sorted( )	Used to sort the given tuple in ascending order. But this method returns the elements in square brackets.
	Syntax `sorted(tuple_name)`
		`>>>t = (32, 45, 25, 33, 55, 89)`
		`>>>sorted(t)`
		`[25, 32, 33, 45, 55, 89]`

index( )	Returns the index of first occurrence of element in the tuple.
	Syntax `tuple_name.index(element)`
		`>>>t = (45, 89, 9, 'The', 23, 25)`
		`>>>t.index('The')`
		`3`

tuple( )	Used to convert string and list into tuple.
	Syntax `tuple(list/string)`
		`>>>name = "RIYA"`
		`>>>tuple (name)`
		`('R', 'I', 'Y', 'A')`

sum( )	Used to calculate the sum of elements of tuple. The elements of tuple must be integer.
	Syntax `sum(tuple_name)`
		`>>>marks = (78, 98, 80, 65, 75, 80)`
		`>>>sum(marks)`
		`476`

reversed( )	Allows us to process the items in a sequence in reverse order.
	Syntax `iterator = reversed(sequence)`
		`>>>marks = (23, 45, 36, 50, 49)`
		`>>>t = reversed (marks)`
		`>>>for i in t:`
		`    print(t)`
		Output
		49
		50
		36
		45
		23

Quick Test 3

1. x, y, z,w,q = (34,56,True,"Rashmi",98.9).
   What is happening in given line of code ?
2. Given t=(10,20,30,40,55,70,80).
   Write a statement to print : (10,30 , 55).
3. Which of the following statements is incorrect?
   (a) T=(5,)
   (b) T=tuple([23,45,56,78])
   (c) Given : T= (1,12,23,45,56) , T[3]=100
4. Write the uses of following functions on a tuple :
   (a) sorted( )
   (b) index( )

2.13 Dictionary

In Python, dictionary is an unordered collection of data values that store the key : value pair instead of single value as an element.

Keys of a dictionary must be unique and of immutable data types such as strings, tuples etc.

Dictionaries are also called **mappings** or **hashes** or **associative arrays**.

Create a Dictionary

Syntax

```
dictionary_name = {key1 : value1,
                   key2 : value2, …}
```

Each key is separated from its value by a colon (:) while each element is separated by commas.

In which, key will be a single element and values can be a list or list within a list, numbers etc.

e.g.
```
>>>Employees = {"Abhi" : "Manger", "Manish"
: "Project Manager", "Aasha" : "Analyst",
"Deepak" : "Programmer", "Ishika" :
"Tester"}
>>>Employees
```

Output

{'Abhi': 'Manager', 'Manish' : 'Project Manager',

'Aasha' : 'Analyst', 'Deepak' : 'Programmer', 'Ishika' : 'Tester'}

Here is the example of a dictionary named Employees in which Employee names are stored as keys and designation stored as values of respected keys.

We can separate these dictionaries as follows:

Key : Value Pair	Key	Value
"Abhi" : "Manager"	"Abhi"	"Manager"
"Manish" : "Project Manager"	"Manish"	"Project Manager"
"Aasha" : "Analyst"	"Aasha"	"Analyst"
"Deepak" : "Programmer"	"Deepak"	"Programmer"
"Ishika" : "Tester"	"Ishika"	"Tester"

We can also create empty dictionary

e.g. `dict1 = {}`

Accessing elements from a Dictionary

In Python, to access the elements from a dictionary, keys are used.

Syntax `dictionary_name [key]`

To access the respective value of key, that key has to be given in square bracket with dictionary name.

e.g.
```
>>>print(Employees["Abhi"])
   Manager
>>>print(Employees["Ishika"])
   "Tester"
```

Traversing a Dictionary

Traversing a dictionary means access each and every element of it. We can traverse a dictionary using for loop.

e.g.
```
dic = {1 : "Math", 2 : "Science", 3 :
  "English", 4 : "Music"}
```

There are multiple ways to iterate over (traversing) a dictionary in Python as follows:

Traversing through the keys	for a in dic : print (a, end="")	1 2 3 4
Traversing through the values	for a in dic : print(dic[a], end="")	Math Science English Music
Traversing through the keys and values	for a in dic : print(a, ':', dic[a])	1 : Math 2 : Science 3 : English 4 : Music

Add Elements to Dictionary

In dictionary, adding of elements extend it with single pair of values. One value at a time can be added to a dictionary by defining value along with the key.

Syntax `dictionary_name[Key] = value`

e.g.
```
>>>Teacher = {'Neha' : 'Hindi', 'Akshay' :
  'Math', 'Parul' : 'English'}
>>>Teacher ['Nisha'] = 'Computer'
```

```
>>>Teacher
{'Akshay' : 'Math', 'Nisha' : 'Computer',
'Neha' : 'Hindi', 'Parul' : 'English'}
```

Updating Elements in a Dictionary

You can update elements that are already exist in a dictionary.

Syntax `dictionary_name [key] = value`

e.g.
```
>>>Student = {11 : 'Ashi', 12 : 'Shivam',
              13 : 'Shrey', 14 : 'Vicky'}
>>>Student [12] = 'Nishant'
>>>Student
{11 : 'Ashi', 12 : 'Nishant', 13 : 'Shrey',
                               14 : 'Vicky'}
```

Deletion from a Dictionary

There are following ways to delete elements from a dictionary as follows

1. Using del Keyword

del keyword is used to delete the key that is present in the dictionary.

Syntax `del dictionary_name [key]`

e.g.
```
>>>Teacher = {"Name" : "Ashi", "Subject":
"Math", "Id" : 2546, "Salary": 25000}
>>>Teacher
{'Subject': 'Math', 'Name': 'Ashi',
              'Salary' : 25000, 'Id' : 2456}
>>>del Teacher ['Id']
>>>Teacher
{'Subject' : 'Math', 'Name' : 'Ashi',
                          'Salary' : 25000}
```

2. Using pop() method

This method is used to delete key and respective value from dictionary.

Syntax `dictionary_name.pop (key)`

e.g.
```
>>>Teacher = {'Name' : 'Ashi', 'Subject' :
     'Math', 'Id' : 2546, 'Salary' : 25000}
>>>Teacher
{'Subject' : 'Math', 'Name' : 'Ashi',
              'Salary' : 25000, 'Id' : 2546}
>>>Teacher.pop ('Id')
2546
>>>Teacher
{'Subject' : 'Math', 'Name' : 'Ashi',
                          'Salary' : 25000}
```

2.14 Built-in Methods in Dictionary

Some built-in methods of dictionary are

Function	Description	Example

len( )	Used to return the total length of the dictionary.
	Syntax `len(dictionary_name)`
		`>>>dic1 = {1 : 'One', 2 : 'Two', 3 : 'Three'}`
		`>>>len(dic1)`
		`3`

clear( )	Used to remove the elements of the dictionary. It produces an empty dictionary.
	Syntax `dictionary_name.clear()`
		`>>>dic1 = {1 : 'One', 2 : 'Two', 3 : 'Three', 4 :'Four'}`
		`>>>dic1.clear()`
		`>>>dic1`
		`{}`

get( )	Returns the value for the given key, if present in the dictionary.
	Syntax `dictionary_name.get (key[, value])`
		`>>>S = {'Name' : 'Riya', 'Rollno' : 23, 'Class' : 12}`
		`>>>S.get('Rollno')`
		`23`

items( )	Returns a view object that displays a list of dictionary's (key, value) tuple pairs.
	Syntax `dictionary_name.items()`
		`>>>dic1 = {1 : 'One', 2 : 'Two', 3 : 'Three', 4 : 'Four'}`
		`>>>print(dic1.items())`
		`dict_items([(1, 'One'), (2, 'Two'), (3, 'Three'), (4, 'Four')])`

keys( )	Returns a view object that displays a list of all the keys in the dictionary.
	Syntax `dictionary_name.keys()`
		`>>>dic1 = {1 : 'One', 2 : 'Two', 3 : 'Three', 4 : 'Four'}`
		`>>>print(dic1.keys())`
		`dict_keys ([1, 2, 3, 4])`

Function	Description	Example

values( )	Returns a view object that displays a list of all the values in the dictionary.
	Syntax `dictionary_name.values()`
		`>>>dic1 = {1 : 'One', 2 : 'Two', 3 : 'Three', 4 : 'Four'}`
		`>>>print(dic1.values())`
		`dict_values(['One', 'Two', 'Three', 'Four'])`

update( )	Updates the dictionary with the elements from the another dictionary object or from an iterable of key/value pairs.
	Syntax
	`dictionary_name1.update(dictionary_name2)`
		`>>>dic1 = {1 : 'One', 2 : 'Two', 3 : 'Three', 4 : 'Four'}`
		`>>>dic2 = {1 : 'Once', 5 : 'Five'}`
		`>>>dic1.update(dic2)`
		`>>>print(dic1)`
		`{1 : 'One', 2 : 'Two', 3 : 'Three', 4 : 'Four', 5 : 'Five'}`

sorted( )	Returns a sorted sequence of the keys in the dictionary.
	Syntax `sorted(dictionary_name)`
		`>>>dic1 = {1 : 'One', 2 : 'Two', 3 : 'Three', 4 : 'Four'}`
		`>>>sorted(dic1)`
		`[1, 2, 3, 4]`

Quick Test 4

1. Write the appropriate function names in the boxes provided.

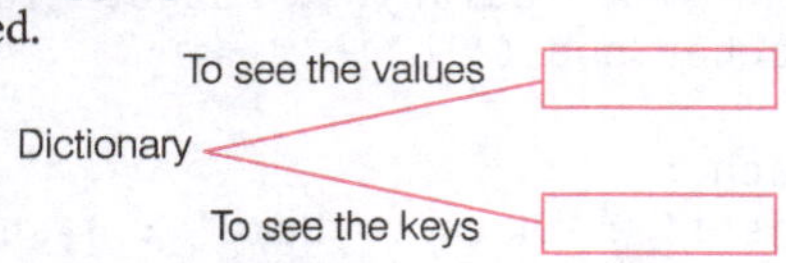

2. Write the use of update function for a dictionary.
3. The method that displays both the keys and values of a dictionary is ....
4. The .... function returns the value against a key.
5. Write two differences between a dictionary and a list.
6. Give output:

```
>>> dic1 = {1 : 'A', 2 : 'B', 3 : 'C'}
>>> dic1.get(2)
```

2.15 Module

A Python module is a file containing Python code (functions, classes, or variables) saved with the extension .py. Modules help organize code logically and contain runnable code.

Structure of a Module

- Docstring: Documentation enclosed in triple quotes.
- Variables: Labels for data in the program.
- Classes: Templates for creating objects.
- Objects: Instances of classes (data + methods).
- Statements: Logical instructions executable by the Python interpreter.
- Functions: Blocks of code performing specific tasks.

Importing Modules

Modules can be imported to use their functions or objects in a program.

1. **Import Entire Module**

```
import module_name
module_name.function_name
```

e.g.
```
import math
print(math.sqrt(16))  # Output: 4.0
```

2. **Import Specific Objects**

```
from module_name import object_name
```

e.g.
```
from math import sqrt
print(sqrt(16))  # Output: 4.0
```

3. **Import Multiple Objects**

```
from module_name import object1, object2
```

e.g.
```
from math import sqrt, pi
```

4. **Import All Objects**

```
from module_name import *
```

Processing of Import Statements

import module_name

- Executes and interprets the module's code.
- Sets up a new namespace for the module's objects.

from module_name import object_name

- Executes and interprets the module's code.
- Adds only the specified objects to the current namespace.

Math Module in Python

Math Module is an in-built Python library made to simplify mathematical tasks in Python.

It consists of various mathematical constants and functions that can be used after importing the math module. The list of all mathematical functions in math module, you can use them when you need it in program:

Function	Description	Syntax	Example

sqrt()	Returns the square root of a number.	`math.sqrt(x)`	`import math`
			`result = math.sqrt(16)`
			`print(result)`
			Output 4.0

pow()	Returns x raised to the power y. Optionally, computes modulus (x^y % z).	`pow(x, y) or pow(x, y, z)`	`import math`
			`result = pow(2, 3)`
			`print(result)`
			Output 8
			`result = pow(2, 3, 5)`
			`print(result)`
			Output 3

fabs()	Returns the absolute value of a number (always a float).	`math.fabs(x)`	`import math`
			`result = math.fabs(-3.5)`
			`print(result)`
			Output 3.5

ceil()	Returns the smallest integer greater than or equal to a given number.	`math.ceil(x)`	`import math`
			`result = math.ceil(4.2)`
			`print(result)`
			Output 5

floor()	Returns the largest integer less than or equal to a given number.	`math.floor(x)`	`import math`
			`result = math.floor(4.8)`
			`print(result)`
			Output 4

Random Functions

There are different random functions in the Random Module of Python. Look at the table below to learn more about these functions:

Function	Description	Syntax	Example

randrange()	Returns a randomly selected element from a range. It can specify a start, stop, and step.	`random.randrange(start, stop, step)`	`import random`
			`result = random.randrange (1, 10, 2)`
			`print(result)`

randint()	Returns a random integer within a specified range (inclusive).	`random.randint(a, b)`	`import random`
			`result = random.randint(1, 10)`
			`print(result)`

random()	Returns a random float number between 0 and 1.	`random.random()`	`import random`
			`result = random.random()`
			`print(result)`

choice()	Returns a randomly selected element from a non-empty sequence (e.g., list, tuple).	`random.choice(sequence)`	`import random`
			`result = random.choice([1, 2, 3, 4, 5])`
			`print(result)`

choices()	Returns a list of randomly selected elements from a sequence, with optional weights and number of selections.	`random.choices (sequence, weights=None, k=1)`	`import random`
			`result = random.choices([1, 2, 3, 4, 5], k=3)`
			`print(result)`

2.16 Errors

An error is a flaw, fault, or failure in a computer program that causes it to produce an incorrect or unexpected result or behave in unintended ways.

Most bugs arise from mistakes and errors made by people in:

- The program's source code
- Its design
- Frameworks and environments used by the program

Types of Errors

1. **Compile-Time Errors** Detected and displayed by the compiler or interpreter during the compilation phase. There are two types of compile time errors
   (i) **Syntax Errors** Violations of the programming language's grammar rules.
   e.g.
   - Missing keywords (e.g., if, for)
   - Incorrect placement of keywords
   - Missing symbols (e.g., colons, commas, brackets)
   - Misspelled keywords
   - Incorrect indentation
   - Empty blocks

   (ii) **Semantic Errors** Statements that are grammatically correct but lack meaning within the program's logic.
   e.g.
   - Using an uninitialized variable
   - Errors in mathematical expressions
   - Unknown references
   - Type incompatibility (e.g., trying to add a number to a string)
2. **Run-Time Errors** Occur while the program is running, even after successful compilation.
   e.g.
   - Division by zero
   - Operations on incompatible data types
   - Using undefined identifiers
   - Accessing non-existent list elements, dictionary values, or object attributes
   - Trying to access a non-existent file
3. **Logical Errors** The program runs without errors but produces incorrect output.
   Programming mistakes like
   - Using the wrong variable name
   - Incorrect indentation levels
   - Incorrect operator precedence
   - Mistakes in boolean expressions

2.17 Exceptions

An exception is an abnormal situation that can occur in a program.

A situation that was not predicted earlier and made the program to behave abnormally producing abnormal outputs.

Exception Handling

The act of writing code in such a manner that, even if an exception occurs, the program does not abnormally terminate, is called exception handling.

Whenever we try to read a file or get input from a user, there is a chance that something unexpected will happen as the file may have been moved or deleted and the user may enter data which is not in the right format.

Such situations can be handled by exception handling.

Syntax

```
try :
   {Run this code}
except:
   {Run this code if an exception occurs}
```

e.g.

```
try:
   age = int (input ("Please enter your
                                     age: "))
   print (" I see that you are % d years
                             old. " % age)
except:
   print (" Hey, that was not a number !!")
```

Python will try to process all the statements inside the try block.

If an ErrorValue occurs at any point as it is executing them, the flow of control will immediately pass to the except block and any remaining statements in the try block will be skipped.

Python Built-in Exceptions

Python provides some basic exception classes which are already defined and can be used in generic cases.

Exception Class	Event
Exception	Base class for all exceptions.
ArithmeticError	Raised when numeric calculations fails.
AssertionError	Raised when Assert statement fails.
FloatingPointError	Raised when a floating point calculation fails.
ImportError	Raised when the imported module is not found.
IndexError	Raised when index of a sequence is out of range.
IndentationError	Raised when there is incorrect indentation.
IOError	Raised when an input / output operation fails.
KeyboardInterrupt	Raised when the user interrupts program execution, generally by pressing Ctrl + C.
KeyError	Raised when the specified key is not found in the dictionary.
OverflowError	Raised when result of an arithmetic operation is too large to be represented.
NameError	Raised when an identifier is not found in the local or global namespace.
RuntimeError	Raised when a generated error does not fall into any category.
SyntaxError	Raised by parser when syntax error is encountered.
TypeError	Raised when a function or an operation is applied to an object of incorrect type.
ValueError	Raised when a function gets argument of correct type but improper value.
ZeroDivisionError	Raised when division or module by zero takes place for all numeric types.
StopIteration	Raised when the next ( ) method of an iterator does not point to any object.
AttributeError	Raised in case of failure of attribute reference or assignment.
EOFError	Raised when there is no input from either raw_input ( ) or input ( ) function and the end of file is reached.

The finally block

finally block can use with the try block in which, it can move the important code which must be executed before the try statement throws an exception.

Syntax

```
try:
   # block of code
   # this may throw an exception
finally:
   # block of code
   # this will always be executed
```

Quick Test 5

1. What is debugging?
2. When are bugs arise in the program?
3. Give one difference between syntax error and semantic error.
4. Where is finally block used?
5. What is the use of break point()?

Mind Map

PYTHON REVISION TOUR II

Lists
It contains a sequence of heterogeneous elements which store integer, string as well as object.

Built-in Methods

Function	Syntax
append( )	list_name.append (element)
insert( )	list_name.insert(index, element)
extend( )	list1_name.extend(list2_name)
sum( )	sum(list_name)
count( )	list_name.count(element)
len( )	len(list_name)
index( )	list_name.index(element)
min( )	min(list_name)
max( )	max(list_name)
pop( )	list_name.pop(index)
remove( )	list_name.remove(element)
clear( )	list_name.clear()
sort( )	list_name.sort()

List Manipulation

Updating Elements in a List

Syntax

L[index]=<new value>

Deleting Elements from a List

Syntax

del list_name [index]

Or

del list_name [start : stop]

Dictionary
Unordered collection of data values that store the key : valuepair instead of single value as an element.

Built-in Methods

Function	Description
len( )	len(dictionary_name)
clear( )	dictionary_name.clear()
get( )	dictionary_name.get (key[, value])
items( )	dictionary_name.items()
keys( )	dictionary_name.keys()
values( )	dictionary_name.values()
update( )	dictionary_name1.update(dictionary_name2)
sorted( )	sorted(dictionary_name)

Dictionary Manipulation

Add Elements to Dictionary

Syntax dictionary_name[Key] = value

Updating Elements in a Dictionary

Syntax dictionary_name [key] = value

Deletion from a Dictionary

Using del Keyword

Syntax

del dictionary_name [key]

Using pop() method

Syntax

dictionary_name.pop (key)

Strings
A sequence of characters is called string.

Built-in Methods

Method	Syntax
capitalize( )	string.capitalize()
center( )	string.center (length [,fillchar])
count( )	string.count(substring, start, end)
endswith( )	string.endswith(suffix, start, end)
find( )	string.find(substring, start, end)
index( )	string.index(substring, start, end)
isalnum( )	string.isalnum()
isalpha( )	string.isalpha()
isdigit( )	string.isdigit()
islower( )	string.islower()
isupper( )	string.isupper()
isspace( )	string.isspace()
len( )	len(string)
lower( )	string.lower()
upper( )	string.upper()
max( )	max(string)
min( )	min(string)

Errors
Errors are problems in a program that causes the program to stop its execution. **Types**– Compile-Time Errors, Run-Time Errors, Logical Errors

Tuples
Sequence of elements of different data types, such as integer, float, string, list or even a tuple.

Built-in Methods

Function	Description
len( )	len(tuple_name)
count( )	tuple_name.count(element)
any( )	any(tuple_name)
max( )	max(tuple_name)
min( )	min(tuple_name)
sorted( )	sorted(tuple_name)
index( )	tuple_name.index(element)
tuple( )	tuple(list/string)
sum( )	sum(tuple_name)
reversed( )	iterator = reversed(sequence)

Note *Packing tuple is the process of assigning multiple objects to a tuple while unpacking tuple is the process of extracting the values from a tuple and assigning them to variables.*

Module
A Python module is a file containing Python code (functions, classes, or variables) saved with the extension .py.

Math Module Math Module is an in-built Python library made to simplify mathematical tasks.

Function	Syntax
sqrt()	math.sqrt(x)
pow()	pow(x, y) or pow(x, y, z)
fabs()	math.fabs(x)
ceil()	math.ceil(x)
floor()	math.floor(x)

Random Module To perform random actions such as generating random numbers, printing random a value for a list or string, etc.

Function	Syntax
randrange()	random.randrange(start,stop,step)
randint()	random.randint(a, b)
random()	random.random()
choice()	random.choice(sequence)
choices()	random.choices (sequence, weights=None, k=1)

Exceptions
An exception is an abnormal situation that can occur in a program.

File Handling Way of handling abnormals situations in a program-run, is known as exception handling.

Python built-in exceptions The built-in exception can be generated by the interpreter or built-in functions. Some built-in exceptions are EOFError, IOError, NameError, IndexError, TypeError etc.

finally block It always executes after normal termination of try block or after block terminates due to some exception.

Traversing It is a technique to iterate the elements/characters of the string/list/tuples. There are various ways to iterate over string/list/tuples

(i) 'for' loop (ii) 'for' loop with range

IMPORTANT POINT **Slicing** In Python, slicing is a way to get specific parts of a string/list/tuples by using start, end and step values.

Syntax of string slicing Substring = s[start : end : step]

Syntax of list slicing list_name [start : end : step]

Syntax of tuple slicing tuple [start : end : step]

Operations We can perform various operations on different sequence (string/list/tuple)

e.g. Concatenation(+), Replication(*), Comparison (==, !=, <, >, >=, < =), membership (in, not in), identity(is, is not).

EXAM PATTERN QUESTIONS

Objective Type Questions

Multiple Choice Questions

1. Consider the statements given below and then choose the correct output from the given options. CBSE SQP 2023-24

```
pride="#G20 Presidency"
print(pride[-2:2:-2])
```

(a) ndsr (b) ceieP0
(c) ceieP (d) yndsr

2. Consider the statements given below and then choose the correct output from the given options : CBSE 2024

```
myStr = "MISSISSIPPI"
print(myStr[ : 4] + "#"+ myStr[-5 : ] )
```

(a) MISSI#SIPPI (b) MISS#SIPPI
(c) MISS#IPPIS (d) MISSI#IPPIS

3. Select the correct output of the code. CBSE 2023

```
S= "Amrit Mahotsav @ 75"
A=S.partition (" ")
print(A)
```

(a) ('Amrit Mahotsav', '@', '75')
(b) ['Amrit','Mahotsav', '@', '75']
(c) ('Amrit', 'Mahotsav @ 75')
(d) ('Amrit', ' ', 'Mahotsav @ 75')

4. Which of the following statement(s) would give an error after executing the following code? CBSE SQP 2022-23

```
S="Welcome to class XII"    # Statement 1
print(S)                    # Statement 2
S="Thank you"               # Statement 3
S[0]='@'                    # Statement 4
S=S+"Thank you"             # Statement 5
```

(a) Statement 3
(b) Statement 4
(c) Statement 5
(d) Statement 4 and 5

5. For a given declaration in Python as s= "WELCOME" Which of the following will be the correct output of print (S [1 : : 2])? CBSE 2021-22 Term I

(a) WEL (b) COME
(c) WLOE (d) ECM

6. Given the Python declaration S1 = "Hello". Which of the following statement will give an error? CBSE 2021-22 Term I

(a) print (S1 [4]) (b) S2=S1
(c) S1 =S1[4] (d) S1[4]="Y"

7. Which of the following is not a valid Python string operation? CBSE 2021-22 Term I

(a) 'Welcome' + '10' (b) 'Welcome' * 10
(c) 'Welcome' * 10.0 (d) "10" + 'Welcome'

8. Select the correct output of the code. CBSE SQP 2023-24

```
s = "Python is fun"
l = s.split()
s_new = "-".join([l[0].upper(), l[1],
l[2].capitalize()])
print (s_new)
```

(a) PYTHON-IS-Fun (b) PYTHON-is-Fun
(c) Python-is-fun (d) PYTHON-Is -Fun

9. Identify the output of the following Python statement. CBSE 2021-22 Term I

```
S = "GOOD MORNING"
print(S.capitalize() ,S.title() ,end="!")
```

(a) GOOD MORNING! Good morning
(b) Good Morning!Good morning
(c) Good morning! Good Morning!
(d) Good morning Good Morning!

10. Identify the output of the following code snippet: CBSE SQP 2024-25

```
text = "PYTHONPROGRAM"
text=text.replace('PY','#')
print(text)
```

(a) #THONPROGRAM (b) ##THON#ROGRAM
(c) #THON#ROGRAM (d) #YTHON#ROGRAM

11. What is the output of the expression? CBSE SQP 2024-25

```
str='International'
Page: 2/10
print(str.split("n"))
```

(a) ('I', 'ter', 'atio', 'al')
(b) ['I', 'ter', 'atio', 'al']
(c) ['I', 'n', 'ter', 'n', 'atio', 'n', 'al']
(d) Error

12. **Select the correct output of the code:**

```
a = "Year 2022 at All the best"
a = a . split ('2')
b = a [0] + " ." + a [1] + " . " + a [3]
print (b)
```

(a) Year . 0. at All the best
(b) Year 0. at All the best
(c) Year . 022. at All the best
(d) Year . 0. at all the best

13. **Select the correct output of the following code :** CBSE 2024

```
event = "G20 Presidency@2023"
L = event. split ( ' ' )
print (L [ : : -2 ])
```

(a) 'G20' (b) ['Presidency@2023']
(c) ['G20'] (d) 'Presidency@2023'

14. **Identify the statement from the following which will raise an error.** CBSE 2024

(a) print ("A" *3) (b) print (5*3)
(c) print ("15" + 3) (d) print ("15" + "13")

15. **Find the output of the following code:**

```
Name="PythoN3@1"
R=" "
for x in range(len(Name)):
    if Name[x].isupper():
        R=R+Name[x].lower()
    elif Name[x].islower():
        R=R+Name[x].upper()
    elif Name[x].isdigit():
        R=R+Name[x-1]
    else:
        R=R+"#"
        print(R)
```

(a) pYTHOn##@ (b) pYTHOnN3#
(c) pYTHOn#3 (d) pYTHOnN3@

16. **What will be the output for the following Python statement?** CBSE 2021-22 Term I

```
L = [10, 20, 30, 40, 50]
L = L + 5
print(L)
```

(a) [10, 20, 30, 40, 50, 5] (b) [15, 25, 35, 45, 55]
(c) [5, 10, 20, 30, 40, 50] (d) Error

17. **Identify the output of the following Python statement.** CBSE SQP 2021-22 Term I

```
x = [[10.0, 11.0, 12.0],[13.0, 14.0, 15.0]]
y = x[1][2]
print(y)
```

(a) 11.0 (b) 12.0
(c) 14.0 (d) 15.0

18. **Consider the statements given below and then choose the correct output from the given options:** CBSE 2025

```
L=['TIC', 'TAC']
print(L[::-1])
```

(a) ['CIT', 'CAT'] (b) ['TIC', 'TAC']
(c) ['CAT', 'CIT'] (d) ['TAC', 'TIC']

19. **Which function returns the sum of all elements of a list?** CBSE 2023

(a) count () (b) sum () (c) total () (d) add ()

20. **Identify the output of the following Python statement.** CBSE 2021-22 Term I

```
L = [ ]
for i in range (4):
        L. append (2*i+1)
print (L[: :-1])
```

(a) [7,5,3,1] (b) [9, 7, 5, 3] (c) [4,3,2,1] (d) [1,2,3,4]

21. **Identify the output of the following Python statement.** CBSE 2021-22 Term I

```
L1, L2 = [10,15, 20, 25], [ ]
for i in range(len(L1)) :
        L2. insert ( i, L1 . pop( ))
print (L1, L2,sep="&")
```

(a) [ ] &[25, 20, 15, 10]
(b) [10,15,20, 25]&[25, 20, 15, 10]
(c) [10, 15, 20, 25]&[10, 15, 20, 25]
(d) [25, 20, 15, 10]&[ ]

22. **Which of the following option can be the output for the following Python code?** CBSE 2021-22 Term I

```
L1 = [10, 20, 30, 20, 10]
L2 = [ ]
for i in L1:
        if i not in L2:
            L2.append(i)
print (L1, L2, sep="&")
```

(a) [10, 20, 30, 20, 10] & [10, 20, 30, 20,10]
(b) [10, 20, 30, 20, 10] [10, 20, 30, 20, 10] &
(c) [10, 20, 30, 20, 10] & [30, 20, 10]
(d) [10, 20, 30, 20, 10] & [10, 20, 30]

23. **What will be the output of the following Python code?** CBSE 2021-22 Term I

```
L = [10 , 20]
L1=[30, 40]
L2=[50, 60]
L. append (L1)
L.extend(L2)
print(L)
```

(a) [60, 50, 40, 30, 20, 10] (b) [10,20,30, 40, 50, 60]
(c) [10, 20, 30, 40, [50, 60]] (d) [10, 20, [30, 40], 50, 60]

24. **Identify the output of the following Python statement.** CBSE SQP 2021 Term I

```
lst1 = [10, 15, 20, 25, 30]
lst1.insert( 3, 4)
lst1.insert( 2, 3)
print (lst1[-5])
```

(a) 2 (b) 3
(c) 4 (d) 20

25. **What does the list.remove(x) method do in Python?** CBSE SQP 2024-25

(a) Removes the element at index x from the list
(b) Removes the first occurrence of value x from the list
(c) Removes all occurrences of value x from the list
(d) Removes the last occurrence of value x from the list

26. **What will be the output of the following code?** CBSE SQP 2024-25

```
tuple1 = (1, 2, 3)
tuple2 = tuple1
tuple1 += (4,)
print(tuple1 == tuple2)
```

(a) True (b) False
(c) tuple1 (d) Error

27. **Consider the declaration L = (1, 'Python', '3.14'). What will be the data type of L?** CBSE SQP 2021 Term I

(a) list (b) tuple
(c) dictionary (d) string

28. **Given the following Tuple** CBSE 2023

```
Tup=(10,20,30,50)
```

Which of the following statements will result in an error?

(a) print (Tup[0]) (b) Tup.insert (2, 3)
(c) print(Tup[1:2]) (d) print(len (Tup)·)

29. **Which of the following is not a tuple in Python?** CBSE 2021-22 Term I

(a) (1,2, 3)
(b) ("One" , "Two", "Three")
(c) (10 ,)
(d) ("One")

30. **Which of the following statement(s) would give an error during execution of the following code?** CBSE SQP 2023-24

```
tup = (20,30,40,50,80,79)
print(tup)              #Statement 1
print(tup[3]+50)        #Statement 2
print(max(tup))         #Statement 3
tup[4]=80               #Statement 4
```

(a) Statement 1 (b) Statement 2
(c) Statement 3 (d) Statement 4

31. **What will be the output for the following Python statement?** CBSE 2021-22 Term I

```
T= (10, 20, [30, 40, 50], 60,70)
T[2] [1]= 100
print(T)
```

(a) (10, 20, 100, 60, 70)
(b) (10, 20, [30, 100, 50], 60, 70)
(c) (10, 20, [100, 40, 50], 60, 70)
(d) Error

32. **Nitish has declared a tuple T in Python as following** CBSE 2021-22 Term I, Competency Based Que.

T = (10, 20, 30)

Now, he wants to insert an element 40 after these three elements of T so that the tuple may contain (10, 20, 30, 40). Which of the following statement shall Nitish write to accomplish the above task?

(a) T = T + 40 (b) T = T + (40)
(c) T = T + (40,)
(d) Nitish cannot insert 40 into the tuple since tuples are immutable.

33. **Given an object obj1= (10, 20, 30, 40, 50, 60, 70, 80, 90). What will be the output of print(obj1[3:7:2])?** CBSE SQP 2021-22 Term I

(a) (40,50,60,70,80)
(b) (40,50,60,70)
(c) (40,50,60)
(d) (40,60)

34. **Given an object obj1 = (10, 15, 25, 30). Identify the statement that will result in an error.** CBSE SQP 2021-22 Term I

(a) print(obj1[2]) (b) obj1[2] = 20
(c) print(min(obj1)) (d) print(len(obj1))

35. **What will be the output of the following code?** CBSE SQP 2021-22 Term I

```
tup1 = (1,2,[1,2],3)
tup1[2][1]=3.14
print(tup1)
```

(a) (1,2,[3.14,2],3) (b) (1,2,[1,3.14],3)
(c) (1,2,[1,2],3.14) (d) Error message

36. **If my_dict is a dictionary as defined below, then which of the following statements will raise an exception?**

```
my_dict = {'apple': 10, 'banana': 20,
'orange': 30}
```

CBSE SQP 2024-25

(a) my_dict.get('orange')
(b) print(my_dict['apple', 'banana'])
(c) my_dict['apple']=20
(d) print(str(my_dict))

37. Identify the invalid Python statement from the following. CBSE 2024

(a) d = dict ( ) (b) e = { } (c) f = [ ] (d) g = dict { }

38. Which of the following will delete key-value pair for key = "Red" from a dictionary D1? CBSE SQP 2023-24

(a) delete D1("Red") (b) del D1["Red"]
(c) del.D1["Red"] (d) D1.del["Red"]

39. Which of the following built-in function/method returns a dictionary? CBSE 2025

(a) dict() (b) values () (c) keys () (d) items ()

40. Which of the following statement(s) would give an error after executing the following code? CBSE 2023

```
Stud= {"Murugan":100, "Mithu ":95}
                                  # Statement 1
print(Stud [95])                  # Statement 2
Stud["Murugan"]=99                # Statement 3
print(Stud.pop( ))                # Statement 4
print(Stud)                       # Statement 5
```

(a) Statement 2 (b) Statement 3
(c) Statement 4 (d) Statement 2 and 4

41. What will be the output for the following Python statement? CBSE 2021-22 Term I

```
D= {"AMIT":90, "RESHMA":96, "SUKHBIR":92,
"JOHN":95}
print("JOHN" in D, 90 in D, sep = "#")
```

(a)True#False (b) True#True
(c) False#True (d) False#False

42. Consider the statements given below and then choose the correct output from the given options: CBSE 2025

```
D={'S01':95, 'S02':96}
for I in D:
    print(I,end='#')
```

(a) S01#S02# (b) 95#96#
(c) S01,95#S02,96% (d) S01#95#S02#96#

43. Identify the output of the following Python statement. CBSE 2021-22 Term I

```
D= { }
T=("ZEESHAN", "NISHANT", "GURMEET", "LISA")
for i in range (1, 5):
    D[i]=T[i-1]
    print(D)
```

(a) {"ZEESHAN", "NISHANT" , "GURMEET", "LISA"}
(b) "ZEESHAN", "NISHANT", "GURMEET", "LISA"
(c) {[1,"ZEESHAN"], [2, "NISHANT"], [3, "GURMEET"], [4, "LISA"]}
(d) {1: "ZEESHAN" , 2 : "NISHANT" , 3 : "GURMEET" , 4 : "LISA" }

44. Given the following dictionaries. CBSE SQP 2022-23

```
dict_exam={"Exam" : "AISSCE", "Year" : 2023}
dict_result={"Total" : 500, "Pass_Marks" : 165}
```

Which statement will merge the contents of both dictionaries?

(a) dict_exam.update(dict_result)
(b) dict_exam + dict_result
(c) dict_exam.add(dict_result)
(d) dict_exam.merge(dict_result)

45. Which of the following statement is false in the context of dictionary? CBSE SQP 2021-22 Term I

(a) The values of a dictionary can be accessed using keys.
(b) The keys of a dictionary can be accessed using values.
(c) Elements in a dictionary are in form of key:value pairs.
(d) Dictionaries are mutable.

46. Identify the output of the following Python code. CBSE 2021-22 Term I

```
D={1:"One", 2 : "Two", 3 : "Three"}
L=[]
for K,V in D.items():
  if V[0]=="T":
      L.append (K)
print(L)
```

(a) [1, 2, 3] (b) ["One", "Two", "Three"]
(c) [2, 3] (d) ["Two", "Three"]

47. What will be the output of the following Python code? CBSE 2021-22 Term I

```
S= "UVW";L= [10 , 20, 30] ;D= { }
N=len (S)
for I in range(N):
  D[L[I]] = S[I]
for K, V in D. items ( ) :
  print (K,V, sep="*", end = ", ")
```

(a) U*10, V*20, W*30, (b) 10*U, 20*V, 30*W,
(c) 10, 20, 30, U*V*W* (d) Error

48. What possible output(s) will be obtained when the following code is executed? CBSE SQP 2023-24

```
import random
myNumber=random.randint(0,3)
COLOR=["YELLOW","WHITE","BLACK","RED"]
for I in range (1, myNumber):
    print(COLOR[I], end = "*")
    print()
```

(a) RED*
WHITE*
BLACK*

(b) WHITE*
BLACK*

(c) WHITE* WHITE*
BLACK* BLACK*

(d) YELLOW*
WHITE*WHITE*
BLACK* BLACK* BLACK*

49. Which of the following is not a function/method of the random module in Python? CBSE 2021-22 Term I

(a) randfloat () (b) randint ()
(c) random () (d) randrange ()

50. Identify the correct possible output for the following Python code. CBSE 2021-22 Term I

```
import random
for N in range (2, 5, 2) :
  print (random. randrange (1, N) ,end="#")
```

(a) 1 # 3 # 5 # (b) 2 # 3 #
(c) 1 # 4 # (d) 1 # 3 #

51. Which of the following option can be the output for the following code? CBSE SQP 2021-22 Term I

```
import random
List=["Delhi","Mumbai","Chennai","Kolkata"]
for y in range(4):
        x = random.randint(1,3)
        print(List[x],end="#")
```

(a) Delhi#Mumbai#Chennai#Kolkata#
(b) Mumbai#Chennai#Kolkata#Mumbai#
(c) Mumbai#Mumbai#Mumbai#Delhi#
(d) Mumbai#Mumbai#Chennai#Mumbai

52. What possible output from the given options is expected to be displayed when the following Python code is executed? CBSE 2024

```
import random
Signal = ['RED', 'YELLOW', 'GREEN']
for K in range (2, 0, -1) :
  R = random, randrange (K)
  print(Signal[R], end = '#')
```

(a) YELLOW # RED #
(b) RED # GREEN #
(c) GREEN # RED #
(d) YELLOW # GREEN #

53. Consider the statements given below and then choose the correct output from the given options: CBSE 2025

```
N = 5
try :
print ('WORD' + N, end = '#')
except :
print ('ERROR', end = ' #')
finally:
print ('OVER')
```

(a) ERROR#
(b) WORD5#OVER
(c) WORD5#
(d) ERROR#OVER

54. Which type of error causes abnormal termination of program while it is executing?

(a) Syntax error (b) Logical error
(c) Runtime error (d) None of these

55. A .... produces an undesired output but without abrupt termination of the execution of the program.

(a) Syntax error (b) Logical error
(c) Runtime error (d) None of these

56. Rohan writes a program of printing "I am new programming developer" but he forget to close the bracket of print () statement. What type of error is this?

(a) Syntax error (b) Logical error
(c) Runtime error (d) None of these

Fill in the Blanks

57. not in operator is the opposite of .... operator.

58. (+) operator is used to .... two strings.

59. The index should be an/a ....

60. .... function same as .... method, but raise an exception if substring is not found.

61. .... returns True if string contains only digits and False otherwise.

62. The index of list should be an/a ....

63. Syntax to concatenate two lists ....

64. .... is performed on lists with the use of colon(:).

65. .... is used to calculate the total length of list.

66. .... integer value which determines the increment between each index for slicing.

67. .... integer where the slicing of the object starts.

68. Travering a tuple is also called ....

69. Tuples are .... by design which means they cannot be changed after creation.

70. * operator is used to .... the tuple.

71. To display elements from beginning to a range use ....

72. .... means they cannot be changed after creation.

73. .... means putting a dictionary inside another dictionary.

74. Key will be a .... element.

75. To access the elements from a dictionary .... are used.

76. User can also add elements into an empty dictionary by ....

77. Errors are also called as ....

78. .... type of error indicates an improper use of Python statements.

79. A/An .... statement allows the programmer to force a specific exception to occur.

80. To handle possible exceptions, we use a .... block.

State whether True or False

81. The first character of string is represented by index 1.

82. list () method is used to create list from an existing sequence.

83. Merging a list is a technique to access an individual element of that list.

84. "A Python List must always contain all its elements of same data type." **CBSE 2025**

85. Slicing operation is performed on tuples with the use of colon (:).

86. Python will try to process all the statements inside the try block.

87. The python interpreter handles logical errors during code execution. **CBSE SQP 2024-25**

88. The finally block in python is executed only if no exception occurs in the try block. **CBSE SQP 2024-25**

89. While handling exceptions in python, name of the exception has to be compulsorily added with except clause. **CBSE 2024**

90. An exception may be raised even if the program is syntactically correct. **CBSE SQP 2023-24**

Assertion and Reason Based Questions

Assertion (A) and Reason (R) Type questions. Choose the correct option as:

(a) Both Assertion (A) and Reason (R) are true, and Reason (R) is the correct explanation of Assertion (A)

(b) Both Assertion (A) and Reason (R) are true, but Reason (R) is not the correct explanation of Assertion (A)

(c) Assertion (A) is True, but Reason (R) is False

(d) Assertion (A) is False, but Reason (R) is True

91. Assertion (A) String is a sequence which is made up of one or more UNICODE characters.

Reason (R) A string can be created by enclosing one or more characters in single, double or triple quote.

92. Assertion (A) Python allows an index value to be positive only.

Reason (R) Negative indices are used when we want to access the characters of the string from right to left.

93. Assertion (A) Strings in Python are mutable.

Reason (R) The first character has the index 0 and the last character has the index n-1 where n is the length of the string.

94. Assertion (A) Lists can be change after creation.

Reason (R) Lists are mutable.

95. Assertion (A) Dictionary is an unordered collection of data values that stores the key: value pair.

Reason (R) Immutable means they cannot be changed after creation.

96. Assertion (A) A list can have elements of different data types

Reason (R) Elements of a list are enclosed in square brackets and are separated by comma.

97. Assertion (A) If list1 = [1,3,5,7,9] and list2 = [2,4,6,8,10] then list1 + list2 gives the result: [1, 3, 5, 7, 9, 2, 4, 6, 8, 10]

Reason (R) Python allows us to join two or more lists using concatenation operator depicted by the symbol +.

98. Assertion (A) math.pow(2,4) gives the output: 16.0

Reason (R) The math.pow() method receives two float arguments, raises the first to the second and returns the result.

99. Assertion (A) Operator * repeats a list by specified number of times.

Reason (R) Operator * concatenates one list to the end of other list.

100. Assertion (A) The expression "Hello".sort() in python will give an error.

Reason (R) sort() does not exist as a method/function for strings in python.

Answers

1. (b) ceieP0
2. (b) MISS#SIPPI
3. (d) ('Amrit', ' ', 'Mahotsav @ 75')
4. (b) Statement 4
5. (d) ECM
6. (d) S1[4]="Y"
7. (c) 'Welcome' * 10.0
8. (b) PYTHON-is-Fun
9. (d) Good morning Good Morning!
10. (a) #THONPROGRAM
11. (b) ['I', 'ter', 'atio', 'al']
12. (a) Year . 0. at All the best
13. (b) ['Presidency@2023']
14. (c) print ("15" + 3)
15. (b) pYTHOnN3#
16. (d) Error
17. (d) 15.0
18. (d) ['TAC', 'TIC']
19. (b) sum ()
20. (a) [7,5,3,1]
21. (a) [ ] &[25, 20, 15, 10]
22. (d) [10, 20, 30, 20, 10] & [10, 20, 30]
23. (d) [10, 20, [30, 40], 50, 60]
24. (b) 3
25. (b) Removes the first occurrence of value x from the list
26. (b) False
27. (b) tuple
28. (b) Tup.insert (2, 3)
29. (d) ("One")
30. (d) Statement 4
31. (b) (10, 20, [30, 100, 50], 60, 70)
32. (d) Nitish cannot insert 40 into the tuple since tuples are immutable.
33. (d) (40,60)
34. (b) obj1[2] = 20
35. (b) (1,2,[1,3.14],3)
36. (b) print(my_dict['apple', 'banana'])
37. (d) g = dict { }
38. (b) del D1["Red"]
39. (a) dict()
40. (d) Statement 2 and 4
41. (a)True#False
42. (a) S01#S02#
43. (d) {1: "ZEESHAN" , 2 : "NISHANT" , 3 : "GURMEET" , 4 : "LISA" }
44. (a) dict_exam.update(dict_result)
45. (b) The keys of a dictionary can be accessed using values.
46. (c) [2, 3]
47. (b) 10*U, 20*V, 30*W,
48. (b) WHITE*
    BLACK*
49. (a) randfloat ()
50. (d) 1 # 3 #
51. (b) Mumbai#Chennai#Kolkata#Mumbai#
52. (a) YELLOW # RED #
53. (b) WORD5#OVER
54. (c) Runtime error
55. (b) Logical error
56. (a) Syntax error
57. in
58. merge
59. integer
60. index(), find()
61. isdigit()
62. integer
63. list = list1 + list2
64. Slice operation
65. len()
66. step
67. start
68. iterate over a tuple
69. immutable
70. replicate
71. [: index]
72. Immutable
73. Nested dictionary
74. single
75. keys
76. dictionary_name [key] = value
77. bugs
78. Semantic Error
79. raise
80. try-except
81. False
82. True
83. False
84. True
85. True
86. True
87. False
88. False
89. False
90. True
91. (b) Both Assertion (A) and Reason (R) are true, but Reason (R) is not the correct explanation of Assertion (A)
92. (d) Assertion (A) is False, but Reason (R) is True
93. (d) Assertion (A) is False, but Reason (R) is True
94. (a) Both Assertion (A) and Reason (R) are true, and Reason (R) is the correct explanation of Assertion (A)
95. (b) Both Assertion (A) and Reason (R) are true, but Reason (R) is not the correct explanation of Assertion (A)
96. (b) Both Assertion (A) and Reason (R) are true, but Reason (R) is not the correct explanation of Assertion (A)
97. (a) Both Assertion (A) and Reason (R) are true, and Reason (R) is the correct explanation of Assertion (A)
98. (a) Both Assertion (A) and Reason (R) are true, and Reason (R) is the correct explanation of Assertion (A)
99. (c) Assertion (A) is True, but Reason (R) is False
100. (a) Both Assertion (A) and Reason (R) are true, and Reason (R) is the correct explanation of Assertion (A)

Subjective Type Questions

Very Short Answer Type Questions

1. Write a block of code to input any string and to find the number of words in the string.

Ans.
```
str = raw_input("Enter a string")
words = str.split()
print (len(words))
```

2. What is a string slice ? How is it used?

Ans. Substring obtained from within a string is called a string slice. It is done by using <stringname>[n:m]. Python will then return characters at indices n,n+1,n+2……m-1.

3. What will be the output of the following code snippet? CBSE SQP 2024-25

```
str= "World Peace"
print(str[-2::-2])
```

Ans. ce lo

4. Write the use of identity operator.

Ans. Identity operators in Python are used to determine whether a value is of a certain class or type.

5. Find the output.

```
>>>l1 = [1, 2, 3, 4]
>>>l2 = [2, 3, 4, 5]
>>>l1 > l2
```

Ans. False

6. Write the syntax of slicing a list.

Ans. `Variable = list_name (start : stop : step)`

7. What is the use of count() function?

Ans. count() function is used to calculate total occurrence of given elements of list.

Syntax `list_name.count(element)`

8. If a = [5,4,3,2,2,2,1] evaluate the following expressions:

(a) a[-1]

(b) a [a [a [a [2] +1]]]

Ans. (a) 1 (b) 2

9. Given the lists L=[1,3,6,82,5,7,11,92], write the output of print(L[2:5])

Ans. [6,82,5]

10. If L1=[1,2,3,2,1,2,4,2, . . .], and L2=[10,20,30, . . .], then CBSE SQP 2024-25, Competency Based Que.

(I) (A) Write a statement to count the occurrences of 4 in L1.

Or **(B) Write a statement to sort the elements of list L1 in ascending order.**

(II) (A) Write a statement to insert all the elements of L2 at the end of L1.

Or **(B) Write a statement to reverse the elements of list L2.**

Ans. (I) (A) L1.count(4) *Or* (B) L1.sort()

(II) (A) L1.extend(L2) *Or* (B) L2.reverse()

11. Why tuples are called immutable?

Ans. Tuples are called immutable because they cannot be changed after creation.

12. What are nested tuples?

Ans. Nested tuples are tuple objects where the elements in the tuples can be tuples themselves.

13. What is the use of less than or equal to (<=) operator in tuple?

Ans. Less than or equal to operator returns True only if the value on the left is either less than or equal to that on the right of the operator.

14. Observe the output of given code.

```
>>>t=["T", "U", "P", "L", "E"]
>>>t2 = tuple(t)
>>>t2
```

Ans. ('T', 'U', 'P', 'L', 'E')

15. What is the property of dictionary?

Ans. More than one entry per key is not allowed in dictionary.

16. Write a statement in Python to declare a dictionary whose keys are 1, 2, 3 and values are Monday, Tuesday and Wednesday respectively. CBSE SQP 2020, Competency Based Que.

Ans. Day={1:'monday',2:'tuesday',3:'wednesday'}

17. Why can't we apply slicing and concatenation on dictionaries?

Ans. Slicing and concatenation operations depend on a specific order while dictionaries are unordered.

18. What is the difference between objects stored in list and dictionaries?

Ans. Objects stored in list are ordered while those in dictionaries are unordered.

19. What is the difference between key and values in a dictionary?

Ans. Any key of the dictionary is associated to a value while the values of a dictionary can be any python data type.

20. How can you remove key : value pairs from a dictionary?

Ans. (i) `del <dictionary>[<key>]`

(ii) `<dictionary>. pop(<key>)`

21. **Consider the following dictionaries, D and D1:** **CBSE 2025**

```
D={"Suman": 40, "Raj":55, "Raman":60}
D1={"Aditi":30, "Amit":90, "Raj":20}
```

(Answer using built-in Python functions only)

(i) (a) **Write a statement to display/return the value corresponding to the key "Raj" in the dictionary D.**

Or

(b) **Write a statement to display the length of the dictionary D1.**

(ii) (a) **Write a statement to append all the key-value pairs of the dictionary D to the dictionary D1.**

Or

(b) **Write a statement to delete the item with the given key "Amit" from the dictionary D1.**

Ans. (i) (a) print(D["Raj"])

Or (b) print(len(D1))

(ii) (a) D1.update(D)

Or (b) del D1["Amit"]

22. **Name the Python Library modules which need to be imported to invoke the following functions:**

(i) **floor()** (ii) **randint()**

Ans. (i) math module

(ii) random module

23. **Identify the correct output(s) of the following code. Also write the minimum and the maximum possible values of the variable b.** **CBSE SQP 2024-25**

```
import random
a="Wisdom"
b=random.randint(1,6)
for i in range(0,b,2):
    print(a[i],end='#')
```

(a) W# (b) W#i#

(c) W#s# (d) W#i#s#

Ans. The randint() function will return values from 1 to 6. Permissible values for the loop variable i are 0,2,4. Hence the outputs can be options (a) or (c) .

24. **What possible output(s) are expected to be displayed on screen at the time of execution of the following program :** **CBSE 2023**

```
import random
M=[5,10,15,20,25,30]
for i in range(1,3):
    first=random.randint(2,5) - 1
    sec=random.randint(3,6) - 2
    third=random.randint(1,4)
    print(M[first],M[sec],M[third],sep="#")
```

(i) 10#25#15
20#25#25

(ii) 5#25#20
25#20#15

(iii) 30#20#20
20#25#25

(iv) 10#15#25#
15#20#10#

Ans. (i) (iv)

25. **What is ceil() function?**

Ans. ceil() function returns ceiling value of x i.e. the smallest integer not less than x.

26. **Write the syntax to import a module.**

Ans. `import module_name`

27. **How can you say that a tuple is an ordered sequence?**

Ans. Elements of a tuple can be accessed using ordinal index and every time same value is returned for a given index. Hence we can say tuple is an ordered sequence.

28. **If we try to access character which is out of range of index, then which type of error will be occurred?**

Ans. IndexError

29. **Name the types of compile time error.**

Ans. (i) Syntax errors

(ii) Semantic errors

30. **Give any two run time errors.**

Ans.
- Division by zero
- Trying to access a file which does not exist

31. **Write one example of each of the following in Python:** **CBSE 2025**

(i) **Syntax Error**

(ii) **Implicit Type Conversion**

Ans. (i) `print("Hello"`

(ii) `x = 10 + 5.5` → `x becomes 15.5`

32. **How is a mutable object different from an immutable object in Python? Identify one mutable object and one immutable object from the following:**
(1,2), [1,2], {1:1,2:2}, '123' **CBSE SQP 2024-25**

Ans. An object that can be changed is mutable.While,an object that cannot be changed after its creation is immutable.

Mutable object: [1,2] or {1:1,2:2} (Any one)

Immutable object: (1,2) or '123' (Any one)

Short Answer Type I Questions

33. How to traverse a string using for loop?

Ans. for statement can iterate over the elements of a sequence or string. It is used when you want to traverse all characters of string.

e.g.
```
sub = "PYTHON"
for i in sub:
      print (i, ' ', end = " ")
```

Output P Y T H O N

34. Predict the output

```
str = "Python Program"
```

(i) `str [3 : 5]` (ii) `str [- 10]`
(iii) `str [5 : ]` (iv) `str [- 28]`

Ans. (i) 'ho' (ii) 'o'
(iii) 'n Program' (iv) IndexError

35. Observe the output

(i) `>>> x = 'Sum' * '3'`
(ii) `>>> x = 'Sum' + '3'`

Ans. (i) It will give TypeError and correct code is x = 'Sum' * 3
(ii) Sum3

36. Write the short note on

(i) isupper() (ii) join()

Ans. (i) **isupper()** Returns True if string has atleast one case character and all case characters are in uppercase and False otherwise.

Syntax `string.isupper()`

(ii) **join()** Returns a string in which the elements of sequence have been joined by string separator.

Syntax `string.join(iterable)`

37. Write a Python program to form a new string made of the first two and last two characters from a given string.

Ans.
```
string1 = input ("Enter string:")
cn = 0
for i in string1:
      cn = cn + 1
new = string1 [0 : 2] + string1
                          [cn-2 : cn]
print ("Newly formed string is :")
print (new)
```

38. Rewrite the following code in Python after removing all syntax error(s). Underline each correction done in the code.

```
STRING = " WELCOME"
NOTE " "
for S in range[0, 8]:
  print (STRING(S))
  print (S STRING)
```

Ans.
```
STRING = " WELCOME "
NOTE = " "
for S in range (0, 8) :
  print (STRING [ S ])
  print (S + STRING)
```

39. Write the output on execution of the following Python code : CBSE 2024

```
S = "Racecar Car Radar"
L = S.split()
for W in L:
    x = W.upper()
    if x == x[::-1]:
        for I in x:
            print(I, end="*")
    else:
        for I in W:
            print(I, end="#")
    print()
```

Ans.
```
R*A*C*E*C*A*R*
C#a#r#
R*A*D*A*R*
```

40. (a) Given is a Python string declaration: CBSE SQP 2022-23

```
myexam="@@CBSE Examination 2022@@"
```

Write the output of: `print (myexam [: :-2])`

(b) Write the output of the code given below:

```
my_dict = {"name" : "Aman", "age" : 26}
my_dict ['age'] = 27
my_dict['address'] = "Delhi"
print(my_dict.items())
```

Ans. (a) `@20 otnmx SC@`

(b) `dict_items([('name', 'Aman'), ('age', 27), ('address', 'Delhi')])`

The age is updated to 27 and a new key 'address' has been added with value 'Delhi'

41. What is the output of below questions?

```
l1 = [23, 45, 19, 77, 10, 22]
```

(i) `l1.sort()`
(ii) `max(l1)`

Ans. (i) [10, 19, 22, 23, 45, 77] (ii) 77

42. Find the output

```
L = [10, 19, 45, 77, 10, 22, 2]
```

(i) `L [3 : 5]`
(ii) `L [:: -2]`

Ans. (i) [77, 10] (ii) [2, 10, 45, 10]

43. **Find the error(s).**

```
L1 = [7, 2, 3, 4]        L2 = L1 + 2
L3 = L1 * 2               L = L1.pop(7)
```

Ans. **Error 1** L2 = L1 + 2 because + operator cannot add list with other type as number or string.

Error 2 L = L1.pop(7) parentheses puts index value instead of element. In the given list, maximum index value is 3 and 7 is out of index range.

44. (a) **Given is a Python list declaration** **CBSE 2023**

```
Listofnames =["Aman", "Ankit", "Ashish",
                        "Rajan", "Rajat"]
```

Write the output of

```
print(Listofnames[-1: - 4: -1 ])
```

(b) **Consider the following tuple declaration**

```
tup1=(10,20,30,(10,20,30),40)
```

Write the output of :

```
print(tup1.index(20))
```

Ans. (a) Output

["Rajat", "Rajan", "Ashish"]

(b) Output

0

45. **Observe the following tuple and answer the questions that follow:**

```
t1 = (70, 56, 'Hello', 22, 2, 'Hi', 'The',
                        'World', 3)
```

(i) `t1[2 : 4]` (ii) `t1[- 6]`

Ans. (i) ('Hello', 22) (ii) 22

46. **Define sum() method with an example.**

Ans. sum() method is used to calculate the sum of elements of tuple. The elements of tuple must be integer.

Syntax `sum(tuple_name)`

e.g.

```
>>>t = (78, 98, 88, 65, 75, 80, 100)
>>>sum(t)
576
```

47. **Observe the following tuples and answer the questions that follow.**

```
t1=(4, 7, 8, 9)
t2=(0, 4, 3)
```

(i)

```
>>>t=t1+t2
>>>print(t)
```

(ii)

```
>>>t=t1*t2
>>>print(t)
```

Ans. (i) (4, 7, 8, 9, 0, 4, 3)

(ii) It gives TypeError because can't multiply sequence by non-int of type 'tuple'.

48. **Define packing and unpacking tuples.**

Ans. Refer to text on page no. 37 (packing and unpacking tuples).

49. **Write the output from the following code:**

```
T1=(10,20,30,40,50)
T2=(100,200,300)
T3=T1+T2
print (T3)
```

Ans. (10, 20, 30, 40, 50, 100, 200, 300)

50. **Find the output from the following code:**

```
t=tuple()
t = t +('Python',)
print (t)
print (len(t))
t1=(10,20,30)
print (len(t1))
```

Ans. ('Python',)

1

3

51. **Define the update() method with its syntax.**

Ans. update() method is used to update the dictionary with the elements from the another dictionary object or from an iterable of key/value pair.

Syntax

```
dictionary_name1.update(dictionary_name2)
```

52. **Find the output.**

```
Student = {1 : 'Aman', 2 : 'Bablu', 3 :
                        'Chandan'}
Student [2] = 'Sahil'
print(Student)
Student[4] = 'Aasha'
print (Student)
```

Ans. {1 : 'Aman', 2 : 'Sahil', 3 : 'Chandan'}

{1 : 'Aman', 2 : 'Sahil', 3 : 'Chandan', 4 : 'Aasha'}

53. **What is the advantage of pop( ) method over a del keyword?**

Ans. Advantage of pop( ) method over a del keyword is that it provides the mechanism to print desired value if tried to remove a non-existing dictionary pair.

Syntax

```
dictionary_name.pop(key, 'Text')
```

54. **Write a program to sort the list alphabetically in a dictionary.**

Ans.

```
dict = {
"L1" : [78, 54, 65, 89, 11],
"L2" : [22, 65, 45, 78, 95],
"L3" : [32, 4, 89, 45, 2]
}
print("\n Before sorting:")
for i in dict.items():
```

```
    print(i)
  print("\n After sorting:")
  for a, b in dict.items()
    dict1 = {a.sorted(b)}
    print(dict1)
```

55. Write the output from the following codes:

```
A={10:1000,20:2000,30:3000,40:4000,50:5000}
print (A.items())
print (A.keys())
print (A.values())
```

Ans. dict_items([(10, 1000), (20, 2000), (30, 3000), (40, 4000), (50, 5000)])

dict_keys([10, 20, 30, 40, 50])

dict_values([1000, 2000, 3000, 4000, 5000])

56. Find errors in the following code and rewrite the correct code

(i) myTuple1=(1,2,3) myTuple1.append(4) print (myTuple1)

(ii) myDictionary2 ={10:1, 20:2, 30:3} print (myDictionary2[1])

Ans. (i) Tuples are immutable so can't be appended.

```
myTuple1=(1,2,3)
myTuple2=(4,)
myTuple3 = myTuple1 + myTuple2
print (myTuple3)
```

(ii) It will give an error myDictionary2 keyError:1

The correct code will be.

```
myDictionary2 = {10:1, 20:2,30:3}
print (myDictionary2[10])
```

57. Find the errors from the following code:

```
c=dict()
  n=input(Enter total number )
i=1
while i<=n:
  a=input("enter place")
  b=input("enter number")
  c[a]=b
i=i+1
  print ("place","\t","number")
for i in c:
  print (i,"\t",c[a[i]])
```

Ans.

```
c=dict()
n=int(input("Enter total number"))
i=1
while i<=n:
  a=input("enter place")
  b=input("enter number")
  c[a]=b
i=i+1
  print ("place","\t","number")
for i in c:
  print (i,"\t",c[i])
```

58. Write the output of the following Python program code:

```
Data =['D','o','','I','t','','@','','1',
                               '2','3','','!']
for i in range(len(Data)-1):
if (Data[i].isupper()):
  Data[i]=Data[i].lower()
elif (Data[i].isspace()):
  Data[i]=Data[i+1]
print (Data)
```

Ans. ['d', 'o', 'I', 'i', 't', '@', '@', '1', '1', '2', '3', '!', '!']

59. Define the following

(i) Tuples

(ii) Dictionaries

Ans. (i) **Tuples** Tuples are immutable Python sequences, i.e. you cannot change elements of a tuple in place. Tuples' items are indexed. Tuples store a reference at each index. Tuples can be indexed sliced and its individual items can be indexed. len (T) returns count of tuple elements.

Tuple manipulation functions are len ( ), max ( ), min, tuple ( ) etc.

(ii) **Dictionaries** Dictionaries in Python are a collection of some key value pairs. These are mutable and unordered collection with elements in the form of a key: value pairs that associate keys to values. The keys of dictionaries are immutable type and unique. To manipulate dictionaries functions are: len ( ), clear ( ), has_key ( ), items ( ), keys ( ), values ( ), update ( ) etc.

60. Write the output displayed on execution of the following Python code : CBSE 2024

```
LS = ["HIMALAYA", "NILGIRI", "ALASKA", "ALPS"]
D = {}
for S in LS:
    if len(S) % 4 == 0:
        D[S] = len(S)
for K in D:
    print(K, D[K], sep="#")
```

Ans. HIMALAYA#8

ALPS#4

61. What possible output(s) are expected to be displayed on screen at the time of execution of the program from

the following code ? Also specify the minimum values that can be assigned to each of the variables BEGIN and LAST.

```
import random
VALUES=[10,20,30,40,50,60,70,80]
BEGIN=random.randint(1,3)
LAST=random.randint(BEGIN,4)
for I in range(BEGIN,LAST+1):
  print VALUES[I],"-",
```

(a) 30 - 40 - 50 –
(b) 10 - 20 - 30 - 40 -
(c) 30 - 40 - 50 - 60 –
(d) 30 - 40 - 50 - 60 - 70 -

Ans. Minimum value for BEGIN:1
Minimum value for LAST:1

62. What possible output from the given options is expected to be displayed when the following code is executed? **CBSE 2025**

```
import random
Cards=["Heart", "Spade", "Club", "Diamond"]
for i in range (2):
  print(Cards [random.randint(1,i+2)],
                              end="#2") 102
```

(a) Spade#Diamond# (b) Spade#Heart#
(c) Diamond#Club# (d) Heart#Spade#

Ans. Random output, but from random.randint(1, i+2), possibilities for 2 iterations:

```
i=0 → randint(1,1) → 1
i=1 → randint(1,3) → any index 1 to 3
```

So expected output varies. One possible correct option: (a) Spade#Diamond#

Short Answer Type II Questions

63. Distinguish between tuple and list.

Ans. Differences between tuple and list are as follows

Tuple	List
Elements of a tuple are immutable.	Elements of a list are mutable.
Tuple is declared in parenthesis ().	List is declared in square brackets [].
Tuples cannot be changed after creation.	Lists can be changed after creation.
Iterating over the elements of a tuple is fast.	Iterating over the elements of a list is slow.

64. Differentiate between a logical error and syntax error. Also, give suitable examples of each in Python.

Ans. Differences between logical error and syntax error are as follows:

Logical Error	Syntax Error
It occurs because of wrong implementation of logic.	It occurs when statements are wrongly written violating rules of the programming language.
With logical errors, the code is syntactically correct and compiler will not show any error message.	With syntax errors, the code is not syntactically correct and compiler will show the error messages.
It produces the output, but undesired.	It does not produce any output.
e.g. in place of (c = a * b); if by mistake (c = a + b); is written, it will be a logical error.	e.g. in place of (a == b); if by mistake (a == b); is written, it will be a syntax error.

65. (A) **I. When is ZeroDivisionError exception raised in Python?**

II. Give an example code to handle ZeroDivisionError? The code should display the message "Division by Zero is not allowed" in case of ZeroDivisionError exception, and the message "Some error occurred" in case of any other exception.

Or

(B) **I. When is NameError exception raised in Python?**

II. Give an example code to handle NameError? The code should display the message "Some name is not defined" in case of NameError exception, and the message "Some error occurred" in case of any other exception.

Ans. (A) (I) ZeroDivisionError exception is raised whenever a number is divided by zero.

(II)
```
try:
a=int(input("Enter the numerator: "))
b=int(input("Enter the denominator: "))
print("Division is : ",a/b)
except ZeroDivisionError:
    print("Division by Zero is not
                                allowed")
except:
    print("Some other Error Ocurred")
```

Or

(B) (I) NameError is raised when the identifier being accessed is not defined in the local or global scope.

(II)
```
try:
   p= input("Enter a word : ")
```

```
        print("Replica :" , q*3)
    except NameError:
        print("Some name is not defined")

    except:
    print("Some Error Ocurred")
```

Long Answer Type Questions

66. Write a program that takes a string with multiple words and capitalizes the first letter of each word and forms a new string out of it.

Ans.

```
str1 = input("Enter a string: ")
l = len(str1)
a = 0
newstr = ""
while a < l:
    if a == 0:
        newstr += str1[0].upper()
        a += 1
    elif str1[a] == ' ' and a + 1 < l and
                            str1[a+1] != ' ':
        newstr += str1[a]
        newstr += str1[a+1].upper()
        a += 2
    else:
        newstr += str1[a]
        a += 1
print("Original string:", str1)
print("New string:", newstr)
```

67. Find the output.

(i)
```
str='Hello'
str1='World'
str[-3]
str1[-5]
str+str1
str1[0]
```

(ii)
```
str='Hello'
str1='World'
str[-2 : - 4]
str1[: - 6]
str*2
str1[-7 :]
```

(iii)
```
str='Hello'
str1='World'
str[-2]+str1[4]
str1[: - 6]+str[0]
str1*3
str1[-7 :]+str[3]
```

(iv)
```
str='Hello'
str1='World'
str[-2]+str1[4:-1]
str1[1:-6]+str
                [0:4]
str1+str
str1[-7 : - 10]
            +str[3:]
```

Ans. (i) l
W
HelloWorld
W

(ii) ' '
' '
HelloHello
World

(iii) ld
H
WorldWorldWorld
Worldl

(iv) l
Hell
WorldHello
lo

68. Observe the code and write the output.

(i) `'arihant publication'.capitalize()`
(ii) `'arihant publication'.count('hant', 0, 10)`
(iii) `'arihant publication'.endswith('ion.')`
(iv) `'Arihant Publication'.find('The')`
(v) `'Arihant Publication'.index('cat')`
(vi) `'Arihant Publication'.isalpha()`
(vii) `'Arihant Publication'.isdigit()`
(viii) `'Arihant Publication'.lower()`

Ans. (i) 'Arihant publication'
(ii) 1
(iii) False
(iv) –1
(v) 13
(vi) False
(vii) False
(viii) 'arihant publication'

69. Write a program to calculate the sum and mean of the elements which are entered by user.

Ans.

```
list1 = list()
sum = 0
num = int(input("Enter the size of the
                              list:"))
print("Enter the number:")
for i in range (int(num)):
    l = int(input(" "))
    list1.append(int(l))
    sum = sum + list1[i]
mean = sum/num
print("Sum = ", sum)
print("Mean = ", mean)
```

70. Write a program to count the frequency of elements in a list entered by user.

Ans.

```
a = []
n = int(input("Enter number of
                        elements:"))
for i in range(1, n + 1):
    b = int(input("Enter element:"))

    a.append (b)
k = 0
num = int(input("Enter the number to be
                         counted:"))
for j in a :
```

```
        if (j == num):
            k = k + 1
print ("Number", num, "is appear", k,
                                    "times.")
```

71. **Answer the following questions**

(i)
```
t1 = (1, 2, 3, (4, 5), 6)
len(t1)
```
(ii)
```
t2 = (1, (2, 3), 4, 5, 6)
t2.count(4)
```
(iii)
```
t1 = (4,)
t2 = ()
t = t1 + t2
any(t)
```
(iv)
```
t3 = (1, 2, 'Hello', 'The', 3, 4)
max(t3)
```

Ans. (i) 5 (ii) 1 (iii) True (iv) TypeError

72. **Write a Python program to search an element with its index number.**

Ans.
```
tuple1=(12,65,78,-63,-2,3,78,-12)
sm=0
x = int(input("Enter number to be
                                    search:"))
found = False
for i in range(len(tuple1)):
  if(tuple1[i] == x):
    found = True
    print("%d found at %dth position"%(x,i))
    break
if(found == False):
  print("%d is not in tuple"%x)
```

73. **Write a Python program to count the frequencies in a list using dictionary.**

Ans.
```
lst = []
n = int(input("Enter number of
                                  elements:"))
for i in range(0, n):
    ele = int(input())
    lst.append(ele)
print("Original List:", lst)
print("Elements with their frequency")
freq = {}
for item in lst :
    if(item in freq):
       freq[item] + = 1
    else:
       freq[item] = 1
for key, value in freq.item():
    print("%d : %d", % (key, value))
```

74. **Predict the output.**

(i)
```
dic = {}
dic[1] = 1
dic['1'] = 2
dic[1.0] = 4
sum = 0
for i in dic:
    sum = sum + dic[i]
print(sum)
```
(ii)
```
dic = {}
dic [(1, 2, 4)] = 8
dic [(4, 2, 1)] = 10
dic [(1, 2)] = 24
sum = 0
for i in dic :
    sum = sum + dic [i]
print (sum)
print (dic)
```

Ans. (i) 6

(ii) 42

{(1, 2) : 24, (4, 2, 1) : 10, (1, 2, 4) : 8}

75. **Write Python program to test if dictionary contains unique keys and values.**

Ans.
```
dict1 = {'Manish' : 1, 'Akshat' : 2, 'Akansha'
                               : 3, 'Nikuj' : 1}
print("The original dictionary : " +
str(dict1))
flag = False
val = dict()
for keys in dict1:
  if dict1[keys] in val:
     flag = True
     break
else :
  val[dict1[keys]] = 1
print("Does dictionary contain repetition:"
                               + str(flag))
```

76. **(A) Write the Python statement for each of the following tasks using built-in functions/methods only:** CBSE 2024

(i) **To remove the item whose key is "NISHA" from a dictionary named Students.**
For example, if the dictionary Students contains {"ANITA": 90, "NISHA": 76, "ASHA": 92}, then after removal the dictionary should contain {"ANITA": 90, "ASHA": 92}

(ii) **To display the number of occurrences of the substring "is" in a string named message.**

For example if the string message contains "This is his book", then the output will be 3.

Or

(B) A tuple named subject stores the names of different subjects. Write the Python commands to convert the given tuple to a list and thereafter delete the last element of the list.

Ans. (A) (i) Students.pop("NISHA")

(ii) print(message.count("is"))

Or (B)
```
subject_list = list(subject)
# Delete an element, for example, "Science"
subject_list.remove("Science")
print(subject_list)
```

77. **Define the following exception classes.**

(a) NameError

(b) RuntimeError

(c) OverflowError

(d) IOError

Ans. (a) **NameError** exception raised when an identifier is not found in the local or global namespace.

(b) **RuntimeError** exception raised when a generated error does not fall into any category.

(c) **OverflowError** exception raised when result of an arithmetic operation is too large to be represented.

(d) **IOError** exception raised when an input/output operation fails.

Case Study Based Questions

Case Study 1

Answer the below questions to execute the below program successfully :

```
string = input ("Please enter your string:")
str1 =" "
for i in _____ :
    str1 = _____ + str1
    print ("String in reverse order :", _____ )
if ( _____ ) :
    print ("This is a palindrome string")
_____
    print ("This is not a palindrome string")
```

(i) **What will come in Line 3 to fill the blank?**

(ii) **Which value will be add to str1?**

(iii) **Fill the blank in Line 5.**

(iv) **Fill the blank in Line 6.**

(v) **Fill the blank in Line 8.**

Ans. (i) string (ii) i

(iii) str1 (iv) string = = str1

(v) else :

Case Study 2

Consider the following program to take in two strings and display the larger string without using built-in functions.

```
str1=input("Enter first string:")      #Line 1
str2=input("Enter second string:")     #Line 2
c1 = 0                                 #Line 3
c2 = _                                 #Line 4
for i in str1:                         #Line 5
    c1 = c1+1                          #Line 6
for j in str2:                         #Line 7
    c2 = c2+1                          #Line 8
if(__):                                #Line 9
    print("Larger string is:")         #Line 10
    print(str2)                        #Line 11
elif(__):                              #Line 12
    print("Both strings are equal.")   #Line 13
__                                     #Line 14
    print("Larger string is:")         #Line 15
    print(__)                          #Line 16
```

Based on the above program, answer the following questions.

(i) **Which could be assigned to variable c2?**

(a) -1 (b) 1

(c) 0 (d) Any integer

(ii) **Which condition will be used in the if statement?**

(a) c1 > c2 (b) c1 < c2

(c) c1 == c2 (d) c1 != c2

(iii) **Which condition will be used in the elif statement?**

(a) c1 > c2 (b) c1 < c2

(c) c1 == c2 (d) c1 != c2

(iv) **Fill in the blank in Line 14.**

(a) if c1 > c2:

(b) elif c1 == c2:

(c) else:

(d) if c1 < c2:

(v) **What value will be printed in the last line?**
(a) str1 (b) str2
(c) c1 (d) c2

Ans. (i) (c) 0 (ii) (b) c1 < c2
(iii) (c) c1 == c2 (iv) (c) else:
(v) (a) str1

Case Study 3

Program to check if elements of a list are same or not, it read from front or back

```
a = [1, 2, 3, 3, 2, 1]
i = ______
mid = (len (a))/2
same = True
while ______
      if a[i] ! = ______ :
            print ("No")
            same = False
            break
      ______
if same = = ______ :
      print ("Yes")
```

(i) **Which value will be assign to variable i.**
(ii) **Fill the blank in Line 5.**
(iii) **Fill the blank in Line 6.**
(iv) **Fill the blank in Line 10.**
(v) **What value will be come to satisfy the condition if in Line 11.**

Ans. (i) 0 (ii) i < mid :
(iii) a [len (a) − i−1] (iv) i = i+1
(v) True

Case Study 4

A Python list is a versatile data structure that allows you to store a collection of items. It's like a dynamic array, capable of holding elements of various data types, including integers, strings, and even other lists. Lists are mutable, meaning you can modify their contents after creation.

Based on the above information, answer the following questions.

(i) **Which of the following is a correct way to create a list in Python?**
(a) list1 = list() (b) list1 = [1, 2, 3, 4]
(c) Both (a) and (b) (d) None of these

(ii) **Which of the following is true about Python lists?**
(a) Lists are immutable.
(b) List size must be declared beforehand.
(c) List elements are stored contiguously in memory.
(d) The size(list1) function is used to find the size of a list.

(iii) **Which of the following Python code snippets will result in an error?**
(a) list1 = [] (b) list1 = [] * 3
(c) list1 = [2, 8, 7] (d) None of these

(iv) **What is the output of the following code?**

```
L = [1, 2, 3, 4, 5, [6, 7, 8]]
print(L[5])
```

(a) [6, 7, 8] (b) 6
(c) Error (d) None of these

(v) **Consider the following list:**

```
L1 = [10, 56, 23, 45, 55, 23, 11, 65, 47,
                                   [15, 13], 75]
```

What will be the output of the following statement?

```
print(L1[::-3])
```

(a) [75, 65, 55, 56] (b) [75, 65, 55, 10]
(c) [75, 65, 55, 56, 10] (d) Error

(vi) **Which of the following operations will sort a list in descending order?**
(a) list_name.sort() (b) max(list_name)
(c) list_name.reverse() (d) list_name[-1]

Ans. (i) (c) Both (a) and (b)
(ii) (c) List elements are stored contiguously in memory.
(iii) (d) None of the above
(iv) (a) [6, 7, 8]
(v) (a) [75, 65, 55, 56]
(vi) (c) list_name.reverse ()

Case Study 5

Priyank is a software developer with a reputed firm. He has been given the task to computerise the operations for which he is developing a form which will accept customer data as follows:

The DATA TO BE ENTERED IS :
Name
Age
Items bought (all the items that the customer bought)
Bill amount **[CBSE Question Bank]**

(i) **Choose the most appropriate data type to store the above information in the given sequence.**
(a) string, tuple, float, integer
(b) string, integer, dictionary, float
(c) string, integer, integer, float
(d) string, integer, list, float

(ii) **Now the data of each customer needs to be organised such that the customer can be identified by name followed by the age, item list and bill**

amount. Choose the appropriate data type that will help Priyank accomplish this task.

(a) List (b) Dictionary

(c) Nested Dictionary (d) Tuple

(iii) Which of the following is the correct way of storing information of customers named 'Paritosh' and 'Bhavesh' with respect to the option chosen above?

(a) customers= {'Paritosh':24,['Printed Paper', ' Penstand'], 3409, 'Bhavesh': 45,['A4 Rim','Printer Cartridge', 'Pen Carton', 'Gift Wrap'], 8099.99 }

(b) customers={'Paritosh':[24,['Printed Paper', ' Penstand'], 3409], 'Bhavesh': [45,['A4 Rim','Printer Cartridge', 'Pen Carton', 'Gift Wrap'], 8099.99] }

(c) customers= ['Paritosh':24,'Printed Paper', ' Penstand', 3409, 'Bhavesh': 45,'A4 Rim','Printer Cartridge', 'Pen Carton', 'Gift Wrap', 8099.99]

(d) customers=('Paritosh':24,['Printed Paper', ' Penstand'], 3409, 'Bhavesh': 45,['A4 Rim','Printer Cartridge', 'Pen Carton', 'Gift Wrap'], 8099.99)

(iv) In order to calculate the total bill amount for 15 customers, Priyank

Statement 1 must use a variable of the type float to store the sum.

Statement 2 may use a loop to iterate over the values.

(a) Both statements are correct.

(b) Statement 1 is correct, but statement 2 is not.

(c) Both statements are incorrect.

(d) Statement 1 is incorrect but statement 2 is correct.

Ans. (i) (d) string, integer, list, float

(ii) (c) Nested Dictionary

(iii) (b) customers={'Paritosh':[24,['Printed Paper', ' Penstand'], 3409], 'Bhavesh': [45,['A4 Rim','Printer Cartridge', 'Pen Carton', 'Gift Wrap'], 8099.99] }

(iv) (a) Both statements are correct.

Case Study 6

You are tasked with managing student records in a Python application using tuples. Each student record is represented as a tuple containing the student's name, age, and a nested tuple of their exam scores. All the student records are stored together in a single tuple called class_records.

Consider the following code snippet:

```
student1 = ("Amit", 15, (88, 92, 79))
student2 = ("Ravi", 16, (90, 85, 94))
student3 = ("Ronit", 15, (85, 87, 91))
class_records = (student1, student2, student3)
```

Based on the above information, answer the following multiple-choice questions:

(i) Which of the following statements about the class_records tuple is TRUE?

(a) class_records is mutable and can be modified after creation.

(b) class_records is immutable, meaning its contents cannot be changed once created.

(c) class_records is partially mutable; only its nested tuples can be modified.

(d) class_records can be modified, but its elements cannot be accessed using indexing.

(ii) What is the result of the expression student1[2][1]?

(a) 15 (b) 92

(c) (88, 92, 79) (d) "Amit"

(iii) Which built-in function is used to determine the number of student records in class_records?

(a) len(class_records)

(b) class_records.count()

(c) class_records.index()

(d) sum(class_records)

(iv) Given the statement name, age, scores = student2, what will be the value of scores?

(a) "Ravi"

(b) 16

(c) (90, 85, 94)

(d) The entire tuple student2

(v) To access Ronit's third exam score, which of the following expressions is correct?

(a) class_records[2][2][2]

(b) class_records[3][2][1]

(c) class_records[2][1][2]

(d) class_records[2][2][1]

Ans. (i) (b) class_records is immutable, meaning its contents cannot be changed once created.

(ii) (b) 92

(iii) (a) len(class_records)

(iv) (c) (90, 85, 94)

(v) (a) class_records[2][2][2]

SELF ASSESSMENT TEST

Multiple Choice Questions

1. To access the individual element of a string, ... is used.

(a) indexing (b) accessing
(c) traversing (d) sequencing

2. .... contains a sequence of heterogeneous elements.

(a) List (b) Array (c) Tuple (d) String

3. Which operator is used as index operator?

(a) () (b) {} (c) : : (d) []

Fill in the Blanks

4. .... function is used to return the total length of the dictionary.

5. Membership operators return .... as per the conditions met.

6. .... method is used to create list from an existing sequence.

7. .... errors occur due to mistakes of the programmer.

State Whether True and False

8. The first character of string is represented by index 1.

9. list () method is used to create list from an existing sequence.

Assertion and Reason Based Questions

Assertion (A) and Reason (R) Type questions. Choose the correct option as

(a) Both Assertion (A) and Reason (R) are true, and Reason (R) is the correct explanation of Assertion (A)
(b) Both Assertion (A) and Reason (R) are true, but Reason (R) is not the correct explanation of Assertion (A)
(c) Assertion (A) is True, but Reason (R) is False
(d) Assertion (A) is False, but Reason (R) is True

10. Assertion (A) A sequence of characters is called string.

Reason (R) Strings are used by programming languages to manipulate text such as words and sentences.

11. Assertion (A) To access the list's elements, index number is used.

Reason (R) Use the index operator () to access the elements of a list.

Very Short Answer Type Questions

12. Predict the output

```
>>>a = '2' + 3
>>>print(a)
```

13. Write an example of mixed data type list.

14. Write the output of given code.

```
>>>t = tuple("HELLO")
>>>t
```

15. Tuples are immutable. Explain.

Short Answer Type Questions

16. Which function is used to remove the first element of a set and the last element of a list?

17. Explain the parameters of given syntax

```
l = list_name[start : stop : step]
```

18. Find the output.

(i) `'program_22'.isalpha()`

(ii) `'*** Hello***'.lstrip('*')`

19. Write a program to count the even numbers in a list.

Long Answer Type Question

20. Write a program to create two dictionaries and swap their values.

Case Study Based Questions

21. A text analysis tool needs to process a large text file, count the occurrences of specific words, and identify the longest word in the file.

The tool should also be able to handle different text encodings and remove punctuation.

(i) To read and process the text file, which Python data type would be most suitable?

(a) List (b) Tuple
(c) String (d) Dictionary

(ii) To count the occurrences of specific words, which string method would be useful?

(a) find() (b) replace()
(c) count() (d) split()

(iii) To remove punctuation from the text, which string operation would be most effective?

(a) String concatenation
(b) String slicing
(c) String replacement
(d) String traversal

(iv) To find the longest word, the tool needs to perform:
(a) String concatenation
(b) String slicing
(c) String traversal and comparison
(d) String formatting

(v) Handling different text encodings is part of:
(a) String methods (b) Handling strings
(c) String operations (d) Traversing a string

22. **A library wants to create a system to track books that are currently checked out. The system should allow librarians to store book titles and the member IDs of those who borrowed them, identify overdue books, and calculate the total number of books checked out.**

(i) Which Python data type would be most suitable for storing book titles and member IDs?
(a) Dictionary (b) Tuple
(c) String (d) List

(ii) To calculate the total number of books checked out, the system needs to perform:
(a) List sorting
(b) List traversal and counting
(c) List slicing
(d) List concatenation

(iii) To identify overdue books, the system should use:
(a) List sorting
(b) List concatenation
(c) List traversal and conditional checks
(d) List slicing

(iv) If the librarian wants to add a new book to the system, which list method would be used?
(a) sort() (b) pop()
(c) append() (d) remove()

(v) To store details for multiple copies of the same book, the system would use:
(a) Tuples
(b) Single list
(c) Dictionaries
(d) Nested lists

23. **A teacher wants to create a system to store and manage student information. The system should store student names, roll numbers, and grades. The teacher needs to access, modify, and traverse this information efficiently.**

(i) Which Python data structure is most suitable for storing student information?
(a) List (b) Tuple
(c) Dictionary (d) Set

(ii) To access a student's grade using their roll number, the teacher should use:
(a) List indexing (b) Dictionary keys
(c) Tuple slicing (d) Set iteration

(iii) To add a new student's information to the system, the teacher would use:
(a) append()
(b) insert()
(c) Dictionary key assignment
(d) extend()

(iv) To get a list of all student roll numbers, the teacher should use:
(a) values() (b) items()
(c) keys() (d) get()

(v) To remove a student's information from the system, the teacher can use:
(a) popitem() or del (b) remove()
(c) discard() (d) clear()

Answers

1. (a) 2. (a) 3. (d) 4. len()
5. Boolean values (True & False) 6. list()
7. Syntax 8. False
9. True 10. (a) 11. (c)
21. (i) → (c), (ii) → (c), (iii) → (c), (iv) → (c), (v) → (b)
22. (i) → (d), (ii) → (b), (iii) → (c), (iv) → (c), (v) → (d)
23. (i) → (c), (ii) → (b), (iii) → (c), (iv) → (c), (v) → (a)

03

CHAPTER

A function provides better modularity for you applications and a high degree of code reusing.

▼ **YOUR STUDY GOALS**

3.1 Types of Python Function
3.2 Parameters and Arguments
3.3 Passing Parameters
3.4 Scope of Variables
3.5 Namespace

▼ **YOUR PRACTICE GOAL**

- Objective Type Questions
  (48 Qs ; MCQs, True or False, Fill in the Blanks, Assertion and Reason)
- Subjective Type Questions
  (47 Qs ; VSA, SA, LA)
- Case Based Questions
  (Objective Case Studies-2 Subjective Case Study 1)

Functions

A function can be defined as the organized block of reusable code, which can be called whenever required. It is basically named unit of a group of proper statements.

Python allows us to divide a large program into the basic building blocks known as a **function**. A function can be called multiple times to provide reusability and modularity to the Python program.

Function Declaration To declare a function ,we use following syntax

Keyword → `def`; Function name → `function_name`; Parameter → `parameters`

```
def function_name(parameters):
    # statement      → Body of statement
    return expression
```

`return` → Function return

There are the following advantages of Python functions

- Using functions, we can avoid rewriting the same logic/code again and again in a program.
- We can track a large Python program easily when it is divided into multiple functions.
- Reusability is the main achievement of Python functions.

3.1 Types of Python Function

There are three types of functions in Python, which are given below

1. Built-in Function

Built-in functions are known as **library functions**. These are pre-defined functions in Python programming system that are always available for use.
e.g. type(), input(), print() etc.

2. User Defined Functions

Python provides facility for programmers to define their own functions according to their requirements. Those functions defined by programmers are known as user defined functions.
e.g. Function for finding factorial, function for checking whether a number isprime or not, etc.

3. Function Defined in Modules

In Python, there are some functions that are pre-defined in specific modules. To access or use these functions, we have to import their module first then access.
e.g. sin(), cos() are contained in math module, mean(),mode() are in statistics module etc.

Defining a Function

Some basic rules to define function in Python are given below

- Function contain 'def' keyword to provide the required functionality. The def keyword is followed by the function name and parentheses ().
- Any input parameters or arguments should be placed within these parentheses. You can also define parameters inside these parentheses.
- There is a colon (:) at the end of def line. Then, the indented statements form the body of function.
- The first statement of a function can be an optional string.
- Function body can contain argument, some set of statements that return result etc.

Syntax

```
def function_name (parameters):
'''Anydocstring'''
    function_body
    return
```

e.g.

```
def fun1(str):
'''Pass a string to print statement'''
    print(str)
    return
```

Calling a Function

Function definition part only define the name of function and specify the parameters.

Now, to execute that function follows the various rules

- Write function_name, which function you want to use.
- In function_name parentheses, pass the parameters. Parameters are the values you pass to the function to tell it what should do and how to do it.
- Function can be called multiple times with different expressions as the actual parameters.

Syntax

```
function_name ()
```

or

```
function_name (parameters)
```

e.g.

```
def fun1(str):
    '''Pass a string to print statement'''
    print(str)
    return
fun1("Hello, it is function calling")
```

Output

Hello, it is function calling

Example 1 To multiply two numbers with the help of function.

```
def mul ():
      x = 4
      y = 5
      Multiply = x * y
      print ("Multiplication is", Multiply)
mul()     # call mul function after run
```

Output

Multiplication is 20

Example 2 To subtract two numbers through a function.

```
def subtract (a,b):
      sub = a - b
      return sub
 n1 = int (input ("Enter first number"))
 n2 = int (input ("Enter second number"))
sub = subtract (n1,n2)
print ("Subtraction of given two numbers",
                                        sub)
```

Output

Enter first number 67
Enter second number 89
Subtraction of given two numbers −22

3.2 Parameters and Arguments

A **parameter** is a variable used to define a particular value during a function definition.

An **argument** is a value passed to the function during the function call which is received for corresponding parameter defined in function header.

Arguments are used to pass the value of a variable to a function. The number of arguments in a function call must be same as the number of parameters in the function definition. Also, the order of argument values must be the same as defined in the function prototype.

The structure of a function passing parameters is shown below

```
                    Parameters
def addition (a, b):              #Function definition
    print (a+b)                   #Body of function
                                  #After press F5 call the function
x=5
                 Arguments
addition(10, x)          #Function calling
```

In the above program, the program execution begins from the function call, it calls addition( ). The call to a function follows a structure very similar to its definition as shown below:

```
addition(a, b):
         \  \
addition(10, x):
```

The parameters in the function declaration have a clear correspondence to the arguments passed in the function call.

The call passes two values, 10 and x, to the function, these correspond to the parameters a and b, declared for the function addition ().

Now, all the processing under addition( ) will be performed on the values 10 and x.

Example 3 To multiply two numbers with passing parameters to function.

```
def mul(a,b):
    mul = a * b
    print ("Value of Multiplication", mul)
                                    #call mul function after run
mul(10, 2)
```

Output

Value of Multiplication 20

Quick Test 1

1. What is a function?
2. When function does provide reusability?
3. Name the three categories of functions.
4. What are parameters?
5. Is parameter same as argument?
6. Find the error in the following lines of code. Also suggest the correct code.
```
def minus(total_decrement)
output = total_decrement
```
7. Why do we define a function ?

3.3 Passing Parameters

Python provides various parameter passing methods that have been discussed below

1. Default Parameter Values

A default parameter is a part of function declaration (not definition).

It instructs the compiler what value to pass for a parameter if the programmer deliberately misses the matching argument of that parameter in the function call statement.

e.g. The function showing the default parameter values.

```
my_func(a, b, c = 10):
```

This function takes three arguments, out of which the last argument c has a default value (i.e. 10).

The programmer may call this function in two ways

(a) **my_func (5, 6, 8)**

In this case, the parameter 'a' gets argument 5, 'b' gets 6 and 'c' gets 8.

(b) **my_func (5, 6)**

In this case, the parameter 'a' gets argument 5, 'b' gets 6 and since the third argument is missing, it will take the default value 10 for 'c'.

One important thing related to default argument is that, any parameter cannot have a default value unless all passing arguments appearing on its right have their default value.

e.g.
```
def invite( x, y = 50, z)          #illegal
def invite(x, y = 50, z = 20)      #legal
```

- This type of declaration can be used in situation where some parameters always have the same value.
- They can be used to combine similar functions into one.

2. Keyword (Named) Arguments

Python also provides another possibility to pass additional parameters. Using keyword argument, you can declare values using name.

Python provides a way of writing function calls where you can write any argument in any order, but value should be in right form.

e.g
```
def func (Book, Page, Prize):
    print ('Book name is :', Book)
    print ('Page:', Page)
    print ('Prize:' , Prize)
#function calling
```

```
func (Book = 'SSC', Page = 1000, Prize = 500)
func (Page = 350, Book = 'English', Prize = 250)
func (Prize = 400, Page = 500, Book = 'Maths')
```

Output

Book name is: SSC
Page: 1000
Prize: 500
Book name is: English
Page: 350
Prize: 250
Book name is: Maths
Page: 500
Prize: 400

As you can see in the above function output, Python has matched all actual parameters that were preceded by identifiers.

3. Positional Arguments

Positional arguments are arguments that need to be included in the proper position or order.

The first position argument always needs to be listed first when the function is called. The second positional argument needs to be listed second and the third positional argument listed third etc.

e.g. Positional argument can be seen in Python's complex () function. This function returns a complex number with a real term and an imaginary term. The order that numbers are passed to the complex () function determines which number is real term and which number is an imaginary term.

e.g. `complex (4, 8)`

Output

(4+8j)

Using Multiple Argument Types Together

In Python, you can pass multiple argument types together in a function call.

We defined the func(Book, Page, Prize), below the statement for function calling in which we will use two different arguments together

```
func('Python Programming', Page = 400,
                                Prize = 550)
```

In above function call, we pass three arguments in which first argument represents the positional argument and remaining two arguments represent keyword arguments.

Returning Values from Functions

In Python, functions may or may not return a value. Python provides two types of functions for this

1. Functions Returning Some Value (Non-void Functions)

This function is used to create a specific task. After completion that task it returns some result in term of value. Non-void functions are also known as fruitful functions. Non-void function can return value in various form.

Syntax `return < value>`

- **Function without Arguments and with Return Values** This function does not receive the data values or variables as arguments from the caller functions, but these functions are able to send back the result to the caller function.

  e.g.
  ```
  def work () :
      print ("Program")
      return
  work ()
  ```

  Output

  Program

- **Function with Arguments and with Return Values** These functions are most valuable type of the functions. These functions receive the data from the caller function for processing and then send back the result to the caller function.

  e.g.
  ```
  def work (a, b):
      s = a + b
      print ("Sum is", s)
      return
  work  (5, 20)
  ```

  Output

  Sum is 25

2. Functions not Returning Any Value (Void Functions)

When a function does not return a value, we can say it is a void function. Void functions are also known non-fruitful functions. Methods in Python do not return any value.

Void function describes in two ways

- **Function without Arguments and without Return Values** Function without arguments means it does not take any data from caller function at the time of function called and without return values means the called function does not send back any data values to the function after processing when its statement is over.

e.g.
```
def work ():
        print ("Program")
```

- **Function with Arguments and without Return Values** In this type of function, the caller function gives the data to the called function but the called function does not send the result back to the caller function.

e.g
```
def work (a, b):
        print ("Sum of a and b", a + b)
```

Returning Multiple Values

In Python, we can return multiple values from a function. Following are different ways:

Using List

When a function takes a list as an argument, it implements a function that operates on an arbitrary number of objects. e.g. The following function computes the mean (average) of a list of integers

```
def mean (* args):
   total = 0.0
   for v in args :
           total + = v
   return (total / len (args))
print (mean(* [1, 2, 3, 4]))
```

Output

2.5

Using String

String can pass to the function by following example

```
def str (* a):
  for i in a:
       print(i)
str ( * ["Hello"])
```

Output

Hello

Using Tuple

Tuples can pass to the function by following example

```
def tup (a) :
  for i in a :
       print (i)
tup ((2, 3, 4, 5, 6))
```

Output

2
3
4
5
6

Using Dictionary

Dictionary can also be pass to the function by following example

e.g.
```
def dic (a) :
  for i in a :
       print (i, ":" , a [i])
dic ({1 : "One", 2 : "Two", 3 : "Three"})
```

Output

1 : One
2 : Two
3 : Three

3.4 Scope of Variables

A variable defined inside a function cannot be accessed outside it. Every variable has a well defined accessibility. The part of the program where a variable is accessible can be defined as the scope of that variable.

Scope of variables in Python program, shows the area where you can use it. The variables are treated differently in different functions.

Generally, we can have only one variable with a name. Python language does not allow to create any two variables with same name in a function, but the two variables with same name may be found in separate function. There are two kinds of scope of variable in Python, which are described below:

1. Local Variable (Local Scope)

A variable that is defined inside any function or a block is known as a local variable. A local variable can be accessed only by the statements of that function, in which these are declared. Any other function of the program cannot use them without receiving as the argument.

The local variables are also called as the **internal variables**. In a function, no two local variables can be declared using same name, but the local variable of two function may be declared with the same name. The local variables retain their values in memory till the complete execution of that function in which these are declared.

e.g
```
def msg() :
  message = "Hello !!!"
      # the variable message is local to the
      # function itself
  print (message)
msg()
print (message)   # this will cause an error since a local
                    variable cannot be accessible here
```

Output

Hello !!!

NameError: Trackback (most recent call last) in line 7 print (message)

NameError : name 'message' is not defined

2. Global Variable (Global Scope)

A variable declared outside of all functions in a program has global scope and is known as global variable. Global variable is usable for all the functions of Python program without declaration in their body or without receiving as the arguments. The global variables are also called as external variables.

If a variable is declared global, it retains its value in the memory of computer system throughout the execution of complete program.

e.g.
```
total = 0   # This is global variable.
            # Function definition is here
def sum (a, b):
          # Add both the parameters and return them.
    total = a + b
          # Here total is local variable.
    print("Inside the function local
                  total: ", total)
          # return total
          # Now you can call sum function
sum(45,13)
print("Outside the function global
                  total: ", total)
```

Output

Inside the function local total: 58

Outside the function global total: 0

3.5 Namespace

A namespace is basically a system to make sure that all the names in a program are unique and can be used without any conflict. Python implements namespaces as dictionaries.

There is a name to object mapping, with the names as keys and the objects as values. Multiple namespaces can use the same name and map it to different objects.

In Python, the **LEGB** rule is used to decide the order in which the namespaces are to be searched for scope resolution.

The scopes are listed below in terms of hierarcy (highest to lowest / narrowest to broadest)

- **Local (L)** : Defined inside function/class.
- **Enclosed (E)** : Defined inside enclosing functions (nested function concept).
- **Global (G)** : Defined at the uppermost level.
- **Built-in (B)** : Reserved names in Python built in modules.

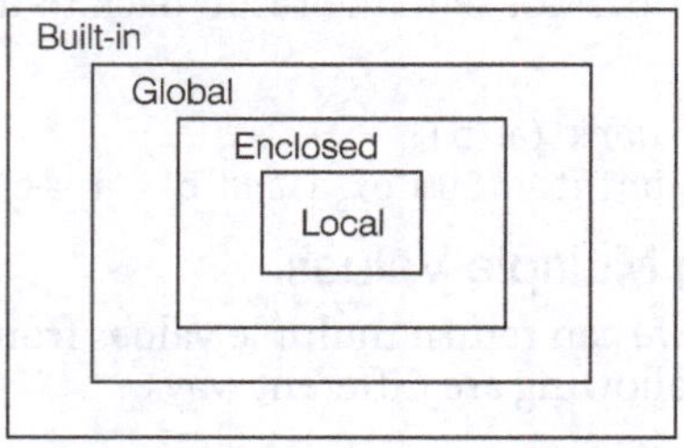

There are three types of namespaces as follows

(i) **Local Namespace** This namespace includes local names inside a function. When a function is called, this namespace is created and it only lasts until the function returns.

(ii) **Global Namespace** This namespace includes names from various imported modules that you are using in a project. When the module is included in the project, it is created and it lasts until the script ends.

(iii) **Built-in Namespace** This namespace includes built-in functions and built-in exception names.

Quick Test 2

1. What do you mean by default parameter value?
2. Where is positional argument used?
3. Void functions are also known as what?
4. Can we called local variables same as external variables?
5. What is the full form of LEGB rule?
6. What do you understand by local and global scope of variables? How can you access a global variable inside the function, if function has a variable with same name. **CBSE SQP 2020**
7. What are keyword arguments?
8. From the function calls given below for a function defined as def fun(p,t,r=7, c=8): determine which is valid and which one is invalid. Give reasons.
   (i) fun(p=5, t=2)
   (ii) fun(c=2, r=7)
   (iii) fun (80,p=7,r=2)

Mind Map

Keyword (Named) Arguments Allow to caller to specify the argument name with values so that the caller does not need to remember the order of parameters.

Default Parameter Values It is a parameter that assumes a default value if a value is not provided int he function call for that argument.

Positional Arguments Arguments that need to be included in the proper position or order.

Function Defined in Modules Functions that are pre-defined in specific modules. e.g. sin(), cos() are contained in math module, mean(),mode() are in statistics module etc.

Function with Arguments and with Return Values These functions receive the data from the caller function for processing and then send back the result to the caller function.

Parameter It is a variable used to define a particular value during a function definition.

User Defined Functions Functions defined by programmers are known as user defined functions.

Argument It is a value passed to the function during the function call which is received for corresponding parameter defined in function header.

Built-in Function pre-defined functions that are always available for use.

Function without Arguments and with Return Values This function does not receive the data values or variables as arguments from the caller functions, but these functions are able to send back the result to the caller function.

Functions Returning Some Value (Non-void Functions) Can return value in various form and it is also known as fruitful functions.
Syntax `return < value>`

Types of Function

Parameters and Arguments

Functions not Returning Any Value (Void Functions) Methods in Python do not return any value and it is also known as non-fruitful functions.

Returning Values from Functions

FUNCTIONS

Python allows us to divide a large program into the basic building blocks known as a function.

Function without Arguments and without Return Values Function without arguments means it does not take any data from caller function at the time of function called and without return values means the called function does not send back any data values to the function after processing when its statement is over.

Scope of Variables The location where we can find a variable and also access it (if required) is called the scope of a variable.

Namespace basically a system to make sure that all the names in a program are unique and can be used without any conflict.

Function with Arguments and without Return Values In this type of function, the caller function gives the data to the called function but the called function does not send the result back to the caller function.

Local Variable It cannot be accessed outside of the function.
e.g.
```
def f():
        S="Arihant" # Local variable
        print(S)
    f()
```

Local Namespace This namespace includes local names inside a function.

Global Variables It defined and declared outside of any function and are not specified to any function.
e.g.
```
def f():
        print(S)
S = "Arihant" # Global variable
f()
```

Built-in Namespace This namespace includes built-in functions and built-in exceptionnames.

Global Namespace This namespace includes names from various imported modules that you are using in a project.

EXAM PATTERN QUESTIONS

Objective Type Questions

Multiple Choice Questions

1. The collection of functions creates a

(a) program (b) software (c) recursion (d) library

2. The def keyword is followed by the function name and

(a) parameter (b) argument
(c) parentheses (d) classes

3. Which of the following components are part of a function header in Python? CBSE SQP 2021-22 Term I

(i) function name **(ii) return statement**
(iii) parameter list **(iv) def keyword**

(a) Only (i) (b) Both (i) and (iii)
(c) Both (iii) and (iv) (d) (i), (iii) and (iv)

4. Aarav created a function to calculate average marks, but it throws an error when only one argument is passed. Which fix is most appropriate? Competency Based Que

```
def avg(m1, m2, m3):
return (m1 + m2 + m3)/3
```

(a) Add default values for m2 and m3
(b) Remove one parameter
(c) Convert it into a lambda function
(d) Use only positional arguments

5. Which of the following is/are built-in function(s)?

(a) type () (b) input ()
(c) print () (d) All of these

6. For a function header as follows CBSE 2021-22 Term I

`def Calc(X, Y=20) :`

Which of the following function calls will give an Error?

(a) Calc(15,25) (b) Calc(X=15,Y=25)
(c) Calc (Y=25) (d) Calc (X=25)

7. Which of the following is the correct way to call a function? CBSE SQP 2021-22 Term I

(a) my_func() (b) def my_func()
(c) return my_func() (d) call my_func()

8. ……… are used to pass the value of a variable to a function.

(a) Arguments (b) Parentheses
(c) Classes (d) Objects

9. Non-void functions are also known as

(a) Non functions (b) Valid functions
(c) Fruitful functions (d) Invalid functions

10. Which of the following is not correct in context of Positional and Default parameters in Python functions? CBSE 2021-22 Term I

(a) Default parameters must occur to the right of Positional parameters.
(b) Positional parameters must occur to the right of Default parameters.
(c) Positional parameters must occur to the left of Default parameters.
(d) All parameters to the right of a Default parameter must also have Default values.

11. Which of the following function header is correct? CBSE SQP 2021-22 Term I

(a) `def cal_si(p=100, r, t=2):`
(b) `def cal_si(p=100, r=8, t):`
(c) `def cal_si(p, r=8, t):`
(d) `def cal_si(p, r=8, t=2):`

12. A teacher made a grading function and called it as grade(name="Anu", 85) but got an error. Why? Competency Based Que.

(a) Too many arguments
(b) Positional argument follows keyword argument
(c) Wrong data type
(d) Default value missing

13. A variable declared in a block is local to that block and is known as

(a) Global variable (b) Local variable
(c) Multi variable (d) Single variable

14. You are writing a function to calculate the total cost of items in a shopping cart. The function should take the price of each item as an argument and return the total sum. Which of the following function definitions would correctly calculate the total? Competency Based Que.

(a) def total_cost(price1, price2): return price1 + price2
(b) def total_cost(price): return sum(price)
(c) def total_cost(price1, price2, price3): total = price1 + price2; return total
(d) def total_cost(price1, price2): total = price1 + price2; print(total)

15. **Consider the code given below** **CBSE SQP 2023-24**

```
b=100
def test(a):
    ........          # missing statement
    b=b+a
    print (a,b)
test(10)
print(b)
```

Which of the following statements should be given in the blank for #Missing Statement, if the output produced is 110?

(a) global a
(b) global b=100
(c) global b
(d) global a=100

16. **Which of the following is not correct in context of scope of variables?** **CBSE 2021-22 Term I**

(a) global keyword is used to change value of a global variable in a local scope.
(b) local keyword is used to change value of a local variable in a global scope.
(c) Global variables can be accessed without using the global keyword in a local scope.
(d) Local variables cannot be used outside its scope.

17. **What is the mean of L in LEGB rule for scope resolution?**

(a) Local (b) Last
(c) Least (d) Library

18. **What will be the output of the following code?** **CBSE SQP 2024-25**

```
c = 10
def add():
    global c
    c = c + 2
    print(c,end='#')
add()
c=15
print(c,end='%')
```

(a) 12%15# (b) 15#12%
(c) 12#15% (d) 12%15#

19. **Observe the given Python code carefully :** **CBSE 2024**

```
a = 20
def convert (a) :
  b = 20
  a = a + b
  convert(10)
print(a)
```

Select the correct output from the given options :

(a) 10 (b) 20
(c) 30 (d) Error

20. **What will be the output of the following Python code?** **CBSE 2021-22 Term I**

```
S="WELCOME"
def Change(T) :
    T="HELLO"
    print (T, end= '@')
Change(S)
print(S)
```

(a) WELCOME@HELLO (b) HELLO@HELLO
(c) HELLO@WELCOME (d) WELCOME@WELCOME

21. **What will be the output of the following Python code?** **CBSE 2021-22 Term I**

```
def FunStr(S):
    T = " "
    for i in S:
        if i. isdigit ():
            T = T + i
    return T
X = "PYTHON 3.9"
Y = FunStr(X)
print (X, Y, sep="*")
```

(a) PYTHON 3.9 (b) PYTHON 3.9*3.9
(c) PYTHON 3.9*39 (d) Error

22. **What will be the output of the following Python code?** **CBSE 2021-22 Term I**

```
V = 50
def Change (N) :
    global V
    V, N = N, V
    print(V, N, sep="#",end="@")
Change (20)
print (V)
```

(a) 20#50@20 (b) 50@20#50
(c) 50#50#50 (d) 20@50#20

23. **What is the output of the following Python code?** **CBSE 2021-22 Term I**

```
def ListChange() :
    for i in'range(len(L)):
        if L[i]%2 == 0:
            L[i]=L[i]*2
        if L[i]%3 == 0:
            L[i]=L[i]*3
        else :
            L[i]=L[i]*5
L = [2, 6, 9, 10]
ListChange ( )
for i in L:
    print(i, end="#")
```

(a) 4#12#27#20# (b) 6#18#27#50#
(c) 20#36#27#100# (d) Error

24. **What will be the output of the following Python code?** CBSE 2021-22 Term I

```
V = 25
def Fun (Ch) :
    V=50
    print (V, end=Ch)
    V *= 2
    print (V, end=Ch)
print (V, end="*")
Fun ("!")
print (V)
```

(a) 25*50!100!25 (b) 50*100!100!100
(c) 25*50!100!100 (d) Error

25. **What will be the output of the following Python code?** CBSE SQP 2021-22 Term I

```
def add (num1, num2):
        sum = num1 + num2
sum = add(20,30)
print(sum)
```

(a) 50 (b) 0 (c) Null (d) None

26. **What will be the output of the following code?** CBSE SQP 2021-22 Term I

```
def my_func(var1=100, var2=200):
    var1+=10
    var2 = var2 - 10
    return var1+var2
print(my_func(50),my_func())
```

(a) 100 200 (b) 150 300
(c) 250 75 (d) 250 300

27. **What will be the output of the following code?** CBSE SQP 2021-22 Term I

```
value = 50
def display(N):
    global value
    value = 25
    if N%7==0:
        value = value + N
    else:
        value = value - N
print(value, end="#")
display(20)
print(value)
```

(a) 50#50 (b) 50#5 (c) 50#30 (d) 5#50#

28. **What is the output of the following code snippet?** CBSE SQP 2021-22 Term I

```
def ChangeVal(M,N):
    for i in range(N):
        if M[i]%5 == 0:
            M[i]//=5
        if M[i]%3 == 0:
            M[i]//=3
L = [25,8,75,12]
ChangeVal(L,4)
for i in L:
    print(i,end="#")
```

(a) 5#8#15#4# (b) 5#8#5#4#
(c) 5#8#15#14# (d) 5#18#15#4#

29. **What will be the output of the following code?** CBSE SQP 2021-22 Term I

```
x = 3
def myfunc():
    global x
    x+=2
    print(x, end=' ')
print(x, end=' ')
myfunc()
print(x, end=' ')
```

(a) 3 3 3 (b) 3 5 3 (c) 3 3 5 (d) 3 5 5

30. **Consider the statements given below and then choose the correct output from the given options.** CBSE 2025

```
def Change (N):
  N = N + 10
  print (N, end='$$')
N = 15
Change (N)
print (N)
```

(a) 25$$15 (b) 15$$25 (c) 25$$25 (d) 2525$$

Fill in the Blanks

31. Python allows us to divide a large program into the basic building blocks known as ....

32. .... inside the function are not executed until the function is called.

33. The order of .... values must be the same as defined in the function prototype.

34. A variable declared outside of all functions in a program has global scope and is known as ....

35. .... namespace includes names from various imported modules that are using in a project.

36. In Python, ... is used to decide the order in which the namespaces are to be searched for scope resolution.

State Whether True or False

37. Built-in functions are known as library functions.

38. Function definition part only define the name of function and specify the parameters.

39. Argument is a variable used to define a particular value during a function definition.

40. Positional arguments are arguments that need to be included in the proper position or order.

41. While defining a function in Python, the positional parameters in the function header must always be written after the default parameters. **CBSE 2024**

42. A variable that is defined inside any function or block is known as a global variable.

Assertion and Reason Based Questions

Assertion (A) and Reason (R) Type questions. Choose the correct option as

(a) Both Assertion (A) and Reason (R) are true, and Reason (R) is the correct explanation of Assertion (A)
(b) Both Assertion (A) and Reason (R) are true, but Reason (R) is not the correct explanation of Assertion (A)
(c) Assertion (A) is True, but Reason (R) is False
(d) Assertion (A) is False, but Reason (R) is True

43. Assertion (A) A function is a block of organized and reusable code that is used to perform a single, related action.

Reason (R) Function provides better modularity for your application and a high degree of code reusability.

44. Assertion (A) Built in function are predefined in the language that are used directly.

Reason (R) print () and input () are built in functions

45. Assertion (A) Python standard library consists of number of modules. **CBSE SQP 2023-24**

Reason (R) A function in a module is used to simplify the code and avoids repetition.

46. Assertion (A) Keyword arguments are related to the function calls.

Reason (R) When you use keyword arguments in a function call, the caller identifies the arguments by the parameter name.

47. Assertion (A) If the arguments in function call statement match the number and order of arguments as defined in the function definition, such arguments are called positional arguments.

Reason (R) During a function call, the argument list first contains default argument(s) followed by positional argument(s). **CBSE SQP 2022-23**

48. Assertion (A) In the case of positional arguments, the function call and function definition statements match in terms of the number and order of arguments. **CBSE SQP 2024-25**

Reason (R) During a function call, positional arguments should precede keyword arguments in the argument list.

Answers

1. (a) program
2. (c) parentheses
3. (d) (i), (iii) and (iv)
4. (a) Add default values for m2 and m3
5. (d) All of these
6. (c) Calc (Y=25)
7. (a) my_func()
8. (a) Arguments
9. (c) Fruitful functions
10. (b) Positional parameters must occur to the right of Default parameters.
11. (d) def cal_si(p, r=8, t=2):
12. (b) Positional argument follows keyword argument
13. (b) Local variable
14. (b) def total_cost(price): return sum(price)
15. (c) global b
16. (b) local keyword is used to change value of a local variable in a global scope.
17. (a) Local
18. (c) 12#15%
19. (b) 20
20. (c) HELLO@WELCOME
21. (c) PYTHON 3.9*39
22. (a) 20#50@20
23. (c) 20#36#27#100#
24. (a) 25*50!100!25
25. (d) None
26. (d) 250 300
27. (b) 50#5
28. (b) 5#8#5#4#
29. (d) 3 5 5
30. (a) 25$$15
31. Function
32. Statements
33. argument
34. Global variable
35. Global
36. LEGB rule
37. True
38. True
39. False
40. True
41. False
42. False
43. (a) Both Assertion (A) and Reason (R) are true, and Reason (R) is the correct explanation of Assertion (A).
44. (a) Both Assertion (A) and Reason (R) are true, and Reason (R) is the correct explanation of Assertion (A).
45. (b) Both Assertion (A) and Reason (R) are true, but Reason (R) is not the correct explanation of Assertion (A).
46. (a) Both Assertion (A) and Reason (R) are true, and Reason (R) is the correct explanation of Assertion (A).
47. (c) Assertion (A) is True, but Reason (R) is False.
48. (b) Both Assertion (A) and Reason (R) are true, but Reason (R) is not the correct explanation of Assertion (A).

Subjective Type Questions

Very Short Answer Type Questions

1. Which statement correctly represent the function body in the given code?

```
def fun (num):
    # function body
print (fun (25))
```

Ans. Complete code is:

```
def fun(num):
    return num
print (fun(25))
```

2. Is built-in function known as library function?

Ans. Yes, built-in functions are known as library functions.

3. Is docstring necessary in user defined function?

Ans. No, docstring is not necessary in user defined function.

4. Mention two advantages of user defined function.

Ans. (i) User defined functions help to decompose a large program into small segments which make program easy to understand, maintain and debug.

(ii) Programmers working on large project can divide the workload by making different functions.

5. Name the category of the function that contains those function which provide the facility for doing some predefined operations. **Competency Based Que.**

Ans. Standard library functions or built-in functions.

6. What are different ways a function can be called?

Ans. A function can be called in two different ways as

(i) call by value

(ii) call by reference

7. Find and write the output of the following Python code. **CBSE SQP 2020**

```
a=10
def call():
    global a
    a=15
    b=20
    print(a)
call()
```

Ans. 15

8. What are parameters?

Ans. Parameters are variables listed within parentheses of a function header that receive the values passed during function call.

9. What is the general syntax for defining a function in Python?

Ans.

```
def <function name> ([parameters]):
    ["""<functions docstrings>"""]
<statement>
    [<statement>]
```

10. What is the difference between arguments and parameters?

Ans. Value that are being passed in a function call are called arguments and values that are received by the called function are called parameters.

11. What will be the output of the following code?

```
def addEm(x,y,z):
    return(x+y+z)
def prod(x,y,z):
    return x*y*z
a = addEm(6,16,26)
b= prod(2,3,6)
print(a,b)
```

Ans. 48 36

12. What is a global statement?

Ans. Global statement is a declaration which holds for the entire current code block. It means that identifiers are to be interpreted as global.

13. (A) Write a user defined function in Python named showGrades (S) which takes the dictionary S as an argument. The dictionary, S contains Name: [Eng, Math, Science] as key:value pairs. The function displays the corresponding grade obtained by the students according to the following grading rules: **CBSE 2024**

Average of Eng, Math, Science	Grade
> = 90	A
< 90 but > = 60	B
< 60	C

For example : Consider the following dictionary

S = {"AMIT": [92, 86, 64], "NAGMA": [65, 42, 43], "DAVID": [92, 90, 88]}

The output should be :

AMIT – B

NAGMA – C

DAVID – A

Or

(B) **Write a user defined function in Python named Puzzle (W, N) which takes the argument W as an English word and N as an integer and returns the string where every Nth alphabet of the word W is replaced with an underscore (" _ ").**

For example : if W contains the word "TELEVISION" and N is 3, then the function should return the string "TE_EV_SI_N". Likewise for the word "TELEVISION" if N is 4, then the function should return "TEL_VIS_ON".

Ans. (A)
```
def showGrades(S):
    for K,V in S.items():
        if(sum(V)/3)>=90:
            Grade="A"
        elif(sum(V)/3)>=60:
            Grade="B"
        else:
            Grade="C"
        print(K,"-",Grade)
S={"AMIT":[92,86,64],"NAGMA":[65,42,43],
                    "DAVID":[92,90,88]}
showGrades(S)
```

Or

(B)
```
def Puzzle(W, N):
    result = list(W)  # Convert the string to
                      a list to allow modifications
    for i in range(N-1, len(W), N):
        result[i] = "_"  # Replace every Nth
                        character with an underscore
    return "".join(result)  # Join the list
                            back into a string
print(Puzzle("TELEVISION", 3))
                    # Output: "TE_EV_SI_N"
print(Puzzle("TELEVISION", 4))
                    # Output: "TEL_VIS_ON"
```

14. Write a function countNow(PLACES) in Python, that takes the dictionary, PLACES as an argument and displays the names (in uppercase)of the places whose names are longer than 5 characters. **CBSE SQP 2023-24**

For example, Consider the following dictionary

```
PLACES={1:"Delhi",2:"London",3:"Paris",4:"New
York",5:"Doha"}
```

The output should be

LONDON

NEW YORK

Or

Write a function, lenWords(STRING), that takes a string as an argument and returns a tuple containing length of each word of a string.

For example, if the string is "Come let us have some fun", the tuple will have (4, 3, 2, 4, 4, 3)

Ans.
```
PLACES={1:"Delhi",2:"London",3:"Paris",4:"New
York",5:"Dubai"}
def countNow(PLACES):
    for i in PLACES.values():
        if len(i)>5:
            print(i.upper())
countNow(PLACES)
```

Or

```
def lenWords(STRING):
    T=()
    L=STRING.split()
    for word in L:
        length = len(word)
        T=T+(length,)
    return T
print (lenWords("Come let us have some fun"))
```

15. Predict the output of the following code **CBSE SQP 2023-24**

```
def Changer(P,Q=10):
    P=P/Q
    Q=P%Q
    return P
A=200
B=20
A=Changer(A, B)
print(A,B,sep = '$')
B=Changer(B)
print (A,B,sep='$',end='###')
```

Ans. 10.0$20,
10.0$2.0###

16. Atharva is a Python programmer working on a program to find and return the maximum value from the list. The code written below has syntactical errors. Rewrite the correct code and underline the corrections made. **Competency Based Que. CBSE 2023**

```
def max_num (L) :
    max=L(0)
    for a in L :
        if a > max
            max=a
    return max
```

Ans. Correct code is

```
def max_num(L):
    max = L[0]
    for a in L :
        if a > max :
            max = a
    return max
```

17. (a) **Write the output of the code given below** CBSE 2023

```
def short_sub(lst,n):
    for i in range(0, n):
        if len(lst)>4 :
            lst [i]=lst [i]+lst[i]
        else:
            lst[i]=lst[i]
subject=['CS','HINDI','PHYSICS','CHEMISTRY',
'MATHS']
short_sub(subject,5)
print(subject)
```

Or

(b) **Write the output of the code given below**

```
a = 30
def call(x):
    global a
    if a%2==0:
        x+=a
    else:
        x-=a
    return x
x=20
print(call(35), end="#")
print(call(40), end="@")
```

Ans. (a) **Output**

['CSCS', 'HINDIHINDI', PHYSICSPHYSICS, 'CHEMISTRYCHEMISTRY', 'MATHSMATHS']

Or

(b) **Output**

65#70@

18. **Predict the output of the code given below** CBSE 2023

```
def makenew(mystr):
    newstr=" "
    count=0
    for i in mystr:
        if count%2!=0:
            newstr=newstr+str(count)
        else:
            if i.lower( ):
                newstr=newstr+i.upper ( )
            else:
                newstr=newstr+i
        count+=1
    print (newstr)
makenew("No@1")
```

Ans. N1@3

19. **Rao has written a code to input a number and check whether it is prime or not. His code is having errors. Rewrite the correct code and underline the corrections made.** Competency Based Que. CBSE SQP 2022-23

```
def prime () :
  n=int(input("Enter number to check : : ")
  for i in range (2, n//2):
    if n%i=0:
      print("Number is not prime \n')
    break
    else:
      print("Number is prime \n')
```

Ans.

```
def prime() :
  n=int(input("Enter number to check ::"))
  for i in range (2, n//2):
    if n%i==0:
      print("Number is not prime \n")
      break
    else:
      print("Number is prime \n")
```

20. **Write the output of the code given below:** CBSE SQP 2022-23

```
p=5
def sum(q,r=2):
      global p
      p=r+q**2
      print(p, end= '#')
a=10
b=5
sum(a,b)
sum(r=5,q=1)
```

Ans. 105#6#

21. **What does the return statement do in a function? Explain with the help of an example.** CBSE 2025

Ans. The return statement exits a function and sends back a value in main program.

```
def add(a, b):
return a + b
```

Short Answer Type I Questions

22. **What are keyword arguments?**

Ans. If there is a function with many parameters and we want to specify only some of them in function call, then value for such parameters can be provided by using their names instead of the positions.

These are called keyword arguments keyword arguments need not be specified in any particular order.

e.g.,

```
def simpleinterest(p, n=2, r=0.6):
def simpleinterest(p, r=0.2, n=3):
```

23. What is a default parameter? How is it specified?

Ans. A parameter having default value in the function header is known as a default parameter.

A parameter can be specified as default only if all the parameters on its right are specified as default. To specify a default parameter syntax is

```
def<function header> (arg1, arg2---arg x
=<value>):
```

argx will now be a default parameter with default value as the value specified.

24. Explain Scope of Variables.

Ans. All variables in a program may not be accessible at all locations in that program. This depends on where you have declared a variable.

The scope of a variable determines the portion of the program where you can access a particular identifier. There are two basic scopes of variables in Python:

(i) Global variables

(ii) Local variables

25. What do you understand by local and global scope of variables? How can you access a global variable inside the function, if function has a variable with same name.

Ans. A global variable is a variable that is accessible globally i.e everywhere in the program. A local variable is one that is only accessible to the current scope, such as temporary variables used in a single function definition. A variable declared outside of the function or in global scope is known as global variable. This means, global variable can be accessed inside or outside of the function where as local variable can be used only inside the function. We can access a global variable by declaring variable as global.

26. What will be the output of following code?

```
a =45
def Fun1 ():
    global a
    print ("Value of a is", a)
    a = 5
    print ("Changed global a to", a)
Fun1 ()
print ("Value of a is", a)
```

Ans. Output

Value of a is 45

Changed global a to 5

Value of a is 5

27. What will be the output of the following? Explain.

```
def f1 ()
  n = 44
def f2 ()
  n = 77
  print (" Value of n", n)
  Print (" Value of n", n)
```

Ans. Firstly call the function

f1()

f2()

Then output will be look like as:

Value of n 77

Value of n 77

28. The code given below accepts five numbers and displays whether they are even or odd :
Observe the following code carefully and rewrite it after removing all syntax and logical errors : **CBSE 2024**

Underline all the corrections made.

```
def EvenOdd ( )
  for i in range (5) :
     num = int (input ("Enter a number")
     if num/2== 0 :
        print ("Even")
     else:
     print ("Odd")
EvenOdd ( )
```

Ans.

```
def EvenOdd():
  for i in range(5):
     num = int(input("Enter a number: "))
     if num % 2 == 0:
        print("Even")
     else:
        print("Odd")
EvenOdd()
```

29. Write a function, c_words ( ) in Python that separately counts and displays the number of uppercase and lowercase alphabets in a text file, Words. txt. **CBSE 2024**

Ans.

```
def c_words():
    with open("Words.txt", "r") as f:
        Txt = f.read()
    CL = CU = 0
    for i in Txt:
        if i.islower():
            CL += 1
        elif i.isupper():
            CU += 1
    print(CL, CU)
c_words()
```

30. Predict the output of the following code : **CBSE 2024**

```
def callon(b=20, a=10):
    b = b + a
    a = b - a
    print(b, "#", a)
    return b
x = 100
y = 200
x = callon(x, y)
```

```
    print(x, "@", y)
    y = callon(y)
    print(x, "@", y)
```

Ans. 300#100
300@200
210#200
300@210

31. The code given below accepts a number as an argument and returns the reverse number. Observe the following code carefully and rewrite it after removing all syntax and logical errors. Underline all the corrections made. **CBSE SQP 2023-24, Competency Based Que.**

```
define revNumber(num):
    rev=0
    rem=0
    While num>0:
        rem == num %10
        rev = rev*10 + rem
        num = num//10
        return rev
print(revNumber(1234))
```

Ans. Correct code is

```
def revNumber(num):
    rev=0
    rem=0
    while num>0:
        rem=num %10
        rev=rev*10+rem
        num=num//10
    return rev
print (revNumber(1234))
```

32. Write a function EOReplace() in Python, which accepts a list L of numbers. Thereafter, it increments all even numbers by 1 and decrements all odd numbers by 1. **CBSE 2023**

Example:
If Sample Input data of the list is
L=[10,20,30,40,35,55]
Output will be:
L=[11,21,31,41,34,54]

Ans.
```
def EOReplace(L):
    for i in range(len(L)):
        if L[i]%2==0:
            L[i]=L[i]+1
        else:
            L[i]=L[i]-1
    print(L)
    EOReplace(L)
```

33. Write a function INDEX_LIST(L), where L is the list of elements passed as argument to the function. The function returns another list named 'indexList' that stores the indices of all Non-Zero Elements of L. **CBSE SQP 2022-23**

For example:
If L contains [12, 4, 0, 11, 0, 56]
The indexList will have - [0, 1, 3, 5]

Ans.
```
def INDEX_LIST(L) :
    indexList=[]
    for a in range(0,len(L)):
        if not L[a]==0:
            indexList.append(a)
    return indexList
    print (INDEX_LIST(L))
```

34. Predict the output of the Python code given below: **CBSE SQP 2022-23**

```
def Diff(N1, N2):
    if N1>N2:
        return N1-N2
    else:
        return N2-N1
NUM = [10, 23, 14, 54, 32]
for CNT in range (4, 0, - 1):
    A=NUM[CNT]
    B=NUM[CNT-1]
    print(Diff(A,B),'#',end=' ')
```

Ans. 22 # 40 # 9 # 13 #

35. Write a Python method/function Count3 and 7(N) to find and display the count of all those numbers which are between 1 and N, which are either divisible by 3 or by 7. **CBSE SQP 2021-22 Term I**

For example:
If the value of N is 15
The count should be displayed as 7
(as 3,6,7,9,12,14,15 in between 1 to 15 are either divisible by 3 or 7)

Ans.
```
def Count3and7(N):
    c=0
    for i in range(1,N+1):
        if i%3==0 or i%7==0:
            c=c+1
            print c
```

36. The code given below accepta N as an integer argument and returns the sum of all integers from 1 to N. Observe the following code carefully and rewrite it after removing all syntax and logical errors. Underline all the corrections made. **CBSE 2025**

```
def Sum (N)
  for I in range (N):
S = S+I
  return S
print (Sum (10)
```

Ans. Corrected code

```
def Sum(N) :
    S = 0
    for I in range( 1, N+1 ):
        S = S + I
    return S
print(Sum(10))
```

Short Answers Type II Questions

37. **Observe the following Python code carefully and obtain the output, which will appear on the screen after execution of it.**

Ans.
```
def Findoutput():
    L = "earn"
    X = ""
    count = 1
    for i in L:
        if i in ['a', 'e', 'i', 'o', 'u']:
            X = X + i.swapcase()
        else:
            if count % 2 != 0:
                X = X + str(len(L[:count]))
            else:
                X = X + i
        count = count + 1
    print(X)
Findoutput()
```

38. **Observe the following Python code very carefully and rewrite it after removing all syntactical errors with each correction underlined.**

```
DEF execmain ():
 x = input ("Enter a number")
 if (abs (x) = x):
     print ("You entered a positive number:")
 else:
     x = *- 1
     print ("Number made postive :" x)
execmain ()
```

Ans.
```
def execmain ()
    x = input ("Enter a number")
    if (abs (x) = = x):
        print ("You entered a positive
                                number :")
    else:
        x* = - 1
        print ("Number made positive : " , x)
execmain()
```

39. **Write a user defined function findname (name) where name is an argument in Python to delete phone number from a dictionary phonebook on the basis of the name, where name is the key.**

Ans.
```
def findname(name):
    if name in phonebook:
        del phonebook[name]
    else:
        print("Name not found")
    print("Phonebook Information")
    print("Name\tPhone no")
    for i in phonebook:
        print(i, "\t", phonebook[i])
```

40. **Write a Python function generatefibo (n) where n is the limit, using a generator function Fibonacci (max) (where max is the limit n) that produces Fibonacci series.**

Ans.
```
def Fibonacci (max):
        a = 0
        b = 1
        while a < = max:
            yield a
            a, b = b, a + b
def   generatefibo (n):
        for i in Fibonacci (n):
            print (i)
```

41. **Riya was asked to accept a list of even numbers but she did not put the relevent condition while accepting the list of numbers. You are required to write a user defined function oddtoeven (L) that accepts the list L as an argument and convert all the odd numbers into even by multiplying them by 2.** Competency Based Que.

Ans.
```
def oddtoeven (L):
    for i in range (len(L)):
        if (L [i]% 2! = 0):
            L [i] = L [i] * 2
    print (L)
```

42. **(a) Predict the output of the following code:** CBSE 2025

```
def ExamOn (mystr):
    newstr = " "
    count = 0
    for i in mystr:
        if count%2 ! = 0:
            newstr = newstr + str (count -1)
        else:
            newstr = newstr + i.lower()
        count + = 1
    newstr = newstr + mystr[:2]
    print("The new string is:", newstr)
ExamOn ("GenX")
```

Or

(b) **Write the output on execution of the following Python code:**

```
def Change (X):
    for K,V in X.items() :
        L1.append(K)
        L2.append (V)
D = (1:"ONE", 2:"TWO", 3:"THREE")
L1 = []
L2 = []
Change (D)
print (L1)
print (L2)
print (D)
```

Ans. (a) The new string is : g0n2Ge

Or (b)
```
[1, 2, 3]
['ONE', 'TWO', 'THREE']
{1: 'ONE', 2: 'TWO', 3: 'THREE'}
```

43. How can you return multiple values from a function. Write its different ways.

Ans. Refer to text on page no 69. (Returning Multiple Values)

Long Answer Type Questions

44. Rahul and Aryan both are friends. They want to display addition of age, subtraction of height, multiply of weight and division of IQ. **Competency Based Que.**

Description as follows:

Rahul	Description
Age	32
Height	175 cm
Weight	75 kg
IQ	100

Aryan	Description
Age	25
Height	165 cm
Weight	75 kg
IQ	50

Firstly, define the function add (), sub (), mul () and div ().

Ans.
```
def add (a, b):
    print("ADDING % d + % d" % (a, b))
    return a + b
def subtract (a, b):
    print("SUBTRACTING % d - % d" % (a, b))
    return a - b
def multiply (a, b):
    print ("MULTIPLYING % d*% d" %(a, b))
    return a * b
def divide (a, b):
    print ("DIVIDING % d / % d" % (a, b))
    return a/b
```

Now call these functions:

```
>>> age = add (32, 25)
ADDING  32 + 25
>>> age
57
>>> height = subtract (175, 165)
SUBTRACTING 175 - 165
>>> height
10
>>> weight = multiply (75, 70)
MULTIPLYING 75 * 70
>>> weight
5250
>>> IQ = divide (100, 50)
DIVIDING 100/50
>>> IQ
2
```

45. Differentiate between actual parameter(s) and formal parameter(s) with a suitable example for each.

Ans. The list of identifiers used in a function call is called actual parameter(s) whereas the list of parameters used in the function definition is called formal parameter(s).

Actual parameter may be value / variable or expression.

Formal parameter is an identifier.

Example:

```
def area(side): # line 1
    return side*side
print(area(5)) # line 2
```

In line 1, side is the formal parameter and in line 2, while invoking area() function, the value 5 is the actual parameter.

A formal parameter, i.e. a parameter, is in the function definition. An actual parameter, i.e. an argument, is in a function call.

46. What is the difference between local variable and global variable ? Also, give a suitable Python code to illustrate both.

Ans. The differences between a local variable and a global variable are given below:

Local Variable	Global Variable
These are declared within a function.	These are declared outside all functions.
Local variable is accessible only within a function in which it is declared.	Global variable is accessible throughout the program.

Local Variable	Global Variable
It is also called an internal variable.	It is also called an external variable.
The local variable of two functions may be declared with same name.	No two global variables in a program may have same name.

e.g.
```
a = 10                #global variable
def value (i) :
    c = 0             #local variable
    c = a + i
    return c
```
Now call the function value
```
>>> value (5)
```
Output

15

47. Explain the use of global key word used in a function with the help of a suitable example.

Ans. In Python, global keyword allows the programmer to modify the variable outside the current scope.

It is used to create a global variable and make changes to the variable in local context. A variable declared inside a function is by default local and a variable declared outside the function is global by default. The keyword global is written inside the function to use its global value. Outside the function, global keyword has no effect.

Example
```
c = 10  # global variable
def add():
    global c
    c = c + 2 # global value of c is incremented by 2
    print("Inside add():", c)
add()
c=15
print("In main:",c)
```
Output

Inside add(): 12

In main: 15

Case Study Based Questions

Case Study 1

These are the values provided in function call/ invoke statement. Required arguments are the arguments passed to a function in correct positional order. Keyword arguments are related to the function calls. When you use keyword arguments in a function call, the caller identifies the arguments by the parameter name. A default argument is an argument that assumes a default value, if a value is not provided in the function call for that argument.

(i) How many types of arguments are there in functions?

(a) 2 (b) 3 (c) 4 (d) 5

(ii) Which argument is an argument that assumes a default value?

(a) Default argument (b) Positional argument
(c) Keyword argument (d) None of the above

(iii) Which arguments are also known as positional arguments?

(a) Keyword argument
(b) Default argument
(c) Required argument
(d) Variable length argument

(iv) Which of these is/are formal argument (s)?

(a) Required argument (b) Keyword argument
(c) Default argument (d) All of these

(v) ………… are the values provided in function call/invoke statement.

(a) Functions (b) Arguments
(c) Preprocessor (d) Models

Ans. (i) (c) There are four arguments in functions as:
- Required arguments/Positional arguments.
- Keyword arguments
- Default arguments
- Variable length arguments

(ii) (a) A default arguments is an arguments that assumes a default value, if a value is not provided in the function call for that argument.

(iii) (c) Required arguments are also known positional argument. These arguments are the arguments passed to a function in correct positional order.

(iv) (d) Formal arguments are the values provided in function call/invoke statement. You can call a function by using the following types of formal arguments as
- Required arguments
- Key word arguments
- Default arguments
- Variable length arguments

(v) (b) Argument are the values provided in function call/invoke statement. A function is a block of organised and reusable code that is used to perform a single, related action.

Case Study 2

A function is a block of organised and reusable code that is used to perform a single, related action. Functions provide better modularity for your application and a high degree of code reusability. The function blocks begin with the keyword def followed by the function name and parentheses (). Any input parameters or arguments should be placed within these parentheses. You can also define parameters inside these parentheses.

(i) Which keyword is used to define function?

(ii) Which type of bracket is placed after name of function?

(iii) A/An .... is a block of organised and reusable code.

(iv) Parameters are defined inside ....

(v) Function is used to perform .... related action.

Ans. (i) A function is a block of organised and reusable code that is used to perform a single, related action. The function block begins with the keyword def followed by the function name.

(ii) The function blocks begin with the keyword def followed by the function name and parentheses (). Any input parameters or arguments should be placed within these parentheses.

(iii) A function is a block of organised and reusable code that is used to perform a single, related action. Functions provide better modularity for your application and a high degree of code reusability.

(iv) Parameters are defined inside parentheses to function are references to object, which are passed value. When you pass a variable to a function, Python passes the reference to the object to which the variable refers.

(v) Function is used to perform related action. A function is a block by code which only runs when it is called. You can pass data, known as parameters into a function.

Case Study 3

Here is the function to find the sum of arguments

```
total = _____                  # Line 1
def sum (arg1, arg2) __        # Line 2
    total = arg1 + _____       # Line 3
    print (total)
    return _____               # Line 5
total = sum (10, 20)
print ( _____ )                # Line 7
```

(i) Which value or constant will be equal to variable total in line 1?

(a) 1 (b) 0
(c) 2 (d) None

(ii) Which symbol is used to terminate the function def in line 2?

(a) ; (b) .
(c) : (d) ,

(iii) Fill the blank in line 3

(a) sum (b) 1
(c) arg2 (d) 0

(iv) Which value will be return in line 5?

(a) sum (b) total
(c) True (d) False

(v) Fill the blank in line 7.

(a) sum (b) True
(c) False (d) total

Ans. (i) (b) Here total is the variable whose value is fixed during the execution of the program

(ii) (c) Python provides the def keyword to define the function the function def in line 2 is terminated with symbol:

(iii) (c) Total is defined the sum of arg 1 and arg 2.

(iv) (b) This function will return the value of variable total.

(v) (d) Line 7 will print the value of total which is the sum of arg 1 and arg

SELF ASSESSMENT TEST

Multiple Choice Questions

1 There is .... at the end of the def line.

(a) colon (:) (b) semicolon (;)
(c) comma (,) (d) blank ()

2 A default argument is a part of

(a) keyword (b) function declaration
(c) function definition (d) positional argument

3 How many kind of scope are there in Python?

(a) One (b) Three (c) Two (d) Four

4 Which of the following scope is defined at the uppermost level?

(a) Built-in (b) Global
(c) Enclosed (d) Local

Fill in the Blanks

5 .... always begins at the first statement of the program.

6 Argument refers to any expression within the parentheses of a ....

7 .... or named argument is one of types of passing argument.

State Whether True or False

8 Built-in functions are known as library functions.

9 Function definition part only define the name of function and specify the parameters.

Assertion and Reason Based Questions

Assertion (A) and Reason (R) Type questions. Choose the correct option as

(a) Both Assertion (A) and Reason (R) are true, and Reason (R) is the correct explanation of Assertion (A)
(b) Both Assertion (A) and Reason (R) are true, but Reason (R) is not the correct explanation of Assertion (A)
(c) Assertion (A) is True, but Reason (R) is False
(d) Assertion (A) is False, but Reason (R) is True

10 **Assertion (A)** Function contain def keyword to provide the required functionality.

Reason (R) There is a semicolon (;) at the end of the def line.

11 **Assertion (A)** Scope of variables in Python program, shows the area where you can use it.

Reason (R) The part of the program where a variable is accessible can be defined as the scope of that variable.

Very Short Answer Type Questions

12 Write the syntax for calling a function.

13 What is the difference between parameters and arguments?

14 Can multiple namespaces use the same name?

Short Answer Type Questions

15 How to define a function?

16 What is mean by keyword arguments?

17 How can you pass string to functions?

18 Explain the term scope of variables.

Long Answer Type Questions

19 What is function? Also, define its types in Python.

20 Explain the local variable with an example.

Case Based Type Question

21. Shrey wrote the program to perform binary search. Help him to execute following program successfully.

```
def Search (a, data):
    lb = 0
    ub = len (a) - 1
    pos = ........
    while .......... :
        mid = int ((ub + lb)/2)
        if (a[mid] = = data) :
            pos = ........
            return
            break
        elif .......... :
            lb = mid + 1
        else :
            ..........
```

(i) Fill the blank in Line 4.
(ii) Which condition will be use in while loop?
(iii) Which value should be assign to pos in Line 8?
(iv) Fill the blank in Line 11 to satisfy the condition elif.
(v) Fill the blank in last line.

Answers

1. (a) 2. (c) 3. (d) 4. (a) 5. Keywords
6. Function call 7. Execution 8. True
9. False 10. (a) 11. (c)
21. (i) → 1, (ii) → lb< = ub, (iii) → mid, (iv) → a[mid] < data (v) → ub = mid-1

04

CHAPTER

File handling is the process of opening, reading, writing and closing files in a program.
It is used to store data in a computer permanently and to perform tasks like data processing, storage and retrieval.

File Handling

▼ **YOUR STUDY GOALS**

4.1 Data File
4.2 Working with Text Files
4.3 Working with Binary Files
4.4 Working with CSV Files

▼ **YOUR PRACTICE GOAL**

- Objective Type Questions (77 Qs ; MCQs, True or False, Fill in the Blanks, Assertion and Reason)
- Subjective Type Questions (65 Qs ; VSA, SA, LA)
- Case Based Questions (Subjective Case Studies-2, Objective Case Study-2)

Most of the computer applications work with files, as files help in storing the information permanently.

A file is a named location on a secondary storage media where data are permanently stored for later access.

Each programming language has some provision to use and create files through programs. Python also supports file handling and allows user to handle files, i.e. to read and write files, along with many other file handling options.

4.1 Data File

Data files are the files that store and preserve data released to a particular application.

Computers store every file as a collection of 0s and 1s, i.e. in binary form. Therefore, every file is basically just a series of bytes stored.

Python language supports three types of data files; text files, binary files, csv files are as follows

Text File

It is a sequence of characters consisting of alphabets, numbers and other special symbols. It stores information in ASCII characters. In text file, each line of text is terminated with a special character known as EOL (End of Line) or delimiter. When this EOL character is read or written, certain internal translations take place.

The default EOL character in Python is the newline (\n). Contents in a text file are usually separated by whitespace, but comma (,) and tab (\t) are also commonly used to separate values in a text file. The file extension of text file is .txt.

Binary File

It is a file that contains information in the same format as it is held in memory. In binary files, no delimiters are used for a line and no translations occur here. They represent the actual content such as image, audio, video, executable files, etc. These files are not human readable. The file extension of binary file is .dat.

CSV File

CSV (Comma Separated Values) format is one of the most simple and common ways to store data in tabular form. It stores tabular data in plain text. Each line of the file is a data record.

Each record consists of one or more fields separated by commas. To represent a CSV file, it must be saved with the .csv file extension.

4.2 Working with Text Files

In every programming language, there are two basic principles to handle file, open and close. Before working with file in Python language, you need to open it in a specific mode as per the file manipulation task you want to perform.

Opening a File

In file handling, the first requirement is opening a file. Once a file is opened, read, write, append, close, etc., can be performed on the file.

To open a file, open() method is used in Python.

Syntax

```
FileObject=open(file_name[,access_mode])
```

Parameters

- **file_name** The file_name argument is a string value that contains the name of the file to be opened.
- **access_mode** The access_mode determines the mode in which the file has to be opened, i.e., read, write, append, etc. This is optional parameter and the default file access mode is read(r).

Text File Access Mode

The file access modes and their description are as follows

Mode	Description
r	Opens a file for reading only. The file pointer is placed at the beginning of the file. This is the default mode.
r+	Opens a file for both reading and writing. The file pointer placed at the beginning of the file.
w	Opens a file for writing only. Overwrites the file if the file exists. If the file does not exist, it creates a new file for writing.
w+	Opens a file for both writing and reading. Overwrites the file if the file exists. If the file does not exist, creates a new file for reading and writing.
a	Opens a file for appending. The file pointer is placed at the end of the file if the file exists. If the file does not exist, it creates a new file for writing.
a+	Opens a file for both appending and reading. The file pointer is placed at the end of the file if the file exists. If the file does not exist, it creates a new file for reading and writing.

The File Object Attributes

File objects are used to read and write data to a file on disk. Once a file is opened and you have one file object, you can get various information related to that file.

All attributes related to file object are as follows

Attribute	Description
file.closed	Returns True if the file is closed, otherwise False.
file.mode	Returns the access mode in which file was opened.
file.name	Returns name of the file.

Example 1. To open the file using open() method.

```
f=open("file.txt","w")
print("Name of the file : ",f.name)
print("Closed or not : ", f.closed)
print("Opening mode : ", f.mode)
```

Output

Name of the file : file.txt

Closed or not: False

Opening mode: w

Opening a File Using with Clause in Python

In Python, the with statement is used to simplify the process of opening and closing files. Python will automatically close the file once the block of code is done—even if there's an error while working with the file. This helps prevent file damage and also removes the need to write file.close() manually.

Syntax
```
with open("filename.txt", "mode") as
file_object:
```
e.g.
```
with open("example.txt", "r") as f:
    content = f.read()
    print(content)
```

Closing a File

It is important to close files as soon as you have finished your work with file. Opened file is closed by calling the close() method of its file objects.

Python automatically closes a file when the reference object of a file is reassigned to another file. It is a good practice to use the close() method to close a file.

Syntax `FileObject.close()`

Python makes sure that any unwritten or unsaved data is flushed off to the file before it is closed.

Example 2 To close the file using close() method.
```
f=open("file.txt","w")
print("of the file: ",f.name)
print("Closed or not: ",f.closed)
print("Opening mode: ",f.mode)
f.close()
```
Output

Name of the file: file.txt
Closed or not: False
Opening mode: w

Writing into Files

For writing to a file, we first need to open it in write or append mode. If we open an existing file in write mode, the previous data will be erased and the file object will be positioned at the beginning of the file.

On the other hand, in append mode, new data will be added at the end of the previous data as the file object is at the end of the file.

In Python, there are two methods of file objects which are used to write data into a files.

(a) write()

write() method takes a string and writes it into the file. This method does not add a newline character ('\n') to the end of the string.

Syntax
```
<FileHandle>.write(str1)
```
Here, str1 is file referenced by <FileHandle>.

<FileHandle> is the file-object holding open file's reference.

Example 3 To write a employee's name in a text file using write() method.
```
f=open("employee.txt","w")
  if not f :
    print("File does not created")
  else :
    for i in range(6):
      name=input("Enter name of employee:")
      f.write(name)
  f.close()
```
Output

Enter name of employee : Shreya
Enter name of employee : Khushi
Enter name of employee : Ashmit
Enter name of employee : Kiyaan
Enter name of employee : Kiran
Enter name of employee : Rahul

User can see the created file in the same folder where Python program is saved.

Created File

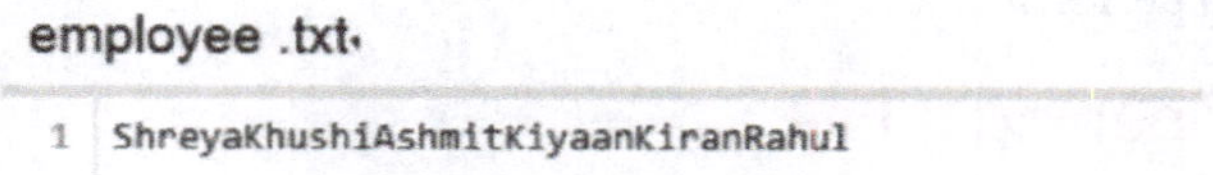

You can also hold some data in separate lines using write () method with the help of new line character '\n' as

e.g.
```
f = open ("employee.txt","w")
  if not f :
    print("File does not created")
  else :
    for i in range (6) :
      name = input ("Enter name of
                          employee:")
      f.write(name + '\n')
  f.close ()
```
Output

Enter name of employee : Shreya
Enter name of employee : Khushi
Enter name of employee : Ashmit
Enter name of employee : Kiyaan
Enter name of employee : Kiran
Enter name of employee : Rahul

Created File

employee .txt

```
Shreya
Khushi
Ashmit
Kiyaan
Kiran
Rahul
```

If numeric data are to be written to a text file, the data need to be converted into string before writing to the file.

e.g.
```
f=open("hello.txt","w")
Salary=12500
f.write(str(Salary))
print("Successfully compiled")
f.close()
```

Output

Successfully compiled

Created File

hello.txt

```
12500
```

(b) writelines ()

Whenever, we have to write a sequence of string to a file, we will use writelines() instead of write().

Syntax <FileHandle>.writelines(L)

Here, all strings in list L as lines to file referenced by <FileHandle>.

Example 4 To write a teacher's name line by line in a text file using writelines() method.

```
c=int(input("How many records do you
                                   want :"))
f=open("Teacher.txt","w")
if not f:
   print("File does not created")
else:
   L=[]
   for i in range(c):
      name=input("Enter name of teacher:")
      L.append(name+'\n')
   f.writelines(L)
f.close()
```

Output

How many records do you want :5

Enter name of teacher : Sidhaaratha Sharma

Enter name of teacher : Nisha Mishra

Enter name of teacher : Soniya Verma

Enter name of teacher : Kiran Gupta

Enter name of teacher : Ansh Sharma

Created File

Teacher.txt

```
Sidhaaratha Sharma
Nisha Mishra
Soniya Verma
Kiran Gupta
Ansh Sharma
```

Reading from Files

After writing information into a file, you must need to read that data at some point. Python provides mainly four types of read methods to read data from file.

Here, the content of file 'arihant.txt' is as follows

Welcome to Arihant!

Welcome to your one-step solutions for all your study, practice and assessment needs for various competitive & recruitment examinations and school segment.

These methods are as follows

(a) read()

This method returns a string containing all characters in a file.

Syntax <FileHandle>.read()

Here, <FileHandle> is the file object holding open file's reference. We are using a file namely "arihant.txt" storing some content.

Example 5 To read entire data from text file.

```
myfile=open('arihant.txt','r')
s=myfile.read()
print(s)
myfile.close()
```

Output

Welcome to arihant!

Welcome to your one-step solutions for all your study, practice and assessment needs for various competitive & recruitment examinations and school segment.

(b) read([size])

This method specifies how many characters the string should return.

Syntax <FileHandle>.read(n)

Here, <FileHandle> is the file object holding open file's reference and 'n' determines number of characters.

If no argument is specified, it reads a complete line and returns string.

Example 6 To read n bytes from text file.

```
myfile=open ('arihant.txt','r')
s=myfile.read(15)
print(s)
myfile.close()
```

Output

Welcome to arih

Example 7 To read n bytes and then reading some more bytes from the last position in text file.

```
myfile=open('arihant.txt','r')
s=myfile.read(10)
print(s)
s1=myfile.read(30)
print(s1)
myfile.close()
```

Output

Welcome to
arihant!
Welcome to your one

(c) readline()

The readline() method will read from a file line by line. For readline(), a line is terminated by '\n' or End of Line (EOL) (i.e. new line character). When end of file is reached, readline() will return an empty string.

Syntax <FileHandle>.readline()

Example 8 To read a file's first three lines line by line.

```
f=open('arihant.txt','r')
str=f.readline()
print(str)
str=f.readline()
print(str)
str=f.readline()
print(str)
f.close()
```

Output

Welcome to arihant!

Welcome to your one-step solutions for all your study, practice and assessment needs for various competitive &

Example 9 To read a entire file line by line.

```
myfile=open('arihant.txt','r')
while True:
    s=myfile.readline()
    if(len(s)<=0):
        break
    print(s)
myfile.close()
```

Output

Welcome to arihant!

Welcome to your one-step solutions for all your study, practice and assessment needs for various competitive & recruitment examinations and school segment.

(d) readlines()

This method will return a list of strings, each separated by '\n'.

This method reads all rows and retains the newlines character that is at the end of every row.

Syntax <FileHandle>.readlines()

Example 10 To read complete file in a list from text file.

```
myfile=open('arihant.txt','r')
s=myfile.readlines()
print(s)
myfile.close()
```

Output

['Welcome to arihant!\n', 'Welcome to your one-step solutions for all your study, \n', 'practice and assessment needs for various competitive & \n', 'recruitment examinations and school segment.']

Example 11 To show the size of a file after removing End of Line (EOL) characters and blank spaces and also print the size of entire file.

```
f=open('arihant.txt','r')
str=" "
s=0
ts=0
while str:
    str=f.readline()
    ts=ts+len(str)
    s=s+len(str.strip())
print("Size of file after removing all EOL
            characters & blank spaces : ",s)
print("Total size of the file: ",ts)
f.close()
```

Output

Size of file after removing all EOL characters & blank spaces: 172

Total size of the file: 175

Example 12 To print the size of entire file in bytes.

```
f=open('student.txt','r')
str=f.read()
```

```
    s=len(str)
    print ("Size of the file is")
    print (s, "bytes")
    f.close()
```

Output

Size of the file is

175 bytes

Example 13 To print the number of line of entire file.

```
f=open('student.txt','r')
s=f.readlines()
lcount=len(s)
print("Number of lines in file is: ",lcount)
f.close()
```

Output

Number of lines in file is: 4

Use of os module

Python's os module provides a unified interface to a number of operating system methods. The os module automatically loads the right implementation module when it is first imported. Before using these modules, you must have to import the os module.

Renaming and Deleting Files

The Python OS module enables interaction with the operating system.

The OS module provides the function that are involved in the file processing operations, like renaming, deleting, etc.

rename() method

This method is used to rename the file. This method does not return any value.

Syntax

```
os.rename(old_FileName,new_FileName)
```

We are using a file namely 'student.txt' storing the content.

S01, Rahul Verma, First division

S02, Reetesh Deshmukh, First division

S03, Aaditya Mishra, Second division

S04, Aradhaya Sinha, Third division

S05, Manish Sharma,Third division

Example 14 To display the content of file after changing the name of file.

```
import os
f= 'student.txt'
if os.path.isfile(f):
    os.rename('student.txt','student1.txt')
    f1='student1.txt'
    ob=open(f1,'r')
    print("Content of new file…")
    for i in ob:
        print(i.rstrip())
    ob.close()
else:
    print("Source file does not exist")
```

Output

Content of new file…

S01,Rahul Verma, First division

S02,Reetesh Deshmukh,First division

S03,Aaditya Mishra,Second division

S04,Aradhaya Sinha,Third division

S05,Manish Sharma,Third division

remove() method

This method is used to remove the existing file. This method does not return any value.

Syntax `os.remove(FileName)`

Example 15 To remove the file and print the status about the file that it exist or not.

```
import os
print("Enter the file name which you
                        want to be deleted:")
f=input()
if os.path.isfile(f):
    os.remove(f)
    print("File successfully deleted")
else:
    print("File does not exist")
```

Output

Enter the file name which you want to be deleted:

'sub'

File does not exist

....

Enter the file name which you want to be deleted:

'sub.txt'

File successfully deleted

Appending Data into a File

In order to append a new line in your existing file, you need to open the file in append mode, by setting 'a' as the mode.

With file access mode 'a', open () function first checks if file exists or not. If the file does not exist, then it creates an empty file and opens it.

Whereas if file exists then opens it. You can also use file access mode 'a+' to open file in reading as well as writing mode.

Syntax

```
FileObject = open('filename', 'a' or 'a+')
```

The content of 'computer.txt' file

Computer science

Head

Authors

Proofreaders

Example 16 To append data into text file.

```
f = open("computer.txt","a")
f.write("\n Welcome to our company")
f.write ("\n I hope you will learn more here")
print ("Append the data")
f.close()
```

Output

Append the data

Content of file after appending the data :

Computer science

Head

Authors

Proofreaders

Welcome to our company

I hope you will learn more here

Quick Test 1

1. In which form, data are stored in binary file?
2. What is file?
3. What is the use of access mode?
4. What is the difference between write() and writelines()?
5. How can you terminate the line?
6. When is os module used in Python program?

flush() Method

This method will force out any unsaved data that exists in a program buffer to the actual file.

Typically, this means that the data will be copied from the program buffer to the operating system buffer(file).

Python automatically flushes the files when closing them. But you may want to flush the data before closing any file.

Syntax `FileObject.flush()`

Example 17 To write the data into file using flush() method.

```
file1=open("flush.log","w+")
file1.write("Status is \n")
file1.write("overall good")
file1.flush()
```

Created File

flush.log

```
1  Status is
2  overall good
```

The flush() method ensures that whatever is held in output buffer, written on the actual file on disk.

Random Access Methods

When you read from file or write in a file, then by default the access is sequential. This means, the read() method always reads data from the beginning of a file and write() method always writes data at the end of data.

File pointer specifies the current position in the file where writing or reading will take place.

Python provides two methods to perform random access operations in a file. These methods help you to manipulate the position of file pointer and thus you can read and write from desired position in the file.

tell() Method

This method tells you the current position within the file, measured in bytes from the beginning of the file.

Syntax `FileObject.tell()`

where, FileObject is the handle of open file.

Now, we are using a file namely 'computer.txt' storing the content.

Computer science

Head

Authors

Proofreaders

Example 18 To know the current position in a text file.

```
import os
tfile='computer.txt'
if os.path.isfile(tfile):
    f=open(tfile,'r+')
    cs=f.readline()
    print("This is first line: ",cs)
```

```
        pos=f.tell()
        print("Current position is :",pos)
        f.close()
    else:
        print("File does not exist")
```

Output

This is first line: Computer science

Current position is :17

seek() Method

This method can be used to change the current position in a file. This method does not return any value.

Syntax

```
FileObject.seek(offset[,mode])
```

Parameters

- **offset** This argument indicates the number of bytes to be moved.
- **mode** This is a number 0 or 1 or 2 signifying. If mode is set to 0, it means use the beginning of the file as the reference position, 1 means use the current position of file as reference position and 2 means use end of file would be taken as the reference position.

Example 19 Check the position of file pointer after first line and print the data of current position and then read the 35th position data from the file.

```
import os
tfile='computer.txt'
if os.path.isfile(tfile):
    f=open(tfile, 'r+')
    cs=f.readline()
    print ("This is first line : ",cs)
    pos=f.tell()
    print("Current position is :",pos)
    f.seek(pos)
    cs=f.readline()
    print("Current position data: ",cs)
    f.seek (35)
    cs=f.readline()
    print("35th position data: ",cs)
    f.close()
else:
    print("File does not exist")
```

Output

This is first line: Computer science
Current position is: 17
Current position data: Head
35th position data: readers

Relative and Absolute Path

A **relative path** is the path that is relative to the working directory location on your computer. Relative path does not start with a leading forward slash and is interpreted from the perspective of the current working directory.

An **absolute path** is the path that contains the entire path to the file or directory that you need to access. This path will begin at the home directory of your computer and end with the file or directory that you want to access. This path starts with a leading forward slash.

getcwd()

This method returns the current working directory of a process.

Syntax `str = os.getcwd()`

Example 20 To display the current working directory.

```
import os
s=os.getcwd()
print("Working folder is %s ",s)
```

Output

Working folder is

C:\Users\Arihant

abspath()

This method returns a normalised absolutised version of the pathname path that means returns the complete path name of the data file.

Syntax

```
FileObject=os.path.abspath(FileName)
```

Example 21 To display the complete path name of the data file.

```
import os
f='computer.txt'
p=os.path.abspath(f)
print("Complete path is ",p)
```

Output

Complete path is

C:\Users\Arihant\computer.txt

Standard File Streams

The standard file streams are simply pre-opened Python file objects that are automatically connected to the program's standard streams when Python starts up.

There are three basic I/O connections : standard input, standard output and standard error.

- **sys.stdin** It stands for standard input. To read a line from a user (keyboard/input device), you must be call sys.stdin.readline().
- **sys.stdout** It stands for standard output. To write a line to a user (monitor). You must be call sys.stdout.write().
- **sys.stderr** It stands for standard error. This file object is used for error message only, even though its output goes for same destination as stdout.

e.g.
```
import sys
f = open ("computer.txt")
l1 = f.readline()
l2 = f.readline()
sys.stdout.write(l1)
sys.stdout.write(l2)
sys.stderr.write ("is no error")
```

Output

Computer science

Head

There is no error

Quick Test 2

1. When Python does automatically flush the files?
2. What is the use of tell() method?
3. Write the syntax of seek() method.
4. Name any two I/O connections.

4.3 Working with Binary Files

Python object handles the binary files. Python provides a special module-the **pickle module** which can be used to store any kind of object in file.

Binary File Access Mode

Binary file access modes and their description are as follows

Mode	Description
rb	Opens a file for reading only in binary format. The file pointer is placed at the beginning of the file. This is the default mode.
rb+	Opens a file for both reading and writing in binary format. The file pointer is placed at the beginning of the file.
wb	Opens a file for writing only in binary format. Overwrites the file if the file exists. If file does not exist, creates a new file for writing.
wb+	Opens a file for both writing and reading in binary format. Overwrites the file if the file exists. If file does not exist, it creates a new file for reading and writing.
ab	Opens a file for appending in binary format. The file pointer is at the end of the file if the file exists. If file does not exist, it creates a new file for writing.
ab+	Opens a file for both appending and reading in binary format. The file pointer is at the end of the file if the file exists. If file does not exist, it creates a new file for appending and writing.

Opening and Closing Binary Files

Opening binary file is same as opening text file that means binary files can be opened by open() method.

Syntax
```
FileObject=open(FileName[,access_mode])
```

After finishing your working in file, it is important to close it. For closing a opening binary file can be used close( ) method like as text file.

Syntax
```
FileObject.close()
```

e.g.
```
file1=open("bin.dat","wb+")
print("Name of the file : ",file1.name)
print("Closed or not: ",file1.closed)
print("Opening mode : ",file1.mode)
file1.close()
```

Output

Name of the file: bin.dat

Closed or not: False

Opening mode: wb+

Using Pickle Module

To save any types of data (object structure), Python provides a module called pickle. The pickle module is used for serializing and de-serializing any Python object structure.

Serialization is the process of transforming data or an object in memory (RAM) to a stream of bytes called byte stream. Serialization process is also called pickling.

De-serialization or unpickling is the inverse of pickling process where a byte stream is converted back to Python object.

In Python, pickle module provides two main methods dump( ) and load( ) for writing and reading in binary files.

Using dump( ) Method

This method is used to write objects to a file. Before use the dump( ) method, you first have to import the pickle module.

Syntax

```
import pickle
   ......
   ......
   ......
pickle.dump(object_to_pickle, FileObject)
```

Parameters

- **pickle** is the module which can be used to store any kind of object in file.
- **object_to_pickle** is either a variable, an instance of class or list, tuple, etc.
- **FileObject** is the name of file in which you want to write.

e.g.
```
import pickle
number_of_data = int(input('Enter the
                                     number of data:'))
list1 = []
for i in range(number_of_data):
   r = input('Enter data '+str(i+1)+' : ')
   list1.append(r)
file = open('imp.dat', 'wb')
pickle.dump(list1, file)
print("Data entered in file")
file.close()
```

Output

Enter the number of data: 5

Enter data 1 : 12

Enter data 2 : 65

Enter data 3 : 45

Enter data 4 : 86

Enter data 5 : 57

Data entered in file

Using load() Method

This method is used to load data from a binary file.

Syntax

```
import pickle
   ......
   ......
   ......
object=pickle.load(FileObject)
```

It is important to know that pickle.load() method would raise EOFError when you reach end of file while reading from file.

e.g.
```
import pickle
file = open('imp.dat', 'rb')
list1 = pickle.load(file)
file .close()
print('Showing the pickled data:')
cnt = 1
for item in list1:
   print('The data', cnt, ' is : ', item)
   cnt += 1
```

Output

Showing the pickled data:

The data 1 is: 12

The data 2 is: 65

The data 3 is: 45

The data 4 is: 86

The data 5 is: 57

Some Basic File Operations on Text and Binary Files in Python

Basic file operations like searching, inserting, deleting and updating on text file and binary file are same. So, we will discuss these operations only on text file.

Searching a File

When you are searching through data in a file, it is a very common pattern to read through a file, ignoring most of the lines and only processing lines which meet particular criteria.

Now, we are using a file namely 'school.txt' storing the content.

School

Teachers

Students

Labs

Sports

Example 22 To search any string in text file.

```
def check ():
   datafile = open ('school.txt')
   found = input("Enter any string to be
   searched: ")
   f=False
   for line in datafile:
         if found in line:
            f = True
            break
```

```
datafile. close()
    return f
f=check()
if(f==True):
    print("True")
else:
    print("False")
```

Output

Enter any string to be searched:

'School'

True

Enter any string to be searched:

'Faculty'

False

Inserting Data into File

Inserting data in already existing file can be happen in two ways:

Insertion at the end of file or insertion in the middle of the file. But there is no way to insert data in the middle of file in Python.

Now, we are using a file namely 'college.txt' storing the content.

College
Class
Lecturer
Students
Staff

Example 23 To insert element or data into an existing text file.

```
def insert():
    import pickle
    file1 = open('college.txt', 'ab')
    while True:
        y = input("Enter something: ")
        pickle.dump(y,file1)
        ans=input("Want to enter more data Y/N")
        if ans.upper()== 'N':
            break
    file1.close()
insert()
```

Output

Enter something: 'Subject'

Want to enter more data Y / N Y

Enter something: 'Study'

Want to enter more data Y / N N

Delete Data from File

Deleting the data from an already existing file, can be happen in two ways are as follows:

Type 1 For small file, which can fit into memory, i.e. a few Mb's.

Now, we are using a file namely 'company.txt' storing the content.

Company
Department
Manager
Employee
Project

Example 24 To delete the second word from a text file.

```
def delete():
    with open('company.txt', 'r') as f:
        l = f.readlines()
    print(l)
    del l[1]
    print("After deletion", l)
    f=open('company.txt','w')
    f.writelines(l)
    f.close()
delete()
```

Output

['Company\n', 'Department\n', 'Manager\n', 'Employee\n', 'Project']

After deletion:

['Company\n', 'Manager\n', 'Employee\n', 'Project']

Type 2 For using files, which will not fit into memory of computer. For this we will need two files.

Here, we are using a file namely 'python.txt' storing the content.

1. Get the data value to be deleted.
2. Open the file for reading from it.
3. Read the complete file into a list.
4. Delete the data from the list.
5. Close the file.
6. Open same file for writing into it.
7. Write the modified list into file.
8. Close the file.

Example 25 To delete the line(s) having word(passed as argument).

```
import os
def filedel(word):
    file1 = open("python.txt","r")
```

```
    nfile = open("algo1.txt", "w")
    while True:
        line = file1.readline()
        if not line:
            break
        else:
            if word in line:
                pass
            else:
                print(line)
                nfile.write(line)
        file1.close()
        nfile.close()
filedel('Write')
```

Output

1. Get the data value to be deleted.
2. Open the file for reading from it.
3. Read the complete file into a list.
4. Delete the data from the list.
5. Close the file.
6. Open same file for writing into it.
8. Close the file.

Created File

algo1.txt

```
1. Get the data value to be deleted
2. Open the file for reading from it
3. Read the complete file into a list
4. Delete the data from the list
5. Close the file
6. Open same file for writing into it
8. Close the file
```

Updating a File

Updating a file in Python can be happen in many ways, but we will discuss about to replace a particular word with another word.

Here, we are using a file namely 'server.log' storing the content.

1. Get the data value to be inserted with its position.
2. Open the original file in reading mode.
3. Open another (temporary) file for writing in it.
4. Start reading original file sequentially, simultaneously writing it in the temporary file.
5. This is to be repeated till you reach the position of insertion of new data value.
6. Write the new value in temporary file.
7. Repeat step 4 for remaining data of original file.
8. Delete original file.
9. Change the name of temporary file to original file.

Example 26 To replace a word with another word.

```
import os
import sys
import fileinput
f=0
print("Text to search for:")
textToSearch = input(">")
print("Text to replace it with:")
textToReplace = input(">")
tempFile = open( "server .log" , 'r+')
for line in fileinput.input("server.log"):
    if textToSearch in line:
        tempFile.write(line.replace(textToSea
        rch, texttoReplace)
        print("Match is found and
        modification done successfully")
        f=1
        break
if(f==0):
    print("Match is not found")
tempFile.close()
```

Output

Text to search for:
>'inserted'
Text to replace it with:
>'entered'
Match is found and modification done successfully
After replacing the update file is as follows

Created File

server.log

```
1. Get the data value to be entered with its position.
2. Open the original file in reading mode.
3. Open another (temporary) file for writing in it.
4. Start reading original file sequentially, simultaneously writing it in the temporary file.
5. This is to be repeated till you reach the position of insertion of new data value.
6. Write the new value in temporary file.
7. Repeat step 4 for remaining data of original file.
8. Delete original file.
9. Change the name of temporary file to original file.
```

Now, we are using a file namely 'sample.txt' storing the content.

The next few lessons will involve downloading a web page from the Internet and reorganising the contents into useful chunks of information.

You will be **going** most of your work using Python code written and executed in Komodo Edit.

going into

into **going**

Example 27 To replace a more than one same word with another word.

```
from tempfile import mkstemp
from shutil import move
from os import remove, close
def replace(file_path, pattern, subst):
    f=0
    #Create temp file
    fh, abs_path = mkstemp()
        with open(abs_path, 'w') as new_file:
            with open(file_path) as old_file:
                for line in old_file:
                    new_file.write(line.replace
                                   (pattern, subst))
        close(fh)
        #Remove original file
        remove(file_path)
        #Move new file
        move(abs_path, file_path)
replace("sample.txt", "going", "doing")
print("Replace successfully")
```

Output

Replace successfully

Created File

sample.txt

```
The next few lessons will involve downloading

a web page from the Internet and reorganizing

the contents into useful chunks of information.

You will be doing most of your work using Python

code written and executed in Komodo Edit.

doing into

into doing
```

Quick Test 3

1. What is the another name of pickling?
2. pickle module deals with which type of files?
3. Why is need to close the file after pickling?
4. How many ways are there for deletion data from file?
5. When does pickle.load() method would raise EOFError?

4.4 Working with CSV Files

csv files are used to store a large number of variables or data. They are incredibly simplified spreadsheets. Each line in a csv file is a data record.

Import CSV Module

csv module is a built-in function that allows Python to parse these types of files. The csv module implements classes to read and write tabular data in csv format. The csv module's reader and writer objects read and write the sequences respectively.

To pull information from csv files, we use loop and split methods to get data from individual columns.

The csv module explicitly exists to handle this task, making it much easier to deal with csv formatted files. csv module includes all the necessary built-in functions. They are

- csv.reader
- csv.writer
- csv.register_dialect
- csv.unregister_dialect
- csv.get_dialect
- csv.list_dialects
- csv.field_size_limit

Open a CSV File

To work with csv file, the first thing to do is to open it. You can open a file using open() method with its name. It is same as a text file.

Syntax `f=open(FileName,access_mode)`

CSV File Access Mode

There are different file access modes to open the csv file as follows

Character	Mode	Description
r	Read	It is default mode and opens a file for reading only
w	Write	Opens a file for writing only. Overwrites the file if the file exists. If file does not exist, it creates a new file for writing.
a	Append	Opens a file for appending. The file pointer is at the end of the file if it exists. If file does not exist, it creates a new file.

Character	Mode	Description
r+	Read + Write	Opens a file for both reading and writing. The file pointer placed at the beginning of the file.
x	Create	Creates a new file

Close a CSV File

When you are finished with work in files, it must to close the file as soon as possible. To close a file, close() method is used.

Syntax `FileName.close()`

Read from CSV File Using csv.reader()

To read data from csv files, you must use the reader() function to generate a reader object. This function returns a reader object which is an iterator of lines in the csv file. We can use a for loop to display lines in the file. The file should be opened in 'r' mode.

Syntax `csv.reader(<FileHandle>)`

Here, we are using a file namely 'designation.csv' storing the content.

Manager, Kiyaan Sharma, 38000, Delhi

Analyst, Kirti Sinha, 35000, Delhi

Programmer, Shreya Sharma, 35000, Pune

DBA, Ashmit Gupta, 32000, Banglore

e.g.
```
import csv
with open('designation.csv') as f:
    reader = csv.reader(f)
    for i in reader:
        print(i)
f.close()
```

Output

['Manager', 'Kiyaan Sharma', '38000', 'Delhi']

['Analyst', 'Kirti Sinha', '35000', 'Delhi']

['Programmer', 'Shreya Sharma', '35000', 'Pune']

['DBA', 'Ashmit Gupta', '32000', 'Banglore']

Write into a CSV File Using csv.writerow()

To write an existing file, you must first open the file in one of writing modes (w, a or r+) first. For this, writerow() function is used in Python for csv files.

This function writes items in a sequence (list, tuple or string) separating them by comma character.

e.g.
```
import csv
with open ('emp.csv','w') as f:
    writer = csv.writer(f)
    writer.writerow(['Analyst','Aditya
                    Mehra', '30000', 'Pune'])
    writer.writerow(['Tester', 'Rahul
                   Sharma', '28000', 'Delhi'])
    writer.writerow(['Project Manager',
             'Mahi Sexena', '36000', 'Noida'])
print("Data successfully add")
f.close()
```

Output

Data successfully add

Created File

emp.csv

```
1  Analyst,Aditya Mehra,30000,Pune
2
3  Tester,Rahul Sharma,28000,Delhi
4
5  Project Manager,Mahi Sexena,36000,Noida
6
7
```

Quick Test 4

1. What is the full form of CSV?
2. How to open a CSV file?
3. Write about X mode of CSV file.
4. Which function is used for writing in csv file?
5. How to pull information from CSV files?

NCERT Folder

1. Differentiate between:

(a) text file and binary file
(b) readline() and readlines()
(c) write() and writelines()

Ans.

Category	Description
(a) Text File vs Binary File	**Text File** Contains human-readable characters encoded in formats like ASCII or UTF-8. It can be opened and read as a sequence of text lines (using newline characters like \n). **Binary File** Contains raw data in binary format. The content is not human-readable and can store data in any form (images, audio, etc.), and is handled as raw bytes without any encoding.
(b) readline() vs readlines()	**readline()** Reads one line from the file at a time. It returns a string (including the newline character) for each line. **readlines()** Reads all lines in a file and returns them as a list of strings, each string representing a line in the file.
(c) write() vs writelines()	**write()** Writes a single string to the file. It doesn't add a newline automatically, so you must manually include \n if you need it. **writelines()** Writes a sequence of strings (like a list or tuple) to the file. Each string in the sequence is written one after the other without adding any newline unless explicitly included.

2. Write the use and syntax for the following methods:

(a) open() (b) read()
(c) seek() (d) dump()

Ans. (a) **open()**

The open() method is used to open a file in a specific mode (e.g., reading, writing, appending, etc.) so that you can interact with the file (e.g., read or write).

Syntax

```
file_object = open(file_name, mode)
```

- **file_name** The name of the file (including path if necessary).
- **mode** The mode in which to open the file. Common modes are:
  - **'r'** Read (default mode).
  - **'w'** Write (creates a new file or overwrites an existing file).
  - **'a'** Append (adds content to the end of the file).
  - **'b'** Binary mode.
  - **'x'** Exclusive creation (fails if file already exists).

Example

```
file = open('example.txt', 'r')
```

(b) **read()**

The read() method is used to read the entire content of a file (or a specified number of bytes) into a string.

Syntax

```
content = file_object.read(size=-1)
```

- **size** Optional. The number of bytes to read. If not specified or set to -1, it reads the entire file.

Example

```
content = file.read() # Reads the entire file
```

(c) **seek()**

The seek() method is used to move the file pointer to a specific position within the file. This is useful for random access to files.

Syntax

```
file_object.seek(offset, whence=0)
```

- **offset** The number of bytes to move the pointer. Positive numbers move forward, negative numbers move backward.
- **whence** Optional. Specifies from where the offset is applied. It can be:
  - **0 (default)** Beginning of the file.
  - **1** Current file position.
  - **2** End of the file.

Example

```
file.seek(10)  # Moves the pointer to the 10th
                 byte from the start.
file.seek(-5, 2)  # Moves the pointer 5 bytes
                    before the end of the file.
```

(d) **dump()**

The dump() method is not a built-in method for file objects in Python, but rather part of the pickle module. It is used to serialize an object and write it to a file.

Syntax

```
import pickle
with open('file.pkl', 'wb') as file:
    pickle.dump(obj, file)
```

- **obj** The object to serialize (e.g., list, dictionary, etc.).
- The file must be opened in binary write mode ('wb') for dump() to work.

Example

```
import pickle
```

```
my_dict = {'name': 'Alice', 'age': 25}
with open('data.pkl', 'wb') as file:
    pickle.dump(my_dict, file)
```

3. Write the file mode that will be used for opening the following files. Also, write the Python statements to open the following files:

(a) a text file "example.txt" in both read and write mode

(b) a binary file "bfile.dat" in write mode

(c) a text file "try.txt" in append and read mode

(d) a binary file "btry.dat" in read only mode.

Ans. (a) a text file "example.txt" in both read and write mode

- **File Mode** 'r+' (read and write mode for text files).
- **Python Statement**
  `file = open('example.txt', 'r+')`

(b) a binary file "bfile.dat" in write mode

- **File Mode** 'wb' (write mode for binary files).
- **Python Statement**
  `file = open('bfile.dat', 'wb')`

(c) a text file "try.txt" in append and read mode

- **File Mode** 'a+' (append and read mode for text files).
- **Python Statement**
  `file = open('try.txt', 'a+')`

(d) a binary file "btry.dat" in read-only mode

- **File Mode** 'rb' (read-only mode for binary files).
- **Python Statement**
  `file = open('btry.dat', 'rb')`

4. Why is it advised to close a file after we are done with the read and write operations? What will happen if we do not close it? Will some error message be flashed? **Competency Based Qus.**

Ans. It is advised to close a file after read and write operations to release system resources, ensure data is properly saved, and allow other processes to access the file.

If you don't close the file:

- Data might not be written to the file (leading to data loss).
- System resources like file handles may be exhausted.
- No immediate error message is flashed, but potential issues like locked files or failed file access may occur.

5. What is the difference between the following set of statements (a) and (b):

(a) P = open("practice.txt","r") P.read(10)

(b) with open("practice.txt", "r") as P: x = P.read()

Ans. (a)
- The file is explicitly opened with open().
- After reading, the file must be manually closed using P.close().

(b)
- The file is automatically opened and closed using the with statement.
- The file is closed automatically when the block is finished, even if an error occurs.

6. Write a command(s) to write the following lines to the text file named hello.txt. Assume that the file is opened in append mode. " Welcome my class" "It is a fun place" "You will learn and play"

Ans. To write the given lines to a file named hello.txt in append mode, you can use the following Python commands:

```
with open("hello.txt", "a") as file:
    file.write("Welcome my class\n")
    file.write("It is a fun place\n")
    file.write("You will learn and play\n")
```

7. Write a Python program to open the file hello.txt used in question no 6 in read mode to display its contents. What will be the difference if the file was opened in write mode instead of append mode?

Ans.
```
with open("hello.txt", "r") as file
    content = file.read()
    print(content)
```

Difference between Write Mode and Append Mode

- **Write Mode ("w")** Overwrites the file's content if it exists, replacing it with new data.
- **Append Mode ("a")** Adds new content to the end of the file without modifying the existing data.

8. Write a program to accept string/sentences from the user till the user enters "END" to. Save the data in a text file and then display only those sentences which begin with an uppercase alphabet.
Define pickling in Python. Explain serialization and deserialization of Python object.

Ans.
```
# Open the file in write mode to save user input
with open("user_data.txt", "w") as file:
    while True:
        sentence = input("Enter a sentence (type
'END' to stop): ")
        if sentence == "END":
            break
        file.write(sentence + "\n")
# Open the file in read mode to display sentences
starting with an uppercase letter
with open("user_data.txt", "r") as file:
    for line in file:
        if line[0].isupper():
            print(line.strip())
```

Pickling in Python is the process of converting Python objects (like lists, dictionaries, classes, etc.) into a byte stream. This byte stream can then be stored in a file or transmitted over a network.

Serialization is the general term for converting an object into a format suitable for storage or transmission.

Deserialization is the reverse process of converting the stored or transmitted data back into the original Python object.

9. Write a program to enter the following records in a binary file:

Item No	**integer**
Item_Name	**string**
Qty	**integer**
Price	**float**

Number of records to be entered should be accepted from the user. Read the file to display the records in the following format:

Item No:
Item Name :
Quantity:
Price per item:
Amount: (to be calculated as Price * Qty)

Ans.

```
import struct
# Function to write records to a binary file
def write_to_binary_file(filename, num_records):
    with open(filename, "wb") as file:
        for _ in range(num_records):
            # Accepting input for each record
            item_no = int(input("Enter Item No
                          (integer): "))
            item_name = input("Enter Item Name
                          (string): ")
            qty = int(input("Enter Quantity
                          (integer): "))
            price = float(input("Enter Price
                          (float): "))
            # Pack the data into binary format
              (integer, string, integer, float)
            record = struct.pack('i20sif',
                item_no, item_name.encode('utf-8'),
                                        qty, price)
            file.write(record)
# Function to read and display records from
                                   the binary file
def read_from_binary_file(filename):
    with open(filename, "rb") as file:
        while True:
            record = file.read
                  (struct.calcsize('i20sif'))
            if not record:
                break
            # Unpack the data from binary format
            item_no, item_name, qty, price =
                struct.unpack('i20sif', record)
            item_name = item_name.decode
                ('utf-8').strip()  # Decoding
                    and stripping extra spaces
            # Calculate the amount
            amount = qty * price
            # Display the record in the
                                 specified format
            print(f"\nItem No: {item_no}")
            print(f"Item Name: {item_name}")
            print(f"Quantity: {qty}")
            print(f"Price per item: {price}")
            print(f"Amount: {amount}")
            print('-' * 30)
# Main program
num_records = int(input("Enter the number of
                       records to be entered: "))
filename = "items.dat"  # File to store the
                                     binary data
# Write records to the binary file
write_to_binary_file(filename, num_records)
# Read and display records from the binary file
      print("\nDisplaying records from the binary
                                          file:")
read_from_binary_file(filename)
```

Mind Map

FILE HANDLING

It is the process of opening, reading, writing and closing files in a program.

Data File

Files that store and preserve data released to a particular application. Python language supports three types of data files – text, binary, csv.

Text File

It is a sequence of characters consisting of alphabets, numbers and other special symbols.

Writing

write() method takes a string and writes it into the file. It does not add a newline character ('\n') to the end of the string.
Syntax `<FileHandle>.write(str1)`

writelines () method Whenever, we have to write a sequence of string to a file, we will use writelines() instead of write().
Syntax `<FileHandle>.writelines(L)`

Reading

read() method returns a string containing all characters in a file.
Syntax `<FileHandle>.read()`

read([size]) method specifies how many characters the string should return.
Syntax `<FileHandle>.read(n)`

readline() method will read from a file line by line. For readline(), a line is terminated by '\n' or End of Line (i.e. new line character).
Syntax `<FileHandle>.readline()`

readlines() method will return a list of strings, each separated by '\n'. It reads all rows and retains the newlines character that is at the end of every row.
Syntax `<FileHandle>.readlines()`

Opening and Closing of Text, Binary and CSV Files

Opening

open() method uses two arguments : filename and mode of a file and returns a file object.
Syntax
`FileObject=open (file_name[,access_mode])`

Closing

close() method frees up the resources that were tied with the file.
Syntax `FileObject.close()`

Binary File

It is a file that contains information in the same format as it is held in memory. They represent the actual content such as image, audio, video, executable files,etc.

Writing

dump() method of pickle module is used to write objects to a binary file. It takes Python object and file object as arguments.
Syntax

```
import pickle
......
......
pickle.dump(object_to
 _pickle,FileObject)
```

Reading

load() method of pickle module is used to read an object from a binary file. It takes file object as a parameter and returns Python object which is read from the binary file.
Syntax

```
import pickle
......
......
object=pickle.load(FileObject)
```

Note To use these methods, we have to first import the pickle module.

CSV File

CSV (Comma Separated Values) format is a way to store data in tabular form. It stores tabular data in plain text. Each line of the file is a data record and record consists of one or more fields separated by commas.

Reading

reader() method returns a reader object which is an iterator of lines in the csv file.
Syntax `csv.reader(<FileHandle>)`

Writing

csv.writer() method It returns a writer object that converts the user's data into a delimited string which can be written into a CSV file using the writerow() and writerows() methods.

- **writerow() method** used to write a single row to a CSV file.
  Syntax `csv.writerow(<FileHandle>)`
- **writerows() method** used to write multiple rows to a CSV file.
  Syntax `csv.writerows(<FileHandle>)`

Note To read/write from/into a CSV file with custom delimiter we use the delimiter parameter in writer method.

File Modes of Text, Binary and CSV Files

r mode	It opens a file for reading only. This is default mode.
rb mode	It opens a file for reading only in binary format.
r+ mode	It opens a file for both reading and writing.
rb + mode	It opens a file for both reading and writing in binary format.
w mode	It opens a file for writing only. Overwrites the file if the file exists.
wb mode	It opens a file for writing only in binary format.
w+ mode	It opens a file for both writing and reading.
wb + mode	It opens a file for both writing and reading in binary format.
a mode	It opens a file for appending. The file pointer is at the end of the file.
ab mode	It opens a file for appending in binary format.
a + mode	It opens a file for both appending and reading.
ab + mode	It opens a file for both appending and reading in binary format.
x mode	It creates a new file.

Accessing and Manipulating Location of File Pointer

File pointer specifies the current position in the file where writing or reading will take place. Python provides two methods to perform random access operations in a file

tell() Method tells you the current position within the file, measured in bytes from the beginning of the file.
Syntax `FileObject.tell()`

seek() Method can be used to change the current position in a file. It does not return any value.
Syntax `FileObject.seek(offset[,mode])`

File Path

Relative path is the path that is relative to the working directory location on your computer. Relative path does not start with a leading forward slash and is interpreted from the perspective of the current working directory.

Absolute path is the path that contains the entire path to the file or directory that you need to access. This path will begin at the home directory of your computer and end with the file or directory that you want to access. This path starts with a leading forward slash.

EXAM PATTERN QUESTIONS

Objective Type Questions

Multiple Choice Questions

1. It is a convenient way to deal with large quantities of data.

(a) Data file (b) Program file
(c) Executable file (d) All of these

2. Text file is a file that stores information in

(a) UNICODE characters (b) BCD characters
(c) ASCII characters (d) ISCII characters

3. In which file, no delimiters are used for line and no translations occur?

(a) Text file (b) Binary file
(c) csv file (d) None of these

4. Which attribute is used to return access mode with that file was opened?

(a) mode.file (b) mode.file.name
(c) file.mode (d) file.mode.type

5. .... method takes a string and writes it in the file.

(a) writelines() (b) write()
(c) writerow() (d) writer()

6. For readline(), a line is terminated by

(a) '\n' (b) EOF
(c) Either (a) or (b) (d) None of these

7. A text file 'student.txt' is stored in the storage device. Identify the correct option out of the following options to open the file in read mode. Competency Based Que.

(i) myfile = open('student.txt','a')
(ii) myfile = open('student.txt','w')
(iii) myfile = open('student.txt','r')
(iv) myfile = open('student.txt')

(a) Only (i)
(b) Both (i) and (iv)
(c) Both (iii) and (iv)
(d) Both (i) and (iii)

8. Which of the following mode in file opening statement results or generates an error if the file does not exist?

(a) a+ (b) r+
(c) w+ (d) None of these

9. Which of the following mode keeps the file offset position at the end of the file? CBSE 2023

(a) r+ (b) r
(c) w (d) a

10. If the following statement is used to read the contents of a textfile object F:

```
X=F. readlines ()
```

Which of the following is the correct data type of x? CBSE 2021-22 Term I

(a) string (b) list
(c) tuple (d) dictionary

11. Which of the following statement is not correct? CBSE 2021-22 Term I

(a) We can write content into a text file opened using 'w' mode.
(b) We can write content into a text file opened using 'w+' mode.
(c) We can write content into a text file opened using 'r' mode.
(d) We can write content into a text file opened using 'r +' mode.

12. Which of the following option is the correct Python statement to read and display the first 10 characters of a text file "Notes. txt"? CBSE 2021-22 Term I

(a) `F = open('Notes.txt');`
`print(F.load(10))`
(b) `F = open ('Notes.txt');`
`print (F.dump(10))`
(c) `F = open('Notes.txt');`
`print(F.read(10))`
(d) `F = open('Notes.txt');`
`print(F.write (10))`

13. Which of the following is not a correct Python statement to open a text file "Notes. txt" to write content into it ? CBSE 2021-22 Term I

(a) `F = open('Notes.txt', 'w')`
(b) `F = open ('Notes.txt', 'a')`
(c) `F = open('Notes.txt', 'A')`
(d) `F = open ( 'Notes. txt', 'w+')`

14. A text file opened using the following statement

```
MyFile = open ('Notes.txt' )
```

Which of the following is the correct Python statement to close it ? **CBSE 2021-22 Term I**

(a) `MyFile=close ( 'Notes.txt')`
(b) `MyFile. close ( 'Notes.txt')`
(c) `close. MyFile ( )`
(d) `MyFile.close( )`

15. Suppose the content of a text file "Rhymes.txt" is as follows **CBSE 2021-22 Term I**

Jack & Jill
went up the hill

What will be the output of the following Python code?

```
F = open ("Rhymes.txt")
L = F.readlines()
for i in L:
    S=i. split ()
    print(len(S),end="#")
```

(a) 2#4#　(b) 3#4#
(c) 2#　(d) 7#

16. Suppose the content of "Rhymes.txt" is

Baa baa black sheep,
have you any wool?

What will be the output of the following Python code? **CBSE 2021-22 Term I**

```
F = open ("Rhymes.txt")
S = F.read ()
L=S.split ()
for i in L :
    if len(i) %3 != 0:
        print (i, end= " ")
```

(a) Baa baa you any
(b) black have wool?
(c) black sheep, have wool?
(d) Error

17. Suppose the content of "Rhymes.txt" is **CBSE 2021-22 Term I**

One, two, three, four, five
Once I caught a fish alive.

What will be the output of the following Python code?

```
F = open ("Rhymes. txt")
S = F. read ( )
print(S.count('e' ,20))
```

(a) 20　(b) 1
(c) 3　(d) 6

18. Suppose the content of "Rhymes. txt" is

Good Morning Madam **CBSE 2021-22 Term I**

What will be the output of the following Python code?

```
F = open ("Rhymes.txt")
L = F.read().split ()
for W in L:
    if W. lower ( )== W [: : -1] . lower ():
        print (W)
```

(a) Good　(b) Morning
(c) Madam　(d) Error

19. Which of the following statement is not correct? **CBSE SQP 2021-22 Term I**

(a) If we try to read a text file that does not exist, an error occurs.
(b) If we try to read a text file that does not exist, the file gets created.
(c) If we try to write on a text file that does not exist, no error occurs.
(d) If we try to write on a text file that does not exist, the file gets created.

20. Which of the following option can be used to read the first line of a text file "Myfile.txt"? **CBSE SQP 2021-22 Term I**

(a) `myfile = open('Myfile.txt'); print(myfile.read(line))`
(b) `myfile = open('Myfile.txt','r'); print(myfile.read(1))`
(c) `myfile = open('Myfile.txt'); print(myfile.readline())`
(d) `myfile = open('Myfile.txt'); print(myfile.readlines())`

21. Assume that the position of the file pointer is at the beginning of 3rd line in a text file. **CBSE SQP 2021-22 Term I**

Which of the following option can be used to read all the remaining lines?

(a) myfile.read(n-3)　(b) myfile.read(n)
(c) myfile.readline()　(d) myfile.readlines()

22. Suppose the content of file "Myfile.txt" is **CBSE SQP 2021-22 Term I**

Twinkle twinkle little star How I wonder what you are Up above the world so high Like a diamond in the sky

What will be the output of the following code?

```
myfile = open("Myfile.txt")
data = myfile.readlines()
print(len(data))
myfile.close()
```

(a) 3　(b) 4
(c) 106　(d) 22

23. **Suppose the content of file "Myfile.txt" is** CBSE SQP 2021-22 Term I

Humpty Dumpty sat on a wall Humpty Dumpty had a great fall All the king's horses and all the king's men Couldn't put Humpty together again

What will be the output of the following code?

```
myfile = open("Myfile.txt")
record = myfile.read().split()
print(len(record))
myfile.close()
```

(a) 24 (b) 25
(c) 26 (d) 27

24. **Suppose the content of file "Myfile.txt" is** CBSE SQP 2021-22 Term I

Ek Bharat Shreshtha Bharat

What will be the output of the following code?

```
myfile = open("Myfile.txt")
vlist = list("aeiouAEIOU")
vc=0
x = myfile.read()
for y in x:
if(y in vlist):
vc+=1
print(vc)
myfile.close()
```

(a) 6 (b) 7
(c) 8 (d) 9

25. **Assume the content of the text file "Myfile.txt" is** CBSE SQP 2021-22 Term I

Arjun Kumar Ismail Khan Joseph B Hanika Kiran

What will be the data type of data_rec?

```
myfile = open("Myfile.txt")
data_rec = myfile.readlines()
myfile.close()
```

(a) string (b) list
(c) tuple (d) dictionary

26. **Suppose the content of file "`Myfile.txt`" is**

Honesty is the best policy.

What will be the output of the following code? CBSE SQP 2021-22 Term I

```
myfile = open("Myfile.txt")
x = myfile.read()
print(len(x))
myfile.close()
```

(a) 5 (b) 25
(c) 26 (d) 27

27. **Suppose the content of "Rhymes.txt" is** CBSE 2021-22 Term I

Hickory Dickory Dock
The mouse went up the clock

What will be the output of the following Python code?

```
F = open ("Rhymes.txt")
L = F.readlines()
X = ["the", "ock"]
for i in L:
    for W in i.split():
if W in X:
    print(W, end = "*")
```

(a) the* (b) Dock*The*the*clock*
(c) Dock*the*clock* (d) Error

28. **Consider the following Python statement:** CBSE 2024

```
F = open ('CONTENT.TXT')
```

Which of the following is an invalid statement in Python ?

(a) F. seek (1, 0) (b) F. seek (0, 1)
(c) F. seek (0, –1) (d) F. seek (0, 2)

29. **Which of the following functions changes the position of file pointer and returns its new position?** CBSE SQP 2023-24

(a) flush() (b) tell()
(c) seek() (d) offset()

30. **The syntax of seek ( ) is** CBSE 2023

```
file_object.seek(offset[,reference_point])
```

What is the default value of reference _point?

(a) 0 (b) 1
(c) 2 (d) 3

31. **Which of the following option is the correct usage for the tell( ) of a file object?** CBSE 2021-22 Term I

(a) It places the file pointer at a desired offset in a file.
(b) It returns the entire content of a file.
(c) It returns the byte position of the file pointer as an integer.
(d) It tells the details about the file.

32. **What is the significance of the seek( ) method?** CBSE 2021-22 Term I

(a) It seeks the absolute path of the file.
(b) It tells the current byte position of the file pointer within the file.
(c) It places the file pointer at a desired offset within the file.
(d) It seeks the entire content of the file.

33. Suppose the content of a text file 'Notes.txt' is "The way to get started is to quit talking and begin doing"
What will be the output of the following Python code? CBSE 2021-22 Term I

```
F = open ("Notes. txt")
F. seek(29)
S = F.read()
print(S)
```

(a) The way to get started is to
(b) quit talking and begin doing
(c) The way to get started is to quit talking and begin doing
(d) gniod nigeb dna gniklat tiuq ot si detrats teg ot yaw ehT

34. What is the significance of the tell() method? CBSE SQP 2021-22 Term I

(a) Tells the path of the file.
(b) Tells the current position of the file pointer within the file.
(c) Tells the end position within the file.
(d) Checks the existence of a file at the desired location.

35. Syntax of seek() function in Python is myfile.seek(offset, reference_point) where myfile is the file object. What is the default value of reference_point? CBSE SQP 2021-22 Term I

(a) 0 (b) 1
(c) 2 (d) 3

36. The correct syntax of seek() is CBSE SQP 2021-22 Term I

(a) file_object.seek(offset [, reference_point])
(b) seek(offset [, reference_point])
(c) seek(offset, file_object)
(d) seek.file_object(offset)

37. Which path does not start with a leading forward slash?

(a) Relative (b) Absolute
(c) Both (a) and (b) (d) None of these

38. Consider the following directory structure:

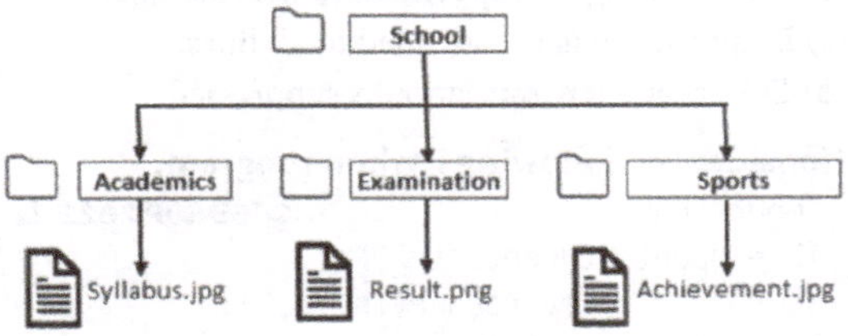

Suppose root directory (School:\) and present working directory are the same. What will be the absolute path of the file 'Syllabus.jpg'? CBSE SQP 2021-22 Term I

(a) School/Syllabus.jpg
(b) School/Academics/Syllabus.jpg
(c) School/Academics/../Syllabus.jpg
(d) School/Examination/Syllabus.jpg

39. It is a way to convey a Python object into a character stream.

(a) Pickling (b) Unpickling
(c) dump() method (d) load() method

40. Which of the following is a function/method of the pickle module? CBSE 2021-22 Term I

(a) reader ( ) (b) writer ( )
(c) load( ) (d) read ( )

41. Which of the following statement is incorrect in the context of pickled binary files? CBSE 2021-22 Term I

(a) csv module is used for reading and writing objects in binary files.
(b) pickle module is used for reading and writing objects in binary files.
(c) load () of the pickle module is used to read objects.
(d) dump () of the pickle module is used to write objects.

42. Which of the following Python module is imported to store and retrieve objects using the process of serialisation and deserialisation? CBSE 2021-22 Term I

(a) csv (b) binary
(c) math (d) pickle

43. Consider the following directory structure

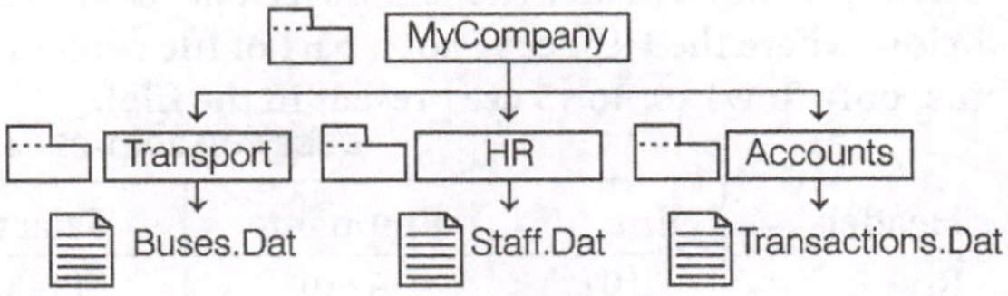

Suppose the present working directory is MyCompany. What will be the relative path of the file Transactions. Dat? CBSE 2021-22 Term I

(a) MyCompany /Transactions .Dat
(b) MyCompany/Accounts/Transactions.Dat
(c) Accounts/Transactions. Dat
(d) . . /Transactions.Dat

44. Which of the following statement is incorrect in the context of binary files? CBSE SQP 2021-22 Term I

(a) Information is stored in the same format in which the information is held in memory.
(b) No end of line (EOL) character translation takes place.
(c) Every line ends with a new line character.
(d) Pickle module is used for reading and writing.

45. Which of the following statement is true? CBSE SQP 2021-22 Term I

(a) Pickling creates an object from a sequence of bytes.
(b) Pickling is used for object serialization.
(c) Pickling is used for object deserialization.
(d) Pickling is used to manage all types of files in Python.

46. Which of the following statement opens a binary file 'record.bin' in write mode and writes an object lst1 = [1,2,3,4] on the binary file? CBSE SQP 2021-22 Term I

(a)
```
with open('record.bin','wb') as myfile:
    pickle.dump(lst1,myfile)
```
(b)
```
with open('record.bin','wb') as myfile:
    pickle.dump(myfile,lst1)
```
(c)
```
with open('record.bin','wb+') as myfile:
    pickle.dump(myfile,lst1)
```
(d)
```
with open('record.bin','ab') as myfile:
    pickle.dump(myfile,lst1)
```

47. Raghav is trying to write an object obj1 = (1,2,3,4,5) on a binary file "test.bin". Consider the following code written by him. CBSE SQP 2021-22 Term I

```
import pickle
obj1 = (1,2,3,4,5)
myfile = open("test.bin",'wb')
pickle.________ #Statement 1
myfile.close()
```

Identify the missing code in Statement 1.

(a) dump(myfile,obj1) (b) dump(obj1, myfile)
(c)write(obj1,myfile) (d) load(myfile,obj1)

48. The content of a binary file "employee.dat" is shown below, where the Header is not a part of file content (i.e. only Row1 to Row5 are present in the file). CBSE SQP 2021-22 Term I

Header ⟶	Empno	Empname	Salary
Row 1 ⟶	101	Anuj	50000
Row 2 ⟶	102	Arijita	40000
Row 3 ⟶	103	Hanika	30000
Row 4 ⟶	104	Firoz	60000
Row 5 ⟶	105	Vijaylakshmi	40000

```
def display(eno):
    f=open("employee.dat", "rb")
    totSum=0
    try:
        whiule True:
            R=pickle.load(f)
            if R[0]==eno:
                ________           #Line1
            totSum=totSum+R[2]
    except:
        f.close()
    print(totSum)
```

When the above mentioned function, display (103) is executed, the output displayed is 190000. Which of the following statement should be used in the blank space of the line marked as Line1 to obtain the above output? CBSE SQP 2021-22 Term I

(a) jump (b) break (c) continue (d) return

49. Which character is used to create a new file in csv?

(a) r (b) w (c) r+ (d) x

50. Which of the following is not a function/method of the csv module in Python?

(a) read() (b) reader() (c) writer() (d) writerow()

51. Which of the following is the correct expansion of CSV? CBSE 2021-22 Term I

(a) Comma Separated Values
(b) Centrally Secured Values
(c) Computerised Secured Values
(d) Comma Secured Values

52. Which of the following is the default character for the newline parameter for a CSV file object opened in write mode in Python IDLE? CBSE 2021-22 Term I

(a) \n (b) \t (c) , (d) ;

53. Which of the following function is used with the csv module in Python to read the contents of a csv file into an object ? CBSE 2021-22 Term I

(a) readrow( ) (b) readrows( )
(c) reader( ) (d) load( )

54. Which of the following characters act as default delimiter in a CSV file? CBSE SQP 2021-22 Term I

(a) Colon (:) (b) Hyphen) (-)
(c) Comma (,) (d) Vertical line (|)

55. Given below is one way of opening a filem "Student.csv" in write mode. CBSE SQP 2021-22 Term I

```
myfile = open("Student.csv","w",newline=' ').
```

What is the importance of newline=' '?

(a) A new line gets added to the file.
(b) Empty string gets appended to the first line.
(c) Empty string gets appended to all lines.
(d) EOL character translation is suppressed.

56. Consider the following Python program: CBSE SQP 2021-22 Term I

```
import csv
fh = open("Student.csv","r")
stureader = csv.reader(fh)
for rec in stureader:
print(rec)
```

What will be the data type of rec?

(a) string (b) list (c) tuple (d) dictionary

Fill in the Blanks

57. Each line of the file is a ....

58. In text files, each line of text is terminated with a special character is known as ....

59. .... are used to read and write data to a file on disk.

60. Opened file is closed by calling the .... method of its file objects.

61. .... method specifies how many characters the string should return.

62. seek() method can be used to change the .... position in a file.

63. .... path starts with a leading forward slash.

64. The file extension of binary file is ....

65. .... method is used to read a pickled object hierarchy from a string.

66. .... are used to store a large number of variables or data.

State Whether True or False

67. Text file is a sequence of characters consisting of alphabets, numbers and other special symbols.

68. w mode creates a new file for reading if the file does not exist.

69. For readline(), a line is terminated by '\n' or End of Line.

70. seek() tells you the current position within the file, measured in bytes from the beginning of the file.

71. CSV file contains information in the same format as it is held in memory.

Assertion and Reason Based Questions

Assertion (A) and Reason (R) Type questions. Choose the correct option as:

(a) Both Assertion (A) and Reason (R) are true, and Reason (R) is the correct explanation of Assertion (A)
(b) Both Assertion (A) and Reason (R) are true, but Reason (R) is not the correct explanation of Assertion (A)
(c) Assertion (A) is True, but Reason (R) is False
(d) Assertion (A) is False, but Reason (R) is True

72. **Assertion (A)** Text file stores information in ASCII or unicode characters.

Reason (R) In text file, there is no delimiter for a line.

73. **Assertion (A)** Access mode 'a' opens a file for appending.

Reason (R) The file pointer is at the end of the file if the file exists

74. **Assertion (A)** For a binary file opened using 'rb' mode, the pickle.dump () method will display an error. **CBSE 2025**

Reason (R) The pickle. dump () method is used to read from a binary file.

75. **Assertion (A)** CSV stands for comma separated value.

Reason (R) CSV files are a common file format for transferring and storing data.

76. **Assertion (A)** CSV file is a human readable text file where each line has a number of fields, separated by comma or some other delimiter. **CBSE 2024**

Reason (R) writerow ( ) method is used to write a single row in a CSV file.

77. **Assertion (A)** CSV (Comma Separated Values) is a file format for data storage which looks like a text file. **CBSE SQP 2022-23**

Reason (R) The information is organized with one record on each line and each field is separated by comma.

Answers

1. (a) Data file
2. (c) ASCII characters
3. (b) Binary file
4. (c) file.mode
5. (b) write()
6. (c) Either (a) or (b)
7. (c) Both (iii) and (iv)
8. (b) r+
9. (d) a
10. (b) list
11. (c) We can write content into a text file opened using 'r' mode.
12. (c) `F = open('Notes.txt'); print(F.read(10))`
13. (c) `F = open('Notes.txt', 'A')`
14. (d) `MyFile.close( )`
15. (b) 3#4#
16. (b) black have wool?
17. (c) 3
18. (c) Madam
19. (b) If we try to read a text file that does not exist, the file gets created.
20. (c) `myfile = open('Myfile.txt'); print(myfile.readline())`
21. (c) myfile.readline()
22. (b) 4
23. (c) 26
24. (c) 8
25. (b) list
26. (d) 27
27. (d) Error
28. (c) F. seek (0, –1)
29. (c) seek()
30. (a) 0

31. (c) It returns the byte position of the file pointer as an integer.
32. (c) It places the file pointer at a desired offset within the file.
33. (b) quit talking and begin doing
34. (b) Tells the current position of the file pointer within the file.
35. (a) 0
36. (a) file_object.seek(offset [, reference_point])
37. (a) Relative
38. (b) School/Academics/Syllabus.jpg
39. (a) Pickling
40. (c) load( )
41. (a) csv module is used for reading and writing objects in binary files.
42. (d) pickle
43. (b) MyCompany/Accounts/Transactions.Dat
44. (b) No end of line (EOL) character translation takes place.
45. (b) Pickling is used for object serialization.
46. (a) `with open('record.bin','wb') as myfile: pickle.dump(lst1,myfile)`
47. (b) dump(obj1, myfile)
48. (c) continue
49. (d) x
50. (a) read()
51. (a) Comma Separated Values
52. (a) \n
53. (c) reader( )
54. (c) Comma (,)
55. (d) EOL character translation is suppressed.
56. (b) list
57. data record
58. EOL (End of Line)
59. File objects
60. close()
61. read ([size])
62. current
63. Absolute
64. .dat
65. load()
66. csv files
67. True
68. False
69. True
70. False
71. False
72. (c) Assertion (A) is True, but Reason (R) is False
73. (a) Both A and R are true and R is the correct explanation for A.
74. (c) Assertion (A) is True, but Reason (R) is False
75. (a) Both (A) and (R) are true and (R) is the correct explanation for (A).
76. (a) Both (A) and (R) are true and (R) is the correct explanation for (A).
77. (a) Both A and R are true and R is the correct explanation for A.

Subjective Type Questions

Very Short Answer Type Question

1. Name the types of data files.

Ans. (i) Text file (ii) Binary file (iii) CSV file

2. Which access mode can be used for opening a file for both appending and reading in a text file?

Ans. a+

3. Which attribute is used to return access mode with that file was opened?

Ans. file.mode

4. When we want to write the data line by line then what syntax should be used?

Ans. Whenever we have to write a sequence of string line by line then we should use writelines( ) method.

Syntax `FileObject.writelines(L)`

Here, all string in list L as lines to file referenced by FileObject.

5. How is read( ) method different from read ([size])?

Ans. read ( ) method returns a string containing all characters in a file. While read ([size]) method specifies how many characters the string should return.

6. Differentiate between the following:

(i) `File1=open('employee. txt', 'a')`

(ii) `File1=open('employee. txt', 'r')`

Ans. (i) This statement opens a 'employee.txt' file for appending only.

(ii) This statement opens a 'employee.txt' file for reading only.

7. What is the use of file object?

Ans. File objects are used to read and write the data to a file on disk.

8. Observe the following code and answer the questions that follow:

```
File = open("Mydata","a")
.........# Blank1
File.close()
```

(i) What type (Text/Binary/CSV) of file is Mydata?

(ii) Fill in the Blank1 with statement to write "ABC" in the file "Mydata".

Ans. (i) Text File

(ii) File.write ("ABC")

9. Differentiate between file modes r+ and w+ with respect to Python.

Ans. r+ opens a text file for both reading and writing.

w+ opens a text file for both reading and writing. It overwrites the file if it exists.

10. Differentiate between file modes r+ and rb+ with respect to Python.

Ans. r+ opens text files in read mode & write mode.

rb + opens binary files in read mode & write mode.

11. Write a statement in Python to perform the following operations:

(i) To open a text file "MYPET.TXT" in write mode.

(ii) To open a text file "MYPET.TXT" in read mode.

Ans. (i) f1 = open ('MYPET.TXT', 'w')

(ii) f2 = open ('MYPET.TXT', 'r')

12. Write a statement in Python to perform the following operations:

(i) To open a text file "LOG.TXT" in read mode.

(ii) To open a text file "LOG.TXT" in write mode

Ans. (i) fileobj=open("LOG.TXT", 'r')

(ii) fileobj=open("LOG.TXT", 'w')

13. How is method write() different from writelines() in python?

Ans. write(str) writes a string into a file while writelines(sequence) writes a list of strings to the file

```
Ex: str = "Hello"
f.write(str)
strlist = ["I","love","Python"]
f.writelines(strlist)
```

14. Write the missing statement to complete the following code: **CBSE SQP 2024-25**

```
file = open("example.txt", "r")
data = file.read(100)
____________________  #Move the file
pointer to the beginning of the file
next_data = file.read(50)
file.close()
```

Ans. file.seek(0)

15. If we do not use flush( ) method then what will be happen?

Ans. If we do not use flush( ) method then write statements strings may still be pending to be written on the disk because flush( ) method ensures that whatever is held in output buffer, is written on the actual file on disk.

16. Riya intends to position the file pointer to the beginning of a text file. Write a Python statement for the same assuming F is the FileObject. **Competency Based Que.**

Ans. F.seek(0)

17. What do you mean by abspath()?

Ans. abspath() method returns a normalised version of the pathname that means returns the complete path name of the data file.

18. Which standard file streams are used in Python?

Ans. (i). `stdin`

(ii) `.stdout`

(iii) `.stderr`

19. What do you mean by sys.stderr?

Ans. Here, stderr stands for standard error. This file object is used for error message only, even though its output goes for same destination as stdout.

20. What is the importance of sys.stdout in Python?

Ans. sys.stdout stands for standard output. It is used to write a line to a user (monitor).

21. Differentiate between w+ and wb+ mode in Python file.

Ans. w+ opens a file in text format and wb+ in binary format, for both writing and reading.

22. Write the full form of CSV.

Ans. Comma separated values

23. Write any two names for built-in functions included by csv module.

Ans. csv.reader, csv.writer

Short Answer Type I Questions

24. Write a user defined function in Python that displays the number of lines starting with 'H' in the file Para.txt.

e.g.

If the file content is Hello...How are you? Hi...I am fine. What are you doing now? Hmm...nothing special. Then the line count should be 3.

Ans.

```
def countH():
    f = open ("Para.txt","r")
    lines = 0
    l=f.readlines()
    for i in l:
        if i[0] = = 'H':
            lines+=1
    print("No.of lines is",lines)
```

25. A text file "Quotes.txt" has the following data written in it:

Living a life you can be proud of Doing your best Spending your time with people and activities that are important to you Standing up for things that are right even when it's hard Becoming the best version of you Write a user defined function to display the total number of words present in the file.

Ans.
```
def countwords():
    s=open("Quotes.txt","r")
    f=s.read()
    z=f.split()
    count=0
    for i in z:
        count=count+1
    print("Total number of words:",count)
```

26. Write a function countmy() in Python to read the text file "Data.txt" and count the number of times "my" occurs in the file.

For example if the file contents are My first book was Me and My Family. It gave me chance to be known to the world. The output of the function should be No. of times "my" occur : 2

Ans.
```
def countmy():
    f=open("Data.txt","r")
    count=0
    x=f.read()
    word=x.split()
    for i in word:
        if(i=="my"):
            count=count+1
    print("No. of times my occur :",
                                  count)
countmy()
```

27. Write a code to read 10 bytes from text file 'detail.txt'.

Ans.
```
myfile=open("detail.txt","r")
s=myfile.read(10)
print(s)
myfile.close()
```

28. Write a code to remove a file and print the status about the file that it exist or not. If it is not exist, display proper message.

Ans.
```
import os
print("Enter the file name which you want
                          to be removed")
f=input()
if os.path.isfile(f):
    os.remove(f)
    print("File successfully deleted")
else:
    print("File does not exist")
```

29. Write a function Del() to delete the 4th word from a text file school.txt.

Ans.
```
def Del():
    with open('school.txt','r') as f:
        l = f.readlines()
    print(l)
    if len (l) > 3:
    print(l)
    f = open ('school.txt', 'w')
    f.writelines(l)
    f.close()
```

30. Write a program to read the content of "percentage.txt" file. The "percentage.txt" file contains Id, Name and Percentage fields. Assume that first field of the student status (between Id and Name) is separated with a comma(,).

Ans.
```
import os
f="percentage.txt"
if os.path.isfile(f):
    fob=open(f)
    print("Student Status")
    print("-----")
    for per in fob:
        print (per)
    fob.close()
else:
    print("File does not exist")
```

31. Write a function countEU() in Python, which should reads each character of a text file. IMP.TXT, should count and display the occurrence of alphabets E and U (including small cases e and u too).

e.g. if the file content is as follows : Pinaky has gone to his friend's house. His friend's name is Ravya. Her house is 12 km from Pinaky's house. The countEU() function should display the output as E : 8 U : 3

Ans.
```
def countEU():
    f=open("IMP.TXT")
    e=0
    u=0
```

```
while True:
   l=f.readline()
   if not l:
      break
   for i in l:
      if(i=='E' or i=='e'):
         e=e+1
      elif(i=='U' or i=='u'):
         u=u+1
            print("E :",e)
            print("U :",u)
            f.close()
```

32. Write a Python program to find the longest word in file "status.txt". If contents of status.txt are

> Welcome to your one-step solutions for all your study, practice and assessment needs for various competitive & recruitment examinations and school segment. We have been working tirelessly for over a decade to make sure that you have best in class study resources because you deserve SUCCESS AND NOTHING LESS...
>
> Output should be :
>
> Longest word : examinations

Ans.
```
def Longest():
    f=open("status.txt")
    words=f.read().split()
    f. close ()
    max_len=len(max(words, key=len))
    for word in words:
       if(len(word)==max_len):
          print("Longest word:",word)
```

33. Write a program to check the position of file pointer after first line and print the data of current position and then read the 15th position data from the file.

Ans.
```
import os
tfile = 'school.txt'
if os.path.isfile(tfile):
    f=open(tfile,'r+')
    cs=f.readline()
    print("First line:",cs)
    pos=f.tell()
    print("Current position :",pos)
    f.seek(pos)
    cs=f.readline()
    print("Current position data :",cs)
    f.seek(15)
    cs=f.readline()
    print("15th position data :",cs)
    f.close()
else:
    print("File does not exist")
```

34. A text file "PARA.txt" contains a paragraph. Write a function that searches for a given character and reports the number of occurrences of the character in the file.

Ans.
```
def count_character_in_file(filename,
                                    char_to_search):
    try:
        with open(filename, 'r') as file:
            content = file.read()
            count = content.count(char_to_search)
            print(f"The character '{char_to_search}'
      appears {count} times in the file '{filename}'.")
    except FileNotFoundError:
        print(f"The file '{filename}' does not exist.")
count_character_in_file("PARA.txt", 'a')
```

35. Write a function in Python to count the number of lowercase and uppercase characters in a text file "Book.txt".

Ans.
```
def count_case_in_file(filename):
    try:
        with open(filename, 'r') as file:
            content = file.read()
            lower_count = sum(1 for char in
                       content if char.islower())
            upper_count = sum(1 for char in
                       content if char.isupper())
            print(f"In the file '{filename}':")
            print(f"Number of lowercase
                    characters: {lower_count}")
            print(f"Number of uppercase
                    characters: {upper_count}")
    except FileNotFoundError:
        print(f"The file '{filename}' does not
                                          exist.")
count_case_in_file("Book.txt")
```

36. (A) Write a Python function that displays all the words containing @cmail from a text file "Emails.txt". **CBSE SQP 2024-25**

***Or* (B) Write a Python function that finds and displays all the words longer than 5 characters from a text file "Words.txt".**

Ans. (A)
```
def show():
    f=open("Email.txt",'r')
    data=f.read()
    words=data.split(' ')
    for word in words:
        if '@cmail' in word:
         print(word,end=' ')
 f.close()
```

Or

(B)
```
def display_long_words():
  with open("Words.txt", 'r') as file:
      data=file.read()
```

```
        words=data.split()
        for word in words:
            if len(word)>5:
                print(word,end=' ')
```

37. Write a function in Python to read a text file, Alpha.txt and displays those lines which begin with the word 'You'. CBSE SQP 2023-24

Or

Write a function, vowelCount() in Python that counts and displays the number of vowels in the text file named Poem.txt.

Ans.
```
def Para():
    fobj = open("Alpha.txt","r")
    data = fobj.readlines()
    for i in data:
        L = i.split()
        if L[0] == "You":
            print(i)
    fobj.close()
```

Or

```
def countVowel():
    fobj = open("Poem.txt","r")
    data = str(fobj.read())
    count=0
    for i in data:
        if i in "aeiouAEIOU":
            count = count+1
    print(count)
    fobj.close()
countVowel()
```

38. Write a method COUNTLINES() in Python to read lines from text file 'TESTFILE.TXT' and display the lines which are not starting with any vowel. CBSE SQP 2022-23

> Example
>
> If the file content is as follows:
>
> An apple a day keeps the doctor away.
>
> We all pray for everyone's safety.
>
> A marked difference will come in our country.
>
> The COUNTLINES() function should display the output as:
>
> The number of lines not starting with any vowel - 1

Or

Write a function ETCount() in Python, which should read each character of a text file "TESTFILE.TXT" and then count and display the count of occurrence of alphabets E and T individually (including small cases e and t too).

> Example
>
> If the file content is as follows:
>
> Today is a pleasant day.
>
> It might rain today.
>
> It is mentioned on weather sites
>
> The ETCount() function should display the output as:
>
> E or e: 6
>
> T or t : 9

Ans.
```
def COUNTLINES():
    file=open('TESTFILE.TXT','r')
    lines=file readlines()
    count=0
    for w in lines:
        if (w[0]).lower() not in 'aeoiu':
            count = count + 1
    print ("The number of lines not
starting with any vowel: ", count)
    file.close()
COUNTLINES()
```

Or

```
def ETCount():
    f=open("TESTFILE.TXT")
    e=0
    t=0
    while True:
        l=f.readline()
        if not l:
            break
        for i in l:
            if(i=='E' or i=='e'):
                e=e+1
            elif(i=='T' or i=='t'):
                t=t+1
print("E :",e)
print("T :",t)
f.close()
```

39. (a) Write a Python function that displays all the lines containing the word 'vote' from a text file "Elections.txt". For example, if the file contains:

> In an election many people vote to choose their representative. The candidate getting the maximum share of votes stands elected.
>
> Normally, one person has to vote once.
>
> The process of voting may vary with time and region.
>
> Then the output should be:
>
> In an election many people vote to choose their representative.
>
> Normally, one person has to vote once.

Or

(b) **Write a Python function that displays all the words starting and ending with a vowel from a text file "Report.txt". The consecutive words should be separated by a space in the output. For example, if the file contains:** CBSE 2025

Once there was a wise man in a village.
He was an awesome story-teller.
He was able to keep people anchored while listening to him.
Then the output should be:
Once a a awesome able

Ans. (a)
```
def find_vote_lines():
    with open("Elections.txt", "r") as f:
        for line in f:
            if "vote" in line.lower():
                print(line.strip())
```

Or

(b)
```
def find_vowel_words():
    vowels = ['a', 'e', 'i', 'o', 'u']
    result = []
    with open('Report.txt', 'r') as file:
        for line in file:
            words = line.split()
            for word in words:
                stripped =
word.strip(",.!?") # Remove punctuation
                if stripped:
first = stripped[0].lower()
last = stripped[-1].lower()
if first in vowels and last in vowels:
result.append(stripped)
    print(" ".join(result))
```

40. Consider the following code :

```
f = open ("mytry","+")
f.write("0123456789abcdef")
f.seek(-3,2)   //statement1
print(f.read(2)) //statement2
```

Explain statement1 and give output of statement2.

Ans. Statement1 uses seek() method that can be used to position the file object at particular place in the file. It's syntax is :

```
FileObject.seek(offset[,from_what])
```

So, f.seek(-3, 2) positions the FileObject to 3 bytes before end of file.

Output of statement2 : de

41. Consider a binary file Employee.dat containing details such as empno:ename:salary (separator ':'). Write a Python function to display details of those employees who are earning between 20000 and 40000. (Both values inclusive)

Ans.
```
def Readfile():
    i=open("Employee.dat","+")
    x=i.readline()
    while(x):
        l=x.split(':')
    if (20000>=float(l[2])<=40000):
      print(x)
    x=i.readline()
```

42. Differentiate between text file and binary file.

Ans. Differences between text file and binary file are as follows

Text File	Binary file
(i) In text file, data are stored as line of characters with each line terminated by a new line character ('\n').	(i) In binary file, data are stored on the disk in the same way as they are presented in the computer memory.
(ii) Text files are in human readable form and they can be created and read using any text editor.	(ii) Binary files are not in human readable form and they can be created and read only by specific program written for them.
(iii) In text files, newline is stored as a combination of carriage return '\r' and linefeed '\n'.	(iii) In binary files, newline is stored only as '\n'.

43. Write a Python program that read the data from file 'original.dat' and delete the line(s) having word (passed as an argument). Then write these data after removing lines into file 'duplicate.dat'.

Ans.
```
import os
def Delete (word):
        file1=open('original.dat','rb')
        nfile=open('duplicate.dat','wb')
        while True :
           line=file1.readline()
           if not line :
              break
           else :
              if word in line :
                 pass
              else:
                 print(line)
                 nfile.write(line)
        file1.close()
        nfile.close()
```

44. Differentiate between text file and CSV file.

Ans. Differences between text file and CSV file are as follows

Text file	CSV file
(i) It is a file that stores information in ASCII characters.	(i) It is a file that stores data in tabular form.
(ii) The file extension of text file is .txt.	(ii) The file extension of CSV file is .csv.

45. A csv file "Happiness.csv" contains the data of a survey. Each record of the file contains the following data:

Competency Baed Que. CBSE SQP 2024-25

- **Name of a country**
- **Population of the country**
- **Sample Size (Number of persons who participated in the survey in that country)**
- **Happy (Number of persons who accepted that they were Happy)**

For example, a sample record of the file may be:

Signiland, 5673000, 5000, 3426

Write the following Python functions to perform the specified operations on this file:

(I) Read all the data from the file and display all those records for which the population is more than 5000000.

(II) Count the number of records in the file.

Ans. (I)
```
import csv
def show():
 f=open("happiness.csv",'r')
 records=csv.reader(f)
 next(records, None) #To skip the Header row
 for i in records:
     if int(i[1])>5000000:
         print(i)
f.close()
```

(II)
```
import csv
def Count_records():
    f=open("happiness.csv",'r')
    records=csv.reader(f)
    next(records, None) #To skip the
                                Header row
    count=0
    for i in records:
      count+=1
    print(count)
    f.close()
```

46. Vedansh is a Python programmer working in a school. For the Annual Sports Event, he has created a CSV file named Result.csv, to store the results of students in different sports events. The structure of Result.csv is :

CBSE SQP 2023-24

[St_Id, St_Name, Game_Name, Result]

Where

Competency Based Que.

- **St_Id is Student ID (integer)**
- **ST_name is Student Name (string)**
- **Game_Name is name of game in which student is participating(string)**
- **Result is result of the game whose value can be either 'Won', 'Lost' or 'Tie'**

For efficiently maintaining data of the event, Vedansh wants to write the following user defined functions

- **Accept() – to accept a record from the user and add it to the file Result.csv. The column headings should also be added on top of the csv file.**
- **wonCount() – to count the number of students who have won any event.**

As a Python expert, help him complete the task.

Ans.
```
import os
def Accept():
      St_Id = int(input("Enter the student ID: "))
      St_Name = input("Enter student name: ")
    Game_Name = input("Enter the name of the game: ")
      Result = input("Enter Result (Won/Lost/Tie): ")
  header = ["St_Id", "St_Name", "Game_Name", "Result"]
    data = [St_Id, St_Name, Game_Name, Result]
      file_exists = os.path.isfile("Result.csv")
      fobj = open("Result.csv", "a", newline="")
      writer = csv.writer(fobj)
      if not file_exists:
writer.writerow(header) # Add header if file does not
exist
writer.writerow(data)
fobj.close()
def wonCount():
fobj = open("Result.csv", 'r')
      rd = csv.reader(fobj, delimiter=',')
      header = next(rd) # Skip header
      print("Header:", header)
      for row in rd:
If row[3].strip().lower() == "won":
     # Case-insensitive match
print(row)
         fobj.close()
         Accept()
wonCount()
```

Short Answer Type II Questions

47. Aman is a Python programmer. He has written a code and created a binary file record.dat with employeeid, ename and salary. The file contains 10 records.

He now has to update a record based on the employee id entered by the user and update the salary. The updated record is then to be written in the file temp.dat. The records which are not to be updated also have to be written to the file temp.dat. If the employee id is not found, an appropriate message should to be displayed. **Competency Based Que. CBSE SQP 2022-23**

As a Python expert, help him to complete the following code based on the requirement given above:

```
import ______                    #Statement 1
def update_data():
  rec={}
  fin=open("record.dat","rb")
  fout=open("____________")       #Statement 2
  found=False
  eid=int(input("Enter employee id to update
                            their salary :: "))
  while True:
    try:
      rec = ____________          #Statement 3
      if rec["Employee id"]= =eid:
          found=True
          rec["Salary"]=int(input("Enter new
                                salary :: "))
          pickle.________         #Statement 4
      else:
          pickle.dump(rec, fout)
      except:
          break
    if found= =True:
      print("The salary of employee id ",eid,"
                         has been updated.")
    else:
      print("No employee with such id is not
                                    found")
    fin.close()
    fout.close()
```

(i) Which module should be imported in the program? (Statement 1)

(ii) Write the correct statement required to open a temporary file named temp.dat. (Statement 2)

(iii) Which statement should Aman fill in Statement 3 to read the data from the binary file, record.dat and in Statement 4 to write the updated data in the file, temp.dat?

Ans. (i) pickle

(ii) "temp.dat","wb"

(iii) pickle.load(fin), pickle.dump(rec,fout)

48. A csv file "P_record.csv" contains the records of patients in a hospital. **CBSE 2025**

Each record of the file contains the following data:

- Name of a patient
- Disease
- Number of days patient is admitted
- Amount

For example, a sample record of the file may be :

["Gunjan", "Jaundice", 4,15000]

Write the following Python functions to perform the specified operations on this file:

(i) Write a function read_data() which reads all the data from the file and displays the details of all the 'Cancer' patients.

(ii) Write a function count_rec() which counts and returns the number of records in the file.

Ans. (i)

```
def read_data():
 import csv
 with open("P_record.csv", "r") as f:
     reader = csv.reader(f)
     for row in reader:
         if row[1] == "Cancer":
             print(row)
```

(ii)

```
def count_rec():
 with open("P_record.csv", "r") as f:
   return sum(1 for _ in f)
```

49. Sangeeta is a Python programmer working in a computer hardware company. She has to maintain the records of the peripheral devices. She created a csv file named Peripheral. csv, to store the details. The structure of Peripheral. csv is : **CBSE 2024**

[P_id, P_name, Price] **Competency Based Que.**

where

- P_id is Peripheral device ID (integer)
- P_name is Peripheral device name (String)
- Price is Peripheral device price (integer)
- Sangeeta wants to write the following user defined functions :
- Add_Device ( ) To accept a record from the user and add it to a csv file, Peripheral. csv.
- Count_Device ( ) To count and display number of peripheral devices whose price is less than 1000.

Ans.

```
import csv
def Add_Device():
```

```
    with open("Peripheral.csv", "a", newline='')
as F:
        W = csv.writer(F)
  P_id = int(input("Enter the Peripheral ID: "))
  P_name = input("Enter Peripheral Name: ")
        Price = int(input("Enter Price: "))
        L = [P_id, P_name, Price]
   W.writerow(L)
def Count_Device():
    with open("Peripheral.csv", "r") as F:
        L = list(csv.reader(F))
        Count = 0
        for D in L:
            if int(D[2]) < 1000:
                Count += 1
        print(Count)
Add_Device()
Count_Device()
```

Long Answer Type Questions

50. Write a program to search a Employee record according to Id from the "emp.txt" file. The "emp.txt" file contains Id, Name and Salary fields. Assume that first field of the employee records (between Id and Name) is separated with a comma(,).

Ans.

```
import os
f1 = "emp.txt"
if os.path.isfile(f1):
   fob = open(f1)
   eid = int(input("Enter employee id: "))
  flag = False
     for emp in fob:
         emp = emp.strip()
         parts = emp.split(',')
         if len(parts) >= 3:
             nid = int(parts[0])
              # directly converting to int
             if eid == nid:
           print("Employee found:", emp)
               flag = True
               break
     fob.close()
     if not flag:
        print("Record not found")
else:
    print("File does not exist")
```

51. Write a program to read the content from a text file "status.txt", count and display the total number of lines and blank spaces present in it. e.g. if the "status.txt" file contains the following lines:

> Welcome to your one-step solutions for all your study, practice and assessment needs for various competitive & recruitment examinations and school segment. We have been working tirelessly for over a decade to make sure that you have best in class study resources because you deserve SUCCESS AND NOTHING LESS...
>
> The output will be:
>
> The status file contents are
>
> Total lines in file are: 6
>
> Total spaces in file are: 43

Ans.

```
import os
tfile='status.txt'
if os.path.isfile(tfile):
    fob=open(tfile,'r')
    blankspaces=total_lines=0
    print("The status file contents are").
    print("-------")
    while True:
        aline=fob.readline()
        if not aline:
            break
        else:
            total_lines=total_lines+1
            aline=aline.rstrip()
            for i in aline:
                if i.isspace():
                    blankspaces=blankspaces+1
    print("Total lines in file are: %d"
                               %total_lines)
    print("Total space in file are: %d" %
                               blankspaces)
    fob.close()
else:
    print("File does not exist")
```

52. Write a program with method countand( ) to count the word 'and' or 'And' as an independent word in a text file "status.txt". e.g. if the content of the file "status. txt" is as follows:

> Welcome to your one-step solutions for all your study, practice and assessment needs for various competitive & recruitment examinations and school segment. We have been working tirelessly for over a decade to make sure that you have best in class study resources because you deserve SUCCESS AND NOTHING LESS...
>
> Then the output of the program should be: Count of _and_ in file is/are: 3

Ans.

```
import os
def countand():
    if os.path.isfile("status.txt"):
       fob=open("status.txt", 'r')
       c=0
```

```
        while True:
            Str=fob.readline()
            if not Str:
                break
            Str=Str.rstrip().lower().split()
            for i in range(len(Str)):
                if (Str[i]=='and'):
                    c=c+1
        print("Count of_and_in file is/are
                                            : ",c)
    else:
        print("File does not exist")
countand()
```

53. **Write a method countopen( ) to count and display the number of lines starting with the word 'OPEN'(including small cases and upper cases) present in a text file "start. txt".**

> e.g. If the file "start.txt" contains the following lines:
>
> Get the data value to be deleted,
> Open the file for reading from it.
> Read the complete file into a list
> Delete the data from the list
> Open the file
> Open same file for writing into it
> Write the modified list into file.
> Close the file.
> The method should display
> Total lines started with word 'OPEN' is/are: 3

Ans.
```
import os
def countopen():
    if os.path.isfile("start.txt"):
        f = open("start.txt", "r")
        c = 0
        print("The lines are:")
        while True:
            l = f.readline()
            if not l:
                break
            l = l.rstrip()
            print(l)
        words = l.upper().split()
if len(words) > 0 and words[0] == "OPEN":
            c += 1
        if c > 0:
print("Total lines started with the word
'OPEN' is/are:", c)
        else:
print("There is no line started with the
word 'OPEN'")
        f.close()
    else:
print("File does not exist")
countopen()
```

54. **Write a function countHisHer() in Python, which reads the contents of a text file diary.txt and count the words His and Her (not case sensitive).**

> **e.g.** If the file contains
> Pinaky has gone to his friend's house.
> His friend's name is Ravya. Her house is 12 km from Pinaky's house.
> The function should display the output as :
> Count for His : 2
> Count for Her : 1

Ans.
```
import os
def countHisHer():
    if os.path.isfile("diary.txt"):
        f=open("diary.txt")
        c1=0
        c2=0
        while True:
            l=f.readline()
            if not l:
                break
        l=l.rstrip().lower().split()
        for i in range(len(l)):
            if(l[i]=='HIS' or l[i]=='his'):
                c1=c1+1
            elif(l[i]=='HER' or l[i]=='her'):
                c2=c2+1
        print("Count for His :",c1)
        print("for Her :",c2)
    else:
        print("File does not exist")
```

55. **(A) Write a user defined function in Python named showInLines( ) which reads contents of a text file named STORY. TXT and displays every sentence in a separate line.** **CBSE 2024**

Assume that a sentence ends with a full stop (.), a question mark (?), or an exclamation mark (!).

For example, if the content of file STORY. TXT is as follows:

> Our parents told us that we must eat vegetables to be healthy. And it turns out, our parents were right! So, what else did our parents tell?
>
> Then the function should display the file's content as follows:
>
> Out parents told us that we must eat vegetables to be healthy.
>
> And it turns out, our parents were right!
> So, what else did our parents tell?

Or

(B) Write a function, c_words ( ) in Python that separately counts and displays the number of uppercase and lowercase alphabets in a text file, Words. txt.

Ans. (A)
```
def showInLines():
  F = open("STORY.TXT", 'r')
  S = F.read()
  F.close()
  sentence = ""
  for ch in S:
      sentence += ch
      if ch in ['.', '?', '!']:
        print(sentence.strip())
        sentence = ""
```

Or

(B)
```
def c_words():
    with open("Words.txt", "r") as f:
        Txt = f.read()
    CL = CU = 0
    for i in Txt:
        if i.islower():
            CL += 1
elif i.isupper():
            CU += 1
    print(CL, CU)
c_words()
```

56. (a) **Write the definition of a Python function named LongLines ( ) which reads the contents of a text file named 'LINES. TXT' and displays those lines from the file which have at least 10 words in it. For example, if the content of 'LINES. TXT' is as follows:** **CBSE 2023**

Once upon a time, there was a woodcutter He lived in a little house in a beautiful, green wood. One day, he was merrily chopping some wood. He saw a little girl skipping through the woods, whistling happily. The girl was followed by a big gray wolf. Then the function should display output as : He lived in a little house in a beautiful, green wood. He saw a little girl skipping, through the woods, whistling happily.

Or

(b) **Write a function count_Dwords( ) in Python to count the words ending with a digit in a text file "Details.txt".**

Example It the file content is as follows: On seat2 VIP1 will sit and On seat1 VVIP2 will be sitting Output will be: Number of words ending with a digit are 4

Ans. (a)
```
def LongLines() :
    f = open("LINES.TXT",'r')
    data= f.readlines()
    for i in data :
      a = i.split ()
      if len(a)>=10 :
        print(i)
    f.close ()
```

Or

(b)
```
def count_Dwords():
    f=open("Details.txt",'r')
    data=f.read()
      a=data.split()
      count=0
      for i in a:
        if i [-1].isDigit():
          count=count+1
      print ("Number of words ending with a digit
                                    are", count)
      f.close()
```

57. Given a file "dept.dat", containing records of departments with following attributes:

Candidate: Name of the candidates Department: Department name like: Computer, Physics, Math, Biology, etc. Write a method copy that would read contents from the file "dept.dat" and creates a file named "com.dat" copying only those records from "dept.dat" where the department name is "Computer". Assume that '-' is a field separator in "dept.dat". **Competency Based Que.**

Ans.
```
import os
def copy():
    f1="dept.dat"
    if not os.path.isfile(f1):
      print(f1, "does not exist")
    else:
      dobj=open("dept.dat","rb")
      cobj=open("com.dat","wb")
      for c in dobj:
        status=c.rstrip()
        ncom=status.split ('-')
        size=len(ncom)
        name=ncom[0]
        dept=ncom[1]
```

```
        if(dept=='Computer'):
            cobj.write(name.upper() + "-"
            + dept.upper() + "\n")
    dobj.close()
    cobj.close()
```

58. **Write a Python program that read a data from file "info.dat" and replace a word with another word.**

Ans.
```
import os
import sys
import fileinput
f=0
print("Text to search for:")
sch=input()
print("Text to replace it with :")
rep=input()
myfile=open("info.txt","r+")
for l in fileinput.input("info.txt"):
    if sch in l:
        L=(l.replace(sch,rep))
        print("Match is found")
        f=1
        break
if(f==0):
    print("Match not found")
myfile.close()
```

59. **(A) (i) Differentiate between 'w' and 'a' file modes in Python.** **CBSE 2024**

(ii) Consider a binary file, items. dat, containing records stored in the given format :

`{item_id: [item_name,amount]}`

Write a function, Copy_new ( ), that copies all records whose amount is greater than 1000 from items. dat to new_items. dat.

Or

(B) (i) What is the advantage of using with clause while opening a data file in Python ? Also give syntax of with clause.

(ii) A binary file, EMP. DAT has the following structure :

`[Emp_Id, Name, Salary]`

where

Emp_Id : Employee id

Name : Employee Name

Salary : Employee Salary

Write a user defined function, disp_Detail ( ), that would read the contents of the file EMP.DAT and display the details of those employees whose salary is below 25000.

Ans. (A) (i)

'w'	'a'
Open the file in write mode.	Open the file in append mode.
If the file doesn't exist, then a new file will be created. The file pointer is in the beginning of the file.	If the file doesn't exist, then a new file will be created. The file pointer is at the end of the file.
If the file exists, the contents of the file, if any, are lost/truncated and the new data is added as fresh data into the file.	If the file exists, the new data is added at the end of the file without deleting the previous contents of the file.

(ii)
```
import pickle
def Copy_new():
  try:
      with open("items.dat", "rb") as F1:
          Data1 = pickle.load(F1)
          Data2 = {}
          for K, V in Data1.items():
              if V[1] > 1000:
                  Data2[K] = V
      with open("new_items.dat", "wb") as F2:
pickle.dump(Data2, F2)
  except FileNotFoundError:
      print("File not found!")
  except Exception as e:
      print(f"An error occurred: {e}")
Copy_new()
```

(B) (i) The advantage of using with clause is that any file that is opened using this clause is closed automatically, once the control comes outside the with clause.
The syntax of with clause is:
with open (file_name, access_mode) as file_object:

(ii)
```
import pickle
def disp_Detail():
  try:
      with open("EMP.DAT", "rb") as F:
          Data = pickle.load(F)
          for D in Data:
              if D[2] < 25000:
                  print(D)
  except FileNotFoundError:
      print("File Not Found!!!")
  except EOFError:
      pass  # End of file reached
  except Exception as e:
      print(f"An error occurred: {e}")
disp_Detail()
```

60. **(i) Differentiate between r+ and w+ file modes in Python.** **CBSE SQP 2023-24**

(ii) Consider a file, SPORT.DAT, containing records of the following structure

[SportName, TeamName, No_Players]

Write a function, copyData(), that reads contents from the file SPORT.DAT and copies the records with Sport name as "Basket Ball" to the file named BASKET.DAT. The function should return the total number of records copied to the file BASKET.DAT.

***Or* (Option for part (ii) only)**

A Binary file, CINEMA.DAT has the following structure:

{MNO:[MNAME, MTYPE]}

Where

- **MNO – Movie Number**
- **MNAME – Movie Name**
- **MTYPE is Movie Type**

Write a user defined function, findType(mtype), that accepts mtype as parameter and displays all the records from the binary file CINEMA.DAT, that have the value of Movie Type as mtype.

Ans. (i) Differences between r+ and w+ modes are as follows

r+	w+
Opens a file for both reading and writing. The file pointer placed at the beginning of the file.	Opens a file for both writing and reading. Overwrites the existing file if the file exists.

(ii)
```
def copyData():
  fobj1=open("SPORT.DAT","rb")
  fobj2=open("BASKET.DAT","wb")
  count=0
  try:
      while True:
          data = pickle.load(fobj1)
          print(data)
          if data[0] == "Basket Ball":
              pickle.dump(data, fobj2)
    count+=1
  except EOFError :
    pass
    finally :
  return count
      fobj1.close()
      fobj2.close()
```

Or

```
def findType(mtype):
  fobj = open("CINEMA.DAT","rb")
  try:
    while True:
        data = pickle.load(fobj)
        if data[2] == mtype:
            print("Movie number:",data[0])
            print("Movie Name:",data[1])
            print("Movie Type:",data[2])
  except EOFError:
    fobj.close()
```

61. **Shreyas is a programmer, who has recently been given a task to write a user defined function named write_bin ( ) to create a binary file called Cust_file.dat containing customer information – customer number (c_no), name (c_name), quantity (qty), price (price) and amount (amt) of each customer.** **CBSE 2023**

The function accepts customer number, name, quantity and price. Thereafter, it displays the message 'Quantity less than 10 .... Cannot SAVE', if quantity entered is less than 10. Otherwise the function calculates amount as price * quantity and then writes the record in the form of a list into the binary file.

```
import pickle
def write_bin( ):
    bin_file = ______                          # Statement 1
    while True:
       c_no=int (input ("enter customer number"))
    c_name=input ("enter customer name")
    qty=int.(input ("enter qty"))
    price=int(input ("enter price"))
    if. _____                                  # Statement 2
       print("Quantity less than 10..Cannot SAVE")
    else :
       amt=price * qty
       c_detail = [c_no, c_name, qty, price, amt]
                                               # Statemnet 3
       _____
       ans=input ("Do you wish to enter more records
                                              y/n")
if ans.lower ( )= ='n':
                                               # Statement 4
                                               # Statement 5
    __________
                                               # Statement 6
__________
```

(i) Write the correct statement to open a file 'Cust_file.dat' for writing the data of the customer.

(ii) Which statement should Shreyas fill in Statement 2 to check whether quantity is less than 10.

(iii) Which statement should Shreyas fill in Statement 3 to write data to the binary file and in Statement 4 to stop further processing if the user does not wish to enter more records.

Or (Option for part (iii) only)

(iii) **What should Shreyas fill in Statement 5 to close the binary file named Cust_file.dat and in Statement 6 to call a function to write data in binary file?**

Ans. (i) `open ("cust_file.dat", "ab")`

(ii) `qty <10 :`

(iii) Statement 3 → `pickle. dump (c_detail, bin_file)`

Statement 4 → `break`

Or

(iii) Statement 5 → `bin_file. close ()`

Statement 6 → `write_bin()`

62. **A file, PASSENGERS. DAT, stores the records of passengers using the following structure:** **CBSE 2025**

[PNR, PName, BRDSTN, DESTN, FARE]

where:

- **PNR - Passenger Number (string type)**
- **PName - Passenger Name (string type)**
- **BRDSTN - Boarding Station Name (string type)**
- **DESTN - Destination Station Name (string type)**
- **FARE - Fare amount for the journey (float type)**

Write user defined functions in Python for the following tasks:

(i) **Create () to input data for passengers and write it in the binary file PASSENGERS. DAT.**

(ii) **SearchDestn (D) to read contents from the file PASSENGERS.DAT and display the details of those Passengers whose DESTN matches with the value of D.**

(iii) **UpdateFare () to increase the fare of all passengers by 5% and rewrite the updated records into the file PASSENGERS. DAT.**

Ans. (i)

```
import pickle
def Create():
with open("PASSENGERS.DAT", "ab") as
file:
      while True:
  pnr = input("Enter PNR: ")
 name = input("Enter Passenger Name: ")
            brostn = input("Enter
Boarding Station Name: ")
            destn = input("Enter
Destination Station Name: ")
        fare = float(input("Enter Fare: "))
            record = {
                "PNR": pnr,
                "Name": name,
                "BROSTN": brostn,
                "DESTN": destn,
                "FARE": fare
            }
        pickle.dump(record, file)
        cont = input("Add another passenger?
                            (y/n): ").lower()
              if cont != 'y':
                  break
```

(ii)

```
def SearchDestn(D):
        with open("PASSENGERS.DAT", "rb")
                                    as file:
            while True:
                try:
                record = pickle.load(file)
                if record["DESTN"] == D:
print(f"PNR: {record['PNR']}, Name:
{record['Name']}, Boarding:
{record['BROSTN']}, Destination:
{record['DESTN']}, Fare:
{record['FARE']}")
            except EOFError:
                break
```

(iii)

```
def UpdateFare():
    records = []
    with open("PASSENGERS.DAT", "rb")
 as file:
        while True:
            try:
records.append(pickle.load(file))
            except EOFError:
                break
    for record in records:
        record["FARE"] *= 1.05
with open("PASSENGERS.DAT", "wb") as
file:
        for record in records:
        pickle.dump(record, file)
```

63. **Surya is a manager working in a recruitment agency. He needs to manage the records of various candidates. For this he wants the following information of each candidate to be stored:** **CBSE SQP 2024-25**

Competency Based Que.

Candidate_ID – integer
Candidate_Name – string
Designation – string
Experience – float

You, as a programmer of the company, have been assigned to do this job for Surya. Suggest:

(I) **What type of file (text file, csv file, or binary file) will you use to store this data? Give one valid reason to support your answer.**

(II) Write a function to input the data of a candidate and append it in the file that you suggested in part (I) of this question.

(III) Write a function to read the data from the file that you suggested in part (I) of this question and display the data of all those candidates whose experience is more than 10.

Ans. (I) csv file. Csv files store data is simple format exchangeable across different platforms

(II)
```
import csv
def add_data():
    with open("Candidates.csv",'a') as f:
        cwriter = csv. writer(f)
    cid=input("Enter Candidate ID: ")
    cnm=input("Enter Candidate name: ")
    cdg=input("Enter Designation: ")
    cexp=input("Enter Experience: ")
    rec=[cid,cnm,cdg,cexp]
    cwriter.writerow(rec)
```

(III)
```
import csv
    with open('Candidates.csv ', 'r')as file:
    csvFile = csv.reader(file)
    for rec in csvFile:
        if int(rec[3])> 10:
            print(rec)
```

64. (a) **Write one difference between CSV and text files. Write program in Python that defines and calls the following user defined functions** **CBSE 2023**

(i) COURIER_ADD ( ): It takes the values from the user and adds the details to a csv file 'courier. csv '. Each record consists of a list with field elements as cid, s_name , Source, destination to store Courier ID, Sender name, Source and destination address respectively.

(ii) COURIER_SEARCH ( ) : Takes the destination as the input and displays all the courier records going to that destination.

Or

(b) **Why it is important to close a file before exiting? Write a program in Python that defines and calls the following user defined functions :**

(i) Add_Book() : Takes the details of the books and adds them to a csv file 'Book.csv'. Each record consists of a list with field elements as book_ID, B_name and pub to store book ID, book name and publisher respectively.

(ii) Search_Book() : Takes publisher name as input and counts and displays number of books published by them.

Ans. (a) Differences between CSV and text files are as follows

CSV files	Text files
A comma-separated values (CSV) file contains tabular data (numbers and text) in plain-text form. An Excel spreadsheet can be saved as a CSV file.	A text file (TXT) is a computer file that stores a typed document as a series of alphanumeric characters and does not contain special formatting.

(i)
```
import csv
def COURIER_ADD():
    fobj=open("courier.csv", "a")
    wrt=csv. writer(fobj)
    cid=int(input("Enter the id:"))
    s_name=input("Enter the sender name:")
    source=input("Enter the source:")
    destination=input("Enter the destination:")
    result=[cid,s_name,source,destination]
    wrt.writerow (result)
    fobj.close()
COURIER_ADD()
```

(ii)
```
import csv
def COURIER_SEARCH():
    fobj=open("courier.csv","r")
    rd=csv.reader(fobj)
    destn=input("Enter the destination to
                                        display:")
    for i in rd:
        if i[3]==destn :
            print(i)
    fobj.close()
COURIER_SEARCH()
```

Or

(b) Files are limited resources managed by the operating system, making sure files are closed after use will protect against hard-to-debug issues like running out of file handles or experiencing corrupted data. The best defense is always to open files with a context manager.

(i)
```
import csv
def Add_Books():
    fobj=open("Books.csv","a")
    wrt=csv.writer(fobj)
    book_id=int(input("Enter the book id:"))
    B_name=input("Enter the book name:")
    pub=input("Enter the publisher:")
    res=[book_id, B_name,pub]
    wrt.writerow(res)
    fobj.close()
Add_Books()
```

(ii)
```
import csv
def Search_Book ():
    fobj=open ("Books.csv","r")
```

```
    rd=csv.reader(fobj)
    pub=input("Enter the publisher to display:")
    c=0
    for res in rd:
        if res [2]==pub :
            c=c+1
    print ("Total number of books",c)
    fobj. close ()
Search_Book ()
```

65. **What is the advantage of using a CSV file for permanent storage?** CBSE SQP 2022-23

Write a Program in Python that defines and calls the following user defined functions:

(i) **ADD()** To accept and add data of an employee to a CSV file 'record.csv'. Each record consists of a list with field elements as empid, name and mobile to store employee id, employee name and employee salary respectively.

(ii) **COUNTR()** To count the number of records present in the CSV file named 'record.csv'.

Or

Give any one point of difference between a binary file and a CSV file.

Write a Program in Python that defines and calls the following user defined functions:

(i) **add()** To accept and add data of an employee to a CSV file 'furdata.csv'. Each record consists of a list with field elements as fid, fname and fprice to store furniture id, furniture name and furniture price respectively.

(ii) **search()** To display the records of the furniture whose price is more than 10000.

Ans. It can store data values separated by comma. It provides a record type structures that can be used in database or dataframe format.

(i)
```
import csv
eid=""
ename=""
emob=""
eLst=[]
def ADD():
    with open ('record.csv','w') as f:
        eid=input("Enter employee ID :")
        ename=input("Enter employee
                                name :")
        emob=input("Enter employee
                              mobile :")
        eLst.append(eid)
        eLst.append(ename)
        eLst.append(emob)
    writer=csv.writer(f)
    writer.writerow(eLst)
    f.close()
```

(ii)
```
def COUNTR():
    ctr=0
    with open("record.csv") as f
        reader=csv.reader()
        for rec in reader :
            print(rec)
            ctr+=1
        print("No. of records :",ctr)
    f.close()
def main():
    ADD()
    COUNTR()
main()
```

Or

Binary file A binary file is stored in binary format and easy, fast for the computer to process.

CSV file It is a simple text file storing data in text format in a record structure separating data by comma.

(i)
```
import csv
fid=""
fname=""
fprice=0.0
fLst=[]
def add():
    with open ('furdata.csv','w') as f:
        fid=input("Enter furniture
                              ID :")
        fname=input("Enter
                  furniture name :")
        fprice=input(float("Enter
                 furniture price :"))
        fLst.append(fid)
        fLst.append(fname)
        fLst.append(fprice)
    writer=csv.writer(f)
    writer.writerow(fLst)
    f.close()
```

(ii)
```
def search():
    try:
        f=open('furdata.csv','r')
        reader=csv.reader(f)
        for rec in reader :
            if float(rec[2])>10000:
                print(rec)
        f.close()
    except:
        print("End of file")
def main():
    add()
    search()
main()
```

Case Study Based Questions

Case Study 1

Riya wrote a program to search any string in text file "school". Help her to execute the program successfully.

```
def check () :
    datafile = open (........)
    found = input ("Enter any string to be
     searched : ")
    f = False
    for line in ........ :
        if found in line :
            f = ........
            break
    return f
f = check ()
if (f = = ........) :
    print ("True")
else :
    print (........)
```

(i) **Riya should open which file to search any string?**

(ii) **Fill the blank in Line 5.**

(iii) **Which value will assign to f in Line 7?**

(iv) **Fill the blank in Line 11.**

(v) **Which variable or value will be print by last line?**

Ans. (i) school.txt (ii) datafile

(iii) True (iv) True

(v) "False"

Case Study 2

Below is a program to delete the line having word (passed as argument). Answer the questions that follow to execute the program successfully.

```
import ........
def filedel (word) :
    file1 = open ("Python. txt "," ........")
    nfile = open ("algo1.txt", "w")
    while True :
        line = file1.readline()
        if not line :
            break
        else :
            if word in line :
                ..........
            else :
                print (line)
                nfile. ........ (line)
        file1. close ()
        ........ . close ()
filedel ('write')
```

(i) **Name the module that should import in Line 1.**

(ii) **In which mode, above program should open the file to delete the line?**

(iii) **Fill the blank in Line 11.**

(iv) **Fill the blank in Line 14**

(v) **Fill the blank in Line 16 to close the file.**

Ans. (i) os

(ii) r

(iii) pass

(iv) write

(v) nfile

Case Study 3

Rohit, a student of Class 12th, is learning CSV File Module in Python. During examination, he has been assigned an incomplete Python code (shown below) to create a CSV File 'Student.csv' (content shown below). Help him in completing the code which creates the desired CSV File.

CSV File

1,AKSHAY,XII,A

2,ABHISHEK,XII,A

3,ARVIND,XII,A

4,RAVI,XII,A

5,ASHISH,XII,A

Incomplete Code

```
import_____                                          #Statement 1
fh = open(____, ____, newline=' ')                   #Statement 2
stuwriter = csv._____                                #Statement 3
data = []
header = ['ROLL_NO', 'NAME', 'CLASS', 'SECTION']
data.append(header)
for i in range(5):
    roll_no = int(input("Enter Roll Number : "))
    name = input("Enter Name : ")
    class = input(": ")
    section = input("Enter Section : ")
    rec = [_____]                                    #Statement 4
    data.append(rec)
stuwriter. _____ (data)                              #Statement 5
fh.close()
```

(i) **Identify the suitable code for blank space in line marked as Statement 1.**

(a) csv file (b) CSV

(c) csv (d) Csv

(ii) Identify the missing code for blank space in line marked as Statement 2.

(a) "School.csv","w"
(b) "Student.csv","w"
(c) "Student.csv","r"
(d) "School.csv","r"

(iii) Choose the function name (with argument) that should be used in the blank space of line marked as Statement 3.

(a) reader(fh)
(b) reader(MyFile)
(c) writer(fh)
(d) writer(MyFile)

(iv) Identify the suitable code for blank space in line marked as Statement 4.

(a) 'ROLL_NO', 'NAME', 'CLASS', 'SECTION'
(b) ROLL_NO, NAME, CLASS, SECTION
(c) 'roll_no','name','class','section'
(d) roll_no,name,class,section

(v) Choose the function name that should be used in the blank space of line marked as Statement 5 to create the desired CSV file?

(a) dump() (b) load()
(c) writerows() (d) writerow()

Ans. (i) (c) csv is the correct code to fill up the blank is Statement 1, which is to be imported.

(ii) (b) This code opens a file student.csv in write mode because append() method is using. So, correct missing code is
"Student.csv", "w"

(iii) (c) writer(fh) should be used in blank space in Statement 3. csv. writer is used to insert data to the CSV file.

(iv) (d) Suitable code for blank space in Statement 4 is roll_no, name, class, section.

(v) (c) writerows() should be used in blank space in Statement 5.
writerows() function writes each sequence in a list as a comma separated line of items in the file.

Case Study 4

Your teacher has given you a method/function FilterWords() in Python which read lines from a text file NewsLetter.TXT and display those words, which are lesser than 4 characters. Your teachers intentionally kept few blanks in between the code and asked you to fill the blanks, so that the code will run to find desired result. Do the needful with the follow **CBSE Question Bank**

```
def FilterWords():
    c=0
    file=open('NewsLetter.TXT', '_____')
                                        #Statement 1
    line = file._____                   #Statement 2
    word = _____                        #Statement 3
    for c in word:
        if _____:                       #Statement 4
            print(c)
    _____                               #Statement 5
FilterWords()
```

(i) Write mode of opening the file in Statement 1?

(a) a (b) ab
(c) w (d) r

(ii) Fill in the blank in Statement 2 to read the data from the file.

(a) File.Read() (b) file.read()
(c) read.lines( ) (d) readlines( )

(iii) Fill in the blank in Statement 3 to read data word by word.

(a) Line.Split()
(b) Line.split()
(c) line.split()
(d) split.word()

(iv) Fill in the blank in Statement 4, which display the word having lesser than 4 characters.

(a) len(c) ==4 (b) len(c)<4
(c) len ( )= =3 (d) len ( )==4

(v) Fill in the blank in Statement 5 to close the file.

(a) file.close() (b) File.Close()
(c) Close() (d) end()

Ans. (i) (d) r mode is used to open the file 'NewsLetter.TXT'. It opens a file in reading mode.

(ii) (b) file.read( ) is used to fill the blank Statement 2 as this method returns a string containing all characters in a file.

(iii) (c) line. split( ) method is used to fill the blank in Statement 3 to read data word-by-word.

(iv) (b) len(c)<4 is used to fill the blank in Statement 4, which display the word having lesser than 4 characters.

(v) (a) file.close() is used to close the file. It is important to close the files as soon as you have finished your work with file.

SELF ASSESSMENT TEST

Multiple Choice Questions

1 The file extension of text file is

(a) .text (b) .txt
(c) .ttx (d) .xtxt

2 Which method specifies how many characters the string should return?

(a) read() (b) read([size])
(c) readline() (d) readlines()

3 Python automatically flushes the files when .... them.

(a) closing (b) opening
(c) processing (d) None of these

4 Which of the following method does not return any value?

(a) remove() (b) read()
(c) write() (d) readline()

5 It opens a file for appending in binary format.

(a) b (b) b+
(c) ab (d) ab+

Fill in the Blanks

6 Python provides mainly .... types of read methods to read data from text file.

7 To write a sequence of string .... method is used.

8 .... method returns the current working directory of a process.

9 .... is the inverse operation, whereby a byte stream is converted back into an object.

10 csv file stores tabular data in ....

State Whether True and False

11. Text file is a sequence of characters consisting of alphabets, numbers and other special symbols.

12. CSV file contains information in the same format as it is held in memory.

Assertion and Reason Based Questions

Assertion (A) and Reason (R) Type questions. Choose the correct option as:

(a) Both Assertion (A) and Reason (R) are true, and Reason (R) is the correct explanation of Assertion (A)
(b) Both Assertion (A) and Reason (R) are true, but Reason (R) is not the correct explanation of Assertion (A)
(c) Assertion (A) is True, but Reason (R) is False
(d) Assertion (A) is False, but Reason (R) is True

13. Assertion (A) In text file, each line of text is terminated with a special character known as EOL.

Reason (R) When this EOL (End of Line) character is read or written, certain internal translations take place.

14. Assertion (A) CSV stores tabular data in plain text.

Reason (R) To represent CSV file, it must be saved with the .cs file extension.

Very Short Answer Type Questions

15 Is the write() method add a newline character to the end of the string?

16 Which method helps you to manipulate the position of file pointer?

17 Which access mode can be used for opening a file for both reading and writing in binary format?

18 Which method is used to read a pickle object hierarchy from a string?

Short Answer Type Questions

19 How can you rename your existing file? Explain with syntax.

20 How is readline () method different from readlines() method in Python?

21 Write a function in Python to read the content of a text file PLACES. TXT and display all those lines on screen, which are either starting with 'P' or starting with 'S'. e.g. The contents of file are

```
Pihu is in class XI
Shorya is also in same class.
Both are friends and good in studies.
Shreya is mutual of them.
```

The output should be 3.

22 Consider the following code:

```
f=open("data","w+")
f.write("ABCDE@12345678")
f.seek(-2,1) //statement1
print (f.read(3)) //statement2
```

Explain statement1 and give output of statement2.

23 What is the use of pickle module? Explain with an example.

24 How are binary files different from csv files in Python?

Long Answer Type Questions

25 Write a program to enter Employee ID, Name and Department into a file called "Employee.txt". Assume that first field of the employee records (between ID and Name) is separated with a comma(,).

26 Write a method count() to count and display the number of lines which contain Python (including small cases and upper cases) present in a text file "start.txt".
e.g. if the file start.txt contains the following lines :

```
Python is a general purpose language
It was developed by Python Software
Foundation
It is based on two programming languages
Python was designed to be highly extensible
```

Output should be : 3

27 How to read from CSV file using csv.reader()? Explain with an example.

Case Based Type Question

28 Program to open a file status.txt to read each character and print the occurrence of alphabets A and N. Answer the following questions to execute the program.

```
def countAN():
      f = open ("status. txt", "r")
      a = 0
      n = 0
      while ........ :
          l = f. readline ( )
          if not l :
              break
          for i in ........ :
              if (i = = 'A' or i = = 'a'):
                      a = + 1
              elif (..........):
                      n = ..........
    print ("A :", a)
    print ("N :", n)
    .......... . close ()
```

(i) Which condition satisfy in while loop?
(ii) Fill the blank in Line 9.
(iii) Fill the blank in Line 12.
(iv) Which value will be assign to variable n?
(v) Fill the blank in Line 16 to close the file.

Answers

1. (b) 2. (b) 3. (a) 4. (c) 5. (c)
6. CSV 7. writelines () 8. 3 9. getcwd ()
10. Deserialization 11. True 12. False
13. (a) 14. (c)
28. (i) → True, (ii) → l, (iii) → i=='N' or i=='n', (iv) → n+=1, (v) → f

05

CHAPTER

Data Structures

Data structures are widely used in almost every aspect of computer science i.e. operating system, compiler design, artificial intelligence, graphics and many more.

YOUR STUDY GOALS

5.1 Need of Data Structure
5.2 Types of Data Structure
5.3 Common Data Structures
5.4 Stack

YOUR PRACTICE GOAL

- Objective Type Questions (36 Qs ; MCQs, True or False, Fill in the Blanks, Assertion and Reason)
- Subjective Type Questions (28 Qs ; VSA, SA, LA)
- Case Study Based Questions (Objective Case Studies-2 Subjective Case Study-1)

In earlier chapters, we explored basic Python data types like Strings, Lists, Tuples, and Sets, which help store and manage collections of elements. Data structures extend this idea by organizing data systematically, enabling efficient access, manipulation, and storage.

A data structure is a way to organize and store data in a computer so it can be used effectively.

By grouping related data elements—whether of the same type or different types—data structures allow us to handle large volumes of information efficiently and perform operations like searching, sorting, or modifying data with ease.

5.1 Need of Data Structure

Data structures are essential for efficiently organizing, storing, and accessing data.

They help in optimizing the performance of algorithms by improving speed and memory usage. By using appropriate data structures, we can:

1. **Increase Efficiency** Enable faster data retrieval and processing.
2. **Optimize Resource Usage** Reduce memory consumption.
3. **Simplify Problem-Solving** Make complex tasks easier, such as sorting, searching,.and updating data.
4. **Enhance Scalability** Ensure the system can handle larger data sets effectively.

5.2 Types of Data Structure

There are two types of data structure as follows

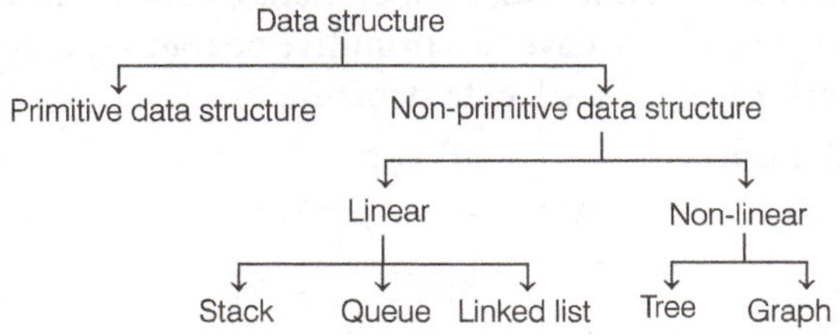

(i) **Primitive data structures** Data structures that are directly operated by machine level instructions are known as primitive data structures. Integer, real, character, pointer and reference are primitive data structures.

(ii) **Non-primitive data structures** These are more complex data structures. These data structures are derived from the primitive data structures. They include formation of sets of homogeneous and heterogeneous data elements.

The non-primitive data structure is divided into two types:

(a) **Linear data structures** These are single level data structures, having their elements in a sequence.

Example array, stack, queue and linked list.

(b) **Non-linear data structures** These are multilevel data structures.

Example tree and graph.

Data structures can also be classified as

(i) **Static data structures** These data structures are those whose size, structure and associated memory locations are fixed at compile time.

Example array.

(ii) **Dynamic data structures** These data structures are those, which can shrink or expand as required during the program execution and their associated memory locations can be changed.

Example linked list.

5.3 Common Data Structures

Common data structures are as follows

(i) **Array** It refers to the name of list of elements in a specific order, typically all elements are of the same type. Elements are accessed using index number. Arrays may be fixed length or resizable.

(ii) **Stack** It is limited form of array based on LIFO (Last In First Out), where insertion and deletion of elements take place at one end called the top of the stack.

It serves as a collection of elements with two principal operations: Push, which adds an element to the collection and Pop, which removes the last element that was added.

(iii) **Queue** It is also a limited form of array based on FIFO (First In First Out), where insertion of elements take place at one end called the Front and deletion of elements take place at the other end called the Rear.

(iv) **Linked list** It is a data structure which consists of a set of data records (nodes) linked together and organized by references (links or pointers). Every node has a data field and an address field. The link between data can also be called a connector.

It is a collection of structures ordered not by their physical placement in memory but by logical links that are stored as part of the data in the structure itself. It is not necessary that it should be stored in the adjacent memory locations.

Operations on Data Structure

The basic operations that are performed on data structure areas follows

(i) **Insertion** It means addition of a new data element in a data structure.

(ii) **Deletion** It means removal of a data element from a data structure. The data element is searched before its removal.

(iii) **Searching** It involves searching for the specific data element in a data structure.

(iv) **Traversal** Traversal of a data structure means visiting each element one by one.

(v) **Sorting** Arranging data elements of a data structure in a specific order (ascending or descending) is called sorting.

(vi) **Merging** Combining elements of two similar data structures to form a new data structure of same type is called merging.

In this chapter, we will study about stack, its implementation using Python as well as its applications.

Quick Test 1

1. What are data structures?
2. Differentiate static and dynamic data structures.
3. What are the different operations on data structures?
4. Give examples of non – primitive data structures.
5. Name some common data structures.

5.4 Stack

Stacks are a type of data structure that operates on the principle of LIFO: Last In, First Out. This means that the last element added to the stack will be the first one to be removed.

A stack is a list where insertion and deletion can take place only at one end called Top. A stack can be implemented using array and using linked list structure, depending upon the requirement.

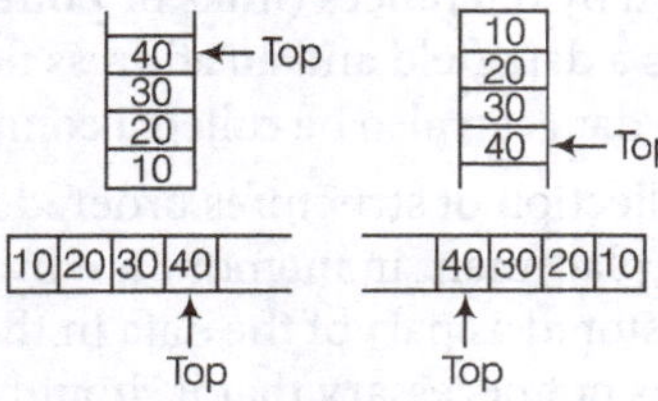

Different forms of stack

Stacks are used extensively at every level of a modern computer system.

e.g. Imagine a stack of books placed one on top of the other. To remove the book at the bottom of the stack, you must first remove all the books above it. Similarly, the last book that was placed on the top of the stack will be the first to be taken out. This concept perfectly demonstrates the LIFO principle.

Some of the other examples of stack in real life are

- Stack of coins.
- Plates placed one above another.
- Pile of clothes in an almirah.
- Multiple chairs in a vertical pile.

In programming, stacks are widely used in scenarios like function call management, undo operations in text editors, and expression evaluation.

Basic Operations and Implementation of Stack

Stack is open at one end, so operations can be performed on single end. We have two primitive operations that can be performed on stack data structure:

(i) Push (ii) Pop

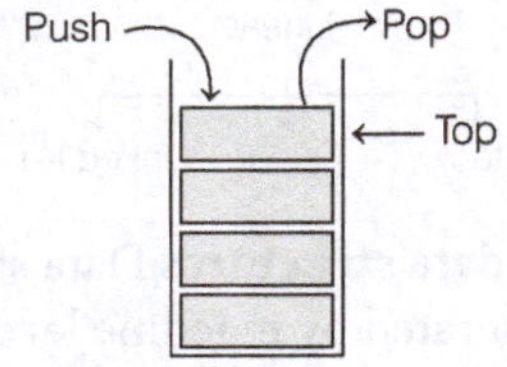

Stack

(i) Push Operation

Whenever we add any element "data" in the list then it will be called as Push operation on stack.

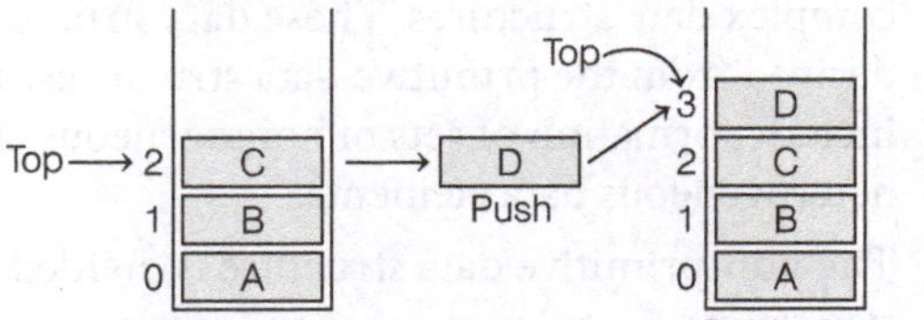

Stack before Stack after

Before every Push operation, the value of "Top" is incremented by one and then value is inserted at the Topof the stack.

(ii) Pop Operation

Whenever we try to remove elements from the stack then the operation is called as Pop operation on stack.

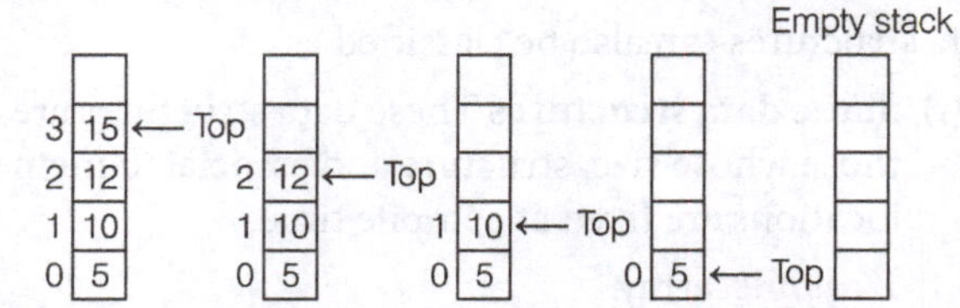

Stack intially Pop (15) Pop (12) Pop (10) Pop (5)

After every Pop operation, the value of "Top" is decremented by one and then value is deleted from the Top of the stack.

Some basic terms are given below

Terms	Definition
Peek	Refer to inspecting the value at the stack's top without moving it. It is also sometimes referred as inspection.
Stack Top	Points at the top most position or point to the last item in stack.

Terms	Definition
Stack Push	The procedure of inserting a new element to the top of the stack is known as Push operation.
Stack Overflow	Any attempt to insert a new element in already full stack results shows overflow.
Stack Pop	The procedure of removing element from the top of the stack is called Pop operation.
Stack Underflow	Any attempt to delete an element from already empty stack results as underflow.

Insertion in a Stack as a List (Pushing)

Before inserting a new data into the stack, it is necessary to check that the stack is full (overflow) or not.

If it is not full then the Push operation can be performed otherwise not.

This test is performed by comparing the value of Top with value MAX-1, the largest index.

Algorithm for Push Operation

In this algorithm, we insert an element called ITEM on the Top of the linear stack called data [MAX], which can hold maximum of MAX elements.

The variable Top is the counter pointing to the topmost element of stack.

Algorithm Steps

```
1. if (Top == (MAX–1))
    write "Stack is full" and go
    to step 4
2. Top  = Top + 1
3. data [Top] = ITEM
4. Stop
```

Deletion in a Stack as a List (Poping)

Before removing a data from the stack, it is necessary to check that the stack is empty (underflow) or not. If it is not empty then the Pop operation can be performed otherwise not.

Algorithm for Pop Operation

In this algorithm, we remove an element from the stack and copy the contents of topmost element into a variable called ITEM.

Algorithm Steps

```
1. if (Top == – 1)
       write "Stack is empty" and go to step 4
2. ITEM = data [Top]
3. Top = Top – 1
4. Stop
```

Traversal in a Stack as an Array

Moving through the elements of the stack is known as traversal.

Traversing is the basic operation to display elements in a stack.

Algorithm Steps to Display all the Elements of the Stack

```
1. Start
2. if (Top == – 1)go to step 3
   else go to step 4
3. Print "Stack is empty" and go to step 7
4. Print the Top element of the stack
5. Decrement Top by 1
6. if (Top == – 1) go to step 7
   else go to step 4
7. Stop
```

> **Mistak Alert!**
>
> Sometimes students confuse between append() and insert() method.

Program 1 To illustrate the basic operation of stack, i.e. Push, Pop and Show elements of stack.

```
def Empty(s):
    if s==[]:
        return True
    else:
        return False
def Push(s,x):
    s.append(x)
    Top=len(s) - 1
def Pop(s):
    if Empty(s):
        return "Underflow"
    else:
        x=s.Pop()
        if len(s)==0:
            Top=None
        else:
            Top=len(s) - 1
        return x
def Show(s):
    if Empty(s):
        print("Stack is Empty")
    else:
        Top=len(s)
        for i in range(Top-1,-1,-1):
            print(s[i])
#------ Main -------
```

```
stk=[]
Top=None
a="y"
while a=="y":
    print("1. Push")
    print("2. Pop")
    print("3. Show")
    print("4. Exit")
    choice=int(input("Enter your choice :"))
    if choice==1:
        x=int(input("Enter the number :"))
        Push(stk,x)
    elif choice==2:
        x=Pop(stk)
        if x=="Underflow":
            print("Stack is Empty")
        else:
            print("Popped element is :",x)
    elif choice==3:
        print("---Stack---",)
        Show(stk)
    elif choice==4:
        break
    else:
        print("Wrong input")
```

Output

1. Push
2. Pop
3. Show
4. Exit

Enter your choice :1

Enter the number :23

1. Push
2. Pop
3. Show
4. Exit

Enter your choice :1

Enter the number :56

1. Push
2. Pop
3. Show
4. Exit

Enter your choice :1

Enter the number :45

1. Push
2. Pop
3. Show
4. Exit

Enter your choice :3

---Stack---

45

56

23

1. Push
2. Pop
3. Show
4. Exit

Enter your choice :2

Popped element is : 45

1. Push
2. Pop
3. Show
4. Exit

Enter your choice :3

---Stack---

56

23

1. Push
2. Pop
3. Show
4. Exit

Enter your choice :1

Enter the number :78

1. Push
2. Pop
3. Show
4. Exit

Enter your choice :3

---Stack---

78

56

23

1. Push
2. Pop
3. Show
4. Exit

Enter your choice :6
Wrong input
1. Push
2. Pop
3. Show
4. Exit
Enter your choice :4

Item Node in Stack

Stored element or item in the stack is called item node. Item node can be of different types as

- When item nodes are integer types, stack will be mentioned as stack of integers.
- When item nodes are string types, stack will be mentioned as stack of string.
- When item nodes are list types, stack will be mentioned as stack of lists.

Applications of Stack

A stack is a LIFO structure, so it is a useful data structure for applications in which information must be stored and later retrieved in reverse order. Stacks are used by operating systems, application softwares as well as compilers.

Some applications of the stack in computer data processing are as follows

1. Processing of Method (Subprogram) Calls

Stacks are frequently used to keep track of the order of execution of the methods called by a main program. It is used to store information about the active subroutines of a computer program.

2. Matching Parentheses

The compilation process is very complex as the compiler checks the syntax minutely. The compiler has to ascertain if the number of left parentheses is equal in number with that of right parentheses and for every left bracket, there is a right bracket. This matching is performed by using a stack.

3. Polish String for Arithmetic Expression

An arithmetic expression is an expression having variables, constants and operators. Assume that an expression has only constants (numeric and logical) and operators (arithmetic-exponentiation, multiplication, division, addition and subtraction or logical-NOT, AND and OR).

Hierarchy of these operations is given below:

Arithmetic Operators	**Precedence**
Exponentiation (∧ or ↑)	Highest
Multiplication and Division (* , /)	Middle
Addition and Subtraction (+, –)	Lowest
Logical Operators	**Precedence**
NOT	Highest
AND	Middle
OR	Lowest

Operations at the same level are executed in a left to right order. Operators may be enclosed within parentheses to override the above rules of hierarchy.

There are three different but equivalent ways of writing expressions: Infix, Postfix and Prefix.

The differences are highlighted below:

Notation	Expression for x + y	Description
Infix	x + y	Operators are placed between operands.
Prefix (Polish)	+ x y	Operators are placed before operands.
Postfix	x y +	Operators are placed after operands.

Benefits of Prefix and Postfix Notations

These notations do not require parentheses to clarify precedence, making them suitable for machine parsing (e.g., stack-based algorithms).

Prefix and Postfix eliminate the need for operator precedence and parentheses, making parsing simpler compared to infix notation.

TEACHER TIP

Students should be careful about the operator precedence while converting.

Conversion from Infix to Postfix Notation

Infix expressions are easier for humans to understand, but require applying operator precedence (BODMAS) for evaluation. For example, in the expression x + y / z, we evaluate y / z first, then add x.

Postfix expressions (Reverse Polish Notation) avoid this issue by arranging operators in the order of evaluation, making it easier for computers to evaluate with a single left-to-right pass.

The Use of Postfix Notation

- **No need for parentheses** Operator precedence and associativity are inherently handled.
- **Simpler computation** It eliminates ambiguity, making it easier for computers to parse and evaluate expressions.

In this section, we will focus on converting an arithmetic expression written in infix notation to its equivalent postfix notation using a stack.

Algorithm: Conversion of Infix Expression to Postfix Expression

1. **Initialize**
   - STACK = empty stack
   - EXP = empty string (output postfix expression)
   - TOP = -1 (initially empty stack)
2. **For each character C in the infix expression**
   - If C is an operand (A-Z, a-z, 0-9):
     - Append C to EXP
   - If C is '(':
     - Push C onto STACK (increase TOP)
     - If C is ')':
     - While STACK is not empty and TOP is not '(':
       - Pop from STACK and append the popped operator to EXP
       - Pop '(' from STACK
   - If C is an operator (+, -, *, /, etc.):
     - While STACK is not empty and the operator at TOP has higher or equal precedence than C:
       - Pop from STACK and append the popped operator to EXP
       - Push C onto STACK (increase TOP)
3. **After processing all characters in the infix expression**
   - While STACK is not empty:
   - Pop from STACK and append the popped operator to EXP
4. **Return EXP as the postfix expression**

By following this algorithm, the infix expression is converted into its corresponding postfix form, which can then be evaluated efficiently.

Example 1 Let us now use this algorithm to convert a given infix expression (x + y)/(z*8) into equivalent postfix expression using a stack. Figure below shows the steps to be followed on encountering an operator or an operand in the given infix expression. Note here that stack is used to track the operators and parentheses, and a string variable contains the equivalent postfix expression.

Initially both are empty. Each character in the given infix expression is processed from left to right and the appropriate action is taken as detailed in the algorithm. When each character in the given infix expression has been processed, the string will contain the equivalent postfix expression.

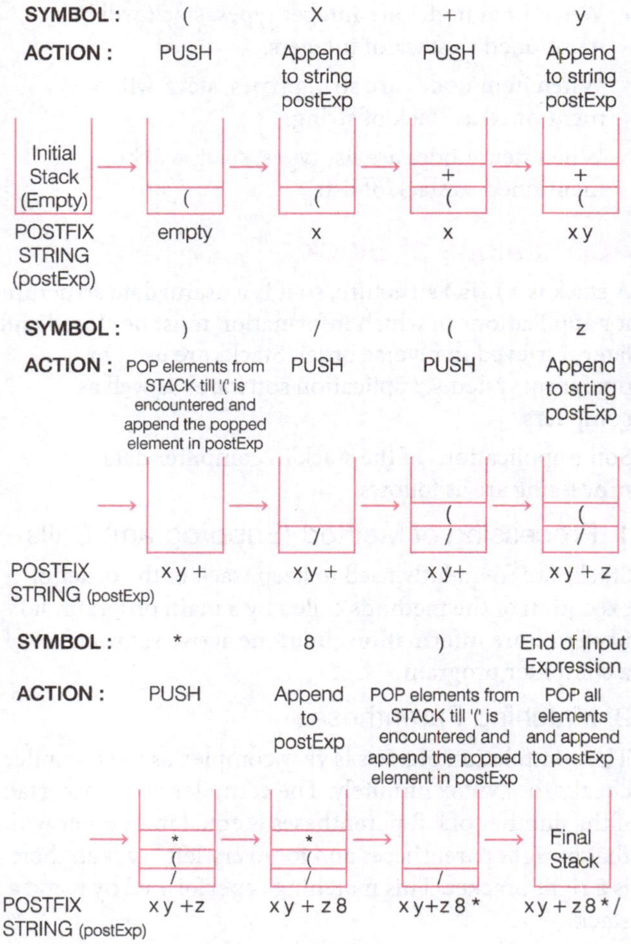

Evaluation of Postfix Expressions

Stacks are commonly used to evaluate expressions written in postfix notation. In postfix notation, also known as Reverse Polish Notation (RPN), the operator follows its operands. This eliminates the need for parentheses to enforce operator precedence.

Algorithm: Evaluation of Postfix Expression

1. Input the postfix expression into a variable, say postExp.
2. For each character in postExp, repeat the following steps:
   - If the character is an operand (a number or variable), push it onto the stack.
   - If the character is an operator (e.g., +, -, *, /):
   - Pop two elements from the stack.
   - Apply the operator on the popped elements (perform the operation).
   - Push the computed result back onto the stack.
3. After processing all characters, if the stack contains exactly one element:
   - Pop the element from the stack and output it as the final result of the postfix expression.
4. Else, if the stack does not contain exactly one element, output "Invalid Postfix Expression".

Example 2 Figure below shows the step-by-step process of evaluation of the postfix expression 7 8 2 * 4 / + using Algorithm.

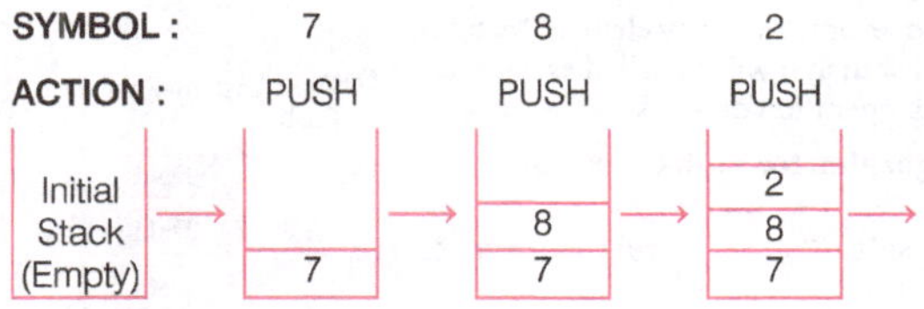

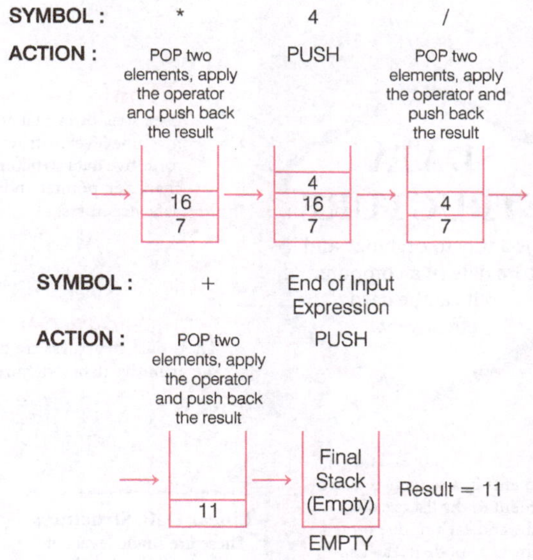

Quick Test 2

1. Can the size of stack increase?
2. Write two examples of stack.
3. What is stack Top?
4. Give any example of postfix expression.
5. During the execution of arithmetic expression, if operations are at same level, then how will these operations be executed?

Mind Map

DATA STRUCTURE
It is a way to organize and store data in a computer so it can be used effectively.

Primitive Data Structures
Data structures that are directly operated by machine level instructions are known as primitive data structures. Integer, real, character, pointer and reference are primitive data structures.

Non-primitive Data Structures
These data structures are derived from the primitive data structures.

Non-linear Data Structures
This means that the data elements are not arranged in a single level, and there are multiple paths to reach any given element.

Tree It is a hierarchical structure that is used to represent and organize data in the form of parent child relationship.

Graph It is used to represent relationship between entities and also used in many practical problems.

Linear Data Structures
These are single level data structures, having their elements in a sequence.

Linked List Stores data elements in a sequence. Each element in the list is called a node, and each node points to the next node in the list.

Queue Stores a collection of elements in a First In First Out (FIFO) order.

Array Stores a collection of elements of the same type in contiguous memory locations.

Stack Stores a collection of elements in a Last In First Out (LIFO) order.

Operations Performed on Stack
Stack is open at one end, so operations can be performed on single end. We have two primitive operations that can be performed on stack data structure.

Push Operation
Whenever we add any element "data" in the list then it will be called as Push operation on stack.

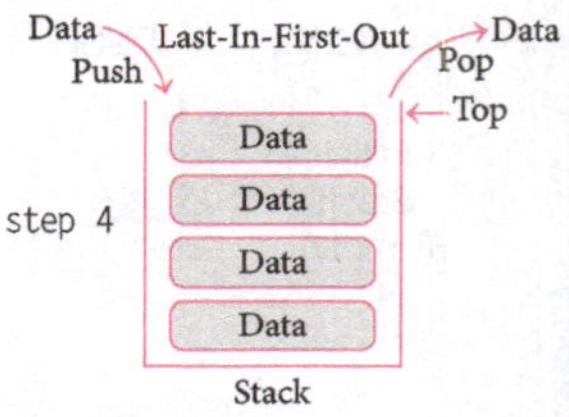

Algorithm for Push Operation

```
1. if (Top == (MAX))
   write "Stack is full" and go to step 4
2. Top = Top + 1
3. data [Top] = ITEM
4. Stop
```

Pop Operation
Whenever we try to remove elements from the stack then the operation is called as Pop operation on stack.

Algorithm for Pop Operation

```
1. if (Top == - 1 )
   write "Stack is empty" and go to step 4
2. ITEM = data [Top]
3. Top = Top - 1
4. Stop
```

Terms	Definition
Peek	Refer to the inspecting the value at the stack's top without moving it. It is also sometimes referred as inspection.
Stack Top	Points at the top most position or point to the last item in stack.
Stack Push	The procedure of inserting a new element to the top of the stack is known as Push operation.
Stack Overflow	Any attempt to insert a new element in already full stack results shows overflow.
Stack Pop	The procedure of removing element from the top of the stack is called Pop operation.
Stack Underflow	Any attempt to delete an element from already empty stack results as underflow.

Applications of Stack
A stack is an appropriate data structure on which information is stored and then later retrieved in reverse order. The application of stack are as follows

- Processing of Method (Subprogram) Calls
- Matching Parentheses
- Polish String for Arithmetic Expression
  - Polish and Reverse Polish Notation
    - Infix Notation
    - Prefix Notation
    - Postfix Notation

- **Infix** It is a way of writing mathematical and logical expressions where the operator is placed between the operands. e.g. a × b, 2 + 2, etc.
- **Prefix** It is also known as polish notation and it is a way to represent mathematical expressions in data structures. e.g. A + B × C would be written as + A × BC, etc.
- **Postifix** It is also known as reverse polish notation and it is a mathematical notation used in data structures to evaluate expressions efficiently.
  e.g. A + (B × C) would be written as ABC × +, etc.

NCERT Folder

1. State TRUE or FALSE for the following cases:

(a) Stack is a linear data structure

(b) Stack does not follow LIFO rule

(c) PUSH operation may result into underflow condition

(d) In POSTFIX notation for expression, operators are placed after operands

Ans. (a) TRUE

(b) FALSE

(c) FALSE

(d) TRUE

2. Find the output of the following code:

(a) result=0
numberList=[10,20,30]
numberList.append(40)
result=result+numberList.pop()
result=result+numberList.pop()
print("Result=",result)

(b) answer=[];
output='' answer.append('T')
answer.append('A')
answer.append('M')
ch=answer.pop()
output=output+ch
ch=answer.pop()
output=output+ch
ch=answer.pop()
output=output+ch
print("Result=",output)

Ans. (a)

1. numberList starts as [10, 20, 30].
2. numberList.append(40) adds 40 to the list, so numberList becomes [10, 20, 30, 40].
3. numberList.pop() removes and returns the last item (40), so result = 0 + 40 = 40.
4. numberList.pop() removes and returns the last item (30), so result = 40 + 30 = 70.
5. The final print statement outputs Result= 70.

(b) The list answer starts as ['T', 'A', 'M'].

The pop() method removes the last element from the list and appends it to output.

The order of pops is:

1. 'M' is popped first, then added to output.
2. 'A' is popped, added to output.
3. 'T' is popped, added to output.

Thus, the result is 'M A T'.

3. Write a program to reverse a string using stack.

Ans.
```
def reverse_string(s):
    stack = []
# Push all characters of the string onto the stack
    for char in s:
        stack.append(char)
# Pop characters from the stack to get the reversed string
    reversed_str = ''
    while stack:
        reversed_str += stack.pop()
    return reversed_str
input_str = "hello"
print("Reversed string:",
reverse_string(input_str))
```

4. For the following arithmetic expression:
((2+3)*(4/2))+2
Show step-by-step process for matching parentheses using stack data structure.

Ans. The step-by-step process for matching parentheses in the expression ((2+3)*(4/2))+2 using a stack data structure:

1. **Initialize an empty stack**
   Stack: []
2. **Iterate through the expression, character by character**
   - Character: (
     - Action: Push the opening parenthesis onto the stack.
     - Stack: [(
   - Character: (
     - Action: Push the opening parenthesis onto the stack.
     - Stack: [(, (
   - Character: 2
     - Action: Ignore, as it's not a parenthesis.
     - Stack: [(, (
   - Character: +
     - Action: Ignore, as it's not a parenthesis.
     - Stack: [(, (
   - Character: 3
     - Action: Ignore, as it's not a parenthesis.
     - Stack: [(, (
   - Character:)
     - Action: Pop the topmost opening parenthesis from the stack.
     - Stack: [(

- Character: *
  - Action: Ignore, as it's not a parenthesis.
  - Stack: [(
- Character: (
  - Action: Push the opening parenthesis onto the stack.
  - Stack: [(, (
- Character: 4
  - Action: Ignore, as it's not a parenthesis.
  - Stack: [(, (
- Character: /
  - Action: Ignore, as it's not a parenthesis.
  - Stack: [(, (
- Character: 2
  - Action: Ignore, as it's not a parenthesis.
  - Stack: [(, (
- Character:)
  - Action: Pop the topmost opening parenthesis from the stack.
  - Stack: [(
- Character:)
  - Action: Pop the topmost opening parenthesis from the stack.
  - Stack: []
- Character: +
  - Action: Ignore, as it's not a parenthesis.
  - Stack: []
- Character: 2
  - Action: Ignore, as it's not a parenthesis.
  - Stack: []

3. **Check if the stack is empty**

   The stack is empty, indicating that all parentheses are matched correctly.

   Conclusion

   The given arithmetic expression ((2+3) * (4/2)) + 2 has correctly matched parentheses.

5. Evaluate following postfix expressions while showing status of stack after each operation given A=3, B=5, C=1, D=4

(a) A B + C * (b) A B * C / D *

Ans. (a) A B + C *:

Step-by-step Evaluation:

1. Push A (3) to the stack
   Stack: [3]
2. Push B (5) to the stack
   Stack: [3, 5]
3. Apply the "+" operator:
   Pop the top two values (5 and 3), add them: 3 + 5 = 8
   Push the result (8) back onto the stack.
   Stack: [8]
4. Push C (1) to the stack
   Stack: [8, 1]
5. Apply the "*" operator:
   Pop the top two values (1 and 8), multiply them: 8 * 1 = 8
   Push the result (8) back onto the stack.
   Stack: [8]
   Final Result : 8

(b) A B * C / D *:

Step-by-step Evaluation:

1. Push A (3) to the stack
   Stack: [3]
2. Push B (5) to the stack
   Stack: [3, 5]
3. Apply the "*" operator:
   Pop the top two values (5 and 3), multiply them: 3 * 5 = 15
   Push the result (15) back onto the stack.
   Stack: [15]
4. Push C (1) to the stack
   Stack: [15, 1]
5. Apply the "/" operator:
   Pop the top two values (1 and 15), divide them: 15 / 1 = 15
   Push the result (15) back onto the stack.
   Stack: [15]
6. Push D (4) to the stack
   Stack: [15, 4]
7. Apply the "*" operator:
   Pop the top two values (4 and 15), multiply them: 15 * 4 = 60
   Push the result (60) back onto the stack.
   Stack: [60]
   Final Result : 60

6. Convert the following infix notations to postfix notations, showing stack and string contents at each step.

(a) A + B - C * D

(b) A * ((C + D)/E)

Ans. (a) A + B - C * D

Expression	Stack	Postfix
A		A
+	+	A
B	+	A B
-	-	A B +

Expression	Stack	Postfix
C	-	A B + C
*	- *	A B + C
D	- *	A B + C D
		A B + C D * -

(b) A * ((C + D)/E)

Expression	Stack	Postfix
A		A
*	*	A
(	*(	A
(	*((	A
C	*((	A C
+	*((+	A C
D	*((+	A C D
)	*(	A C D +
/	*(/	A C D +
E	*(/	A C D + E
)	*	A C D + E /
		A C D + E / *

7. Write a program to create a Stack for storing only odd numbers out of all the numbers entered by the user. Display the content of the Stack along with the largest odd number in the Stack.

(Hint. Keep popping out the elements from stack and maintain the largest element retrieved so far in a variable. Repeat till Stack is empty)

Ans.
```
# Function to create a Stack for odd numbers
def store_odd_numbers():
    stack = []
    n = int(input("Enter the number of
                                      elements: "))
# Input numbers and push only odd numbers to stack
    for_ in range(n):
        num = int(input("Enter a number: "))
        if num % 2 != 0:
            stack.append(num)
# Display stack content and find the largest odd number
    print("Stack contents (Odd numbers):",
                                          stack)
# Finding the largest odd number
    largest_odd = None
    while stack:
        current = stack.pop()
        if largest_odd is None or current >
                                      largest_odd:
            largest_odd = current
    print("Largest odd number in the
                              Stack:", largest_odd)
# Call the function
store_odd_numbers()
```

EXAM PATTERN QUESTIONS

Objective Type Questions

Multiple Choice Questions

1. Which of the following is/are linear data structure(s)?

(a) Array (b) Stack
(c) Queue (d) All of these

2. ………… of data structure means processing all the data elements of it.

(a) Traversal (b) Searching
(c) Insertion (d) Merging

3. Process of inserting an element in stack is called

(a) Create (b) Push
(c) Evaluation (d) Pop

4. Process of removing an element from stack is called

(a) Create (b) Push
(c) Evaluation (d) Pop

5. In a stack, if a user tries to remove an element from empty stack is called

(a) Underflow (b) Overflow
(c) Empty (d) Garbage collection

6. Pushing an element into stack already having five elements and stack size of 5, then stack becomes

(a) Overflow (b) Uses flow
(c) Crash (d) Underflow

7. The data structure required to check whether an expression contains balanced parentheses is
(a) Queue (b) Array (c) Stack (d) Tree

8. Which data structure is needed to convert infix notation to postfix notation?
(a) Branch (b) Tree (c) Queue (d) Stack

9. What is the result of the following operation?
```
Top (Push (s, x))
```
(a) x (b) Null (c) s (d) None of these

10. Which of the following is not an inherent application of stack ?
(a) Reversing a string
(b) Evaluation of postfix expression
(c) Implementation of recursion
(d) Job scheduling

Fill in the Blanks

11. Integer, real, character data, pointer and reference are ....

12. .... means addition of a new data element in a data structure.

13. Stack is limited form of array based on ....

14. A stack is a/an .... data type.

15. Moving through the elements of the stack is known as ....

16. Pile of books is an example of ......

17. In infix notation, operators are written in .... their operands.

18. Prefix notation is also known as ....

State Whether True or False

19. Data structure is a way of storing and organising information in the computer.

20. Non-linear data structure are array, stack, queue etc.

21. Data structures that are directly operated by machine level instructions are known as non-primitive data structure.

22. Insertion of a data structure means processing all the data elements of it.

23. Stack is a list where insertion and deletion can take place only at one end called Top.

Assertion and Reason Based Questions

Assertion (A) and Reason (R) Type questions. Choose the correct option as:

(a) Both Assertion (A) and Reason (R) are true, and Reason (R) is the correct explanation of Assertion (A)
(b) Both Assertion (A) and Reason (R) are true, but Reason (R) is not the correct explanation of Assertion (A)
(c) Assertion (A) is True, but Reason (R) is False
(d) Assertion (A) is False, but Reason (R) is True

24. Assertion (A) A data structure is a named group of data types.
Reason (R) A data structure has a well defined operations, behaviour and properties.

25. Assertion (A) Simple data structures are built from primitive data types.
Reason (R) Stacks and queues are simple data structures.

26. Assertion (A) Lists are sequences just like strings.
Reason (R) Lists are mutable.

27. Assertion (A) Joining two lists is just like adding two strings.
Reason(R) The concatenation operator + is used to add two strings.

28. Assertion (A) Using append(), many elements can be added at a time.
Reason (R) For adding more than one element, extend() method can be used.

29. Assertion (A) A stack is a linear data structure that stores items in First in first out.
Reason (R) New element is added at one end and an element is removed from that end only.

30. Assertion (A) push (A) removes the element from stack
Reason (R) The time complexity of push () is O(1).

31. Assertion (A) Stacks and queues are linear data structures
Reason (R) Lists, tuples, dictionaries, sets are Python built-in linear data structures.

32. Assertion (A) LIFO is a technique to access data from queues
Reason (R) LIFO stands for Last In First Out

33. Assertion (A) The element in stack is removed from the top.
Reason (R) The process of removal is called POP.

34. Assertion (A) An error occurs when one tries to delete an empty stack.
Reason (R) This situation is called as inspection.

35. Assertion (A) A stack is a LIFO structure. **CBSE 2023**
Reason (R) Any new element pushed into the stack always gets positioned at the index after the last existing element in the stack.

36. Assertion (A) The postfix form of (A + B) * C is AB + C *.
Reason (R) Postfix notation refers to when operator is placed after its operands.

Answers

1. (d) All of these
2. (a) Traversal
3. (b) Push
4. (d) Pop
5. (a) Underflow
6. (a) Overflow
7. (c) Stack
8. (d) Stack
9. (a) x
10. (d) Job scheduling
11. primitive data structures
12. Insertion
13. LIFO (Last In First Out)
14. abstract
15. traversal
16. stack
17. between
18. polish notation
19. True
20. False
21. False
22. False
23. True
24. (a) Both Assertion (A) and Reason (R) are true, and Reason (R) is the correct explanation of Assertion (A)
25. (c) Assertion (A) is True, but Reason (R) is False
26. (b) Both Assertion (A) and Reason (R) are true, but Reason (R) is not the correct explanation of Assertion (A)
27. (a) Both Assertion (A) and Reason (R) are true, and Reason (R) is the correct explanation of Assertion (A)
28. (d) Assertion (A) is False, but Reason (R) is True
29. (d) Assertion (A) is False, but Reason (R) is True
30. (d) Assertion (A) is False, but Reason (R) is True
31. (c) Assertion (A) is True, but Reason (R) is False
32. (d) Assertion (A) is False, but Reason (R) is True
33. (a) Both Assertion (A) and Reason (R) are true, and Reason (R) is the correct explanation of Assertion (A)
34. (c) Assertion (A) is True, but Reason (R) is False
35. (a) Both Assertion (A) and Reason (R) are true, and Reason (R) is the correct explanation of Assertion (A)
36. (a) Both Assertion (A) and Reason (R) are true, and Reason (R) is the correct explanation of Assertion (A)

Subjective Type Questions

Very Short Answer Type Questions

1. What is data structure ?

Ans. Data structure is a way of storing and organising information in the computer, so that it can be retrieved and used most productively.

2. Name any two non-primitive data structures.

Ans. Array, linked list

3. Define any two operations on data structure.

Ans. Two operations on data structure are as follows

(i) **Insertion** It means addition of a new data element in a data structure.

(ii) **Searching** It involves searching for the specific data element in a data structure.

4. What is the minimum number of stacks of size n required to implement a queue of size n?

Ans. Two

5. If the elements A, B, C and D are placed in a stack and are deleted one at a time, in what order will they be removed ?

Ans. D C B A

6. What is the condition of stack underflow?

Ans. Any attempt to delete an element from already empty stack results into stack underflow.

7. Write the applications of stack.

Ans. There are some applications of stack are as follows

- Infix to postfix conversion using stack.
- Evaluation of postfix expression.
- Reverse a string using stack.
- Implement two stacks in an array.

8. Give any two characteristics of stacks.

CBSE SQP 2021-22 Term II

Ans. A stack is an abstract data type that holds an ordered, linear sequence of items. The characteristics of stacks are:

(i) It is a Last In First Out (LIFO) data structure which means the item which is inserted last in the stack will be the first one to delete from the stack.

(ii) The insertion and deletion happens at one end i.e. from the top of the stack.

9. What is the value of the postfix expression?

6 3 2 4 + − *

Ans. Postfix expression is : (6 * (3 − (2 + 4)))
= (6 * (3 − 6))
= (6 * (−3))
= − 18

Short Answer Type I Questions

10. Consider the following stack of characters, where STACK is allocated N = 8 memory cells.

STACK : A, C, D, F, K, ..., ..., ...

Describe the STACK at the end of the followingoperations. Here, Pop and Push are algorithmsfor deleting and adding an element to the stack.

(i) Pop (STACK, ITEM)
(ii) Pop (STACK, ITEM)
(iii) Push (STACK, L)
(iv) Push (STACK, P)
(v) Pop (STACK, ITEM)
(vi) Push (STACK, R)
(vii) Push (STACK, S)
(viii) Pop (STACK, ITEM)

Ans. The stack contents will be as follows after the operationsof stack

(i) STACK : A, C, D, F
(ii) STACK : A, C, D
(K is deleted) (F is deleted)
(iii) STACK : A, C, D, L
(iv) STACK: A, C, D, L, P
(L is inserted) (P is inserted)
(v) STACK : A, C, D, L
(vi) STACK : A, C, D, L, R
(P is deleted) (R is inserted)
(vii) STACK : A, C, D, L, R, S
(S is inserted)
(viii) STACK : A, C, D, L, R
(S is deleted)

11. Convert the following Infix expression to its equivalent Postfix expression, showing the Stack contents for each step of conversion.

A + B * C ^ D - E

Ans. ((A + (B * (C ^ D))) - E)

Infix to Postfix table

Sr No	Expression	Stack	Postfix
0	(	(	
1	(	((	
2	A	((	A
3	+	((+	A
4	(	((+(	A
5	B	((+(	AB
6	*	((+(*	AB
7	(	((+(*(	AB
8	C	((+(*(	ABC
9	^	((+(*(^	ABC
10	D	((+(*(^	ABCD
11	)	((+(*	ABCD^
12	)	((+	ABCD^*
13	)	(	ABCD^*+
14	-	(-	ABCD^*+
15	E	(-	ABCD^*+E
16	)		ABCD^*+E-
17			ABCD^*+E-

12. Evaluate the following Postfix expression.

20, 10, -, 15, 3, /, +, 5, *

Ans.

Symbol	Operation	Stack	Result
20	Push	20	
	Push	20,10	
	Pop (10) Pop (20) Push (20-10) =10	10	
15	Push	10,15	
3	Push	10,15,3	
/	Pop (3) Pop (15) Push (15/3) = 5	10,5	
+	Pop (5) Pop (10) Push (10+5) =15	15	
5	Push	15,5	
	Pop (5) Pop (15) Push (15*5) = 75	75	75

Result = 75

13. (A) You have a stack named BooksStack that contains records of books. Each book record is represented as a list containing book_title, author_name, and publication_year. Competency Based Que.

Write the following user-defined functions in Python to perform the specified operations on the stackBooksStack: CBSE SQP 2024-25

(I) push_book(BooksStack, new_book): This function takes the stack BooksStack and a new book recordnew_book as arguments and pushes the new book record onto the stack.

(II) **pop_book(BooksStack)** This function pops the topmost book record fromthe stack and returns it.

If the stack is already empty, the function should display "Underflow".

(III) **peep(BookStack)** This function displays the topmost element of the stackwithout deleting it. If the stack is empty, the function should display 'None'.

Or

(B) Write a Python program to input an integer and display all its prime factors in descending order, using a stack.

For example, if the input number is 2100, the output should be: 7 5 5 3 2 2 (because prime factorization of 2100 is 7×5×5×3×2×2)

Hint Smallest factor, other than 1, of any integer is guaranteed to be prime.

Ans. (A)

(I)
```
def push_book(BooksStack, new_book):
        BooksStack.append(new_book)
```

Here the stack is implemented using a stack.

Hence the append() function is used to add the new element at the top of the stack.

(II)
```
def pop_book(BooksStack):
  if not BooksStack:
  print("Underflow")
else:
  return(BookStack.pop())
```

Here the stack is implemented using a stack .

The pop() function removes and displays the last element of a list. Hence the pop() function is used here to take out the topmost element of the stack.

(III)
```
def peep(BooksStack):
if not BooksStack:
  print("None")
else:
  print(BookStack[-1])
```

Since the topmost element has to be displayed without removing , the pop() function cannot be used here. Instead the BookStack[-1] statement prints the last element of the list that has index -1.

Or

(B)
```
n=int(input("Enter an integer: "))
s=[] #stack
f=2
while n>1:
  if n%f==0:
      s.append(f)
      n//=f
  else: f+=1
while s:
  print(s.pop(),end=' ')
```

To find the prime factorization the number is repeatedly divided to find the clear division, starting from f=2. When no longer divisible by 2 it is divided by the next prime factor and so on. All such factors are pushed into the stack. Finally the stack contents are popped.

14. Consider a list named Nums which contains random integers. CBSE 2024

Write the following user defined functions in Python and perform the specified operations on a stack named BigNums.

(i) PushBig ( ) It checks every number from the list Nums and pushes all such numbers which have 5 or more digits into the stack, BigNums.

(ii) PopBig ( ) It pops the numbers from the stack, BigNums and displays them. The function should also display "Stack Empty" when there are no more numbers left in the stack.

For example: If the list Nums contains the following data :

Nums = [213, 10025, 167, 254923, 14, 1297653, 31498, 386, 92765]

Then on execution of PushBig ( ), the stack BigNums should store :

[10025, 254923, 1297653, 31498, 92765]

And on execution of PopBig ( ), the following output should be displayed :

92765
31498
1297653
254923
10025
Stack Empty

Ans. # Define the stack and input list

```
Nums = [1234, 12345, 67890, 12, 567890, 123]
BigNums = []
```

(i)
```
def PushBig():
    for N in Nums:
        if N >= 10000:
# Check if the number is 10000 or greater
            BigNums.append(N)
```

(ii)
```
def PopBig():
    while BigNums:
        print(BigNums.pop())
    print("Stack Empty")
# Test the functions
    PushBig()
    PopBig()
```

15. **A list, NList contains following record as list elements:** **CBSE SQP 2023-24**

[City, Country, distance from Delhi]

Each of these records are nested together to form a nested list. Write the following user defined functions in Python to perform the specified operations on the stack named travel.

(i) Push_element(NList) It takes the nested list as an argument and pushes a list object containing name of the city and country, which are not in India and distance is less than 3500 km from Delhi.

(ii) Pop_element() It pops the objects from the stack and displays them. Also, the function should display "Stack Empty" when there are no elements in the stack.

For example: If the nested list contains the following data

```
NList=[["New York", "U.S.A.", 11734],
["Naypyidaw", "Myanmar", 3219],
["Dubai", "UAE", 2194],
["London", "England", 6693],
["Gangtok", "India", 1580],
["Columbo", "Sri Lanka", 3405]]
```

The stack should contain

```
['Naypyidaw', 'Myanmar'],
['Dubai', 'UAE'],
['Columbo', 'Sri Lanka']
```

The output should be

['Columbo', 'Sri Lanka']
['Dubai', 'UAE']
['Naypyidaw', 'Myanmar']
Stack Empty

Ans.

```
travel = []
(i) def Push_element(NList):
        for i in NList:
            if i[1]!="India" and i[2]<3500:
                travel.append([i[0],i[1]])
(ii) def Pop_element():
        while len(travel):
            print(travel.pop())
        else:
            print("Stack Empty")
```

16. **(a) A list contains following record of customer:**

[Customer_name, Room Type]

Write the following user defined functions to perform given operations on the stack named 'Hotel' **CBSE 2023**

(i) Push_Cust () To Push customers' names of those customers who are staying in 'Delux' Room Type.

(ii) Pop_Cust () To Pop the names of customers from the stack and display them. Also, display "Underflow" when there are no customers in the stack.

For example:

If the lists with customer details are as follows :

```
[" Siddarth","Delux" ]
["Rahul","Standard"]
["Jerry","Delux"]
```

The stack should contain

Jerry
Siddharth

The output should be:

Jerry
Siddharth
Underflow

Or

(b) Write a function in Python, Push (Vehicle) where, Vehicle is a dictionary containing details of vehicles - {Car_Name : Maker}.

The function should push the name of car manufactured by 'TATA' (including all the possible cases like Tata, TaTa, etc.) to the stack.

For example:

If the dictionary contains the following data

```
Vehicle={"Santro" : "Hyundai", "Nexon" :
 "TATA", "Safari" : "TaTa"}
```

The stack should contain

Safari
Nexon

Ans. (a)

```
L = [['Siddharth', 'Delux'], ['Rahul',
                    'Standard'], ['Jerry', 'Delux']]
Hotel = []
(i) def Push_Cust():
        for cust in L:
            if cust[1] =='Delux':
                Hotel.append(cust [0])
(ii) def Pop_Cust():
        while len(Hotel)>0:
            print(Hotel.pop())
            print("Underflow")
    Push_Cust()
    Pop_Cust()
```

Or

(b)

```
Vehicle={"Santro":"Hyundai","Nexon":"TATA",
                            "Safari":"TaTa"}
stack = []
def Push (V):
```

```
  for i in V:
     if V[i].upper()== "TATA":
        stack.append(i)
  print(stack)
Push(Vehicle)
```

17. **A list contains following record of a customer:**
[Customer_name, Phone_number, City]
Write the following user defined functions to perform given operations on the stack named 'status': CBSE SQP 2022-23

(i) **Push_element() - To Push an object containing name and Phone number of customers who live in Goa to the stack**

(ii) **Pop_element() - To Pop the objects from the stack and display them. Also, display 'Stack Empty' when there are no elements in the stack.**

For example:
If the lists of customer details are:

```
["Gurdas", "99999999999", "Goa"]
["Julee", "8888888888", "Mumbai"]
["Murugan", "77777777777", "Cochin"]
["Ashmit", "1010101010", "Goa"]
```

The stack should contain
["Ashmit", "1010101010"]
["Gurdas", "9999999999"]
The output should be:
["Ashmit", "1010101010"]
["Gurdas", "9999999999"]
Stack Empty

Or

Write a function in Python, Push(SItem) where , SItem is a dictionary containing the details of stationary items- {Sname:price}.
The function should push the names of those items in the stack who have price greater than 75. Also display the count of elements pushed into the stack.
For example:
If the dictionary contains the following data:

```
Ditem={"Pen":106,"Pencil":59,"Notebook":
                                80,"Eraser":25}
```

The stack should contain
Notebook
Pen
The output should be:
The count of elements in the stack is 2

Ans. (i)

```
def Push_element(custLst):
    for rec in custLst:
        if rec[2]=="Goa":
            status.append[rec[0],
                          rec[1]]
```

(ii)

```
def Pop_element(custLst):
    for a in
range(-1,-1*len(custLst)-1,-1):
        print(custLst[a])
    print("Stack Empty")
```

Or

```
stackItem=[]
def Push(SItem):
    count=0
    for k in SItem:
        if (SItem[k]>=75):
            stackItem.append(k)
            count=count+1
    print("The count of elements in
the stack is : ",count)
```

18. **Julie has created a dictionary containing names and marks as key value pairs of 6 students. Write a program, with separate user defined functions to perform the following operations** CBSE SQP 2022 Term II

- **Push the keys (name of the student) of the dictionary into a stack, where the corresponding value (marks) is greater than 75.** Competency Based Que.
- **Pop and display the content of the stack.**

For example
If the sample content of the dictionary is as follows

```
R={"OM":76, "JAI":45, "BOB":89, "ALI":65,
                     "ANU":90, "TOM":82}
```

The output from the program should be
TOM ANU BOB OM

Or **Alam has a list containing 10 integers. You need to help him create a program with separate user defined functions to perform the given operations based on this list.**

- **Traverse the content of the list and push the even numbers into a stack.**
- **Pop and display the content of the stack.**

For example,
If the sample content of the list is as follows

```
N=[12, 13, 34, 56, 21, 79, 98, 22, 35, 38]
```

Sample Output of the code should be:

```
38 22 98 56 34 12
```

Ans.

```
R={"OM":76, "JAI":45, "BOB":89, "ALI":65,
"ANU":90, "TOM":82}
def PUSH(S,N):
  S.append(N)
def POP(S):
  if S!=[]:
```

```
        return S.pop()
    else:
        return None
ST=[ ]
for k in R:
    if R[k]>=75:
        PUSH(ST,k)
while True:
    if ST!=[]:
        print(POP(ST),end=" ")
    else:
        break
```

Or

```
N=[12, 13, 34, 56, 21, 79, 98, 22, 35, 38]
def PUSH(S,N):
    S.append(N)
def POP(S):
    if S!=[]:
        return S.pop()
    else:
        return None
ST=[ ]
for k in N:
    if k%2==0:
        PUSH(ST,k)
while True:
    if ST!=[]:
        print(POP(ST),end=" ")
    else:
        break
```

19. Sukanya has created a dictionary containing names and marks as key value pairs of 6 students. Write a program, with separate user defined functions to perform the following operations :

Competency Based Que.

(A) (i) Push the keys (name of the student) of the dictionary into a stack, where the corresponding value (marks) is greater than 75.

(ii) Pop and display the content of the stack.

For example If the sample content of the dictionary is as follows

```
R={"OM":76, "JAI":45, "BOB":89,
      "ALI":65, "ANU":90, "TOM":82}
```

The output from the program should be

TOM ANU BOB OM

Or

(B) Write a program to accept as many city names from the user and push them into a stack , only if the city names are palindromes.

(A palindrome is a word which is same as its reverse).

Ans. (A) (i)

```
R={"OM":76, "JAI":45, "BOB":89,
            "ALI":65, "ANU":90, "TOM":82}
def PUSH(S,N):
  S.append(N)
```

(ii)
```
def POP(S):
  if S!=[]:
    return S.pop()
  else:
    return None
ST=[ ]
for k in R:
    if R[k]>=75:
      PUSH(ST,k)
while True:
  if ST!=[]:
    print(POP(ST),end=" ")
  else:
    break
```

Or

(B)
```
palinstack=[]
def pushcity(n) :
    palinstack.append(n)
ans='y'
while ans=='y':
      n=input("Enter a city :")
     if n== n[::-1]:
pushcity(n)
ans=input("Add more(y/n)")
```

20. The stack Admissionstack[] is a list implement stack comprising of student records of the following structure : [Rno , Name , Class , Grade]

Define functions for the following :

(a) enterstack(slst) : Function to push a student record to the stack only if the student has grade "A".

(b) getstack() : Function to pop and show the topmost student of the stack.

(c) peepstack() : Function t display all the student records without removing any record.

Or

(i) Define the operations possible on a stack.

(ii) Define a function push2_5() to push numbers into a stack , only if the numbers end with 2 or 5

Ans. (a)
```
def enterstack(slst):
        if slst[3]=="A":
            Admissionstack.append(slst)
```

(b)
```
def getstack():
    if Admissionstack==[] :
        print("No students")
    else:
        Admissionstack.pop()
```
(c)
```
def peepstack():
    if Admissionstack==[] :
        print("No students")
    else:
        p= len(Admissionstack)-1
        while p>=0:
            print(Admissionstack[p])
            p-=1
```

Or

(i) A stack allows the following operations :

Push() This function pushes an element into the stack keeping the LIFO principle, which means the element is pushed to the top of the stack.

Pop() This function takes out the topmost element from the stack and displays it .

Traversal () This function displays each of the stack contents from top index to 0 with the LIFO principle . It does not remove the elements.

(ii)
```
stack=[]
def push2_5(n) :
    if n%10==2 or n%10==5:
        stack.append(n)
```

21. Write a program to print a string in reverse order using the following functions

(a) pushstack(stack , character) : Function to push a character into the stack

(b) popstack(stack) : Function pop all the elements from the stack

(c) isempty( ) – Function to check whether the stack is empty or not.

Or

(i) Define a stack.

(ii) Give few applications of stack.

(iii) Give any two characteristics of stacks.

Ans. (a)
```
def pushstack(stack, ch):
    stack.append(ch)
        top=len(stack)-1
        return
```
(b)
```
def popstack(stack):
        if isempty(stack):
            return
        else:
            top=len(stack)-1
            for a in range(top, -1, -1):
                print (stack[a])
        return
```
(c)
```
def isempty(stack):
        if stack==[]:
            return True
        else:
    return False
#----------main---------
stk=[]
top=None
str=input("Enter a string")
for a in str:
pushstack(stk, a)
print ("------Reverse------")
popstack(stk)
```

Or

(i) A stack is a data structure that allows addition and removal of elements in a particular order. Every time an element is added, it goes on the top of the stack and the only element that can be removed is the element that was at the top of the stack.

(ii) Applications of stack

1. Expression evaluation
2. Backtracking (game playing, finding paths, exhaustive searching).
3. Memory management, run-time environment for nested language features.

(iii) Characteristics of Stacks:

- It is a LIFO data structure.
- The insertion and deletion happens at one end i.e. from the top of the stack.

22. (a) **A stack, named ClrStack, contains records of some colors. Each record is represented as a tuple containing four elements ColorName, RED, GREEN, BLUE. ColorName is a string and RED, GREEN, BLUE are integers. For example, a record in the stack may be ('Yellow', 237, 250, 68)**

Write the following user-defined functions in Python to perform the specified operations on ClrStack:

(i) **push_Clr (ClrStack, new_Clr)** This function takes the stack ClrStack and a new record new_Clr as arguments and pushes this new record onto the stack.

(ii) **pop_Clr (ClrStack)** This function pops the topmost record from the stack and returns it. If the stack is already empty, the function should display the message "Underflow".

(iii) **isEmpty (ClrStack)** This function checks whether the stack is empty. If the stack is empty, the function should return True, otherwise the function should return False.

Or

(b) **Write the following user-defined functions in Python:**

(i) **push_trail (N,myStack)** Here N and mystack are lists and myStack represents a stack. The function should push the last 5 clements from the list N onto the stack myStack. For example, if the list N is [1,2,3,4,5,6,7], then the function push_trail() should push the elements 3,4,5,6,7 onto the stack. Therefore the value of stack will be [3,4,5,6,7]. Assume that N contains at least 5 elements.

(ii) **pop_one (myStack)** The function should pop an element from the stack myStack, and return this element. If the stack is empty, then the function should display the message 'Stack Underflow', and return None.

(iii) **display_all (myStack)** The function should display all the elements of the stack myStack, without deleting them. If the stack is empty, the function should display the message 'Empty Stack'.

Ans. (a) (i)
```
def push_Clr(ClrStack, new_Clr):
    ClrStack.append(new_Clr)
```
(ii)
```
def pop_Clr(ClrStack):
    if isEmpty(ClrStack):
        print("Underflow")
        return None
    return ClrStack.pop()
```
(iii)
```
def isEmpty(ClrStack):
    return len(ClrStack) == 0
```
Or

(b) (i)
```
def push_trail(N, myStack):
    p = [-5:]  # This slice will be an
                                empty list
    myStack.extend(p)
```
(ii)
```
def pop_one(myStack):
    if len(myStack) == 0:
        print("Stack underflow")
        return None
    else:
        item = myStack.pop()
        return item
```
(iii)
```
def display_all(myStack):
    if len(myStack) == 0:
        print("Stack is Empty")
    else:
        top = len(myStack) - 1
        print("top ->", top)
        for p in range(top - 1, -1, -1):
            print(myStack[p])
```

Short Answer Type II Questions

23. Alam has a list containing 10 integers. You need to help him create a program with separate user defined functions to perform the given operations based on this list.

Traverse the content of the list and push the even numbers into a stack.

Pop and display the content of the stack.

For example, If the sample content of the list is as follows

N=[12, 13, 34, 56, 21, 79, 98, 22, 35, 38]

Sample Output of the code should be:

38 22 98 56 34 12

N=[12, 13, 34, 56, 21, 79, 98, 22, 35, 38]

Ans.
```
def PUSH(S,N):
    S.append(N)
def POP(S):
    if S!=[]:
        return S.pop()
    else:
        return None
ST=[ ]
for k in N:
    if k%2==0:
        PUSH(ST,k)
while True:
    if ST!=[]:
        print(POP(ST),end=" ")
    else:
        break
```

24. Write a function in Python PUSH(Arr), where Arr is a list of numbers. From this list push all numbers divisible by 5 into a stack implemented by using a list. Display the stack if it has at least one element, otherwise display appropriate error message.

Ans. Python function PUSH(Arr) that pushes numbers divisible by 5 into a stack (list) and displays the stack or an error message:
```
def PUSH(Arr):
    stack = []
# Initialize an empty stack
    for num in Arr:
        if num % 5 == 0:
# Check if the number is divisible by 5
            stack.append(num)
# Push the number into the stack
    if stack:
# If the stack contains at least one element
        print("Stack:", stack)
```

```
    else:
        print("Error: No numbers divisible
                                    by 5.")
```

Example:

PUSH([1, 5, 10, 7, 15])

Output:

Stack: [5, 10, 15]

If there are no numbers divisible by 5 in the list:

PUSH([1, 2, 3, 7])

Output:

Error: No numbers divisible by 5.

Long Answer Type Questions

25. Write Add new(Book) and Remove(Book) methods in Python to Add a new Book and Remove a Book from a List of Books, considering them to act as PUSH and POP operations of the data structure stack.

Ans.
```
books=[]
defAddnew (books,name):
   books.append (name)
   print("bookl:",name,"inserted")
def remove(books):
   if books==[]:
     print("stack is empty")
   else:
     print("book:",books.pop (), "deleted ")
```

26. Write a function to push any student's information to stack.

Ans.
```
def push(stack):
   s=[]
   print ("STACK BEFORE PUSH")
   display(stack)
   s.append(input ("Enter student rollno?"))
   s.append(input ("Enter student name"))
   s.append (input ("Enter student grade"))
   stack.append(s)
def display (stack):
   l=len (stack)
   print ("STACK CONTENTS")
   for i in range (L-1,-1,-1):
   print stack [i]
stack=[]
print "Creating stack"
n = input ("Enter the number of students")
for i in range(n):
  push (stack)
display (stack)
```

27. Write a program to implement a stack for these book details (bookno, bookname). That is, now each item node of the stack contains two types of information –a bookno and its name. Just implement push and display operations.

Ans.
```
def isempty(stk):
   if stk==[]
     returnTrue
   else:
     return False
def pushbook (stk, item):
   stk.append(item)
   top=len (stk)-1
def displaybook(stk):
   if isempty(stk):
     print("Stack Empty")
   else:
     top=len (stk)-1
     print ("book no… book name")
     for a in range (top,-1,-1) :
        print (stk[a])
stk=[]
top=None
while True:
   print ("book")
   print("1. add a book")
   print ("2. display list")
   print ("3. exit")
   ch=int (input("enter your choice 1-3:"))
 if ch==1:
   bno=input("enter book no:")
   bname=input ("enter book name")
   item=[bnp, bname]
   pushbook (stk, item)
   input()
 elif ch==2:
   displaybook(stk)
   input()
 elif ch=3:
   break
 else:
   print("invalid choice!")
   input()
```

28. Write the following user-defined functions in Python to perform the specified operations on the stack NumStack:

(I) push_num(NumStack, new_num): This function takes the stack NumStackand a new number as arguments and pushes the new number onto the stackonly if it is even

(II) pop_num(NumStack): This function pops the topmost number from the stack and returns it. If

the stack is already empty, the function should display "Underflow".

(III) peep(NumStack): This function displays the topmost element of the stack without deleting it. If the stack is empty, the function should display 'None'.

Ans. (I)
```
def push_num(NumStack, new_num)
  if new_num%2==0:
    NumStack.append(new_num)
```
(II)
```
def pop_num(NumStack):
  if not NumStack:
    print("Underflow")
  else:
    return NumStack.pop()
```
(III)
```
def peep(NumStack):
  if not NumStack:
    print("None")
  else:
    print(NumStack[-1])
```

Case Study Based Questions

Case Study 1

Read the following and answer the question that follow.

Lists are the container which store the heterogeneous elements of any type as integer, character, floating point elements of a list are represented by enclosing them in square brackets [ ].

Consider following list for python language

```
L=[13, 3.45, "Tree", 'Amar', [10, 8.91,
                          "Apple"], 456]
```

(i) The output of L[-2] will be
   (a) 10 (b) 8.91
   (c) [10, 8.91, 'Apple'] (d) 3.45

(ii) To get value 8.91 from the list, the python statement will be
   (a) L[4][1] (b) L[-2][-2]
   (c) Both a) and b) (d) None of these

(iii) The length of the list is
   (a) 6 (b) 8
   (c) 18 (d) None of these

(iv) print(len(L[2])==len(L[3])) will print
   (a) False (b) True
   (c) Error (d) None of these

(v) The output of print (L[1 : 5 : 2]) will be
   (a) [3.45, 'Amar']
   (b) [3.45, 'Amar', 456]
   (c) [3.45, 'Tree', 'Amar', 10, 8.91]
   (d) Error

Ans. (i) (c) As it is list within a list.

(ii) (c) Both are correct as L[4][1] and L[-2] [-2] access the same value from the list as 8.91.

(iii) (a) As the list inside another list is taken as one element, thus there are 6 total items in the list L.

(iv) (b) As both len(L[2] and len(L[3]) represents same length so the output on the screen will be true.

(v) (a) The output of the print command will be [3.45, 'Amar'] as the indexing corresponds to this items in the list.

Case Study 2

Millions of computer science students have taken a course on algorithms and data structures, typically the second course after the initial one introducing programming. One of the basic data structures in such a course is the stack. The stack has a special place in the emergence of computing as a science, as argued by Michael Mahoney, the pioneer of the history of the theory of computing. The stack can be used in many computer applications, few are given below:

- In recursive function
- When function is called.
- Expression conversion such as – Infix to Postfix, Infix to Prefix, Postfix to Infix, Prefix to Infix.

In stack, insertion operation is known as Push whereas deletion operation is known as Pop.

Code 1

```
def push (Country, N):
  Country.______(len (Country),N))
                                    # Statement 1
#Function Calling
Country=[]
C=['Indian', 'USA', 'UK', 'Canada', 'Sri
Lanka']
for i in range (0, len(C), _____):
                                    # Statement 2
  push (Country, C[i])
print (Country)
```

Output

['Indian', 'UK', 'Sri Lanka']

Code 2

```
def pop (Country):
  if ______ :                      # Statement 3
     return "Under flow"
  else:
     return Country. ______() # Statement 4
# Function Calling
for i in range (len (Country) + 1):
  print (______)                   # Statement 5
```

Output

Sri Lanka

UK

Indian

Under flow

Fill the above statements based on given questions. **[CBSE Question Bank]**

(i) Identify the suitable code for the blank of Statement 1.

(a) .append()
(b) .insert()
(c) .extend()
(d) .append(len(Country),N)

(ii) Fill the Statement 2, to insert the alternate element from Country list.

(a) 3 (b) 0
(c) – 1 (d) 2

(iii) Fill the Statement 3, to check the stack is empty.

(a) Country=[] (b) Country.isEmpty()
(c) len(Country)==0 (d) None of these

(iv) Fill the Statement 4, to delete an element from the stack.

(a) pop(1) (b) pop()
(c) del country[1] (d) Country.delete(1)

(v) Fill the Statement 5, to call the pop function.

(a) pop(C)
(b) pop(Country)
(c) call pop(Country)
(d) def pop(Country)

Ans. (i) (*b*) The Statement 1 used under the push() operation. The Push operation of stack is used to insert element in the stack.

(ii) (*d*) The alternate element from the country list C will be 2 because the list starts with 0.

(iii) (*c*) The stack will be considered as empty, if all the elements are popped up from stack and its length has become 0.

(iv) (*b*) Statement 4 is a part of pop function. If condition is used to check whether stack is empty or not. If not then code will execute else part and pop element from stack.

(v) (*b*) The Statement 5 will call pop function, which is already declared as Code 2 and taking a parameter country list

Case Study 3

Read the following passage and answer the question that follow.

Lists are the container which store the heterogeneous elements of any type a integer character, floating point that store in square brackets [ ].

Consider following list for python language.

```
L=["Suresh", 3.45, "Tree", 'Amar', [10,
        8.91, "Apple"], 456]
```

(i) The output of L[4][–2] will be ....

(ii) The output of len(L[4]) is ....

(iii) What will the statement L[2] = 234 do?

(iv) print(len(L[0]+L[–1]) will print?

(v) The output of print(L[1:5:3]) will be ....

Ans. (i) Since L[4][-2] corresponds to the sub-list item 8.91 so the output will be 8.91.

(ii) The length of the sublist is 3 so the output of the length of sublist is 3.

(iii) The item in the list that corresponds to the index 2 will be replaced by 234, i.e. The list item tree will be replaced by 234.

(iv) It will display an error message as the len() method takes only list as its argument and not any operator in it.

(v) [3.45, [10, 8.91, 'Apple']]

SELF ASSESSMENT TEST

Multiple Choice Questions

1 Which of the following is/are example(s) of non-primitive data structure?

(a) Array (b) Linked list
(c) Stack (d) All of the above

2 Which data structure is used in breadth first search of a graph to hold nodes?

(a) Array (b) Tree (c) Stack (d) Queue

3 What is the result of the following operation?

```
Top (Push (st, a))
```

(a) Null (b) st
(c) a (d) None of these

4 In postfix notation, operators are written .... their operand.

(a) between (b) after (c) before (d) anywhere

Fill in the Blanks

5 .... **are used in almost every program or software.**

6 .... **are multilevel data structures. e.g. tree, graph, etc.**

7 The link between data can also be called a ....

8 A/An .... is an expression having variables, constants and operators.

State Whether True or False

9. The primary operations associated with a stack data structure are "push" to add an element and "pop" to remove an element.

10. A stack follows the First-In, First-Out (FIFO) principle.

Assertion and Reason Based Questions

Assertion (A) and Reason (R) Type questions. Choose the correct option as

(a) Both Assertion (A) and Reason (R) are true, and Reason (R) is the correct explanation of Assertion (A)
(b) Both Assertion (A) and Reason (R) are true, but Reason (R) is not the correct explanation of Assertion (A)
(c) Assertion (A) is True, but Reason (R) is False
(d) Assertion (A) is False, but Reason (R) is True

11. Assertion (A) A data structure is a group of data that have different data types which can be accessed as a unit.

Reason (R) Data structure has well defined operations, properties and behaviours.

12. Assertion (A) Array refers to the name of list of elements in a specific order, typically all elements are of the same type.

Reason (R) Stack is limited form of array based on FIFO (First In First Out).

Very Short Answer Type Questions

13 What are the conditions that must be checked before doing the Push and Pop operations in the stack?

14 If the operators are placed before/in between/after the operands, what are these type of expressions called?

15 What is the difference between prefix notation and postfix notation?

Short Answer Type Questions

16 Evaluate the following postfix expression with the help of a stack and show the contents of the stack after each operation.

```
100, 8, 3, *, 50, 2, –, +,–
```

17 Convert the following infix expression into postfix form

```
a + b * c + (d * e + f)
```

18 Evaluate the following postfix notation. Show the status of stack after every step of evaluation (i.e. after each operator)

```
True, False, NOT, AND, True, False, AND, OR
```

Long Answer Type Question

19 A linear stack called status contains the following information:

- **Phone number of Teacher**
- **Name of Teacher**

Write the following methods to perform given operations on the stack status:

(i) **Push_element() To Push an object containing Phone number of Teacher and Name of Teacher into the stack.**

(ii) **Pop_element() To Pop an object from the stack and to release the memory.**

Case Based Type Question

20 **Below is a push operation of stack containing names of items. Notice that name should only accept characters, spaces and periods (.) except digits. Answer the below questions to execute program successfully.**

```
def input1():
  name = re.compile (r" ______")
  while:
     n = input ("Enter name:")
     while name. _____(n) :
        print ("Invalid name")
        print ("Enter name correctly")
        n = ______
     Sname. ______(n)
     c = input ("Enter more name <y/n>").
                                    upper ()
     if (______) :
        break
```

(i) **Fill the blank in Line 3.**

(ii) **Which function is used with name in Line 5?**

(iii) **Which value or function will be assign to variable n?**

(iv) **Fill the blank in Line 9.**

(v) **Which condition will be used in if condition?**

Answers

1. (d) 2. (d) 3. (c) 4. (b) 5. Pointer

6. Non-linear data structures 7. Data Structure

8. Expression 9. True 10. False

11. (d) 12. (c)

20. (i) ^[A-Za-z.]+$ (ii) match

(iii) input ("Enter name") (iv) append(n)

(v) c=='n':

06

CHAPTER

Computer networks have revolutionized use of computers. They are used in our everyday life from Automated Teller Machine (ATM) to airline reservation system to electronic mail services.

▼ **YOUR STUDY GOALS**

6.1 Evolution of Networking
6.2 Type of Networks
6.3 Network Devices
6.4 Network Topology
6.5 WWW or World Wide Web
6.6 XML
6.7 Domain Names System
6.8 Web Server
6.9 Web Hosting
6.10 Web Browser
6.11 Website
6.12 Web Page

▼ **YOUR PRACTICE GOAL**

- Objective Type Questions (60 Qs ; MCQs, True or False, Fill in the Blanks, Assertion and Reason)
- Subjective Type Questions (63 Qs ; VSA, SA, LA)
- Case Based Questions (Objective Case Studies-3)

Computer Network

A **computer network** is a collection of computers and other hardware interconnected by communication channels that allows sharing of resources and information.

A computer networking is the practice for exchanging information between two or more computer devices together for the purpose of data sharing. These devices can include computers, servers, printers, and other hardware. Networks allow for the efficient exchange of data, enabling various applications such as email, file sharing, and internet browsing.

Advantages of Network

Computer networks offer many advantages, including:

(i) **File Sharing** Networking of computer helps the user to share data files.

(ii) **Hardware Sharing** Users can share devices such as printers, scanners, CD-ROM drives, hard drives, etc. in a computer network.

(iii) **Application Sharing** Applications can be shared over the network and this allows implementation of client/server applications.

(iv) **User Communication** This allows users to communicate using E-mail, newsgroups, video conferencing within the network.

(v) **Access to Remote Database** This allows users to access remote database, e.g. airline reservation database may be accessed for ticket booking.

Disadvantages of Network

Some of the main disadvantages of comptuer network are discussed below:

(i) If network are badly managed, services can become unusable and productivity fails.

(ii) If software and files held centrally, it may be impossible to carry out any work if the central server fails.

(iii) File security is more important especially if connected to WAN e.g., protection from viruses.

(iv) To handle network of organisation you may need specialist staff to run the network.

6.1 Evolution of Networking

Evolution of networking is described below:

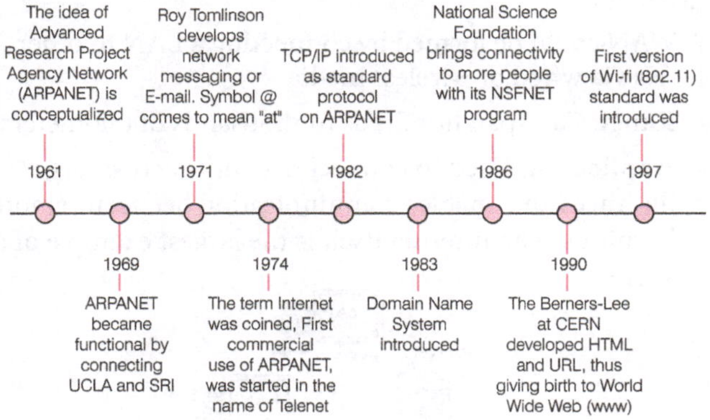

ARPANET (Advanced Research Agency Network)

- ARPANET was the network that became the basis for the Internet.
- It was the first network that came into existence in 1969, which was designed and named by the Advanced Research Projects Agency (ARPA) and US Department of Defence (DoD).
- It was where a bunch of PCs were associated at various colleges and US DoD for sharing of information and messages and associating with individuals to share their perspectives.

NSFNET (National Science Federation Network)

- In mid 80's another federal agency, NSFNET (National Science Federation Network) created a new network which was more capable than ARPANET and became the first backbone infrastructure for the commercial public Internet.
- Its main aim was to use network only for academic research and not for any kind of private business activity. Later, many privately owned/ businesses with their very own private systems joined with ARPANET and NSFNET to make more capable and wide network, the Internet.

Internet

- The Internet is a worldwide network of computer networks that developed from the first network ARPANET.
- The internet is made up of many small networks each run by different companies and interconnected at the peering point (Point where two networks connect or exchange data). It is an interconnection of large and small networks around the globe.
- The Internet allows users to communicate with another user which is connected to another network.
- The internet is a super network it allows all the computers to exchange information with each other. Internet uses a common set of rules to communicate which are called **Protocols** and the internet uses a set of protocols called **TCP/IP** (Transmission Control Protocol / Internet Protocol).

6.2 Type of Networks

Based on the geographical area covered and data transfer rate, computer networks are broadly categorised as:

1. PAN (Personal Area Network)

A Personal Area Network (PAN) is a small network typically used for connecting devices within a very limited range, such as within a room or an individual's workspace.

- **Range** Usually up to 10 meters (about 30 feet).
- **Application** Commonly used to connect personal devices like smartphones, tablets, laptops, and printers. Bluetooth and infrared connections are typical examples of PAN technologies.

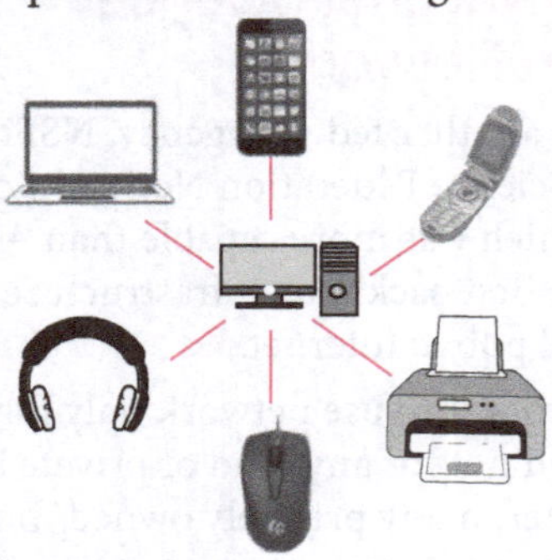

Example Connecting your smartphone to a wireless headset via Bluetooth.

2. LAN (Local Area Network)

A Local Area Network (LAN) is a network that connects computers and devices within a specific area, such as a home, office, or school.

- **Range** Typically spans from a few meters to hundred of meters.
- **Application** Used to share resources like files, printers, and internet access within a building or campus. LANs can be wired (using Ethernet cables) or wireless (using Wi-Fi).

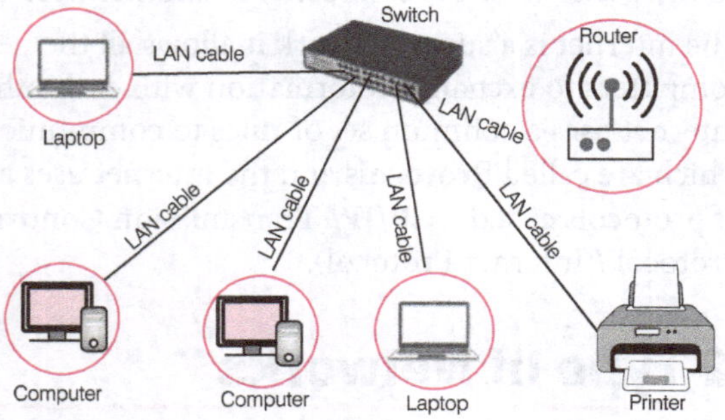

Example The network in your school that connects all computers and printers in the computer lab.

3. MAN (Metropolitan Area Network)

A Metropolitan Area Network (MAN) covers a larger geographic area than a LAN but is smaller than a WAN. It connects computers within a metropolitan area, such as a large city, multiple cities or a large area with multiple buildings.

- **Range** Generally spans from a few kilometers to several tens of kilometers.
- **Application** Used to connect multiple LANs within a city or large campus. It supports high-speed data transfer and is often used by businesses, educational institutions, and government organizations.

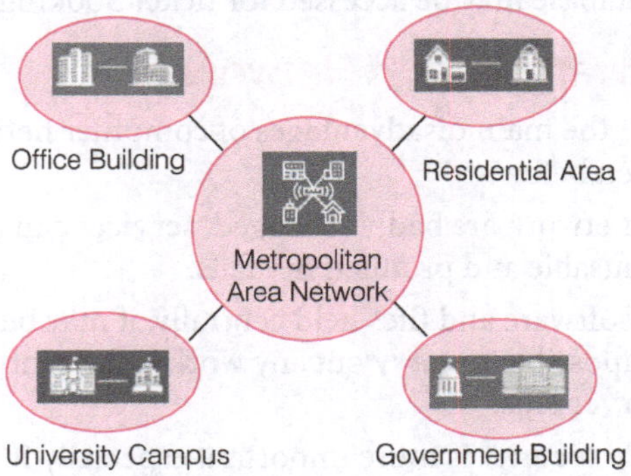

Example The network that connects several branch offices of a company within a city.

4. WAN (Wide Area Network)

A Wide Area Network (WAN) covers a vast geographic area, often spanning cities, countries, or even continents. It connects multiple LANs and MANs over large distances.

A WAN could be formed by connecting a LAN to other LANs via wired or wireless media.

- **Range** Can span hundreds to thousands of kilometers.
- **Application** Used to connect networks across large distances and enables communication between remote locations. The Internet itself is the largest example of a WAN.

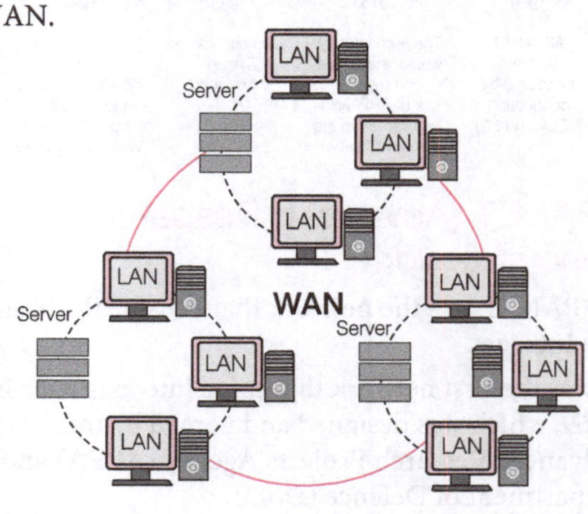

Example The network connecting a company's headquarters with its branches located in different countries.

6.3 Network Devices

Hardware device that are used to connect computers, printers, fax machines and other electronic devices to a network are called **network device**. There are many types of network devices used in networking and some of them are described below:

Repeater

It is a hardware device which is used to amplify or regenerate signals in a network to extend the distance they can travel without degradation. Commonly used in long-distance data transmission to ensure signal strength remains strong.

Hub

A hub is a device that broadcasts data to all devices on a network. It acts as a centralised connection to several computers with the central node or server.

There are two types of hub:

(i) **Active Hub** It acts as repeaters. It amplifies the signal as it moves from one device to another.

(ii) **Passive Hub** It simply passes the signal from one connected device to another.

Switch

A switch is a hardware device, which is used to connect devices or segments of the network into smaller subsets of LAN segments and forwards data based on MAC addresses, enabling efficient internal communication within a network.

Gateway

A gateway is a device, which is used to connect dissimilar networks. A device that acts as a "gate" between two different networks, translating data between different protocols. It allows communication between networks using different architectures or formats (e.g., between a local network and the internet).

Router

It is a hardware device, which is designed to take incoming packets, analyse the packets, moving and converting the packets to another network interface, dropping the packets, directing packets to the appropriate locations, etc.

RJ45 Connector

RJ45 stands for Registered Jack-45. It is an eight wire connector. RJ45 connector is used to connect computers onto a Local Area Network (LAN).

It is commonly used in telephony applications and networking. It is also used for serial connections.

Ethernet Card

An ethernet card is a kind of network adapter. These adapters support the ethernet standard for high-speed network connections *via* cables. Ethernet cards are sometimes known as **Network Interface Cards** (NICs).

Wi-Fi Card

These are small and portable cards that allow to connect to the Internet through a wireless network.

In these cards, transmission is done through radio waves. Many newer computers, mobile devices, etc., are equipped with wireless networking capability and do not require a Wi-Fi card.

Modem (MOdulator DEModulator)

It is a device that converts digital signal to analog signal (modulator) at the sender's site and converts back analog signal to digital signal (demodulator) at the receiver's end, in order to make communication possible via telephone lines.

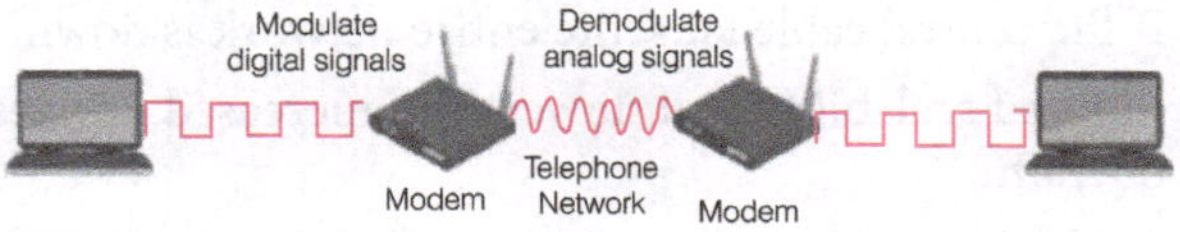

Modems are of two types:

(i) **Internal Modem** Fixed within a computer.

(ii) **External Modem** Connected externally to a computer.

Quick Test 1

1. Write the full form of ARPANET, NSFNET.
2. Why Internet is called network of networks?
3. Which type of network would use phone line?
4. Which device joins multiple computers together within one LAN?
5. A group of computers connected together with the help of cables within an office building is called what?
6. What is hub?
7. What is the use of repeater in a network?

6.4 Network Topology

The arrangement of computers and other peripherals in a network is called its **topology**.

The main network topologies are as follows:

1. Bus Topology (Linear Topology)

In bus topology all the devices are connected to a single central cable (the bus), and data travels along this cable to all devices.

However, only single workstation can transmit a message at a time in bus topology.

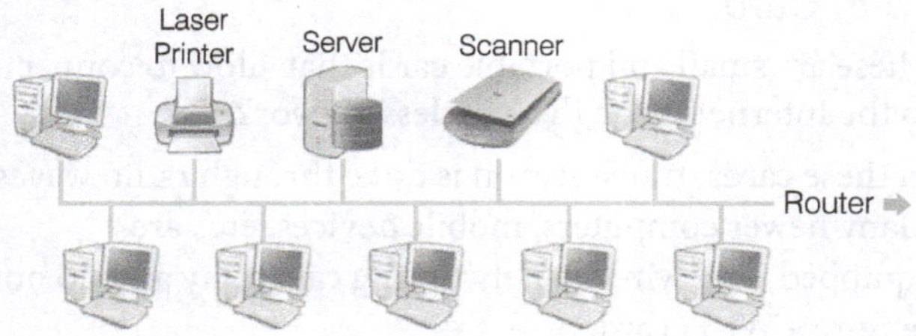

Bus topology

Advantages of Bus Topology

- Simple and cost-effective.
- Easy to install and requires less cabling.

Disadvantages of Bus Topology

- If the central cable fails, the entire network is down.
- Limited scalability and slower with increased devices or traffic.
- Difficult to troubleshoot issues.

2. Star Topology

In star topology, the devices are connected to a central node which is networking device like a hub or switch, which manages the data flow.

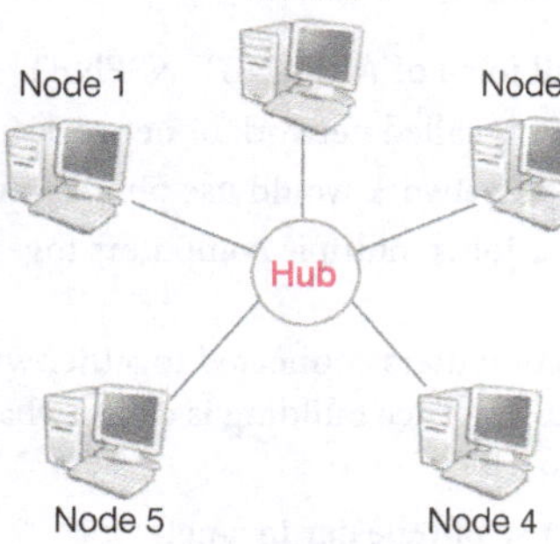

Star topology

Advantages of Star Topology

- Easy to install, manage and troubleshoot.
- A failure in one device or cable doesn't affect the rest of the network.
- Allows several types of cables in same network.

Disadvantages of Star Topology

- Requires more cable length than bus topology.
- If hub or server fails, the entire network will be disabled.
- Difficult to expand, as the new node has to connect all the way to central node.

3. Tree Topology

A tree topology is an extension and variation of bus topology. It's a hierarchical network combining elements of star and bus topologies. Groups of star-configured networks are connected to a central bus backbone.

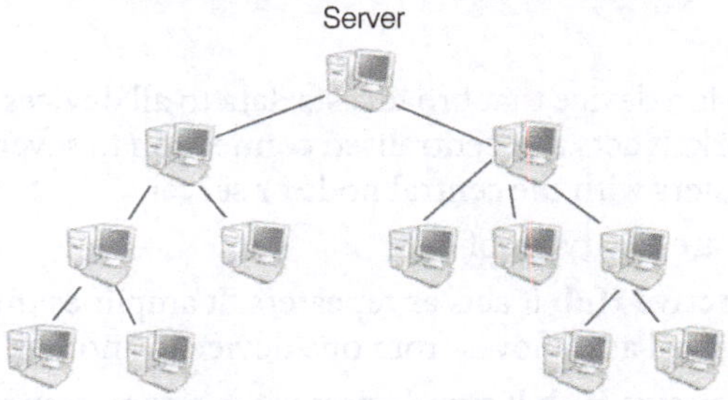

Tree topology

Advantages of Tree Topology

- Highly scalable, suitable for larger networks.
- We can easily extend the network.
- Faulty nodes can easily be isolated from the rest of the network.

Disadvantages of Tree Topology

- Long cables are required.
- There are dependencies on the root node.
- Installation and reconfiguration is very difficult.

Mobile Technologies

Mobile communication has evolved significantly, from 1G's basic voice calls to the advanced 5G networks of today. Each generation (1G, 2G, 3G, 4G, 5G) brought advancements like digital voice, faster data speeds, and improved reliability. This evolution has transformed how we communicate, enabling features like SMS, MMS, high-speed internet access, and the foundation for technologies like the Internet of Things (IoT) and smart devices. 5G, with its ultra-fast speeds, is poised to revolutionize industries like autonomous vehicles and M2M communication.

6.5 WWW or World Wide Web

The World Wide Web (WWW), often called the web, is a system of interconnected webpages and information that you can access using the Internet.

It was created to help people share and find information easily, using links that connect different pages together. The web allows us to browse websites, watch videos, shop online, and connect with others around the world through our computers and phones.

It is a project created, by **Tim Berner Lee** in **1989**, for researchers to work together effectively at **CERN**. It is an organization, named the **World Wide Web Consortium** (W3C), which was developed for further development of the web. This organization is directed by Tim Berner's Lee, aka the father of the web.

World Wide Web is based on client/server software design. A client/server software design requires two types of software to work in communication environment as shown in figure.

(i) **Client Software** It is a type of software, which is used by a client (or user) to request some information from web server. e.g. Web browsers

(ii) **Server Software** It is a type of software, which is used by the server to answer the requests and provide the required information. e.g. Microsoft, Oracle, etc.

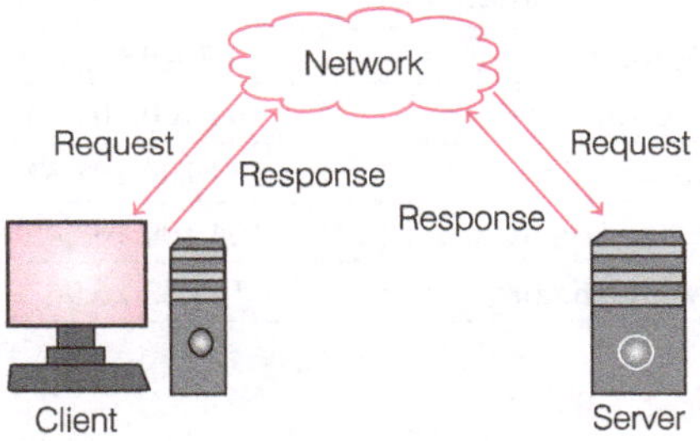

It is possible to use your local computer as a server but usually you want to have a fixed server, which runs 24×7 hours. So, more advanced and large systems are used as a server instead of local computers.

Mistake Alert!

Students might get confused by the difference between Internet and WWW that is the Internet is the infrastructure that connects devices, while the WWW is an information space built on that infrastructure, consisting of web pages and applications.

In 1990, by defining three fundamentals technologies that lead to creation of web.

1. **HTML** (HyperText Markup Language) is a standard language used for designing and structuring web pages. It enables web content to be displayed consistently across different devices and platforms globally. HTML uses tags to define how content is presented in a web browser. The basic structure of every webpage is built using HTML, making it the foundation for web design.
2. **HTTP** (HyperText Transfer Protocol) is a set of rules used for retrieving and transferring web pages and other resources across the web. Its more secure and encrypted version is HTTPS (HyperText Transfer Protocol Secure), which ensures secure communication over the internet by encrypting data.
3. **URI** (Uniform Resource Identifier) is a unique identifier used to locate a resource on the web. It can identify a resource (whether hardware or software) by its location, its name, or both.

A URL (Uniform Resource Locator) is a specific type of URI that not only identifies the resource but also provides the method (protocol) and location for accessing it. It's a unique identifier that identifies the location of a resource on the Internet.

URLs are often referred to as web addresses or website addresses because web pages are the most common resource that end users use URLs to find. Other resources include CSS documents, videos, and images. Every file stored on a server has a unique URL, which tells a web browser how and where to retrieve that resource.

We actively use web addresses by typing them into the web browser's address bar. End users also interact with web addresses when they click a hyperlink on web pages, bookmark lists, or emails.

Components of a URL

There are several parts of a URL; some are present in all web addresses and others are optional. However, each part has a specific purpose to help you access anything online.

Consider the following URL structure:

https://www.example.com:8080/products/page1.html?search=keyword#section1

Where,

- **Protocol** https://
- **Subdomain** www
- **Domain** example.com
- **Port** 8080
- **Path** /products/page1.html
- **Query parameters** ?search=keyword
- **Fragment identifier** #section1

TEACHER TIP
The Domain Name System (DNS) is like the internet's phone book. It helps you find websites by translating easy-to-remember names (like www.example.com) into the numerical IP addresses (like 192.0.2.1) that computers use to locate each other on the internet. Without DNS, you would have to remember long strings of numbers to visit your favorite websites.

Note *These days it is not mandatory to mention protocol and subdomain while entering a URL. The browser automatically prefixes it.*

Types of URL

There are two types of URL

1. Absolute URL

An absolute URL provides the complete path to a resource, including the protocol, domain, and the file or resource location.

Example https://www.example.com/images/logo.png

2. Relative URL

A relative URL provides a path relative to the current page or directory. It does not include the domain or protocol.
Example /images/logo.png

It is commonly used within a website to link to resources on the same domain.

6.6 XML

XML, or eXtensible Markup Language, is a flexible and structured way to store and transport data. Unlike HTML, which is designed primarily for displaying data in web browsers, XML focuses on describing data and its structure.

It uses tags to define elements and attributes, allowing users to create their own custom tags that are meaningful to their specific needs.

This makes XML versatile and widely used for data exchange between different systems, such as web services and databases. XML files are human-readable and can be easily parsed by computers, making them ideal for data storage and transmission in various applications, including web development, configuration files, and data interchange formats.

6.7 Domain Names System

The Domain Name System (DNS) is a crucial component of the Internet, often likened to a phone book that translates user-friendly domain names into numerical IP addresses. This process allows users to easily navigate the web without memorizing complex numeric addresses.

However, remembering names is easier than memorizing numbers.

That's why each computer server hosting a website or web resource is assigned a name linked to its IP address. These names are known as domain names or hostnames, corresponding to the unique IP addresses assigned to each server.

Think of it like a phonebook: instead of remembering every person's phone number, we use names to identify them. Similarly, domain names are easier to recall than IP addresses.

For example, here are the IP addresses and domain names of some websites:

Domain Name	IP Address
ncert.nic.in	164.100.60.233
cbse.nic.in	164.100.107.32
mhrd.gov.in	164.100.163.45
wikipedia.org	198.35.26.96

Need for DNS

While every device connected to the internet is identified by its unique IP address, these addresses can be cumbersome and prone to change.

DNS serves as an essential intermediary that converts these domain names into their corresponding IP addresses, making it easier for users to access websites. Without DNS, accessing a site like www.ncert.in would require remembering its IP address (e.g., 164.100.60.233), let's understand the various types of domains:

Types of Domains

1. **Generic Domains**
   - .com (commercial)
   - .edu (educational)
   - .mil (military)
   - .org (nonprofit organization)
   - .net (network-related)
2. **Country Code Domains**
   - .in (India)
   - .us (United States)
   - .uk (United Kingdom)
3. **Inverse Domain** This refers to the process of finding the domain name associated with a given IP address, known as reverse DNS lookup.

DNS Server

DNS (Domain Name System) is a system that translates human-readable domain names (like www.arihant.com) into IP addresses (like 192.0.2.1). This translation is essential because, while humans prefer to use easy-to-remember names, computers communicate using numerical IP addresses.

Working of Domain Name Resolution

1. **User Action** When you type a URL into your web browser (e.g., www.arihant.com), your browser needs to find out the corresponding IP address to access the website.
2. **DNS Query** The browser sends a request to a DNS server to resolve the domain name to an IP address.
3. **DNS Server Response**
   - If the DNS server has the IP address for the domain name cached (stored in memory), it returns the IP address directly to the browser.
   - If the server does not have the IP address cached, it will query other DNS servers, potentially following a chain of queries through multiple servers until it finds the address or confirms that the domain does not exist.
4. **Loading the Website** Once the browser receives the IP address, it can make an HTTP request to the web server at that address, retrieving the desired web page and loading it in your browser.

DNS Server Hierarchy

The DNS system is organized hierarchically:

1. **Root Servers** At the top of the hierarchy there are 13 root DNS servers. These servers do not store the IP addresses for domain names directly but instead direct queries to the appropriate TLD (Top-Level Domain) servers based on the domain extension (like .com, .org, .net).
2. **TLD Servers** Below the root servers are TLD servers, which handle specific top-level domains. For example, the .com TLD server knows the IP addresses of all domains that end in .com.
3. **Authoritative DNS Servers** At the next level are authoritative DNS servers, which contain the actual IP addresses for specific domain names. These servers can either directly provide the IP address or delegate the query to another server that has the information.

6.8 Web Server

Web server is a program which processes the network requests of the users and serves them with files that create web pages. This exchange takes place using Hypertext Transfer Protocol (HTTP).

Basically, web servers are computers used to store HTTP files which makes a website and when a client requests a certain website, it delivers the requested website to the client.

For example, you want to open Facebook on your laptop and enter the URL in the search bar of google. Now, the laptop will send an HTTP request to view the Facebook webpage to another computer known as the webserver. This computer (webserver) contains all the files (usually in HTTP format) which make up the website like text, images, gif files, etc. After processing the request, the webserver will send the requested website-related files to your computer and then you can reach the website as shown in figure.

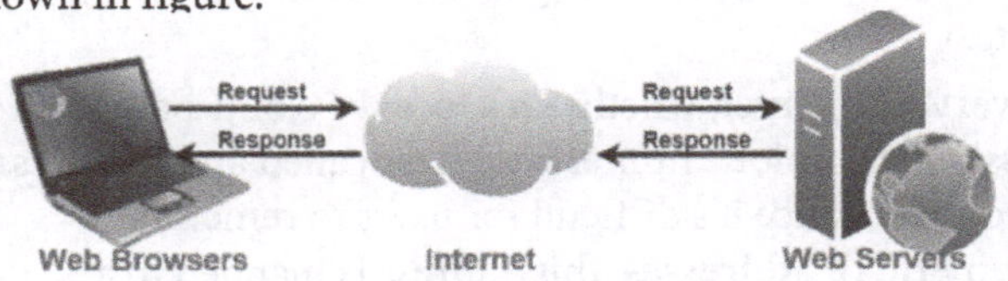

A web server provides several key services, including:

1. **Hosting Websites** Serves HTML, CSS, JavaScript, and multimedia content to users' web browsers.
2. **File Storage and Management** Allows users to upload, download, and manage files, including images, videos, and documents.

3. **Processing Dynamic Content** Supports the execution of server-side scripts (e.g., PHP, Python, ASP.NET) to generate dynamic web pages.
4. **HTTP Request Handling** Manages incoming HTTP or HTTPS requests and sends appropriate responses (e.g., web pages, API data).
5. **Security Services** Provides SSL/TLS encryption for secure data transmission, and implements security measures like firewalls, authentication, and access controls.
6. **Logging and Monitoring** Tracks server activity, including user access, errors, and performance metrics for analysis.
7. **Load Balancing** Distributes incoming traffic across multiple servers to ensure optimal performance and availability.
8. **Database Connectivity** Facilitates communication between web applications and databases to retrieve and store data.

6.9 Web Hosting

Web hosting is a service that allows a website or web page to be accessible via the Internet, making it part of the World Wide Web. To host a website, you need to upload the site's files (HTML, CSS, JavaScript, images, databases, etc.) from your local computer onto a server that is connected to the Internet. This can be done either using your own server or by renting server resources like CPU, RAM, and storage from a cloud service provider.

The web hosting service typically requires a payment to access resources such as RAM, disk space, and bandwidth. These resources can be scaled based on the website's needs, depending on the traffic and loads on the site.

Every web server, whether it's local or cloud-based, is assigned a unique numeric address called an IP address. However, since it's difficult for users to remember numeric **IP addresses**, this address is mapped to a domain name, a more user-friendly textual identifier. The domain name is entered into a browser's URL bar to access the website, and it must be registered with an authorized agency.

To host a website, follow these key steps:

1. **Select a Web Hosting Service** Choose a reliable web hosting provider. The provider will offer web server space and essential services like database support, bandwidth, backups, firewall, and email services. The selection depends on the features and services you want to offer on your website.
2. **Register a Domain Name** Pick a suitable domain name for your website, and register it through a domain name registrar. The domain name is essentially the website's address on the internet (e.g., www.example.com).
3. **Configure Web Space** After purchasing web hosting, create login credentials with the required access rights for managing your hosting account. Note down the IP address of the server where your site will be hosted.
4. **Upload Your Website** Develop your website and upload it to the web server using tools like FTP or file management provided by the host. You can use CMS platforms like WordPress if you're not building the site from scratch.
5. **Link Domain to Web Hosting** Connect your domain name to your hosting provider by updating DNS settings. This ensures that when someone types your domain name, they are directed to your hosted website.
6. **Test and Launch** Once everything is set up, test your website to ensure it works correctly. After testing, your site is live for users worldwide!

6.10 Web Browser

The web browser is an application software to explore WWW (World Wide Web). It provides an interface between the server and the client and it requests to the server for web documents and services. It works as a compiler to render HTML which is used to design a webpage.

Whenever we search for anything on the internet, the browser loads a web page written in HTML, including text, links, images, and other items such as style sheets and JavaScript functions. Google Chrome, Microsoft Edge, Mozilla Firefox, and Safari are examples of web browsers.

There are two types of web browsers

(i) **Text-Based Web Browsers** are the web browsers that support text only, i.e. these browsers do not support graphics. e.g. Linux.

(ii) **Graphical-Based Web Browsers** provide a Graphical User Interface (GUI) where the user can jump from one web page to another by clicking on the hyperlink on a web page. e.g. Chrome, Internet Explorer, Mozilla Firefox, etc.

Web Browser Toolbar

A major part of the user interface for a browser is the toolbar. This appears at the top of the browser window, above the viewing pane and it can perform a number of critical functions.

Major functions of browser toolbar are as follows

(i) **Back** This takes you one step back in your history, to the page you were on before the current page.

(ii) **Forward** It allows you to move forward through your history, to where you were before you used the Back button.

(iii) **Address Bar** This is a text box that displays the URL of the current page.

(iv) **Stop** This will be found either just inside the address bar or just next to it. It only appears when the page is currently in the process of loading. If you click it, the page will stop loading.

(v) **Refresh** The Refresh or Reload button looks like a circular arrow. This button repeats the request that led to the current page, which usually cause the same page to load into the browser again.

(vi) **Bookmark** This allows you to bookmark the URL, saving it to you browser.

Some Popular Web Browsers

Here is a list of 6 popular web browsers:

1. Google Chrome
2. Mozilla Firefox
3. Apple Safari
4. Microsoft Edge
5. Tor Browser
6. Opera

> **Additional Information** Mosaic was the first web browser developed by the National Centre for Supercomputing Application (NCSA). The initial web browsers like Mosaic used to support HTML documents containing plain text (static website) only, but nowadays with the advancement of technology, modern web browsers allow us to view interactive and dynamic websites.

6.11 Website

A website is a collection of interconnected web pages written in HTML (HyperText Markup Language). To be accessible to users globally, a website must be hosted on a web server, which is a computer connected to the internet.

Key characteristics of a website include:

- **Hyperlinks and Hypertext** Web pages are linked together, allowing users to navigate seamlessly.
- **Common Design and Interface** Websites typically share a consistent look and feel across all pages.
- **Additional Content** Websites may include images, videos, and other digital assets that enhance the user experience.

In today's digital age, websites serve various purposes, acting as environments that provide information, promote interaction, and support organizational goals.

Types of Website

Static Website Displays fixed content; pages are pre-designed and do not change based on user interaction. e.g. A basic company portfolio.

Dynamic Website Displays content that changes dynamically based on user interaction or database inputs. e.g. Social media platforms.

Components of a Website

1. **Web Host** This is the physical location where the website resides, typically on a web server. It consists of a group of linked webpages that are licensed as a website when hosted.
2. **Address (URL)** The URL is the address users enter into their web browsers to access a website. The web server delivers the requested website based on this address.
3. **Homepage** This is the first page that visitors see when they access a website. The homepage is crucial as it establishes the website's look and feel and provides links to other pages.
4. **Design** The design encompasses the overall aesthetic of the website, achieved through elements like navigation menus, graphics, and layout.
5. **Content** The content includes all the text, images, and multimedia found on the website's pages. High-quality content is vital for attracting and engaging visitors.

6. **Navigation Structure** This defines how the pages are organized and linked. A well-structured navigation menu helps users easily find information on the site.

6.12 Web Page

A webpage is a digital document linked to the World Wide Web that can be viewed by anyone with internet access and a web browser. It can include various types of information, such as text, images, graphics, animations, videos, sounds, and more.

Webpages are primarily written in HTML (HyperText Markup Language), allowing them to be displayed on the internet.

Users can access a webpage by entering its URL (Uniform Resource Locator) in the address bar of a web browser.

Types of Web Page

Static Web Page

A web page which displays same kind of information whenever a user visits, is known as a static web page. A static web page generally has .htm or .html as extension.

Example A page that contains school or company information. The content of this page will not change every day unless the HTML file is manually edited by a programmer who maintains it.

Dynamic Web Page

An interactive web page is a dynamic web page. A dynamic web page uses scripting languages to display changing content on the web page. Such a page generally has .php, .asp or .jsp as extension.

Example When you login to your Yahoo e-mail account to check and to send e-mails. Moreover, the list of e-mail messages changes as it arrives or as the list is deleted or is moved to another folder.

Quick Test 2

1. If you connected your computer network in the form of star or bus topology, which topology will require more cable length?
2. Which topology is ideal for long distance networking?
3. What is DNS? What is a DNS server?
4. Distinguish between web browser and web server.
5. Define the following terms: **CBSE SQP 2021-22 Term II**
   (a) WWW
   (b) Web hosting
6. Differentiate between URL and domain name with the help of an appropriate example. **CBSE 2023**

Mind Map

COMPUTER NETWORK

Collection of computers and other hardware interconnected by communication channels that allows sharing of resources and information.

Network Topologies

Geometric representation of all the nodes in a network.

Bus All devices are connected to a single cable, with terminators at each end.

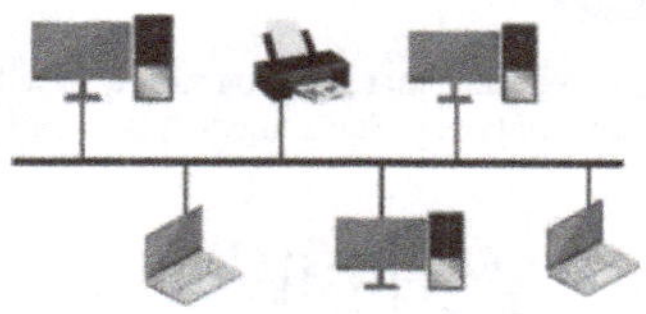

Star A star topology is based on a central node acts as a hub.

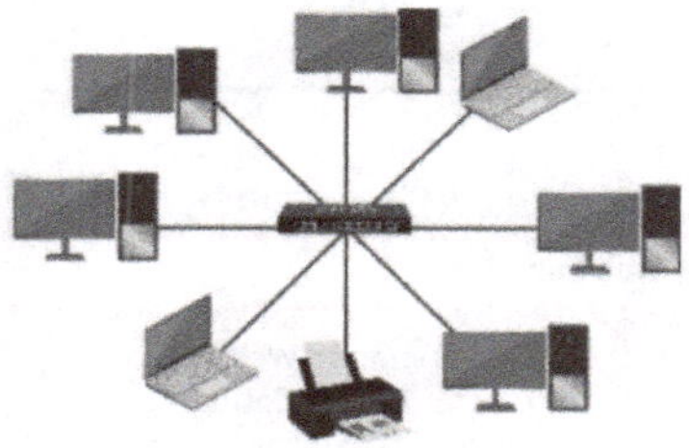

Tree Devices are connected in a hierarchical structure. This topology is known as a Star Bus topology because it combines several star topologies into a single bus.

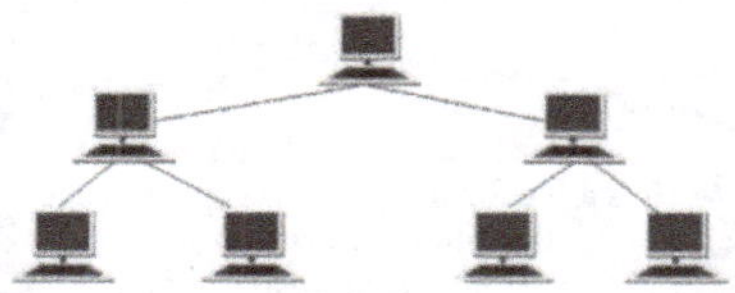

Network Devices

Hub Redirects the received information to all the connected nodes.

Switch Filters and forwards data packets across a network.

Repeater It is used to amplify and regenerate a signal which is on its way through a communication channel.

Router Forwards data packets by finding the shortest route.

Gateway Connects dissimilar networks (different hardware and software configurations) with different protocols.

Modem Converts digital signal into analog signal and *vice-versa*.

RJ45 Connector RJ45 stands for Registered Jack-45. It is an eight wire connector. It is used to connect computers onto a LAN.

Ethernet Card These adapters support the ethernet standard for high-speed network connections *via* cables. It is additionally called Network Interface Cards (NICs).

Wi-Fi Card A Wi-Fi card also known as a wireless network card, is a hardware component that allows a computer to connect to the internet through a wireless network.

Network devices are physical devices that allow hardware on a computer network to interact and communicate with one another.

Evolution of Networking

1969 **ARPANET (Advanced Research Agency Network)** was the first network and the base of the Internet.

1985 **NSFNET (National Science Federation Network)** was the first backbone infrastructure for the commercial public Internet.

1983 **Internet** is made up of many small networks each run by different companies and interconnected at the peering point.

Types of Network

PAN **Personal Area Network** It is a small network typically used for connecting devices within a very limited range, such as within a room or an individual's workspace.

LAN **Local Area Network** It is a network that connects computers and devices within a specific area, such as a home, office, or school.

MAN **Metropolitan Area Network** It connects computers within a metropolitan area, such as a large city, multiple cities or a large area with multiple buildings.

WAN **Wide Area Network** It covers a vast geographic area, often spanning cities, countries or even continents. A WAN could be formed by connecting a LAN to other LANs *via* wired or wireless media.

Mind Map

WEB SERVICE

A web service is a software module that is designed to perform a certain set of tasks.

Web Browser It provides an interface between the server and the client and it requests to the server for web documents and services.

Types of Web Browsers

Text-Based Web Browsers are the web browsers that support text only, i.e. these browsers do not support graphics. e.g. Lynx.

Graphical-Based Web Browsers provide a Graphical User Interface (GUI) where the user can jump from one web page to another by clicking on the hyperlink on a web page. e.g. Chrome, Internet Explorer, Mozilla Firefox, etc.

Website
A website is a collection of interconnected web pages written in HTML (HyperText Markup Language).

Types of Website

Static Website Displays fixed content; pages are pre-designed and do not change based on user interaction. e.g. A basic company portfolio.

Dynamic Website Displays content that changes dynamically based on user interaction or database inputs. e.g. Social media platforms.

Web Page It is a digital document linked to the World Wide Web that can be viewed by anyone with internet access and a web browser.

Types of Web Page

Static Web Page
Displays same kind of information whenever a user visits, is known as a static web page. A static web page generally has .htm or .html as extension.

Dynamic Web Page
Uses scripting languages to display changing content on the web page. Such a page generally has .php, .asp or .jsp as extension.

XML (eXtensible Markup Language)
It is a file format and markup language that allows users to store, transmit and reconstruct data.

Web server
It is software and hardware that stores, processes, and delivers webpages to users.

WWW (World Wide Web) It often called the web, is a system of interconnected web pages and information that you can access using the Internet.

Components of WWW

HTML (HyperText Markup Language) is a standard language used for designing and structuring web pages.

HTTP (HyperText Transfer Protocol) is a set of rules used for retrieving and transferring web pages and other resources across the web.

URI (Uniform Resource Identifier) is a unique identifier used to locate a resource on the web.

A URL (Uniform Resource Locator) is a specific type of URI that not only identifies the resource but also provides the method (protocol) and location for accessing it. Types of URL – Absolute, Relative.

Domain Names System (DNS)

It is used to translating easy-to-remember names (like www.example-com) into the numerical (like 192.0.2.1) that computers use to locate each other on the internet.

Working of DNS

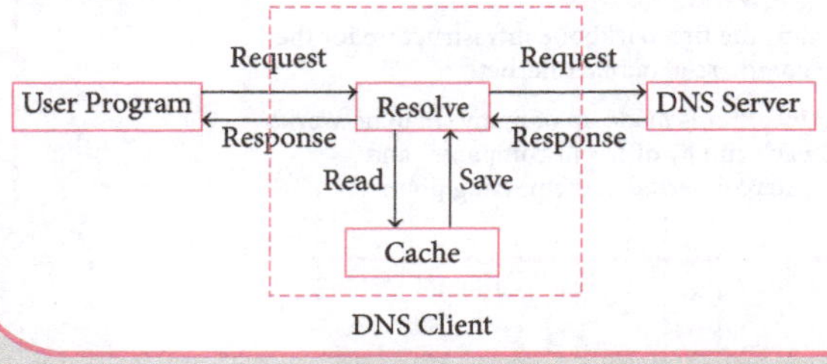

NCERT Folder

1. Explore and find out the minimum internet speed required to make a video call.

Ans. The minimum internet speed required to make a video call is not same, it varies depending on the quality of the video and the number of participants.

Here are some general guidelines:

- **Standard Video Call** 1 Mbps upload speed for standard video conferencing.
- **High-Quality Video Call (480p)** 0.6-1.5 Mbps download and upload speed.
- **HD Video Call (720p)** 1.2-2.5 Mbps download and upload speed.
- **Full HD Video Call (1080p)** 3-4 Mbps download and upload speed.
- **Group Video Call** 8 Mbps per person for good quality.

2. It is possible to access your bank account from any part of the world. Whether the bank's network is a LAN, MAN, WAN or any other type?

Ans. Yes, It's possible to access your bank account from anywhere in the world, regardless of the bank's network type (LAN, MAN, WAN, etc.).

3. How will a Bus topology behave in case a Node is down?

Ans. In a bus topology, if a node goes down, the entire network is affected. Data transmission stops until the failed node is repaired or replaced. The network splits into two separate segments, with nodes on either side unable to communicate. It's difficult to detect and correct errors due to the lack of redundancy.

4. You are encouraged to take up any area of concern where you think IoT can be immensely beneficial and discuss it with your peers. An example for the same can be preventing road accidents.

Ans. IoT can be immensely beneficial in these areas highlighting the potential of IoT to enhance safety, efficiency, and sustainability across industries.

- **Preventing Road Accidents** IoT enables vehicle-to-vehicle (V2V) communication, smart traffic systems, and real-time monitoring of vehicle health, reducing accidents by providing predictive insights and alerts.
- **Healthcare Monitoring** IoT-powered wearable devices can monitor minor signs in real-time, detecting potential health risks early, and sending alerts to both users and their respect doctors.
- **Energy Efficiency** Smart grids and IoT sensors can optimize energy usage, reduce wastage, and ensure efficient distribution of power, leading to sustainable energy management.
- **Agriculture** IoT in smart farming allows real-time monitoring of soil conditions, weather data, and crop health, leading to increased productivity and resources efficiency.

5. Write down the names of few commonly used networking devices.

Ans. The names of few commonly used networking devices are as follow:

- **Wired Devices** Hub, Switch, Router, Gateway, Modem, Firewall
- **Wireless Devices** Wireless Router (WR), Wi-Fi Adaptor, Wireless Range Extender
- **Network Connectivity Devices** Ethernet Card, Fibre Optic Cable, Network Cable (RJ-45), Network Adapters (USB, PCI)

6. Two universities in different States want to transfer information. Which type of network they need to use for this?

Ans. To transfer information between two universities in different states, they would need to use a Wide Area Network (WAN).

7. Define the term topology. What are the popular network topologies?

Ans. The arrangement of computers and other peripherals in a network is called its topology.

The main network topologies are:

- Bus Topology
- Star Topology
- Tree Topology

8. Identify the type of topology from the following:

(a) Each node is connected with the help of a single cable.

(b) Each node is connected with central switching through independent cables.

Ans. (a) Bus Topology (b) Star Topology

9. Explain the following devices:

(a) Switch **(b) Repeater**

(c) Router **(d) Gateway**

(e) NIC

Ans. (a) **Switch** A switch is network device connecting multiple devices, forwarding data packets between them. It operates at the data link layer of the OSI model. Switches increase network efficiency, reduce data collisions, and improve overall performance.

(b) **Repeater** It is a hardware device which is used to amplify or regenerate signals in a network to extend the distance they can travel without degradation. Repeaters operate at physical Layer of the OSI model, ensuring reliable data transmission over long distances.

(c) **Router** A router connects multiple networks, directing traffic between them. It operates at network layer of the OSI model, using IP addresses to route data packets. Routers enable communication between different networks, manage traffic, and provide security features.

(d) **Gateway** A gateway connects a network to an external network or the internet. It translates data formats, protocols, and addresses between networks. Gateway operate at multiple OSI layers, and often provide security and firewall functionality.

(e) **NIC** A NIC (Network Interface Card) is a hardware component that connects a computer to a network. NICs enable computers to communicate with networks, facilitating internet access, file sharing, and communication.

10. Draw a network layout of star topology and bus topology connecting five computers.

Ans. Refer to network layout on page no. 160 (Bus topology, star topotogy).

11. Among LAN, MAN, and WAN, which has the highest speed and which one can cover the largest area?

Ans. LAN (Local Area Network) has high-speed data transfer rates from about (100Mbps to 10Gbps), and WAN (Wide Area Network) covers large geographical area (e.g., city, country, continent).

EXAM PATTERN QUESTIONS

Objective Type Questions

Multiple Choice Questions

1. The one which is a collection of independent computers and other hardware interconnected by communication channels?

(a) Computer (b) Networking
(c) Sharing (d) None of these

2. Which of the following is an advantage of networking?

(a) Application sharing (b) File sharing
(c) User communication (d) All of these

3. Network formed between computers which are spread across the continents is called

(a) LAN (b) WAN
(c) MAN (d) WLAN

4. Riya wants to transfer pictures from her mobile phone to her laptop. She uses Bluetooth Technology to connect two devices. Which type of network will be formed in this case? CBSE SQP 2023-24

(a) PAN (b) LAN
(c) MAN (d) WAN

5. Modulation and demodulation is performed by

(a) microwave (b) satellite
(c) modem (d) gateway

6. A modem is connected in between a telephone line and a

(a) computer (b) serial port
(c) network (d) communication adapter

7. The device which may operate at different network speeds depending on the protocol standard they support?

(a) Router (b) Ethernet card
(c) RJ45 Connector (d) None of these

8. Which network device is used to connect two networks that use different protocols? CBSE SQP 2024-25

(a) Modem (b) Gateway
(c) Switch (d) Repeater

9. Fill in the blank.

The modem at the sender's computer end acts as a .... CBSE SQP 2023-24

(a) Model (b) Modulator
(c) Demodulator (d) Convertor

10. Which of the following networking devices is used to regenerate and transmit the weakened signal ahead? CBSE 2025

(a) Hub (b) Ethernet Card
(c) Repeater (d) Modem

11. **Geometric arrangement of devices on the network is called**
(a) topology (b) protocols
(c) media (d) LAN

12. **In which of the topology, network components are connected to the same cable?**
(a) Star (b) Ring
(c) Bus (d) Mesh

13. **HTML is a markup language for describing web document. HTML uses**
(a) pre-specified tags
(b) user defined tags
(c) tags only for linking
(d) fixed tags defined by the language

14. **Which of the following components is NOT a part of a URL?**
(a) Protocol (b) Fragment identifier
(c) Domain (d) MIME type

15. **The basic purpose of URL is to locate**
(a) Web server (b) IP address
(c) Web page (d) Node

16. **Which of the following statements are true about URL?**
(a) URL means Uniform Resource Locator
(b) You can enter URL into address bar
(c) An example of URL is we@fg.com
(d) Both (a) and (b)

17. **What is the expanded form of XML?**
(a) Extended Markup Language
(b) Extensible Markup Language
(c) Extra Markup Language
(d) None of these

18. **Which of the following is a unique name that identifies a particular website and represents the name of the server?**
(a) XML (b) Domain Name
(c) HTML (d) None of these

19. **Which is used to translate domain name into IP address?**
(a) Domain name (b) URL
(c) Domain name system (d) None of these

20. **What does the acronym DNS stand for?**
(a) Domain Name Server (b) Digital Network System
(c) Domain Name System (d) Data Network Service

21. **Each computer connected to the Internet must**
(a) be a pentium machine (b) have a unique IP address
(c) have a web browser (d) have a modem connection

22. **IP address are converted into**
(a) a binary string (b) alphanumeric string
(c) a hierarchy of domain name (d) a hexadecimal string

23. **What is the main function of a web server?**
(a) Store HTML files only
(b) Process network requests and serve files
(c) Design web pages
(d) Host domain names

24. **A ____________ is program running on the server which accepts request from a browser and send HTML.**
(a) Web server (b) Web transmitter
(c) Web intermediate (d) Web multitasker

25. **Which of the following service is a type of Internet hosting service that allows individuals and organisations to make their website accessible via the WWW?**
(a) Web server (b) Website
(c) Web hosting (d) None of these

26. **What type of web browser does not support graphics?**
(a) Graphical-Based Web Browser
(b) Hybrid Web Browser
(c) Text-Based Web Browser
(d) Multimedia Web Browser

27. **A collection of web pages linked together in a random order is**
(a) a website (b) a web server
(c) a search engine (d) a web browser

28. **Mozilla is a free internet software that include**
(a) Web browser (b) email client
(c) HTML editor (d) All of these

29. **Which of the following web page displays same kind of information whenever a user visits?**
(a) Dynamic web page (b) Static web page
(c) Both (a) and (b) (d) None of these

Fill in the blanks

30. ……… is private because it guarantees privacy inside the organisation.

31. ……… was the world's first operational packet switching network.

32. ……… acts as a centralised connection to several computers with the central node or server.

33. Hub is associated with ……… network.

34. The antenna transmits the radio signals to those equipment, which has ……… .

35. The ……… is a collection of millions of files stored on thousands of computers all over the world.

36. The design of .... focuses on documents, it is widely used for the representation of arbitrary data structures.

37. The character based naming system by which server are identified is known as ....

38. The .... can refer to either the hardware or the software that helps to deliver web content, accessible through the Internet.

State whether True or False

39. A computer network allows for the efficient exchange of data, enabling applications such as email, file sharing, and internet browsing.

40. A hub amplifies and regenerates signals as it broadcasts data to all devices on a network.

41. A gateway is used to connect dissimilar networks and allows communication between networks using different architectures or formats.

42. A router only analyzes packets and directs them to their destination; it does not alter the packets.

43. Wi-Fi cards are necessary for devices to connect to the internet if they are equipped with wireless networking capability.

44. A tree topology combines elements of both star and bus topologies, with groups of star-configured networks connected to a central bus backbone.

45. The World Wide Web (WWW) is a collection of hypertext documents that are accessed using the Internet.

46. HTML is used to describe the structure and layout of a web page, while XML is designed to store and transport data.

47. A domain name is the same as a URL and does not include any additional information like protocol or path.

48. A web server is software that processes requests for web pages and delivers them to a user's web browser.

49. Web browsers are responsible for hosting websites on the Internet.

Assertion and Reason Based Questions

Assertion (A) and Reason (R) Type questions. Choose the correct option as:

(a) Both Assertion (A) and Reason (R) are true, and Reason (R) is the correct explanation of Assertion (A)

(b) Both Assertion (A) and Reason (R) are true, but Reason (R) is not the correct explanation of Assertion (A)

(c) Assertion (A) is True, but Reason (R) is False

(d) Assertion (A) is False, but Reason (R) is True

50. Assertion (A) A router is primarily used to connect dissimilar networks and ensure efficient data transmission between them.

Reason (R) Routers analyze incoming packets and determine the best path for data to travel to its destination.

51. Assertion (A) A modem converts digital signals to analog signals to facilitate communication over telephone lines.

Reason (R) Modems are used to connect devices to local networks and the internet.

52. Assertion (A) An access point is a device that connects dissimilar networks.

Reason (R) Access point broadcast wireless signals that wifi cards can detect.

53. Assertion(A) A gateway connects dissimilar networks.

Reason (R) Gateway establishes a connection between local network and external network.

54. Assertion (A) In a star topology, if the central hub fails, the entire network goes down.

Reason (R) Star topology connects all devices to a central node, which manages data flow.

55. Assertion (A) The World Wide Web was created by Sir Tim Berners-Lee in 1990 to help researchers share information easily.

Reason (R) The World Wide Web allows users to browse websites, watch videos, and connect with others through interconnected webpages.

56. Assertion (A) HTML is the standard language used for designing and structuring web pages.

Reason (R) XML is primarily designed for displaying data in web browsers.

57. Assertion (A) An absolute URL provides the complete path to a resource, including the domain and protocol.

Reason (R) A relative URL can be used to link to resources on the same domain without specifying the protocol or domain.

58. Assertion (A) The Domain Name System (DNS) translates user-friendly domain names into numerical IP addresses.

Reason (R) DNS is necessary because memorizing IP addresses is easier than remembering names.

59. Assertion (A) The hierarchical structure of DNS includes root servers, TLD servers, and authoritative DNS servers.

Reason (R) All servers in the DNS hierarchy store the IP addresses for every domain name.

60. Assertion (A) Web servers process network requests and serve files that create web pages.

Reason (R) Web servers only store static content and do not process dynamic requests.

Answers

1. (b) Networking
2. (d) All of these
3. (b) WAN
4. (a) PAN
5. (c) modem
6. (a) computer
7. (b) Ethernet card
8. (b) Gateway
9. (b) Modulator
10. (c) Repeater
11. (a) topology
12. (c) Bus
13. (d) fixed tags defined by the language
14. (d) MIME type
15. (b) IP address
16. (d) Both (a) and (b)
17. (b) Extensible Markup Language
18. (b) Domain Name
19. (c) Domain name system
20. (c) Domain Name System
21. (b) have a unique IP address
22. (c) a hierarchy of domain name
23. (b) Process network requests and serve files
24. (a) Web server
25. (c) Web hosting
26. (c) Text-Based Web Browser
27. (a) a website
28. (d) All of these
29. (b) Static web page
30. VPN
31. ARPANET
32. Hub
33. Star
34. Wi-Fi cards
35. World Wide Web
36. XML
37. Domain name system
38. web server
39. True
40. False
41. True
42. False
43. False
44. True
45. True
46. True
47. False
48. True
49. False
50. (a) Both A and R are true, and R is the correct explanation of A.
51. (c) Assertion (A) is True, but Reason (R) is False.
52. (a) Both A and R are true, and R is the correct explanation of A.
53. (a) Both A and R are true, and R is the correct explanation of A.
54. (a) Both A and R are true, and R is the correct explanation of A.
55. (a) Both A and R are true, and R is the correct explanation of A.
56. (c) Assertion (A) is True, but Reason (R) is False.
57. (a) Both A and R are true, and R is the correct explanation of A.
58. (d) Assertion (A) is True, but Reason (R) is False.
59. (c) Assertion (A) is True, but Reason (R) is False.
60. (d) Assertion (A) is True, but Reason (R) is False.

Subjective Type Questions

Very Short Answer Type Questions

1. Name the term defined by given below statement: "A group of computers connected to each other by a link."

Ans. Computer network is defined as a group of computers connected to each other by a link.

2. What was the role of ARPANET in the computer network?

Ans. ARPANET (Advanced Research Projects Agency Network) goal was to connect computers at different universities and US defense. ARPANET started with a handful of computers but it expanded rapidly.

3. Which cable networks are used for LAN connections?

Ans. Twisted pair and fibre optic cables are used for LAN connections.

4. How is crossover Ethernet cable different from rest of the Ethernet cables?

Ans. A crossover cable is a special type of Ethernet cable specially designed for connecting two computers, whereas most Ethernet cable are designed to connect one computer to a router or a switch.

5. List down the types of computer networks.

Ans. Following are the three main types of computer networks, based upon the geographical area as follows:

(i) Local Area Network (LAN)
(ii) Metropolitan Area Network (MAN)
(iii) Wide Area Network (WAN)

6. Which type of network (out of LAN, PAN and MAN) is formed, when you connect two mobiles using bluetooth to transfer a picture file?

Ans. When two mobiles are connected using bluetooth to transfer a picture file, a PAN (Personal Area Network) is created.

7. Arrange the following network in ascending order of their area:

LAN, PAN, WAN, MAN

Ans. PAN < LAN < MAN < WAN

8. What is the purpose of switch in a network?

Ans. A switch is a networking device, which is used to connect different LAN segments of a network. A switch also supports packet filtering and forwarding between LAN segments.

9. Beauty lines fashion incorporation is a fashion company with design unit and market unit 135 m away from each other. The company recently connected their LANs using Ethernet cable to share the stock related information. But after joining their LANís they are not able to show the information due to loss of signal in between. Which device out of the following should you suggest to be installed for a smooth communication?

(i) Modem (ii) Repeater (iii) UPS

Ans. They should use repeater. As repeater is a device used to amplify the signals.

10. Name any two components required for networking.

Ans. Switch/hub and repeaters.

11. Why is a switch called an intelligent hub?

Ans. A switch is also known as intelligent hub because a hub forwards each incoming packet (data) to all the hub ports. Whereas, a switch forwards each incoming packet to the specified recipient.

12. What is the advantage of using switch over hub?

Ans. Switch provides a dedicated line at full bandwidth between two devices but hub doesnít provide a dedicated line. Hub share the bandwidth.

13. Give one function of a gateway.

Ans. The gateway is a node in a network, which serves as a proxy server and a firewall system, that prevents the unauthorised access.

14. What is a modem?

Ans. Modem stands for Modulator/Demodulator, which converts analog signal into digital signal and again digital signal into analog signal. It is used to connect the computers and transmit data using telephone lines.

15. A company wants to form a network on their five computers to a server within the company premises. Represent star and ring topologies diagrammatically for this network.

Ans.

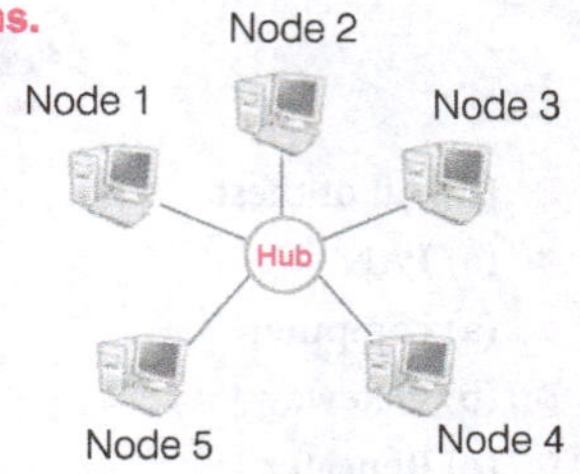

Star topology

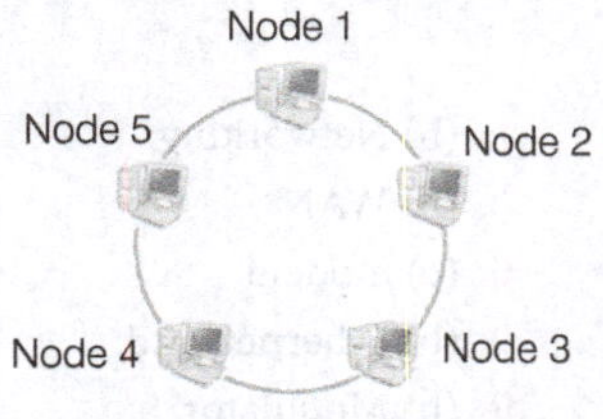

Ring topology

16. What is difference between star topology and bus topology of network?

Ans. In star topology, nodes are connected to server individually whereas in bus topology all nodes are connected to server along a single length of cable.

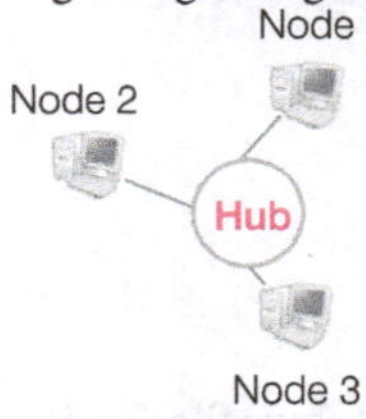

Star topology

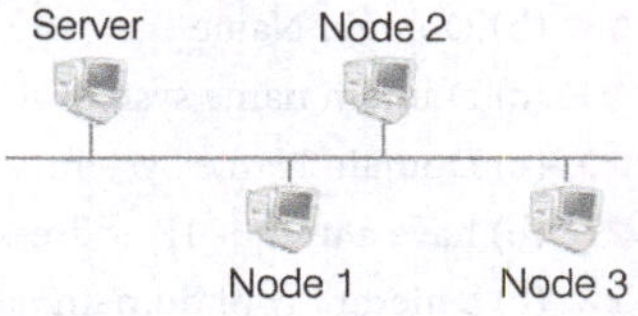

Bus toplogy

17. HTTP stands for? NCERT

Ans. HTTP stands for Hypertext Transfer Protocol

18. What is WWW?

Ans. WWW (World Wide Web) is a system of Internet servers that supports hypertext and multimedia to access several Internet protocols on a single interface.

19. Give one suitable example of each URL and domain name.

Ans. URL - http : // www.gabsclasses.com/aboutus

Domain name - www.gabsclasses.com

20. How is a domain name different from a URL?

Ans. Domain names are used in URLs to identify particular web servers, For example, in the URL http://www.cbse.nic.in/welcome.htm, the domain name is www.cbse.nic.in

21. Can we use URL to access a web page? How?

Ans. Yes, as a location on a web server, which is called a website and each website has a unique address known as URL. So, URL can be used to access a web page.

22. Write the full form of the following

(i) GNU (ii) XML

Ans. (i) GNU - Gnu's Not Unix

(ii) XML - eXtensible Markup Language

23. Write two points of difference between XML and HTML. CBSE SQP 2022-23, 2023-24

Ans. XML is designed for data storage and transport, focusing on data structure and custom tags. HTML is used for displaying content on the web, with predefined tags for formatting and layout.

XML is case-sensitive and allows user-defined tags. HTML is not case-sensitive and uses a fixed set of tags defined by the language.

24. **(i) Expand the following terms** CBSE SQP 2023-24

POP3 , URL

(ii) Give one difference between XML and HTML.

Ans. (i) Post Office Protocol 3, Uniform Resource Locator

(ii) HTML (HyperText Markup Language) use pre-defined tags while XML (eXtensible Markup Language) use user-defined tags.

25. **When a user browsers a website, the web server sends a text file to the web browser. What is the name of this?**

Ans. Cookies

26. **Briefly discuss the role of a web browser in Internet surfing.**

Ans. A web browser is a software program that allows a user to locate and display web pages, acts as Internet surfing.

27. **Name one commonly used open source Internet browser and one commonly used open source operating system.**

Ans. Open source internet browser - Chromium

Open source operating system - Linux

28. **(i) Define the term web hosting.**

(ii) Name any two web browsers. CBSE 2024

Ans. (i) Web hosting is a service that allows users to put a website or a webpage onto the Internet, and make it a part of the World Wide Web.

(ii) Google Chrome,Microsoft Edge

29. **Define the following terms:** CBSE SQP 2022 Term II

(a) WWW **(b) Web hosting**

Ans. (a) WWW is a set of protocols that allow you to access any document on the internet through the naming systems based on URLs.

(b) Web hosting is a service that allows organisations and individuals to post a website or web page onto the server, which can be viewed by everyone on the Internet.

30. **MR. Lal owns a factory which manufactures automobile spare parts. Suggest him the advantages of having a web page for his factory.**

Ans. The web page provides the information to the clients about his factory of spare parts. Moreover, he can receive the order on the Internet from the client using the web page.

Short Answer Type I Questions

31. **Write the name of benefits of networking.**

Ans. Some of the benefits of networking are

(i) File sharing
(ii) Hardware sharing
(iii) Application sharing
(iv) User communication
(v) Access to remote database

32. **Differentiate between the terms Internet and Intranet.**

Ans. Differences between Internet and Intranet are as follows:

Internet	Intranet
Access by an individual with dial-up access.	Access by only Authorized employees.
Information on Internet could be general, public and advertisement.	Information on Intranet could be specific, corporate and proprietary.

33. **Write any two uses of Internet.**

Ans. Two uses of Internet are as follows:

(i) Internet is used for communication and information sharing.

(ii) Business use the Internet to provide access to complex databases.

34. **Identify the following devices**

(i) An intelligent device that connects several nodes to form a network and redirects the received information only to intended node(s).

(ii) A device that regenerates (amplifies) the received signal and re-transmits it to its destinations.

Ans. (i) Switch

(ii) Repeater

35. **Define repeaters with its two types.**

Ans. Repeaters are used to amplify the signals, when they are transported over a long distance.

Repeaters are of two types

(i) Amplifier It amplifies or boosts the incoming signals. So, it amplifies both the signal and any concurrent noise.

(ii) Signal repeater It only amplifies the signal and filters out the noise signals. So, we get only the clear signal at the receiver end.

36. **When the computer network uses telephone lines as communication channel then MODEM is used as a data communication device. Now, explain the working of MODEM.**

Ans. MODEM performs the task of modulation at sender's site and DEModulation at the receiver's site. Basically, our computer generates data in the form of digital signals, which need to be forwarded to the receiver through telephone lines.

Since, telephone lines can carry only analog signals. So, digital signals need to be converted to analog signals at sender's site, this is called modulation. At receiver's site, again analog signals should be converted back to the original digital signals, then this is called demodulation.

37. List one advantage and one disadvantage of star topology. CBSE SQP 2024-25

Ans. **Advantage of star topology** Error detection and isolation is easy.

Disadvantage of star topology Costly due to independent cables.

38. Write two points of difference between XML and HTML. CBSE SQP 2022-23, 2023-24

Ans.

XML	HTML
Tags are user defined	Tags are predefined
Tags are case sensitive	Tags are not case sensitive

39. Expand the following terms :

XML, PPP

Ans. XML – eXtensible Markup Language

PPP – Point-to-Point Protocol

40. Differentiate between XML and HTML.

Ans. XML was designed to describe data and to focus on what data is. HTML was designed to display data and to focus on how data looks.

HTML is about displaying information while XML is about describing information.

41. Distinguish between website and web browser.

Ans. Website is a place on the net servers to keep web pages. Web browser is a software application for retrieving, presenting and traversing information on the world wide web.

Short Answer Type II Questions

42. Mr. GopiNath Associate Manager of Unit Nations corporate recently discovered that the communication between his company's accounts office and HR office is extremely slow and signals drop quite frequently. These offices are 120 metre away from each other and connected by an Ethernet cable.

(i) Suggest him a device which can be installed in between the office for smooth communication.

(ii) What type of network is formed by having this kind of connectivity out of LAN, MAN and WAN?

Ans. **(i) The device that can be installed between the office for smooth communication is repeater.**

(ii) The type of network is Local Area Network (LAN).

43. Write a short note on LAN and PAN.

Ans. **LAN** A Local Area Network is a computer network covering a small geographical area like a home, office or small group of building such as building in a school. Computer connected to a LAN can share information and peripheral equipments.

PAN It stands for Personal Area Network. It is a computer network used for communication among computer and different technological devices close to it. Technologies such as bluetooth and infrared communication form a wireless PAN around the device.

44. Which device is used to connect dissimilar networks?

Ans. A gateway is a device, which is used to connect dissimilar networks. The gateway establishes an intelligent connection between a local network and external network, which are completely different in structure. Gateway also serve as proxy server and a firewall system that prevents the unauthorised access.

45. Define hub and write its functions and types.

Ans. A hub connects several computers together and acts as a central node or server.

Function of a hub

(i) Interconnects number of computers or users.

(ii) All the incoming data packets received by the hub are send to all hub ports and from their, the data is sent to all the computers, connected in a hub network.

Hub are of two types

(i) Active hub It acts as repeater. It amplifies the signal as these move from one device to another.

(ii) Passive hub It simply passes the signal from one connected device to another.

46. What is the difference between star topology and bus topology of network?

Ans. Differences between star topology and bus topology are as follows :

Star Topology	Bus Topology
All the nodes are directly connected with the central node or server.	There is a single length of transmission medium on which various nodes are attached and the server can be anywhere in the transmission cable.
Easy to detect faults.	Faults cannot be easily detected.
It is fast in transmission.	Becomes slow with increase in node.

47. Define tree topology. Also, write down its two limitations.

Ans. A tree topology is an extension and variation of bus topology. Its basic structure is like an inverted tree, where the root acts as a server.

Limitations

- Long cables are required for this kind of topologies.
- There is the dependence on the root node.

48. Give two advantages and two disadvantages of star topology. CBSE 2022, CBSE SQP 2024-25

Ans. Advantages of Star Topology are

- Ease of service All the data passes through the hub. The hub makes it easy to troubleshoot by offering a single point for error connection.
- Centralized control Computers are connected by cable segments to centralized component, called a hub or switch.

Disadvantages of Star Topology are

- Long cable length Requires more cable than a linear bus.
- Difficult to expand Extra hardware is required (hubs or switches) which adds to cost.

49. Sahil, a class X student, has just started understanding the basics of Internet and web technologies. He is a bit confused in between the terms "World Wide Web" and "Internet". Help him in understanding both the terms with the help of suitable examples of each.

Ans. Internet and World Wide Web are not the same thing. Let's break down the difference:

- **Internet** A global network of interconnected computers that allows information to be shared and accessed worldwide.
- **World Wide Web (WWW)** A system of interconnected documents accessed through the internet using hypertext links.
- **Example** The internet is like the highway whereas World Wide Web is like the specific destinations on that highway.

50. What is the difference between domain name and IP address?

Ans. Difference between domain name and IP address are as follows:

IP address	Domain name
IP address is an identifier for a computer or device on a TCP/IP network.	A domain name is a name that identifies one or more IP addresses.
e.g. 1.160.10.240 could be an IP address.	e.g. The domain name microsoft.com represents about a dozen IP addresses.

51. Write a short note on IP address and give its characteristics.

Ans. Internet internally follows number based addressing system. Numeric address of a computer is called IP address by a scheme called Domain Name System (DNS).

The IP address consists of four numbers from 0 to 255 separated by dots.

The characteristics of an IP address are as follows

(i) IP addresses are unique.
(ii) IP addresses are global and standardised.

52. Discuss the functioning of a web browser and web server.

Ans. A web browser acts as a link/ interface between a client and a server. Its primary function is to display various web documents to the clients requesting them. A web server functions to accept browser requests, generate responses, maintain the web apps, and accept the client data.

53. What is the difference between a webpage and website?

Ans.

Web Page	Website
A single document accessible on the internet.	A collection of related web pages under a single domain.
Can contain text, images, videos, and links.	Comprises multiple web pages linked together.
Typically identified by a unique URL.	Identified by a main domain name (e.g., www.arihant.com).
Example An article or a blog post.	**Example** The entire blog or news site.

Long Answer Type Questions

54. Granuda consultants are setting up a secured network for their office campus at Faridabad for their day-to-day office and web based activities. They are planning to have connectivity between 3 buildings and the head office situated in Kolkata.
Answer the questions (i) to (v) after going through the building positions in the campus and other details, which are given below. Competency Based Que.

Distance between various buildings

Building RAVI to Building JAMUNA	120 m
Building RAVI to Building GANGA	50 m
Building GANGA to Building JAMUNA	65 m
Faridabad Campus to Head Office	1460 km

Number of computers

Building RAVI	25
Building JAMUNA	150
Building GANGA	51
Head Office	10

(i) Suggest the most suitable place (i.e. block) to house the server of this organisation. Also, give a reason to justify your suggested location.

(ii) Suggest a cable layout of connections between the building inside the campus.

(iii) Suggest the placement of the following devices with justification:

(a) Switch (b) Repeater

(iv) The organisation is planning to provide a high speed link with its head office situated in the Kolkata using a wired connection. Which of the following cable will be most suitable for this job?

(a) Optical fibre (b) Co-axial cable
(c) Ethernet cable

(v) Consultancy is planning to connect its office in Faridabad which is more than 10 km from Head office. Which type of network will be formed?

Ans. (i) The most suitable place to house the server is JAMUNA because it has maximum number of computers.

(ii)

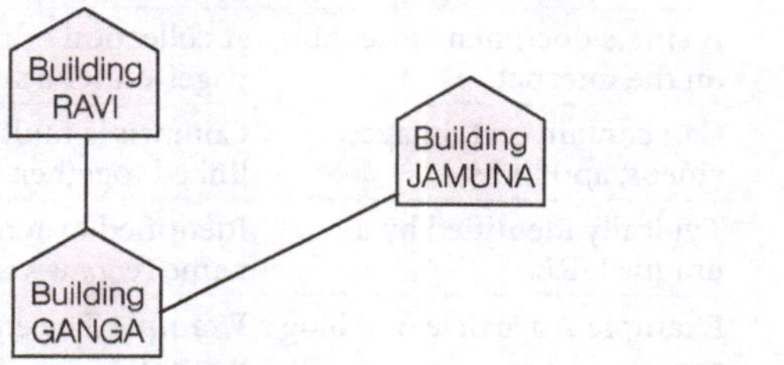

(iii) (a) Switches are needed in every building to share bandwidth in every building.

(b) Repeaters may be skipped as per above layout, (because distance is less than 100 m) however, if building RAVI and building JAMUNA are directly connected, we can place a repeater there as the distance between these two buildings is more than 100 m.

(iv) (b) Co-axial cable.

(v) MAN

55. Trine Tech Corporation (TTC) is a professional consultancy company. The company is planning to set up their new offices in India with its hub at Hyderabad. As a network adviser, you have to understand their requirement and suggest them the best available solutions. Their queries are mentioned as (i) to (v) below. **Competency Based Que.**

Physical locations of the blocks of TTC

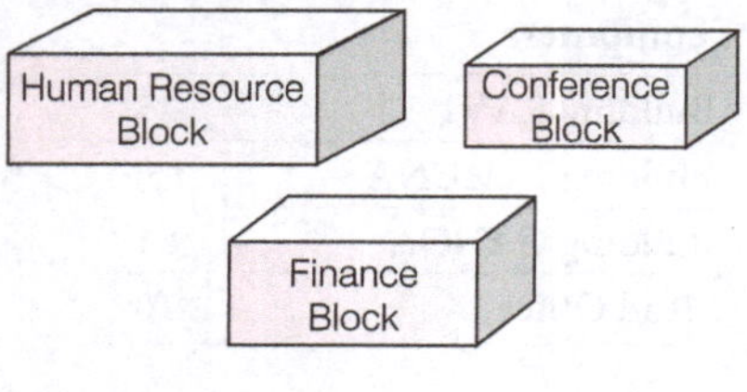

Block to block distance (in m)

Block (From)	Block (To)	Distance
Human Resource	Conference	110
Human Resource	Finance	40
Conference	Finance	80

Expected number of computers to be in each block

Block	Computers
Human Resource	25
Finance	120
Conference	90

(i) Which will be the most appropriate block, where TTC should plan to install their server?

(ii) Draw a block to block cable layout to connect all the buildings in the most appropriate manner for efficient communication.

(iii) What will be the best possible connectivity out of the following, you will suggest to connect the new set up of offices in Bengalore with its London based office.

- Satellite Link
- Infrared
- Ethernet

(iv) Which of the following device will be suggested by you to connect each computer in each of the buildings?

- Switch
- Modem
- Gateway

(v) Company is planning to connect its offices in Hyderabad which is less than 1 km. Which type of network will be formed?

Ans. (i) TTC should install its server in finance block as it is having maximum number of computers.

(ii)

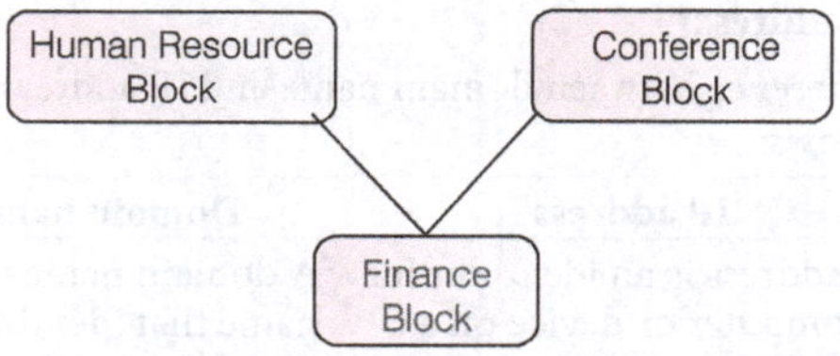

The above layout is based on minimum cable length required, which is 120 metres in the above case.

(iii) Satellite Link.

(iv) Switch.

(v) LAN

56. **Freshminds University of India is starting its first campus in Ana Nagar of South India with its centre admission office in Kolkata. The university has three major blocks comprising of Office block, Science block and Commerce block is in 5 km area campus.** **Competency Based Que.**

As a network expert, you need to suggest the network plan as per (i) to (v) to the authorities keeping in mind the distance and other given parameters.

Expected wire distance between various locations

Office Block to Science Block	90 m
Office Block to Commerce Block	80 m
Science Block to Commerce Block	15 m
Kolkata Admission Office to Ana Nagar Campus	450 km

Expected number of computers to be installed at various locations in the university are as follows:

Office Block	10
Science Block	140
Commerce Block	30
Kolkata Admission Office	8

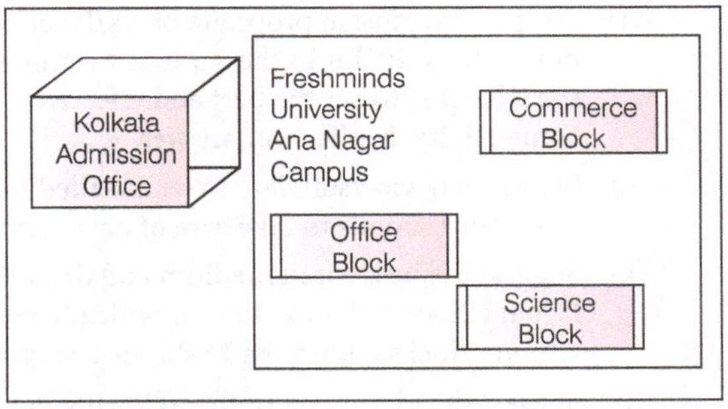

(i) Suggest the authorities, the cable layout amongst various blocks inside university campus for connecting the blocks.

(ii) Suggest the most suitable place (i.e. block) to house the server for this university with a suitable reason.

(iii) Suggest an efficient device form the following to be installed in each of the block to connect all the computers.

(a) Modem

(b) Switch

(c) Gateway

(iv) Suggest the most suitable (very high speed) service to provide data connectivity between admission office located in Kolkata and the campus located in Ana Nagar form the following options:

- Telephone line
- Fixedline dial-up connection
- Co-axial cable network
- GSM
- Leased line
- Satellite connection.

(v) University is planning to connect its campus in Kolkata which is more than 100 km. Which type of network will be formed?

Ans. (i)

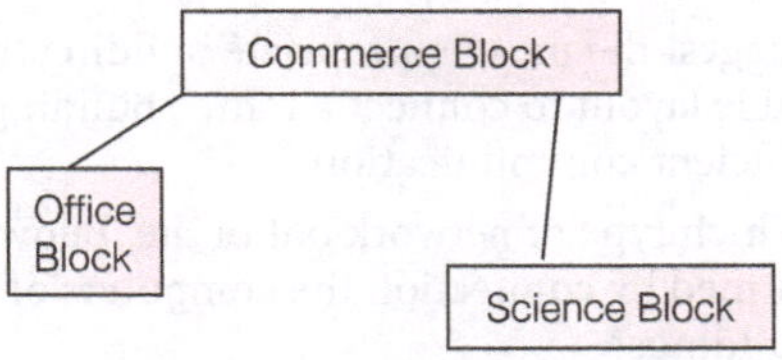

(ii) The most suitable place to house the server is Science Block as it has maximum number of computers. Thus, reducing the cabling cost and increases efficiency of network.

(iii) (b) Switch is the device to be installed in each of the blocks to connect all the computers.

(iv) Satellite connection.

(v) MAN

57. **Expertia Professional Global (EPG) in an online corporate training provider company for IT related courses. The company is setting up their new campus in Mumbai. You as a network expert have to study the physical locations of various buildings and the number of computers to be installed. In the planning phase, provide the best possible answers for the queries (i) to (v) raised by them.** **Competency Based Que.**

Physical locations of the buildings of EPG

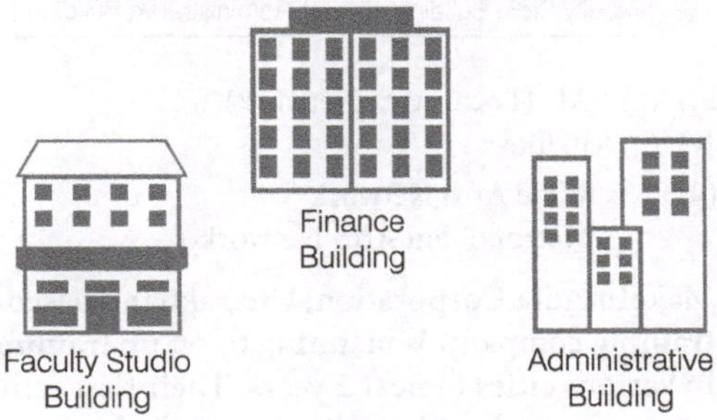

Building to building distance (in metre)

From	To	Distance
Administrative Building	Finance Building	60
Administrative Building	Faculty Studio Building	120
Finance Building	Faculty Studio Building	70

Expected computers to be installed in each building

Buildings	Computers
Administrative Building	20
Finance Building	40
Faculty Studio Building	120

(i) Suggest the most appropriate building, where EPG should plan to install the server.

(ii) Suggest the most appropriate building to building cable layout to connect all three buildings for efficient communication.

(iii) Which type of network out of the following is formed by connection the computers of these three buildings?

(a) LAN (b) MAN
(c) WAN

(iv) Which wireless channel out of the following should be opted by EPG to connect to students of all over the world?

(a) Infrared (b) Microwave
(c) Satellite

(v) Expand the following

- WAN
- MAN

Ans. (i) EPG should install the server in the Faculty Studio Building as it has maximum number of computers.

(ii)

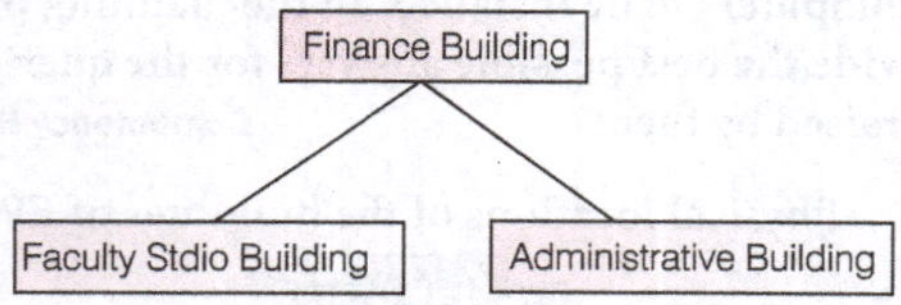

(iii) (a) LAN (Local Area Network).

(iv) (c) Satellite.

(v) • Wide Area Network
• Metropolitan Area Network

58. **MakeInIndia Corporation, Uttarakhand based IT training company, is planning to set up training centres in various cities in next 2 years. Their first campus is coming up in Kashipur district. At Kashipur campus, they are planning to have 3 different blocks for App development, Web designing and Movie editing. Each block has number of computers, which are required to be connected in a network for communication, data and resource sharing. As a network consultant of this company, you have to suggest the best network related solutions for them for issues/problems raised in question nos. (i) to (v), keeping in mind the distances between various blocks/locations and other given parameters.** **Competency Based Que.**

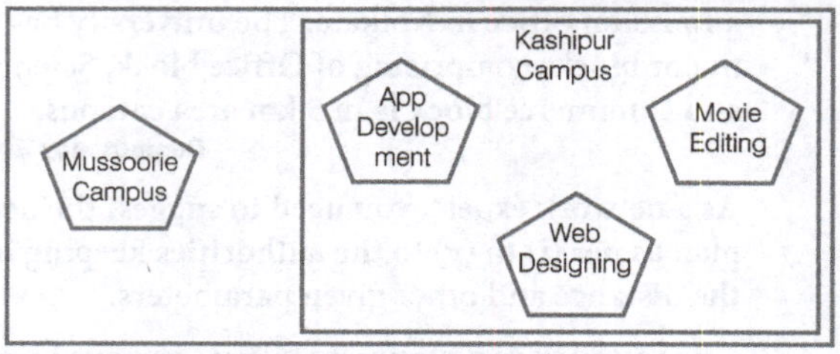

Distance between various blocks/locations:

Block	Distance
App development to Web designing	28 m
App development to Movie editing	55 m
Web designing to Movie editing	32 m
Kashipur Campus to Mussoorie Campus	232 m

Number of computers

Block	Number of Computers
App development	75
Web designing	50
Movie editing	80

(i) Suggest the most appropriate block/location to house the SERVER in the Kashipur campus (out of the 3 blocks) to get the best and effective connectivity. Justify your answer.

(ii) Suggest a device/software to be installed in the Kashipur Campus to take care of data security.

(iii) Suggest the best wired medium and draw the cable layout (Block to Block) to economically connect various blocks within the Kashipur Campus.

(iv) Suggest the placement of the following devices with appropriate reasons:

(a) Switch / Hub (b) Repeater

(v) Suggest a protocol that shall be needed to provide Video Conferencing solution between Kashipur Campus and Mussoorie Campus.

Ans. (i) Movie Editing block , as it has the maximum number of computers.

(ii) Firewall

(iii) Optical fibre cable

Cable Layout

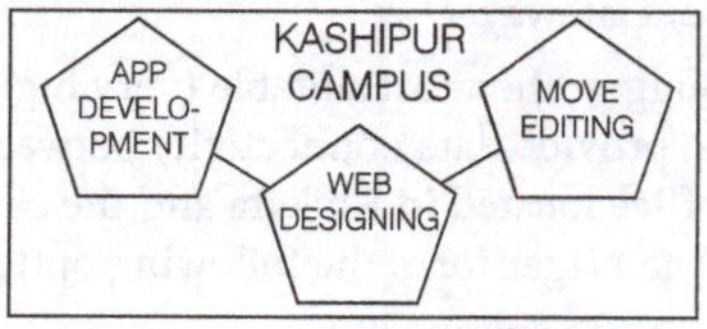

(iv) (a) Switch/Hub to be placed in all buildings , as all have multiple computers that need to be connected.

(b) Repeater to be placed between App Development and Movie Editing blocks as the distance between them is larger.

(v) VoIP – Voice over Internet Protocol.

59. Quickdev, an IT based firm, located in Delhi is planning to set up a network for its four branches within a city with its Marketing department in Kanpur. As a network professional, give solutions to the questions (i) to (v), after going through the branches locations and other details which are given below

Competency Based Que.

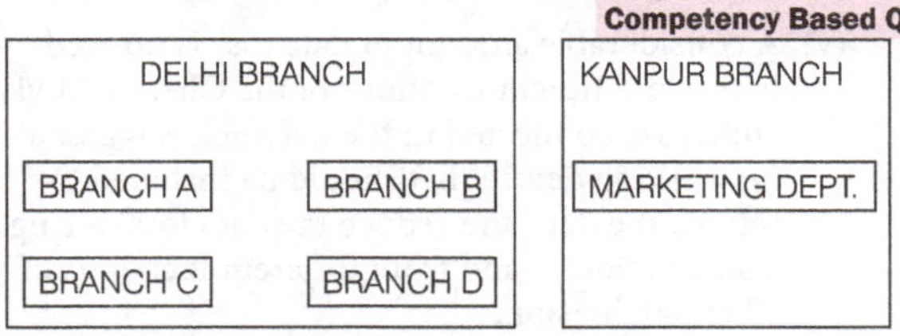

Distance between various branches is as follows

Branch	Distance
Branch A to Branch B	40 m
Branch A to Branch C	80 m
Branch A to Branch D	65 m
Branch B to Branch C	30 m
Branch B to Branch D	35 m
Branch C to Branch D	15 m
Delhi Branch to Kanpur	300 km

Number of computers in each of the branches

Branch	Number of Computers
Branch A	15
Branch B	25
Branch C	40
Branch D	115

(i) Suggest the most suitable place to install the server for the Delhi branch with a suitable reason.

(ii) Suggest an ideal layout for connecting all these branches within Delhi.

(iii) Which device will you suggest, that should be placed in each of these branches to efficiently connect all the computers within these branches?

(iv) Delhi firm is planning to connect to its Marketing department in Kanpur which is approximately 300 km away. Which type of network out of LAN, WAN or MAN will be formed? Justify your answer.

(v) Suggest a protocol that shall be needed to provide help for transferring of files between Delhi and Kanpur branch. **CBSE 2023**

Ans. (i) Branch D is the most suitable place to install the server for the Delhi branch because it has maximum number of computer.

(ii)

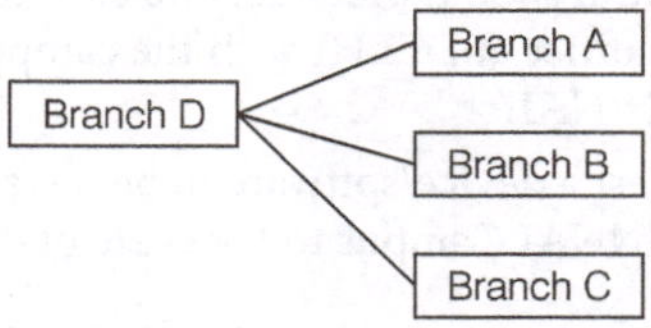

(iii) Switch (iv) WAN (Wide Area Network)

(v) FTP (File Transfer Protocol)

60. Meticulous EduServe is an educational organization. It is planning to setup its India campus at Chennai with its head office at Delhi. The Chennai campus has 4 main buildings – ADMIN, ENGINEERING, BUSINESS and MEDIA

CBSE SQP 2023-24, Competency Based Que.

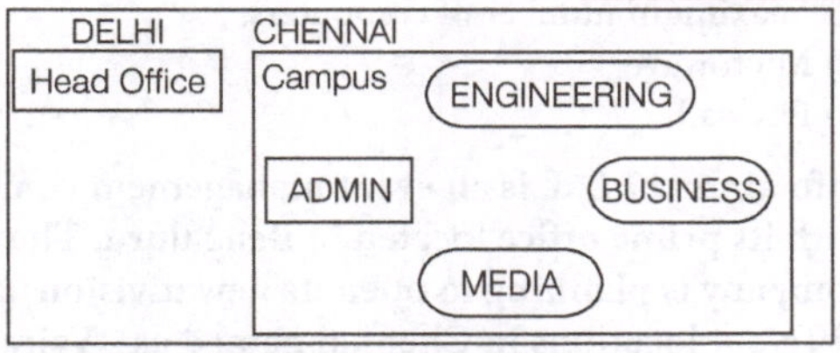

Block to Block distances (in metre)

From	To	Distance
ADMIN	ENGINEERING	55 m
ADMIN	BUSINESS	90 m
ADMIN	MEDIA	50 m
ENGINEERING	BUSINESS	55 m
ENGINEERING	MEDIA	50 m
BUSINESS	MEDIA	45 m
DELHI HEAD OFFICE	CHENNAI CAMPUS	2175 km

Number of computers in each of the blocks/Center is as follows:

ADMIN	110
ENGINEERING	75
BUSINESS	40
MEDIA	12
DELHI HEAD	20

(a) Suggest and draw the cable layout to efficiently connect various blocks of buildings within the CHENNAI campus for connecting the digital devices.

(b) Which network device will be used to connect computers in each block to form a local area network?

(c) Which block, in Chennai Campus should be made the server? Justify your answer.

(d) Which fast and very effective wireless transmission medium should preferably be used to connect the head office at DELHI with the campus in CHENNAI?

(e) Suggest a device/software to be installed in the CHENNAI Campus to take care of data security.

Ans. (a)

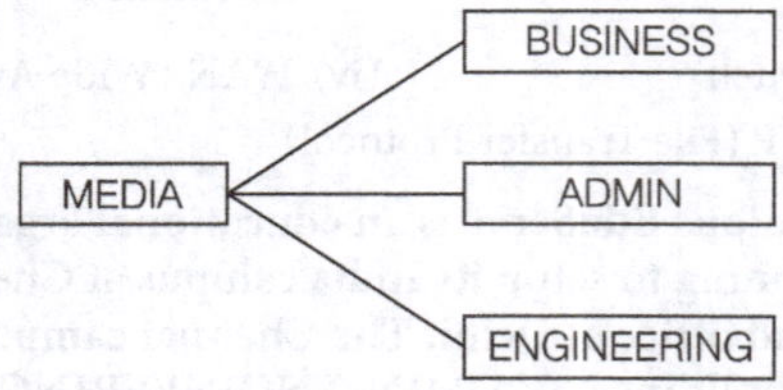

(b) Switch

(c) ADMIN block should be made the server because it has maximum number of computers.

(d) Microwave

(e) Firewall

61. Infotainment Ltd. is an event management company with its prime office located in Bengaluru. The company is planning to open its new division at three different locations in Chennai named as - Vajra, Trishula and Sudershana. **CBSE 2024**

You, as a networking expert need to suggest solutions to the questions in part (i) to (v), keeping in mind the distances and other given parameters.

Competency Based Que.

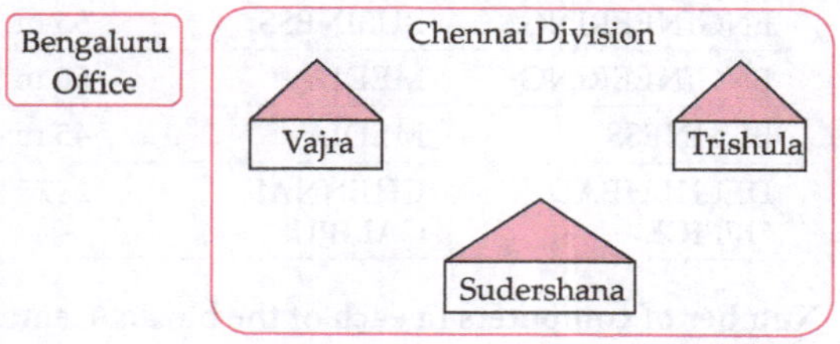

Distances between various locations :

Vajra to Trishula	350 m
Trishula to Sudershana	415 m
Sudershana to Vajra	300 m
Bengaluru Office to Chennai	2000 km

Number of computers installed at various locations :

Vajra	120
Sudershana	75
Trishula	65
Bengaluru Office	250

(i) Suggest and draw the cable layout to efficiently connect various locations in Chennai division for connecting the digital devices.

(ii) Which block in Chennai division should host the server? Justify your answer.

(iii) Which fast and effective wired transmission medium should be used to connect the prime office at Bengaluru with the Chennai division?

(iv) Which network device will be used to connect the digital devices within each location of Chennai division so that they may communicate with each other?

(v) A considerable amount of data loss is noticed between different locations of the Chennai division, which are connected in the network. Suggest a networking device that should be installed to refresh the data and reduce the data loss during transmission to and from different locations of Chennai division.

Ans. (i)

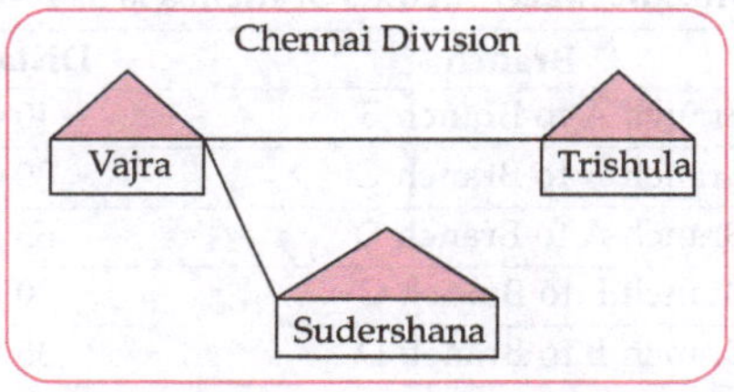

(ii) Vajra can host the server as it has a maximum number of computers.

(iii) Optical Fibre

(iv) Switch/Hub/Router

(v) Repeater

62. Event Horizon Enterprises is an event planning organization. It is planning to set up its India campus in Mumbai with its head office in Delhi. The Mumbai campus will have four blocks/buildings - ADMIN, FOOD, MEDIA, DECORATORS. You, as a network expert, need to suggest the best network-related solutions for them to resolve the issues/problems mentioned in points (I) to (V), keeping in mind the distances between various blocks/buildings and other given parameters. **CBSE SQP 2024-25**

Competency Based Que.

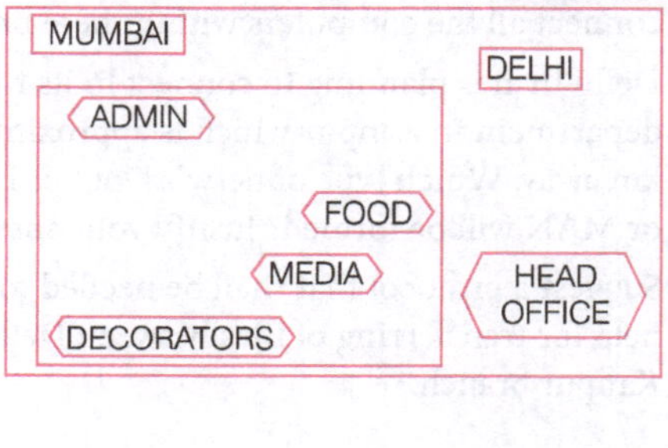

Block to Block distances (in Mtrs.)

From	To	Distance
ADMIN	FOOD	42 m
ADMIN	MEDIA	96 m
ADMIN	DECORATORS	48 m
FOOD	MEDIA	58 m
FOOD	DECORATORS	46 m
MEDIA	DECORATORS	42 m

Distance of Delhi Head Office from Mumbai Campus = 1500 km

Number of computers in each of the blocks/Center is as follows

ADMIN	25
FOOD	18
MEDIA	30
DECORATORS	20
DELHI HEAD OFFICE	18

(I) Suggest the most appropriate location of the server inside the MUMBAI campus. Justify your choice.

(II) Which hardware device will you suggest to connect all the computers within each building?

(III) Draw the cable layout to efficiently connect various buildings within the MUMBAI campus. Which cable would you suggest for the most efficient data transfer over the network?

(IV) Is there a requirement of a repeater in the given cable layout? Why/ Why not?

(V) (A) What would be your recommendation for enabling live visual communication between the Admin Office at the Mumbai campus and the DELHI Head Office from the following options:

(a) Video Conferencing

(b) Email

(c) Telephony

(d) Instant Messaging

Or

(B) What type of network (PAN, LAN, MAN, or WAN) will be set up among the computers connected in the MUMBAI campus?

Ans. (I) MEDIA : As it houses the maximum number of computers.

(II) Switch : A Switch is an intelligent device that can connect multiple nodes.

(III) Cable layout

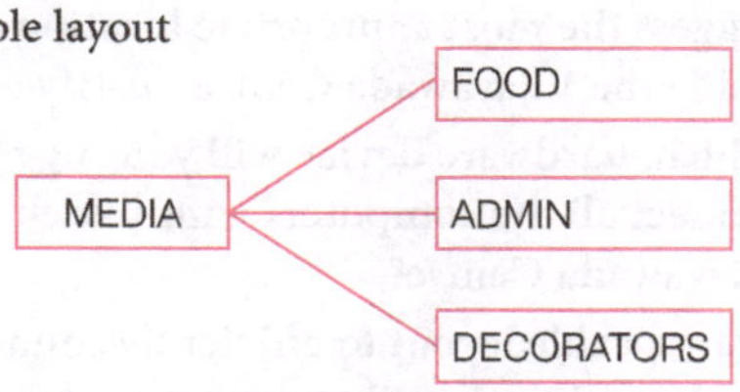

Optical fibre cable should be used

(IV) Yes , between MEDIA and Admin as the distance is 96m.

(V) (A) Video conferencing

Or

(B) LAN

63. **'Swabhav' is a big NGO working in the field of psychological treatment and counselling, having its head office in Nagpur. It is planning to set up a centre in Vijayawada. The Vijayawada Center will have four blocks -ADMIN, PSYCHIATRY, PSYCHOLOGY, and ICU. You, as a network expert, need to suggest the best network-related solutions for them to resolve the issues/problems mentioned in questions (i) to (v), keeping the following parameters in mind:**

CBSE 2025, Competency Based Que.

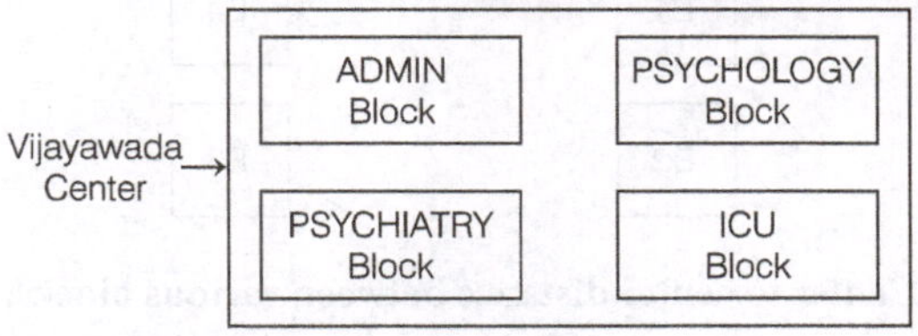

Block to Block distances (in metres):

From	To	Distance
ADMIN	PSYCHIATRY	65 m
ADMIN	PSYCHOLOGY	65 m
ADMIN	ICU	65 m
PSYCHIATRY	PSYCHOLOGY	100 m
PSYCHIATRY	ICU	50 m
PSYCHOLOGY	ICU	50 m

Distance of Nagpur head office from Vijayawada Centre = 700 km

Number of computers in each block is as follows:

Block	No. of Computers
ADMIN	16
PSYCHIATRY	40
PSYCHOLOGY	19
ICU	20

(i) **Suggest the most appropriate location of the server inside the Vijayawada Centre. Justify your choice.**

(ii) **Which. hardware device will you suggest to connect all the computers within each block of Vijayawada Centre?**

(iii) **Draw a cable layout to efficiently connect various blocks within the Vijayawada Centre.**

(iv) **Where should the router be placed to provide internet to all the computers in the Vijayawada Centre?**

(v) (a) **The Manager at Nagpur wants to remotely access the computer in admin block in Vijayawada. Which protocol will be used for this?**

Or (b) **Which type of network (PAN, LAN, MAN or WAN) will be set up among the computers connected with Vijayawada Centre?**

Ans. (i) PSYCHIATRY block (highest no. of computers)

(ii) SWITCH

(iii) ADMIN → PSYCHIATRY (65m)
ADMIN → PSYCHOLOGY (65m)
ADMIN → ICU (65m)

(iv) ADMIN

(v) (a) FTP *Or* (b) LAN

Case Study Based Questions

Case Study 1

A company ABC Enterprises has four blocks of buildings as shown below:

Center to center distance between various blocks:

B3 to B1	50 m
B1 to B2	60 m
B2 to B4	25 m
B4 to B3	170 m
B3 to B2	125 m
B1 to B4	90 m

Number of computers in each block:

B1	150 m
B2	15 m
B3	15 m
B4	25 m

Computers in each block are networked but blocks are not networked. The company has now decided to connect the blocks also. **[CBSE Question Bank]**

(i) **Suggest the most appropriate topology for the connections between the blocks.**
(a) Ring topology (b) Star topology
(c) Mesh topology (d) Bus topology

(ii) **The company wants Internet accessibility in all the blocks. The suitable and cost-effective technology for that would be**
(a) satellite (b) lease line
(c) telephone line (d) broadband

(iii) **Which one of the following device will you suggest for connecting all the computers with in each of their blocks?**
(a) Switch/Hub (b) Modem
(c) Telephone (d) Repeater

(iv) **The company is planning to link its head office situated in New Delhi with the offices in hilly areas. Suggest a way to connect it economically.**
(a) Microwaves (b) Coaxial cable
(c) Fibre optic (d) Radiowaves

(v) **Suggest the most appropriate location of the server, to get the best connectivity for maximum number of computers.**
(a) Block B2 (b) Block B1
(c) Block B4 (d) Block B3

Ans. (i) (*b*) By using star topology, all the blocks can be connected with each other using hub or switch in low cost.

(ii) (*d*) The most suitable way to connect all blocks are to use broadband. As the distance between some blocks are greater than 100m, therefore lease line or cables will not be suitable. Also, the speed of broadband will be good in comparison to other cable options due to use of fibre optics.

(iii) (*a*) Switch/Hub are the network connecting device which are used to connect all the devices with each other in the form of generally star topology.

(iv) (*d*) The most suitable wireless channel for hilly areas are radio waves. Due to the property that it can penetrate walls, plants etc.

(v) (*b*) Block B1 is the most suitable block to install server as it has the maximum computers.

Case Study 2

Meerut school in Meerut is starting up the network between its different wing. There are four buildings named S,J,A and H. The distance between various buildings is as follows:

A to S	**200m**
A to J	**150m**
A to H	**50m**
S to J	**250m**
J to H	**350m**

Number of computers in each Buildings

S	**130**
J	**80**
A	**160**
H	**50**

(i) What type of topology is best suited for above network?

(a) Star topology (b) Bus topology

(c) Ring topology (d) Mesh topology

(ii) Suggest the most suitable place (i.e. buiding) to house the server of this school.

(a) Building S (b) Building J

(c) Building A (d) Building H

(iii) Which one of the following devices will you suggest for connecting all the computers with in each of their buildings?

(a) Switch/Hub (b) Modem

(c) Telephone (d) Repeater

(iv) The school is planning to link its head office situated in New Delhi with the offices in hilly areas. Suggest a way to connect it economically.

(a) Micro waves (b) Coaxial cable

(c) Fibre optic (d) Radio waves

(v) The company wants interest acessibility in all the blocks. The suitable and cost-effective technology for that would be:

(a) Satellite (b) Lease line

(c) Telephone (d) Broadband

Ans. (i) (a) Star topology

(ii) (c) Building A

(iii) (a) Switch/Hub

(iv) (d) Radio waves

(v) (d) Broadband

Case Study 3

A group of entrepreneurs is planning to launch a new online education platform called "LearnSmart." They want to create an interactive website where students can access courses, submit assignments, and communicate with instructors. To achieve this, they need to understand several key concepts related to web services.

(i) What should the entrepreneurs consider when choosing a domain name for their website?

(a) It should be easy to remember.

(b) It should include keywords relevant to education.

(c) It should be unique and not infringe on existing trademarks.

(d) All of the above

(ii) Which of the following is a valid URL for accessing the homepage of the LearnSmart website?

(a) www.learnsmart.com/home

(b) learnsmart homepage

(c) http://learnsmart.com

(d) Both (a) and (c)

(iii) When designing the website, which markup language will the entrepreneurs use to structure the content on their web pages?

(a) XML (b) HTML

(c) JSON (d) CSS

(iv) Which software application will users need to access the LearnSmart website from their devices?

(a) Web Server (b) Web Hosting

(c) Web Browser (d) HTML Editor

(v) To make the LearnSmart website accessible on the internet, which service will they need to acquire?

(a) Domain registration

(b) Web Hosting

(c) Web Development Tools

(d) All of the above

Ans. (i) (d) All of the above

(ii) (d) Both a and c

(iii) (b) HTML

(iv) (c) Web Browser

(v) (b) Web Hosting

SELF ASSESSMENT TEST

Multiple Choice Questions

1. Which of the following is considered the precursor to the modern internet?
(a) NSFNET (b) WWW
(c) ARPANET (d) HTML
2. Which of the following is a primary difference between HTML and XML?
(a) HTML focuses on describing document structure, while XML focuses on data storage and transport.
(b) HTML allows the use of user-defined tags, while XML does not.
(c) HTML is a language for defining data, while XML is for creating websites.
(d) XML is only used in web browsers, while HTML is used in web servers.
3. It is an Internet service, which allows a particularly configured server computer to distribute documents across the Internet.
(a) HTML (b) WWW (c) XML (d) URL
4. A web browser functions by sending requests to web servers. What protocol does a web browser typically use to request web pages?
(a) File Transfer Protocol (FTP)
(b) Simple Mail Transfer Protocol (SMTP)
(c) Hypertext Transfer Protocol (HTTP)
(d) Domain Name System (DNS)
5. Google chrome is an example of
(a) Web browser (b) Web server
(c) HTTP (d) WWW
6. Which of the following scripting language is used for creating dynamic and interactive websites?
(a) ASP (b) VB Script
(c) PHP (d) All of these

Fill in the Blanks

7. The address of location of the document on WWW is called ....
8. ________ is a markup language designed to store and transport data, often used for data exchange between different systems.
9. The process of making a website available on the internet through a server is known as ________.
10. .... basically refers to the transition from static HTML web pages to a more dynamic web.

State Whether True or False

11. Mobile computing transports data, voice and video over a network via a mobile device.
12. Domain names are used to translate IP addresses into user-friendly names for websites.
13. A web browser is a type of network device used to connect computers in a local area network.

Assertion and Reason Based Questions

Assertion (A) and Reason (R) Type questions. Choose the correct option as:

(a) Both Assertion (A) and Reason (R) are true, and Reason (R) is the correct explanation of Assertion (A)
(b) Both Assertion (A) and Reason (R) are true, but Reason (R) is not the correct explanation of Assertion (A)
(c) Assertion (A) is True, but Reason (R) is False
(d) Assertion (A) is False, but Reason (R) is True

14. **Assertion** The World Wide Web (WWW) is a system that allows users to access information over the internet using hyperlinks and web pages.
Reason The WWW uses the HTTP protocol to transfer data between web servers and web browsers.
15. **Assertion** HTML (Hyper Text Markup Language) is primarily used for creating the structure of web pages.
Reason HTML allows the inclusion of images, videos, and hyperlinks to create interactive web pages.
16. **Assertion** A domain name is a human-readable address used to locate websites on the internet.
Reason A domain name translates to an IP address, which is used by the DNS to route traffic to the correct web server.

Very Short Answer Type Questions

17. Write the difference between 1G and 2G.
18. What can a user do with WWW?
19. Name any two common web browsers.

Short Answer Type Questions

20. What is the difference between HTML and XML?
21. What are the functions of web browser?
22. Explain the uses of web browser.

Long Answer Type Questions

23. Explain the role of HTML, XML, and URLs in the functioning of web services. How do they contribute to the structure and accessibility of websites?
24. What is the significance of domain names and web hosting in the operation of a website? Discuss their role in website accessibility and online presence.
25. Differentiate between web browsers and web servers, and explain their roles in the interaction between users and websites.

Case Study Based Question

26. A company named "TechSolutions" is planning to build a website for their new online software store. They need to ensure that the website is easily accessible to users worldwide. The website should be compatible with various web browsers and offer a smooth user experience. To make this happen, TechSolutions is considering different aspects such as domain names, URLs, HTML, XML, web servers, and web hosting services.

In this context, answer the following questions:

(i) Which of the following components is essential for creating a structured webpage that can be rendered in web browsers?
(a) XML (b) HTML
(c) URL (d) Web Hosting

(ii) What does a URL represent in the context of web services?
(a) A unique identifier for a website's server
(b) A protocol used for data transmission
(c) A standard markup language used for web pages
(d) The address used to access a website or resource on the web

(iii) Which markup language is primarily used for storing and transporting data, typically used in web services for data exchange between systems?
(a) HTML (b) CSS
(c) XML (d) JavaScript

(iv) If TechSolutions wants to ensure their website is accessible worldwide, which of the following would be critical for this task?
(a) Web Hosting (b) XML
(c) HTML (d) Domain Name

(v) Which of the following is responsible for storing and serving the content of a website on the internet?
(a) Web Server (b) Web Browser
(c) URL (d) HTML

Answers

1. (c) 2. (a) 3. (b) 4. (c) 5. (a)
6. (d) 7. URL 8. XML 9. Web hosting
10. Web 2.0 11. True 12. True
13. False 14. (a) 15. (b) 16. (a)
26. (i) → (b), (ii) → (d), (iii) → (c), (iv) → (d), (v) → (a)

07

CHAPTER

Data Communication as the process of sharing information (data) between two or more devices. Just like you talk to your friends, computers and other devices also need ways to "talk" to each other.

YOUR STUDY GOALS

7.1 Concept of Data Communication
7.2 Measuring Capacity of Communication Media
7.3 Switching Techniques
7.4 Transmission Media
7.5 Identifying Nodes in a Networked Communication
7.6 Network Protocols

YOUR PRACTICE GOAL

- Objective Type Questions (25 Qs ; MCQs, True or False, Fill in the Blanks, Assertion and Reason)
- Subjective Type Questions (31 Qs ; VSA, SA, LA)
- Case Based Questions (Objective Case Study-1)

Data Communication

Data Communication as the process of sending and receiving information (data) electronically between two or more devices. This is the foundation of how we connect with each other and access information in today's digital world. We'll be exploring the key concepts and technologies that make this happen, from the basic building blocks of communication to the different ways data travels and the rules (protocols) that ensure smooth and reliable exchange.

7.1 Concept of Data Communication

The term "Data Communication" comprises two words: Data and Communication. Data can be any text, image, audio, video, and multimedia files. Communication is an act of sending or receiving data.

Thus, data communication refers to the exchange of data between two or more networked or connected devices. These devices must be capable of sending and receiving data over a communication medium. Examples of such devices include personal computers, mobile phones, laptops, etc.

Components of Data Communication

There are mainly five components of a data communication system.

There are five key components:

1. **Message** The data or information, which is to be communicated. It can be in various forms, such as text, audio, or video files.
2. **Sender** The device or system that originates and sends the message. Examples include computers, mobile phones, or video cameras.

3. **Receiver** The device or system that receives the message. Similar to the sender, this could be a computer, mobile phone, or other communication devices.
4. **Communication Media** The physical or wireless path through which the message travels from the sender to the receiver. It can be guided media like cables (e.g., twisted pair, fiber optic) or unguided media like radio waves and microwaves.
5. **Set of Rules (Protocol)** The set of predefined rules that ensure proper communication between devices. Protocols manage data formats, transmission speed, and error handling, and are necessary to ensure devices can understand and respond to each other correctly.

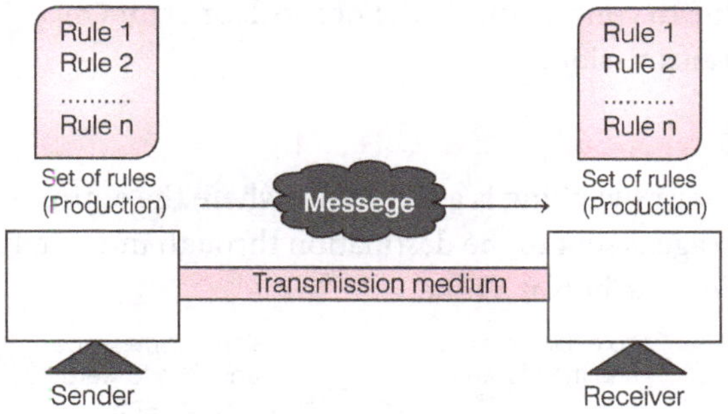

The **type of data transmission** determines the direction in which data moves between the sender and receiver. There are three types of data transmission:

- **Simplex** Data is sent from sender to receiver.
- **Half-duplex** Data can be transmitted in both directions, but not simultaneously.
- **Full-duplex** Data can be transmitted in both directions at the same time.

7.2 Measuring Capacity of Communication Media

In data communication, the transmission medium is also known as channel. A data channel is the medium used to carry information /data from one point to another.

The capacity of communication media is measured in terms of bandwidth and data transfer rate:

Bandwidth

The maximum amount of data that can be transmitted over a communication link in a given amount of time. It's measured in hertz (Hz) and represents the range of frequencies available for data transmission. A higher bandwidth means a higher data transfer rate.

Data Transfer Rate

The number of bits transmitted between a source and destination in one second. It's also known as bit rate and is measured in bits per second (bps).

Note MBps stands for Megabyte per second whereas Mbps stands for Megabit per second.

Measurement of Data Transfer Rate

- One **Kilobit Per Second** (Kbps) equals 1000 bits per second (bps). (Kbps is sometimes also written as 'kbps' both carry the same meaning.)
- One **Megabit Per Second** (Mbps) equals 1000 kbps or one million bps.
- One **Gigabit Per Second** (Gbps) equals 1000 mbps or one million kbps or one billion bps.
- One **Terabit Per Second** (Tbps) equals 1000 gbps or one million mbps or one billion kbps or one trillion bps.

Data rates for non-network equipment are sometimes shown in Bytes Per Second (BPS) rather than bits per second. In those cases:

- One KBPS equals one kilobyte per second.
- One MBPS equals one megabyte per second.
- One GBPS equals one gigabyte per second.
- One TBPS equals one terabyte per second.
- One kilobyte per second equals 8 kilobits per second.

7.3 Switching Techniques

Switching techniques are used for transmitting data across networks. Different types of switching techniques are employed to provide communication between two computers.

These are three types of switching techniques:

(i) Circuit Switching

Circuit switching is a method of communication where a dedicated communication path or circuit is established between two devices before data transmission begins. This circuit remains exclusively reserved for the two communicating parties for the duration of the session, ensuring a continuous, direct connection.

This approach is most commonly associated with traditional telephone systems, where a stable connection is maintained for the entire call. Once the communication session ends, the circuit is released for use by others.

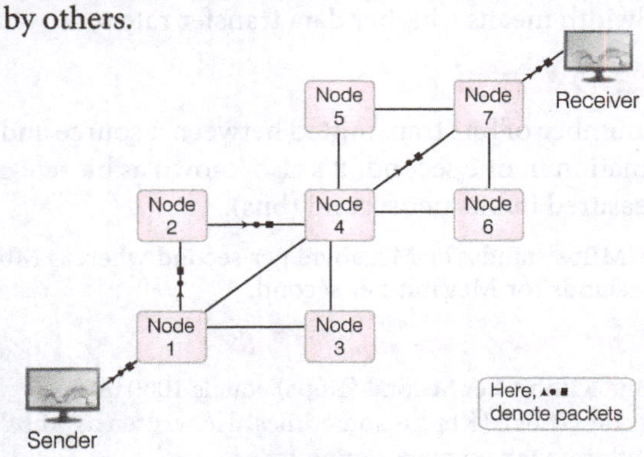

Circuit switching

Advantages of Circuit Switching

- **Dedicated bandwidth** Guarantees consistent communication quality with minimal delays.
- **Low latency** Ideal for real-time communication like voice calls.

Disadvantages of Circuit Switching

- **Inefficient for data transmission** Resources are tied up even during silence or idle periods.
- **Fixed path** Does not adapt dynamically to network congestion.

(ii) Packet Switching

Packet switching is a communication technique used in computer networks where data is divided into small, manageable units called **packets** before being transmitted. These packets are independently routed through the network and may follow different paths to reach the same destination.

At the destination, the packets are reassembled in the correct order to recreate the original message.

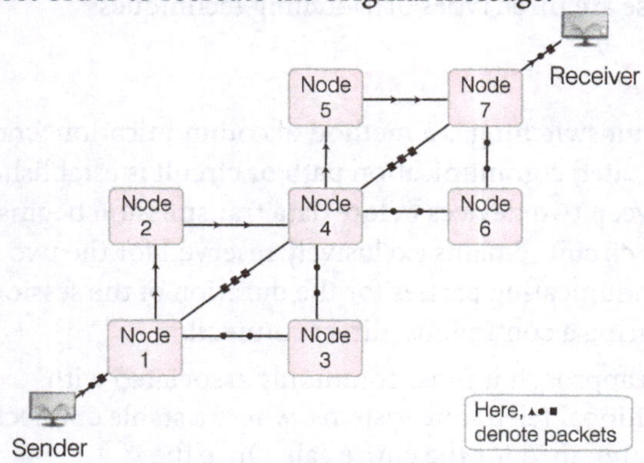

Packet switching

Advantages of Packet Switching

- **Efficient use of bandwidth** Packet switching is efficient because bandwidth is shared among multiple users, and resources are allocated only when data needs to be transmitted.
- **Flexible** Packet switching is flexible and can handle a wide range of data rates and packet sizes.

Disadvantages of Packet Switching

- **Higher latency** Packet switching has higher latency than circuit switching because packets must be routed through multiple nodes, which can cause delay.
- **Packet loss** Packet switching can result in packet loss due to congestion on the network or errors in transmission.

(iii) Message Switching

Message switching is a technique where the entire message is sent to the destination through intermediate nodes, one hop at a time.

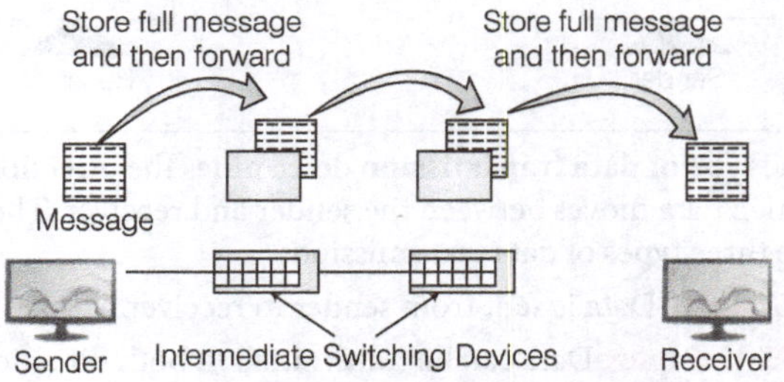

Message switching

Each intermediate node stores the complete message temporarily and forwards it to the next node when the path is available. It is also known as a **store-and-forward network**.

Advantages of Message Switching

- **Efficient Use of Bandwidth** Since the path is not dedicated to one communication, multiple messages from different sources can use the same path, optimizing network resource usage.
- **No Need for Continuous Connection** Unlike circuit switching, the sender and receiver do not need to establish a continuous connection, making message switching flexible, especially for systems where communication might be delayed or interrupted.

Disadvantages of Message Switching

- **Higher Delay** Since messages need to be stored and forwarded at each intermediate node, it can cause significant delays, especially if the network is congested or the nodes are busy.
- **Need for Large Storage** Intermediate nodes must have large storage capacities to hold entire messages, which can be inefficient for longer messages or large networks.

Comparison between the various switching techniques

Criteria	Circuit Switching	Message Switching	Packet Switching
Path established in advance	Yes	No	No
Store and forward technique	No	Yes	Yes
Message follows multiple routes	No	Yes	Yes

Quick Test 1

1. What is meant by data communication? Explain its components.
2. Write about data transfer rate.
3. Find out how many hertz is 10 Megahertz.
4. Which of the following switching services are appropriate for setting up
   (i) a voice communication and
   (ii) internet service respectively?

7.4 Transmission Media

A transmission medium is a physical path between the transmitter (source) and the receiver (destination) i.e. it is the channel through which data is sent from one place to another. Transmission media is broadly classified as guided or unguided. Below figure shows the classification of transmission media:

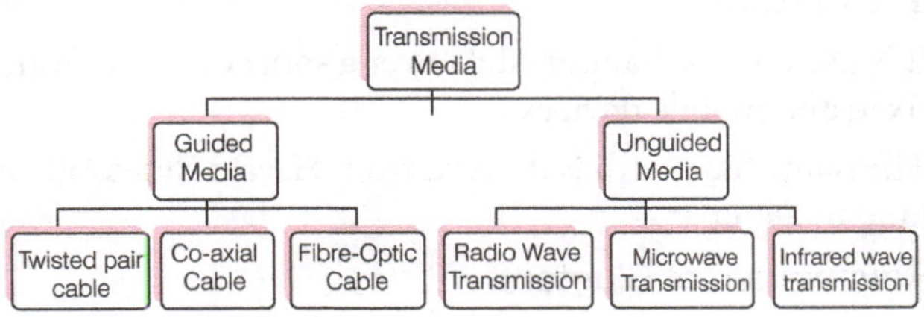

Guided Media or Wired Technologies

In wired technologies, the computers in a network are connected through wire or cable. The data signal physically gets transferred from the transmitting computer to the receiving computer through the wired transmission medium.

Some of guided media are given below:

Ethernet Cable or Twisted Pair Cable

In twisted pair cable, we have pairs of copper wires twisted together to reduce interference. One of the wire is used to carry signals to the receiver and the other is used only as a ground reference. e.g. Local Area Networks (LAN's) are used twisted pair cable.

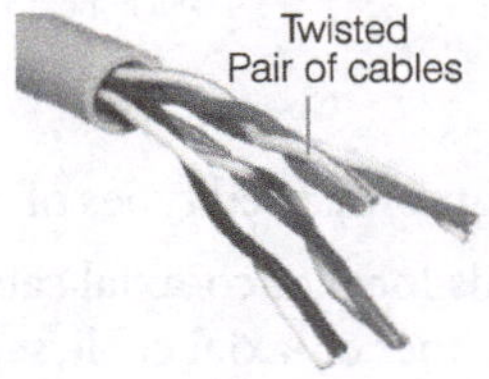

There are two types of twisted pair cables

(i) **Shielded Twisted Pair (STP) Cable** It has shielding of the individual pair of wires, which protects it from external interference and crosstalk.

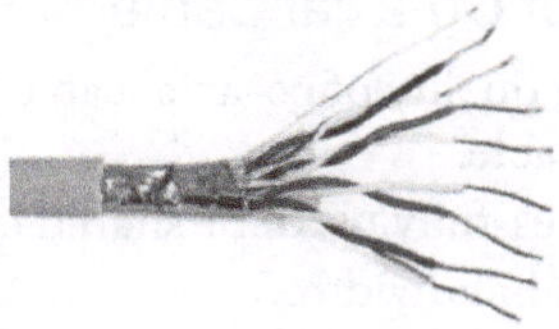

(ii) **Unshielded Twisted Pair (UTP) Cable** It has two unshielded wires twisted around each other.

UTP cables are found in many LAN networks and telephone systems.

Advantages of Twisted Pair Cable

- Simple structure
- Physically flexible
- Easy to install
- Very inexpensive

Disadvantages of Twisted Pair Cable

- Due to high attenuation, signals cannot be transported
- Over a long distance without using repeaters
- Due to low bandwidth, it is unsuitable for broadband application.
- Data rates supported 1 Mbps to 10 Mbps

Co-axial Cable

A single copper conductor surrounded by insulation, shielding, and an outer protective layer. Co-axial cable is commonly used in transporting multi-channel television signals in cities.

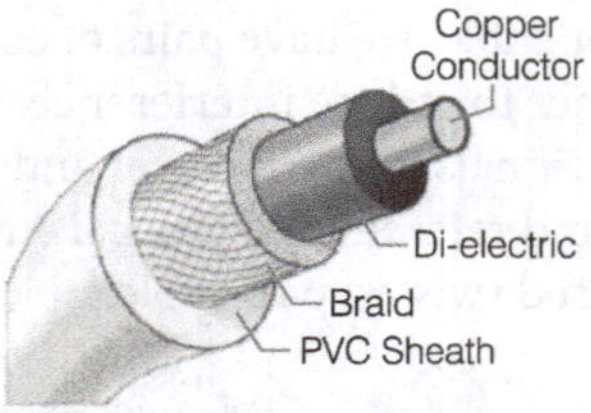

Co-axial cable

The two most commonly used types of co-axial cable are:

(i) **Thicknet** This form of co-axial cable is thick. The length of thicknet co-axial cable segments can be upto 500 metre long.

(ii) **Thinnet** This form of co-axial cable is thinner and using this cable, nodes having maximum distance of 185 metre can be joined.

Advantages of Co-axial Cable

- Transmission quality of co-axial cable is better than twisted pair cable.
- It can be successfully used for shared cable network.
- IT offers high bandwidth.

Disadvantages of Co-axial Cable

- It is expensive compared to twisted pair cable.
- These are difficult to manage and reconfigure as compared to twisted pair cable.

Optical Fibre

Optical Fibre transmits data as light signals through glass or plastic Fibres.

There are three main parts in optical Fibre:

(i) **Core** It is the section through which data travels in the form of light.

(ii) **Cladding** The cladding is covering of the core. Its function is to reflect back the light into the core, as it is a denser medium.

(iii) **Protective Coating** It is the outer cover of cladding for the protection of the optical Fibre.

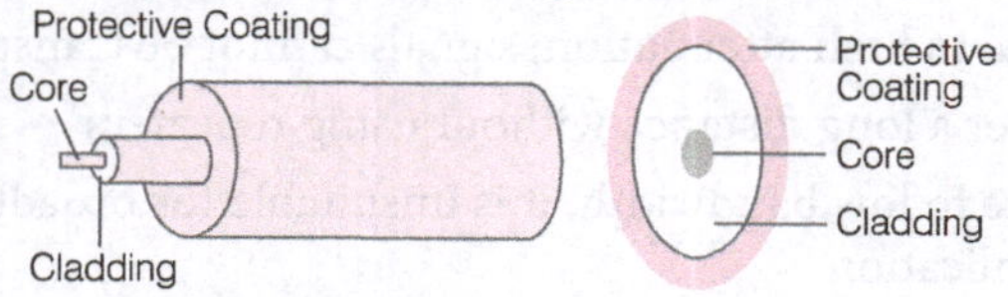

Optical fibre

There are two types of Fibre optic cables:

(i) **Single Mode** It supports a segment length of upto 2 kms and bandwidth of upto 100 Mbps.

(ii) **Multi Mode** The maximum segment length of multimode is upto 100 kms and bandwidth of upto 2 Gbps.

Note Such types of cables are usually used in backbone networks. Backbone networks interconnect different segments of the network and provide a path to exchange information between different LANs or subnetworks.

Advantages of Optical Fibre Cable

- It is immune to electrical and magnetic fields. So, the data does not get disturbed and pure data is retrieved on the other end.
- Highly suitable for harsh industrial environment.
- It guarantees secure transmission and has a very high transmission capacity.
- Bandwidth is upto 10 Gbps.

Disadvantages of Optical Fibre Cable

- Connecting two Fibres together or a light source to Fibre is different.
- Optical cables are expensive to install but last longer than copper cables.
- Optical Fibres require more protection around the cable as compared to copper cables.
- Fibre optic cables are quite fragile and may need special care to make them sufficiently robust for an office environment.

Unguided Media or Wireless Technologies

When the computers in a network are interconnected and data is transmitted through waves, then they are said to be connected through unguided media. Some of the unguided media are given below:

1. Bluetooth

It is used for exchanging data over a short distance from fixed and mobile devices.

The name bluetooth is derived from Harald Bluetooth, a king in Denmark.

Advantages of Bluetooth

(i) We are able to share data without any cord.

(ii) We are able to share data without disclosing our private data.

(iii) We can use bluetooth on many different devices, as it is available in all devices such as laptops, cell phones, music players, hand sets, printers and a lot more other products.

Disadvantages of Bluetooth

(i) Battery consumption
(ii) Data transfer is very slow

2. Infrared

It is the frequency of light that is not visible to human eye. These high frequencies allow high speed data transmission.

Infrared communiucation requires a transceiver (a combination of transmitter and receiver) in both devices that communicate.

Infrared communication is playing an important role in wireless data communication due to the popularity of laptop computers, personal digital assistants (PDAs), digital cameras, mobile phones, pagers and other devices but being a line-of-sight transmission, it is sensitive to fog and other atmospheric conditions.

Advantages of Infrared

(i) Power consumption is less.
(ii) Circuitry cost is less.
(iii) Circuitry is simple.
(iv) Secure mode of transmission.

Disadvantages of Infrared

(i) Line of sight, need to be in a straight line for communication.
(ii) Limited in a short range.
(iii) Can be blocked by common materials like walls, people, plants, etc.

3. Radiowave

When two terminals communicate by using radio frequencies, then such type of communication is known as radiowave transmission.

Radiowave transmission set-up has two parts; Transmitter and Receiver.

(i) Devices which transmits signals are termed as **transmitter.**
(ii) Devices which receives signals are termed as **receiver.**

Both the transmitter and receiver use antennas to radiate and capture the radio signal.

Advantages of Radiowave

(i) Cheaper than wired network.
(ii) Provides mobility.
(iii) Easy to use over difficult terrain.

Disadvantages of Radiowave

(i) Insecure communication can be easily taped.
(ii) It is affected by the weather conditions such as rain, storms, thunder, etc.

4. Microwave

It permits data transmission rates of about 16 gigabits per second. This type of transmission uses high frequency radio signals to transmit data through space. Like radio waves, microwaves can pass through obstacles viz. buildings, mountains etc. Microwaves offer a line of sight method of communication.

A transmitter and receiver of a microwave system are mounted on very high towers and both should be visible to each other (line of sight).

In case of microwave transmission, curvature of the earth, mountains and other structures often block the line of sight.

Hence several repeater stations are required for long distance transmission thereby increasing the cost considerably.

It is generally used for long distance telephonic communications.

Advantages of Microwave

(i) Microwave transmission does not require the expense of laying cables.
(ii) It can carry 25000 voice channels at the same time.
(iii) Since no cables are to be laid down so it offers ease of communication over difficult terrains like hilly areas.

Disadvantages of Microwave

(i) Signals become weak after travelling a certain distance and require amplification. To overcome this problem, repeaters are used at regular intervals (25-30 kms).

The data signals are received, amplified and then retransmitted. This makes it a very expensive mode of communication

(ii) Installation and maintenance of microwave links is very expensive.
(iii) The transmission is affected by weather conditions like rain, thunderstorms etc.

7.5 Identifying Nodes in a Networked Communication

Nodes in a networked communication are identified by IP addresses on the internet and MAC addresses on local Ethernet networks. These addresses allow messages to be routed and delivered to the correct recipient.

MAC Address

- It stands for **Media Access Control**, and also known as **Physical address, hardware address**, or **BIA (Burned In Address)**.
- It is globally unique; it means two devices cannot have the same MAC address. It is represented in a hexadecimal format on each device, such as **00:0a:95:9d:67:16**.
- It is 12-digit, and 48 bits long, out of which the first 24 bits are used for **OUI**(Organization Unique Identifier), and 24 bits are for NIC/vendor-specific.
- It works on the data link layer of the OSI model.
- It is provided by the device's vendor at the time of manufacturing and embedded in its NIC, which is ideally cannot be changed.
- The **ARP protocol** is used to associate a logical address with a physical or MAC address.

IP Address

An Internet Protocol (IP) address is a unique numerical identifier for every device or network that connects to the internet.

Typically assigned by an internet service provider (ISP), an IP address is an online device address used for communicating across the internet.

There are two versions of IP addresses that are commonly used on the internet: IPv4 and IPv6. An IPv4 address is expressed as a set of four dotted decimal numbers, where each octet is separated by a period, such as 192.168.35.4.

The three digits in the first octet represent a particular network on the internet while the rest of the digits represent the actual host address within the local network, such as a workstation or a server.

An IPv6 address represents eight groups of four hexadecimal digits separated by colons, such as 2620:cc:8000:1c82:544c:cc2e:f2fa:5a9b.

7.6 Network Protocols

Protocol refers to the set of rules applicable for a network. The protocol defines standardised format for the data packet to be transmitted through the network.

Some of the commonly used protocols are as follows

HTTP (HyperText Transfer Protocol)

HTTP is an application layer protocol. It is widely used protocol. This protocol is used by the world wide web. HTTP defines how messages are formatted and transmitted and what actions web servers and browsers should take in response to various commands. It is a request/response standard between a client (end-user) and a server (website). e.g. when you enter a URL in your browser, this actually sends an HTTP command to the web server directly to fetch and transmit the requested web page. It is generic, stateless and object oriented protocol.

HTTPS (HyperText Transfer Protocol Secure)

HTTPS is the secure version of **HTTP**. It encrypts the data transferred between your web browser and the website to ensure that sensitive information (like passwords and credit card numbers) is kept safe from hackers. This added layer of security is crucial when you are sharing personal information online. Websites using HTTPS can be recognized by a **padlock icon** in the address bar.

TCP/IP (Transmission Control Protocol/Internet Protocol)

TCP/IP is the communication protocol for the Internet. It defines the rules, computers must follow to communicate with each other over the Internet. The TCP/IP is a protocol used in E-mail transmission.

The TCP/IP is a protocol, which is responsible for finding path for the destination. It also splits the message into several datagrams, if it does not fit in one datagram.

Therefore, these datagrams are sent through different alternate paths towards the destination. The TCP makes sure that the datagram arrives at the destination correctly. While IP is responsible for moving packet of data from source to destination. It handles the address part of each packet so that it reaches to the right destination.

PPP (Point-to-Point Protocol)

It is a data link layer protocol, which encapsulates other network layer protocols for transmission on synchronous and asynchronous communication lines. The PPP is used with dial-up Internet connections including ISDN. It is a layered protocol, which is used for transmitting the IP data packets over usual telephone lines.

It encapsulates packets into PPP frames and then forwards them to the server over the serial transmission lines.

PPP defines the format of frame to be exchanged between devices on one or multiple links and also defines the authenticity of the two devices.

FTP (File Transfer Protocol)

It is a standard network protocol used to transfer files from one host to another host over a TCP-based network, such as the Internet.

FTP is based on client/server principle. It establishes two connections between the hosts. One connection is used for data transfer, which is opened and closed for each file transfer and the other for control information, which remains connected during the entire interactive FTP session.

Remote Login (Telnet)

Telnet is a protocol used for creating a connection with a remote computer. Once your telnet client establishes a connection to the remote host, telnet client becomes a virtual terminal, allowing you to communicate with the remote host from your computer.

It establishes a connection either with command line client or with a programmatic interface. Telnet provides an error free connection, which is always faster than the latest conventional modems.

Protocols used in Email

Email protocols are standardized rules that govern how emails are sent and received over the internet. They ensure that email clients (like Outlook or Gmail) can communicate effectively with mail servers (the computers that store and manage email). The two basic types of email protocols are:

SMTP (Simple Mail Transfer Protocol)

SMTP is a protocol used for sending emails over the internet. It operates on the TCP/IP network and is responsible for transferring email messages from the sender's mail server to the recipient's mail server. When you send an email, SMTP ensures that the message is properly delivered to the correct address.

POP3 (Post Office Protocol Version 3)

POP3 is a protocol used to retrieve emails from a remote mail server. When you check your email, POP3 allows you to download your messages to your local device (like a computer or smartphone). Once downloaded, the emails can typically be accessed offline. POP3 is helpful for users who want to manage their emails without needing a constant internet connection.

VOIP

VoIP (Voice over Internet Protocol) is a technology that enables voice calls over the internet instead of traditional phone lines, converting voice signals into digital data. Popular services include Skype, Zoom, WhatsApp, and Google Meet.

Advantages of VoIP

- Reduces communication costs, especially for long-distance calls.
- Works from any location with internet access, on various devices.
- Offers features like video calls, voicemail, and conference calls without extra charges.
- Easy to scale for businesses with minimal hardware changes.
- Can integrate with other tools like email and chat for unified communication.

Disadvantages of VoIP

- Requires a stable, fast internet connection.
- Does not work during outages without backup power.
- Call quality can suffer from delays and packet inconsistency.
- Vulnerable to hacking and eavesdropping, requiring encryption.
- May have unreliable access to emergency services like 911.

Quick Test 2

1. Give two examples of communication technology.
2. What is the importance of communication channel?
3. Name two transmission media for networking.
4. Which protocol is also known as remote login?
5. Distinguish between FTP and Telnet.
6. Name any two Internet protocol used by web.

Mind Map

Identifying Nodes in a Networked Communication

- **MAC (Media Access Control) Address** also known as Physical address, hardware address, or BIA (Burned In Address). It is globally unique; it means two devices cannot have the same MAC address. It is represented in a hexadecimal format on each device, such as 00:0a:95:9d:67:16.
- **IP (Internet Protocol) Address** is a unique numerical identifier for every device or network that connects to the internet. There are two versions of IP addresses that are commonly used on the internet: IPv4 and IPv6.

Components of Data Communication

Message The information being sent, such as text, numbers, photos, sound, or video.
Sender The device that sends the message, such as a computer, phone, or tablet.
Receiver The device that receives the message, such as a computer, television, or printer.
Transmission medium The physical path the message travels, such as a wire, fiber optic cable, or wireless.
Protocol The set of rules that govern the communication between the sender and receiver.

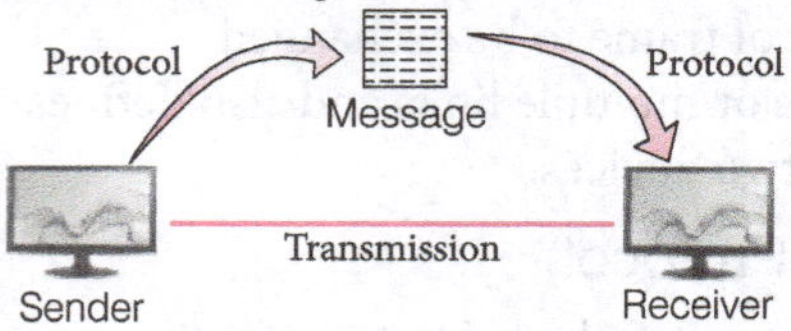

DATA COMMUNICATION

Data Communication comprises two words: **Data** and **Communication**. Data can be any text, image, audio, video, and multimedia files. Communication is an act of sending or receiving data.

Switching Techniques

Circuit Switching In this technique, connection is established between the source and destination before communication.

Packet Switching In this technique, data is divided into small, manageable units called packets before being transmitted.

Types of Data Communication

- **Simplex** Data is sent from sender to receiver.
- **Half-duplex** Data can be transmitted in both directions, but not simultaneously.
- **Full-duplex** Data can be transmitted in both directions at the same time.

Measuring Capacity of Communication Media

- **Bandwidth** of a channel is the range of frequencies available for data transmission. A higher bandwidth means a higher data transfer rate.
- **Data Transfer Rate** The number of bits transmitted between a source and destination in one second. It's also known as bit rate and is measured in bits per second (bps).

Transmission Media

Guided Media or Wired Technologies In this technology, the computers in a network are connected through wire or cable.

- **Ethernet Cable or Twisted Pair Cable** Twisted pair cables have two conductors that are generally made up of copper and each conductor has insulation. There are two types of twisted pair cables– Shielded Twisted Pair (STP) Cable, Unshielded Twisted Pair (UTP) Cable.

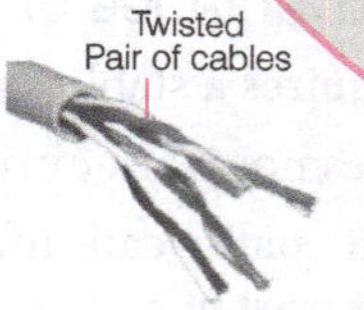

- **Co-axial Cable** A single copper conductor surrounded by insulation, shielding, and an outer protective layer. Co-axial cable is commonly used in transporting multi-channel television signals in cities. The two most commonly used types of co-axial cable are– Thicknet, Thinnet.

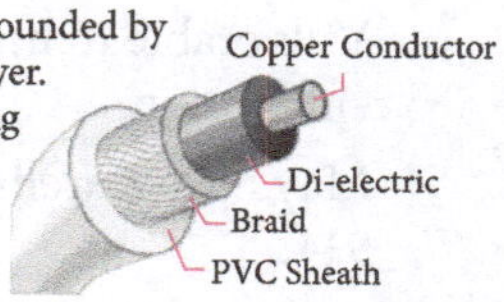

- **Optical Fibre** It transmits data as light signals through glass or plastic Fibres. Three main parts in optical fibre are Core, Cladding and Protective Coating.

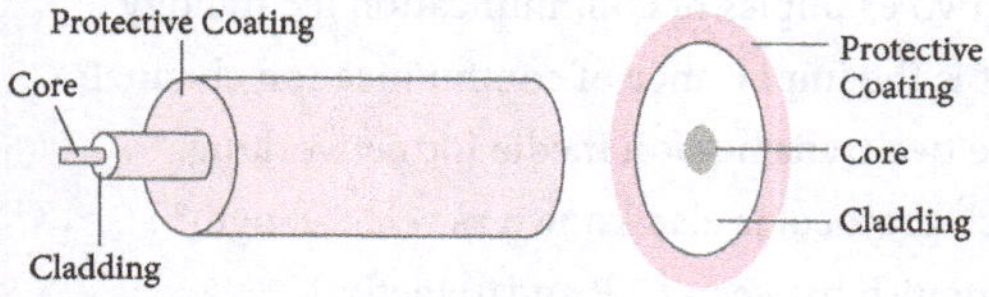

There are two types of Fibre optic cables – Single Mode, Multi Mode

Unguided Media or Wireless Technologies
When the computers in a network are interconnected and data is transmitted through waves, then they are said to be connected through unguided media.

- Bluetooth
- Infrared
- Radiowave
- Microwave

NETWORK PROTOCOLS

HTTP	HyperText Transfer Protocol
TCP/IP	Transmission Control Protocol/Internet Protocol
FTP	File Transfer Protocol
VOIP	Voice over Internet Protocol
HTTPS	HyperText Transfer Protocol Secure
PPP	Point-to-Point Protocol
RDP	Remote Login (Telnet)

NCERT Folder

1. Do mobile phones have a MAC address? Is it different from the IMEI number of mobile phones?

Ans. Yes, mobile phones have a MAC (Media Access Control) address, but it's not directly related to the IMEI (International Mobile Equipment Identity) number. MAC address, typically represented by 12-digit hexadecimal code (e.g., 00:11:22:33:44:55).

In contrast, the IMEI is a 15-digit numerical identifier (e.g., 987892365389002) that uniquely identifies the device at an international level, tied to its hardware. While the MAC address is used for device authentication and security within the local networks

2. List various types of senders on a network.

Ans. In a network, various types of senders (or devices that transmit data) include:

- **Computers (PCs, Laptops)** These are common devices that sends data packets over a network to other devices or servers.
- **Servers** It sends the data to the client in client-server models, such as web servers or database servers.
- **Mobile Devices** Smartphones and tablets that sends the data through Wi-Fi or cellular networks.
- **IoT Devices** Sensors and smart devices that sends the data continuously, often in small packets.
- **Routers and Switches** It sends routing information and forward data packets between network segments.
- **Printers/Scanners** Network-enabled printers or scanners that send data to devices like computers.

3. Find out how many hertz in 10 Megahertz.

Ans. 1MHz = 1,000,000 Hz

So, 10 MHz = 10 × 1,000,000 Hz = 10,000,000 Hz

4. Explore how 5G can impact society.

Ans. 5G has the ability to significantly impact society by enabling faster, more reliable communication and supporting a wide range of new technologies.

Main areas of impact include:

- **Enhanced Connectivity** 5G offers faster data speeds and lower latency, improving internet access and connectivity for smart cities, IoT devices, and remote areas.
- **Healthcare** Remote surgeries, telemedicine, and real-time patient monitoring can be easily done with 5G, improving healthcare delivery and outcomes.
- **Industry and Automation** 5G will accelerate industry 4.0 by enabling more advanced automation, real-time monitoring, and the use of AI in manufacturing, logistics, and supply chains.
- **Entertainment and Media** 5G will enable higher-quality streaming, VR, and AR experiences, transforming gaming, education and other industries.
- **Transportation** Autonomous vehicles and smart traffic systems will benefit from 5G's high-speed communication, improving safety and reducing congestion.

5. Mention any two main advantages of using a network of computing devices.

Ans. The two main advantages of using a network of computing devices are as following:

1. Network of computing devices enhanced collaboration and communication, it enables:
   - Real-time data sharing and synchronization.
   - Video conferencing and online meetings.
   - Instant messaging and email.
   - Collaborative work on projects and documents.
2. Network of computing devices increased flexibility and scalability as a result:
   - It's easy to add new devices and users.
   - Network architecture can be modified or expanded as needed.
   - Network architecture can grow or shrink as organization needs change.
   - Users can easily access network resources from anywhere, at any time.

6. What is the significance of MAC address?

Ans. A MAC (Media Access Control) address is a unique identifier assigned to network devices, ensuring accurate data transmission and network security. MAC addresses prevent data misrouting, enable secure communication, and simplify troubleshooting. They are essential for various network technologies, including Ethernet, Wi-Fi, and Bluetooth.

7. How is IP address different from MAC address? Discuss briefly.

Ans. IP address different from MAC address are as follows

IP Address	MAC Address
An IP address is a logical address used for routing data packets between networks.	A MAC address is a physical address assigned by the device manufacturer for local network communication.
It is assigned by a network administrator and changes with each network connection.	It is unique and permanent identifier, remaining static across networks.

IP Address	MAC Address
An IP address is typically 32 bits (IPv4) or 128 bits (IPv6) in length.	A MAC address is 48 bits (6 bytes) in length and represented in hexadecimal format.
IP addresses function at the network layer.	MAC address operate at the data-link layer.

8. What is data communication? What are the main components of data communication?

Ans. Refer to text on page no. 188. (Data communication, components of Data communication)

9. Which communication mode allows communication in both directions simultaneously?

Ans. Full Duplex (FDX)

10. What are three categories of wired media? Explain them.

Ans. Refer to text on page no. 191 (Guided media or wired technologies).

11. Which transmission media carries signals in the form of light?

Ans. Optical Fibre Cable carries signals in the form of light.

12. List out the advantages and disadvantages of optical fiber cable.

Ans. Refer to text on page no.192 (Optical fibre)

13. What is the range of frequency for radio waves?

Ans. Radio Frequency have a frequency range of: 3KHz to 300 GHz

14. 18 Gbps is equal to how many Bits per second?

Ans. 1 Gbps = 1,000,000,000 bps

So, 18 Gbps = 18 × 1,000,000,000 bps

= 18,000,000,000 bps or 18 billion bits per second.

15. A composite signal contains frequencies between 500 MHz and 1GHz. What is the bandwidth of a signal?

Ans. Highest frequency (fH) = 1 GHz = 1000 MHz

Lowest frequency (fL) = 500 MHz

Bandwidth (BW) = fH – fL

= 1000 MHz – 500 MHz

= 500 MHz

So, the bandwidth of the signal is: 500 MHz or 0.5 GHz.

EXAM PATTERN QUESTIONS

Objective Type Questions

Multiple Choice Questions

1. Frequency is measured in

(a) Cycles per second (b) Hertz
(c) Both (a) and (b) (d) None of these

2. Which transmission media is commonly used in transporting multi-channel television signals in cities?

(a) Optical Fibre (b) Co-axial cable
(c) Ethernet cable (d) None of these

3. A medium that is used in the transmission of a message from one point to another?

(a) Baud rate (b) Communication channel
(c) Network (d) Bandwidth

4. _______ is used for point-to-point communication or unicast communication such as radar and satellite. CBSE 2023

(a) INFRARED WAVES (b) BLUETOOTH
(c) MICROWAVES (d) RADIOWAVES

5. Which protocol is used to ensure secure communication over the internet?

(a) HTTP (b) FTP (c) HTTPS (d) TCP

6. Fill in the blank:

_______ is a communication methodology designed to deliver both voice and multimedia communications over Internet protocol. SQP 2022-23

(a) VoIP (b) SMTP (c) PPP (d) HTTP

7. Which of the following is the communication protocol that sets the standard used by every computer that accesses web based information?

(a) XML (b) HTML
(c) HTTP (d) None of these

8. Which part of TCP/IP is responsible for dividing a file or message into very small parts, at the source computer?

(a) TCP (b) IP
(c) Both (a) and (b) (d) None of these

9. Which protocol out of the following is used to send and receive emails over a computer network? **CBSE 2024**
   (a) PPP (b) HTTP (c) FTP (d) SMTP
10. Which protocol is used to transfer files over the Internet? **CBSE 2024**
   (a) HTTP (b) FTP (c) PPP (d) HTTPS
11. Which of the following options is the correct protocol used for phone calls over the internet? **CBSE 2025**
   (a) PPP (b) FTP (c) HTTP (d) VoIP

Fill in the Blanks

12. One Tbps equals ……… gbps or one ……… mbps.
13. Telnet is a ……… based computer protocol.
14. ……… is the amount of digital data that is moved from one place to another in a given time.
15. …… is a set of rules that needs to be followed by the communicating parties in order to have a successful and reliable data communication over a network. **CBSE 2024**
16. E-mail is the process of sending and receiving messages ……… .

State whether True or False

17. Circuit switching is a communication method where a dedicated path is established and used for the entire session, even if no data is being transmitted.
18. The primary disadvantage of packet switching is its low latency, which makes it ideal for real-time communication like voice calls.
19. ARPANET was the first operational packet-switching network and laid the foundation for modern Internet technologies like TCP/IP.
20. Message switching involves a continuous, dedicated connection between the sender and receiver for the entire message transmission.

Assertion and Reason Based Questions

Assertion (A) and Reason (R) Type questions. Choose the correct option as:

(a) Both Assertion (A) and Reason (R) are true, and Reason (R) is the correct explanation of Assertion (A)
(b) Both Assertion (A) and Reason (R) are true, but Reason (R) is not the correct explanation of Assertion (A)
(c) Assertion (A) is True, but Reason (R) is False
(d) Assertion (A) is False, but Reason (R) is True

21. **Assertion (A)** Packet switching is more efficient in utilizing bandwidth than circuit switching.
    Reason (R) In packet switching, data is divided into packets that are transmitted independently, allowing multiple users to share the same network resources.
22. **Assertion (A)** Circuit switching is well-suited for real-time communication, such as voice calls.
    Reason (R) Circuit switching uses store-and-forward techniques to handle data transmission.
23. **Assertion (A)** Message switching causes higher delays compared to circuit switching.
    Reason (R) In message switching, the entire message is stored at intermediate nodes before being forwarded, leading to potential delays.
24. **Assertion (A)** Full-duplex communication allows data to be sent and received simultaneously.
    Reason (R) In full-duplex communication, data flows in only one direction at a time.
25. **Assertion (A)** The TCP/IP protocol is responsible for ensuring that data packets are delivered to the correct destination.
    Reason (R) TCP/IP splits messages into multiple datagrams and routes them based on network conditions.

Answers

1. (c) Both (a) and (b)
2. (b) Co-axial cable
3. (b) Communication channel
4. (c) MICROWAVES
5. (c) HTTPS
6. (a) VoIP
7. (c) HTTP
8. (a) TCP
9. (d) SMTP
10. (b) FTP
11. (d) VoIP
12. 1000, million
13. Text
14. Data Transfer Rate (DTR)
15. Protocol
16. electronically
17. True
18. False
19. True
20. False
21. (a) Both Assertion (A) and Reason (R) are true, and Reason (R) is the correct explanation of Assertion (A).
22. (c) Assertion (A) is True, but Reason (R) is False.
23. (a) Both Assertion (A) and Reason (R) are true, and Reason (R) is the correct explanation of Assertion (A).
24. (c) Assertion (A) is True, but Reason (R) is False.
25. (a) Both Assertion (A) and Reason (R) are true, and Reason (R) is the correct explanation of Assertion (A).

Subjective Type Questions

Very Short Answer Type Questions

1. What is the difference between video conferencing and chat?

Ans. Chat generally involves one-to-one communication. On the other hand, video conferencing means more than two persons are involved in a discussion.

2. Two people, one knowing only English and other knowing only Chinese are talking to each other. Can we call it a communication?

Ans. No, because only a meaningful exchange of information between two living beings is called communication.

3. Name two switching techniques used to transfer data between two terminals (computers).

Ans. Switching techniques used to transfer data between two terminals are

(i) Circuit switching (ii) Packet switching

4. Which switching technique breaks data into smaller packets for transmission, allowing multiple packets to share the same network resources. CBSE SQP 2024-25

Ans. Packet Switching

5. Write down the name of communication channel used for telephone line and TV.

Ans. Communication channel for telephone line is twisted pair cable and for TV is co-axial cable.

6. Which guided media provides secure transmission amongst all of them?

Ans. Optical fibre provides secure transmission as compared to twisted pair and co-axial cable. As, it is more immune to tapping than copper cables.

7. Give one basic difference between guided and unguided transmission channels.

Ans. In guided transmission media, cables (or wires) are used for communicating data while in unguided transmission, in place of cables, signals travel through air.

8. Which wireless technology is commonly used in mobile phones.?

Ans. Bluetooth is commonly used as a wireless technology in mobile phones and laptops.

9. Give one major disadvantage of bluetooth.

Ans. Only short range communication is possible using bluetooth.

10. Name the protocol, which helps you to communicate between a web server and web browser.

Ans. HTTP

11. Expand the following terms CBSE SQP 2023-24

POP3 , URL

Ans. Post Office Protocol 3, Uniform Resource Locator

12. (a) Expand and explain the term URL CBSE 2025

***Or* (b) Expand the term PPP. What is the use of PPP?**

Ans. (a) URL: Uniform Resource Locator (web address).

Or

(b) PPP: Point-to-Point Protocol (used for direct communication between two nodes).

Short Answer Type I Questions

13. What is the difference between e-mail and chat?

Ans. In order to chat, you need have an account on the same service as the person you are chatting with e.g. on the other hand in case of E-mail, it is not necessary, i.e. you can have an account from any provider and you can establish your own.

14. Explain the term

(i) Bandwidth (ii) Broadband

Ans. (i) Bandwidth It is the communication capacity of a network. It refers to the data carrying capacity of a channel or medium.

(ii) Broadband It is a wide bandwidth data transmission with an ability to simultaneously transport multiple signals and traffic types.

15. In twisted pair cable, two insulated wires are twisted around each other which provides protection against noise. Explain.

Ans. Twisting the cables keep them close together so that, any external magnetic fields must cross both cable at the same time, so the interference created in one cable is cancelled by the almost exact opposite amount of interference in the other.

16. Write two advantages of using an optical fibre cable over an ethernet cable to connect two service stations, which are 190 m away from each other.

Ans. **Low power** Because signals in optical fibres degrade less, lower power transmitters can be used.

Higher data rate Due to higher bandwidth, data rate of optical fibre is more than the data rate of ethernet cable (upto 1 Gbps).

17. Explain two problems that can occur during transmission of data.

Ans. Two problems that can occur during transmission of data are as follows:

(i) **Crosstalk** Disturbance caused by the electric or magnetic fields of one signal in an adjacent signal.

(ii) **Attenuation** During transmission, the signal strength is reduced, this phenomenon is called attenuation.

18. Differentiate between wired and wireless transmission. CBSE 2023

Ans. Differences between wired and wireless transmission are as follows

Wired Transmission		Wireless Transmission	
(i)	These are also called guided media.	(i)	These are also called unguided media.
(ii)	In this media, the computers in a network are connected through wire or cable.	(ii)	In this media, the computers in a network are connected through waves.

19. Write two characteristics of Wi-Fi.

Ans. Characteristics of Wi-Fi are as follows:

(i) It is a wireless solution for getting connected to the Internet.

(ii) It is handy as well as available throughout the journey.

20. (a) **Differentiate between Wired and wireless transmission.**

Or

(b) **Differentiate between URL and domain name with the help of an appropriate example.** CBSE 2023

Ans. (a) Differences between wired and wireless transmission are as follows

Wired Transmission		Wireless Transmission	
(i)	These are also called guided media.	(i)	These are also called unguided media.
(ii)	In this media, the computers in a network are connected through wire or cable.	(ii)	In this media, the computers in a network are connected through waves.

Or

(b) Differences between URL and domain name are as follows

URL	Domain name
URL is a specific character string that constitutes a reference to a resource.	Domain name is a unique name that identifies a particular website and represents the name of the server, where the web pages store.
e.g. https://en.example.org/wiki/ Main_Page	**e.g.** arihant.com

21. What is VoIP?

Ans. VoIP (Voice over Internet Protocol) is simply the transmission of voice traffic over IP based networks. VoIP has been around in one form or another, since 1973 when it began as an experiment by US.

22. What is protocol? Which protocol is used to copy a file from/to a remote server?

Ans. Protocol is a set of rules that two or more computers must follow to communication on network. FTP (File Transfer Protocol) is used to copy a file from/to a remotely located server.

23. (i) **Expand the following** CBSE 2022

(a) SMTP, (b) XML

(ii) **Out of the following, which is the fastest wired and wireless medium of transmission?**

Infrared, Coaxial cable, Optical fibre, Microwave, Ethernet cable

Ans. (i) (a) SMTP stands for Simple Mail Transfer Protocol. It is an internet standard communication protocol for electronic mail transmission.

(b) XML stands for eXtensible Markup Language. It consists of a set of codes, or tags, that describe the text in a digital document where the tags are not predefined.

(ii) Wired -> Optical fibre

Wireless -> Microwave

24. (a) **Write the full forms of the following** CBSE 2023

(i) HTML (ii) TCP

(b) **What is the need of protocols?**

Ans. (a) (i) HTML – HyperText Markup Language

(ii) TCP– Transmission Control Protocol

(b) Protocol allows connected devices to communicate with each other, regardless of any differences in their internal processes, structure or design.

25. Expand the term SMTP. What is the use of SMTP?

Ans. SMTP Simple mail transfer protocol .

SMTP is a common language used to send email. It's a universal set of rules that allow servers and email clients to communicate via the internet. Think of SMTP as the language your computer uses to tell a server where an email goes, what's in the email, what's attached, and more.

Short Answer Type II Questions

26. What is chatting? Is it necessary to be online while chatting?

Ans. Chatting is the textual or multimedia conversation over the Internet. It is a real communication between two users via computer. It is widely interactive text based communication process that takes places over the Internet. Yes, it is necessary to be online while chatting.

27. Explain the three main parts of an optical fibre cable.

Ans. The three main parts of an optical fibre cable are as follows

(i) Core It is the section through which the data travel in the form of light.

(ii) Cladding It is the covering part of core. Its function is to reflect back the light into the core, as it is a denser medium.

(iii) Protective Coating It is the outer cover of cladding for the protection of optical fibre from damage and moisture.

28. Explain wireless technology and give a brief note on the following

(a) Bluetooth

(b) Radiowave

Ans. Wireless technology is also known as unguided media. This media does not use any wires or cable for its connectivity in the network. It uses electromagnetic waves. Some of the wireless technologies are:

(i) Bluetooth
(ii) Radiowave
(iii) Infrared
(iv) Microwave
(v) Satellite communication

(a) Bluetooth It is used for exchanging data over a short distance from fixed and mobile devices. This type of media comes under PAN (Personal Area Network).

(b) RadiowaveWhen two terminals are connected by using radio frequencies, then such type of communication is known as radiowave transmission. Radiowave transmission set-up has two parts.

- **Transmitter** Devices, which transmit signals are termed as transmitter.
- **Receiver** Devices, which receive signals are known as receiver.

29. (i) Give two advantages and two disadvantages of star topology. **CBSE 2022, CBSE SQP 2024-25**

(ii) How is packet switching different from circuit switching? **CBSE SQP 2022-2023, CBSE 2024**

Ans. (i) **Advantages of Star Topology are**

- Ease of service All the data passes through the hub. The hub makes it easy to troubleshoot by offering a single point for error connection.
- Centralized control Computers are connected by cable segments to centralized component, called a hub or switch.

Disadvantages of Star Topology are

- Long cable length Requires more cable than a linear bus.
- Difficult to expand Extra hardware is required (hubs or switches) which adds to cost.

(ii) The differences between Packet Switching and Circuit Switching are as follows:

Packet Switching	Circuit Switching
Data is broken into packets and transmitted independently.	A dedicated communication path is established for the entire duration of the call.
More efficient for bursty data traffic, as the network resources are shared.	Less efficient, as the dedicated path remains unused if no data is being sent.
Connection is established as needed, with no constant connection required.	A fixed, continuous connection is maintained throughout the session.
Suitable for data, email, and internet traffic.	Suitable for voice calls and video conferences.
Example The internet, where packets are routed based on the current network conditions.	**Example** Traditional telephone networks.

Long Answer Type Questions

30. What is switching techniques? Explain any two switching technique.

Ans. Refer to text on page no 189 (Switching techniques).

31. Explain the twisted pair cable in details.

Ans. Refer to text on page no 191 (Ethernet cable or twisted pair cable).

Case Study Based Question

Case Study

A small company, "Creative Designs," has been experiencing consistently slow internet speeds in their office. They have several computers connected to a wireless router provided by their internet service provider (ISP).

They primarily use the internet for web browsing, sending emails with attachments, and occasionally uploading large design files to a cloud storage service. Employees have been complaining about the time it takes to load web pages and the frequent delays in sending and receiving emails.

(i) What is the most probable cause of slow internet speeds experienced by multiple users connected to the same wireless router in the office?

(a) Problems with the physical wiring outside the office building.

(b) Inefficient routing protocols used by the ISP.

(c) Overcrowding of the wireless channel or interference from other devices.

(d) Incorrect IP address configurations on the individual computers.

(ii) If Creative Designs frequently uploads large design files, which factor related to their internet connection would most directly impact the time it takes for these uploads?

(a) The type of web browser used by the employees.

(b) The upload speed provided by their internet service plan.

(c) The domain name of their cloud storage service.

(d) The type of email client software they are using.

(iii) The office uses email extensively, often with attachments. Which network protocol is primarily responsible for sending these emails from their computers?

(a) HTTP (b) FTP

(c) SMTP (d) POP3

(iv) If some employees are closer to the wireless router and experience faster speeds than those farther away, what could be a contributing factor to this difference?

(a) The IP addresses assigned to the closer computers are prioritized.

(b) The wired connection to the ISP is experiencing intermittent issues.

(c) The signal strength of the wireless network weakens with distance.

(d) The web servers of the websites they are visiting are located farther away.

(v) Creative Designs' ISP provided a wireless router. What is the primary function of this router in their local network?

(a) To store all the company's files and applications.

(b) To translate domain names into IP addresses.

(c) To facilitate communication between the computers on the local network and provide access to the internet.

(d) To manage the email accounts of all the employees.

Ans. (i) (c) Overcrowding of the wireless channel or interference from other devices.

(ii) (b) The upload speed provided by their internet service plan.

(iii) (c) SMTP

(iv) (c) The signal strength of the wireless network weakens with distance.

(v) (c) To facilitate communication between the computers on the local network and provide access to the internet.

SELF ASSESSMENT TEST

Multiple Choice Questions

1. Which of the following is NOT considered a basic component of data communication?
   (a) Sender (b) Receiver
   (c) Transmission medium (d) Operating system
2. The capacity of a communication media is typically measured by its:
   (a) Data transfer rate (b) IP address
   (c) Circuit switching (d) Network protocol
3. In which switching technique is the communication channel established for the entire duration of the transmission?
   (a) Packet switching (b) Circuit switching
   (c) IP addressing (d) Routing
4. Which of the following transmission media uses light pulses to transmit data?
   (a) Twisted pair cable (b) Co-axial cable
   (c) Fiber-optic cable (d) Radio waves
5. Which e-mail protocol is a client/server protocol in which e-mail is received and held for you by your internet server?
   (a) POP3 (b) SMTP
   (c) TCP (d) None of these

Fill in the Blanks

6. A unique numerical label assigned to each device participating in a computer network for communication is known as an __________.
7. The process of dividing data into smaller units for transmission across a network is called __________.
8. __________ is a wired communication medium that consists of two insulated wires twisted together to help reduce electromagnetic interference.
9. __________ is a network protocol primarily used for sending email.

State Whether True or False

10. Bandwidth refers to the actual speed at which data is transferred over a communication medium at a specific point in time.
11. Microwaves are a type of wired communication media commonly used for long-distance terrestrial communication towers.
12. POP3 is a client/ server protocol in which E-mail is received and held for you by your Internet server.
13. SMTP is the protocol used for receiving E-mail over the Internet.

Assertion and Reason Based Questions

Assertion (A) and Reason (R) Type questions. Choose the correct option as:

(a) Both Assertion (A) and Reason (R) are true, and Reason (R) is the correct explanation of Assertion (A)
(b) Both Assertion (A) and Reason (R) are true, but Reason (R) is not the correct explanation of Assertion (A)
(c) Assertion (A) is True, but Reason (R) is False
(d) Assertion (A) is False, but Reason (R) is True

14. **Assertion (A)** Circuit switching is well-suited for applications that require a dedicated and guaranteed bandwidth throughout the communication.
    Reason (R) In circuit switching, a physical path is established between the sender and receiver before the data transmission begins and is maintained for the entire duration of the communication.
15. **Assertion (A)** Fiber-optic cables are less susceptible to electromagnetic interference compared to copper cables.
    Reason (R) Data in fiber-optic cables is transmitted as pulses of light rather than electrical signals.
16. **Assertion (A)** HTTP is the underlying protocol used by the World Wide Web.
    Reason (R) HTTP defines how messages are formatted and transmitted between web browsers and web servers.

Very Short Answer Type Questions

17. What is the main purpose of an IP address?
18. Name one advantage of using fiber-optic cable for data transmission.
19. What is the primary function of a network protocol?

Short Answer Type Questions

20. Briefly explain the difference between bandwidth and data transfer rate in the context of measuring communication media capacity.
21. Contrast circuit switching and packet switching as methods for data transmission, highlighting one key characteristic of each.

22. Explain HTTPs.
23. Name two different types of wireless communication media mentioned and provide a brief example of their application.

Long Answer Type Questions

24. Explain the core differences between circuit switching and packet switching. Describe a scenario where each switching method would be most suitable and briefly justify your choice based on their operational characteristics.
25. Discuss the significance of both physical transmission media (wired and wireless) and network protocols in enabling data communication. Provide one key advantage and one key disadvantage for a specific wired medium (e.g., fiber-optic) and a specific wireless medium (e.g., radio waves).
26. Describe the roles of IP addresses and at least two different network protocols (e.g., HTTP and SMTP) in internet communication. Explain how these elements work together to enable a user to send an email from their computer.

Case Study Based Questions

27. Tech Solutions requires a reliable network for their new office. They need to connect approximately 20 computers for internet access, email communication, and sharing files on a local server.

    They are considering different wired and wireless options and need to ensure efficient data transfer and a stable internet connection. They also need to assign unique identifiers to each computer on the network for communication.

    (i) For establishing a wired local area network (LAN) within their office to connect the 20 computers, which of the following would be a common and cost-effective choice of transmission media?
    (a) Radio waves (b) Microwaves
    (c) Twisted pair cable (d) Fiber-optic cable

    (ii) To enable the computers in the office to communicate with each other and access the internet, which fundamental network protocol suite is required?
    (a) HTTP (b) SMTP
    (c) FTP (d) TCP/IP

    (iii) Each computer on the new office network will need a unique identifier for communication within the local network. What is this identifier called?
    (a) Domain Name (b) URL
    (c) IP Address (d) Web Server

    (iv) If Tech Solutions wants to allow employees to easily transfer files between their computers and the local server, which of the following network protocols would be most suitable for this purpose?
    (a) HTTP (b) SMTP
    (c) FTP (d) POP3

    (v) To access websites on the internet from their office computers, which of the following application layer protocols will be primarily used by the web browsers?
    (a) SMTP (b) FTP (c) HTTP (d) TCP

Answers

1. (d) 2. (a) 3. (b) 4. (c) 5. (a)
6. IP address 7. packetization
8. Twisted pair cable 9. SMTP
10. False 11. False 12. True 13. False 14. (a)
15. (a) 16. (a)
27. (i) → (c), (ii) → (d), (iii) → (c), (iv) → (c), (v) → (c)

08 CHAPTER

A database is a collection of interrelated data that helps in the efficient retrieval, insertion, and deletion of data from the database and organizes the data in the form of tables, view, schemas, reports, etc.

Database Concept

YOUR STUDY GOALS

8.1 Database Management System (DBMS)
8.2 File Sytem
8.3 Data Abstraction
8.4 Data Independence
8.5 Data Models

YOUR PRACTICE GOAL

- Objective Type Questions (49 Qs ; MCQs, True or False, Fill in the Blanks, Assertion and Reason)
- Subjective Type Questions (30 Qs ; VSA, SA, LA)
- Case Based Questions (Objective Case Study-1)

A **database** can be defined as a collection of organised information in such a way that user can retrieve data quickly.

A database has the following properties

- It is a collection of related data elements representing real-world information.
- It is logical, coherent and internally consistent.

Needs of Database

A database is a collection of data, usually stored in electronic form. A database is typically designed so that it is easy to store and access information.

The various reasons a database is important are

- **Accurate** A database is accurate as it has all sorts of build in constraints, checks etc. This means that the information available in a database is guaranteed to be correct in most cases.
- **Security of data** Databases have various methods to ensure security of data. There are user logins required before accessing a database and various access specifiers. These allow only authorised users to access the database.
- **Data integrity** This is ensured in databases by using various constraints for data. Data integrity in databases makes sure that the data is accurate and consistent in a database.
- **Easy to research data** It is very easy to access and research data in a database. This is done using Data Query Languages (DQL) which allow searching of any data in the database and performing computations on it.

8.1 Database Management System (DBMS)

A Database Management System is a set of programs that enables users to define, create and maintain the database and provides controlled access to this database.

The primary goal of a DBMS is to provide a way to store and retrieve database information that is both convenient and efficient.

Data in a database can be added, deleted, changed, sorted, searched, etc., using a DBMS. e.g. MySQL, Ingres, MS-Access, Oracle, etc., are the most popular DBMS softwares.

The purpose of a DBMS is to bridge the gap between the information and data. The data stored in memory or on a disk must be converted to usable information.

Advantages of DBMS

The advantages of database management systems are:

1. **Reduces Redundancy** Integrates all files into a single database, eliminating duplicate data and saving memory.

   Example Duplicate student records in library and exam systems are unified in a DBMS.
2. **High Security** Ensures data is secure with controlled access for authorized users only.
3. **Data Integrity** Maintains accurate and consistent data by reducing redundancy and inconsistency.
4. **Supports Multiple Users** Allows multiple users to access the database simultaneously without conflicts.
5. **Data Consistency** Updates data across files consistently, unlike traditional file systems.
6. **Shared Data** Authorized users can share data; admin manages access rights.
7. **Restricts Unauthorized Access** Protects data from unauthorized users.
8. **Backup and Recovery** Automates backups and recovers data efficiently, saving time and resources.

Disadvantages of DBMS

There are many advantages and disadvantages of DBMS (Database Management System). The disadvantages of DBMS are explained below.

1. **Complexity** Requires understanding of its complex functionality to avoid poor design decisions.
2. **Large Size** Occupies significant disk space.
3. **Performance Issues** May not always meet desired performance speed.
4. **System Vulnerability** Centralized resources mean failure impacts all users and applications.

8.2 File Sytem

A file can be understood as a container to store data in a computer. Files can be stored on the storage device of a computer system. Contents of a file can be texts, computer program code, comma separated values (CSV), etc. Likewise, pictures, audios/videos, web pages are also files.

Files stored on a computer can be accessed directly and searched for desired data. But to access data of a file through software.

DBMS vs File Processing System

Database Management System (DBMS)	File Processing System
A database management system coordinates both physical and logical access to the data.	File processing system coordinates only the physical access.
A database management system is a collection of applications, i.e. dedicated for managing data stored in a database.	A file processing system is a collection of raw data files stored in the hard drive of a system.
A database management system is designed to allow flexible access to data (i.e. queries).	File processing system is designed to allow predetermined access to data (i.e. compiled programs).
A database management system is designed to coordinate multiple users accessing the same data at the same time.	A file processing system is usually designed to allow one or more programs to access different data files at the same time.

8.3 Data Abstraction

Database systems use abstraction to hide irrelevant details, simplifying database design and improving efficiency.

Levels of Data Abstraction

1. Physical or Internal Level

- Lowest level, defines how data is stored in memory.
- Includes access methods (sequential/random) and file organization (e.g., B+ trees, hashing).
- Details like memory blocks and storage sizes are hidden from users.
- **Example** Employee data stored in memory blocks.

2. Logical or Conceptual Level

- Describes actual data stored (tables and relationships).
- Focuses on simple structures but hides physical complexities.
- Physical Data Independence: Changes in physical schema do not affect the logical schema.
- Used by database administrators for schema design.
- **Example** Employee attributes and relationships (e.g., manager-employee).

3. View or External Level

- Highest level, provides user-specific views of the database.
- Users interact via rows, columns, or GUI/CLI.
- Hides logical and physical details to simplify interaction.
- Multiple views can exist for different users.
- **Example** Customer data displayed as tables or forms.

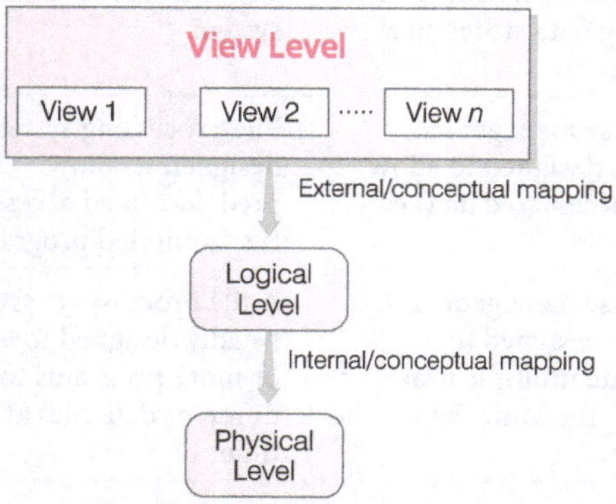

Three levels of data abstraction

8.4 Data Independence

Ability to modify a schema at one level without affecting other levels. Reduces cost and effort when altering the database.

Types of Data Independence

1. Physical Level Data Independence

- Changes in physical storage do not affect logical schema.
- **Examples** New storage devices, file organization changes, or altering indexes.

2. Logical Level Data Independence

- Changes in logical schema do not affect external views or programs.
- **Examples** Adding/removing attributes, modifying table structures or relationships.

Quick Test 1

1. What is a Database Management System (DBMS)?
2. Mention one advantage and one disadvantage of DBMS.
3. What is the difference between a file system and a DBMS?
4. Define the three levels of data abstraction in DBMS.

8.5 Data Models

Data model can be defined as an integrated collection of concepts for describing and manipulating data, relationship between data and constraints on the data in an organisation. A data model provides a way to describe the design of a database at the internal, conceptual and external level. The three data models, that are used for database management system:

Hierarchical Data Model

The hierarchical Model is one of the oldest models in the data model which was developed by IBM, in the 1950s. In this data model, data is organised in a tree-like structure. There is a hierarchy of parent and child data segments.

It comprises a set of records connected to one another through links. The link is an association between two or more records. To create links between these records, the hierarchical model uses parent child relationship. In a hierarchical database, the parent child relationship is One-to-Many.

This restricts a child segment to having only one parent segment but a parent segment can have one or more child segments. Top of the structure consists of a single segment and known as root segment. The operations that can be performed on hierarchical model are retrieval, insertion, deletion and modification of records. The following figure represents a hierarchical structure:

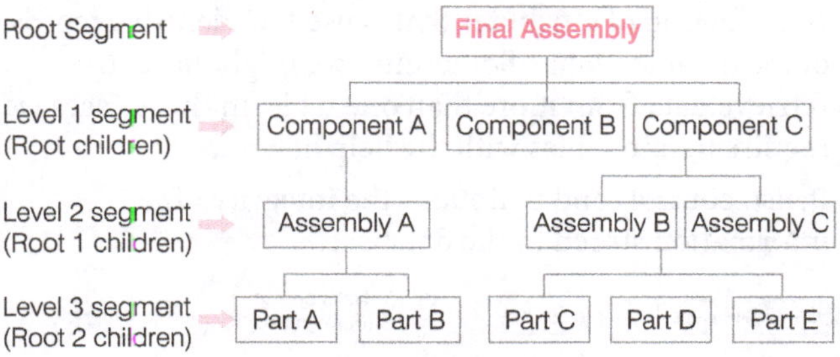

Hierarchical data model

Network Data Model

In network data model, the data is represented by collection of records and relationships among data by links like hierarchical data model.

The only difference is that in the network data model, records are organised as arbitrary graphs rather than trees.

In this model, the parent child relationship is Many-to-Many, i.e. one child segment can have multiple parent segments.

Example 1 A supplier S1 supplies three items I4, I5 and I7 in the quantities 20, 20 and 10 respective.

Now, this relationship has been shown in the following figure

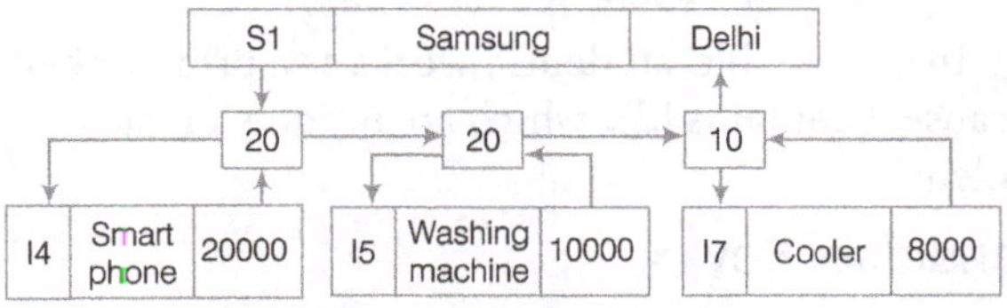

Network data model

The operations that can be performed on a network model include find, insert, delete, modify, etc. The inserting or removing records involve connect, disconnect and reconnect operations.

Relational Data Model

The relational data model uses a collection of tables to represent both data and the relationship among data. A table is a collection of records and each record in a table contains the same fields.

Each record (rows) in the table represents an entity and a field (columns) represents an attribute of entity. The tables are referred to as relations in a relational data model.

Properties of relational data model

(i) Values are atomic.

(ii) Each row is unique.

(iii) Column values are of the same kind.

(iv) The sequence of columns and rows is insignificant.

(v) Each column has a unique name.

Example 2 The following figure shows the relational data model of book-publication, which contains the tables for Book, Author and Publisher.

Table : Author

Author_id	Name	Dob
A001	Henry Korth	6/7/55
A002	Ivan Byross	23/6/65
A003	R.J. Patel	10/10/75

Table : Publisher

Pub_id	Name	City
P001	TTM	Delhi
P002	BPB	Mumbai
P003	Atul	Ahemdabad

Book_id	Author_id	Pub_id	Book_title
B001	A001	P001	DBMS
B002	A002	P002	SQL,PL/SQL
B003	A003	P003	Programming in C

Table : Book

Relational data model

In the relational data model, the relationship between two tables is implemented through a common attribute in the tables.

In the above figure, the relationship between tables Author and Book is implemented by the common attribute Author_id and the relation between tables Publisher and Book is implemented by common attribute Pub_id.

Relational Database

In a relational database, data is stored in different tables with relationships to each other.

These tables communicate and share information, which facilitates data search ability, organisation and reporting.

Various terms related to relational database are as follows

Relation

A relation is a table with columns and rows, which represent the data items and relationships among them. Relations have three important properties as name, cardinality and degree.

These properties help us to further define and describe relations:

(1) **Name** The first property of a relation is its name, which is represented by the title or the entity identifier.

(2) **Cardinality** The second property of a relation is its cardinality, which refers to the number of tuples (rows) in a relation.

(3) **Degree** The third property of a relation is its degree, which refers to the number of attributes (columns) in each tuple.

Relational Database Management System (RDBMS)

A Relational Database Management System (RDBMS) is a database management system. It is developed by Dr. E.F. Codd, of IBM's SAN Jose Research Laboratory.

RDBMS stores data in the form of related tables. RDBMS are powerful because they require few assumptions about how data is related or how it will be extracted from the database.

An important feature of relational system is that a single database can be spread across several tables. Today, popular RDBMS include Oracle, Microsoft SQL Server, MySQL, PostgreSQL, etc.

Domain

A domain is a collection of all possible values from which the values for a given column or an attribute is drawn. A domain is said to be atomic if elements are considered to be indivisible units.

e.g. In Book table, the domain of attribute Book_id contains following values: 100, 101 and 102.

Attributes

The heading of columns of a table are known as attributes. Each attribute of a table has a distinct name.

Tuples

The rows in a relation are also known as tuples. Each row or tuple has a set of permitted values for each attribute.

Attributes

Book_id	Author_id	Emp_Salary	Years
100	Jim	20000	2
101	James	21000	1
102	Anne	21001	3

Tuples

Table : Book

Keys

The key is defined as the column or attribute or a combination of attributes that is used to identify records of the database table. Sometimes we might have to retrieve data from more than one table, in those cases we require to join tables with the help of keys.

It also controls and maintains the integrity of information stored in the database.

Candidate Keys | Alternate Key | Relationship (Foreign Key) | Primary Key

studentId	firstname	lastname	courseId
L0002345	Jim	Black	C002
L0001254	James	Harradine	A004
L0002349	Amanda	Holland	C002
L0001198	Simon	McCloud	S042
L0023487	Peter	Murray	P301
L0018453	Anne	Norris	S042

Primary Key

Student table

courseId	courseName
A004	Accounts
C002	Computing
P301	History
S042	Short Course

Course table

There are various types of keys, which are as follows:

Primary Key

The primary key of a relational table uniquely identifies each record in the table. In some tables, combination of more than one attributes is declared as primary key. In that case, primary key is known as composite key. The value of primary key should be unique and not null. Every relation does have a primary key.

e.g. In above table, studentId works as a primary key because it contains Id's, which are unique for each student.

Candidate Key

The set of all attributes, which can uniquely identify each tuple of a relation are known as candidate keys. Each table may have one or more candidate keys and one of them will become the primary key.

e.g. columns studentId and the combination of firstname and lastname work as the candidate keys for the given Student table.

Alternate Key

From the set of candidate keys after selecting one of the keys as primary key, all other remaining keys are known as alternate keys. These keys are also unique but they allow nulls. e.g. from the candidate keys (studentId, firstname and lastname), studentId chosen as a primary key then the firstname and lastname column work as a alternate key.

Foreign Key

A foreign key is a non-key attribute, whose value is derived from the primary key of another table. The relationship between two tables is established with the help of foreign key. A table may have multiple foreign keys and each foreign key can have different referenced table.

Foreign key play an essential role in database design, when tables are broken apart then foreign keys make it possible for them to be reconstructed. e.g. courseId column of Student table work as a foreign key for Student table, as well as a primary key for Course table (referenced table).

Quick Test 2

1. Why foreign keys are allowed to have NULL values? Explain with an example. **NCERT**
2. Differentiate between: **NCERT**
   (a) Database state and database schema
   (b) Primary key and foreign key
   (c) Degree and cardinality of a relation
3. Explain the use of 'Foreign Key' in a Relational Database Management System. Give example to support your answer. **SQP 2022-2023**
4. Explain the concept of candidate keys with the help of an appropriate example.

NCERT Folder

1. Give the terms for each of the following:

(a) Collection of logically related records.

(b) DBMS creates a file that contains description about the data stored in the database.

(c) Attribute that can uniquely identify the tuples in a relation.

(d) Special value that is stored when actual data value unknown for an attribute.

(e) An attribute which can uniquely identify tuples of the table but is not defined as primary key of the table.

(f) Software that is used to create, manipulate and maintain a relational database.

Ans. (a) Table (b) Data Dictionary
(c) Primary key (d) NULL
(e) Alternate key (f) DBMS

2. Compared to a file system, how does a database management system avoid redundancy in data through a database?

Ans. A Database Management System (DBMS) avoids redundancy through normalization, which organizes data into tables to eliminate duplicate data and dependencies.

It enforces relationships and constraints, ensuring that data is stored once and referenced rather than duplicated, thereby maintaining data integrity and consistency.

3. What are the limitations of file system that can be overcome by a relational DBMS?

Ans. Limitations of File Systems Overcome by Relational DBMS

(1) **Data Redundancy** Relational DBMS minimizes duplication through normalization.

(2) **Data Integrity** DBMS enforces constraints to maintain accurate data, unlike file systems.

(3) **Data Access** DBMS provides complex querying capabilities using SQL, while file systems require manual data handling.

(4) **Concurrency Control** DBMS supports multiple users accessing data simultaneously, ensuring data consistency.

(5) **Data Security** DBMS offers advanced security features, including user permissions and encryption, which file systems lack.

4. A school has a rule that each student must participate in a sports activity. So each one should give only one preference for sports activity. Suppose there are five students in a class, each having a unique roll number. The class representative has prepared a list of sports preferences as shown below.

Table : Sports Preferences

Roll_no	Preference
9	Cricket
13	Football
17	Badminton
17	Football
21	Hockey
24	NULL
NULL	Kabaddi

Answer the following:

(a) Roll no 24 may not be interested in sports. Can a NULL value be assigned to that student's preference field?

(b) Roll no 17 has given two preferences in sports. Which property of relational DBMS is violated here? Can we use any constraint or key in the relational DBMS to check against such violation, if any?

(c) Kabaddi was not chosen by any student. Is it possible to have this tuple in the Sports Preferences relation?

Ans. (a) No, a NULL value cannot be assigned because every student must give one preference, and NULL violates this rule.

(b) Roll no 17 violates the uniqueness property of the primary key (Roll_no). To prevent this, we can use the PRIMARY KEY constraint to ensure each roll number appears only once.

(c) No, since Kabaddi wasn't chosen by any student, the tuple should not exist in the relation as it violates the rule of each student providing a sports preference.

5. In another class having 2 sections, the two respective class representatives have prepared 2 separate Sports Preferences tables, as shown below: Sports preference of section 1 (arranged on roll number column)

Table : Sports Preferences

Roll_no	Sports
9	Cricket
13	Football
17	Badminton
21	Hockey
24	Cricket

Sports preference of section 2 (arranged on Sports name column, and column order is also different)

Table : Sports Preferences

Sports	Roll_no
Badminton	17
Cricket	9
Cricket	24
Football	13
Hockey	21

Are the states of both the relations equivalent? Justify.

Ans. Yes, the states of both the tables are same as the order of rows and columns does not matter and data is just the same in both the tables.

6. The school canteen wants to maintain records of items available in the school canteen and generate bills when students purchase any item from the canteen. The school wants to create a canteen database to keep track of items in the canteen and the items purchased by students. Design a database by answering the following questions:

(a) To store each item name along with its price, what relation should be used? Decide appropriate attribute names along with their data type. Each item and its price should be stored only once. What restriction should be used while defining the relation?

(b) In order to generate bill, we should know the quantity of an item purchased. Should this information be in a new relation or a part of the previous relation? If a new relation is required, decide appropriate name and data type for attributes.

Also, identify appropriate primary key and foreign key so that the following two restrictions are satisfied:

(i) The same bill cannot be generated for different orders.

(ii) Bill can be generated only for available items in the canteen.

(c) The school wants to find out how many calories students intake when they order an item. In which relation should the attribute 'calories' be stored?

Ans. (a) Relation for items and prices:

- **Relation** CanteenItems
- **Attributes** ItemID (INT, Primary Key), ItemName (VARCHAR), Price (DECIMAL)
- **Restriction** Use a Unique constraint on ItemName to ensure each item is stored only once.

(b) Relation for purchases and billing:

- A new relation is required: PurchaseRecords
- Attributes: BillID (INT, Primary Key), ItemID (INT, Foreign Key referencing CanteenItems), Quantity (INT)
- Restrictions:

(i) **Primary Key** BillID (to ensure unique bills).

(ii) **Foreign Key** ItemID (to ensure items are available in the canteen).

(c) **Storing calories**

- The attribute Calories should be stored in the CanteenItems relation since it is related to each item.
- Attribute: Calories (INT).

7. An organisation wants to create a database EMPDEPENDENT to maintain following details about its employees and their dependent.

EMPLOYEE(AadharNumber, Name, Address, Department,EmployeeID)

DEPENDENT(EmployeeID, DependentName, Relationship)

(a) Name the attributes of EMPLOYEE, which can be used as candidate keys.

(b) The company wants to retrieve details of dependent of a particular employee. Name the tables and the key which are required to retrieve this detail.

(c) What is the degree of EMPLOYEE and DEPENDENT relation?

Ans. (a) Candidate keys for EMPLOYEE: AadharNumber, EmployeeID

(b) Tables: EMPLOYEE, DEPENDENT; Key: EmployeeID

(c) Degree of EMPLOYEE: 5, Degree of DEPENDENT: 3

8. School uniform is available at M/s Sheetal Private Limited. They have maintained SCHOOL_UNIFORM Database with two relations viz. UNIFORM and COST. The following figure shows database schema and its state.

School Uniform Database

Attributes and Constraints

Table : UNIFORM

Attribute	UCode	Uname	UColor
Constraints	Primary Key	Not Null	–

Table : COST

Attribute	UCode	Size	Price
Constraints	Composite	Primary Key	>0

Table : UNIFORM

UCode	UName	UColor
1	Shirt	White
2	Pant	Grey
3	Skirt	Grey
4	Tie	Blue
5	Socks	Blue
6	Belt	Blue

Table : COST

UCode	Size	COST Price
1	M	500
1	L	580
1	XL	620
2	M	810
2	L	890
2	XL	940
3	M	770
3	L	830
3	XL	910
4	S	150
4	L	170
5	S	180
5	L	210
6	M	110
6	L	140
6	XL	160

(a) Can they insert the following tuples to the UNIFORM Relation? Give reasons in support of your answer.

(i) 7, Handkerchief, NULL

(ii) 4, Ribbon, Red (iii) 8, NULL, White

(b) Can they insert the following tuples to the COST Relation? Give reasons in support of your answer.

(i) 7, S, 0 (ii) 9, XL, 100

Ans. (a) (i) Yes, it can be inserted.

(ii) Yes, it can be inserted.

(iii) No, it cannot be inserted as UName cannot be NULL.

(b) (i) No, it can not be inserted as the price is greater than 0.

(ii) Yes, it can be inserted.

9. In a multiplex, movies are screened in different auditoriums. One movie can be shown in more than one auditorium. In order to maintain the record of movies, the multiplex maintains a relational database consisting of two relations viz. MOVIE and AUDI respectively as shown below:

Movie(Movie_ID, MovieName, ReleaseDate)

Audi(AudiNo, Movie_ID, Seats, ScreenType, TicketPrice)

(a) Is it correct to assign Movie_ID as the primary key in the MOVIE relation? If no, then suggest an appropriate primary key.

(b) Is it correct to assign AudiNo as the primary key in the AUDI relation? If no, then suggest appropriate primary key.

(c) Is there any foreign key in any of these relations?

Ans. (a) Yes, assigning Movie_ID as the primary key in the MOVIE relation is correct, as it uniquely identifies each movie.

(b) No, assigning AudiNo alone as the primary key in the AUDI relation is not correct, as an auditorium can screen multiple movies. A composite key of AudiNo and Movie_ID would be more appropriate to uniquely identify each record.

(c) Yes, Movie_ID in the AUDI relation is a foreign key referencing the Movie_ID in the MOVIE relation.

10. For the above given database STUDENT-PROJECT, answer the following:

Student Project Database

Table : STUDENT

Roll No	Name	Class	Section	Registration_ID
11	Mohan	XI	1	IP-101-15
12	Sohan	XI	2	IP-104-15
21	John	XII	1	CS-103-14
22	Meena	XII	2	CS-101-14
23	Juhi	XII	2	CS-101-10

Table : PROJECT

ProjectNo	PName	Submission Data
101	Airline Database	12/01/2018
102	Library Database	12/01/2018
103	Employee Database	15/01/2018
104	Student Database	12/01/2018
105	Inventory Database	15/01/2018
106	Railway Database	15/01/2018

Table : PROJECT ASSIGNED

Registration_ID	ProjectNo
IP-101-15	101
IP-104-15	103
CS-101-14	102
CS-101-14	105
CS-101-10	104

(a) Name primary key of each table.

(b) Find foreign key(s) in table PROJECT-ASSIGNED.

(c) Is there any alternate key in table STUDENT? Give justification for your answer.

(d) Can a user assign duplicate value to the field RollNo of STUDENT table? Jusify.

Ans. (a) STUDENT: RollNo

PROJECT: ProjectNo

PROJECT ASSIGNED: Registration_ID

(b) ProjectNo

(c) Name can be an alternate key as it stores unique values for each row.

(d) No, RollNo being the primary key must be unique for each row.

Mind Map

Terminologies

Relation

A relation is a table with columns and rows, which represent the data items and relationships among them.

- **Name** It is represented by the title or the entity identifier.
- **Cardinality** It refers to the number of tuples (rows) in a relation.
- **Degree** It refers to the number of attributes (columns) in each tuple.

Domain

A domain is a collection of all possible values from which the values for a given column or an attribute is drawn.

Tuples

The rows in a relation are also known as tuples. Each row or tuple has a set of permitted values for each attribute.

Attributes

The heading columns of a table are known as attributes. Each attribute of a table has a distinct name.

Keys

Used to uniquely identify and record or row of data from the table.

- **Primary Key** is a column or set of columns in a table that uniquely identifies each row in the table.
- Minimal set of attributes that can uniquely identify a tuple is known as a **candidate key**.
- An **alternate key** is any candidate key in a table that is not chosen as the primary key.
- A **foreign key** is an attribute in one table that refers to the primary key in another table.

Relational Database

In a relational database, data is stored in different tables with relationships to each other.

DBMS

A Database Management System is a collection of programs that enables users to create, maintain and use a database.

DATABASE

Collection of related data that has been recorded, organized and made available for searching is called a Database.

DATA

Data is a collection of raw facts which have not been processed to reveal useful information.

DATABASE CONCEPTS

Relational Data Model

The relational data model uses a collection of tables to represent both data and the relationship among data. A table is a collection of records and each record in a table contains the same fields.

Network Data Model

In network data model, the data is represented by collection of records and relationships among data by links like hierarchical data model. In this model, the parent child relationship is Many-to-Many.

Hierarchical Data Model

In this data model, data is organised in a tree-like structure. There is a hierarchy of parent and child data segments. In a hierarchical database, the parent child relationship is One-to-Many.

DATA MODEL

It is a conceptual framework used to define and organize the structure, relationships and rules of data in a database.

View of Data

The views of data are the different ways to present the data to users. These views are created to hide the complexity of the data structure from the end-user.

View Level

View 1 | View 2 | ····· | View n

External/conceptual mapping

Logical Level

Internal/conceptual mapping

Physical Level

- **Internal/Physical view** Deals with the physical storage of the data.
- **Conceptual view** Describes the logical structure and relationships of the data.
- **External view** Also known as the view level, this view provides customized data access for individual users or groups.

EXAM PATTERN QUESTIONS

Objective Type Questions

Multiple Choice Questions

1. A collection of interrelated records is called a
(a) utility file
(b) management information system
(c) database
(d) spreadsheet

2. What is the overall term for creating, editing, formatting, storing, retrieving text document?
(a) Word processing
(b) Spreadsheet design
(c) Web design
(d) Database management system

3. Which of the following component of database system consists of various secondary storage devices on which data is stored?
(a) Hardware
(b) User
(c) Data
(d) Software

4. The database administrator's function in an organisation is
(a) to be responsible for the technical aspects of managing the information contained in organisational database
(b) to show the relationship among entity classes in a data warehouse
(c) to define which data mining tools must be used to extract data
(d) None of the above

5. An advantage of the database management approach is
(a) data is dependent on programs
(b) data redundancy increases
(c) data is integrated and can be accessed by multiple programs
(d) All of the above

6. Which of the following is the drawback of DBMS?
(a) Improvement in data
(b) Backup and recovery
(c) Complexity
(d) Maintenance of data integrity

7. Which type of database model, organised the data in the form of tree with nodes?
(a) Network data model
(b) Hierarchical data model
(c) Relational data model
(d) Multiple data model

8. In a relational data model, a data structure that organises the information about a single topic into rows and columns is
(a) block (b) record
(c) tuple (d) table

9. Which of the following was first network database?
(a) SYSTEM 2000 (b) DBTG Codasyl
(c) SYSTEM Codasyl (d) DBTG 2000

10. The cardinality property of a relation, refers to the
(a) number of database (b) number of columns
(c) number of rows (d) number of tables

11. Fill in the blank
______ is a number of tuples in a relation. **CBSE 2023**
(a) Attribute (b) Degree
(c) Domain (d) Cardinality

12. Rows of a relation are called
(a) relation (b) tuples
(c) data structure (d) an entity

13. A set of possible data values is called
(a) attribute (b) degree
(c) tuple (d) domain

14. A RDBMS must comply with at least ________rules.
(a) 4 (b) 5
(c) 6 (d) 7

15. How many rules were laid down by EF codd?
(a) 10 (b) 13
(c) 12 (d) 15

16. The purpose of the primary key in a database is to
(a) unlock the database
(b) provide a map of the data
(c) uniquely identify a record
(d) establish constraints on database operations

17. In files, there is a key associated with each record which is used to differentiate among different records. For every file, there is atleast one set of keys that is unique. Such a key is called

(a) unique key (b) prime attribute
(c) index key (d) primary key

18. Key to represent relationship between tables is called

(a) primary key (b) secondary key
(c) foreign key (d) composite key

19. Which of the following statements is FALSE about keys in a relational database? CBSE SQP 2023-24

(a) Any candidate key is eligible to become a primary key.
(b) A primary key uniquely identifies the tuples in a relation.
(c) A candidate key that is not a primary key is a foreign key.
(d) A foreign key is an attribute whose value is derived from the primary key of another relation

20. Fill in the blank

__________ is a non-key attribute, whose values are derived from the primary key of some other table. CBSE SQP 2022-23

(a) Primary Key (b) Foreign Key
(c) Candidate Key (d) Alternate Key

Fill in the Blanks

21. In the ...., data is stored in the form of files.

22. .... are the users who may communicate with the database directly via online terminal.

23. The purpose of .... is to bridge the gap between the information and data.

24. .... contains metadata, which means, it contains the database descriptions used by the DBMS.

25. .... is the lowest level of abstraction that describes how the data is physically stored and organised on storage medium.

26. .... is the ability to change the conceptual schema without affecting the external schema.

27. .... component of database system acts as an interface between the user and the database.

28. Degree refers to the number of .... in each tuple.

29. Oracle is an example of ....

30. A candidate key that is not the primary key is known as ....

State Whether True or False

31. A Database Management System (DBMS) eliminates data redundancy and inconsistency.

32. In the file processing system, handling new queries is easy and does not require changes in application programs.

33. A Foreign Key is a non-key attribute whose value is derived from the primary key of another table.

34. The conceptual level of data abstraction describes how data is physically stored.

35. Relational databases store data in tables called relations, where data can be reorganized and accessed flexibly.

36. The referential integrity rule states that a foreign key value must always reference a primary key value in another table or be null.

Assertion and Reason Based Questions

Assertion (A) and Reason (R) Type questions. Choose the correct option as:

(a) Both Assertion (A) and Reason (R) are true, and Reason (R) is the correct explanation of Assertion (A)
(b) Both Assertion (A) and Reason (R) are true, but Reason (R) is not the correct explanation of Assertion (A)
(c) Assertion (A) is True, but Reason (R) is False
(d) Assertion (A) is False, but Reason (R) is True

37. Assertion (A) A database is a collection of unorganized data.

Reason (R) A database allows users to retrieve data quickly and efficiently.

38. Assertion (A) DBMS stands for Database Management Service.

Reason (R) A DBMS is an interface that helps users interact with data stored in databases.

39. Assertion (A) Data redundancy is a benefit of using a database management system (DBMS).

Reason (R) DBMS eliminates duplicate data entries, enhancing data integrity.

40. Assertion (A) Data models provide a way to describe the design of a database at various levels.

Reason (R) The three types of data models are hierarchical, network, and relational data models.

41. Assertion (A) Limitations faced in file system can be overcome by storing the data in a database.

Reason (R) We can organise related data logically in a database.

42. Assertion (A) Recording of relationship implementation in network model is very complex since pointers are used.

Reason (R) DBTG codasyl was the first network database.

43. **Assertion (A)** A primary key can contain duplicate values in a relational database.

Reason (R) A primary key uniquely identifies each record in a table.

44. **Assertion (A)** In a hierarchical data model, data is organized in a tree-like structure.

Reason (R) Each child segment can have multiple parent segments in a hierarchical data model.

45. **Assertion (A)** In a relational data model, each table is referred to as a relation.

Reason (R) A relation in a relational data model is structured as rows and columns.

46. **Assertion (A)** The columns of a relation are the attributes.

Reason (R) Tuples are also referred as fields.

47. **Assertion (A)** The maximum set of attributes that are uniquely identify a tuple is known as a candidate key.

Reason(R) Out of one or more candidate keys, the attribute chosen by the database designer to uniquely identify the tuples in relation is called primary key of that relation.

48. **Assertion (A)** A foreign key is used to uniquely identify each record in a table.

Reason (R) A foreign key derives its value from the primary key of another table.

49. **Assertion (A)** We can retrieve records from more than one table in MySQL. **CBSE 2025**

Reason (R) Foreign key is used to establish a relationship between two tables.

Answers

1. (c) database
2. (d) Database management system
3. (a) Hardware
4. (a) to be responsible for the technical aspects of managing the information contained in organisational database
5. (c) data is integrated and can be accessed by multiple programs
6. (c) Complexity
7. (b) Hierarchical data model
8. (d) table
9. (b) DBTG Codasyl
10. (c) number of rows
11. (d) Cardinality
12. (b) tuples
13. (d) domain
14. (c) 6
15. (c) 12
16. (c) uniquely identify a record
17. (d) primary key
18. (c) foreign key
19. (c) A candidate key that is not a primary key is a foreign key.
20. (b) Foreign Key
21. file processing system
22. Online users
23. DBMS
24. Data dictionary
25. Internal level
26. Logical data independence
27. Software
28. attributes (columns)
29. RDBMS
30. alternate key
31. True
32. False
33. True
34. False
35. True
36. True
37. (d) Assertion (A) is False, but Reason (R) is True
38. (d) Assertion (A) is False, but Reason (R) is True
39. (d) Assertion (A) is False, but Reason (R) is True
40. (a) Both Assertion (A) and Reason (R) are true, and Reason (R) is the correct explanation of Assertion (A)
41. (a) Both Assertion (A) and Reason (R) are true, and Reason (R) is the correct explanation of Assertion (A)
42. (b) Both Assertion (A) and Reason (R) are true, but Reason (R) is not the correct explanation of Assertion (A)
43. (d) Assertion (A) is False, but Reason (R) is True
44. (c) Assertion (A) is True, but Reason (R) is False
45. (a) Both Assertion (A) and Reason (R) are true, and Reason (R) is the correct explanation of Assertion (A)
46. (c) Assertion (A) is True, but Reason (R) is False
47. (d) Assertion (A) is False, but Reason (R) is True
48. (d) Assertion (A) is False, but Reason (R) is True
49. (a) Both Assertion (A) and Reason (R) are true, and Reason (R) is the correct explanation of Assertion (A)

Subjective Type Questions

Very Short Answer Type Questions

1. What is a database?

Ans. A database is a collection of data that is organised so that its contents can be easily accessed, managed and updated.

2. What is database schema?

Ans. The design of the database is known as the database schema.

3. What do you understand by data redundancy?

Ans. Data redundancy means duplication of data.

4. Name the various data models available for database system.

Ans. There are generally three data models available

(i) Relational (ii) Network
(iii) Hierarchical

5. Write an example of hierarchical database.

Ans. SYSTEM 2000 is an example of hierarchical database.

6. Mention two disadvantages of hierarchical model.

Ans. (i) Complex to implement
(ii) Difficult to manage

7. Write one difference between degree and cardinality.

Ans. Degree refers to the number of columns and cardinality refers to the number of rows in a relation.

8. If R1 is a relation with 8 rows and 5 columns, then what will be the cardinality of R1?

Ans. The cardinality of R1 will be 8.

9. Who developed RDBMS?

Ans. The Relational Database Management System was created by Dr. E.F. Codd.

10. List different types of keys used in a table in DBMS.

Ans. There are various types of keys used in a table in DBMS such as

(i) Primary key (ii) Candidate key
(iii) Alternate key (iv) Foreign key

Short Answer Type I Questions

11. List some commonly used DBMS software packages.

Ans. Some commonly used DBMS software packages are

(i) MySQL (ii) Oracle
(iii) Postgre (iv) DB2
(v) MS-SQL (vi) Sybase

12. Mention the various advantages of DBMS.

Ans. DBMS has the following advantages:

(i) Reduced data redundancy
(ii) Elimination of inconsistency
(iii) Data sharing
(iv) Data integrity
(v) Data security
(vi) Ease of application development

13. Write some advantages of DBMS over file system?

Ans. Advantags are:

(i) No redundant data (ii) Data security
(iii) Easy access of data
(iv) Data consistency and integrity

14. (a) Consider the table MOVIEDETAILS given below:

CBSE SQP 2021-22 Term II

Table : MOVIEDETAILS

MOVIEID	TITLE	LANGUAGE	RATING	PLATFORM
M001	Minari	Korean	5	Netflix
M004	MGR Magan	Tamil	4	Hotstar
M010	Kaagaz	Hindi	3	Zee5
M011	Harry Potter and the Chamber of Secrets	English	4	Prime Video
M015	Uri	Hindi	5	Zee5
M020	Avengers: Endgame	English	4	Hotstar

(i) Identify the degree and cardinality of the table.

(ii) Which field should be made the primary key? Justify your answer.

Or

(b) **(i) Identify the candidate key(s) from the table MOVIEDETAILS.**

(ii) Consider the table SCHEDULE given below.

Table : SCHEDULE

SLOTID	MOVIEID	TIMESLOT
S001	M010	10 AM to 12 PM
S002	M020	2 PM to 5 PM
S003	M010	6 PM to 8 PM
S004	M011	9 PM to 11 PM

Which field will be considered as the foreign key if the tables MOVIEDETAILS and SCHEDULE are related in a database?

Ans. (a) (i) Degree is 5. Cardinality is 6.

(ii) MOVIEID should be made the primary key as it uniquely identifies each record of the table.

Or

(b) (i) MOVIEID and TITLE are the candidate keys in table MOVIEDETAILS.

(ii) MOVIEID is the foreign key if the tables MOVIEDETAILS and SCHEDULE are related in a database.

15. What is the difference between degree and cardinality of a table? What is the degree and cardinality of the following table?

Eno	Name	Salary
101	John Fedrick	45000
103	Raya Mazumdar	50600

Ans. **Degree** The number of attributes or columns in a table is called the degree of the table.

The degree of the given table is 3

Cardinality The number of rows or records in a table is called the cardinality of the table. The cardinality of the given table is 2.

16. A table CUSTOMER has 10 columns but no row. Later, 10 new rows are inserted and 3 rows are deleted in the table. What is the degree and cardinality of the table CUSTOMER.

Ans. Degree = 10 (No. of columns)

Cardinality = 10-3 = 7(No. of rows)

17. Differentiate between an attribute and a tuple with an example.

Ans. The columns of a table are referred to as attributes. It is also known as field which is reserved for a specific piece of data. The rows of a table are referred to as tuples.

Attributes

S. No.	Name	Class
1	Raj	10
2	Ajay	12
3	Rahul	11

Tuples

18. Describe the following terms:

(i) Domain **(ii) DB2**

Ans. (i) **Domain** It is a set of possible values for an attribute. A domain is said to be atomic if elements of the domain are considered as indivisible units.

(ii) **DB2** It is a Relational Database Management System (RDBMS), fully featured, high performance database capable of handling large quantities of data and concurrently serving many users.

19. What do you understand by primary key? Give a suitable example of primary key from a table containing some meaningful data.

Ans. A primary key is a set of one or more attributes that can uniquely identify tuples within the relation.

Example

TABLE: ITEM

ItemNo	Name	State	City
11	Pastry	10	Ajmer
12	Pizza	15	Delhi
13	Cake	5	Pune
14	Burger	35	Delhi

The attribute ItemNo is a primary key in ITEM table as it contains unique value for each tuple in a relation.

20. Observe the following table carefully and write the names of the most appropriate columns, which can be considered as (i) candidate keys and (ii) primary key.

Table : Product

CID	CNAME	AMOUNT	COUNTRY	ITEM
101	ALLE	100000	JMEKA	SHOES
111	BEN	20000	FRANCE	HELMET
110	RIKI	25000	AMERICA	BAG
011	BRETT LEE	105000	AUSTRALIA	BAT

Ans. (i) Candidate Keys CID, ITEM

(ii) Primary key CID

Short Answer Type II Questions

21. Why does the need of the database system arise? Give the reason.

Ans. The need of the database system arose in the early 1960s in response to traditional file processing system. To overcome the disadvantages of file processing system, the database system was designed.

Some of the major disadvantage of file processing system are given below:

(i) Data redundancy

(ii) Data inconsistency

(iii) Lack of security features

(iv) Handling new queries is difficult.

22. Mention atleast three limitations of DBMS.

Ans. Some limitations of DBMS are given below

(i) **High Cost** DBMS requires various software, hardware and highly intelligent people for operating and maintaining the database system. It increases its cost.

(ii) **Database Failure** If database is corrupted due to power failure or any other reason, our valuable data may be lost or whole system stops.

(iii) **Data Quality** With increased number of users accessing data directly. There are enormous opportunities for users to damage data. So, it is not easy to provide a strategy to support multiple users to update data simultaneously.

23. In which data model, data is organised in a tree like structure. Explain, them.

Ans. Refer to the text on page no. 208-209 (Hierarchical data model).

24. What are primary and alternate key in a database? Give suitable example to explain each.

Ans. **Primary Key** It is a column or set of columns which helps to identify row uniquely.

Examples In table Student, RollNo of all students are different. So, RollNo is a primary key helps to identify the information of all students uniquely.

Alternate Key It is a column or set of columns that can act as a primary key but not selected as a primary key.

Table : Student

AdmNo	RollNo	Name	Marks
1000	1	Akash	85
1201	2	Neha	90
850	3	Babita	70
1255	4	Himanshu	75

Example In table Student, RollNo and AdmNo of all students are different. Both of them can be selected as a primary key.

Suppose, we have selected RollNo as a primary key then AdmNo is called as alternate key.

25. Give an example of a table which has one Primary key and two alternate keys. How many Candidate keys will this table have? **CBSE SQP 2024-25**

Ans. A table with one primary key and two alternate keys will have three candidate keys.

For example:

StudentID (Primary Key)	Email (Alternate Key)	PhoneNumber (Alternate Key)	Name
101	abc@example.com	1234567890	John
102	xyz@example.com	0987654321	Sarah

Here, StudentID, Email, and PhoneNumber are all candidate keys (with StudentID being the primary key).

26. Give suitable example of a table with sample data and illustrate primary and candidate keys in it.

Ans. **Candidate key** It is a set of all attributes that uniquely identifies records in a table. Each table may have one or more candidate keys.

Example In Student table, AdmNo and RollNo both can identify records uniquely. So, both are candidate key.

Primary Key It is a set of one or more attributes that can uniquely identify each tuple of a relation. A relation can have only one primary key.

Example In Student Table, AdmNo of all students are different. So, we have created AdmNo as primary key.

Table : Student

AdmNo	RollNo	Name	Class	Marks
2715	1	Ram	12	90
2816	2	Shyam	11	95
2404	3	Ajay	10	92
2917	4	Tarun	12	94

27. Explain the concept of "Alternate Key" in a Relational Database Management System with an appropriate example. **CBSE 2023**

Ans. An Alternate Key in a Relational Database Management System (RDBMS) is a candidate key that is not chosen as the primary key.

It is still unique and can be used to identify records, but it is secondary to the primary key.

Example In a table of employees, the Employee ID could be the primary key, while the Email address (which is also unique) would be an alternate key. Both can uniquely identify a record, but only one is the primary key.

28. Explain the use of 'Foreign Key' in a Relational Database Management System. Give example to support your answer. **SQP 2022-23**

Ans. A foreign key is a linking field between two tables and brings corresponding or matching values from the two tables.

Example Consider the tables Bank_Account and Branch

Table : Bank_Account

ACode	Name	Type
A01	Amrita	Savings
A02	Parthodas	Current
A03	Miraben	Current

Table : Branch

ACode	City
A01	Delhi
A02	Mumbai
A03	Nagpur

To display the City of Amrita , the Acode field has to be used to link the tables. Acode is the foreign key in Bank_Account table.

Long Answer Type Questions

29. Explain database and DBMS in detail.

Ans. Database The database is a shared collection of logically related data, designed to meet the information needs of an organisation. A database is a computer based record keeping system whose over all purpose is to record and maintains information.

The database holds not only the organisation's operational data but also a description of this data. For this reason, a database is also defined as a self-describing collection of integrated records. The description of the data is known as the data dictionary or metadata (data about data).

DBMS A Database Management System (DBMS) is a collection of programs that enables users to store, modify and extract information from a database as per the requirements. It acts as an interface between the application program and the operating system to access or manipulate the database.

A database management system is a piece of software that provides services for accessing a database, while maintaining all the required features of the data.

Commercially available database management system in the market are dbase, FoxPro, Oracle, MySQL and DB2 etc.

30. Write down some differences between a primary key and candidate key.

Ans. Differences between primary key and candidate key:

Primary Key	Candidate Key
Uniquely identifies each record in a table.	A set of fields that can uniquely identify a record.
Only one primary key is allowed per table.	A table can have multiple candidate keys.
Cannot contain NULL values.	Candidate keys can also not contain NULL values.
It is the main key chosen among candidate keys.	All candidate keys are eligible to be primary.
Automatically enforced by the database system.	Not enforced unless one is chosen as primary.
Used to define relationships with other tables.	Used for internal uniqueness, not necessarily for relationships.

Case Study Based Questions

Case Study 1

Answer the following questions on the basis of following table:

Table: Student

Stud_id	Stut_name	Class	Fees
1	Aman	IX	3000
2	Anil	X	3200

Table: Teacher

T_id	T_name	T_sal	Stus_id
3210	Mr. Kumar	60000	1
3211	Mr. Sethi	70000	2

(i) **What is the degree of Student table and Teacher table?**
(a) 4,4
(b) 2,2
(c) 4,2
(d) 2,4

(ii) **Which field should be the primary key for the Student table?**
(a) Stud_id, Stud_name (b) Stud_name
(c) Stud_id (d) Stud_id, class

(iii) **What is the cardinality of Student table and Teacher table?**
(a) 4,4 (b) 3,2
(c) 4,2 (d) 2,2

(iv) **What will be the foreign key for Teacher table?**
(a) Stud_id, Stud_name (b) Stud_name
(c) Stud_id (d) Stud_id, class

(v) **Which field should be the primary key for the Teacher table?**
(a) T_id, Stud_id (b) Stud_id
(c) T_id (d) T_id, T_name

Ans. (i) (a) 4,4 (ii) (c) Stud_id
(iii) (d) 2,2 (iv) (c) Stud_id
(v) (c) T_id

SELF ASSESSMENT TEST

Multiple Choice Questions

1 Which of the following type of users who need not be aware of the presence of the database system?

(a) Specialised users (b) DBA
(c) Naive users (d) Online users

2 Which type of data contains the structure and format of queries, reports and other application component?

(a) Application Data (b) User Data
(c) Meta Data (d) None of these

3 Which of the following level presents a logical view of the database?

(a) Internal level (b) Conceptual level
(c) External level (d) None of these

4 In which type of data model, the data is represented by collection of records and relationship among data that are represented by links?

(a) Relational data model
(b) Network data model
(c) Hierarchical data model
(d) None of the above

5 The set of all attributes, which are uniquely identify each tuple of a relation are known as

(a) Candidate key (b) Alternate key
(c) Primary key (d) Foreign key

Fill in the Blanks

6 A .... can be defined as a collection of organised information in such a way that user can retrieve data quickly.

7 The .... are the people who manages the database and perform different operations on it.

8 .... means that the data contained in the database is accurate and consistent.

9 .... is the highest level of database abstraction and also known as view level or user view.

10 A .... is a collection of all possible values from which the values for a given column is drawn.

State Whether True and False

11. Data in a database can be added, deleted, changed, sorted, searched etc., using DBMS.

12 The heading of columns of a table is known as tuples.

Assertion and Reason Based Questions

Assertion (A) and Reason (R) Type questions. Choose the correct option as:

(a) Both Assertion (A) and Reason (R) are true, and Reason (R) is the correct explanation of Assertion (A)
(b) Both Assertion (A) and Reason (R) are true, but Reason (R) is not the correct explanation of Assertion (A)
(c) Assertion (A) is True, but Reason (R) is False
(d) Assertion (A) is False, but Reason (R) is True

13 **Assertion (A)** Database is a collection of related data elements representing real-world information.

Reason (R) Database is logical, coherent and internally consistent.

14 **Assertion (A)** The data dictionary also called a system catalog is an important part of the DBMS.

Reason (R) It contains metadata, which means, it contains the database descriptions used by the DBMS.

Very Short Answer Type Questions

15 Write any one advantage of DBMS.

16 Who is the application programmer in database?

17 Name three levels of data abstraction.

18 Name the process by which the system hides certain details of how data is stored and maintained from the user.

Short Answer Type Questions

19 How will you explain data sharing and data integrity?

20 Explain the relational database.

21 Distinguish between physical data independence and logical data independence.

22 Write down the difference between DBMS and file processing system.

23 How attribute is different from domain? Give example of it.

Long Answer Type Questions

24 Define the following terms:

(i) Hierarchical data model (ii) Attribute
(iii) Relation (iv) Key

25 Describe the components of DBMS in detail.

Case Study Based Question

26. **ABC School is maintaining a student database. They created a table named STUDENT to store student information. The structure of the table is as follows:**

RollNo	Name	Class	Age	Email	Section	ClassTeacherID
101	Aanya	10	15	aanya@gmail.com	A	T01
102	Rohan	10	14	rohan@gmail.com	A	T01
103	Sanya	10	15	sanya@gmail.com	B	T02

The school wants to ensure data is stored without repetition and maintains relationships between different tables like STUDENT, TEACHER, and CLASS.

Answer the following Questions:

(i) **What is the need for using a database in this scenario?**
(a) To store more data only
(b) To prevent loss of data during power failure
(c) To manage data efficiently and avoid duplication
(d) To print reports only

(ii) **In the STUDENT table, RollNo uniquely identifies each student. What is it known as?**
(a) Foreign Key (b) Primary Key
(c) Candidate Key (d) Alternate Key

(iii) **Which of the following would be considered a Candidate Key in the STUDENT table?**
(a) RollNo only
(b) Name only
(c) RollNo and Email
(d) Class and Section

(iv) **If Email is not selected as the primary key but is unique, then what is it called?**
(a) Foreign Key
(b) Composite Key
(c) Alternate Key
(d) Redundant Key

(v) **In another table TEACHER, the field TeacherID is the primary key. In the STUDENT table, ClassTeacherID refers to this. What type of key is ClassTeacherID in the STUDENT table?**
(a) Primary Key
(b) Alternate Key
(c) Candidate Key
(d) Foreign Key

Answers

1. (c) 2. (c) 3. (b) 4. (b) 5. (a)
6. Database 7. DBA
8. Data integrity 9. External schema
10. domain 11. True 12. False 13. (a) 14. (a)
26. (i) → (c), (ii) → (b), (iii) → (c), (iv) → (c), (v) → (d)

09

CHAPTER

SQL is a standard language used to store, retrieve and manipulate data in relational database.
It perform tasks like creating, updating and deleting database.

YOUR STUDY GOALS

9.1 SQL Statements
9.2 SQL Data Types
9.3 DDL Statements/Commands
9.4 DML Statements/Commands
9.5 Working with NULL Values
9.6 SQL Functions
9.7 GROUP BY Statement
9.8 HAVING Clause
9.9 Cartesian Product on Two Tables
9.10 Join

YOUR PRACTICE GOAL

- Objective Type Questions (50 Qs ; MCQs, True or False, Fill in the Blanks, Assertion and Reason)
- Subjective Type Questions (77 Qs ; VSA, SA, LA)
- Case Based Questions (Objective Case Study-1 Subjective Case Studies-2)

Structured Query Language

Structured Query Language (SQL) is the most popular query language used by major relational database management systems such as MySQL, ORACLE, SQL Server, etc. SQL is easy to learn as the statements comprise of descriptive english words and are not case sensitive.

SQL provides statements for defining the structure of the data, manipulating data in the database, declaring constraints and retrieving data from the database in various ways, depending on your requirements.

SQL provides variety of tasks such as

- Querying data.
- Creating, replacing, altering and dropping tables.
- Inserting, updating and deleting rows in a table.
- Controlling access to the database.
- Guaranteeing database consistency and integrity.

Advantages of SQL

- It is not platform dependent, it can be used in all types of devices; PCs, laptops and even mobile phones also.
- SQL queries can be used to retrieve large amount of records from a database quickly and efficiently.
- SQL generally consists of english language statements and it is very easy to learn and understand.
- SQL is used for relational database.
- SQL can do both the jobs of being a programming language as well as an interactive language at the same time.
- SQL provides client-server architecture. It is used for linking front end computers and back end databases.

- With the emergence of object based programming, object storage capabilities are extended to relational database.

Disadvantages of SQL

- Interfacing a SQL database is more complex than adding a few lines of code.
- Although SQL databases confirm to ANSI and ISO standards, some databases go for proprietary extensions to standard SQL to ensure vendor lock-in.

9.1 SQL Statements

SQL command or statement is a special kind of sentence that contains clauses and all end with a semicolon(;) just as a sentence ends with a period.

There are four types of SQL statements

DDL (Data Definition Language)

It provides statements for creation and deletion of the database tables, views, etc.

The DDL provides a set of definitions to specify the storage structure in a database system.

Some DDL statements are as follows

CREATE	Used to create new table in the database.
DROP	Used to delete tables from the database.
ALTER	Used to change the structure of the database table. This statement can add up additional column, drop existing, and even change the data type of columns involved in a database table.
RENAME	Used to rename a table.

DML (Data Manipulation Language)

It provides statements for manipulating the database objects. It is used to query the databases for information retrieval.

Some DML statements are as follows

INSERT	Used to insert data into a table.
SELECT	Used to retrieve data from a database.
UPDATE	Used to update existing data within a table.
DELETE	Used to delete all records from a table.

DCL (Data Control Language)

It is used to assign security levels in database, which involves multiple user setups. They are used to grant defined role and access privileges to the users.

Some DCL statements are as follows

GRANT	Used to give user's access privileges to database.
REVOKE	Used to withdraw access privileges given with grant command.

TCL (Transaction Control Language)

It is used for controlling the transactions in a database system. These are also used to manage the changes made by DML.

Some TCL statements are as follows

COMMIT	Used to save the work done.
SAVEPOINT	Used to identify a point in a transaction to which you can later rollback.
ROLLBACK	Used to restore database to original since the last COMMIT.
SET TRANSACTION	Establishes properties for the current transactions.

*In this chapter, we will discuss only **DDL and DML** statements.*

Rules for SQL Commands

Rules for SQL commands are given below

(i) SQL statements can be typed in lowercase or uppercase letter. SQL statements are not case sensitive.

(ii) The statements can be typed in single line or multiple lines.

(iii) A semicolon (;) is used to terminate the SQL statements.

(iv) The statements may be distributed across the line but keywords cannot be.

(v) A comma (,) is used to separate parameters without a clause.

(vi) Characters and date constants or literals must be enclosed in single quotes ('A').

(vii) A command can be typed either full or first four characters.

9.2 SQL Data Types

Data types are declared to identify the type of data that will be stored in a particular field or variable.

The following list of general SQL data types are given below

Data Type	Syntax	Explanation (if applicable)
INTEGER	INTEGER or INT	A 32-bit signed integer value and its range from –2147483648 to 2147483647.
SMALLINT	SMALLINT	A 16-bit signed integer value and its range from –32768 to 32767.
NUMERIC	NUMERIC (p,s)	Where, p is a precision value and s is a scale value. e.g. numeric (6,2) is a 6 digit number that has 4 digit before the decimal and 2 digit after the decimal.
DECIMAL	DECIMAL (p,s)	Where, p is a precision value and s is a scale value. (same as NUMERIC)
REAL	REAL	Single-precision floating point number.
DOUBLE PRECISION	DOUBLE PRECISION	Double-precision floating point number.
FLOAT	FLOAT(p)	Where, p is a precision value.
CHARACTER	CHAR(x)	Where, x is the number of characters to be stored. This data type will occupy space for NULL values. It can hold atmost 255 characters.
CHARACTER VARYING	VARCHAR(x)	Where, x is the number of characters to be stored. It will occupy space for NULL values. It can hold atmost 2000 characters and used in ANSI standard.
CHARACTER VARYING	VARCHAR2 (x)	Where, x is the number of characters to be stored. It can hold 4000 bytes of characters and used only in Oracle.
DATE	DATE	Stores year, month and day values.
TIME	TIME	Stores hour, minute and second values.

SQL Command Basics

SQL database is a way of organising a group of tables and table stores the data in the form of rows and columns. To create a bunch of different tables that share a common theme, you would group them into one database to make the management process easier.

So, for manipulating data, we need to know about database commands, which are described below

Creating and Using a Database

Create a Database

Creating database is an easier task. You need to just type the name of the database in a CREATE DATABASE command.

Syntax

`CREATE DATABASE [IF NOT EXISTS]<database_name>;`

CREATE DATABASE command will create an empty database with the specified name and would not contain any table.

IF NOT EXISTS is an optional part of this statement which prevents you from an error if there exists a database with the given name in the database catalog.

e.g. `mysql>CREATE DATABASE BOOK;`

Output Query OK, 1 row affected <0.01 sec>

Select a Database

Creating database is not enough for use. Before working with tables, first you have to select the database.

The only thing need to be considered before selecting a database is that it must already exist. To select a database USE command is used.

Syntax `USE <database_name>;`

e.g. `mysql>USE ENGBOOK;`

Where, USE command makes the specified database as a current working database and EGNBOOK is the database name.

Output Database changed

Show Databases

To check the names of the existing databases on the server you need to use the SHOW command. This will provide you the information about databases and the contents available in it.

Syntax `SHOW DATABASES;`

e.g. `mysql>SHOW DATABASES;`

Output

```
+----------+
| Database |
+----------+
| BOOK     |
| SCHOOL   |
| COPIES   |
| STUDENT  |
+----------+
```

Dropping a Database

Database can be removed or deleted using DROP command. But before deleting a database make sure that you do not need the data stored in different tables of a database because when you delete a database, all its tables also gets removed along with it.

Syntax `DROP DATABASE <database_name>;`

e.g. `mysql>DROP DATABASE SCHOOL;`

Output Query OK, 1 row affected (0.04 sec)

Note
- Drop command permanently removes the database.
- MySQL is not case-sensitive, so you can write SQL commands either in uppercase or lowercase but for UNIX, MySQL is case-sensitive.

Quick Test 1

1. Write two advantages of SQL.
2. Write the short note on DDL.
3. Write use of semicolon(;) in SQL statements
4. Which language is used to query the database for information retrieval?
5. Write two disadvantage of SQL.

9.3 DDL Statements/Commands

Some DDL statements are as follows

CREATE Statement

The CREATE statement is used to create a table in a database. In this command, we need to give information about table like number of columns, rows and its types and constraints.

Syntax

```
CREATE TABLE <table_name>
(
    <column_name1><data_type>[(<size>)] [constraints],
    <column_name2><data_type>[(<size>)] [constraints],
    <column_name3><data_type>[(<size>)] [constraints],
    ....
);
```

The data type specifies what type of data, the column can hold and the size or constraint is optional.

Constraints

Constraints are the conditions that the table must satisfy. These can be enforced on the attributes of a relation. These can be specified at the time of creating table. They are used to ensure integrity of a relation, hence named as integrity constraints.

Some types of constraints are:

- **NOT NULL Constraint** It ensures that a column cannot store NULL value.
- **UNIQUE Constraint** It is used to uniquely identify each record in a database.
- **PRIMARY KEY Constraint** It ensures that a column have an unique identity, which helps to find a particular record in a table and no column that is part of the primary key constraint can contain a NULL value.
- **FOREIGN KEY Constraint** It designates a column or combination of columns as a foreign key and establishes its relationship with a primary key in different tables.
- **CHECK KEY Constraint** It is used to define condition, which column in each row must satisfy.
- **DEFAULT Constraint** It inserts default value into a column.

Example 1 If we want to create a table PERSONS that contains five columns: P_Id, FirstName, LastName, Address and City.

We use the following CREATE statement:

```
CREATE TABLE PERSONS
(
   P_Id INT Primary Key,
   FirstName VARCHAR(25)NOT NULL,
   LastName VARCHAR(25),
   Address VARCHAR(30),
   City VARCHAR(25)
);
```

Displaying the Table Structure

DESCRIPTION or DESC command is used to verify the structure of a table that you have created.

This command display the column names, available data items with their data types.

Syntax `DESCRIBE <table_name>;`

Or `DESC <table_name>;`

e.g. `DESC PERSONS;`

Output

Field	Type	Null	Key	Default	Extra
P_Id	Int	NO	PRI		
FirstName	varchar(25)	NO			
LastName	varchar(25)	YES			
Address	varchar(30)	YES			
City	varchar(25)	YES			

DROP Statement

The DROP statement is used to remove the table definition and all data, constraints and permission specified for that table. You have to be careful while using the DROP command because once the table is deleted, then all the information available in the table would be lost forever. But there is a condition for dropping a table; it must be empty. A table with rows in it cannot be dropped.

Syntax `DROP TABLE table_name;`

e.g. `DROP TABLE EMPLOYEE;`

The above query will delete the table EMPLOYEE and after this, no table with Employee name would exist. We cannot even rollback after dropping a table.

ALTER Statement

The ALTER statement is used to add, delete or modify columns and constraints in the existing table.

To ADD a Column

Syntax `ALTER TABLE table_name ADD column_name data_type;`

e.g. `ALTER TABLE STUDENT ADD Section CHAR;`

The above query will add column Section to STUDENT table, whose data type is character.

To DROP Column

Syntax `ALTER TABLE table_name DROP COLUMN column_name;`

e.g. `ALTER TABLE STUDENT DROP COLUMN location;`

The above query will delete a column location from STUDENT table.

To MODIFY Column Data Type

Syntax

```
ALTER TABLE table_name MODIFY column_name
data_type;
```

e.g. `ALTER TABLE STUDENT MODIFY Fee NUMBER(15,2);`

The above query will modify the data type of Fee column, of STUDENT table.

To DELETE a Constraint

Syntax `ALTER TABLE table_name DROP Constraint_Name;`

e.g. `ALTER TABLE STUDENT DROP Primary Key;`

The above query will delete the primary key constraint from STUDENT table.

RENAME Statement

The RENAME statement is used to rename a table.

Syntax

```
RENAME old_table_name TO new_table_name;
```

e.g. `RENAME STUDENT TO CANDIDATE;`

The above query will rename STUDENT table to CANDIDATE.

9.4 DML Statements/Commands

Some DML statements are as follows

INSERT Statement

The INSERT statement is used to insert a new row/data in a table.

Syntax

```
INSERT INTO table_name VALUES
                    (value1, value2, value3,...);
```

Or

```
INSERT INTO table_name(column1, column2,
column3,...)VALUES(value1, value2,
value3,...);
```

Example 2 If we have the following PERSONS table

P_Id	LastName	FirstName	Address	City
1	Hansen	Ola	Timoteivn 10	Sandnes
2	Svendson	Tove	Borgvn 23	Sandnes
3	Pettersen	Kari	Storgt 20	Stavanger

and we want to insert a new row in the PERSONS table.

We use the following SQL statement

```
INSERT INTO PERSONS VALUES (4,'Nilsen',
Johan', 'Bakken 2', 'Stavanger');
```

Output

P_Id	LastName	FirstName	Address	City
1	Hansen	Ola	Timoteivn 10	Sandnes
2	Svendson	Tove	Borgvn 23	Sandnes
3	Pettersen	Kari	Storgt 20	Stavanger
4	Nilsen	Johan	Bakken 2	Stavanger

Insert Data Only in Specified Columns

It is also possible to add data only in specific columns.

Example 3 The following SQL statement will add a new row, but add data only in the P_Id, LastName and the FirstName columns.

We use the following SQL statement

```
INSERT INTO PERSONS(P_Id, LastName, FirstName)
VALUES(5, 'Tjessem', 'Jakob');
```

Output

P_Id	LastName	FirstName	Address	City
1	Hansen	Ola	Timoteivn10	Sandnes
2	Svendson	Tove	Borgvn 23	Sandnes
3	Pettersen	Kari	Storgt 20	Stavanger
4	Nilsen	Johan	Bakken 2	Stavanger
5	Tjessem	Jakob	NULL	NULL

SELECT Statement

The SELECT statement is used to select data from a database or view table information. The result is stored in a result table, called the result set.

Syntax

To select some specify columns

```
SELECT column_name(s) FROM table_name;
```

Or

To select all columns

```
SELECT * FROM table_name;
```

Where asterisk (*) is a quick way of selecting all columns.

In SQL, SELECT clause is used to list the attributes desired in the result of a query and FROM clause is used to list the relations from which such columns are to be extracted.

Example 4 If we want to select the content of the columns named LastName and FirstName from the PERSONS table.

We have to use the following SELECT statement

```
SELECT LastName,FirstName FROM PERSONS;
```

Output

LastName	FirstName
Hansen	Ola
Svendson	Tove
Pettersen	Kari

Example 5 If we want to select all the columns from the PERSONS table.

We have to use the following SELECT statement

```
SELECT * FROM PERSONS;
```

Output

P_Id	LastName	FirstName	Address	City
1	Hansen	Ola	Timoteivn 10	Sandnes
2	Svendson	Tove	Borgvn 23	Sandnes
3	Pettersen	Kari	Storgt 20	Stavanger

Column Alias

Column alias is used to temporarily rename a table's column for the purpose of a particular query.

This renaming is a temporary change and the actual column name does not change in the database.

Syntax

```
SELECT <column_name1> AS <Alias_name> FROM
<table_name>;
```

Where, Alias_name specifies the reference name of the specified column.

Table: COMPANY

EMP_ CODE	EMP_ NAME	EMP_DEPT _NO	EMP_SAL ARY	Joining_ Date
100	RAHUL SHARMA	D05	25600	2012 -02-06
101	VIKAS MITTAL	D03	26000	2002-12-04
102	PUNEET JAIN	D05	23500	2004-08-06
103	SACHIN VATS	D02	24000	2007-09-06
104	UDAY SINGH	D03	26000	2001-07-06
105	RAVI SHUKLA	D01	26500	2012-05-06
106	VINAY RANA	D03	25500	2001-02-06

Example 6 To select the DOJ of all the employees referenced as Joining_Date from the table COMPANY the query would be like

```
mysql>SELECT DOJ AS Joining_Date FROM COMPANY;
```

Output

```
+--------------+
| Joining_Date |
+--------------+
|  2012-02-06  |
|  2002-12-04  |
|  2004-08-06  |
|  2007-09-06  |
|  2001-07-06  |
|  2012-05-06  |
|  2001-02-06  |
+--------------+
7 rows in set (0.00 sec)
```

Operators in SQL

SQL supports different types of operators, some of them are described below

Arithmetic Operators

These operators are used to perform mathematical calculations, such as addition, subtraction, multiplication, division and remainder.
Some most important arithmetic operators used in SQL are

OPERATOR	DESCRIPTION
+ (Addition)	Add the two arguments together
– (Subtraction)	Subtract the second argument from the first argument
* (Multiplication)	Multiplies the two arguments
/ (Division)	Divide the first argument by the second argument
% (Modulo)	Divide the first argument from the second argument and provides the remainder of that operation

Syntax

```
SELECT <Expression1> <arithmetic operator>
    <Expression2>
    [FROM <table_name>]
    [WHERE <Condition>];
```

Example 7 Query to display **EMP_NAME, EMP_DEPT_NO** and 20% of **EMP_SALARY** for each employee for social fund.

```
mysql> SELECT EMP_NAME, EMP_DEPT_NO,
EMP_SALARY*0.20
FROM COMPANY;
```

Output

EMP_NAME	EMP_DEPT_NO	EMP_SALARY*0.20
Rahul Sharma	D05	5120
Vikas Mittal	D03	5200
Puneet Jain	D05	4200
Sachin Vats	D02	4700
Uday Singh	D03	5200
Ravi Shukla	D01	4700
Vinay Rana	D03	4800

7 rows in set (0.00 sec)

Arithmetic operators can be implemented through simple SELECT statement without any table. This acts like a function.

e.g. `SELECT 35*2+5;`

Output

35*2+5
75

1 row in set (0.03 sec)

Comparison Operators

These operators are used to test or compare the value of two operands, *i.e.*, between two variables or between a variable and a constant.
If the condition is false, then the result is zero (0) and if the condition is true, then the result is non-zero. These operators are also called **relational operators.**

Some of the comparison/relational operators used in SQL are as follows

OPERATOR	DESCRIPTION
=	Equal to
>	Greater than
<	Less than
>=	Greater than or equal to
<=	Less than or equal to
<> or !=	Not equal to (not ISO standard)
!<	Not less than (not ISO standard)
!>	Not greater than (not ISO standard)

Syntax

```
SELECT <column name>|*|expression
FROM <table name> WHERE<expression>
<comparison operator> <expression>;
```

Example 8 Query to display **EMP_NAME** and **EMP_SALARY** for those employees whose salary is greater than or equal to 25000.

```
mysql>  SELECT EMP_NAME,EMP_SALARY
        FROM COMPANY
        WHERE EMP_SALARY> = 25000;
```

Output

EMP_NAME	EMP_SALARY
Rahul Sharma	25600
Vikas Mittal	26000
Uday Singh	26000

3 rows in set (0.00 sec)

When we use relational operators with character data type, '<' means earlier in the alphabet and '>' means later in the alphabet 'Bangalore' < 'Brajil' as 'a' comes before 'r' in alphabet.

Logical Operators

The logical operators compare two conditions at a time to determine whether a row can be selected for the output. Logical operators are also called **boolean operators**, because these operators return a boolean data type value as TRUE, or FALSE.

When retrieving data using a SELECT statement, you can use these operators in the WHERE clause, which allows you to combine more than one condition.

Some of the Boolean/Logical operators used in SQL are as follows

OPERATOR	DESCRIPTION
AND	Logical AND compares two expressions and return true, when both expressions are true
OR	Logical OR compares two expressions and return true, when atleast one of the expressions is true
NOT	NOT takes a single expression as an argument and changes its value from false to true or from true to false. You can use an exclamation point (!) in place of this operator

Syntax

```
SELECT <column name>|*|<expression>
FROM <table name>
WHERE <expressions> <boolean operator>
<expressions>;
```

Example 9 Query to display **EMP_CODE** and **EMP_NAME** for those employees whose **EMP_DEPT_NO** is D05 and **EMP_SALARY** is greater than 22000.

```
mysql> SELECT EMP_CODE,EMP_NAME
       FROM COMPANY
       WHERE (EMP_DEPT_NO='D05'AND
       EMP_SALARY >22000);
```

Output

```
+----------+-----------------+
| EMP_CODE |   EMP_NAME      |
+----------+-----------------+
| 100      | Rahul Sharma    |
+----------+-----------------+
1 rows in set (0.00 sec)
```

Example 10 Query to display **EMP_CODE** and **EMP_NAME** for those employees whose **EMP_DEPT_NO** is D05 or **'EMP_SALARY'** is greater than 22000.

```
mysql> SELECT EMP_CODE, EMP_NAME
       FROM COMPANY
       WHERE(EMP_DEP_NO = 'D05' OR
       EMP_SALARY>22000);
```

Output

```
+----------+--------------------+
| EMP_CODE | EMP_NAME           |
+----------+--------------------+
|   100    | Rahul Sharma       |
|   101    | Vikas Mittal       |
|   102    | Puneet Jain        |
|   103    | Sachin Vats        |
|   104    | Uday Singh         |
|   105    | Ravi Shukla        |
|   106    | Vinay Rana         |
+----------+--------------------+
7 rows in set (0.00 sec)
```

Example 11 Query to display **EMP_CODE** and **EMP_NAME** for the employee whose **EMP_SALARY** is not greater than 22000.

```
mysql> SELECT EMP_CODE, EMP_NAME
       FROM COMPANY
       WHERE(NOT EMP_SALARY>22000);
                   or
mysql> SELECT EMP_CODE, EMP_NAME
       FROM COMPANY
       WHERE !(EMP_SALARY>22000);
```

Output

```
+----------+-----------------+
| EMP_CODE | EMP_NAME        |
+----------+-----------------+
|   102    | Puneet Jain     |
+----------+-----------------+
 1 row in set (0.00 sec)
```

DISTINCT Keyword

In a table, some of the columns may contain duplicate values. This is not a problem, however, sometimes you may want to list only the different (distinct) values in a table. The DISTINCT keyword can be used to return only distinct (different) values in a particular column or a whole table.

Syntax

```
SELECT DISTINCT column_name(s)
FROM table_name;
```

Example 12 If we want to select only the distinct values from the column named "City" from the PERSONS table given in example 2.

We have to use the following SELECT statement

```
SELECT DISTINCT City FROM PERSONS;
```

Output

```
+-----------+
|   City    |
+-----------+
|  Sandnes  |
+-----------+
| Stavanger |
+-----------+
```

ALL Keyword

ALL clause result just the same as that when you do not specify DISTINCT. It will give values of selected attribute from every row of table without considering the duplicate records.

Syntax `SELECT ALL column_name FROM table_name;`

WHERE Clause

The WHERE clause is used to extract only those records that fulfill a specified criteria.

Syntax

```
SELECT column_name(s) FROM table_name
WHERE condition;
```

Example 13 If we want to select only the persons living in the city "Sandnes" from the table PERSONS.

We use the following SELECT statement

```
SELECT * FROM PERSONS
WHERE City='Sandnes';
```

Output

P_Id	LastName	FirstName	Address	City
1	Hansen	Ola	Timoteivn 10	Sandnes
2	Svendson	Tove	Borgvn 23	Sandnes

Quotes Around Text Fields

SQL uses single quotes around text values (most database systems will also accept double quotes).

However, numeric values should not be enclosed in quotes.

For text values,

This is correct

```
SELECT * FROM PERSONS WHERE FirstName='Tove';
```

This is wrong

```
SELECT * FROM PERSONS WHERE FirstName=Tove;
```

For numeric values,

This is correct

```
SELECT * FROM PERSONS WHERE Year=1965;
```

This is wrong

```
SELECT * FROM PERSONS WHERE Year='1965';
```

Operators Allowed in the WHERE Clause

(i) **BETWEEN Operator** selects a range of data between two values. The values can be numbers, text or dates.

Syntax

```
SELECT column_name(s)
FROM table_name
WHERE column_name
BETWEEN value1 AND value2;
```

Example 14 If we want to select the persons with a last name alphabetically between "Hansen" and "Pettersen" from the table PERSONS.

We use the following SELECT statement

```
SELECT * FROM PERSONS
WHERE LastName
BETWEEN 'Hansen' AND 'Pettersen';
```

Output

P_Id	LastName	FirstName	Address	City
1	Hansen	Ola	Timoteivn 10	Sandnes
3	Pettersen	Kari	Storgt 20	Stavanger

(ii) **NOT BETWEEN Operator** selects the data outside the range of data between two values. The values can be text, numbers or dates.

Syntax

```
SELECT column_name(s)
FROM table_name
WHERE column_name
NOT BETWEEN value1 AND value2;
```

Example 15 To display the persons outside the range in the previous example, use NOT BETWEEN operator.

We use the following SELECT statement

```
SELECT * FROM PERSONS
WHERE LastName
NOT BETWEEN 'Hansen' AND 'Pettersen';
```

Output

P_Id	LastName	FirstName	Address	City
2	Svendson	Tove	Borgvn 23	Sandnes

(iii) **LIKE Operator** is used to match a value similar to specific pattern in a column using % and _. The % sign represents zero, one or multiple characters, while _ represents a single character. It is useful when you want to search rows to match a specific pattern, or when you do not know the entire value.

Syntax

```
SELECT column_name FROM table_name
WHERE column_name LIKE "condition";
```

Example 16 To display the FirstName that start with letter "T".

We use the following SELECT statement

```
SELECT FirstName FROM PERSONS
WHERE FirstName LIKE "T%";
```

Output

FirstName
Tove

Example 17. If we want to display the all records, where the LastName's second letter is 'a'.

We use the following SELECT statement

```
SELECT * FROM PERSONS
WHERE LastName LIKE"_a%";
```

Output

P_Id	LastName	FirstName	Address	City
1	Hansen	Ola	Timoteivn 10	Sandnes

(iv) **IN Operator** checks a value within a set of values separated by commas and retrieve the rows from the table which are matching.

The IN operator allows you to specify multiple values in a WHERE clause.

Syntax

```
SELECT column_name(s)
FROM table_name
WHERE column_name IN (value1,value2,...);
```

Example 18 If we want to select the persons with a last name equal to "Hansen" or "Pettersen" from the table PERSONS.

We use the following SELECT statement

```
SELECT * FROM PERSONS
WHERE LastName IN
('Hansen','Pettersen');
```

Output

P_Id	LastName	FirstName	Address	City
1	Hansen	Ola	Timoteivn 10	Sandnes
3	Pettersen	Kari	Storgt 20	Stavanger

ORDER BY Clause

The ORDER BY keyword is used to sort the result set along a specified column with the SELECT command. The ORDER BY keyword sorts the records in ascending order by default.

If you want to sort the records in a descending order, you can use the DESC keyword.

Syntax

```
SELECT column_name(s)
FROM table_name
ORDER BY column_name(s)ASC/DESC;
```

Example 19 If we want to select all the persons from the table PERSONS, however, we want to sort the persons by their last name in ascending order.

We use the following SELECT statement

```
SELECT * FROM PERSONS
ORDER BY LastName ASC;
```

Output

P_Id	LastName	FirstName	Address	City
1	Hansen	Ola	Timoteivn 10	Sandnes
3	Pettersen	Kari	Storgt 20	Stavanger
2	Svendson	Tove	Borgvn 23	Sandnes

UPDATE Statement

The UPDATE statement is used to update existing records in a table.

The WHERE clause in the UPDATE statement specifies, which record or records that should be updated. If you omit the WHERE clause, all records will be updated.

Note *Expressions are also used in the SET clause of the UPDATE command to manipulate the values.*

Syntax

```
UPDATE table_name
SET column1=value1, column2=value2,...
WHERE <condition>;
```

Example 20 If we want to update the person "Ola Hansen" in the PERSONS table.

We use the following SQL statement

```
UPDATE PERSONS
SET Address='Nissestien 67',
City ='Sandnes'
WHERE LastName='Hansen' AND
FirstName='Ola';
```

Output

P_Id	LastName	FirstName	Address	City
1	Hansen	Ola	Nissestien 67	Sandnes
2	Svendson	Tove	Borgvn 23	Sandnes
3	Pettersen	Kari	Storgt 20	Stavanger

SQL UPDATE Warning

Be careful when updating records. If we omit the WHERE clause in the example above, like this:

```
UPDATE PERSONS
SET Address='Nissestien 67',
City='Sandnes';
```

The PERSONS table would have looked like this

P_Id	LastName	FirstName	Address	City
1	Hansen	Ola	Nissestien 67	Sandnes
2	Svendson	Tove	Nissestien 67	Sandnes
3	Pettersen	Kari	Nissestien 67	Sandnes

DELETE Statement

The DELETE statement is used to delete rows in a table. The WHERE clause in the DELETE statement specifies, which records to be deleted. If you omit the WHERE clause, all records will be deleted.

Syntax

```
DELETE FROM table_name WHERE <condition>;
```

Example 21 If we want to delete the person "Kari Pettersen" in the PERSONS table.

We use the following SQL statement

```
DELETE FROM PERSONS
WHERE LastName='Pettersen'
AND FirstName='Kari';
```

Output

P_Id	LastName	FirstName	Address	City
1	Hansen	Ola	Timoteivn 10	Sandnes
2	Svendson	Tove	Borgvn 23	Sandnes

Delete All Rows

It is possible to delete all rows in a table without deleting the table. This means that the table structure, attributes and indexes will be intact.

Syntax `DELETE FROM table_name;`

Quick Test 2

1. SELECT and ALTER are which type of commands?
2. What is unique constraints?
3. Write the syntax to modify the column data type.
4. What is the use of DISTINCT keyword with SELECT statement?
5. Give an example using IN operator.

9.5 Working with NULL Values

In SQL, the empty values are represented as NULL in a table. If a table having null values, then you can display columns with null values or without null values and you can replace NULL values with another value.

To handle NULL values in SQL, you should use the following commands

IS NULL Clause

If we want to search the column whose value is NULL in a table, then we use IS NULL clause.

Syntax

```
SELECT<column_name> FROM <table_name>
WHERE <column_name> IS NULL;
```

Example 22 Let us consider the following table Teacher

T_No	T_Name	T_Salary	DOJ
T01	Aradhna	17000	2013-01-08
T02	Ritika	NULL	2013-12-14
T03	Ravindra	NULL	2013-11-23
T04	Dushyant	16000	2014-01-10
T05	Swati	19000	2014-02-10

Query to display column whose value is NULL.

We use the following SQL statement

```
SELECT * FROM Teacher
WHERE T_Salary IS NULL;
```

Output

T_No	T_Name	T_Salary	DOJ
T02	Ritika	NULL	2013-12-14
T03	Ravindra	NULL	2013-11-23

IS NOT NULL Clause

If we want to search the column whose value is not NULL in a table then we use IS NOT NULL clause.

Syntax

```
SELECT<column name> FROM <table_name>
WHERE <column_name> IS NOT NULL;
```

Example 23 Consider the above table Teacher. Query to display column whose value is not NULL.

We use the following SQL statement

```
SELECT * FROM Teacher
WHERE T_Salary IS NOT NULL;
```

Output

T_No	T_Name	T_Salary	DOJ
T01	Aradhna	17000	2013-01-08
T04	Dushyant	16000	2014-01-10
T05	Swati	19000	2014-02-10

9.6 SQL Functions

A function in SQL performs a specific task and returns one or more values as a result. Functions are powerful tools in SQL queries, allowing us to manipulate data efficiently.

SQL functions can be applied to operate on either single or multiple rows in a table. Based on how they operate, SQL functions are divided into two categories:

1. **Single Row Functions** These operate on individual records and return one result for each row.

2. **Aggregate Functions** These operate on groups of rows and return a single result for the entire group.

In this chapter, we will discuss only aggregate functions.

Aggregate Functions

Aggregate functions are also known as **group functions**, they return a result only in single row based on group of rows, rather than on single row.

It always used with SELECT command and in ORDER BY and HAVING clauses. They are commonly used with the GROUP BY clause in a SELECT statement.

Some of the Aggregate functions are

Function Syntax	Function Use
`SUM( [ALL DISTINCT] expression)`	The total of the (distinct) values in a numeric column/expression.
`AVG([ALL | DISTINCT] expression)`	The average of the (distinct) values in a numeric column/expression.
`COUNT([ALL | DISTINCT] expression)`	The number of (distinct) non-NULL values in a column/expression.
`COUNT(*)`	The number of selected rows.
`MAX(expression)`	The highest value in a column/expression.
`MIN(expression)`	The lowest value in a column/expression.

The SQL aggregate functions return a single value, calculated from values in a column.

9.7 GROUP BY Statement

The GROUP BY statement is used with the aggregate functions to group the result set by one or more columns.

Syntax
```
SELECT column_name,
aggregate_function(column_name)
FROM table_name
WHERE condition
GROUP BY column_name;
```

Consider the following ORDERS table

TABLE: ORDERS

O_Id	OrderDate	OrderPrice	Customer
1	2008/11/12	1000	Hansen
2	2008/10/23	1600	Nilsen
3	2008/09/02	700	Hansen
4	2008/09/03	300	Hansen
5	2008/08/30	2000	Jensen
6	2008/10/04	100	Nilsen

Example 24 If we want to find the total sum (OrderPrice) of each customer from table ORDERS.

We use the following SQL statement
```
SELECT Customer, SUM(OrderPrice)
FROM ORDERS
GROUP BY Customer;
```

Output

Customer	SUM(OrderPrice)
Hansen	2000
Nilsen	1700
Jensen	2000

Let's see what happens if we omit the GROUP BY statement:
```
SELECT Customer,SUM(OrderPrice)
FROM ORDERS;
```
The result set will look like this

Customer	SUM(OrderPrice)
Hansen	5700

In the above case, SELECT statement cannot be used, because the SELECT statement above has two columns specified (Customer and SUM(OrderPrice)).

The "SUM(OrderPrice)" returns a single value (that is the total sum of the "OrderPrice" column), while "Customer" returns 6 values (one value for each row in the "ORDERS" table).

This will therefore not give us the correct result. However, you have seen that the GROUP BY statement solves this problem.

9.8 HAVING Clause

The HAVING clause is used with GROUP BY clause to place condition because the WHERE keyword could not be used with aggregate functions.

Syntax
```
SELECT column_name,
aggregate_function(column_name)
FROM table_name
WHERE condition
GROUP BY column_name
HAVING aggregate_function(column_name)
                              <condition>;
```

Example 25 If we want to find any of the customers have a total order of less than 2000 from table ORDERS.

We use the following SQL statement
```
SELECT Customer,SUM(OrderPrice)
```

```
FROM ORDERS
GROUP BY Customer
HAVING SUM(OrderPrice)<2000;
```

Output

Customer	SUM(OrderPrice)
Nilsen	1700

Example 26 If we want to find the customers 'Hansen' or 'Jensen' have a total order of more than 1500.

We add an ordinary WHERE clause to the SQL statement

```
SELECT Customer,SUM(OrderPrice)
FROM ORDERS
WHERE Customer='Hansen' OR
Customer='Jensen'
GROUP BY Customer
HAVING SUM(OrderPrice)>1500;
```

Output

Customer	SUM(OrderPrice)
Hansen	2000
Jensen	2000

9.9 Cartesian Product on Two Tables

The Cartesian product in SQL refers to the result of a join operation where every row from one table is combined with every row from another table.

This type of join produces a result set that is the product of the number of rows in the first table and the number of rows in the second table.

Consider the following tables Student and Courses

Table : Students

StudentID	Name
1	Rahul
2	Priya
3	Arjun

Table : Courses

CourseID	CourseName
101	Mathematics
102	Science
103	English

Example 27. To get the Cartesian product of the Students and Courses tables, you would use the following SQL query:

```
SELECT *FROM Students, Courses;
```

Output

Table : Students * Courses

StudentID	Name	CourseID	CourseName
1	Rahul	101	Mathematics
1	Rahul	102	Science
1	Rahul	103	English
2	Priya	101	Mathematics
2	Priya	102	Science
2	Priya	103	English
3	Arjun	101	Mathematics
3	Arjun	102	Science
3	Arjun	103	English

9.10 Join

A join is a query that combines rows from two or more tables. In a join query, more than one tables are listed in FROM clause. The function of combining data from multiple tables is called joining. SQL can obtain data from several related tables by performing either a physical or virtual join on the tables.

Joins are used when we have to select data from two or more tables. Joins are used to extract data from two (or more) tables, when we need a relationship between certain columns in these tables.

The SQL Join condition is always used in the WHERE clause of SELECT, UPDATE and DELETE statements.

There are different kind of SQL joins

1. Equi Join 2. Self Join 3. Natural Join

We are discuss only equi join and natural join in this chapter.

Equi Join

Equi join is a simple SQL join condition that uses equal sign as a comparison operator.

Syntax

```
SELECT col1, col2, col3
FROM table1, table2
WHERE table1.col1 = table2.col1;
```

Consider the following tables PERSON and ORDERS

TABLE : PERSON

P_Id	Last_Name	First_Name	City
1	Sharma	Abhay	Mumbai
2	Gupta	Mohan	Delhi
3	Verma	Akhil	Mumbai

TABLE : ORDERS

O_Id	Order_No	P_Id
1	10050	3
2	25000	3
3	5687	1
4	45000	1
5	35000	15

Example 28 To join two tables PERSON and ORDERS using a condition (i.e. P_Id of PERSON table is equal to the P_Id of ORDERS table).

We use the following SQL statement

```
SELECT Last_Name, First_Name, Order_No
FROM PERSON, ORDERS
WHERE PERSON.P_Id=ORDERS.P_Id
ORDER BY PERSON.Last_Name;
```

Output

Last_Name	First_Name	Order_No
Sharma	Abhay	5687
Sharma	Abhay	45000
Verma	Akhil	10050
Verma	Akhil	25000

SQL equi joins are further classified into two categories

(i) Inner Join

The inner join using either of the equivalent queries gives the intersection of two tables, i.e. it returns us the rows, which are common in both the tables.

Syntax

```
SELECT col1, col2
FROM table1 INNER JOIN table2
ON table1.column_name=table2.column_name;
```

Example 29 To perform INNER JOIN on two tables PERSON and ORDERS.

We use the following SQL statement

```
SELECT Last_Name, First_Name FROM
PERSON INNER JOIN ORDERS ON
PERSON.P_Id=ORDERS.P_Id;
```

Output

Last_Name	First_Name
Verma	Akhil
Verma	Akhil
Sharma	Abhay
Sharma	Abhay

(ii) Outer Join

The outer join include rows in a joined result even when they have no match in the joined table. An outer join returns all rows that satisfy the join condition and also returns those rows from one table for which no rows from the other satisfy the join condition.

(a) Left Outer Join

The left outer join returns all the rows from the left table, even if there are no matches in the right table.

Syntax

```
SELECT column 1, column 2
FROM table1 LEFT JOIN table2 ON
table1.column_name = table2.column_name;
```

Example 30 To perform LEFT OUTER JOIN on two tables PERSON and ORDERS.

We use the following SQL statement

```
SELECT P.Last_Name,
P.First_Name,O.Order_No
FROM PERSON P
LEFT JOIN ORDERS O
ON P.P_Id = O.P_Id ORDER BY
P.First_Name;
```

Output

Last_Name	First_Name	Order_No
Sharma	Abhay	5687
Sharma	Abhay	45000
Verma	Akhil	25000
Verma	Akhil	10050
Gupta	Mohan	

(b) Right Outer Join

The right outer join returns all the rows from the right table, even if there are no matches in the left table.

Syntax

```
SELECT column1, column2
FROM table1 RIGHT JOIN table2
ON table1.column_name=table2.column_name;
```

Example 31 To perform RIGHT OUTER JOIN on two tables PERSON and ORDERS.

We use the following SQL statement

```
SELECT P.Last_Name, P.First_Name,
O.Order_No FROM PERSON P RIGHT JOIN ORDERS
ON P.P_Id = O.P_Id
ORDER BY P.Last_Name;
```

Output

Last_Name	First_Name	Order_No
Sharma	Abhay	45000
Sharma	Abhay	5687
Verma	Akhil	25000
Verma	Akhil	10050
		35000

Natural Join

The natural join is a type of equi join and is structured in such a way that, columns with same name of associated tables will appear once only.

Syntax

```
SELECT * FROM table1
NATURAL JOIN table2;
```

Consider the following tables

TABLE: FOODS

Item_Id	Item_Name	Item_Unit	Company_Id
1	Chex Mix	Pcs	16
6	Cheez-it	Pcs	15
2	Biscuit	Pcs	15
3	Munch	Pcs	17
4	Rice	Pcs	15
5	Cake	Pcs	18
7	Snake	Pcs	NULL

TABLE: COMPANY

Company_Id	Company_Name	Company_City
18	Order All	Boston
15	Jack Hill Ltd	London
16	Akas Foods	Delhi
17	Foodies	London
19	Sip_n_Bite	New York

Example 32 To fetch all the unique columns from 'FOODS' and 'COMPANY' tables, after joining these tables.

We use the following SQL statement

```
SELECT * FROM FOODS NATURAL JOIN COMPANY
WHERE FOODS.Company_Id=COMPANY.Company_Id;
```

Output

Item_Id	Item_Name	Item_Unit	Company_Id	Company_Name	Company_City
1	Chex Mix	Pcs	16	Akas Foods	Delhi
6	Cheez-it	Pcs	15	Jack Hill Ltd	London
2	Biscuit	Pcs	15	Jack Hill Ltd	London
3	Munch	Pcs	17	Foodies	London
4	Rice	Pcs	15	Jack Hill Ltd	London
5	Cake	Pcs	18	Order All	Boston

Quick Test 3

1. How to delete all rows from table?
2. Why do we use DISTINCT keyword with COUNT( ) function?
3. Name any two aggregate functions.
4. HAVING keyword is used with which clause?
5. What is the difference between left outer join and right outer join?
6. Write a short note on natural join.

Mind Map

Structured Query Language

Programming language for storing and processing information in a relational database.

Multiple-row Functions

It is also known as **Aggregate functions** and **Group functions**. This functions work with data of multiple-rows at a time and return a single output value.

Single-row Functions

This type of function work with a single-row at a time. It returns a result for each row of the table, on which the query is performed. This is also known as Scalar functions.

Types of SQL Functions

MySQL function performs a pre-defined task and returns a single value such as a numerical, string or date/time value.

Types of Multiple-row Functions

MAX() Returns the maximum value from a set of values.
Syntax `MAX(column_name)`

MIN() Returns the minimum value from a set of values.
Syntax `MAX(column_name)`

AVG() Returns the average value of a numeric column.
Syntax `AVG(column_name)`

SUM() Returns the total sum of a numeric column.
Syntax `SUM(column_name)`

COUNT() Returns the number of rows that match a specified criteria.
Syntax `COUNT(column_name)` *Or* `COUNT(*)`

Or The COUNT DISTINCT function returns the number of unique values in the column or expression.
Syntax `SELECT COUNT(DISTINCT column_name)FROM table_name;`

Working with NULL Values

In SQL, the empty values are represented as NULL in a table.

- If we want to search the column whose value is NULL in a table, then we use **IS NULL** clause.
- If we want to search the column whose value is not NULL in a table then we use **IS NOT NULL** clause.

Clause

- The **ORDER BY clause** sorts the records in ascending order by default. If you want to sort the records in descending order, you can use the DESC keyword.
  Syntax
  ```
  SELECT column_name(s)FROM table_name ORDER BY column_name(s)ASC/DESC;
  ```
- The **GROUP BY clause** can be used with SELECT statement, if we want to select multiple records and group of results by one or more columns.
  Syntax
  ```
  SELECT Empid, SUM(Salary) AS "TotalSalary" FROM PAYMENTS GROUP BY Department;
  ```
- The **HAVING clause** can be used only with the SELECT statement. HAVING is applied to summarised rows (summarised with GROUP BY).
  Syntax
  ```
  SELECT Customer, SUM(OrderPrice) FROM ORDER GROUP BY Customer
  HAVING SUM(OrderPrice)<2000;
  ```
- **JOIN clause** is used to combine rows from two or more tables based on a related column between them.

Data Types of SQL

To identify the type of data that will be stored in a particular field or variable.

Data Type	Syntax
INTEGER	INTEGER or INT
SMALLINT	SMALLINT
NUMERIC	NUMERIC(p,s)
DECIMAL	DECIMAL(p,s)
REAL	REAL
DOUBLE PRECISION	DOUBLE PRECISION
FLOAT	FLOAT(p)
CHARACTER	CHAR(x)
CHARACTER VARYING	VARCHAR(x)
CHARACTER VARYING	VARCHAR2(x)
DATE	DATE
TIME	TIME

SQL Commands

- **Data Definition Language (DDL)** Define the structure of your tables and other objects in the database. **Commands** CREATE, ALTER, DROP, RENAME, TRUNCATE, COMMENT.
- **Data Manipulation Language (DML)** Access and manipulate data in existing database. **Commands** SELECT, INSERT, UPDATE, DELETE.
- **Transaction Control Language (TCL)** Manage transactions in database. **Commands** COMMIT, ROLLBACK and SAVEPOINT.
- **Data Control Language (DCL)** Assign security levels in database. **Commands** GRANT and REVOKE.

SQL Operators

- **Arithmetic Operators**
  +, –, *, /, %
- **Comparison Operators**
  = , > , < , >=, <=, <> or != , !< , !>
- **Logical Operators**
  AND, OR, NOT
- **BETWEEN Operator**
  Used to check range
- **IN Operator**
  Check a value within a set of values.
- **LIKE Operator** Used to search a specific pattern in a column.

Constraints

- **Unique Constraints** No two rows have the same value in the specified columns
- **Default Constraints** Default value is inserted in the field automatically.
- **Primary Key Constraints** Unique identification of each rows and do not allow NULL value.
- **Foreign Key Constraints** It ensures that values in one table match values in another table.
- **Check Constraints** Used to limit the value range that can be placed in a column.
- **Not Null Constraints** Enforces a column to NOT accept NULL values.

NCERT Folder

In-text Questions

1. Which two constraints when applied together will produce a Primary Key constraint?

Ans. The two constraints that, when applied together to a column (or a set of columns), will produce a Primary Key constraint are:

1. **NOT NULL** This constraint ensures that the column(s) cannot contain any null values. Every row must have a value for the primary key.
2. **UNIQUE** This constraint ensures that all values in the column(s) are distinct. No two rows can have the same value for the primary key.

2. Which datatype out of Char and Varchar will you prefer for storing contact number (mobile number)? Discuss.

Ans. 1. **Variable Length** Mobile numbers have a consistent length (e.g., 10 digits in India, but can vary internationally with prefixes).

VARCHAR stores only the actual characters entered, saving space compared to CHAR which would pad shorter numbers with spaces to a fixed length.

2. **Flexibility** While generally consistent, prefixes or extensions might be added in some cases. VARCHAR accommodates this variability without wasting space for the majority of standard-length numbers.
3. **No Performance Advantage for Fixed Length** For this relatively short string, the slight performance advantage CHAR might offer in some scenarios due to its fixed length is negligible and outweighed by the space efficiency of VARCHAR.

3. What are the minimum and maximum income values that can be entered in the income attribute given the data type is INT?

Ans. The INT data type in SQL typically allows values in the range:

- Minimum: –2,147,483,648
- Maximum: 2,147,483,647

(Based on 4-byte signed integer storage)

4. 1. **Which of the two insert statement should be used when the order of data to be inserted are not known?**

2. **Can we insert two records with the same roll number?**

Roll Number	SName	SDateof Birth	GUID
1	Atharv Ahuja	2003-05-15	444444444444
2	Daizy Bhutia	2002-02-28	111111111111
3	Taleem Shah	2002-02-28	
4	John Dsouza	2003-08-18	333333333333
5	Ali Shah	2003-07-05	101010101010
6	Manika P	2002-03-10	466444444666

Ans. 1.
```
INSERT INTO table_name (column1, column2, ...)
VALUES (value1, value2, ...);
```

2. No, if RollNumber is defined as a PRIMARY KEY or has a UNIQUE constraint.

Otherwise, Yes, but it is not recommended as it may lead to duplicate identification issues.

5. The following query selects records of all the employees except Aaliya.

```
mysql> SELECT * FROM EMPLOYEE WHERE NOT Ename
= 'Aaliya';
```

What will happen if in the above query we write "Aaliya" as "AALIYA" or "aaliya" or "AaLIYA"? Will the query generate the same output or an error?

Ans. In MySQL, string comparisons are case-insensitive by default. So, if you write 'AALIYA', 'aaliya', or 'AaLIYA' instead of 'Aaliya',

The query `SELECT * FROM EMPLOYEE  WHERE NOT Ename = 'AALIYA';`

will still work correctly and produce the same output—excluding Aaliya's record, regardless of the case.

6. Can we use arithmetic operators (+, -. *, or /) on date functions?

Ans. Yes, arithmetic operators can be used with date functions, but with some conditions:

You can add or subtract numbers (like days) to/from dates.

Example:

SELECT CURDATE() + 7;   -- Adds 7 days to current date

SELECT '2025-04-08' - INTERVAL 5 DAY;

Multiplication (*) and division (/) are not directly applicable to date functions.

Exercise Questions

1. Answer the following questions:

(a) Define RDBMS. Name any two RDBMS software.

(b) What is the purpose of the following clauses in a select statement?

(i) ORDER BY **(ii) GROUP BY**

(c) **Site any two differences between Single Row Functions and Aggregate Functions.**

(d) **What do you understand by Cartesian Product?**

(e) **Differentiate between the following statements:**

(i) **ALTER and UPDATE**

(ii) **DELETE and DROP**

(f) **Write the name of the functions to perform the following operations:**

(i) **To display the day like "Monday", "Tuesday", from the date when India got independence.**

(ii) **To display the specified number of characters from a particular position of the given string.**

(iii) **To display the name of the month in which you were born.**

(iv) **To display your name in capital letters**

Ans. (a) RDBMS (Relational Database Management System) is a type of database management system that stores data in a structured format using rows and columns, enabling relationships between data items. Two examples of RDBMS software are MySQL and Oracle Database.

(b) (i) **ORDER BY** This clause is used to sort the result set of a query by one or more columns, either in ascending (ASC) or descending (DESC) order.

(ii) **GROUP BY** This clause groups rows that have the same values in specified columns into aggregated data, allowing for functions like COUNT, SUM, AVG, etc., to be applied to each group.

(c)

Single Row Functions	Aggregate Functions
Operates on a single row at a time	Operates on groups of rows
Can be used in SELECT, WHERE, and ORDER BY clause.	Can be used in the SELECT clause only.

(d) A Cartesian Product is the result of combining every row from one table with every row from another table in a database. If Table A has m rows and Table B has n rows, the Cartesian Product will result in m×n rows, which can lead to a large dataset if the tables are not filtered properly.

(e) (i) Differentiate between the ALTER and UPDATE statements:

ALTER	UPDATE
Used to modify the structure of a database object.	Used to modify existing records in a table.
Syntax `ALTER TABLE table_name ADD column_name data_type;`	**Syntax** `UPDATE table_name SET column_name = value WHERE condition;`
Can add, delete, or modify columns and constraints.	Can change the values of one or more columns in existing rows.
Affects the schema of the database.	Affects the data within the rows of a table.
Does not change the existing data types.	Changes the actual data stored in the table.

(ii) Differentiate between DELETE and DROP:

DELETE	DROP
Used to remove specific rows from a table based on a condition.	Used to remove entire tables, views, or databases.
Does not free up the storage space immediately; space is marked for reuse.	Frees up all storage associated with the table or database.
Can be rolled back if within a transaction.	Cannot be rolled back; the data is permanently removed.
Triggers can be activated when using DELETE.	Does not activate triggers since it removes the entire object.
Syntax `DELETE FROM table_name WHERE condition;`	**Syntax** `DROP TABLE table_name;`

(f) (i) datetime.date.strftime()

(ii) str[start:end]

(iii) datetime.date.strftime()

(iv) str.upper()

2. Write the output produced by the following SQL statements:

(a) **SELECT POW(2,3);**

(b) **SELECT ROUND(342.9234,-1);**

(c) **SELECT LENGTH("Informatics Practices");**

(d) **SELECT YEAR("1979/11/26"), MONTH("1979/11/26"), DAY("1979/11/26"), MONTHNAME("1979/11/26");**

(e) **SELECT LEFT("INDIA",3), RIGHT("Computer Science",4), MID("Informatics",3,4), SUBSTR("Practices",3);**

Ans. (a) **Output** 8
(2 raised to the power of 3)

(b) **Output** 340
(Rounded to the nearest ten)

(c) **Output** 21
(Number of characters in the string)

(d) **Output** 1979, 11, 26, November
(Year, Month, Day, and Month Name)

(e) **Output** IND, ence, for, actices
(First 3 letters of "INDIA", last 4 letters of "Computer Science", 4 characters starting from the 3rd position of "Informatics", and substring starting from the 3rd position of "Practices")

3. Consider the following MOVIE table and write the SQL queries based on it.

MovieID	Movie Name	Category	Release Date	Production Cost	Business Cost
001	Hindi_ Movie	Musical	2018-04-23	124500	130000
002	Tamil_ Movie	Action	2016-05-17	112000	118000
003	English_ Movie	Horror	2017-08-06	245000	360000
004	Bengali_ Movie	Adventu re	2017-01-04	72000	100000
005	Telugu_ Movie	Action	-	100000	-
006	Punjabi_ Movie	Comedy	-	30500	-

(a) Display all the information from the Movie table.

(b) List business done by the movies showing only MovieID, MovieName and Total_Earning. Total_Earning to be calculated as the sum of ProductionCost and BusinessCost.

(c) List the different categories of movies.

(d) Find the net profit of each movie showing its MovieID, MovieName and NetProfit. Net Profit is to be calculated as the difference between Business Cost and Production Cost.

(e) List MovieID, MovieName and Cost for all movies with ProductionCost greater than 10,000 and less than 1,00,000.

(f) List details of all movies which fall in the category of comedy or action.

(g) List details of all movies which have not been released yet.

Ans. (a)
```
SELECT * FROM MOVIE;
```
(b)
```
SELECT  MovieID,  MovieName, (ProductionCost +
BusinessCost) AS Total_Earning
FROM  MOVIE;
```
(c)
```
SELECT DISTINCT Category FROM MOVIE;
```
(d)
```
SELECT MovieID, MovieName, (BusinessCost -
ProductionCost) AS NetProfit FROM MOVIE;
```
(e)
```
SELECT MovieID, MovieName, ProductionCost AS
Cost
FROM MOVIE
WHERE ProductionCost > 10000 AND
ProductionCost < 100000;
```
(f)
```
SELECT *
FROM MOVIE
WHERE Category IN ('Comedy', 'Action');
```
(g)
```
SELECT *
FROM MOVIE
WHERE ReleaseDate IS NULL;
```

4. Suppose your school management has decided to conduct cricket matches between students of Class XI and Class XII. Students of each class are asked to join any one of the four teams – Team Titan, Team Rockers, Team Magnet and Team Hurricane. During summer vacations, various matches will be conducted between these teams. Help your sports teacher to do the following:

(a) Create a database "Sports".

(b) Create a table "TEAM" with following considerations:

(i) It should have a column TeamID for storing an integer value between 1 to 9, which refers to unique identification of a team.

(ii) Each TeamID should have its associated name (TeamName), which should be a string of length not less than 10 characters.

(c) Using table level constraint, make TeamID as the primary key.

(d) Show the structure of the table TEAM using a SQL statement.

(e) As per the preferences of the students four teams were formed as given below. Insert these four rows in

TEAM table:

Row 1:	(1, Team Titan)
Row 2:	(2, Team Rockers)
Row 3:	(3, Team Magnet)
Row 3:	(4, Team Hurricane)

(f) Show the contents of the table TEAM using a DML statement.

(g) Now create another table MATCH_DETAILS and insert data as shown below. Choose appropriate data types and constraints for each attribute.

Table: MATCH_DETAILS

Match ID	Match Date	FirstTeam ID	SecondTea mID	FirstTeam Score	SecondTea mScore
M1	2018-07-17	1	2	90	86
M2	2018-07-18	3	4	45	48
M3	2018-07-19	1	3	78	56
M4	2018-07-19	2	4	56	67
M5	2018-07-18	1	4	32	87
M6	2018-07-17	2	3	67	51

Ans. (a) `CREATE DATABASE Sports;`

(b, c)
```
CREATE TABLE TEAM (
TeamID INT CHECK (TeamID BETWEEN 1 AND 9),
TeamName VARCHAR(50) CHECK
(LENGTH(TeamName) >= 10),
PRIMARY KEY (TeamID)
);
```
(d) `DESCRIBE TEAM;`

(e)
```
INSERT INTO TEAM (TeamID, TeamName)
VALUES (1, 'Team Titan');
INSERT INTO TEAM (TeamID, TeamName)
VALUES (2, 'Team Rockers');
INSERT INTO TEAM (TeamID, TeamName)
VALUES (3, 'Team Magnet');
INSERT INTO TEAM (TeamID, TeamName)
VALUES (4, 'Team Hurricane');
```
(f) `SELECT * FROM TEAM;`

(g) Create Table MATCH_DETAILS
```
CREATE TABLE MATCH_DETAILS (
MatchID VARCHAR(2) PRIMARY KEY,
MatchDate DATE,
FirstTeamID INT CHECK (FirstTeamID
BETWEEN 1 AND 4),
SecondTeamID INT CHECK (SecondTeamID
BETWEEN 1 AND 4),
FirstTeamScore INT CHECK (FirstTeamScore
>= 0),
SecondTeamScore INT CHECK
(SecondTeamScore >= 0),
FOREIGN KEY (FirstTeamID) REFERENCES
TEAM(TeamID),
FOREIGN KEY (SecondTeamID) REFERENCES
TEAM(TeamID)
);
```
Insert Data into MATCH_DETAILS
```
INSERT INTO MATCH_DETAILS (MatchID,
MatchDate, FirstTeamID, SecondTeamID,
FirstTeamScore, SecondTeamScore) VALUES
('M1', '2018-07-17', 1, 2, 90, 86),
('M2', '2018-07-18', 3, 4, 45, 48),
('M3', '2018-07-19', 1, 3, 78, 56),
('M4', '2018-07-19', 2, 4, 56, 67),
('M5', '2018-07-18', 1, 4, 32, 87),
('M6', '2018-07-17', 2, 3, 67, 51);
```

5. Using the sports database containing two relations (TEAM, MATCH_DETAILS) and write the queries for the following:

(a) Display the MatchID of all those matches where both the teams have scored more than 70.

(b) Display the MatchID of all those matches where FirstTeam has scored less than 70 but SecondTeam has scored more than 70.

(c) Display the MatchID and date of matches played by Team 1 and won by it.

(d) Display the MatchID of matches played by Team 2 and not won by it.

(e) Change the name of the relation TEAM to T_DATA. Also change the attributes TeamID and TeamName to T_ID and T_NAME respectively.

Ans. (a)
```
SELECT MatchID FROM MATCH_DETAILS WHERE
FirstTeamScore > 70 AND SecondTeamScore > 70;
```
(b)
```
SELECT MatchID FROM MATCH_DETAILS WHERE
FirstTeamScore < 70 AND SecondTeamScore > 70;
```
(c)
```
SELECT MatchID, MatchDate FROM MATCH_DETAILS
WHERE FirstTeamID = 1 AND FirstTeamScore >
SecondTeamScore;
```
(d)
```
SELECT MatchID FROM MATCH_DETAILS WHERE
SecondTeamID = 2 AND SecondTeamScore <=
FirstTeamScore;
```
(e)
```
ALTER TABLE TEAM RENAME TO T_DATA;
ALTER TABLE T_DATA RENAME COLUMN TeamID TO T_ID;
ALTER TABLE T_DATA RENAME COLUMN TeamName TO
T_NAME;
```

6. A shop called Wonderful Garments who sells school uniforms maintains a database SCHOOLUNIFORM as shown below.

Table : Uniform

UCode	UName	UColor
1	Shirt	White
2	Pant	Grey
3	Skirt	Grey
4	Tie	Blue
5	Socks	Blue
6	Belt	Blue

Table : Cost

UCode	Size	Priec
1	M	500
1	L	580
1	XL	620
2	M	810
2	L	890
2	XL	940
3	M	770
3	L	830
3	XL	910
4	S	150
4	L	170
5	S	180
5	L	210
6	M	110
6	L	140
6	XL	160

It consisted of two relations – UNIFORM and COST. They made UniformCode as the primary key for UNIFORM relations. Further, they used UniformCode and Size to be composite keys for COST relation. By analysing the database schema and database state, specify SQL queries to rectify the following anomalies.

(a) M/S Wonderful Garments also keeps handkerchiefs of red colour, medium size of Rs. 100 each.

(b) INSERT INTO COST (UCode, Size, Price) values (7, 'M',100);

When the above query is used to insert data, the values for the handkerchief without entering its details in the UNIFORM relation is entered. Make a provision so that the data can be entered in the COST table only if it is already there in the UNIFORM table.

(c) Further, they should be able to assign a new UCode to an item only if it has a valid UName. Write a query to add appropriate constraints to the SCHOOLUNIFORM database.

(d) Add the constraint so that the price of an item is always greater than zero.

Ans. (a) Insert Handkerchief Details

To insert the handkerchief details into the UNIFORM relation, use the following SQL query:

INSERT INTO UNIFORM (UniformCode, UName, Color, Size) VALUES (7, 'Handkerchief', 'Red', 'M');

(b) Prevent Insertion in COST Without UNIFORM Entry

To ensure that entries in the COST table can only be made if the corresponding entry exists in the UNIFORM table, you can use a foreign key constraint:

```
ALTER TABLE COST
ADD CONSTRAINT fk_uniform
FOREIGN KEY (UCode) REFERENCES
UNIFORM(UniformCode);
```

(c) Ensure Valid UName for New UCode

To enforce that a new UCode can only be assigned if there is a valid UName, you can use a check constraint. Assuming that UName should not be NULL, you can use:

```
ALTER TABLE UNIFORM
ADD CONSTRAINT chk_uname
CHECK (UName IS NOT NULL);
```

(d) Price Must Be Greater Than Zero

To ensure that the price of an item in the COST table is always greater than zero, you can add a check constraint:

```
ALTER TABLE COST
ADD CONSTRAINT chk_price
CHECK (Price > 0);
```

7. Consider the following table named "Product", showing details of products being sold in a grocery shop.

PCode	PName	UPrice	Manufacturer
P01	Washing Powder	120	Surf
P02	Toothpaste	54	Colgate
P03	Soap	25	Lux
P04	Toothpaste	65	Pepsodent
P05	Soap	38	Dove
P06	Shampoo	245	Dove

Write SQL queries for the following:

(a) Create the table Product with appropriate data types and constraints.

(b) Identify the primary key in Product.

(c) List the Product Code, Product name and price in descending order of their product name. If PName is the same, then display the data in ascending order of price.

(d) Add a new column Discount to the table Product.

(e) Calculate the value of the discount in the table Product as 10 per cent of the UPrice for all those products where the UPrice is more than 100, otherwise the discount will be 0.

(f) Increase the price by 12 per cent for all the products manufactured by Dove.

(g) Display the total number of products manufactured by each manufacturer.

Write the output(s) produced by executing the following queries on the basis of the information given above in the table Product:

(h) SELECT PName, avg(UPrice) FROM Product GROUP BY Pname;

(i) **SELECT DISTINCT Manufacturer FROM Product;**

(j) **SELECT COUNT (DISTINCT PName) FROM Product;**

(k) **SELECT PName, MAX(UPrice), MIN(UPrice) FROM Product GROUP BY PName;**

Ans. (a)
```
CREATE TABLE Product (
    PCode VARCHAR(5) PRIMARY KEY,
    PName VARCHAR(50) NOT NULL,
   UPrice DECIMAL(10, 2) CHECK (UPrice >= 0),
    Manufacturer VARCHAR(50) NOT NULL
);
```

(b) The primary key in the Product table is PCode.

(c)
```
SELECT PCode, PName, UPrice
FROM Product
ORDER BY PName DESC, UPrice ASC;
```

(d)
```
ALTER TABLE Product
ADD Discount DECIMAL(10, 2);
```

(e)
```
SELECT PCode, PName,UPrice,Manufacturer,
(UPrice * 10 / 100) * (UPrice > 100) AS
Discount FROM Product;
```

(f)
```
UPDATE Product
SET UPrice = UPrice * 1.12
WHERE Manufacturer = 'Dove';
```

(g)
```
SELECT Manufacturer, COUNT(*) AS
TotalProducts
FROM Product
GROUP BY Manufacturer;
```

(h)

PName	avg(UPrice)
Soap	31.50
Toothpaste	59.50
Washing Powder	120.00
Shampoo	245.00

(i)

Manufacturer
Surf
Colgate
Lux
Pepsodent
Dove

(j)

COUNT(DISTINCT PName)
5

(k)

PName	MAX(UPrice)	MIN(UPrice)
Soap	38	25
Toothpaste	65	54
Washing Powder	120	120
Shampoo	245	245

8. Using the CARSHOWROOM database given below, write the SQL queries for the following:

CarId	Car Name	Price	Model	Year Manufacture	Fueltype
D001	Dzire	582613.00	LXI	2017	Betrol
D001	Dzire	673112.00	VXI	2018	Petrol
B001	Baleno	567031.00	Sigma 1.2	2019	Pertol
B002	Baleno	647858.00	Delta 1.2	2018	Petrol
E001	EECO	355205.00	5 STR STD	2017	CNG
E001	EECO	654914.00	CARE	2018	CNG
S001	SWIFT	514000.00	LXI	2017	Petrol
S002	SEIFT	614000.00	VXI	2018	Petrol

(a) **Add a new column Discount in the INVENTORY table.**

(b) **Set appropriate discount values for all cars keeping in mind the following:**

(i) **No discount is available on the LXI model.**

(ii) **VXI model gives a 10 per cent discount.**

(iii) **A 12 per cent discount is given on cars other than LXI model and VXI model.**

(c) **Display the name of the costliest car with fuel type "Petrol".**

(d) **Calculate the average discount and total discount available on Baleno cars.**

(e) **List the total number of cars having no discount.**

Ans. (a)
```
ALTER TABLE INVENTORY ADD Discount
DECIMAL(5, 2);
```

(b) (i)
```
UPDATE INVENTORY SET Discount = 0 WHERE
model = 'LXI';
```

(ii)
```
UPDATE INVENTORY SET Discount = price *
0.10 WHERE model = 'VXI';
```

(iii)
```
UPDATE INVENTORY SET Discount = price *
0.12 WHERE model NOT IN ('LXI', 'VXI');
```

(c)
```
SELECT name FROM INVENTORY WHERE
fuel_type = 'Petrol' ORDER BY price DESC
LIMIT 1;
```

(d)
```
SELECT AVG(Discount) AS avg_discount,
SUM(Discount) AS total_discount
FROM INVENTORY
WHERE name = 'Baleno';
```

(e)
```
SELECT COUNT(*) FROM INVENTORY WHERE
Discount = 0;
```

EXAM PATTERN QUESTIONS

Objective Type Questions

Multiple Choice Questions

1. Which of the following is an advantage of SQL?

(a) High speed (b) Client/server language
(c) Easy to learn (d) All of these

2. In a table in MySQL database, an attribute A of datatype varchar(20) has the value "Keshav". The attribute B of datatype char(20) has value "Meenakshi". How many characters are occupied by attribute A and attribute B? CBSE SQP 2023-24

(a) 20,6 (b) 6,20 (c) 9,6 (d) 6,9

3. In which datatype the value stored is padded with spaces to fit the specified length. CBSE SQP 2024-25

(a) DATE (b) VARCHAR
(c) FLOAT (d) CHAR

4. In MYSQL, which type of value should not be enclosed within quotation marks? CBSE 2025

(a) DATE (b) VARCHAR
(c) FLOAT (d) CHAR

5. Which of the following command is used to remove the table definition and all data?

(a) Create (b) Select
(c) Drop (d) None of these

6. Which of the following commands will delete the table from MYSQL database? CBSE SQP 2022-23

(a) DELETE TABLE (b) DROP TABLE
(c) REMOVE TABLE (d) ALTER TABLE

7. Which of the following is a correct syntax to add a column in SQL command?

(a) ALTER TABLE table_name ADD column_name data_type;
(b) ALTER TABLE ADD column_name data_type;
(c) ALTER table_name ADD column_name data_type;
(d) None of the above

8. Fill in the blank:

________command is used to remove primary key from the table in SQL. CBSE SQP 2022-23

(a) UPDATE (b) REMOVE
(c) ALTER (d) DROP

9. While creating a table, which constraint does not allow insertion of duplicate values in the table? CBSE 2025

(a) UNIQUE (b) DISTINCT
(c) NOT NULL (d) HAVING

10. Which statement of SQL provides statements for manipulating the database objects?

(a) DDL (b) DML (c) DCL (d) TCL

11. What will be the output of the query? CBSE SQP 2024-25

```
SELECT * FROM products WHERE product_name
LIKE 'App%';
```

(a) Details of all products whose names start with 'App'
(b) Details of all products whose names end with 'App'
(c) Names of all products whose names start with 'App'
(d) Names of all products whose names end with 'App'

12. Which of the following operator displays a record if either the first condition or the second condition is true?

(a) AND (b) BETWEEN
(c) OR (d) None of these

13. Which keyword can be used to return only different values in a particular column or a whole table?

(a) WHERE (b) DISTINCT
(c) ALL (d) BETWEEN

14. Fill in the blank:

The SELECT statement when combined with ______ clause, returns records without repetition. CBSE 2024

(a) DESCRIBE (b) UNIQUE
(c) DISTINCT (d) NULL

15. The .... keyword sorts the records in ascending order by default.

(a) LIKE (b) UPDATE
(c) ORDER (d) ORDER BY

16. Fill in the blank.

__________ clause is used with SELECT statement to display data in a sorted form with respect to a specified column. CBSE 2023

(a) WHERE (b) ORDER BY
(c) HAVING (d) DISTINCT

17. Which of the following is not a DDL command in SQL? CBSE 2024

(a) DROP (b) CREATE
(c) UPDATE (d) ALTER

18. Which of the following is a DML command in SQL? CBSE 2025

(a) UPDATE (b) CREATE
(c) ALTER (d) DROP

19. Aggregate functions are also known as

(a) group functions (b) group method
(c) sum function (d) Add function

20. Which of the following function returns the total number of values?

(a) MAX (b) MIN
(c) COUNT (d) SUM

21. Which function is used to display the total number of records from table in a database? CBSE SQP 2022-23

(a) SUM(*) (b) TOTAL(*)
(c) COUNT(*) (d) RETURN(*)

22. In SQL, the aggregate function which will display the cardinality of the table is .... CBSE 2024

(a) sum ( ) (b) count (*)
(c) avg ( ) (d) sum (*)

23. Which aggregate function can be used to find the cardinality of a table? CBSE SQP 2024-25

(a) sum() (b) count()
(c) avg() (d) max()

24. Which aggregate function in SQL displays the number of values in the specified column ignoring the NULL values? CBSE 2025

(a) len () (b) count()
(c) number() (d) num()

25. Which of the following join gives the intersection of two tables?

(a) Outer join (b) Inner join
(c) Equi join (d) None of these

Fill in the blanks

26. SQL is running in all ....

27. .... provides statements for creation and deletion of the database tables, views.

28. .... data type stores year, month and day values.

29. The SQL .... is used to add, delete or modify columns and constraints in the existing table.

30. The .... clause is used to extract only those records that fulfil a specified criteria.

31. The .... is a quick way of selecting all columns.

32. .... operator is used to match a value similar to specific pattern in a column using % and _ .

33. The .... statement is used with the aggregate functions to group the result set by one or more columns.

34. .... function returns the largest value from the selected column.

35. .... is a simple SQL join condition that uses equal sign as a comparison operator.

State whether True or False

36. When using the ALTER TABLE command in SQL, you can only add new columns to a table, but you cannot remove existing columns or constraints like a primary key.

37. The IN operator in SQL can be used in the WHERE clause to filter results based on a range of values, but it cannot be used with subqueries.

38. The HAVING clause is used in SQL to filter records after aggregation with GROUP BY, and it can also be used to filter on non-aggregated columns, similar to the WHERE clause.

39. In SQL, the NULL value can be compared directly with an equality operator (e.g., = NULL) to check if a column contains a NULL value.

40. In a SQL JOIN operation, a Cartesian product is produced when no ON condition is specified between the two tables, resulting in every row of the first table being combined with every row of the second table.

41. If table A has 6 rows and 3 columns, and table B has 5 rows and 2 columns, the Cartesian product of A and B will have 30 rows and 5 columns. CBSE 2025

Assertion and Reason Based Questions

Assertion (A) and Reason (R) Type questions. Choose the correct option as:

(a) Both Assertion (A) and Reason (R) are true, and Reason (R) is the correct explanation of Assertion (A)
(b) Both Assertion (A) and Reason (R) are true, but Reason (R) is not the correct explanation of Assertion (A)
(c) Assertion (A) is True, but Reason (R) is False
(d) Assertion (A) is False, but Reason (R) is True

42. **Assertion (A)** The VARCHAR(n) data type can store variable-length strings up to n characters.

Reason (R) The CHAR(n) data type is more efficient for storing strings than VARCHAR(n).

43. **Assertion (A)** The CREATE DATABASE statement is used to create a new database in SQL.
Reason (R) SQL databases can only be created if the user has administrative privileges.

44. **Assertion (A)** The SHOW TABLES command displays all the tables in the current database.
Reason (R) The USE database_name command changes the current database context.

45. **Assertion (A)** The PRIMARY KEY constraint ensures that a column cannot have duplicate values.
Reason (R) The UNIQUE constraint allows for one null value in a column.

46. **Assertion (A)** A SELECT command in SQL can have both WHERE and HAVING clauses. **CBSE SQP 2024-25**
Reason (R) WHERE and HAVING clauses are used to check conditions, therefore, these can be used interchangeably.

47. **Assertion (A)** The WHERE clause is used to filter records in a SQL query.
Reason (R) The ORDER BY clause is used to specify the order of the records returned by a query.

48. **Assertion (A)** The NULL value represents a missing or undefined value in SQL.
Reason (R) The IS NOT NULL condition can be used to filter out records that have NULL values.

49. **Assertion (A)** The GROUP BY clause is used to aggregate data in SQL queries.
Reason (R) The HAVING clause is used to filter the results of the aggregated data.

50. **Assertion (A)** The JOIN operation can combine rows from two or more tables based on a related column.
Reason (R) A CARTESIAN PRODUCT results in all possible combinations of rows from the involved tables.

Answers

1. (d) All of these
2. (b) 6,20
3. (d) CHAR
4. (c) FLOAT
5. (c) Drop
6. (b) DROP TABLE
7. (a) ALTER TABLE table_name ADD column_name data_type;
8. (c) ALTER
9. (a) UNIQUE
10. (b) DML (Data Manipulation Language)
11. (a) Details of all products whose names start with 'App'
12. (c) OR
13. (b) DISTINCT
14. (c) DISTINCT
15. (d) ORDER BY
16. (b) ORDER BY
17. (c) UPDATE
18. (a) UPDATE
19. (a) group functions
20. (c) COUNT
21. (c) COUNT(*)
22. (b) count (*)
23. (b) count()
24. (b) count()
25. (b) Inner join
26. Servers
27. DDL (Data Definition Language)
28. DATE
29. ALTER TABLE
30. WHERE
31. *(asterisk)
32. LIKE
33. GROUP BY
34. Max()
35. Equi join
36. False
37. False
38. False
39. False
40. True
41. True
42. (c) Assertion (A) is True, but Reason (R) is False.
43. (a) Both Assertion (A) and Reason (R) are true, and Reason (R) is the correct explanation of Assertion (A).
44. (a) Both Assertion (A) and Reason (R) are true, and Reason (R) is the correct explanation of Assertion (A).
45. (a) Both Assertion (A) and Reason (R) are true, and Reason (R) is the correct explanation of Assertion (A).
46. (c) Assertion (A) is True, but Reason (R) is False
47. (b) Both Assertion (A) and Reason (R) are true, but Reason (R) is not the correct explanation of Assertion (A).
48. (a) Both Assertion (A) and Reason (R) are true, and Reason (R) is the correct explanation of Assertion (A).
49. (b) Both Assertion (A) and Reason (R) are true, but Reason (R) is not the correct explanation of Assertion (A).
50. (b) Both Assertion (A) and Reason (R) are true, but Reason (R) is not the correct explanation of Assertion (A).

Subjective Type Questions

Very Short Answer Type Questions

1. Mention two characteristics of SQL.

Ans. (i) SQL is a very simple and easy to learn.

(ii) SQL allows the users to create, update, delete and retrieve data from a database.

2. Give any two features of SQL. **CBSE 2024**

Ans. Two features of SQL are

- It is used to retrieve and view specific data from a table in a database.
- Each query in SQL ends with a semicolon (;).

3. Expand the following abbreviation:

(i) SQL (ii) DML

Ans. (i) SQL - Structured Query Language

(ii) DML - Data Manipulation Language

4. Name any two DDL and any two DML commands. **CBSE 2023**

Ans. DDL commands : CREATE, ALTER

DML commands : INSERT, UPDATE

5. Name any two DDL commands.

Ans. DDL consists of various commands such as

(i) Create (ii) Alter

6. Name any four Transaction Control Language (TCL) commands.

Ans. *Four TCL commands are listed below:*

(i) Commit

(ii) Rollback

(iii) Savepoint

(iv) Set Transaction

7. What is the use of Set Transaction command?

Ans. Set Transaction command establishes properties for the current transactions.

8. Differentiate between char(n) and varchar(n) data types with respect to databases. **CBSE SQP 2022 Term II, 2023**

Ans. Differentiate between char(n) and varchar(n) are as follows

char(n)	varchar(n)
It stores a fixed length string between 1 and 255 characters.	It stores a variable length string.
If the value is of smaller length, then it adds blank spaces.	No blanks are added by varchar(n) even if value is of smaller length.

9. Which SQL command can change the degree of an existing relation? **CBSE SQP 2024-25**

Ans. Alter table command

10. Give the SQL statement to create a table Student with Roll Number, Name, Age and Marks.

Ans.
```
CREATE TABLE Student (Roll_Number NUMBER(5)
Primary key, Name CHAR (20), Age Number (2),
Marks Number (4));
```

11. Give the syntax of DROP statement.

Ans. `DROP TABLE table_name;`

12. Nisha is assigned the task of maintaining the staff data of an organization. She has to store the details of the staff in the SQL table named EMPLOYEES with attributes as EMPNO, NAME, DEPARTMENT, BASICSAL to store Employee's Identification Number, Name, Department, and Basic Salary respectively. There can be two or more Employees with the same name in the organization. **CBSE 2025**

(i) (a) Help Nisha to identify the attribute which should be designated as the PRIMARY KEY. Justify your answer.

Or

(b) Help Nisha to identify the constraint which should be applied to the attribute NAME such that the Employees' Names cannot be left empty or NULL while entering the records but can have duplicate values.

(ii) (a) Write the SQL command to change the size of the attribute BASICSAL in the table EMPLOYEES to allow the maximum value of 99999.99 to be stored in it.

Or

(b) Write the SQL command to delete the table EMPLOYEES.

Ans. (i) (a) EMPNO should be the PRIMARY KEY

Or

(b) Apply NOT NULL constraint on NAME.

(ii) (a)
```
ALTER TABLE EMPLOYEES MODIFY BASICSAL
DECIMAL (7,2);
```

Or

(b) `DROP TABLE EMPLOYEES;`

13. How will you select the content of the columns named LastName and FirstName from the Employee table.

Ans. `SELECT LastName, FirstName FROM Employee;`

14. What is the use of WHERE clause in SQL?

Ans. The WHERE clause is used to extract only those records that fulfil a specified criteria.

15. Write the query to select all the persons from the table Persons and sort the persons by their last name in ascending order.

Ans. `SELECT * FROM Persons ORDER BY LastName ASC;`

16. Give the syntax of Having clause.

Ans.
```
SELECT column_name, aggregate_function
(column_name)
FROM table_name
WHERE condition
GROUP BY column_name
HAVING aggregate_function (column_name)
<condition>;
```

17. Name any two logical operators.

Ans. And, OR

18. Ms. Veda created a table named Sports in a MySQL database, containing columns Game_id, P_Age and G_name. CBSE 2024

After creating the table, she realized that the attribute, Category has to be added. Help her to write a command to add the Category column. Thereafter, write the command to insert the following record in the table :

Game_id : G42
P_Age : Above 18
G_name : Chess
Category : Senior

Or

Write the SQL commands to perform the following tasks:

(i) View the list of tables in the database, Exam.

(ii) View the structure of table, Term1.

Ans.
```
ALTER TABLE SPORTS ADD CATEGORY VARCHAR(10);
INSERT INTO SPORTS(Game_id, P_Age, G_name,
Category) VALUES("G42","Above
18","Chess","Senior");
```

Or

(i) SHOW TABLES;
(ii) DESCRIBE Term1;

19. (I) (A) What constraint should be applied on a table column so that duplicate values are not allowed in that column, but NULL is allowed. CBSE SQP 2024-25

Or

(B) What constraint should be applied on a table column so that NULL is not allowed in that column, but duplicate values are allowed.

(II) (A) Write an SQL command to remove the Primary Key constraint from a table, named MOBILE. M_ID is the primary key of the table.

Or **(B) Write an SQL command to make the column M_ID the Primary Key of an already existing table, named MOBILE.**

Ans. (I) (A) The Unique constraint does not allow duplicate values but allows NULL values.

Or

(B) The NOT NULL constraint does not allow NULL values but allows duplicate values.

(II) (A) `Alter table MOBILE Drop Primary key(M_ID);`

Or

(B) `Alter table MOBILE ADD Primary key(M_ID);`

20. Differentiate between COUNT() and COUNT(*) functions in SQL with appropriate example. CBSE SQP 2022-23

Or **Categorize the following commands as DDL or DML. INSERT, UPDATE, ALTER, DROP**

Ans. COUNT(*) returns the count of all rows in the table, whereas COUNT() is used with Column_Name passed as argument and counts the number of non-NULL values in a column that is given as argument.

Example

Table : EMPL

EMPNO	ENAME	JOB	SAL	DEPTNO
8369	SMITH	CLERK	2985	10
8499	ANYA	NULL	9870	20
8566	AMIR	SALESMAN	8760	30
8698	BINA	MANAGER	5643	20
8912	SUR	NULL	3000	10

e.g. `SELECT COUNT(*) FROM EMPL;`

Output

COUNT(*)
5

e.g. `SELECT COUNT (JOB) FROM EMPL;`

Output

COUNT(JOB)
3

Since JOB has 2 NULL values.

Or

DDL ALTER , DROP

DML INSERT , UPDATE

21. Write the query to count the total number of employees from Payments table.

Ans. `SELECT COUNT(*) "Employees" FROM Payments;`

22. Write the output of the queries (i) to (iv) based on the table FURNITURE given below. **CBSE SQP 2022 Term II**

Table : FURNITURE

FID	NAME	DATEOFPURCHASE	COST	DISCOUNT
B001	Double Bed	03-JAN-2018	45000	10
T010	Dinning Table	10-MAR-2020	51000	5
B004	Single Bed	19-JUL-2021	22000	0
C003	Long back Chair	30-DEC-2016	12000	3
T006	Console Table	17-NOV-2019	15000	12
B006	Bunk bed	01-JAN-2021	28000	14

(i) `SELECT SUM(DISCOUNT) FROM FURNITURE WHERE COST>15000;`

(ii) `SELECT MAX(DATEOFPURCHASE) FROM FURNITURE;`

(iii) `SELECT * FROM FURNITURE WHERE DISCOUNT>5 AND FID LIKE "T%";`

(iv) `SELECT DATEOFPURCHASE FROM FURNITURE WHERE NAME IN ("Dinning Table", "Console Table");`

Ans. (i)

SUM(DISCOUNT)
29

(ii)

MAX(DATEOFPURCHASE)
19-Jul-2021

(iii)

FID	NAME	DATEOF PURCHASE	COST	DISCOUNT
T006	Console Table	17-NOV-2019	15000	12

(iv)

DATEOFPURCHASE
10-MAR-2020
17-NOV-2019

23. (i) **Which command is used to view the list of tables in a database?** **CBSE SQP 2022 Term II**

(ii) **Give one point of difference between an equi-join and a natural join.**

Ans. (i) SHOW Tables, command is used to view the list of tables in a database.

(ii) The differences between equi-join and natural join :

Equi-Join	Natural Join
Columns from two tables are compared for equality.	Only one of the identical columns existing in both tables is present.
Duplicate columns are shown.	No duplication of columns.

24. Define cartesian product with respect to RDBMS. **CBSE 2024**

Ans. Cartesian Product operation combines rows/tuples from two tables/relations. It results in all the pairs of rows from both the tables. It is denoted by 'X'.

Short Answer Type I Questions

25. Write the disadvantages of SQL.

Ans. Refer to text on page no 225 (Disadvantages of SQL).

26. Which commands are used to control user's privileges and how?

Ans. There are two commands that are used to control a user's privileges

(i) GRANT (ii) REVOKE

The GRANT command is used to give an existing user privileges and REVOKE command is used to remove privileges. If a user does not exist, GRANT will create a new user at the same time and give them all privileges.

27. Differentiate between COMMIT and ROLLBACK command.

Ans. COMMIT command is used to permanent all the changes made by DML commands, while ROLLBACK means that it undoes all changes since the beginning of a transaction or since a save point.

28. What are DDL and DML?

Ans. **DDL (Data Definition Language)** is a part of SQL, which provides commands for creating, altering and dropping the tables. Different DDL commands are CREATE, ALTER, DROP and RENAME.

DML (Data Manipulation Language) is a part of SQL, which provides commands for inserting, deleting and updating the information in a database. Different DML commands are SELECT, UPDATE, INSERT.

29. Describe the four data types in SQL.

Ans. Refer to the text on page no. 226 (SQL Data Types`).

30. How to create a database?

Ans. Refer to text on page no 226 (Create a database).

31. Charu has to create a database named MYEARTH in MySQL.

She now needs to create a table named CITY in the database to store the records of various cities across the globe. The table CITY has the following structure.

Table : CITY

Field Name	Data Type	Remarks
CITYCODE	CHAR(5)	Primary Key
CITYNAME	CHAR(30)	
SIZE	INTEGER	
AVGTEMP	INTEGER	
POPULATIONRATE	INTEGER	
POPULATION	INTEGER	

Help her to complete the task by suggesting appropriate SQL commands. CBSE SQP 2022 Term II

Ans. Command to create database

```
CREATE DATABASE MYEARTH;
```

Command to create table

```
CREATE TABLE CITY(
CITYCODE CHAR(5) PRIMARY KEY,
CITYNAME CHAR(30),
SIZE INT,
AVGTEMP INT,
POPULATIONRATE INT,
POPULATION INT,
);
```

32. (i) A table, ITEM has been created in a database with the following fields ITEMCODE, ITEMNAME, QTY, PRICE Give the SQL command to add a new field, DISCOUNT (of type Integer) to the ITEM table.

(ii) Categorize following commands into DDL and DML commands?

INSERT INTO, DROP TABLE, ALTER TABLE, UPDATE...SET CBSE SQP 2022 Term II

Ans. (i) `ALTER TABLE ITEM ADD Discount INT;`

(ii) DDL means 'Data Definition Language'. It is used to create and modify the structure of database objects in SQL. So, DDL commands are DROP TABLE, ALTER TABLE.

DML is 'Data Manipulation Language' which is used to manipulate data itself.

So, DML commands are INSERT INTO, UPDATE...SET.

33. Consider the table Projects given below: CBSE 2024

Table : Projects

P_id	Pname	Language	Startdate	Enddate
P001	School Management System	Python	2023-01-12	2023-04-03
P002	Hotel Management System	C++	2022-12-01	2023-02-02
P003	Blood Bank	Python	2023-02-11	2023-03-02
P004	Payroll Management System	Python	2023-03-12	2023-06-02

Based on the given table, write SQL queries for the following :

(i) Add the constraint, primary key to column P_id in the existing table Projects.

(ii) To change the language to Python of the project whose id is P002.

(iii) To delete the table Projects from MySQL database along with its data.

Ans. (i) `ALTER TABLE Projects ADD PRIMARY KEY (P_id);`

(ii) `UPDATE Projects SET LANGUAGE= "Python" WHERE P_id = "P002";`

(iii) `DROP TABLE Projects;`

34. Navdeep creates a table RESULT with a set of records to maintain the marks secured by students in Sem 1, Sem2, Sem3 and their division. After creation of the table, he has entered data of 7 students in the table. CBSE SQP 2022-23

ROLL_NO	SNAME	SEM1	SEM2	SEM3	DIV
101	KARAN	366	410	402	I
102	NAMAN	300	350	325	I
103	ISHA	400	410	415	I
104	RENU	350	357	415	I
105	ARPIT	100	75	178	IV
106	SABINA	100	205	217	II
107	NEELAM	470	450	471	I

Based on the data given above answer the following questions:

(i) Identify the most appropriate column, which can be considered as Primary key.

(ii) If two columns are added and 2 rows are deleted from the table result, what will be the new degree and cardinality of the above table?

(iii) Write the statements to:

(a) Insert the following record into the table Roll No- 108, Name- Aadit, Sem1- 470, Sem2-444, Sem3-475, Div- I.

(b) Increase the SEM2 marks of the students by 3% whose name begins with 'N'.

Or (Option for part iii only)

Write the statements to:

(a) Delete the record of students securing IV division.

(b) Add a column REMARKS in the table with datatype as varchar with 50 characters

Ans. (i) ROLL_NO

(ii) Degree : 8 Cardinality : 5

(iii) (a) `INSERT INTO RESULT VALUES(108," Aadit",470,444,475,"I");`

(b) `UPDATE RESULT SET SEM2=SEM2+ (SEM*0.03) WHERE SNAME LIKE "N%";`

Or

(iii) (a) `DELETE FROM RESULT WHERE DIV="IV";`

(b) `ALTER TABLE RESULT ADD COLUMN REMARKS VARCHAR(50);`

35. The school has asked their estate manager Mr. Rahul to maintain the data of all the labs in a table LAB. Rahul has created a table and entered data of 5 labs. **CBSE 2023**

LABNO	LAB_NAME	INCHARGE	CAPACITY	FLOOR
L001	CHEMISTRY	Daisy	20	I
L002	BIOLOGY	Venky	20	II
L003	MATH	Preeti	15	I
L004	LANGUAGE	Daisy	36	III
L005	COMPUTER	Mary Kom	37	II

Based on the data given above answer the following questions :

(i) Identify the columns which can be considered as Candidate keys.

(ii) Write the degree and cardinality of the table.

(iii) Write the statements to

(a) Insert a new row with appropriate data.

(b) Increase the capacity of all the labs by 10 students which are on I Floor.

Or (Option for part (iii) only)

(iii) Write the statements to :

(a) Add a constraints PRIMARY KEY to the column LABNO in the table.

(b) Delete the table LAB.

Ans. (i) LABNO, LAB_NAME

(ii) Degree-5
Cardinality-5

(iii) (a) `INSERT INTO LAB VALUES("L006","COMPUTER", "John",20,"II");`

(b) `UPDATE LAB SET capacity = capacity + 10 WHERE FLOOR = "I";`

Or

(iii) (a) `ALTER TABLE LAB ADD constraint PRIMARY KEY(LAB NO);`

(b) `DROP LAB;`

36. Create a table named Programmers with the following structure :

P_Name	VARCHAR(20)
DOJ	Date
SAL	NUMBER

(i) Display the name of the programmer, which has the highest salary.

(ii) Update the salary of all programmer by 2000, whose name start with letter R.

Ans. (i)
```
SELECT P_Name MAX(SAL)
FROM Programmers;
```
(ii)
```
UPDATE Programmers SET SAL = SAL +
2000  WHERE P_Name LIKE 'R%';
```

37. Explain IS NULL clause in SQL.

Ans. If we want to search the column whose value is NULL in a table, then we use IS NULL clause.

Syntax
```
SELECT <column_name>
FROM <table_name>
WHERE <column_name> IS NULL;
```

38. Consider the following table with their fields

`EMPLOYEE (E_CODE, E_NAME, DESIG, SALARY, DOJ)`

List the names, salary, PF, HRA, DA of all the employees in the EMPLOYEE table. HRA is 25% of salary and DA is 10% of salary. PF is 5% of salary. The result should be in descending order of salary.

Ans.
```
SELECT E_Name, SALARY, SALARY * 0.25
AS HRA, SALARY*0.10
AS DA, SALARY*0.05 AS PF
FROM EMPLOYEE
ORDER BY SALARY DESC;
```

39. **Write a output for SQL queries (i) to (iii), which are based on the table ITEMS.**

TABLE: ITEMS

Code	IName	Qty	Price	Company	TCode
1001	DIGITAL PAD 121	120	11000	XENITA	T01
1006	LED SCREEN 40	70	38000	SANTORA	T02
1004	CAR GPS SYSTEM	50	2150	GEOKNOW	T01
1003	DIGITAL CAMERA 12X	160	8000	DIGICLICK	T02
1005	PEN DRIVE 32 GB	600	1200	STOREHOME	T03

(i) `SELECT MAX(Price), MIN(Price) FROM ITEMS;`

(ii) `SELECT Price * Qty AMOUNT FROM ITEMS WHERE Code=1004;`

(iii) `SELECT DISTINCT TCode FROM ITEMS;`

Ans. (i)

MAX(Price)	MIN(Price)
38000	1200

(ii)

AMOUNT
107500

(iii)

TCode
T01
T02
T03

40. **Give the output of the following SQL statements, which are based on the table APPLICANTS.**

TABLE: APPLICANTS

No.	NAME	FEE	GENDER	C_ID	JOINYEAR
1012	Amandeep	30000	M	A01	2012
1102	Avisha	25000	F	A02	2009
1103	Ekant	30000	M	A02	2011
1049	Arun	30000	M	A03	2009
1025	Amber	40000	M	A02	2011
1106	Ela	40000	F	A05	2010
1017	Nikita	35000	F	A03	2012
1108	Arluna	30000	F	A03	2012
2109	Shakti	35000	M	A04	2011
1101	Kirat	25000	M	A01	2012

(i) `SELECT NAME, JOINYEAR FROM APPLICANTS WHERE GENDER ='F' AND C_ID='A02';`

(ii) `SELECT MIN(JOINYEAR) FROM APPLICANTS WHERE GENDER = 'M';`

(iii) `SELECT AVG(FEE) FROM APPLICANTS WHERE C_ID='A01' OR C_ID='A05';`

Ans. (i)

NAME	JOINYEAR
Avisha	2009

(ii)

MIN (JOINYEAR)
2009

(iii)

AVG (FEE)
31666.666

41. **Write the output for SQL queries (i) to (iii), which are based on the table CUSTOMER.**

TABLE: CUSTOMER

CID	CNAME	GENDER	SID	AREA
1001	R SHARMA	FEMALE	101	NORTH
1002	M R TIWARY	MALE	102	SOUTH
1003	M K KHAN	MALE	103	EAST
1004	A K SINGH	MALE	102	EAST
1005	S SEN	FEMALE	101	WEST
1006	R DUBEY	MALE	104	NORTH
1007	M AGARWAL	FEMALE	104	NORTH
1008	S DAS	FEMALE	103	SOUTH
1009	R K PATIL	MALE	102	NORTH
1010	N KRISHNA MURTY	MALE	102	SOUTH

(i) `SELECT COUNT(*), GENDER FROM CUSTOMER GROUP BY GENDER;`

(ii) `SELECT CNAME FROM CUSTOMER WHERE CNAME LIKE 'L%';`

(iii) `SELECT DISTINCT AREA FROM CUSTOMER;`

Ans. (i)

COUNT (*)	GENDER
4	FEMALE
6	MALE

(ii) No rows selected

(iii)

DISTINCT AREA
NORTH
SOUTH
EAST
WEST

42. **Write the output for SQL queries (i) to (iii), which are based on the table CARDEN.**

TABLE: CARDEN

Ccode	CarName	Make	Color	Capacity	Charges
501	A-star	Suzuki	RED	3	14
503	Indigo	Tata	SILVER	3	12
502	Innova	Toyota	WHITE	7	15
509	SX4	Suzuki	SILVER	4	14
510	C-Class	Mercedes	RED	4	35

(i) `SELECT COUNT(DISTINCT Make) FROM CARDEN;`

(ii) `SELECT COUNT(*) Make FROM CARDEN;`

(iii) `SELECT CarName FROM CARDEN WHERE Capacity = 4;`

Ans. (i)

COUNT (DISTINCT Make)
4

(ii)

Make
5

(iii)

CarName
SX4
C-Class

43. **Consider the table CLUB given below and write the output of the SQL queries that follow.** **CBSE SQP 2023-24**

CID	CNAME	AGE	GENDER	SPORTS	PAY	DOAPP
5246	AMRITA	35	FEMALE	CHESS	900	2006-03-27
4687	SHYAM	37	MALE	CRICKET	1300	2004-04-15
1245	MEENA	23	FEMALE	VOLLEYB ALL	1000	2007-06-18
1622	AMRIT	28	MALE	KARATE	1000	2007-09-05
1256	AMINA	36	FEMALE	CHESS	1100	2003-08-15
1720	MANJU	33	FEMALE	KARATE	1250	2004-04-10
2321	VIRAT	35	MALE	CRICKET	1050	2005-04-30

(i) `SELECT COUNT(DISTINCT SPORTS) FROM CLUB;`

(ii) `SELECT CNAME, SPORTS FROM CLUB WHERE DOAPP<"2006-04-30" AND CNAME LIKE "%NA";`

(iii) `SELECT CNAME, AGE, PAY FROM CLUB WHERE GENDER = "MALE" AND PAY BETWEEN 1000 AND 1200;`

Ans. (i)

COUNT(DISTINCT SPORTS)
4

(ii)

CNAME	SPORTS
AMINA	CHESS

(iii)

CNAME	AGE	PAY
AMRIT	28	1000
VIRAT	35	1050

44. **Consider the table ORDERS given below and write the output of the SQL queries that follow :** **CBSE 2024**

ORDNO	ITEM	QTY	RATE	ORDATE
1001	RICE	23	120	2023-09-10
1002	PULSES	13	120	2023-10-18
1003	RICE	25	110	2023-11-17
1004	WHEAT	28	65	2023-12-25
1005	PULSES	16	110	2024-01-15
1006	WHEAT	27	55	2024-04-15
1007	WHEAT	25	60	2024-04-30

(i) `SELECT ITEM, SUM (QTY) FROM ORDERS GROUP BY ITEM;`

(ii) `SELECT ITEM, QTY FROM ORDERS WHERE ORDATE BETWEEN '2023-11-01' AND '2023-12-31';`

(iii) `SELECT ORDNO, ORDATE FROM ORDERS WHERE ITEM = 'WHEAT' AND RATE > = 60;.`

Ans. (i)

ITEM	SUM (QTY)
RICE	48
PULSES	29
WHEAT	80

(ii)

ITEM	QTY
RICE	25
WHEAT	28

(iii)

ORDNO	ORDATE
1004	2023-12-25
1007	2024-04-30

45. **Consider the table ORDERS as given below, and write the following queries:** CBSE SQP 2024-25

O_Id	C_Name	Product	Quantity	Price
1001	Jitendra	Laptop	1	12000
1002	Mustafa	Smartphone	2	10000
1003	Dhwani	Headphone	1	1500
-	-	-	-	-
-	-	-	-	-
-	-	-	-	-

Note **The table contains many more records than shown here.**

(A) (I) To display the total Quantity for each Product, excluding Products with total Quantity less than 5.

(II) To display the orders table sorted by total price in descending order.

(III) To display the distinct customer names from the Orders table.

Or

(B) (I) To display the total number of orders quantity-wise.

(II) To delete all the orders where the Product is Laptop.

(III) Display the sum of Price of all the orders for which the quantity is null.

Ans. (A) (I)
```
select Product, sum(Quantity) from orders group by product having sum(Quantity)>=5;
```
(II)
```
select * from orders order by Price desc;
```
(III)
```
select distinct C_Name from orders;
```
Or

(B) (I)
```
Select quantity, count(*) from orders group by quantity;
```
(II)
```
Delete from orders where product = "Laptop";
```
(III)
```
Select sum(price) from orders where quantity is null;
```

46. **Write a query on the Salespeople table, whose output will exclude all salespeople with a rating >= 100, unless they are located in Delhi.**

Ans.
```
SELECT * FROM Salespeople
WHERE rating < 100 OR city = 'Delhi';
```
Or
```
SELECT * FROM Salespeople WHERE NOT
rating > = 100 OR city = 'Delhi';
```
Or
```
SELECT * FROM Salespeople WHERE NOT
(rating > = 100 AND city <> 'Delhi');
```

47. **Write a short note on DISTINCT keyword with an example.**

Ans. Refer to the text on page no 231 (DISTINCT keyword).

48. **Explain the use of ORDER BY clause.**

Ans. The ORDER BY keyword is used to sort the result set along a specified column with the SELECT command.

The ORDER BY keyword sorts the records in ascending order by default. If you want to sort the records in a descending order, you can use the DESC keyword.

Syntax
```
SELECT column_name(s)
FROM table_name
ORDER BY column_name(s) ASC/DESC;
```

49. **Define UPDATE command of SQL with its basic syntax.**

Ans. An UPDATE command is used to directly change or modify the value stored in one or more fields in a specified record.

Syntax
```
UPDATE table_name
SET column1 = value1, column2 = value2,...
WHERE <condition>;
```

50. **Consider the table Personal given below:** CBSE SQP 2023-24

Table: Personal

P_ID	Name	Desig	Salary	Allowance
P01	Rohit	Manager	89000	4800
P02	Kashish	Clerk	NULL	1600
P03	Mahesh	Superviser	48000	NULL
P04	Salil	Clerk	31000	1900
P05	Ravina	Superviser	NULL	2100

Based on the given table, write SQL queries for the following:

(i) Increase the salary by 5% of personals whose allowance is known.

(ii) Display Name and Total Salary (sum of Salary and Allowance) of all personals. The column heading 'Total Salary' should also be displayed.

(iii) Delete the record of Supervisors who have salary greater than 25000.

Ans. (i)
```
UPDATE Personal
SET Salary=Salary*0.5
WHERE Allowance IS NOT NULL;
```
(ii)
```
SELECT Name, Salary + Allowance AS "Total
Salary" FROM Personal;
```
(iii)
```
DELETE FROM Personal WHERE Salary > 25000;
```

51. **Write the queries for the following questions using the table Item with the following fields.**

(Item_Code, Item_Name, Quantity, Price)

(i) **Display the price 500 of item having code as I06.**

(ii) **Display the names of all items with quantity greater than 50 and price less than 500.**

(iii) **Display the item code of all items with quantity less than 70.**

Ans. (i)
```
UPDATE ITEM SET Price = Price + 500
WHERE Item_Code = 'I06';
```
(ii)
```
SELECT Item_Name FROM Item
WHERE (Quantity > 50) AND (Price < 500);
```
(iii)
```
SELECT Item_Code FROM Item
WHERE Quantity < 70;
```

Short Answer Type II Questions

52. (a) **Consider the following tables-Bank_Account and Branch:** **CBSE SQP 2022-23**

Table: Bank_Account

ACode	Name	Type
A01	Amrita	Savings
A02	Parthodas	Current
A03	Miraben	Current

Table : Branch

ACode	City
A01	Delhi
A02	Mumbai
A01	Nagpur

What will be the output of the following statement?

```
SELECT * FROM Bank_Account NATURAL JOIN Branch;
```

(b) **Write the output of the queries (i) to (iv) based on the table, TECH_COURSE given below:**

Table: TECH_COURSE

CID	CNAME	FEES	STARTDATE	TID
C201	Animation and VFX	12000	2022-07-02	101
C202	CADD	15000	2021-11-15	NULL
C203	DCA	10000	2020-10-01	102
C204	DDTP	9000	2021-09-15	104
C205	Mobile Application Development	18000	2022-11-01	101
C206	Digital marketing	16000	2022-07-25	103

(i)
```
SELECT DISTINCT TID FROM TECH_COURSE;
```
(ii)
```
SELECT TID, COUNT(*), MIN(FEES) FROM
TECH_COURSE GROUP BY TID HAVING
COUNT(TID)>1;
```
(iii)
```
SELECT CNAME FROM TECH_COURSE WHERE
FEES>15000 ORDER BY CNAME;
```
(iv)
```
SELECT AVG(FEES) FROM TECH_COURSE WHERE
FEES BETWEEN 15000 AND 17000;
```

Ans. (a)

ACode	Name	Type	City
A01	Amrita	Savings	Delhi
A02	Parthodas	Current	Mumbai
A01	Amrita	Savings	Nagpur

(b) (i)

DISTINCT (TID)
101
NULL
102
103
104

(ii)

TID	COUNT(*)	MIN(FEES)
101	2	12000

(iii)

CNAME
Digital Marketing
Mobile Application Development

(iv)

AVG(FEES)
15500

53. (a) **Write the outputs of the SQL queries (i) to (iv) based on the relations Teacher and Placement given below:** **CBSE SQP 2022-23**

Table : Teacher

T_ID	Name	Age	Department	Date_of_join	Salary	Gender
1	Arunan	34	Computer Sc	2019-01-10	12000	M
2	Saman	31	History	2017-03-24	20000	F
3	Randeep	32	Mathematics	2020-12-12	30000	M
4	Samira	35	History	2018-07-01	40000	F
5	Raman	42	Mathematics	2021-09-05	25000	M
6	Shyam	50	History	2019-06-27	30000	M
7	Shiv	44	Computer Sc	2019-02-25	21000	M
8	Shalakha	33	Mathematics	2018-07-31	20000	F

Table : Placement

P_ID	Department	Place
1	History	Ahmedabad
2	Mathematics	Jaipur
3	Computer Sc	Nagpur

(i) `SELECT Department, avg(salary) FROM Teacher GROUP BY Department;`

(ii) `SELECT MAX(Date_of_Join),MIN(Date_of_Join) FROM Teacher;`

(iii) `SELECT Name, Salary, T.Department, Place FROM Teacher T, Placement P WHERE T.Department = P.Department AND Salary>20000;`

(iv) `SELECT Name, Place FROM Teacher T, Placement P WHERE Gender = 'F' AND T.Department = P.Department;`

(b) **Write the command to view all tables in a database.**

Ans. (a)(i)

Department	Avg(Salary)
Computer Sc	16500
History	30000
Mathematics	25000

(ii)

MAX(Date_Join)	MIN(Date_Join)
2021-09-05	2017-03-24

(iii)

NAME	SALARY	DEPARTMENT	PLACE
Randeep	30000	Mathematic	Jaipur
Samira	40000	History	Ahmedabad
Raman	25000	Mathematics	Jaipur
Shyam	30000	History	Ahmedabad
Shiv	21000	Computer Sc	Nagpur

(iv)

NAME	PLACE
Saman	Ahmedabad
Samira	Ahmedabad
Salakha	Jaipur

(b) `SHOW TABLES;`

54. (a) **Consider the following tables - LOAN and BORROWER:** **CBSE 2023**

Table : LOAN

LOAN_NO	B_NAME	AMOUNT
L-170	DELHI	3000
L-230	KANPUR	4000

Table : BORROWER

CUST_NAME	LOAN_NO
JOHN	L-171
KRISH	L-230
RAVYA	L-170

How many rows and columns will be there in the natural join of these two tables?

(b) **Write the output of the queries (i) to (iv) based on the table, WORKER given below:**

Table : WORKER

W_ID	F_NAME	L_NAME	CITY	STATE
102	SAHIL	KHAN	KANPUR	UTTAR PRADESH
104	SAMEER	PARIKH	ROOP NAGAR	PUNJAB
105	MARY	JONES	DELHI	DELHI
106	MAHIR	SHARMA	SONIPAT	HARYANA
107	ATHARVA	BHARDWAJ	DELHI	DELHI
108	VEDA	SHARMA	KANPUR	UTTAR PRADESH

(i) `SELECT F_NAME, CITY FROM WORKER ORDER BY STATE DESC;`

(ii) `SELECT DISTINCT(CITY) FROM WORKER;`

(iii) `SELECT F_NAME, STATE FROM WORKER WHERE L_NAME LIKE '_HA%';`

(iv) `SELECT CITY,COUNT(*) FROM WORKER GROUP BY CITY;`

Ans. (a) rows : 2
columns : 4

(b) (i)

F_NAME	CITY
SAHIL	KANPUR
VEDA	KANPUR
SAMEER	ROOP NAGAR
MAHIR	SONIPAT
MARY	DELHI
ATHARVA	DELHI

(ii)

DISTINCT (CITY)
KANPUR
ROOP NAGAR
DELHI
SONIPAT

(iii)

F_NAME	STATE
SAHIL	UTTAR PRADESH
MAHIR	HARYANA
ATHARVA	DELHI
VEDA	UTTAR PRADESH

(iv)

CITY	COUNT(*)
KANPUR	2
ROOP NAGAR	1
DELHI	2
SONIPAT	1

55. (a) **Write the outputs of the SQL queries (i) to (iv) based on the relations COMPUTER and SALES given below** **CBSE 2023**

Table : COMPUTER

PROD_ID	PROD_NAME	PRICE	COMPANY	TYPE
P001	MOUSE	200	LOGITECH	INPUT
P002	LASER PRINTER	4000	CANON	OUTPUT
P003	KEYBOARD	500	LOGITECH	INPUT
P004	JOYSTICK	1000	IBALL	INPUT
P005	SPEAKER	1200	CREATIVE	OUTPUT
P006	DESKJET PRINTER	4300	CANON	OUTPUT

Table : SALES

PROD_ID	QTY_SOLD	QUARTER
P002	4	1
P003	2	2
P001	3	2
P004	2	1

(i) `SELECT MIN(PRICE), MAX(PRICE) FROM COMPUTER;`

(ii) `SELECT COMPANY, COUNT(*) FROM COMPUTER GROUP BY COMPANY HAVING COUNT(COMPANY) > 1;`

(iii) `SELECT PROD_NAME, QTY_SOLD FROM COMPUTER C, SALES S WHERE C. PROD_ID=S.PROD_ID AND TYPE = 'INPUT';`

(iv) `SELECT PROD_NAME, COMPANY, QUARTER FROM COMPUTER C, SALES S WHERE C.PROD_ID=S.PROD_ID;`

(b) **Write the command to view all databases.**

Ans. (a) (i)

MIN(PRICE)	MAX(PRICE)
200	4300

(ii)

COMPANY	COUNT(*)
LOGITECH	2
CANON	2

(iii)

PROD_NAME	QTY_SOLD
MOUSE	3
KEYBOARD	2
JOYSTICK	2

(iv)

PROD_NAME	COMPANY	QUARTER
MOUSE	LOGITECH	2
LASER PRINTER	CANON	1
KEYBOARD	LOGITECH	2
JOYSTICK	IBALL	1

(b) `SHOW DATABASES;`

56. **Write queries (i) to (iv) based on the tables EMPLOYEE and DEPARTMENT given below** **CBSE SQP 2022 Term II**

Table : EMPLOYEE

EMPID	NAME	DOB	DEPTID	DESIG	SALARY
120	Alisha	23-Jan-1978	D001	Manager	75000
123	Nitin	10-Oct-1977	D002	AO	59000
129	Navjot	12-Jul-1971	D003	Supervisor	40000
130	Jimmy	30-Dec-1980	D004	Sales Rep	
131	Faiz	06-Apr-1984	D005	Dep Manager	65000

Table : DEPARTMENT

DEPTID	DEPTNAME	FLOORNO
D001	Personal	4
D002	Admin	10
D003	Production	1
D004	Sales	3

(i) **To display the average salary of all employees, department wise.**

(ii) **To display name and respective department name of each employee whose salary is more than 50000.**

(iii) **To display the names of employees whose salary is not known, in alphabetical order.**

(iv) **To display DEPTID from the table EMPLOYEE without repetition.**

Ans. (i)
```
SELECT AVG(SALARY)
FROM EMPLOYEE
GROUP BY DEPTID;
```
(ii)
```
SELECT NAME, DEPTNAME
FROM EMPLOYEE, DEPARTMENT
```

```
WHERE
EMPLOYEE.DEPTID=DEPARTMENT.DEPTID
AND SALARY>50000;
```

(iii)
```
SELECT NAME FROM EMPLOYEE
WHERE SALARY IS NULL
ORDER BY NAME;
```

(iv)
```
SELECT DISTINCT DEPTID FROM EMPLOYEE;
```

57. **Consider the tables PRODUCT and BRAND given below:** CBSE SQP 2023-24

Table: PRODUCT

PCode	PName	UPrice	Rating	BID
P01	Shampoo	120	6	M03
P02	Toothpaste	54	8	M02
P03	Soap	25	7	M03
P04	Toothpaste	65	4	M04
P05	Soap	38	5	M05
P06	Shampoo	245	6	M05

Table: BRAND

BID	BName
M02	Dant Kanti
M03	Medimix
M04	Pepsodent
M05	Dove

Write SQL queries for the following.

(i) Display product name and brand name from the tables PRODUCT and BRAND.

(ii) Display the structure of the table PRODUCT.

(iii) Display the average rating of Medimix and Dove brands.

(iv) Display the name, price, and rating of products in descending order of rating.

Ans. (i)
```
SELECT PName, BName FROM PRODUCT P, BRAND B
WHERE P.BID =B.BID;
```

(ii)
```
DESC PRODUCT;
```

(iii)
```
SELECT BName, AVG(Rating) FROM PRODUCT P, BRAND
B WHERE P.BID=B.BID
GROUP BY BName HAVING BName = "Medimix" OR
BName = "Dove";
```

(iv)
```
SELECT PName, UPrice, Rating FROM PRODUCT ORDER
BY Rating DESC;
```

58. **Consider the tables Admin and Transport given below :** CBSE 2024

Table : Admin

S_id	S_name	Address	S_type
S001	Sandhya	Rohini	Day Boarder
S002	Vedanshi	Rohtak	Day Scholar
S003	Vibhu	Raj Nagar	NULL
S004	Atharva	Rampur	Day Boarder

Table : Transport

S_id	Bus_no	Stop_name
S002	TSS10	Sarai Kale Khan
S004	TSS12	Sainik Vihar
S005	TSS10	Kamla Nagar

Write SQL queries for the following :

(i) Display the student name and their stop name from the tables Admin and Transport.

(ii) Display the number of students whose S_type is not known.

(iii) Display all details of the students whose name starts with 'V'.

(iv) Display student id and address in alphabetical order of student name, from the table Admin.

Ans. (i)
```
SELECT S_name, Stop_name FROM Admin,
Transport WHERE Admin.S_id =
Transport.S_id;
```

(ii)
```
SELECT COUNT(*) FROM Admin WHERE S_type
IS NULL;
```

(iii)
```
SELECT * FROM Admin WHERE S_name LIKE
'V%';
```

(iv)
```
SELECT S_id, Address FROM Admin ORDER BY
S_name;
```

59. **Saman has been entrusted with the management of Law University Database. He needs to access some information from FACULTY and COURSES tables for a survey analysis. Help him extract the following information by writing the desired SQL queries as mentioned below.** CBSE SQP 2024-25

Table: FACULTY

F_ID	FName	LName	Hire_Date	Salary
102	Amit	Mishra	12-10-1998	12000
103	Nitin	Vyas	24-12-1994	8000
104	Rakshit	Soni	18-5-2001	14000
105	Rashmi	Malhotra	11-9-2004	11000
106	Sulekha	Srivastava	5-6-2006	10000

Table: COURSES

C_ID	F_ID	CName	Fees
C21	102	Grid Computing	40000
C22	106	System Design	16000
C23	104	Computer Security	8000
C24	106	Human Biology	15000
C25	102	Computer Network	20000
C26	105	Visual Basic	6000

(I) To display complete details (from both the tables) of those Faculties whose salary is less than 12000.

(II) To display the details of courses whose fees is in the range of 20000 to 50000 (both values included).

(III) To increase the fees of all courses by 500 which have "Computer" in their Course names.

(IV) (A) To display names (FName and LName) of faculty taking System Design.

Or

(B) To display the Cartesian Product of these two tables.

Ans. (I)
```
Select * from Faculty A , Courses B
where A.F_ID= B.F_ID and A. Salary
<12000;
```
(II)
```
Select * from Courses where Fees between
20000 and 50000;
```
(III)
```
Update Courses set Fees =Fees + 500
where Cname like "%Computer%";
```
(IV) (A)
```
Select A.Fname, A.Lname from Faculty
A , Courses B where A.F_ID= B.F_ID and
B.CName="System Design";
```
Or

(B) Select * from faculty , courses;

60. **Suman has created a table named WORKER with a set of records to maintain the data of the construction sites, which consists of WID, HNAME, WAGE, HOURS, TYPE and SITEID. After creating the table, she entered data in it, which is as follows:** **CBSE 2025**

WID	WNAME	WAGE	HOURS	TYPE	SITEID
W 01	Ahmed J	1500	200	Unskilled	103
W 11	Naveen S	520	100	Skilled	101
W 02	Jacob B	780	95	Unskilled	101
W 15	Nihal K	560	110	Semiskilled	NULL
W 10	Anju S	1200	130	Skilled	103

(a) Based on the data given above, answer the following questions.

(i) Write the SQL statement to display the names and wages of those workers whose wages are between 800 and 1500

(ii) Write the SQL statement to display the record of workers whose SITEID is not known.

(iii) Write the SQL statement to display WNAME, WAGE and HOURS of all those workers whose TYPE is 'Skilled'.

(iv) Write the SQL statement to change the WAGE to 1200 of the workers where the TYPE is "Semiskilled".

Or

(b) Considering the above given table WORKER, write the output on execution of the following SQL commands:

(i) SELECT WNAME, WAGE * HOURS FROM WORKER WHERE SITEID = 103;

(ii) SELECT COUNT (DISTINCT TYPE) FROM WORKER;

(iii) SELECT MAX (WAGE), MIN (WAGE), TYPE FROM WORKER GROUP BY TYPE;

(iv) SELECT WNAME, SITEID FROM WORKER WHERE TYPE = "Unskilled" ORDER BY HOURS;

Ans. (a) (i)
```
SELECT WNAME, WAGE
FROM WORKER
WHERE WAGE BETWEEN 800 AND 1500;
```
(ii)
```
SELECT *
FROM WORKER
WHERE SITEID IS NULL;
```
(iii)
```
SELECT WNAME, WAGE, HOURS
FROM WORKER
WHERE TYPE = 'Skilled';
```
(iv)
```
UPDATE WORKER
SET WAGE = 1200
WHERE TYPE = 'Semiskilled';
```
Or

(b) (i) Output:

WNAME	WAGE * HOURS
Ahmed J	300000
Anju S	156000

(ii) Output:

```
There are 3 distinct TYPE values:
'Unskilled', 'Skilled', 'Semiskilled'
Answer:
3
```

(iii) Output:

MAX(WAGE)	MIN(WAGE)	TYPE
1500	520	Unskilled
1200	560	Skilled
780	780	Semiskilled

(iv) Output:

WNAME	SITEID
Jocab B	101
Ahmed J	103

61. Assume that you are working in the IT Department of a Creative Art Gallery (CAG), which sells different forms of art creations like Paintings, Sculptures etc. The data of Art Creations and Artists are kept in tables Articles and Artists respectively. Following are few records from these two tables: **CBSE 2025**

Table : Articles

Code	A_Code	Article	DOC	Price
PL001	A0001	Painting	2018-10-19	20000
SC028	A0004	Sculpture	2021-01-15	16000
QL005	A0003	Quilling	2024-04-24	3000

Table : Artists

A_Code	Name	Phone	Email	DOB
A0001	Roy	595923	r@CrAG. com	1986-10-12
A0002	Ghosh	1122334	ghosh@CrAG.com	1972-02-05
A0003	Gargi	121212	Gargi@CrAG.com	1996-03-22
A0004	Mustafa	33333333	Mf@CrAg.com	2000-01-01

Note
- **The tables contain many more records than shown here.**
- **DOC is Date of Creation of an Article.**

As an employee of CAG, you are required to write the SQL queries for the following:

(i) **To display all the records from the Articles table in descending order of price.**

(ii) **To display the details of Articles which were created in the year 2020.**

(iii) **To display the structure of Artists table.**

(iv) (a) **To display the name of all artists whose Article is Painting through Equi Join.**

Or

(b) **To display the name of all Artists whose Article is 'Painting' through Natural Join.**

Ans. (i)
```
SELECT * FROM Articles  ORDER BY
Price DESC;
```

(ii) Since DOC is in YYYY-MM-DD format, we can extract the year using YEAR():
```
SELECT * FROM Articles
WHERE YEAR(DOC) = 2020;
```

Note You can also use LIKE '2020%' if YEAR() is not available in your environment.

(iii)
```
DESC Artists;
```

(iv) (a)
```
SELECT Artists.Name FROM Artists JOIN
Articles ON Artists.A_Code =
Articles.A_Code WHERE
Articles.Article = 'Painting';
```

Or

(b)
```
SELECT Name FROM Artists NATURAL JOIN
Articles WHERE Article = 'Painting';
```

Long Answer Type Questions

62. Answer the questions (i) to (v) on the basis of the following tables SHOPPE and ACCESSORIES.

TABLE: SHOPPE

Id	SName	Area
S001	ABC Computeronics	CP
S002	All Infotech Media	GK II
S003	Tech Shoppe	CP
S004	Geeks Tecno Soft	Nehru Place
S005	Hitech Tech Store	Nehru Place

TABLE: ACCESSORIES

No	Name	Price	Id
A01	Mother Board	12000	S01
A02	Hard Disk	5000	S01
A03	Keyboard	500	S02
A04	Mouse	300	S01
A05	Mother Board	13000	S02
A06	Keyboard	400	S03
A07	LCD	6000	S04
T08	LCD	5500	S05
T09	Mouse	350	S05
T10	Hard Disk	4500	S03

(i) To display Name and Price of all the Accessories in ascending order of their Price.

(ii) To display Id and SName of all Shoppe located in Nehru Place.

(iii) To display Minimum and Maximum Price of each Name of Accessories.

(iv) To display Name, Price of all Accessories and their respective SName, where they are available.

(v) To display name of accessories whose price is greater than 1000.

Ans. (i)
```
SELECT Name, Price
FROM ACCESSORIES
ORDER BY Price;
```
(ii)
```
SELECT Id, SName
FROM SHOPPE
WHERE Area = 'Nehru Place';
```
(iii)
```
SELECT MIN(Price) "Minimum Price",
MAX(Price) "Maximum Price", Name
FROM ACCESSORIES
GROUP BY Name;
```
(iv)
```
SELECT Name, Price, SName
FROM ACCESSORIES A, SHOPPE S
WHERE A.Id = S.Id;
```
but this query enable to show the result because A.Id and S.Id are not identical.

(v)
```
SELECT Name From
ACCESSORIES
WHERE Price>1000;
```

63. Consider the following tables STORE and answer the questions:

TABLE: STORE

ItemNo	Item	Scode	Qty	Rate	LastBuy
2005	Sharpener Classic	23	60	8	31-JUN-09
2003	Balls	22	50	25	01-FEB-10
2002	Gel Pen Premium	21	150	12	24-FEB-10
2006	Gel Pen Classic	21	250	20	11-MAR-09
2001	Eraser Small	22	220	6	19-JAN-09
2004	Eraser Big	22	110	8	02-DEC-09
2009	Ball Pen 0.5	21	180	18	03-NOV-09

Write SQL commands for the following statements:

(i) To display details of all the items in the STORE table in ascending order of LastBuy.

(ii) To display ItemNo and Item name of those items from STORE table, whose Rate is more than ₹ 15.

(iii) To display the details of those items whose Supplier code (Scode) is 22 or Quantity in Store (Qty) is more than 110 from the table STORE.

(iv) To display minimum rate of items for each Supplier individually as per Scode from the table STORE.

(v) To display the item with its quantity which include pen in their name.

Ans. (i)
```
SELECT * FROM STORE ORDER BY LastBuy;
```
(ii)
```
SELECT ItemNo, Item FROM STORE WHERE
Rate>15;
```
(iii)
```
SELECT * FROM STORE WHERE Scode = 22
OR Qty>110;
```
(iv)
```
SELECT MIN(Rate) FROM STORE GROUP BY
Scode;
```
(v)
```
SELECT Item, Qty FROM STORE WHERE Item
LIKE '%Pen%';
```

64. Consider the following tables STUDENT and STREAM. Write SQL commands for the statements (i) to (v).

TABLE: STUDENT

SCODE	NAME	AGE	STRCDE	POINTS	GRADE
101	Amit	16	1	6	NULL
102	Arjun	13	3	4	NULL
103	Zaheer	14	2	1	NULL
105	Gagan	15	5	2	NULL
108	Kumar	13	6	8	NULL
109	Rajesh	17	5	8	NULL
110	Naveen	13	3	9	NULL
113	Ajay	16	2	3	NULL
115	Kapil	14	3	2	NULL
120	Gurdeep	15	2	6	NULL

TABLE: STREAM

STRCDE	STRNAME
1	SCIENCE+COMP
2	SCIENCE+BIO
3	SCIENCE+ECO
4	COMMERCE+MATHS
5	COMMERCE+SOCIO
6	ARTS+MATHS
7	ARTS+SOCIO

(i) To display the name of streams in alphabetical order from table STREAM.

(ii) To display the number of students whose POINTS are more than 5.

(iii) To update GRADE to 'A' for all those students, who are getting more than 8 as POINTS.

(iv) ARTS+MATHS stream is no more available. Make necessary change in table STREAM.

(v) To display student's name whose stream name is science and computer.

Ans. (i)
```
SELECT STRNAME FROM STREAM ORDER BY
STRNAME;
```
(ii)
```
SELECT COUNT(*) FROM STUDENT WHERE
POINTS > 5;
```
(iii)
```
UPDATE STUDENT SET GRADE = 'A' WHERE
POINTS > 8;
```
(iv)
```
DELETE FROM STREAM WHERE STRNAME
    = 'ARTS + MATHS';
```
(v)
```
SELECT NAME FROM STUDENT
WHERE STUDENT.STRCDE = STREAM.STRCDE
AND STRNAME = "SCIENCE + COMP";
```

65. **Consider the following tables GARMENT and FABRIC. Write SQL commands for the statements (i) to (v).**

TABLE: GARMENT

GCODE	DESCRIPTION	PRICE	FCODE	READYDATE
10023	PENCIL SKIRT	1150	F03	19-DEC-08
10001	FORMAL SHIRT	1250	F01	12-JAN-08
10012	INFORMAL SHIRT	1550	F02	06-JUN-08
10024	BABY TOP	750	F03	07-APR-07
10090	TULIP SKIRT	850	F02	31-MAR-07
10019	EVENING GOWN	850	F03	06-JUN-08
10009	INFORMAL PANT	1500	F02	20-OCT-08
10007	FORMAL PANT	1350	F01	09-MAR-08
10020	FROCK	850	F04	09-SEP-07
10089	SLACKS	750	F03	20-OCT-08

TABLE: FABRIC

FCODE	TYPE
F04	POLYSTER
F02	COTTON
F03	SILK
F01	TERELENE

(i) To display GCODE and DESCRIPTION of each GARMENT in descending order of GCODE.

(ii) To display the details of all the GARMENTs, which have READYDATE in between 08-DEC-07 and 16-JUN-08 (inclusive of both the dates).

(iii) To display the average PRICE of all the GARMENTs. Which are made up of FABRIC with FCODE as F03.

(iv) To display FABRIC wise highest and lowest price of GARMENTs from GARMENT table. (Display FCODE of each GARMENT along with highest and lowest price.)

(v) To display garment's description with their price whose fabric is silk.

Ans. (i)
```
SELECT GCODE, DESCRIPTION FROM GARMENT
ORDER BY GCODE DESC;
```
(ii)
```
SELECT * FROM GARMENT
WHERE READYDATE BETWEEN '08-DEC-07'
AND '16-JUN-08';
```
(iii)
```
SELECT AVG(PRICE) FROM GARMENT WHERE
FCODE = 'F03';
```
(iv)
```
SELECT FCODE, MAX(PRICE), MIN(PRICE)
FROM GARMENT GROUP BY FCODE;
```
(v)
```
SELECT DESCRIPTION, PRICE FROM GARMENT
WHERE GARMENT.FCODE = FABRIC.FCODE
AND TYPE = "SILK";
```

66. **Consider the following tables. Write SQL commands for the statements (i) to (v).**

TABLE: SENDER

SenderID	SenderName	SenderAddress	SenderCity
ND01	R Jain	2, ABC Appts	New Delhi
MU02	H Sinha	12, Newtown	Mumbai
MU15	S Jha	27/A, Park Street	Mumbai
ND50	T Prasad	122-K, SDA	New Delhi

TABLE: RECIPIENT

RecID	SenderID	RecName	RecAddress	RecCity
KO05	ND01	R Bajpayee	5, Central Avenue	Kolkata
ND08	MU02	S Mahajan	116, A Vihar	New Delhi
MU19	ND01	H Singh	2A, Andheri East	Mumbai
MU32	MU15	P K Swamy	B5, C S Terminus	Mumbai
ND48	ND50	S Tripathi	13, B1 D, Mayur Vihar	New Delhi

(i) To display the names of all Senders from Mumbai.

(ii) To display the RecID, SenderName, SenderAddress, RecName, RecAddress for every Recipient.

(iii) To display Recipient details in ascending order of RecName.

(iv) To display number of Recipients from each City.

(v) To display the detail of recipients who are in Mumbai.

Ans. (i)
```
SELECT SenderName FROM SENDER WHERE
SenderCity = 'Mumbai';
```
(ii)
```
SELECT RecID, SenderName,
SenderAddress, RecName, RecAddress
FROM RECIPIENT, SENDER WHERE
RECIPIENT.SenderID = SENDER.SenderID;
```
(iii)
```
SELECT * FROM RECIPIENT ORDER BY
RecName;
```
(iv)
```
SELECT COUNT(*) AS "No. of
Recipients", RecCity FROM RECIPIENT
GROUP BY RecCity;
```
(v)
```
SELECT * FROM RECIPIENT
WHERE RecCity = "Mumbai";
```

67. Write the SQL commands for (i) to (v) on the basis of the table HOSPITAL

TABLE: HOSPITAL

No.	Name	Age	Department	Dateofadm	Charges	Sex
1	Sandeep	65	Surgery	23/02/98	300	M
2	Ravina	24	Orthopaedic	20/01/98	200	F
3	Karan	45	Orthopaedic	19/02/98	200	M
4	Tarun	12	Surgery	01/01/98	300	M
5	Zubin	36	ENT	12/01/98	250	M
6	Ketaki	16	ENT	24/02/98	300	F
7	Ankita	29	Cardiology	20/02/98	800	F
8	Zareen	45	Gynaecology	22/02/98	300	F
9	Kush	19	Cardiology	13/01/98	800	M
10	Shailya	31	Nuclear Medicine	19/02/98	400	M

(i) To show all information about the patients of Cardiology Department.

(ii) To list the name of female patients, who are in Orthopaedic Department.

(iii) To list names of all patients with their date of admission in ascending order.

(iv) To display Patient's Name, Charges, Age for male patients only.

(v) To display name of doctor are older than 30 years and charges for consultation fee is more than 500.

Ans. (i)
```
SELECT * FROM HOSPITAL WHERE
Department = 'Cardiology';
```
(ii)
```
SELECT Name FROM HOSPITAL WHERE
Department = 'Orthopaedic' AND Sex
= 'F';
```
(iii)
```
SELECT Name FROM HOSPITAL ORDER BY
Dateofadm;
```
(iv)
```
SELECT Name, Charges, Age FROM
HOSPITAL WHERE Sex = 'M';
```
(v)
```
SELECT NAME FROM HOSPITAL WHERE Age>30
AND Charges>500;
```

68. Write SQL commands for (i) to (v) on the basis of table INTERIORS.

TABLE: INTERIORS

No.	ITEMNAME	TYPE	DATEOF STOCK	PRICE	DISCO-UNT
1	Red rose	Double Bed	23/02/02	32000	15
2	Soft touch	Baby cot	20/01/02	9000	10
3	Jerry's home	Baby cot	19/02/02	8500	10
4	Rough wood	Office Table	01/01/02	20000	20
5	Comfort zone	Double Bed	12/01/02	15000	20
6	Jerry look	Baby cot	24/02/02	7000	19
7	Lion king	Office Table	20/02/02	16000	20
8	Royal tiger	Sofa	22/02/02	30000	25
9	Park sitting	Sofa	13/12/01	9000	15
10	Dine Paradise	Dining Table	19/02/02	11000	15
11	White Wood	Double Bed	23/03/03	20000	20
12	James 007	Sofa	20/02/03	15000	15
13	Tom look	Baby cot	21/02/03	7000	10

(i) To show all information about the Sofa from the INTERIORS table.

(ii) To list the ITEMNAME, which are priced at more than 10000 from the INTERIORS table.

(iii) To list ITEMNAME and TYPE of those items, in which DATEOFSTOCK is before 22/01/02 from the INTERIORS table in descending order of ITEMNAME.

(iv) To insert a new row in the INTERIORS table with the following data
{14, 'TrueIndian', 'Office Table', '25/03/03', 15000, 20}

(v) To display the name of item with their price which have discount more than 20.

Ans. (i)
```
SELECT * FROM INTERIORS WHERE TYPE
= 'Sofa';
```
(ii)
```
SELECT ITEMNAME FROM INTERIORS WHERE
PRICE > 10000;
```
(iii)
```
SELECT ITEMNAME, TYPE FROM INTERIORS
WHERE DATEOFSTOCK < '22/01/02'
ORDER BY ITEMNAME DESC;
```
(iv)
```
INSERT INTO INTERIORS VALUES
(14,'TrueIndian', 'Office Table',
'25/03/03',15000,20);
```
(v)
```
SELECT ITEMNAME, PRICE FROM INTERIORS
WHERE DISCOUNT>20;
```

69. **Given the following tables for a database LIBRARY**

TABLE: BOOKS

Book_Id	Book_Name	Author_Name	Publishers	Price	Type	Qty
F0001	The Tears	William Hopkins	First Publ	750	Fiction	10
F0002	Thunderbolts	Anna Roberts	First Publ	700	Fiction	5
T0001	My First C++	Brain & Brooke	EPB	250	Text	10
T0002	C++ Brainworks	A.W. Rossaine	TDH	325	Text	5
C0001	Fast Cook	Lata Kapoor	EPB	350	Cookery	8

TABLE: ISSUED

Book_Id	Quantity_Issued
F0001	3
T0001	1
C0001	5

Write SQL queries for (i) to (v).

(i) To show Book name, Author name and Price of books of EPB Publishers.

(ii) To list the names from books of Fiction type.

(iii) To display the names and price of the books in descending order of their price.

(iv) To increase the price of all books of First Publ Publishers by 50.

(v) To display the detail of book whose quantity less than 10.

Ans. (i)
```
SELECT Book_Name, Author_Name, Price
FROM BOOKS WHERE Publishers = 'EPB';
```
(ii)
```
SELECT Book_Name FROM BOOKS WHERE Type
= 'Fiction';
```
(iii)
```
SELECT Book_Name, Price FROM BOOKS
ORDER BY Price DESC;
```
(iv)
```
UPDATE BOOKS SET Price = Price + 50
WHERE Publishers = 'First Publ';
```
(v)
```
SELECT * FROM BOOKS
WHERE Qty<10;
```

70. **Write SQL commands for (i) to (v) on the basis of table STUDENT**

TABLE: STUDENT

SNO	NAME	STREAM	FEES	AGE	SEX
1	ARUN KUMAR	COMPUTER	750.00	17	M
2	DIVYA JENEJA	COMPUTER	750.00	18	F
3	KESHAR MEHRA	BIOLOGY	500.00	16	M
4	HARISH SINGH	ENG. DR	350.00	18	M
5	PRACHI	ECONOMICS	300.00	19	F
6	NISHA ARORA	COMPUTER	750.00	15	F
7	DEEPAK KUMAR	ECONOMICS	300.00	16	M
8	SARIKA VASWANI	BIOLOGY	500.00	15	F

(i) List the name of all the students, who have taken stream as COMPUTER.

(ii) To count the number of female students.

(iii) To display the number of students stream wise.

(iv) To display all the records in sorted order of name.

(v) To display the stream of student whose name is Harish.

Ans. (i)
```
SELECT NAME FROM STUDENT WHERE STREAM
='COMPUTER';
```
(ii)
```
SELECT COUNT(*) FROM STUDENT WHERE SEX
= 'F';
```
(iii)
```
SELECT STREAM, COUNT(*) FROM STUDENT
GROUP BY STREAM;
```
(iv)
```
SELECT * FROM STUDENT ORDER BY NAME;
```
(v)
```
SELECT STREAM FROM STUDENT
WHERE NAME LIKE "%HARISH%";
```

71. Given the following family relation. Write SQL commands for questions (i) to (v) based on the table FAMILY

TABLE: FAMILY

No.	Name	Female Members	Male Members	Income	Occupation
1	Mishra	3	2	7000	Service
2	Gupta	4	1	50000	Business
3	Khan	6	3	8000	Mixed
4	Chaddha	2	2	25000	Business
5	Yadav	7	2	20000	Mixed
6	Joshi	3	2	14000	Service
7	Maurya	6	3	5000	Farming
8	Rao	5	2	10000	Service

(i) To select all the information of family, whose Occupation is Service.
(ii) To list the name of family, where female members are more than 3.
(iii) To list all names of family with income in ascending order.
(iv) To count the number of family, whose income is less than 10000.
(v) To display the detail of family whose income is more than 10000 and occupation is mixed type.

Ans. (i)
```
SELECT * FROM FAMILY WHERE Occupation
= 'Service';
```
(ii)
```
SELECT Name FROM FAMILY WHERE
FemaleMembers > 3;
```
(iii)
```
SELECT Name, Income FROM FAMILY ORDER
BY Income;
```
(iv)
```
SELECT COUNT(*) FROM FAMILY WHERE
Income < 10000;
```
(v)
```
SELECT * FROM FAMILY
WHERE INCOME > 10000
AND Occupation = "Mixed";
```

72. Consider the following tables PRODUCT and CLIENT. Write SQL commands for the statement (i) to (v).

TABLE: PRODUCT

P_ID	ProductName	Manufacturer	Price
TP01	Talcom Powder	LAK	40
FW05	Face Wash	ABC	45
BS01	Bath Soap	ABC	55
SH06	Shampoo	XYZ	120
FW12	Face Wash	XYZ	95

TABLE: CLIENT

C_ID	ClientName	City	P_ID
01	Cosmetic Shop	Delhi	FW05
06	Total Health	Mumbai	BS01
12	Live Life	Delhi	SH06
15	Pretty Woman	Delhi	FW12
16	Dreams	Bengaluru	TP01

(i) To display the details of those Clients, whose City is Delhi.
(ii) To display the details of products, whose Price is in the range of 50 to 100 (both values included).
(iii) To display the ClientName, City from table CLIENT and ProductName and Price from table PRODUCT, with their corresponding matching P_ID.
(iv) To increase the Price of all products by 10.
(v) To display the product detail whose manufacturer is ABC and price less than 50.

Ans. (i)
```
SELECT * FROM CLIENT WHERE
City='Delhi';
```
(ii)
```
SELECT * FROM PRODUCT WHERE Price
BETWEEN 50 AND 100;
```
(iii)
```
SELECT ClientName, City, ProductName,
Price FROM CLIENT, PRODUCT
WHERE CLIENT.P_ID = PRODUCT.P_ID;
```
(iv)
```
UPDATE PRODUCT SET Price = Price + 10;
```
(v)
```
SELECT *FROM PRODUCT
WHERE Manufacturer = "ABC"
AND Price < 50;
```

73. Study the following tables DOCTOR and SALARY and write SQL commands for the questions (i) to (v).

TABLE: DOCTOR

ID	NAME	DEPT	SEX	EXPERI-E NCE
101	John	ENT	M	12
104	Smith	ORTHOPEDIC	M	5
107	George	CARDIOLOGY	M	10
114	Lara	SKIN	F	3
109	K George	MEDICINE	F	9
105	Johnson	ORTHOPEDIC	M	10
117	Lucy	ENT	F	3
111	Bill	MEDICINE	F	12
130	Morphy	ORTHOPEDIC	M	15

TABLE: SALARY

ID	BASIC	ALLOWANCE	CONSULTATION
101	12000	1000	300
104	23000	2300	500
107	32000	4000	500
114	12000	5200	100
109	42000	1700	200
105	18900	1690	300
130	21700	2600	300

(i) Display NAME of all doctors who are in MEDICINE department having more than 10yrs experience from the table DOCTOR.

(ii) Display the average salary of all doctors working in ENT department using the tables DOCTOR and SALARY. SALARY = BASIC + ALLOWANCE.

(iii) Display the minimum ALLOWANCE of female doctors.

(iv) Display the highest consultation fee among all male doctors.

(v) To display the detail of doctor who have experience more than 12 years.

Ans. (i)
```
SELECT NAME FROM DOCTOR WHERE DEPT =
'MEDICINE' AND EXPERIENCE > 10;
```
(ii)
```
SELECT AVG(BASIC + ALLOWANCE) FROM
SALARY WHERE SALARY.ID IN(SELECT ID
FROM DOCTOR WHERE DEPT = 'ENT');
```
(iii)
```
SELECT MIN(ALLOWANCE) FROM SALARY
WHERE SALARY.ID IN(SELECT ID FROM
DOCTOR WHERE SEX = 'F');
```
(iv)
```
SELECT MAX(CONSULTATION) FROM SALARY
WHERE SALARY.ID IN(SELECT ID FROM
DOCTOR WHERE SEX = 'M');
```
(v)
```
SELECT * FROM DOCTOR
WHERE EXPERIENCE>12;
```

74. Study the following tables FLIGHTS and FARES and write SQL commands for the questions (i) to (iv).

TABLE: FLIGHTS

FL_NO	STARTING	ENDING	NO_FLIGHT	NO_STOPS
IC301	MUMBAI	DELHI	8	0
IC799	BENGALURU	DELHI	2	1
MC101	INDORE	MUMBAI	3	0
IC302	DELHI	MUMBAI	8	0
AM812	KANPUR	BENGALURU	3	1
IC899	MUMBAI	KOCHI	1	4
AM501	DELHI	TRIVANDRUM	1	5
MU499	MUMBAI	MADRAS	3	3
IC701	DELHI	AHMEDABAD	4	0

TABLE: FARES

FL_NO	AIRLINES	FARE	TAX%
IC701	INDIAN AIRLINES	6500	10
MU499	SAHARA	9400	5
AM501	JET AIRWAYS	13450	8
IC899	INDIAN AIRLINES	8300	4
IC302	INDIAN AIRLINES	4300	10
IC799	INDIAN AIRLINES	10500	10
MC101	DECCAN AIRLINES	3500	4

(i) Display FL_NO and NO_FLIGHT from KANPUR to BENGALURU from the table FLIGHTS.

(ii) Arrange the contents of the table FLIGHTS in the ascending order of FL_NO.

(iii) Display the FL_NO and fare to be paid for the flights from DELHI to MUMBAI using the tables FLIGHTS and FARES, where the fare to be paid = FARE + FARE * TAX % 100.

(iv) Display the minimum fare INDIAN AIRLINES is offering from the table FARES.

(v) To display the detail fares of Indian airlines.

Ans. (i)
```
SELECT FL_NO, NO_FLIGHT FROM FLIGHTS
WHERE STARTING = 'KANPUR' AND ENDING =
'BENGALURU';
```
(ii)
```
SELECT * FROM FLIGHTS ORDER BY FL_NO;
```
(iii)
```
SELECT FL_NO, FARE + FARE * TAX%100
FROM FARES WHERE FL_NO = (SELECT FL_No
FROM FLIGHTS WHERE STARTING = 'DELHI'
AND ENDING = 'MUMBAI');
```
(iv)
```
SELECT MIN(FARE) FROM FARES GROUP BY
AIRLINES HAVING AIRLINES = 'INDIAN
AIRLINES';
```
(v)
```
SELECT * FROM FARES
WHERE AIRLINES = " Indian Airlines";
```

75. Write SQL commands for (i) to (v) on the basis of the table SPORTS

TABLE: SPORTS

STUDENTNO	CLASS	NAME	GAME1	GRADE	GAME2	GRADE1
10	7	Sameer	Cricket	B	Swimming	A
11	8	Sujit	Tennis	A	Skating	C
12	7	Kamal	Swimming	B	Football	B
13	7	Veena	Tennis	C	Tennis	A
14	9	Archana	Basketball	A	Cricket	A
15	10	Arpit	Cricket	A	Athletics	C

(i) **Display the games taken up by the students, whose name starts with 'A'.**

(ii) **Write a query to add a new column named MARKS.**

(iii) **Write a query to assign a value 200 for Marks for all those, who are getting grade 'B' or grade 'A' in both GAME1 and GAME2.**

(iv) **Which command will be used to arrange the whole table in the alphabetical order of NAME?**

(a) `SELECT FROM SPORTS ORDER BY NAME;`

(b) `SELECT*SPORTS ORDER  BY NAME;`

(c) `SELECT*FROM SPORTS ORDER NAME;`

(d) `SELECT*FROM SPORTS ORDER BY NAME;`

(v) **Identify the attribute best suitable to be declared as a primary key.**

Ans. (i)
```
SELECT GAME1, GAME2 FROM SPORTS WHERE
NAME LIKE 'A%';
```
(ii)
```
ALTER TABLE SPORTS ADD(MARKS NUMBER(3));
```
(iii)
```
UPDATE SPORTS SET MARKS = 200
WHERE GRADE = 'A' OR GRADE = 'B' OR
GRADE1 = 'A' OR GRADE1 = 'B';
```
(iv) (d) `SELECT * FROM SPORTS ORDER BY NAME;`

(v) STUDENTNO attribute is best suitable to be declared as a primary key.

76. Write SQL commands for (i) to (v) on the basis of table EMPLOYEE

TABLE: EMPLOYEE

S NO	NAME	BASIC	DEPARTMENT	DATO FAPP	AGE	SEX
1	KARAN	8000	PERSONNEL	27/03/97	35	M
2	DIVAKAR	9500	COMPUTER	20/01/98	34	M
3	DIVYA	7300	ACCOUNTS	19/02/97	34	F
4	ARUN	8350	PERSONNEL	01/01/95	33	M
5	SABINA	9500	ACCOUNTS	12/01/96	36	F
6	JOHN	7400	FINANCE	24/02/97	36	M
7	ROBERT	8250	PERSONNEL	20/02/97	39	M
8	RUBINA	9450	MAINTENANCE	22/02/98	37	F
9	VIKAS	7500	COMPUTER	13/01/94	41	M
10	MOHAN	9300	MAINTENANCE	19/02/98	37	M

(i) **Which command will be used to list the names of the employees, who are more than 34 years old sorted by NAME.**

(a)
```
SELECT NAME FROM EMPLOYEE WHERE
AGE>34 ORDER BY NAME;
```
(b)
```
SELECT * FROM EMPLOYEE WHERE
AGE>34 ORDER BY NAME;
```
(c)
```
SELECT NAME FROM EMPLOYEE WHERE
AGE>34;
```
(d)
```
SELECT NAME FROM EMPLOYEE AGE>34
ORDER BY NAME;
```
(ii) **Write a query to display a report, listing NAME, BASIC, DEPARTMENT and annual salary. Annual salary equals to BASIC * 12.**

(iii) **Insert the following data in the EMPLOYEE table 11, 'VIJAY', 9300, 'FINANCE', '13/7/98', 35, "M"**

(iv) **Write a query to count the number of employees, who are either working in PERSONNEL or COMPUTER department.**

(v) **Write the degree and cardinality of the table EMPLOYEE.**

Ans. (i) (a)
```
SELECT NAME FROM EMPLOYEE WHERE AGE
> 34 ORDER BY NAME;
```
(ii)
```
SELECT NAME, BASIC, DEPARTMENT,
BASIC*12 "Annual Salary" FROM
EMPLOYEE;
```
(iii)
```
INSERT INTO EMPLOYEE VALUES(11, 'VIJAY',
9300, 'FINANCE', '13/7/98', 35,'M');
```
(iv)
```
SELECT COUNT(*) FROM EMPLOYEE
WHERE DEPARTMENT = 'PERSONNEL' OR
DEPARTMENT = 'COMPUTER';
```
(v) Degree of the given table is 7 and cardinality is 10.

77. Write SQL commands for (i) to (v) on the basis of table COLLEGE

TABLE: COLLEGE

No	Name	Age	Department	DateofJoin	Basic	Sex
1	Shalaz	45	Biology	13/02/88	10500	M
2	Sameera	54	Biology	10/01/90	9500	F
3	Yagyen	43	Physics	27/02/98	8500	M
4	Pratyush	34	Chemistry	11/01/93	7500	M
5	Aren	51	Mathematics	22/01/91	8500	M
6	Reeta	27	Chemistry	14/02/94	9000	F
7	Urvashi	29	Biology	10/02/93	8500	F
8	Teena	35	Mathematics	02/02/89	10500	F
9	Viren	49	Mathematics	03/01/88	9000	M
10	Prakash	22	Physics	17/02/92	8000	M

(i) **Write a query to change the Basic salary to 10500 of all those teachers from COLLEGE, who joined the COLLEGE after 01/02/89 and are above the age of 50.**

(ii) **Write a query to display Name, Age and Basic of all those from COLLEGE, who belong to Physics and Chemistry department only.**

(iii) **Which command will be used to delete a row from table COLLEGE, in which NAME is VIREN?**

(iv) **Insert the following data in the given table COLLEGE**

11, 'Saurav', 50, 'Chemistry', '18/05/93', 12000, 'M'

(v) **Identify the attribute best suitable to be declared as a primary key.**

Ans. (i)
```
UPDATE COLLEGE SET Basic = 10500
WHERE DateofJoin >'01/02/89' AND
Age>50;
```

(ii)
```
SELECT Name, Age, Basic FROM COLLEGE
WHERE Department='Physics' OR
Department='Chemistry';
```

(iii)
```
DELETE FROM COLLEGE WHERE Name
= 'VIREN';
```

(iv)
```
INSERT INTO COLLEGE VALUES (11,
'Saurav', 50, 'Chemistry', '18/05/93',
12000, 'M');
```

(v) No attribute is best suitable to be declared as a primary key.

Case Study Based Questions

Case Study 1

Consider the following table Persons and answer the questions that follows

PID	LastName	FirstName	Address	City
101	Hansen	Ola	Timoteivn 10	Sandnes
102	Svendson	Tove	Borgvn 23	Sandnes
103	Petterson	Kari	Storgt 20	Stavanger
104	Nilsen	Johan	Bakken 2	Stavanger
105	Tjessem	Jakob	NULL	NULL

(i) **Write the degree and cardinality of table Persons.**

(ii) **Identify the attribute best suitable to be declared as a primary key.**

(iii) **Which command is used to show the content of table Persons?**

(iv) **To display the detail of persons whose city is Sandnes.**

(v) **Insert the row with value (106, John, Miller, NULL, Sandnes)**

Ans. (i) Degree = 5

cardinality = 5

(ii) PID

(iii)
```
DESC Persons;
```

(iv)
```
SELECT * FROM Persons
WEHRE City="Sandnes";
```

(v)
```
INSERT INTO Persons (106, "John",
"Miller", NULL, "Sandnes");
```

Case Study 2

Consider the table Teacher and answer the questions that follow

PID	Name	Salary	Subject	DOJ
T01	Aradhna	17000	Science	2013-01-08
T02	Ritika	15000	Mathematics	2013-12-14
T03	Ravindra	12000	Science	2013-11-23
T04	Dushyant	15000	English	2014-01-10
T05	Swati	20000	Mathematics	2014-02-10
T06	Shrey	18000	Computer	2014-06-07

(i) **Write the degree and cardinality of table Teacher.**

(ii) **Find the attribute best suitable to be declared as a primary key.**

(iii) **To display the detail of teacher whose subject is computer.**

(iv) **Find the output, SELECT Name FROM Teacher WHERE Salary > 15000;**

(v) **To display the name of teacher whose data of joining is 2014-02-10;**

Ans. (i) Degree = 5 Cardinality = 6

(ii) T_ID

(iii)
```
SELECT * FROM Teacher WHERE Subject =
"Computer";
```

(iv)

Name
Aradhna
Swati
Shrey

(v) SELECT Name FROM Teacher
FROM DOJ = "2014-02-10";

Case Study 3

In a Database, there are two tables with the instances given below:

Table : STUDENTS

ADMNO	NAME	CLASS	SEC	RNO	ADDRESS	PHONE
1211	MEENA	12A	D	4	A-26	3245678
1212	VANI	10A	D	1	B-25	5456789
1213	MEENA	12B	A	1	NULL	NULL
1214	KARISH	10B	B	3	AB-234	4567890

Table : SPORTS

ADMNO	GAME	COACHNAME	GRADE
1215	CRICKET	MR.RAVI	A
1213	VOLLEYBALL	MR.AMANDEEP	B
1211	VOLLEYBALL	MR.GOVARDHAN	A
1212	BASKET BALL	MR. TEWARI	B

CBSE Question Bank

(i) **Choose the command to display name and game of those students whose address is available in STUDENTS table.**

(a) SELECT NAME, GAME FROM STUDENTS, SPORTS WHERE STUDENTS.ADMNO=SPORTS.ADMNO AND ADDRESS IS NOT NULL;

(b) SELECT NAME, GAME FROM STUDENTS, SPORTS WHERE STUDENTS.ADMNO=SPORTS.ADMNO AND ADDRESS IS NULL;

(c) SELECT NAME, GAME FROM STUDENTS, SPORTS WHERE STUDENTS.ADMNO=SPORTS.ADMNO, ADDRESS IS NULL;

(d) SELECT NAME, GAME FROM STUDENTS, SPORTS WHERE STUDENTS.ADMNO=SPORTS.ADMNO NOT ADDRESS IS NULL;

(ii) **Identify the statement to delete a column phone from the table STUDENTS.**

(a) ALTER TABLE STUDENTS DROP PHONE;

(b) DROP PHONE;

(c) UPDATE DROP PHONE;

(d) DELETE FROM STUDENTS WHERE DROP PHONE;

(iii) **Choose the command to display name of the students who are studying in class 12 and their corresponding coach names.**

(a) SELECT NAME, COACHNAME FROM STUDENTS, SPORTS WHERE CLASS LIKE "12%" AND STUDENTS.ADMNO =SPORTS.ADMNO;

(b) SELECT NAME, COACHNAME FROM STUDENTS, SPORTS WHERE CLASS LIKE "12%", STUDENTS.ADMNO= SPORTS.ADMNO;

(c) SELECT NAME, COACHNAME FROM STUDENTS, SPORTS WHERE CLASS LIKE "12%" AND ADMNO.STUDENTS =ADMNO.SPORTS;

(d) SELECT NAME, COACHNAME FROM STUDENTS, SPORTS WHERE CLASS LIKE= "12%" AND STUDENTS=SPORTS;

(iv) **Choose the command to count the number of students who play volleyball.**

(a) SELECT COUNT(*) FROM STUDENTS, SPORTS WHERE GAME="VOLLEYBALL" AND STUDENTS.ADMNO=SPORTS.ADMNO ;

(b) SELECT COUNT(GAME) FROM STUDENTS, SPORTS WHERE GAME="VOLLEYBALL" AND STUDENTS.ADMNO=SPORTS.ADMNO ;

(c) SELECT COUNT(*) FROM STUDENTS, SPORTS WHERE GAME="VOLLEYBALL" ;

(d) SELECT COUNT(*) FROM STUDENTS, SPORTS WHERE SPORTS="VOLLEYBALL" AND STUDENTS.ADMNO=SPORTS.ADMNO

Ans. (i) (*a*) For writing the query it is required to select NAME and GAME field from STUDENTS table and SPORTS table using an equi join operation.

(ii) (*a*) ALTER command is used, if there is any updation required in definition of a table. DROP clause is used with ALTER command to delete a column from a table.

Syntax to delete any column from table is

ALTER TABLE <table_name> DROP <column_name>;

(iii) (*a*) One field is from STUDENTS table and one is from SPORTS table, equi join will be used and to select any kind of pattern in character field LIKE clause is used.

(iv) (*a*) To count number of students play volleyball again we need to apply join and only those students are required to be counted who are present in both tables.

COUNT(*) will count all rows.

SELF ASSESSMENT TEST

Multiple Choice Questions

1 Which of the following is a non-procedural computer language, aimed to store, manipulate and query data in a relational database?

(a) SQL (b) Java
(c) Database (d) None of these

2 Which of the following is used to terminate the SQL statements?

(a) , (b) ; (c) # (d) &

3 Which SQL command used to change the structure of database table?

(a) Create (b) Rename
(c) Alter (d) Drop

4 Which of the following is a correct syntax to drop a column in SQL command?

(a) `ALTER TABLE table_name COLUMN column_name;`
(b) `ALTER TABLE table_name DROP COLUMN column_name;`
(c) `ALTER table_name DROP column_name;`
(d) `ALTER TABLE table_name DROP column_name;`

5 Which of the following operator displays a record if both the first condition and the second condition are true?

(a) OR (b) AND
(c) NOT (d) None of these

Fill in the Blanks

6 SQL is widely used for ....

7 .... statement is used to rename a table.

8 ...... inserts default value into a column.

9 The .... statement is used to select data from a database or view table information.

10 The .... operator selects the data outside the range of data between two values.

State Whether True of False

11 The varchar(n) data type stores variable-length character strings with a maximum length of n.

12 The DELETE command removes a table structure permanently from the database.

13 The IS NULL operator is used to check whether a column has no value (null).

Assertion and Reason Based Questions

Assertion (A) and Reason (R) Type questions. Choose the correct option as:

(a) Both Assertion (A) and Reason (R) are true, and Reason (R) is the correct explanation of Assertion (A)
(b) Both Assertion (A) and Reason (R) are true, but Reason (R) is not the correct explanation of Assertion (A)
(c) Assertion (A) is True, but Reason (R) is False
(d) Assertion (A) is False, but Reason (R) is True

14 **Assertion (A)** The DISTINCT keyword is used in SQL to remove duplicate values from the result set.

Reason (R) DISTINCT helps in retrieving only unique rows by eliminating duplicates.

15 **Assertion (A)** The GROUP BY clause is used to filter records based on a given condition.

Reason (R) GROUP BY is always used with aggregate functions.

Very Short Answer Type Questions

16 Name the various SQL datatypes used in SQL.

17 What is the use of GRANT command?

18 Give the syntax of modify the column data type.

19 Write the example of DISTINCT keyword.

Short Answer Type Questions

20 Write INSERT INTO commands to add two rows in table BANK, which as account number, name, bank name, amount and date of opening.

21 Give the output of the following SQL queries on the basis of table SHOP.

S.No.	P_Name	S_Name	Qty	Cost	City
S1	Biscuit	Priyagold	120	12.00	Delhi
S2	Bread	Britannia	200	25.00	Mumbai
S3	Chocolate	Cadbury	350	40.00	Mumbai
S4	Sauce	Kissan	400	45.00	Chennai

(i) `SELECT * FROM SHOP WHERE Qty BETWEEN 100 AND 400;`

(ii) `SELECT * FROM SHOP ORDER BY Qty;`

(iii) `SELECT S_Name, P_Name, Cost FROM SHOP WHERE Qty < 300;`

Long Answer Type Question

22 Consider the following tables CONSIGNOR and CONSIGNEE and answer (i) to (v).

TABLE: CONSIGNOR

CnorID	CnorName	CnorAddress	City
ND01	R Singhal	24, ABC Enclave	New Delhi
ND02	Anit Kumar	123, Palm Avenue	New Delhi
MU15	R Kohil	5/A, Suth street	Mumbai
MU50	S Kaur	27-K, Westend	Mumbai

TABLE: CONSIGNEE

CneeID	CnorID	CneeName	CneeAddress	CneeCity
MU05	ND01	Rahul Kishore	5, Park Avenue	Mumbai
ND08	ND02	P Dhingra	16/J, Moore Enclave	New Delhi
KO19	MU15	AP Roy	2A, Central Avenue	Kolkata
MU32	ND02	S Mittal	P 245, AB Colony	Mumbai
ND48	MU50	BP Jain	13, Block D,A Vihar	New Delhi

Write SQL commands for the following statements:

(i) To display the names of all CONSIGNORS from Mumbai.

(ii) To display the CneeID, CnorName, CnorAddress, CneeName, CneeAddress for every CONSIGNEE.

(iii) To display CONSIGNEE details in ascending order of CneeName.

(iv) To display number of consignors from each city.

(v) To display the detail of consignor whose city is New Delhi.

Case Study Based Question

23. Consider the table Student and answer the questions that follows

TABLE : STUDENT

Code	Name	Age	Marks	Points
101	Amit	16	76	6
102	Arjun	13	84	4
103	Zaheer	14	73	2
105	Gagan	15	68	1
108	Kumar	17	92	8
109	Rajesh	15	39	8
110	Naveen	13	52	9
113	Ajay	16	76	3
115	Kapil	14	57	2
120	Gurdeep	15	76	6

(i) Identify the attribute best sutiable to be declared as a primary key.

(ii) Write the degree and cardinality of table Student.

(iii) Insert the following row
(121, Shrey, 14, 78, 4)

(iv) To display the name of student whose marks is more than 75.

(v) Write the command to display the content of table student.

Answers

1. (a) 2. (b) 3. (c) 4. (b) 5. (b)
6. Managing database 7. Rename
8. Default 9. SELECT 10. NOT BETWEEN 11. True
12. False 13. True 14. (a) 15. (d)

10

CHAPTER

Interfacing Python with MySQL involves connecting a Python application to a MySQL database to perform operations such as data retrieval, insertion, updating and deletion.

Interface Python with MySQL

▼ **YOUR STUDY GOALS**

10.1 Connecting to MySQL from Python
10.2 To Show the List of Existing Database
10.3 Create the New Database
10.4 Creating Table
10.5 ALTER Table
10.6 INSERT Operation

▼ **YOUR PRACTICE GOAL**

- Objective Type Questions (38 Qs ; MCQs, True or False, Fill in the Blanks, Assertion and Reason)
- Subjective Type Questions (32 Qs ; VSA, SA, LA)
- Case Based Questions (Objective Case Studies-3)

While developing real life applications, we need to connect it with database in order to encounter such situation where the data stored in database need to be manipulated/changed.

Python allows us to connect our application to the databases like MySQL,MongoDB, SQLite and many others.

In this chapter, we will discuss Python - MySQL connectivity and learn to perform different database operations in Python.

10.1 Connecting to MySQL from Python

Before we connect Python program with any database like MySQL we need to build a bridge to connect Python and MySQL.

To build this bridge so that data can travel both ways we need a connector called **"mysql.connector"**.

Install MySQL Connector

The **mysql.connector** is not a built-in module, we need to install it. Execute the following command to install it using pip installer.

```
>python -m pip install mysql-connector
```

If you are using Anaconda Jupyter then type following command on terminal

```
conda install -c anaconda mysql-connector-python
```

Steps for Creating Database Connectivity

There are various steps for creating database connectivity as follows

Step 1 **Import mysql.connector module**

To import mysql.connector module, write the following command :

```
import mysql.connector
```

Or

```
import mysql.connector as mydb
```

Here, mydb is an identifier which can be choose by user.

Step 2 **Create the connection object**

To create a connection between the MySQL database and Python application, use connect() method mysql.connector module is used. Pass the database details like HostName, UserName and database Password. This method returns the connection object.

Syntax

```
Connection_object
        = mysql.connector.connect(
    host = HostName,
    user = UserName,
    passwd = password
)
```

e.g.

```
import mysql.connector
con = mysql.connector.connect(
    host = "localhost",
    user = "root",
    passwd = "arihant"
)
print(con)
```

Output

<mysql.connector.connection.MYSQL Connection object at Ox7fb142edd780>

If you want to connect to specific database, you have to specify the database name in connect() method.

e.g.

```
import mysql.connector
con = mysql.connector.connect(
    host = "localhost",
    user = "root",
passwd = "arihant",
database = "mysql"
)
print(con)
```

Mistake Alert!

Sometimes students change the order of the variables, which results an error.

Step 3 **Creating the cursor object**

The cursor object is used to define as an abstraction that specified in Python DB-API 2.0. It provides the facility to the user to work on multiple separate environment through the same connection to the database. Cursor object can be create using cursor () method of connection object. It is an important term to the database for executing queries.

Syntax

```
cursor_object = connection_object.
                        cursor()
```

e.g.

```
import mysql.connector
con = mysql.connector.connect(
    host = "localhost",
    user = "root",
    password = "arihant",
    database = "mysql"
)
print(con)
cursor = con.cursor()
print(cursor)
```

Output

<mysql.connector.connection.MySQL connection object at O × 7fb142edd780>
MySQLCursor : (Nothing executed yet)

Step 4 **Execute the Query**

After creating the cursor, SQL query can be execute using execute() function.

Syntax `cursor_object.execute (query)`

Step 5 **Clean up the environment**

This is the final step for creating database connectivity. There is necessary to close the connection which you created.

Syntax `connection_object.close()`

e.g. We created the connection con, so to close this connection use following command

```
con.close()
```

10.2 To Show the List of Existing Database

If you want to display the name of all existing database, use following query

Syntax `>show databases`

e.g.
```
import mysql.connector
con = mysql.connector.connect(
host = "localhost",
user = "root",
passwd = "arihant")
cursor = con.cursor()
try:
 db = cursor.execute("show databases")
except:
 con.rollback()
for i in cursor:
 print(i)
con.close()
```

Output

('information_schema',)
('my',)
('mysql',)
('test',)

10.3 Create the New Database

To create the new database ,use following command

Syntax `create database (database_name)`

e.g.
```
import mysql.connector
con = mysql.connector.connect(
host = "localhost",
user = "root",
passwd = "arihant"
)
cursor = con.cursor()
try:
cursor.execute("create database Python DB")
db = cursor.execute("show databases")
except:
con.rollback()
for i in cursor:
  print(i)
con.close()
```

Output

('PythonDB',)
('information_schema',)
('my',)
('mysql',)
('test',)

10.4 Creating Table

We can create a table using CREATE TABLE statement.

Syntax
```
CREATE TABLE Table_Name
(
   column1 datatype constraint,
   column2 datatype constraint,
   :
   columnN datatype
)
```

Here, we will create table Student in database PythonDB with five columns as Name, Class, RollNo, Address and Percentage.

e.g.
```
import mysql.connector
con = mysql.connector.connect
(host = "localhost",
user = "root",
passwd = "arihant",
database = "PythonDB")
cursor = con.cursor()
try:
   db = cursor.execute ("create table
   Student
   (Name Varchar(30)NOT NULL,
   RollNo Int(10) Primary key,
   Class Varchar(5),
   Address Varchar(50),
   Percentage Float (15)))
except:
   con.rollback()
con.close()
```

In Python shell,
```
>>> use PythonDB;
Database changed
>>> desc Student;
```

Field	Type	Null	Key	Default	Extra
Name	Varchar<30>	NO		NULL	
RollNo	Int<10>	NO	PRI	NULL	
Class	Varchar<5>	YES		NULL	
Address	Varchar<50>	YES		NULL	
Percentage	Float<15>	YES		NULL	

```
5 rows in set <0.06 sec>
```

10.5 ALTER Table

If user wants to alter existing table, ALTER TABLE statement is used.

Syntax
```
ALTER TABLE Table_Name ADD ColumnName
Datatype
```

e.g. We will add new column Age in table Student.

```
import mysql.connector
con = mysql.connector.connect
      (host = "localhost",
      user = "root",
      passwd = "arihant",
      database = "PythonDB")
cursor = con.cursor()
try:
   cursor.execute("alter table Student add
   Age int(5) not null")
except :
      con.rollback()
con.close()
```

In Python shell,

```
>>>desc Student;
```

Field	Type	Null	Key	Default	Extra
Name	varchar(30)	NO		NULL	
RollNo	int(10)	NO	PRI	NULL	
Class	varchar(5)	YES		NULL	
Address	varchar(50)	YES		NULL	
Percentage	float(15)	YES		NULL	
Age	int(5)	NO		NULL	

Quick Test 1

1. Write command to install connector for MySQL using pip installer.
2. Which command is used to clean up the environment?
3. Write the statement to execute the query.
4. How to display the name of pre-existing databases?
5. What is the use of cursor() method?

10.6 INSERT Operation

Insert operation is required when you want to create your records into a database's table. INSERT INTO statement is used to add a record.

1. Add Single Record into a Table

In Python, to add single record into a table, we can mention the format specifier (%s) in place of value.

Example Without format specifier

```
import mysql.connector
con = mysql.connector.connect
   (host = "localhost",
   user = "root",
   passwd = "arihant",
   database = "PythonDB")
cursor = con.cursor()
sql = "insert into Student (Name,
RollNo, Class, Address, Percentage,
Age) values ('Riya', 27, 12, 'Delhi',
73, 15)"
try :
   cursor.execute (sql)
   con.commit()
except :
   con.rollback()
con.close()
```

Example With format specifier

```
import mysql.connector
con = mysql.connector.connect
   (host = "localhost",
   user = "root",
   passwd = "arihant",
   database = "PythonDB")
cursor = con.cursor()
sql = "insert into Student (Name,
RollNo, Class, Address, Percentage,
Age )values (%s, %s, %s, %s, %s, %s)"
values = ("Riya", 27, 12, "Delhi", 73, 15)
try :
   cursor.execute(sql, values)
   con.commit()
except:
   con.rollback()
con.close()
```

In Python shell,

```
>>>select *from Student;
```

Name	RollNo	Class	Address	Percentage	Age
Riya	27	12	Delhi	73	15

String template with{} and format()

In this method in place of %s we will use {} and to pass values for these placeholder format() is used. Inside we can optionally give 0,1,2...... values for e.g. {0},{1} but its mandatory.

We can also optionally pass named parameter inside {} so that while passing values through format function we need not to remember the order of value to pass, For e.g. {roll}, {name} etc.

Example With {} and format()

```
import mysql.connector
    con = mysql.connector.connect(
   host="localhost",
   user="root",
```

```
        passwd="arihant",
      database="PythonDB"
    )
      cursor = con.cursor()
sql = "INSERT INTO Student (Name, RollNo,
Class, Address, Percentage, Age) VALUES
('{}', {}, {}, '{}', {}, {})".format(
    "Riya", 27, 12, "Delhi", 73, 15)
try:
    cursor.execute(sql)
    con.commit()
    print("Record inserted successfully!")
except:
    con.rollback()
    print("Error occurred during
insertion.")
     finally:
    con.close()
>>>select *from Student;
```

Assuming the Student table already exists, the output will be:

Name	RollNo	Class	Address	Percentage	Age
Riya	27	12	Delhi	73	15

2. Insert Multiple Rows or Records

You can also insert multiple records at a time. To insert multiple records, use format specifier (%s) makes it easy. For this executemany() is used because it executes more than one statements together.

e.g.

```
import mysql.connector
con = mysql.connector.connect
   (host = "localhost",
   user = "root",
   passwd = "arihant",
   database = "PythonDB")
cursor = con.cursor()
sql = "insert into Student (Name,
   RollNo, Class, Address,
   Percentage, Age) values (%s, %s,
   %s, %s, %s, %s)
values = [("Ayush", 33, 11,
      "Delhi", 97, 14),
      ("Kiran", 22, 11,
      "Pune", 88, 15),
      ("Nisha", 28, 12,
      "Meerut", 95, 16)]
try :
    cursor.executemany(sql,values)
    con.commit()
except:
    con.rollback()
con.close()
```

In Python Shell,

```
>>>select*From Student;
```

Name	RollNo	Class	Address	Percentage	Age
Riya	27	12	Delhi	73	15
Ayush	33	11	Delhi	97	14
Kiran	22	11	Pune	88	15
Nisha	28	12	Meerut	95	16

Update Operation

Update operation means to update one or more records on any database, which are already exist in that database. For this, UPDATE statement is used.

Syntax

```
UPDATE Table_Name SET column_Name = value
WHERE condition
```

Example 1 In Student table, we will update the class of those student whose Roll No is 22.

```
import mysql.connector
con = mysql.connector.connect
(host = "localhost", user = "root",
      passwd = "arihant",
      database= "PythonDB")
cursor = con.cursor()
try :
   cursor.execute ("update Student set
          Class = 12 where RollNo = 22")
   con.commit()
except :
      con.rollback()
con.close()
```

In Python Shell,

```
>>>SELECT *FROM Student;
```

Name	RollNo	Class	Address	Percentage	Age
Riya	27	12	Delhi	73	15
Ayush	33	11	Delhi	97	14
Kiran	22	12	Pune	88	15
Nisha	28	12	Meerut	95	16

Delete Operation

This operation is required when you want to delete some records from the database. For this, DELETE FROM statement is used.

Syntax

```
DELETE FROM Table_Name WHERE condition
```

Example 2

In Student table, we will delete the record of that student whose Roll No is 33.

```
import mysql.connector
con = mysql.connector.connect
(host = "localhost", user = "root",
      passwd = "arihant",
      database = "PythonDB")
cursor = con.cursor()
try:
      cursor.execute ("delete from Student
where RollNo = 33")
      con.commit()
except:
      con.rollback()
con.close()
```

In Python Shell,

```
>>>SELECT *FROM Student;
```

Name	RollNo	Class	Address	Percentage	Age
Riya	27	12	Delhi	73	15
Kiran	22	12	Pune	88	15
Nisha	28	12	Meerut	95	16

Read Operation

This operation is used to fetch some useful information from the database. By following methods, you can fetch the data from database

1. fetchone()

It returns the next row from the result set as tuple. If there are no more rows to retrieve, None is returned.

Example 3 To fetch only one record

```
import mysql.connector
con = mysql.connector.connect
(host = "localhost",
   user = "root",
   passwd = "arihant",database = "PythonDB")
cursor = con.cursor()
try:
   cursor.execute ("Select Name,
   RollNo, Address, Percentage from
      Student")
   display = cursor.fetchone()
   print(display)
except:
   con.rollback()
con.close()
```

Output

('Riya', 27, 'Delhi', 73)

2. fetchmany ([size])

It returns the number of rows specified by the size argument. When called repeatedly this method fetches the next set of rows of a query result and returns a list of tuples. If no more rows are available, it returns an empty list.

Example 4 To fetch many records from database PythonDB

```
import mysql.connector
con = mysql.connector.connect
(host = "localhost", user = "root",
  passwd = "arihant",database = "PythonDB")
cursor = con.cursor()
try:
   size = int(input("Enter the value of
   numbers of rows."))
   cursor.execute("Select*from Student")
   display = cursor.fetchmany(size)
   for i in display:
      print (i)
except:
   con.rollback()
con.close()
```

Output

Enter the value of no. of rows : 2

('Riya', 27, 12, 'Delhi', 73, 15)

('Kiran', 22, 12, 'Delhi', 88, 15)

3. fetchall()

It fetches all the rows of a query result. It returns all the rows as a list of tuples. An empty list is returned if there is no record to fetch.

Example 5 To fetch all records from database PythonDB

```
import mysql.connector
con = mysql.connector.connect
(host = "localhost", user = "root",
   passwd = "arihant",
   database = "PythonDB")
cursor = con.cursor()
try :
   cursor.execute ("select * from
   Student")
   display = cursor.fetchall()
   for i in display :
         print(i)
except :
   con.rollback ()
con.close()
```

Output

('Riya', 27, 12, 'Delhi', 73, 15)
('Kiran', 22, 12, 'Delhi', 88, 15)
('Nisha', 28, 12, 'Meerut', 95, 16)

rowcount

This is read only attribute and returns the number of rows that were affected by an execute() method.

Quick Test 2

1. Which function is used to insert multiple values into a table.
2. The function used to delete a record from a table is ____ ?
3. Differentiate fetchone(() and fetchmany().
4. Write the use of fetchall() method.
5. When rowcount is used?

Mind Map

INTERFACE PYTHON WITH MYSQL

It involves connecting a Python application to a MySQL database to perform operations such as data retrieval, insertion, updating and deletion.

Connecting to MySQL from Python

Steps for Creating Database Connectivity

Step 1 Import mysql.connector module

Syntax
```
import mysql.connector
```
Or
```
import mysql.connector as mydb
```

Step 2 Create the connection object

Syntax
```
Connection_object= mysql.connector.connect
    (
      host = HostName,
      user = UserName,
      passwd = password
    )
```

Step 3 Creating the cursor object

Syntax
```
cursor_object = connection_object.cursor()
```

Step 4 Execute the Query

Syntax
```
cursor_object.execute (query)
```

Step 5 Clean up the environment

Syntax
```
connection_object.close()
```

Install MySQL connector

The mysql.connector is not a built-in module, we need to install it.

Syntax
```
>python -m pip install mysql-connector
```

Parameterized Query

We can pass values to query to perform dynamic search like we want to search for any employee number entered during runtime or to search any other column values.

String template with %s formatting

In this method we will use %s in place of values to substitute and then pass the value for that place.

String template { } and format ( )

In this method in place of %s we will use { } and to pass value for these placeholder format ( ) is used.

DML Queries

CREATE DATABASE

Syntax
```
CREATE DATABASE (database_name)
```

CREATE TABLE

Syntax
```
CREATE TABLE Table_Name
(
column1 datatype constraint,
column2 datatype constraint,
columnN datatype
)
```

ALTER TABLE

Syntax
```
ALTER TABLE Table_Name ADD ColumnName Datatype
```

DDL Command

INSERT INTO Operation

Insert operation is required when you want to create your records into a database's table. INSERT INTO statement is used to add a record.

Syntax
```
INSERT INTO table_name(column_1, column_2, column_3) VALUES
(value_1, value_2, value_3);
```

UPDATE Operation

Update operation means to update one or more records on any database, which are already exist in that database.
For this, UPDATE statement is used.

Syntax
```
UPDATE Table_Name SET column_Name = value WHERE condition
```

DELETE Operation

This operation is required when you want to delete some records from the database. For this, DELETE FROM statement is used.

Syntax
```
DELETE FROM Table_Name WHERE condition
```

Read Operation

Used to fetch some useful information from the database.

fetchone()

It returns the next row from the result set as tuple. If there are no more rows to retrieve, None is returned.

fetchmany ([size])

It returns the number of rows specified by the size argument. When called repeatedly this method fetches the next set of rows of a query result and returns a list of tuples. If no more rows are available, it returns an empty list.

fetchall()

It fetches all the rows of a query result. It returns all the rows as a list of tuples. An empty list is returned if there is no record to fetch.

rowcount

This is read only attribute and returns the number of rows that were affected by an execute() method.

EXAM PATTERN QUESTIONS

Objective Type Questions

Multiple Choice Questions

1. User can write Python script using

(a) MySQL.connector library (b) SQL.connect library
(c) MySQL.connect library (d) Any one of the above

2. Which of the following method is used to create a connection between the MySQL database and Python?

(a) connector ( ) (b) connect ( )
(c) con ( ) (d) cont ( )

3. What is default value of host?

(a) Host (b) localhost
(c) global host (d) None of these

4. To establish a connection between Python and SQL database, connect() is used. Which of the following arguments may not necessarily be given while calling connect() ? SQP 2022-23

(a) host (b) database (c) user (d) password

5. Mandatory arguments required to connect any database from Python

(a) Username, Password, Hostname, Database Name, Port.
(b) Username, Password, Hostname.
(c) Username, Password, Hostname, Database Name.
(d) Username, Password, Hostname, Port.

6. Which command is used to display the name of existing databases?

(a) display databases; (b) result databases;
(c) show databases; (d) output databases;

7. Which method of cursor class is used to insert or update multiple rows using a single query?

(a) cursor.executeall(query, rows)
(b) cursor.execute(query, rows)
(c) cursor.executemultiple (query, rows)
(d) cursor.executemany(query, rows)

8. Which method of cursor class is used to execute database function or stored procedure in Python

(a) cursor.callprocedure('procedureName', [parameters,])
(b) cursor.callproc('procedureName', [parameters,])
(c) cursor.callfunc('procedureName', [parameters,])
(d) cursor.callfunction('procedureName', [parameters,])

9. Exception raised when the relational integrity of the database is affected in Python

(a) IntegrityFailError (b) IntegrityFailure
(c) IntegrityViolationError (d) IntegrityError

10. __________ is the set of records that are retrieved after execution of SQL query over an established database connection.

(a) sqlresult (b) resultset
(c) table (d) tuple

11. .... operation is required when you want to create your records into a database table.

(a) Update (b) Delete (c) Read (d) Insert

12. Which method returns the next row from the result set as tuple?

(a) fetchone ( ) (b) fetchmany ( )
(c) fetchall ( ) (d) rowcount

13. Which method of cursor class is used to fetch limited rows from the table?

(a) cursor.fetchsize(SIZE)
(b) cursor.fetchmany(SIZE)
(c) cursor.fetchall(SIZE)
(d) cursor.fetchonly(SIZE)

14. fetchall() method fetches all rows in a result set and returns a Examination Paper 2023

(a) Tuple of lists (b) List of tuples
(c) List of strings (d) Tuple of strings

15. Which of the following is invalid method for fetching the records from database within Python?

(a) fetchone() (b) fetchmany()
(c) fetchall() (d) fetchmulti()

16. Which method of cursor class is used to get the number of rows affected after any of the insert/ update/delete database operation executed from Python?

(a) cursor.rowcount
(b) cursor.getaffectedcount
(c) cursor.rowscount
(d) cursor.rcount

Fill in the Blanks

17. ...... can connect to MySQL databases from Python.

18. The mysql.connector is .... a built in module.

19. .... method returns the connection object.

20. .... can be create using cursor ( ) method of connection object.

21. .... statement is used to add a record.

State Whether True or False

22. In Python, when using the execute() method with SQL queries, it is mandatory to use a cursor object to execute SQL queries against a connected database.

23. The commit() method in Python's DB-API is used to save changes in the database permanently, but it is unnecessary for read-only operations such as SELECT queries.

24. After executing an INSERT, UPDATE, or DELETE query, the rowcount attribute of the cursor will give the number of rows affected by the query.

25. The fetchone() method in Python's DB-API always returns a list containing all the rows returned by the query execution.

26. In Python's sqlite3 module, using %s format specifier in the execute() method is a valid way to pass parameters for SQL queries, but using format() for parameterized queries is not recommended for security reasons.

Assertion and Reason Based Questions

Directions: In the following questions, A statement of Assertion (A) is followed by a statement of Reason (R). Mark the correct choice as.

(a) Both A and R are true and R is the correct explanation for A.

(b) Both A and R are true and R is not correct explanation for A.

(c) A is true but R is false.

(d) A is false but R is true.

27. Assertion (A) Python Database Connectivity is transfer of data between Python programs and MySQL.

Reason (R) Python MySQL Database Connectivity needs to install MySQL connector.

28. Assertion (A) Database connection is closed at the end of processing.

Reason (R) cursor.close() is given to close the connection.

29. Assertion (A) MySQLdb is an interface for connecting to a MySQL database servers from Python.

Reason (R) exit () method is used to close the connection to the database.

30. Assertion (A) A cursor is a Python object that enables you to work with the database.

Reason (R) To get a cursor you need to call the cursor method on the database object.

31. Assertion (A) connect () function is required in a program to establish connection to a MySQL database.

Reason (R) cursor() instantiates objects that can execute operations such as SQL statements .

32. Assertion (A) A cursor is a control structure that access records.

Reason (R) You can check for connection with using is_connected().

33. Assertion (A) SQL query is executed using parameterized execute statement.

Reason (R) The retrieved records are stored as resultset

34. Assertion (A) c. fetchone () returns the next row of the query result as a sequence.

Reason (R) c.fetchone () raises an exception if there is no result set.

35. Assertion (A) n number of rows can be retrieved from the result set.

Reason (R) fetchmany() method returns n number of records from the resultset.

36. Assertion (A) fetchall() method returns the records one by one.

Reason (R) fetchone() method retrieves one record from the result set.

37. Assertion (A) The result stored in resultset is extracted using fetch methods.

Reason (R) rowcount() is a property of cursor that returns number of rows (depends on the type of query executed).

38. Assertion (A) rowcount() function returns number of rows affected or fetched.

Reason (R) The number of rows from fetch() methods.

Answers

1. (a) MySQL.connector library
2. (b) connect ( )
3. (b) localhost
4. (a) host
5. (c) Username, Password, Hostname, Database Name.
6. (c) show databases;
7. (d) cursor.executemany(query, rows)
8. (b) cursor.callproc('procedureName', [parameters,])
9. (d) IntegrityError
10. (b) resultset
11. (d) Insert
12. (a) fetchone ( )
13. (b) cursor.fetchmany(SIZE)
14. (b) List of tuples
15. (d) fetchmulti()
16. (a) cursor.rowcount
17. MySQL.connector()
18. not
19. connect ( )
20. Cursor object
21. INSERT INTO
22. True
23. True
24. True
25. False
26. True
27. (a) Both A and R are true and R is the correct explanation for A.
28. (c) A is true but R is false.
29. (c) A is true but R is false.
30. (a) Both A and R are true and R is the correct explanation for A.
31. (b) Both A and R are true and R is not correct explanation for A.
32. (b) Both A and R are true and R is not correct explanation for A.
33. (a) Both A and R are true and R is the correct explanation for A.
34. (c) A is true but R is false.
35. (a) Both A and R are true and R is the correct explanation for A.
36. (d) A is false but R is true.
37. (b) Both A and R are true and R is not correct explanation for A.
38. (c) A is true but R is false.

Subjective Type Questions

Very Short Answer Type Questions

1. What is database connection?

Ans. A database connection is a facility in computer science that allows client software to talk to database server software, whether on the same machine or not.

2. What is database connectivity?

Ans. Database connectivity is an application programming interface (API) which allows the programmer to connect and interact with databases.

3. What conditions or terms are included by DB-API?

Ans.
- Importing the API module
- Acquiring a connection with database
- Stored procedures and issuing SQL statements
- Closing the connection

4. How and why do use SQL Server?

Ans. SQL Server is free which means anyone can download and use it. The application uses SQL (Structured Query Language), and it is easy to use.

5. What is the default port for MySQL Server?

Ans. The default port for MySQL Server is 3306. Another standard default port is 1433 in TCP/IP for SQL Server.

6. Which command is used to import mysql.connector package with an identifier?

Ans.
```
import mysql.connector as identifier_name
```
e.g.
```
import mysql.connector as mydb
```

7. How to create a connection object?

Ans.
```
connection_object
          = mysql.connector.connect (
     (host = HostName,
      user = UserName,
    passwd = password)
```

8. Write a checklist before connecting to a database?

Ans. Before connecting to a MySQL database make sure

(i) You have created a database

(ii) You have created a table

(iii) This table has fields

9. What is a cursor?

Ans. A cursor is a Python object that enables you to work with the database. In dataset terms, the cursor is positioned at a particular location within a table or tables in a database.

10. What is a query result set?

Ans. A result set is an object that is returned when a cursor object is used to query a table.

11. Write the command to add a column salary in table Employee.

Ans. ALTER TABLE Employee ADD salary Int(10);

12. How fetchone ( ) method is differ from fetchall() method?

Ans. fetchone ( ) method returns the next row from the result set as tuple while fetchall ( ) fetches all the rows of a query result.

13. Define the fetchmany ([size]).

Ans. fetchmany([size]) returns the number of rows specified by the size argument.
When called repeatedly this method fetches the next set of rows of a query result and returns a list of tuples. If no more rows are available, it returns an empty list.

Short Answer Type I Questions

14. Differentiate between fetchone() and fetchall() methods with suitable examples for each.

Ans. The difference between fetchone() and fetchall() methods:

fetchone()	fetchall()
Fetches a single record from the result set.	Fetches all records from the result set.
Returns a tuple representing a single row.	Returns a list of tuples, each representing a row.
Example cursor.execute("SELECT * FROM students") row = cursor.fetchone() print(row)	**Example** cursor.execute("SELECT * FROM students") rows = cursor.fetchall() print(rows)

15. A resultset is extracted from the database using the cursor object (that has been already created) by giving the following statement.

```
Mydat = cursor.fetchone()
```

(i) How many records will be returned by fetchone() method?

(ii) What will be the datatype of Mydata object after the given command is executed?

Ans. (i) One record (ii) tuple

16. Given a database Inventory, userid – store manager password- welcometostore123

Write Python code to connect to the above database.

Ans.

```
import mysql.connector
  # Connect to the database
conn = mysql.connector.connect
(
    host="localhost",
      # Replace with your host
    user="userid",
      # Replace with your username
    password="welcometostore123",
      # Replace with your password
    database="Inventory"
      # Database name
)
  # Check connection
if conn.is_connected():
    print("Connected to the database")
  # Close the connection
conn.close()
```

17. Consider the following structure of table Hospital.

Hospital

Hospital_id(p)

Hospital_name

Bed_Count

Write Python code to create the above table structure.

Ans.

```
import mysql.connector
  # Establish connection to MySQL
conn = mysql.connector.connect
(
    host="localhost",
    user="your_username",
    password="your_password",
    database="your_database"
)
cursor = conn.cursor()
  # Create table
cursor.execute
(""" CREATE TABLE Hospital
      (
        Hospital_id INT PRIMARY KEY,
        Hospital_name VARCHAR(255),
        Bed_Count INT
      ) """)
  # Commit changes and close connection
conn.commit()
cursor.close()
conn.close()
```

18. **The code given below deletes the record from. the table employee which contains the following record structure:** **CBSE 2023**

E_ code - String

E_name - String

Sal - Integer

City - String

Note the following to establish connectivity between Python and MySQL

- **Username is root**
- **Password is root**
- **The table exists in a MySQL database named emp.**
- **The details (E_code, E_name, Sal, City) are the attributes of the table.**

Write the following statements to complete the code:

Statement 1–to import the desired library.

Statement 2– to execute the command that deletes the record with E_code as 'E101'.

Statement 3–to delete the record permanently from the database.

```
import _____ as mysql                        # Statement 1
def delete( ) :
    mydb=mysql.connect (host="localhost",
    user="root",passwd="root",database="emp")
    mycursor=mydb.cursor( )
    _____________                            # Statement 2
    _________                                # Statement 3
    print ("Record deleted")
```

Or

The code given below reads the following records from the table employee and displays only those records who have employees coming from city 'Delhi'

E_code-String

E_name-String

Sal - Integer

City - String

Note the following to establish connectivity between Python and MySQL :

- **Username is root**
- **Password is root**
- **The table exists in a MySQL database named emp.**
- **The details (E_code, E_name, Sal, City) are the.attributes of the table.**

Write the following statements to complete the code

Statement 1 – to import the desired library.

Statement 2 – to execute the query that fetches records of the employees coming from city 'Delhi'.

Statement 3–to read the complete data of the query (rows whose city is Delhi) into the object named details, from the table employee in the database.

```
import _____ as mysql                        # Statement 1
def display( ) :
    mydb=mysql.connect(host="localhost",
    user="root", passwd="root", database="emp")
    mycursor=mydb.cursor( )
    ______________________                   # Statement 2
    details = _____________                  # Statement 3
    for i in details:
        print(i)
```

Ans. Statement 1 → `mysql.connector`

Statement 2 → `mycursor.execute ('DELETE FROM Employee WHERE E_code= "E101" ')`

Statement 3 → `mydb. commit()`

Or

Statement 1 → `mysql. connector`

Statement 2 → `mycursor.execute ('SELECT * FROM Employee WHERE City = "Delhi" ')`

Statement 3 → `mycursor. fetchall ()`

19. **The code given below inserts the following record in the table Student:** **CBSE SQP 2022-23**

RollNo - integer

Name - string

Class - integer

Marks - integer

Note the following to establish connectivity between Python and MYSQL:

- **Username is root**
- **Password is tiger**
- **The table exists in a MYSQL database named school.**
- **The details (RollNo, Name, Class and Marks) are to be accepted from the user.**

Write the following missing statements to complete the code:

Statement 1-to form the cursor object

Statement 2-to execute the command that inserts the record in the table Student.

Statement 3-to add the record permanently in the database

```
import mysql.connector as mysql
def sql_data():
     con1=mysql.connect(host=
               'localhost",user='root",
password="tiger", database="school")
     mycursor= _________ #Statement 1
     rno=int(input("Enter Roll
                         Number :: "))
     name=input("Enter name :: ")
     clas=int(input("Enter class :: "))
     marks=int(input("Enter Marks :: "))
     querry="insert into student
values({},'{}',{},{})".format
                  (rno,name,clas,marks)
______________________ #Statement 2
______________________ # Statement 3
print("Data Added successfully")
```

Or

The code given below reads the following record from the table named student and displays only those records who have marks greater than 75:

RollNo - integer

Name - string

Class - integer

Marks - integer

Note the following to establish connectivity between Python and MYSQL:

- **Username is root**
- **Password is tiger**
- **The table exists in a MYSQL database named school.**

Write the following missing statements to complete the code:

Statement 1-to form the cursor object

Statement 2-to execute the query that extracts records of those students whose marks are greater than 75.

Statement 3-to read the complete result of the query (records whose marks are greater than 75) into the object named data, from the table student in the database.

```
import mysql.connector as mysql
   def sql_data():
        con1=mysql.connect(host=
                "localhost",user="root",password=
                                   "tiger",
                 database="school")
        mycursor=_________     #Statement 1
        print("Students with marks
                     greater than 75 are : ")
        _________________      #Statement 2
        data =_________        #Statement 3
        for i in data:
           print(i)
        print()
```

Ans. Statement1: con1.cursor()

Statement2:mycursor.execute(querry)

Statement3:con1.commit()

Or

Statement1: con1.cursor()

Statement2:mycursor.execute("Select * from student where marks>75")

Statement3:mycursor.fetchall()

Short Answer Type II Questions

20. Following table represents information on sales representatives for Premiere Products and contains the following data fields for sales representations.

Sales representative's number → SLSRNUMB

Sales representative's name → SLSRNAME

Sales representative's address → SLSRADDR

Total commission paid to the sales representative → TOTCOMM

Sales representative's commission rate → COMMRATE

Write Python code to create the above table

Ans.

```
import mysql.connector
# Establishing the connection to the MySQL
database
connection = mysql.connector.connect(
    host="localhost",
        # Replace with your MySQL host
    user="root",
        # Replace with your MySQL username
    password="password",
        # Replace with your MySQL password
    database="your_database"
        # Replace with your database name
)
cursor = connection.cursor()
# SQL query to create the table
create_table_query = """
```

```
CREATE TABLE SalesRepresentatives (
    SLSRNUMB INT PRIMARY KEY,
    SLSRNAME VARCHAR(100),
    SLSRADDR VARCHAR(255),
    TOTCOMM DECIMAL(10, 2),
    COMMRATE DECIMAL(5, 2)
)
"""
# Executing the query
cursor.execute(create_table_query)
# Committing changes and closing the
connection
connection.commit()
cursor.close()
connection.close()
print("Table 'SalesRepresentatives'
created successfully.")
```

21. Write Python code to create a table Faculty with following fields.

Id, LastName, FirstName, LocationId, phone, rank, stardate Rank should be one of the following

ASSO, FULL, ASST, INST

Ans.

```
import mysql.connector
# Establish the connection
conn = mysql.connector.connect(
    host="localhost",
    user="your_username",
    password="your_password",
    database="your_database"
)
# Create a cursor object
cursor = conn.cursor()
# Create the Faculty table
cursor.execute("""
CREATE TABLE Faculty (
    Id INT PRIMARY KEY,
    LastName VARCHAR(50),
    FirstName VARCHAR(50),
    LocationId INT,
    Phone VARCHAR(15),
    Rank ENUM('ASSO', 'FULL', 'ASST', 'INST'),
    StartDate DATE
)
""")
# Commit and close the connection
conn.commit()
cursor.close()
conn.close()
```

22. Consider the following table Order Details of database sales

Table: Sales

ORDNUMB	PARTNUMB	NUMBORD	QUOTPRIC
12494	CB03	4	175.00
12495	CX11	2	57.95
12498	AZ52	2	22.95
12500	BT04	1	402.99

Ans.

```
import mysql.connector
# Establish the connection
connection = mysql.connector.connect(
    host="your_host",  # e.g., "localhost"
    user="your_user",  # e.g., "root"
    password="your_password",  # your MySQL
password
    database="your_database"  # your
database name
)
cursor = connection.cursor()
# SQL query to insert data
insert_query = """
INSERT INTO Sales (ORDNUMB, PARTNUMB,
NUMBORD, QUOTPRIC)
VALUES (%s, %s, %s, %s)
"""
# Data to be inserted
data = [
    (12494, "CB03", 4, 175.00),
    (12495, "CX11", 2, 57.95),
    (12498, "AZ52", 2, 22.95),
    (12500, "BT04", 1, 402.99)
]
# Inserting data
cursor.executemany(insert_query, data)
# Commit changes to the database
connection.commit()
# Close the connection
cursor.close()
connection.close()
print("Data inserted successfully.")
```

23. Write the following Python function to perform the specified operation: **CBSE SQP 2024-25**

AddAndDisplay(): To input details of an item and store it in the table STATIONERY. The function should then retrieve and display all records from the STATIONERY table where the Price is greater than 120.

Assume the following for Python-Database connectivity:

Host: localhost, User: root, Password: Pencil

Ans.
```
import mysql.connector as mycon
def Add_Item():
mycon=mycon.connect(host="localhost",
            user="root", passwd="Pencil",
                     database="ITEMDB")
mycur= mycon.cursor()
itmno=input("Enter Item Number: ")
itmnm=input("Enter Item Name: ")
itmpr=input("Enter price: ")
itmqty=input("Enter qty: ")
query="Insert into stationery values
                        ({},{}',{},{})"
query=query.format(itmno, itmnm, itmpr,
                                 itmqty)
mycur.execute(query)
mycon.commit()
mycur.execute("select * from stationery
                      where price>120")
for rec in mycur: print(rec)
mycon.close()
```

24. Sunil wants to write a program in Python to update the quantity to 20 of the records whose item code is 111 in the table named shop in MySQL database named Keeper. **CBSE 2024**

The table shop in MySQL contains the following attributes :

- **Item_code: Item code (Integer)**
- **Item_name: Name of item (String)**
- **Qty: Quantity of item (Integer)**
- **Price: Price of item (Integer)**

Consider the following to establish connectivity between Python and MySQL:

- **Username : admin**
- **Password : Shopping**
- **Host : localhost**

Or

Sumit wants to write a code in Python to display all the details of the passengers from the table flight in MySQL database, Travel. The table contains the following attributes:

F_code: Flight code (String)
F_name: Name of flight (String)
Source: Departure city of flight (String)
Destination: Destination city of flight (String)
Consider the following to establish connectivity between Python and MySQL :
Username : root
Password : airplane
Host : localhost

Ans.
```
import mysql.connector
# Establishing the connection to the database
conn = mysql.connector.connect(
    host='localhost',
    user='admin',
    password='Shopping',
    database='Keeper'
)
# Creating a cursor object using the
                            cursor() method
cursor = conn.cursor()
# SQL query to update the quantity of the
                   records with item code 111
update_query = "UPDATE shop SET Qty = 20
                      WHERE Item_code = 111"
try:
    # Executing the SQL command
    cursor.execute(update_query)
    # Commit the transaction
    conn.commit()
    # Print the number of rows affected
    print(cursor.rowcount, "record(s)
                     updated successfully")
except mysql.connector.Error as err:
    # Rollback the transaction in case of
                                    an error
    conn.rollback()
    print(f"Error: {err}")
finally:
    # Closing the cursor and connection
    cursor.close()
    conn.close()
```

Or

```
import mysql.connector
# Establish connection to the MySQL database
conn = mysql.connector.connect(
    host="localhost",
    user="root",
    password="airplane",
    database="Travel"
)
# Create a cursor object
cursor = conn.cursor()
# Execute the SQL query to fetch all
                details from the flight table
query = "SELECT * FROM flight"
cursor.execute(query)
# Fetch all rows from the executed query
rows = cursor.fetchall()
# Print each row
```

```
for row in rows:
    print(row)
# Close the cursor and connection
cursor.close()
conn.close()
```

25. Consider the table Product with following structure.
P_ID, ProductName, Manufacturer, Price.
Write Python code to increase the price of all products by 50.

Ans.
```
import MySQLdb
db = MySQLdb.connect('localhost', 'PId',
"PID@pwd", 'sales')
cursor = db.cursor()
sql = """Update Product set Price =
Price+50"""
try:
    cursor.execute(sql)
    db.commit()
except:
    db.rollback()
    cursor.close()
  db.close()
```

26. A table, named THEATRE, in CINEMA database, has the following structure: **CBSE 2025**

Field	Type
Th_ID	Char (5)
Name	Varchar (15)
City	Varchar (15)
Location	Varchar (15)
Seats	int

Write a function Delete_Theatre (), to input the value of Th_ID from the user and permanently delete the corresponding record from the table.
Assume the following for Python-Database connectivity:
Host: localhost, User: root, Password: Ex2025

Ans.
```
import mysql.connector
def Delete_Theatre():
    th_id = input("Enter Th_ID: ")
    conn = mysql.connector.connect(
        host="localhost",
        user="root",
        password="Ex2025",
        database="CINEMA"
    )
  cursor = conn.cursor()
  query = "DELETE FROM THEATRE WHERE
  Th_ID = %s"
   cursor.execute(query, (th_id,))
    conn.commit()
    print("Theatre deleted
successfully.")
    conn.close()
```

Long Answer Type Questions

27. Create following table using Python code.
Table Name = Customer
Database – xyzcorp
Userid – Adminxyz
Password – Axydm12

CUSTNUMB	CUSTNAME	ADDRESS	BALANCE	CREDLIM	SLSRNUMB
124	TINA ADAMS	481 Tilak lane ,CP,Delhi	41800.75	50,000	3
256	RVENKAT	215 Mylapore ,Chennai	100000.75	80,000	6
567	BHUVNA BALAJI	808 ,Bala Nagar ,Hyderabad	57,000.75	50,000	6
622	PRATHAM JAIN	149,Plot 182,sec-9 Dwarka, Delhi	57,500.75	80,000	12

Ans.
```
import MySQLdb
db=MySQLdb.connect("localhost",
          "Adminxyz", "Axydm12", "xyzcorp")
cursor=db.cursor()
cursor.execute("DROP TABLE IF EXISTS
                                CUSTOMER")
sql="""Create Table Customer (CUSTNUMB
    CHAR(3) NOTNULL, CUSTNAME CHAR(60) NOT
   NULL, ADDRESS CHAR(100), BALANCE Float,
      CREDLIM Float, SLSRNUMB CHAR(2) NOT
                                  NULL)"""
cursor.execute(sql)
cursor.close()
rec_ins=[('124', 'TINA ADAMS', '481 Tilak
   lane , CP, Delhi', 41800.75, 50000, '3'),
('256', 'R VENKAT', '215 Mylapore,
           Chennai', 100000.75, 80000,'6'),
('567', 'BHUVNA BALAJI', '808 BalaNagar,
          Hyderabad' 57000.75, 50000,'6'),
('622', 'PRATHAM JAIN', '149 Plot 182,
 sec-9 Dwarka,Delhi', 57500.75,80000, '12')]
sql_insert= """INSERT INTO Customer
    (CUSTNUMB, CUSTNAME, ADDRESS, BALANCE,
  CREDLIM , SLSRNUMB), (VALUES ('%s', '%s',
                 '%s','%f', '%f', '%s')"""
```

```
cursor=db.cursor(prepared=TRUE)
try:
    cursor.executemany(sql_insert, rec_ins)
    print(cursor.rowcount,
          "Records inserted successfully")
    db.commit()
except:
   db.rollback()
   cursor.close()
db.close()
```

28. **Kabir wants to write a program in Python to insert the following record in the table named Student in MySQL database, SCHOOL** CBSE SQP 2023-24

- **rno(Roll number)- integer**
- **name(Name) - string**
- **DOB (Date of birth) - Date**
- **Fee - float**

Note the following to establish connectivity between Python and MySQL

- **Username - root**
- **Password - tiger**
- **Host - localhost**

The values of fields rno, name, DOB and fee has to be accepted from the user. Help Kabir to write the program in Python.

Ans.

```
import mysql.connector as mysql
con=mysql.connect(host="localhost",user="root",
        password="tiger", database="my_database")
cursor = con.cursor()
rno = int(input("Enter the Roll Number: "))
name = input("Enter the name: ")
DOB = input("Enter date of birth: ")
fee = float(input("Enter Fee: "))
query="INSERT INTO Student VALUES
     ({},'{}','{}',{})".format(rno,name,DOB,fee)
cursor.execute(query)
con.commit()
print("Data entered successfully !!!")
con.close()
```

29. **Write the Python code for (i) and (ii) on the basis of table College.**

No	Name	Age	Department	DateofJoin	Basic	Sex
1	Aren	51	Mathematics	22/01/91	8500	M
2	Reeta	27	Chemistry	14/02/94	9000	F
3	Viren	49	Mathematics	03/01/88	9000	M
4	Prakash	22	Physics	17/02/92	8000	M
5	Shalaz	45	Biology	13/02/88	10500	M
6	Urvashi	29	Biology	10/02/93	8500	F

(i) To insert a new row in the table College with the following data

15, "Atin", 27, "Physics", "15/05/02", 8500, "M"

(ii) To delete a row from table in which name is Viren.

Ans. (i)

```
import mysql.connector as mydb
con = mydb.connect (
    host = "localhost",
    user = "root",
    passwd = "admin@123",
    database = "Management")
cursor = con.cursor ( )
sql = "INSERT INTO College (No, Name,
       Age, Department, DateofJoin,
       Basic, Sex) VALUES
       (15, 'Atin', 27, 'Physics',
       '15/05/02', 8500, 'M')"
cursor.execute (sql)
con.close ( )
```

(ii)

```
import mysql.connector as mydb
con = mydb.connect
     (host = "localhost",
     user = "root",
     passwd = "admin@123",
     database = "Management")
cursor = con.cursor ( )
try:
   cursor.execute ("DELETE FROM
       College WHERE Name = 'Viren' " )
   con.commit ( )
except :
   con.rollback ( )
con.close ( )
```

30. **Create following table using Python code where**

Database — Test
Table — Watches
User name — Root
Password — System

WatchId	WatchName	Price	Type	Qty_store
W001	High Time	10000	Unisex	100
W002	Life Time	15000	Ladies	150
W003	Wave	20000	Gents	200
W004	High Fashion	7000	Unisex	250
W005	Golden Time	25000	Gents	100

Ans.

```
import mysql.connector
my = mysql.connector.connect
  (host = "localhost", user = "Root",
     passwd = "System", database = "Test")
cursor = my.cursor ( )
db = cursor.execute ("CREATE TABLE Watches
    (Watch_Id varchar(5) Primary Key,
                  WatchName char(20) NOT NULL,
```

```
         Price float, Type varchar (20),
           Qty_store  Int(5) NOT NULL))"
sql = "INSERT INTO Watches
    (WatchId, WatchName, Price, Type,
    Qty_store) VALUES (%s, %s, %s, %s, %s)"
val = [("W001", "High Time", 10000,
    "Unisex", 100),
    ("W002", "Life Time", 15000,
    "Ladies", 150),
    ("W003", "Wave", 20000,
    "Gents", 200),
    ("W004", "HighFashion", 7000,
    "Unisex", 250),
    ("W005", "Golden Time", 25000,
    "Gents", 100)]
try:
  cursor. executemany (sql, val)
  my.commit ( )
except :
  my.rollback ( )
my.close ( )
```

31. **Here is a table Club**

MemberId	MemberName	Address	Age	Fee
M001	Sumit	New Delhi	20	2000
M002	Nisha	Gurgaon	19	3500
M003	Niharika	New Delhi	21	2100
M004	Sachin	Faridabad	18	3500

Write the Python code for the following

(i) Update the Address of member whose MemberId is M003 with Noida.

(ii) Delete the record of those member whose name is Sachin.

Ans. (i)

```
import mysql.connector
mycon = mysql.connector.connect
(host = "localhost",
user = "Admin", passwd = "Admin@123",
database = "System")
cursor = mycon.cursor ( )
try:
    cursor.execute ("UPDATE Club SET
    Address = 'Noida' WHERE MemberId
          = 'M003')")
    mycon.commit ( )
except :
    mycon.rollback ( )
mycon.close ( )
```

(ii)

```
import mysql. connector
mycon = mysql. connector.connect
      (host = "localhost",
      user = "Admin",
      passwd = "Admin@123",
      database = "System")
cursor = mycon.cursor ( )
try:
    cursor.execute ("DELETE FROM Club
    WHERE MemberName = 'Sachin'")
    cursor.commit ( )
except:
    mycon.rollback ( )
mycon.close ( )
```

32. **Consider the table MobileMaster**

M_Id	M_Company	M_Name	M_Price	M_Mf_Date
MB001	Samsung	Galaxy	4500	2014-02-12
MB002	Nokia	N1100	2250	2011-04-15
MB003	Sony	Experia M	9500	2017-11-20
MB004	Oppo	SelfieEx	8500	2010-08-21

Write the Python code for the following

(i) To display details of those mobiles whose price is greater than 8000.

(ii) To increase the price of mobile Samsung by 2000.

Ans. (i)

```
import mysql.connector as mydb
mycon = mydb.connect
     (host = "localhost",
     user = "root",
     passwd = "system",
     database = "Admin")
cursor = mycon.cursor ( )
sql = "SELECT * FROM MobileMaster
WHERE M_Price > 8000"
try:
    cursor.execute (sql)
    display = cursor. fetchall ( )
    for i in display:
          print(i)
except:
      mycon.rollback ( )
mycon.close ( )
```

(ii)

```
import mysql.connector as mydb
mycon = mydb.connect
     (host = "localhost",
     user = "root",
     passwd = "system",
     database = "Admin")
cursor = mycon.cursor ( )
sql = "UPDATE MobileMaster SET M_Price
    = M_Price + 2000
    WHERE M_Company = 'Samsung'"
try:
    cursor.execute (sql)
    mycon.commit ( )
except :
    mycon.rollback ( )
mycon.close( )
```

Case Study Based Questions

Case Study 1

Consider the following code:

```
import MySQLdb
db=MySQLdb.connect('localhost', 'LIBMAN',
                          'Admin@pwd','library')
cursor=db.cursor(prepared=TRUE)
sql = """Insert into table('MemId',
     'MemName','MemAdd',)values('%s','%s',
                                  '%s', )"""
insert_value=[('1021', 'Ronit', '12,
           Block A, Kaveri Vihar' ), ('1022',
              'Smriti', '12/9 Indira Puram')]
try:
      cursor.executemany(sql,insert_value)
print(cursor.rowcount,'Records inserted')
      db.commit()
except:
     db.rollback()
     cursor.close()
db.close()
```

(i) **What of the following statement is connecting database server?**

(a) importMySQLdb (b) MySQLdb.connect
(c) db.cursor (d) None of these

(ii) **The role of the statement 'cursor=db.cursor' is:**

(a) Create an instance of a cursor
(b) Moves cursor row wise
(c) Connects cursor to database
(d) Prepares cursor to move

(iii) **Which of the following statement will add the record in the table?**

(a) Insert Into
(b) Insert Value
(c) cursor.executemany(sql,insert_value)
(d) None of these

(iv) **What will be the output of following statement in the given code?**

```
print(cursor.rowcount,"Recordsinser
ted")
```

(a) 0 (b) 1
(c) 2 (d) 3

(v) **What will be the result of 'cursor.close()' ?**

(a) Close the cursor
(b) Reset all results
(c) Deletes all references to the connection
(d) All of these

Ans. (i) (b) The connect() constructor creates a connection to the MySQL server and returns a MySQLConnection object.

(ii) (a) Cursor is a special control structure that created to get access of all the records retrieved as per query.

(iii) (c) The executemany() method is used to insert multiple rows in a table.

Syntax `cursor_object.executemany(statement, arguments)`

Where statement refers to the string containing the query to execute and arguments refers to the sequence containing values to use within insert statement.

(iv) (c) The rowcount() method is used to get number of records affected by query involving any Delete, update & insert command.

(v) (d) close() is used when you are done using a cursor. This method closes the cursor, resets all results, and ensures that the cursor object has no reference to its original connection object.

Case Study 2

Consider the following code:

```
import MySQLdb
db=MySQLdb.connect('localhost','LibMan','i
sspwd','Library')
cursor=db.cursor()
sql="UPDATE BOOK set Status ='ISSUE' where
BookId='%s'"/("1021")
try:
    db.execute(sql)
    db.commit()
except:
    db.rollback()
    db.close()
```

(i) **What is "Library" in the statement MySQLdb.connect('localhost','LibMan','isspwd','Library')**

(a) User (b) Password
(c) Table (d) Database

(ii) **What will be the result of the above code?**

(a) A new record is added
(b) A record with book id '1021' is updated
(c) A record with status 'Issue' is updated
(d) All of these

(iii) **What is the use of try in above code?**

(a) Handles the errors
(b) Try the logic of code
(c) test a block of code for errors
(d) executes the block

(iv) **Which of the following method closes the database connection?**

(a) db.commit() (b) db.rollback()
(c) db.close() (d) None of these

(v) **What is the function of db.rollbback() in the code?**

(a) Returns the database to some previous state
(b) Returns cursor to the previous row
(c) Review the records updated
(d) All of these

Ans. (i) (d) The syntax of connect function is as follows:

```
connect(host = <host-name>, user=<username>,
passwd=<password> , database =<database>)
```

(ii) (b) The sql query "UPDATE BOOK set Status ='ISSUE' where BookId='%s' "/("1021") will execute and the status of record with book id '1021' will be updated as 'Issue'.

(iii) (c) The try block lets you test a block of code for errors and the except block lets you handle the error.

(iv) (c) If the connection to a database is closed by the user with the close() method, any outstanding transactions are rolled back by the database.

(v) (a) When the ROLLBACK command is executed, the changes made to database files, updates, additions, or deletions since the commitment boundary are rolled back and the original entries are put back in the files.

Case Study 3

Consider the following table STUDENT:

Stud	Name	Course	Result
1101	Anubhav Singh	BCom	Awaited
1102	Riya Sharma	BSc	Passed
1103	Kartikey Rana	BSc	Passed
1104	Archana Kapoor	BBA	Awaited
1105	Aarti Sharma	BCom	Awaited
1106	Sanchit Kumar	BCom	Passed

(i) **What will be the query statement to insert a new record with Student id = 1107, name = Sumit Saxena, Course = BBA and result = passed**

(a)
```
sql = "INSERT INTO student (stuid,
   name,course, result) VALUES ('1107',
   'Sumit Saxena', 'BBA', 'Passed')"
```
(b)
```
sql = "INSERT INTO student VALUES ('1107',
   'Sumit Saxena', 'BBA', 'Passed')"
```
(c) Both (a) and (b)
(d) None of these

(ii) **The following sql command has been given:**

```
Sql = "UPDATE student SET result =
'Passed' WHERE course = 'BCom' "
```

The result of which of the following STUID will be changed to "Passed"?

(a) 1101 (b) 1101, 1104
(c) 1101, 1105 (d) 1101, 1104, 1105

(iii) **Consider the following code:**

```
sql = '''SELECT * from STUDENT'''
cursor.execute(sql)
result = cursor.fetchone();
print(result)
```

What will be the output of the above code in reference to the STUDENT table?

(a) 1101, Anubhav Singh, BCom, Awaited
(b) 1106, Sanchit Kumar, BCom, Passed
(c) 1103, Kartikey Rana, BSc, Passed
(d) Both a) and b)

(iv) **Consider the following code:**

```
result = cursor.fetchmany(2);
print(result)
```

What will be the result if it is executed after the code given in (iii)?

(a) 1101, Anubhav Singh, BCom, Awaited
1102, Riya Sharma, BSc, Passed
(b) 1102, Riya Sharma, BSc, Passed
1103, Kartikey Rana, BSc, Passed
(c) 1103, Kartikey Rana, BSc, Passed
1104, Archana Kapoor, BBA, Awaited
(d) None of these

(v) **Consider the following code:**

```
cursor=db.cursor()
query = "DELETE FROM student WHERE course =
         'BCom' AND result = 'Awaited' "
cursor.execute(query)
del_rows= cursor.rowcount
print(del_rows)
```

What will be the output of the above code?

(a) 1 (b) 2 (c) 3 (d) 4

Ans. (i) (c) INSERT INTO statement is used to add new records in a table. For this you need to specify table name, column names and the values.
But if you pass values of a record in the same order of the columns of the table, then you don't need to give column names.

(ii) (c) The rows having STUID 1101 and 1105, both match the condition given with WHERE clause.

(iii) (a) The fetchone() method fetches next row from the result set and returns it as a tuple.

(iv) (b) The fetchmany(n) method fetches the given number of records from the cursor position.

(v) (b) The records of students with StuId 1101 and 1105 are the two rows that meets the criteria given with WHERE clause.

SELF ASSESSMENT TEST

Multiple Choice Questions

1 What is an identifier in following command?

```
import mysql.connector as db
```

(a) import (b) mysql
(c) connector (d) db

2 To add a new column into a table, which command is used?

(a) ALTER TABLE
(b) UPDATE FROM
(c) INSERT INTO
(d) All of the above

3 To insert multiple records into table, which method is used to execute statements?

(a) execute ( )
(b) executemany ( )
(c) executeall ( )
(d) None of the above

4 Which of the following statement is correct?

(a) DELETE INTO (b) DELETE TABLE
(c) DELETE ALL (d) DELETE FROM

5 It fetches all the rows of a query result.

(a) fetchall ( ) (b) fetchmany ( )
(c) fetchwhole ( ) (d) allfetch ( )

Fill in the Blanks

6 Cursor object can be create using ...... method of connection object.

7 After creating the cursor, SQL query can be execute using ....function.

8 To add a record into table, we can mention ...... in place of value.

9 We can create a table using .... statement.

10 ...... can connect to mysql database from Python.

State Whether True and False

11. User can write Python script using mysql.connector library after installing Python MySQL connector.

12. To add single record into a table, we can mention the format specifier (%s) in place of value.

13. fetchone() returns the number of rows specified by the size argument.

Assertion and Reason Based Questions

Assertion (A) and Reason (R) Type questions. Choose the correct option as:

(a) Both A and R are true and R is the correct explanation for A.
(b) Both A and R are true and R is not correct explanation for A.
(c) A is true but R is false.
(d) A is false but R is true.

14. **Assertion (A)** User can write Python script using mysql.connector library after installing Python MySQL connector.

Reason (R) It can connect to MySQL databases from Python.

15. **Assertion (A)** Insert operation is required when you want to create your records into a database's table.

Reason (R) INSERT INTO statement is used to add a record.

Very Short Answer Type Questions

16 Write the command to import the connection of Python with MySQL.

17 Define the fetchone ( ) method.

18 How fetchmany ( ) method is differ from fetchall() method?

19 Write the command to update the table Employee with Salary column, change the salary of those employee who have computer skills with 35000.

20 What do you mean by read operation?

Short Answer Type Questions

21 Create the connection of Python with MySQL, in which

```
database name = System
User = Admin
Password = Admin@123
```

22 Write the code to create a table stationery in database School with following fields.

Fields	Datatype
I_Code	Varchar(3) (P)
I_Name	Char(30)
Qty.	Int
Price	Float

23 Consider the table Employee whose columns' name are `E_ID, EmpName, JoiningDate, Salary, Department`

Write the code to insert the following record into the above table:

E101	Atin	12-10-2009	35000	DBA
E102	Sandeep	7-8-1999	58000	Business Analyst

Long Answer Type Questions

24 Consider the table FLIGHTS

FL_No	Starting	Ending	No_Flight	No_Stops
IC301	Mumbai	Delhi	8	0
IC799	Bengluru	Delhi	2	1
MC101	Indore	Mumbai	3	0
AM812	Kanpur	Bengluru	3	1

Write the Python code for the following

(i) To display details of those flights whose number of flights greater than 5.

(ii) To increase the number of flights of flight Indore to Mumbai by 3.

Case Based Type Question

25 **Riya is developing a Python application for a movie theatre called Movie Magic. The application connects to a MySQL database named CINEMA. It allows the admin to insert new theatre records, update theatre details, delete a theatre, and display all theatres. She uses the mysql.connector module to establish a connection between Python and SQL.**

- **To perform SQL operations, Riya uses:**
- **connect() to connect to the database.**
- **cursor() to create a cursor object.**
- **execute() to run SQL commands.**
- **commit() to save changes like insert/update/delete.**
- **fetchall() and fetchone() to retrieve data.**
- **%s as a placeholder in SQL queries for inserting values securely.**
- **rowcount to check how many rows were affected by a query.**

Here's a sample function she wrote to delete a theatre by its ID:

```
  import mysql.connector def
delete_theatre(th_id):
conn = mysql.connector.connect(host=" local
host", user="root", password="pass123",
database="CINEMA")
      cursor = conn.cursor()
cursor.execute("DELETE FROM THEATRE WHERE
Th_ID = %s", (th_id,))
        conn.commit()
print(cursor.rowcount,"record(s) deleted.")
     conn.close()
```

(i) What is the purpose of conn.commit() in the delete_theatre() function?

(a) To retrieve all records from the database
(b) To execute the SQL command
(c) To save changes permanently in the database
(d) To close the database connection

(ii) What is the role of %s in the cursor.execute() statement?

(a) It is used to insert a string value directly into the SQL query
(b) It is a placeholder for safely inserting values and preventing SQL injection
(c) It replaces the entire SQL command
(d) It is used to convert strings to SQL-compatible format

(iii) Which method should Riya use to retrieve all records from the THEATRE table?

(a) fetchrow() (b) fetchone()
(c) fetchall() (d) commit()

(iv) What does cursor.rowcount return after executing a DELETE query?

(a) The total number of columns in the table
(b) The number of rows deleted by the query
(c) The number of SQL statements in the script
(d) The current row being accessed

(v) What is the correct order of steps for performing a SQL query in Python using mysql.connector?

(a) cursor() → connect() → execute() → fetchall()
(b) connect() → cursor() → execute() → fetchall()/commit()
(c) connect() → execute() → cursor() → fetchall()
(d) execute() → fetchall() → connect() →cursor()

Answers

1. (d) 2. (a) 3. (b) 4. (d)
5. (a) 6. cursor() 7. execute()
8. Values 9. CREATE TABLE
10. Mysql. connector 11. True 12. True
13. False 14. (a) 15. (a)
25. (i) → (c), (ii) → (b), (iii) → (c), (iv) → (b), (v) → (b)

1. PYTHON PROGRAMMING

AIM 1. **Read a text file line by line and display each word separated by a #.**
Text file contains:

Python unlocks endless possibilities!
A thousand lines start with one step.
Fixing bugs is a step to mastery!

Procedure

```
# Open the text file for reading
# Use raw string for file path or escape backslashes
file_path = r"C:\Users\Arihant\Downloads\CODE_WORK\myfile.txt"   # Using raw string
try:
    with open(file_path, "r") as file:
        # Read each line of the file
        for line in file:
            # Split the line into words
            words = line.split()
            # Join the words with '#' and print
            print("#".join(words))
except FileNotFoundError:
    print("The file does not exist.")
```

Output

```
========== RESTART: C:\Users\Arihant\Downloads\CODE_WORK\myprogram.py ==========
Python#unlocks#endless#possibilities!
A#thousand#lines#start#with#one#step.
Fixing#bugs#is#a#step#to#mastery!
>>>
```

AIM 2. **Read a text file and display the number of vowels/consonants/uppercase/lowercase characters in the file.**

Procedure

```
def count_characters(file_path):
    vowels = "aeiouAEIOU"
    consonants = "bcdfghjklmnpqrstvwxyzBCDFGHJKLMNPQRSTVWXYZ"
    uppercase = 0
    lowercase = 0
    vowel_count = 0
    consonant_count = 0
    try:
        with open(file_path, "r") as file:
            # Read through each line of the file
            for line in file:
                # Iterate through each character in the line
                for char in line:
                    if char.isalpha():  # Consider only alphabetic characters
                        if char in vowels:
                            vowel_count += 1
                        elif char in consonants:
                            consonant_count += 1
```

```
                if char.isupper():
                    uppercase += 1
                elif char.islower():
                    lowercase += 1
        # Display the results
        print(f"Vowels: {vowel_count}")
        print(f"Consonants: {consonant_count}")
        print(f"Uppercase Characters: {uppercase}")
        print(f"Lowercase Characters: {lowercase}")
    except FileNotFoundError:
        print("The file was not found. Please check the file path.")
# Replace with the correct file path
file_path = r"C:\Users\Arihant\Downloads\CODE_WORK\myfile.txt"
# Call the function to count the characters
count_characters(file_path)
```

Output

```
============== RESTART: C:/Users/Arihant/Downloads/CODE_WORK/P2.py =============
Vowels: 31
Consonants: 58
Uppercase Characters: 3
Lowercase Characters: 86
>>>
```

AIM 3. **Remove all the lines that contain the character 'a' in a file and write it to another file.**

Procedure

```
def remove_lines_with_a(input_file_path, output_file_path):
    try:
        with open(input_file_path, "r") as infile:
            lines = infile.readlines()
        with open(output_file_path, "w") as outfile:
            for line in lines:
                if 'a' not in line:
                    outfile.write(line)
        print(f"Lines without 'a' have been written to {output_file_path}.")
    except FileNotFoundError:
        print("The input file was not found. Please check the file path.")
# Replace with the correct file paths
input_file_path = r"C:\Users\Arihant\Downloads\CODE_WORK\myfile.txt"
output_file_path = r"C:\Users\Arihant\Downloads\CODE_WORK\myfile1.txt"
# Call the function to remove lines containing 'a'
remove_lines_with_a(input_file_path, output_file_path)
```

Output

```
============== RESTART: C:/Users/Arihant/Downloads/CODE_WORK/P3.py =============
Lines without 'a' have been written to C:\Users\Arihant\Downloads\CODE_WORK\myfile1.txt.
>>> |
```

AIM 4. **Create a binary file with name and roll number. Search for a given roll number and display the name, if not found display appropriate message.**

Procedure

```
import pickle
# Function to create a binary file with names and roll numbers
def create_binary_file(file_path):
    students = [
        ("Ram", 101),
        ("Mohan", 102),
```

```
        ("Sita", 103),
        ("Abhinav", 104)
    ]
    with open(file_path, "wb") as file:
        # Use pickle to serialize the list of students and write to the file
        pickle.dump(students, file)
    print(f"Binary file '{file_path}' has been created.")
# Function to search for a roll number and display the name
def search_roll_number(file_path, roll_number):
    try:
        with open(file_path, "rb") as file:
            # Load the list of students from the binary file
            students = pickle.load(file)
            # Search for the roll number
            for name, roll in students:
                if roll == roll_number:
                    print(f"Roll number {roll_number} corresponds to: {name}")
                    return
            print(f"Roll number {roll_number} not found.")
    except FileNotFoundError:
        print(f"The file {file_path} does not exist.")
# File path for the binary file
file_path = r"C:\Users\Arihant\Downloads\CODE_WORK\myfile2.dat"
# Create the binary file with student data
create_binary_file(file_path)
# Search for a roll number (replace 102 with any roll number to test)
roll_number_to_search = 102
search_roll_number(file_path, roll_number_to_search)
```

Output

```
========================================================== RESTART: C:/Users/Arihant/Downloads/CODE_WORK/P4.py ========
Binary file 'C:\Users\Arihant\Downloads\CODE_WORK\myfile2.dat' has been created.
Roll number 102 corresponds to: Mohan
>>> |
```

AIM 5. Create a binary file with roll number, name and marks. Input a roll number and update the marks.

Procedure

```
import pickle
# Function to create a binary file with roll number, name, and marks
def create_binary_file(file_path):
    students = [
        (101, "Ram", 85),
        (102, "Sita", 90),
        (103, "Mohan", 78),
        (104, "Gita", 88)
    ]
    with open(file_path, "wb") as file:
        # Use pickle to serialize the list of students and write it to the file
        pickle.dump(students, file)
    print(f"Binary file 'C:\\Users\\Arihant\\Downloads\\CODE_WORK\\myfile2.dat' has
                                                                    been created.")

# Function to update marks for a given roll number
def update_marks(file_path, roll_number, new_marks):
    try:
```

```
        with open(file_path, "rb") as file:
            # Load the list of students from the binary file
            students = pickle.load(file)
        # Find the student with the given roll number and update marks
        found = False
        for i, (roll, name, marks) in enumerate(students):
            if roll == roll_number:
                students[i] = (roll, name, new_marks)
                found = True
                break
        if not found:
            print(f"Roll number {roll_number} not found.")
            return
        # Rewrite the updated list back to the binary file
        with open(file_path, "wb") as file:
            pickle.dump(students, file)
        print(f"Marks for roll number {roll_number} have been updated to {new_marks}.")
    except FileNotFoundError:
        print(f"The file {file_path} does not exist.")
# File path for the binary file
file_path = r"C:\Users\Arihant\Downloads\CODE_WORK\myfile2.dat"
# Create the binary file with student data
create_binary_file(file_path)
# Input the roll number and new marks to update
roll_number_to_update = int(input("Enter the roll number to update: "))
new_marks = int(input(f"Enter the new marks for roll number {roll_number_to_update}: "))
# Update the marks for the given roll number
update_marks(file_path, roll_number_to_update, new_marks)
```

Output

```
=================================== RESTART: C:/Users/Arihant/Downloads/CODE_WORK/P5.py ===
Binary file 'C:\Users\Arihant\Downloads\CODE_WORK\myfile2.dat' has been created.
Enter the roll number to update: 103
Enter the new marks for roll number 103: 99
Marks for roll number 103 have been updated to 99.
>>>
```

AIM 6. **Write a random number generator that generates random numbers between 1 and 6 (simulates a dice).**

Procedure

```
import random
# Function to simulate a dice roll
def roll_dice():
    return random.randint(1, 6)
# Example: Roll the dice and display the result
result = roll_dice()
print(f"The dice rolled: {result}")
```

Output

```
=================================== RESTART: C:/Users/Arihant/Downloads/CODE_WORK/P6.py ===
The dice rolled: 2
>>>
=================================== RESTART: C:/Users/Arihant/Downloads/CODE_WORK/P6.py ===
The dice rolled: 3
>>>
=================================== RESTART: C:/Users/Arihant/Downloads/CODE_WORK/P6.py ===
The dice rolled: 5
>>>
```

AIM 7. Write a Python program to implement a stack using list.

Procedure

```
class Stack:
    def __init__(self):
        # Initialize the stack as an empty list
        self.stack = [ ]
    # Push an element to the stack
    def push(self, item):
        self.stack.append(item)
        print(f"{item} has been pushed to the stack.")
    # Pop an element from the stack
    def pop(self):
        if not self.is_empty():
            popped_item = self.stack.pop()
            print(f"{popped_item} has been popped from the stack.")
            return popped_item
        else:
            print("Stack is empty. Cannot pop.")
    # Peek the top element of the stack
    def peek(self):
        if not self.is_empty():
            return self.stack[-1]
        else:
            print("Stack is empty. No elements to peek.")
            return None
    # Check if the stack is empty
    def is_empty(self):
        return len(self.stack) == 0
    # Get the size of the stack
    def size(self):
        return len(self.stack)
# Create a stack and perform some operations
stack = Stack()
stack.push(23)  # Push 23 onto the stack
stack.push(44)  # Push 44 onto the stack
stack.push(99)  # Push 99 onto the stack
print(f"Top element: {stack.peek()}")  # Peek at the top element
print(f"Stack size: {stack.size()}")  # Get the size of the stack
stack.pop()  # Pop the top element
stack.pop()  # Pop another element
print(f"Stack size after pops: {stack.size()}")  # Get the size of the stack after popping
```

Output

```
================================================================ RESTART: C:/Users/Arihant/Downloads/CODE_WORK/P7.py ==
23 has been pushed to the stack.
44 has been pushed to the stack.
99 has been pushed to the stack.
Top element: 99
Stack size: 3
99 has been popped from the stack.
44 has been popped from the stack.
Stack size after pops: 1
>>>
```

AIM 8. **Create a CSV file by entering user-id and password, read and search the password for given userid.**

Procedure

```
import csv
# Function to create a CSV file with user-id and password
def create_csv_file(file_path):
    users = [
        ("user1", "password123"),
        ("user2", "password234"),
        ("user3", "password345"),
        ("user4", "password456")
    ]
    with open(file_path, mode="w", newline="") as file:
        writer = csv.writer(file)
        # Write headers
        writer.writerow(["User-ID", "Password"])
        # Write user data
        writer.writerows(users)
    print(f"CSV file '{file_path}' has been created.")
# Function to search for a password by user ID
def search_password(file_path, user_id):
    try:
        with open(file_path, mode="r", newline="") as file:
            reader = csv.reader(file)
            # Skip the header
            next(reader)
            for row in reader:
                if row[0] == user_id:
                    print(f"Password for user '{user_id}' is: {row[1]}")
                    return
            print(f"User ID '{user_id}' not found.")
    except FileNotFoundError:
        print(f"The file {file_path} does not exist.")
# File path for the CSV file
file_path = r"C:\Users\Arihant\Downloads\CODE_WORK\user_data.csv"
# Create the CSV file with user data
create_csv_file(file_path)
# Input the user ID to search for the password
user_id_to_search = input("Enter the User-ID to search: ")
# Search for the password of the given user ID
search_password(file_path, user_id_to_search)
```

Output

```
==================================================================== RESTART: C:/Users/Arihant/Downloads/CODE_WORK/P8.py =====
CSV file 'C:\Users\Arihant\Downloads\CODE_WORK\user_data.csv' has been created.
Enter the User-ID to search: user2
Password for user 'user2' is: password234
>>> |
```

2. DATABASE MANAGEMENT

AIM 1. **Create a student table and insert data. Implement the following SQL commands on the student table:**
(a) ALTER table to add new attributes / modify data type / drop attribute
(b) UPDATE table to modify data
(c) ORDER By to display data in ascending / descending order
(d) DELETE to remove tuple(s)
(e) GROUP BY and find the min, max, sum, count and average

Procedure **Create the student table**

```
CREATE TABLE student ( student_id INT PRIMARY KEY, student_name VARCHAR(50),
                                              age INT, gender VARCHAR(10), marks FLOAT );
```

Insert sample data into the student table

```
INSERT INTO student (student_id, student_name, age, gender, marks) VALUES
(1, 'Aarav Kumar', 20, 'Male', 85.5),
(2, 'Aditi Sharma', 22, 'Female', 90.0),
(3, 'Rohan Gupta', 21, 'Male', 88.5),
(4, 'Priya Iyer', 23, 'Female', 92.5),
(5, 'Arjun Patel', 24, 'Male', 79.0);
Select * FROM STUDENT;
```

Output

Student Table

student_id	student_name	age	gender	marks
1	Aarav Kumar	20	Male	85.5
2	Aditi Sharma	22	Female	90.0
3	Rohan Gupta	21	Male	88.5
4	Priya Iyer	23	Female	92.5
5	Arjun Patel	24	Male	79.0

(a) ALTER table to add new attributes / modify data type / drop attribute

Add New Attributes (Columns)

```
ALTER TABLE student
ADD address VARCHAR(100);
```

Output

student_id	student_name	age	gender	marks	address
1	Aarav Kumar	20	Male	85.5	NULL
2	Aditi Sharma	22	Female	90.0	NULL
3	Rohan Gupta	21	Male	88.5	NULL
4	Priya Iyer	23	Female	92.5	NULL
5	Arjun Patel	24	Male	79.0	NULL

Modify Data Type of an Existing Column

```
ALTER TABLE student
MODIFY marks DECIMAL(5,2);
```

Drop an Attribute (Column)

```
ALTER TABLE student
DROP COLUMN gender;
```

Output

student_id	student_name	age	marks	address
1	Aarav Kumar	20	85.50	NULL
2	Aditi Sharma	22	90.00	NULL
3	Rohan Gupta	21	88.50	NULL
4	Priya Iyer	23	92.50	NULL
5	Arjun Patel	24	79.00	NULL

(b) UPDATE table to modify data

```
UPDATE student
SET marks = 92
WHERE student_id = 1;
```

Output

student_id	student_name	age	marks	address
1	Aarav Kumar	20	92.00	NULL
2	Aditi Sharma	22	90.00	NULL
3	Rohan Gupta	21	88.50	NULL
4	Priya Iyer	23	92.50	NULL
5	Arjun Patel	24	79.00	NULL

(c) ORDER BY to display data in ascending / descending order

Display Data in Ascending Order by Marks

```
SELECT * FROM student
ORDER BY marks ASC;
```

Output

student_id	student_name	age	marks	address
5	Arjun Patel	24	79.00	NULL
1	Aarav Kumar	20	92.00	NULL
3	Rohan Gupta	21	88.50	NULL
2	Aditi Sharma	22	90.00	NULL
4	Priya Iyer	23	92.50	NULL

Display Data in Descending Order by Marks:

```
SELECT * FROM student
ORDER BY marks DESC;
```

Output

student_id	student_name	age	marks	address
4	Priya Iyer	23	92.50	NULL
1	Aarav Kumar	20	92.00	NULL
2	Aditi Sharma	22	90.00	NULL
3	Rohan Gupta	21	88.50	NULL
5	Arjun Patel	24	79.00	NULL

(d) DELETE to remove tuple(s)

```
DELETE FROM student
WHERE student_id = 3;
```

Output

student_id	student_name	age	marks	address
4	Priya Iyer	23	92.50	NULL
1	Aarav Kumar	20	92.00	NULL
2	Aditi Sharma	22	90.00	NULL
5	Arjun Patel	24	79.00	NULL

(e) GROUP BY and find the min, max, sum, count and average

Student_id	Student_name	age	gender	marks	Grade
1	Aarav Kumar	20	Male	85.5	B
2	Aditi Sharma	22	Female	90.0	A
3	Rohan Gupta	21	Male	88.5	B
4	Priya Iyer	23	Female	92.5	A
5	Arjun Patel	24	Male	79.0	C

Find the Count of Students in Each Grade

```
SELECT grade, COUNT(*) AS count
FROM student
GROUP BY grade;
```

Output

grade	count
A	2
B	2
C	1
D	0

Find the Minimum Marks in Each Grade

```
SELECT grade, MIN(marks) AS min_marks
FROM student
GROUP BY grade;
```

Output

grade	min_marks
A	92.0
B	88.5
C	79.0
D	NULL

Find the Maximum Marks in Each Grade

```
SELECT grade, MAX(marks) AS max_marks
FROM student
GROUP BY grade;
```

Output

grade	max_marks
A	92.5
B	88.5
C	79.0
D	NULL

Find the Sum of Marks in Each Grade

```
SELECT grade, SUM(marks) AS total_marks
FROM student
GROUP BY grade;
```

Output

grade	total_marks
A	182.5
B	174.0
C	79.0
D	NULL

Find the Average Marks in Each Grade

```
SELECT grade, AVG(marks) AS average_marks
FROM student
GROUP BY grade;
```

Output

grade	average_marks
A	91.25
B	87.0
C	79.0
D	NULL

AIM 2. **Integrate SQL with Python by importing suitable module**

Procedure

```
import sqlite3
   # Step 1: Create a connection to the SQLite database
   # This will create a database file named 'student.db' if it doesn't already exist.
conn = sqlite3.connect('student.db')
   # Step 2: Create a cursor object
cursor = conn.cursor()
   # Step 3: Create a student table (if it doesn't already exist)
cursor.execute('''
CREATE TABLE IF NOT EXISTS student (
    student_id INTEGER PRIMARY KEY,
    student_name TEXT,
    age INTEGER,
    marks REAL
)
''')
   # Step 4: Insert data into the student table
cursor.execute('''
INSERT INTO student (student_id, student_name, age, marks)
```

```
VALUES (1, 'Aarav Kumar', 20, 92.00),
       (2, 'Aditi Sharma', 22, 90.00),
       (3, 'Rohan Gupta', 21, 88.50),
       (4, 'Priya Iyer', 23, 92.50),
       (5, 'Arjun Patel', 24, 79.00)
''')
   # Step 5: Commit the changes to the database
conn.commit()
   # Step 6: Query data from the student table
cursor.execute('SELECT * FROM student')
   # Fetch all rows and print them
rows = cursor.fetchall()
for row in rows:
    print(row)
   # Step 7: Close the cursor and connection
cursor.close()
conn.close()
```

Output

```
============= RESTART: C:/Users/Arihant/Downloads/CODE_WORK/sql.py =============
(1, 'Aarav Kumar', 20, 92.0)
(2, 'Aditi Sharma', 22, 90.0)
(3, 'Rohan Gupta', 21, 88.5)
(4, 'Priya Iyer', 23, 92.5)
(5, 'Arjun Patel', 24, 79.0)
>>> |
```

CBSE EXAMINATION PAPER 2025

COMPUTER SCIENCE

Time : 3 Hours | Max. Marks : 70

General Instructions

1. This question paper contains 37 questions.
2. All questions are compulsory. However, internal choices have been provided in some questions. Attempt only one of the choices in such questions.
3. The paper is divided into 5 Sections - A, B, C, D and E.
4. **Section A**, consists of 21 questions (1 to 21). Each question carries 1 Mark.
5. **Section B**, consists of 7 questions (22 to 28). Each question carries 2 Marks.
6. **Section C**, consists of 3 questions (29 to 31). Each question carries 3 Marks.
7. **Section D**, consists of 4 questions (32 to 35). Each question carries 4 Marks.
8. **Section E**, consists of 2 questions (36 to 37). Each question carries 5 Marks.
9. All programming questions are to be answered using Python Language only.
10. In case of MCQ, text of the correct answer should also be written.

SECTION A

(21 × 1 = 21)

1. **State True or False:**

"A Python List must always contain all its elements of same data type."

2. **What will be the output of the following statement?**

```
print(14%3**2*4)
```

(a) 16 (b) 64
(c) 20 (d) 256

3. **Identify the correct output of the following code snippet:**

```
game = "Olympic2024"
print (game.index("C"))
```

(a) 0 (b) 6
(c) −1 (d) ValueError

4. **Which of the following is the correct identifier?**

(a) global (b) Break
(c) def (d) with

5. **Identify the invalid Python statement out of the following options.**

(a) print ("A", 10, end="*")
(b) print ("A", sep="*", 10)
(c) print ("A", 10, sep="*")
(d) print ("A"*10)

6. **Consider the statements given below and then choose the correct output from the given options:**

```
L=['TIC', 'TAC']
print(L[::-1])
```

(a) ['CIT', 'CAT'] (b) ['TIC', 'TAC']
(c) ['CAT', 'CIT'] (d) ['TAC', 'TIC']

7. **Which of the following operator evaluates to True if the variable on either side of the operator points towards the same memory location and False otherwise?**

(a) is (b) is not
(c) and (d) or

8. **Consider the statements given below and then choose the correct output from the given options.**

```
D = {'S01' : 95, 'S02' : 96}
for I in D:
print(I, end = '#')
```

(a) S01#S02# (b) 95#96#
(c) S01,95#S02, 96# (d) S01#95 S02#96#

9. **While creating a table, which constraint does not allow insertion of duplicate values in the table?**

(a) UNIQUE (b) DISTINCT
(c) NOT NULL (d) HAVING

10. **Consider the statements given below and then choose the correct output from the given options:**

```
def Change (N):
N = N + 10
print (N, end='$$')
N = 15
Change (N)
print (N)
```

(a) 25$$15 (b) 15$$25
(c) 25$$25 (d) 2525$$

11. **Consider the statements given below and then choose the correct output from the given options:**

```
N = '5'
try :
print ('WORD' + N, end = '#')
except :
print ('ERROR', end = '#')
finally:
print ('OVER')
```

(a) ERROR# (b) WORD5#OVER
(c) WORD5# (d) ERROR#OVER

12. **Which of the following built-in function/method returns a dictionary?**

(a) dict () (b) keys () (c) values () (d) items ()

13. **Which of the following is a DML command in SQL?**

(a) UPDATE
(b) CREATE
(c) ALTER
(d) DROP

14. **Which aggregate function in SQL displays the number of values in the specified column ignoring the NULL values?**

(a) len () (b) count ()
(c) number () (d) num ()

15. **In MYSQL, which type of value should not be enclosed within quotation marks?**

(a) DATE (b) VARCHAR
(c) FLOAT (d) CHAR

16. **State True or False:**

If table A has 6 rows and 3 columns, and table B has 5 rows and 2 columns, the Cartesian product of A and B will have 30 rows and 5 columns.

17. **Which of the following networking devices is used to regenerate and transmit the weakened signal ahead?**

(a) Hub (b) Ethernet Card
(c) Repeater (d) Modem

18. **Which of the following options is the correct protocol used for phone calls over the internet?**

(a) PPP (b) FTP
(c) HTTP (d) VoIP

19. **Expand ARPANET.**

Directions (Q. Nos. 20 and 21) are Assertion (A) and Reason (R) based questions. Mark the correct choice as

(a) Both Assertion (A) and Reason (R) are true and Reason (R) is the correct explanation for Assertion (A).
(b) Both Assertion (A) and Reason (R) are true and Reason (R) is not the correct explanation for Assertion (A).
(c) Assertion (A) is true, but Reason (R) is false.
(d) Assertion (A) is false, but Reason (R) is true.

20. **Assertion (A) For a binary file opened using 'rb' mode, the pickle.dump () method will display an error.**

Reason (R) The pickle. dump () method is used to read from a binary file.

21. **Assertion (A) We can retrieve records from more than one table in MYSQL.**
Reason (R) Foreign key is used to establish a relationship between two tables.

SECTION B

(7 × 2 = 14)

22. **What does the return statement do in a function? Explain with the help of an example.**

23. **Write one example of each of the following in Python:**

(i) Syntax Error
(ii) Implicit Type Conversion

24. **Consider the following dictionaries, D and D1:**

D = {"Suman" : 40, "Raj" : 55, "Raman": 60}

D1={"Aditi" : 30, "Amit" : 90, "Raj" : 20}

(Answer using built-in Python functions only)

(i) (a) Write a statement to display/return the value corresponding to the key "Raj" in the dictionary D.

Or (b) Write a statement to display the length of the dictionary D1.

(ii) (a) Write a statement to append all the key-value pairs of the dictionary D to the dictionary D1.

Or

(b) Write a statement to delete the item with the given key "Amit" from the dictionary D1.

25. **What possible output from the given options is expected to be displayed when the following code is executed?**

```
import random
Cards=["Heart", "Spade", "Club", "Diamond"]
for i in range (2):
print (Cards [random. randint (1,i+2)], end="#")
```

(a) Spade#Diamond#

(b) Spade#Heart#

(c) Diamond#Club#

(d) Heart#Spade#

26. **The code given below acceptb N as an integer argument and returns the sum of all integers from 1 to N. Observe the following code carefully and rewrite it after removing all syntax and logical errors. Underline all the corrections made.**

```
def Sum (N)
for I in range (N):
S=S+I
return S
print (Sum (10)
```

27. **Nisha is assigned the task of maintaining the staff data of an organisation. She has to store the details of the staff in the SQL table named EMPLOYEES with attributes as EMPNO, NAME, DEPARTMENT, BASICSAL to store Employee's Identification Number, Name, Department, and Basic Salary, respectively. There can be two or more Employees with the same name in the organisation.**

(i) (a) Help Nisha to identify the attribute which should be designated as the PRIMARY KEY. Justify your answer.

Or

(b) Help Nisha to identify the constraint which should be applied to the attribute NAME such that the Employees' Names cannot be left empty or NULL, while entering the records but can have duplicate values.

(ii) (a) Write the SQL command to change the size of the attribute BASICSAL in the table EMPLOYEES to allow the maximum value of 99999.99 to be stored in it.

Or

(b) Write the SQL command to delete the table EMPLOYEES.

28. (a) Expand and explain the term URL.

Or

(b) Expand the term PPP. What is the use of PPP?

SECTION C

(3 × 3 = 9)

29. (a) Write a Python function that displays all the lines containing the word 'vote' from a text file "Elections.txt". For example, if the file contains:

In an election many people vote to choose their representative. The candidate getting the maximum share of votes stands elected.

Normally, one person has to vote once.

The process of voting may vary with time and region.

Then the output should be:

In an election many people vote to choose their representative.

Normally, one person has to vote once.

Or

(b) Write a Python function that displays all the words starting and ending with a vowel from a text file "Report.txt". The consecutive words should be separated by a space in the output. For example, if the file contains:

Once there was a wise man in a village.

He was an awesome story-teller.

He was able to keep people anchored while listening to him.

Then the output should be:

Once a a awesome able

30. (a) A stack, named ClrStack, contains records of some colors. Each record is represented as a tuple containing four elements-ColorName, RED, GREEN, BLUE. ColorName is a string, and RED, GREEN, BLUE are integers. For example, a record in the stack may be ('Yellow', 237, 250, 68)

Write the following user-defined functions in Python to perform the specified operations on ClrStack:

(i) **push_Clr (ClrStack, new_Clr)** This function takes the stack ClrStack and a new record new_Clr as arguments and pushes this new record onto the stack.

(ii) **pop_Clr (ClrStack)** This function pops the topmost record from the stack and returns it. If the stack is already empty, the function should display the message "Underflow".

(iii) **isEmpty (ClrStack)** This function checks whether the stack is empty. If the stack is empty, the function should return True, otherwise the function should return False.

Or

(b) Write the following user-defined functions in Python:

(i) **push_trail (N,myStack)** Here N and mystack are lists, and myStack represents a stack. The function should push the last 5 elements from the list N onto the stack myStack. For example, if the list N is [1,2,3,4,5,6,7], then the function push_trail() should push the elements 3,4,5,6,7 onto the stack. Therefore, the value of stack will be [3,4,5,6,7]. Assume that N contains at least 5 elements.

(ii) **pop_one (myStack)** The function should pop an element from the stack myStack, and return this element. If the stack is empty, then the function should display the message 'Stack Underflow', and return None.

(iii) **display_all (myStack)** The function should display all the elements of the stack myStack, without deleting them. If the stack is empty, the function should display the message 'Empty Stack'.

31. (a) Predict the output of the following code:

```
def ExamOn (mystr):
newstr = " "
count = 0
for i in mystr:
    if count%2 ! = 0:
        newstr = newstr + str (count -1)
    else:
        newstr = newstr + i.lower()
    count + = 1
newstr = newstr + mystr[:2]
print("The new string is:", newstr)
ExamOn ("GenX")
```

Or

(b) Write the output on execution of the following Python code:

```
def Change (X) :
    for K,V in X.items() :
    L1.append(K)
    L2.append(V)
D = (1:"ONE", 2:"TWO", 3:"THREE")
L1 = []
L2 = []
Change (D)
print (L1)
print (L2)
print (D)
```

SECTION D

(4 × 4 = 16)

32. Suman has created a table named WORKER with a set of records to maintain the data of the construction sites, which consists of WID, WNAME, WAGE, HOURS, TYPE and SITEID. After creating the table, she entered data in it, which is as follows:

WID	WNAME	WAGE	HOURS	TYPE	SITEID
W01	Ahmed J	1500	200	Unskilled	103
W11	Naveen S	520	100	Skilled	101
W02	Jacob B	780	95	Unskilled	101
W15	Nihal K	560	110	Semiskilled	NULL
W10	Anju S	1200	130	Skilled	103

(a) Based on the data given above, answer the following questions.

(i) Write the SQL statement to display the names and wages of those workers whose wages are between 800 and 1500.

(ii) Write the SQL statement to display the record of workers whose SITEID is not known.

(iii) Write the SQL statement to display WNAME, WAGE and HOURS of all those workers whose TYPE is 'Skilled'.

(iv) Write the SQL statement to change the WAGE to 1200 of the workers where the TYPE is "Semiskilled".

Or

(b) Considering the above given table WORKER, write the output on execution of the following SQL commands:

(i) SELECT WNAME, WAGE * HOURS FROM WORKER WHERE SITEID = 103;

(ii) SELECT COUNT (DISTINCT TYPE) FROM WORKER;

(iii) SELECT MAX (WAGE), MIN (WAGE), TYPE FROM WORKER GROUP BY TYPE;

(iv) SELECT WNAME, SITEID FROM WORKER WHERE TYPE = "Unskilled" ORDER BY HOURS;

33. A csv file "P_record.csv" contains the records of patients in a hospital.

Each record of the file contains the following data:

- Name of a patient
- Disease
- Number of days patient is admitted
- Amount

For example, a sample record of the file may be :

["Gunjan", "Jaundice", 4,15000]

Write the following Python functions to perform the specified operations on this file:

(i) Write a function read_data() which reads all the data from the file and displays the details of all the 'Cancer' patients.

(ii) Write a function count_rec() which counts and returns the number of records in the file.

34. Assume that you are working in the IT Department of a creative Art Gallery (CAG), which sells different forms of art creations like Paintings, sculptures etc the data of art crestions and Artists are kept in tables Articles and Artists, respectively. Following are few records from these two tables:

Table : Articles

Code	A_Code	Article	DOC	Price
PL001	A0001	Painting	2018-10-19	20000
SC028	A0004	Sculpture	2021-01-15	16000
QL005	A0003	Quilling	2024-04-24	3000

Table : Artists

A_Code	Name	Phone	Email	DOB
A0001	Roy	595923	r@CrAG. com	1986-10-12
A0002	Ghosh	1122334	ghosh@CrAG.com	1972-02-05
A0003	Gargi	121212	Gargi@CrAG.com	1996-03-22
A0004	Mustafa	33333333	Mf@CrAg.com	2000-01-01

Note :

- The tables contain many more records than shown here.
- DOC is Date of Creation of an Article.

As an employee of CAG, you are required to write the SQL queries for the following:

(i) To display all the records from the Articles table in descending order of price.

(ii) To display the details of Articles which were created in the year 2020.

(iii) To display the structure of Artists table.

(iv) (a) To display the name of all artists whose Article is Painting through Equi Join.

Or

(b) To display the name of all Artists whose Article is 'Painting' through Natural Join.

35. A table, named THEATRE, in CINEMA database, has the following structure:

Field	Type
Th_ID	char (5)
Name	varchar (15)
City	varchar (15)
Location	varchar (15)
Seats	int

Write a function Delete_Theatre (), to input the value of Th_ID from the user and permanently delete the corresponding record from the table.

Assume the following for Python-Database connectivity:

Host: localhost, User: root, Password: Ex2025

SECTION E

(2× 5= 10)

36. A file, PASSENGERS. DAT, stores the records of passengers using the following structure:

[PNR, PName, BRDSTN, DESTN, FARE]

where:

PNR - Passenger Number (string type)

PName - Passenger Name (string type)

BRDSTN - Boarding Station Name (string type)

DESTN - Destination Station Name (string type)

FARE - Fare amount for the journey (float type)

Write user defined functions in Python for the following tasks:

(i) **Create ()** to input data for passengers and write it in the binary file PASSENGERS. DAT.

(ii) **SearchDestn (D)** to read contents from the file PASSENGERS.DAT and display the details of those Passengers whose DESTN matches with the value of D.

(iii) **UpdateFare ()** to increase the fare of all passengers by 5% and rewrite the updated records into the file PASSENGERS. DAT.

37. 'Swabhaav' is a big NGO working in the field of Psychological treatment and Counselling, having its Head Office in Nagpur. It is planning to set up a center in Vijayawada. The Vijayawada Center will have four blocks –ADMIN, PSYCHIATRY, PSYCHOLOGY, and ICU. You, as a Network Expert, need to suggest the best network-related solutions for them to resolve the

issues/problems mentioned in questions (i) to (v), keeping the following parameters in mind:

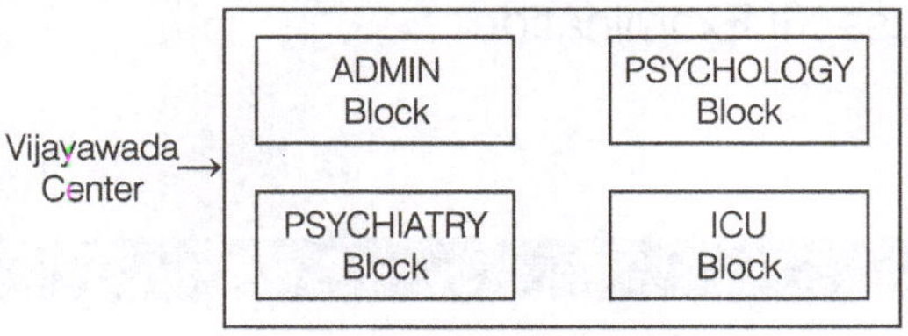

Block to Block distances (in metres):

From	To	Distance
ADMIN	PSYCHIATRY	65 m
ADMIN	PSYCHOLOGY	65 m
ADMIN	ICU	65 m
PSYCHIATRY	PSYCHOLOGY	100 m
PSYCHIATRY	ICU	50 m
PSYCHOLOGY	ICU	50 m

Distance of Nagpur Head Office from Vijayawada Center = 700 km

Number of Computers in each block is as follows:

Block	No. of Computers
ADMIN	16
PSYCHIATRY	40
PSYCHOLOGY	19
ICU	20

(i) Suggest the most appropriate location of the server inside the Vijayawada Center. Justify your choice.

(ii) Which hardware device will you suggest to connect all the computers within each block of Vijayawada Center?

(iii) Draw a cable layout to efficiently connect various blocks within the Vijayawada Center.

(iv) Where should the router be placed to provide internet to all the computers in the Vijayawada Center?

(v) (a) The Manager at Nagpur wants to remotely access the computer in Admin block in Vijayawada. Which protocol will be used for this?

Or

(b) Which type of network (PAN, LAN, MAN or WAN) will be set up among the computers connected with Vijayawada Center?

Answers

1. False 2. (c) 3. (d) 4. (b) 5. (b)
6. (d) 7. (a) 8. (a) 9. (a) 10. (a)
11. (b) 12. (a) 13. (a) 14. (b) 15. (c)
16. True 17. (c) 18. (d)
19. Advanced Research Projects Agency Network
20. (c) 21. (a)
22. Refer to Ques. 21 on page 78 (Very Short Answer Type).
23. Refer to Ques. 31 on page 53 (Very Short Answer Type).
24. Refer to Ques. 21 on page 53 (Very Short Answer Type).
25. Refer to Ques. 62 on page 57 (Short Answer Type I).
26. Refer to Ques. 36 on page 80-81 (Short Answer Type I).
27. Refer to Ques. 12 on page 249 (Very Short Answer Type).
28. Refer to Ques. 12 on page 200 (Very Short Answer Type).
29. Refer to Ques. 39 on page 114-115 (Short Answer Type I).
30. Refer to Ques. 22 on page 149-150 (Short Answer Type I).
31. Refer to Ques. 42 on page 81-82 (Short Answer Type II).
32. Refer to Ques. 60 on page 261 (Short Answer Type II).
33. Refer to Ques. 48 on page 117 (Short Answer Type II).
34. Refer to Ques. 61 on page 262 (Short Answer Type II).
35. Refer to Ques. 26 on page 290 (Short Answer Type II).
36. Refer to Ques. 62 on page 123 (Long Answer Type).
37. Refer to Ques. 63 on page 183-184 (Long Answer Type).

SAMPLE QUESTION PAPER 1

A Highly Simulated Sample Question Paper for CBSE Class XII Examination

COMPUTER SCIENCE

Time : 3 Hours **Max. Marks : 70**

General Instructions

1. This question paper contains 37 questions.
2. All questions are compulsory. However, internal choices have been provided in some questions. Attempt only one of the choices in such questions.
3. The paper is divided into 5 Sections - A, B, C, D and E.
4. **Section A,** consists of 21 questions (1 to 21). Each question carries 1 Mark.
5. **Section B,** consists of 7 questions (22 to 28). Each question carries 2 Marks.
6. **Section C,** consists of 3 questions (29 to 31). Each question carries 3 Marks.
7. **Section D,** consists of 4 questions (32 to 35). Each question carries 4 Marks.
8. **Section E,** consists of 2 questions (36 to 37). Each question carries 5 Marks.
9. All programming questions are to be answered using Python Language only.
10. In case of MCQ, text of the correct answer should also be written.

SECTION A

[21 × 1 = 21]

1. State True or False.
"Lists and dictionaries are mutable."

2. Identify the output from the following options.

```
sub = "PYTHON"
for i in sub:
    print (i, '', end = " ")
```

(a) P Y T H O N

(b) P
Y
T
H
O
N

(c) None

(d) P,Y,T,H,O,N

3. In complex number a + ib, b represents as

(a) real part
(b) imaginary part
(c) special part
(d) None of these

4. Which of the following is a valid Python identifier?

(a) 2ndValue
(b) my-value
(c) class
(d) _myValue

5. What will be the output of the following code snippet :

```
S="Exams@2025"
print(S[-2 : 2 : -2]
```

6. Observe the following tuples and choose the correct option

```
t1=(4, 7, 8, 9)
t2=(0, 4, 3)
    >>>t=t1+t2
    >>>print(t)
```

(a) (4, 7, 8, 9, 0, 4, 3)
(b) (4, 7, 8, 9, 4, 7, 8, 9)
(b) (4, 7, 8, 9)
(d) None of the above

7. Suppose d = {"john":40, "peter":45}, to delete the entry for "john" what command do we use?

(a) d.delete("john":40)
(b) d.delete("john")
(c) del d["john"]
(d) del d("john":40)

8. List, dictionary and sets are

(a) mutable
(b) immutable
(c) Both (a) and (b)
(d) None of these

9. What is the output of the following code?

```
num=4+float(7)/int(2.0)
print("num=",num)
```

(a) num = 7.5
(b) 7.5
(c) num : 7.5
(d) Error

10. **Assume that the position of the file pointer is at the beginning of 3rd line in a text file. Which of the following option can be used to read all the remaining lines?**

(a) myfile.read(n–3)
(b) myfile.read(n)
(c) myfile.readline()
(d) myfile.readlines()

11. **State True or False : The finally block will execute as soon as the exception occurs.**

12. **What will be the output of the last print statement?**

```
x = 50
def func(x):
  print('x is', x)
  x = 2
  print('Changed local x to', x)
func(x)
print('x is now', x)
```

(a) x is now 50 (b) x is now 2
(c) x is now 100 (d) None of these

13. **Write the SQL command that add a new column in existing the table.**

14. **What will be the output of the following query :**

```
Select Dept, Count(*) from Emp Group by Dept;
```

(a) Displays total number of employee records.
(b) Displays number of departments
(c) Displays department wise count of employees.
(d) Displays the unique department names.

15. **Which of the following function returns the total number of values?**

(a) MAX (b) MIN
(c) COUNT (d) SUM

16. **Which operator is used to compare a value to a specified list of values?**

(a) ANY (b) BETWEEN
(c) ALL (d) IN

17. **Which of the following is the communication protocol that sets the standard used by every computer that accesses web based information?**

(a) XML (b) HTML
(c) HTTP (d) None of these

18. **Which among the following is not a protocol.**

(a) TCP (b) PPP (c) SGML (d) HTTPS

19. **Which network protocol ensures that data is sent and received in the correct order, and can handle retransmission of lost packets to maintain data integrity?**

Directions (Q. Nos. 20 and 21) are Assertion (A) and Reason (R) based questions. Mark the correct choice as

(a) Both Assertion (A) and Reason (R) are true and Reason (R) is the correct explanation for Assertion (A).
(b) Both Assertion (A) and Reason (R) are true and Reason (R) is not the correct explanation for Assertion (A).
(c) Assertion (A) is true, but Reason (R) is false.
(d) Assertion (A) is false, but Reason (R) is true.

20. **Assertion (A) Built-in functions are predefined in the system and can be directly used in any program.**

Reason (R) id() and type() are built-in functions in Python.

21. **Assertion (A) The cardinality of a table can be increased by adding fields to the table.**

Reason (R) Cardinality is number of records , adding fields will increase the degree.

SECTION B

[7 × 2 = 14]

22. (i) **Suppose there is a list such that: L=[2,3,4]. If we want to print this list in reverse order with an output of L=[4,3,2], which function/method should be used?**

(ii) **Which clause can sort a list in descending order.**

23. **Give two examples each of membership and identity operators**

24. **Given Empdict={"Eno": "E001","Ename":"Jack","Dept":"Accts"}**

(I) (a) Write a statement to add the salary as 15000 into the dictionary.

Or

(b) Write a statement to modify the "Ename" to "Ananya".

(II) (a) Write a statement to display the keys of the dictionary.

Or

(b) Write a statement to remove the key : value pair of "Dept"

25. **Which of the following can be the possible output of the code given below :**

```
import random
VALUES=[10,20,30,40,50,60,70,80]
BEGIN=random.randint(1,3)
LAST=random.randint(BEGIN,4)
for I in range(BEGIN,LAST+1):
  print (VALUES[I],"-", )
```

(a) 30 - 40 - 50 - (b) 10 - 20 - 30 - 40 -
(c) 30 - 40 - 50 - 60 - (d) 30 - 40 - 50 - 60 - 70 -

26. (a) **Give one point of difference between an equi-join and a natural join.**

(b) **What is cross join?**

27. (I) (a) Differentiate between an attribute and a tuple with an example.

Or (b) Consider the following table with their fields EMPLOYEE (E_CODE, E_NAME, DESIG, SALARY, DOJ)

List the names, salary, PF, HRA, DA of all the employees in the EMPLOYEE table. HRA is 25% of salary and DA is 10% of salary. PF is 5% of salary. The result should be in descending order of salary.

(II) (a) What are foreign keys ? Write its properties.

Or (b) How many primary keys can be defined in a table ? How many foreign keys can be defined in a table?

SECTION C

[3 × 3 = 9]

28. (i) **Expand the following terms:**
MAN, FTP

(ii) **What was the role of ARPANET in the computer network?**

Or (i) **Name two switching techniques used to transfer data between two terminals (computers).**

(ii) **How can a Word document be sent alongwith an E-mail?**

29. **Write a Python program that reads the data from file 'original.dat' and delete the line(s) having word (passed as an argument). Then write these data after removing lines into file 'duplicate.dat'.**

Or **Write a program in Python to open a text file "lines.txt" and display all those words whose length is greater than 5.**

30. **You have a stack of characters, where STACK is allocated N = 8 memory cells.**
STACK : A, C, D, F, K, ..., ..., ...
Describe the STACK at the end of the following operations.Here, Pop and Push are algorithms for deleting and adding an element to the stack.

(i) **Pop (STACK, ITEM)**
(ii) **Pop (STACK, ITEM)**
(iii) **Push (STACK, L)**
(iv) **Push (STACK, P)**
(v) **Pop (STACK, ITEM)**
(vi) **Push (STACK, R)**
(vii) **Push (STACK, S)**
(viii) **Pop (STACK, ITEM)**

Or

Write a Python program to input as many numbers and push them to a stack primestack[ ] using a function pushprimes() , only if the number input is a prime.

31. **Consider the table MOVIEDETAILS given below**

Table : MOVIEDETAILS

MOVIEID	TITLE	LANGUAGE	RATING	PLATFORM
M001	Minari	Korean	5	Netflix
M004	MGR Magan	Tamil	4	Hotstar
M010	Kaagaz	Hindi	3	Zee5
M011	Harry Potter and the Chamber of Secrets	English	4	Prime Video
M015	Uri	Hindi	5	Zee5
M020	Avengers: Endgame	English	4	Hotstar

(A) Write statements to :

(i) Delete the records whose language is "English".

(ii) Add a new record : "M050", "Palki,"Hindi", 5,"Amazon Prime".

(iii) Add a new column "DAYS" of type integer.

(B) (i) Remove the column "RATING".

(ii) Display Title and language of movies played on "Hotstar"

(iii) Increase rating of "Hindi" movies by 2.

SECTION D

[4×4=16]

32. (A) (i) When is the ImportError exception raised?

(ii) Which error is raised by the following code?

```
import pickle as p
try:
     f=open("myfile.dat","w")
 p.dump(["1,"Sachin","Accts"],"a")
    f.close()
except:
   print("Module not found")
```

Or (B) (i) When is ZeroDivisionError exception raised?

(ii) When is the code in else block executed?

33. In a census project Smita has been assigned to write a file handling code that would add aadhar details of people and display certain records from the file. Help Smita in writing a Python program for operating on a CSV file "people.csv" using following functions:

addPeople() To input details of people and add them to a CSV file "people.csv" without removing the previous records. The record structure is as follows :

AdhrNo Name City Age

The file should store only those people whose age is greater than and equal to 18.

getPeople() To open the file "people.csv" and display records whose name starts with "P".

34. Consider the tables Hotel and Room given below :

Table : Hotel

TId	CName	RoomId	DtofArrival	Charges
T1	Ritesh	R1	2016-09-09	1800
T2	Sumana	R2	2020-08-01	2000
T3	Abhi	R3	1995-04-05	3000
T4	Ram	R1	1994-02-02	2500
T5	Nitin	R2	NULL	7000

Table : Room

RoomID	RoomType	FLoor
R1	AC	First
R2	Deluxe	Second
R3	General	Second

With respect to the tables given above, write SQL commands for the following.

(i) Insert the 1st record.

(ii) Display the details of customers who have arrived after 01-05-2005.

(iii) Display names and room types of customers whose charges are between 2000 and 3000.

(iv) (a) Display names of customers staying in First floor.

Or (b) Display name , date of arrival, room types of customers arrived in "September".

35. Write the code to create a table Product in database Inventory with following fields

Fields	Datatype
PID	varchar(5)
PName	char(30)
Price	float
Rank	varchar(2)

Note the following to establish the connection between Python and MySQL:

Host : localhost
Username : system
Password : hello
Database : Inventory

SECTION E

[2×5=10]

36. Mr John is a developer in St. Xavier's college and is assigned to develop a program to accept data of students and add them to a csv file.

He is also supposed to perform reading operation on the csv file to retrieve data of students of a particular city.

Help him to write a program using following functions:

inputStud() To input details of as many students and add them to a csv file "college.csv" without removing the previous records. The file stores the records in following structure.

SrNo Studname City Percentage

readCollege() To open the file "college.csv" and display records whose city is "Kolkata".

37. Sony corporation has set up its 4 offices in the city of Srinagar, with its offices X, Z, Y, U

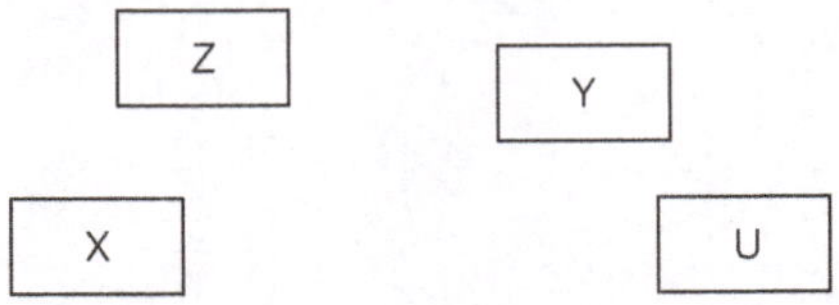

Branch to Branch distance is given below:

X to Z	40 m
Z to Y	60 m
Y to X	135 m
X to U	70 m
Z to U	165 m
Z to U	80 m

Number of computers in each of the offices is as follows:

X	50
Z	130
Y	40
U	15

(i) Suggest a suitable cable layout of connectivity of the offices.

(ii) Suggest placement of server in the network with suitable reason.

(iii) Suggest placement of following devices in the network:

(a) Switch/Hub (b) Repeater

(iv) Suggest a suitable topology for connecting the computers in each building.

(v) (A) Write any one advantage of the topology suggested.

Or

(B) Write any one disadvantage of the topology suggested.

Answers

1. True 2. (a) 3. (b) 4. (d)
5. 22s 6. (a) 7. (c) 8. (a)
9. (a) 10. (d) 11. False 12. (a)
13. ALTER Table table_name ADD column_name data_type
14. (c) 15. (c) 16. (d) 17. (c) 18. (c)
19. TCP 20. (b) 21. (d)

SAMPLE QUESTION PAPER 2

A Highly Simulated Sample Question Paper for CBSE Class XII Examination

COMPUTER SCIENCE

Time : 3 Hours **Max. Marks : 70**

General Instructions

1. This question paper contains 37 questions.
2. All questions are compulsory. However, internal choices have been provided in some questions. Attempt only one of the choices in such questions.
3. The paper is divided into 5 Sections - A, B, C, D and E.
4. **Section A**, consists of 21 questions (1 to 21). Each question carries 1 Mark.
5. **Section B**, consists of 7 questions (22 to 28). Each question carries 2 Marks.
6. **Section C**, consists of 3 questions (29 to 31). Each question carries 3 Marks.
7. **Section D**, consists of 4 questions (32 to 35). Each question carries 4 Marks.
8. **Section E**, consists of 2 questions (36 to 37). Each question carries 5 Marks.
9. All programming questions are to be answered using Python Language only.
10. In case of MCQ, text of the correct answer should also be written.

SECTION A

[21 × 1 = 21]

1. State True or False.

"A tuple is a immutable data type."

2. Given L=[2,3,4,5,6] . The output of print(L[-1:-5]) is

(a) [6,5,4] (b) Error (c) [ ] (d) [6,5]

3.
```
t1=(9,6,7,6)
t2=(2,8,12,20)
```
The output of the statement below is
```
print( min(t1) + max(t2))
```
(a) 26 (b) 25
(c) Error (d) None of these

4. Find the output of the following code:
```
Name="PythoN31"
R=""
for x in range(len(Name)):
    if Name[x].isupper():
        R=R+Name[x].lower()
    elif Name[x].islower():
        R=R+Name[x].upper()
    elif Name[x].isdigit():
        R=R+Name[x-1]
    else:
        R=R+"#"
print(R)
```
(a) pYTHOn##@ (b) pYTHOnN#@
(c) pYTHOn#@ (d) pYTHOnN@#

5. Given : s="Olympic@gmail.com". What will be the output of `print(s[2: :2])`**?**

(a) 'ypcalcm' (b) 'ypcgalcm'
(c) 'ypcglcm' (d) 'pcgalm'

6. Given a tuple t=(2,5,1,6,3). The statement t.sort() returns

(a) (1,2,3,5,6) (b) (6,5,3,2,1)
(c) Error (d) None of these

7. Which of the following errors will result the abnormal termination of program?

(a) Run-time (b) Compile-time
(c) Semantic (d) Syntax

8. Which of the following is not a type of operator in Python?

(a) Identity (b) Shift
(c) Comparison (d) Booleanshift

9. What is the output of "hello"+1+2+3 ?

(a) hello123 (b) hello (c) Error (d) hello6

10. Write the missing statement to place the file pointer at position(10) from beginning of the file.
```
fobj=open("study.txt","r")
fobj.__________
s=fobj.read(20)
print(s)
fobj.close()
```

11. State True or False : IOError exception is raised when a number is divided by 0.

12. Consider the following code and answer the questions that follow:

Book = { 1 : 'Thriller', 2 : 'Mystery', 3 : 'Crime', 4: 'Children Stories')

Library = { '5' : 'Madras Diaries', '6' : 'Malgudi Days'}

Ramesh needs to change the title in the dictionary book from 'Crime' to 'Crime Thriller'. He has written the following command:

Book['Crime']='Crime Thriller'

But he is not getting the answer . Help him choose the correct command:

(a) Book[2]='Crime Thriller'
(b) Book[3]='Crime Thriller'
(c) Book[2]=('Crime Thriller')
(d) Book[3]=('Crime Thriller')

13. Which SQL command is used to add a new column to an existing table? ALTRTABLE table-name ADA COLUMN Col-name

14. What will the following query do?

```
Update School set session =session +1 ;
```

(a) Adds a new column Session to the school table
(b) Updates the column School in the table session.
(c) Changes the session field in the school table by increasing it.
(d) Increases the size of the session column by 1.

15. Which statement of SQL provides statements for manipulating the database objects?

(a) DDL (b) DML (c) DCL (d) TCL

16. The .... command can be used to remove all records of a table along with the table structure.

(a) DELETE TABLE (b) DROP TABLE
(c) REMOVE TABLE (d) None of these

17. Frequency is measured in

(a) Cycles per second (b) Hertz
(c) Both (a) and (b) (d) None of these

18. The main computer in any network is called as

(a) Client (b) Server
(c) Switch (d) Hub

19. Which protocol is used to transfer files from one host to another over a TCP-based network? FTP

Directions (Q. Nos. 20 and 21) are Assertion (A) and Reason (R) based questions. Mark the correct choice as

(a) Both Assertion (A) and Reason (R) are true and Reason (R) is the correct explanation for Assertion (A).
(b) Both Assertion (A) and Reason (R) are true and Reason (R) is not the correct explanation for Assertion (A).
(c) Assertion (A) is true, but Reason (R) is false.
(d) Assertion (A) is false, but Reason (R) is true.

20. Assertion (A) A function with 3 formal parameters must be called with 3 actual parameters.

Reason (R) Since, all the formal parameters are used to produce the output from the function, the function expects the same number of parameters from the function call.

21. Assertion (A) A referential integrity is a system of rules of DBMS.

Reason (R) It ensures that user don't accidently delete or change related data.

SECTION B

[7 × 2 = 14]

22. Write the method to perform the following.

(A) To remove and display an element at a specific index in a list.
(B) To get the number of elements in a list

23. How are lists different from dictionaries? Write two points.

24. Given : l1 = [23, 45, 19, 77, 10, 22]

(i) Write function names for the following with respect to strings.

(a) To make the first letter of a string in capital.

Or (b) To find the index of the 1st occurrence of a string in another.

(ii) (a) Write an appropriate loop for the condition a loop is to be repeated 100 times.

Or

(b) State any two keywords that make the program code jump from one place to other.

25. What possible output(s) are expected to be displayed on screen at the time of execution of the program from the following code? Also specify the maximum values that can be assigned to each of the variables FROM and TO.

```
import random
AR=[20,30,40,50,60,70]
FROM=random.randint(1,3)
TO=random.randint(2,4)
for K in range(FROM,TO+1):
  print (AR[K],end="# ")
```

(a) 10#40#70# (b) 30#40#50#
(c) 50#60#70# (d) 40#50#70#

26. **What do you understand by primary key? Give a suitable example of primary key from a table containing some meaningful data.**

27. (i) Write commands to be used for the following purposes.

(a) To add a constraint to a field of a table.

Or

(b) To change the value in a field.

(ii) Write clauses to be used for the following purposes

(a) To remove a column.

Or (b) To rename a field.

28. **(a) Expand the following terms HTTPS, HTML**

(b) Which cable networks are used for LAN connections?

Or **(a) Write down the name of communication channel used for telephone line and TV.**

(b) Why is a switch called an intelligent hub?

SECTION C

[3 × 3 = 9]

29. **A binary file "emp.dat" contains records of employees as per following structure:**

Eno	Ename	Salary
1	Mr. Raj	85000

....

....

Write a program in Python to open the Binary file "emp.dat" and display only those records where the employee salary is greater than 75000.

Or

Write a program to read the content from a text file "status.txt", count and display the total number of lines and blank spaces present in it. e.g. if the "status.txt" file contains the following lines:

Welcome to your one-step solutions for all your study, practice and assessment needs for various competitive & recruitment examinations and school segment. We have been working tirelessly for over a decade to make sure that you have best in class study resources because you deserve SUCCESS AND NOTHING LESS...

The output will be:

The status file contents are

Total lines in file are: 4

Total spaces in file are: 43

30. **Julie has created a dictionary containing names and marks as key value pairs of 6 students. Write a program, with separate user defined functions to perform the following operations**

Push the keys (name of the student) of the dictionary into a stack, where the corresponding value (marks) is greater than 75.

Pop and display the content of the stack.

For example If the sample content of the dictionary is as follows

R={"OM":76, "JAI":45, "BOB":89, "ALI":65, "ANU":90, "TOM":82}

The output from the program should be

TOM ANU BOB OM

Or

Alam has a list containing 10 integers. You need to help him create a program with separate user defined functions to perform the given operations based on this list.

Traverse the content of the list and push the even numbers into a stack.

Pop and display the content of the stack.

For example, If the sample content of the list is as follows

N=[12, 13, 34, 56, 21, 79, 98, 22, 35, 38]

Sample Output of the code should be:

38 22 98 56 34 12

31. **Consider the table Person :**

P_Id	LastName	FirstName	Address	City
1	Hansen	Ola	Timoteivn 10	Sandnes
2	Svendson	Tove	Borgvn 23	Sandnes
3	Pettersen	Kari	Storgt 20	Stavanger
4	Nilsen	Johan	Bakken 2	Stavanger

(a) Write statements to

(i) Display the Unique Cities.

(ii) Display Firstnames of people who do not have an address.

(iii) Display the last name and city of person whose first name starts with K.

Or (b) (i) Display the person ID and first name who live in Sandnes.

(ii) Change city to "Melbourne" for records whose Firstname ends with "K"

(iii) Increase the width of the column Firstname to varchar(45)

SECTION D

[4 × 4 = 16]

32. (A) (i) What are Semantic errors. Give an example.

(ii) What output will the following code produce :

```
try:
file1=open("Dairy.txt","r")
     try:
     file1.write("Python Programming")
     finally:
     file1.close()
     print("Diary file closed")
     except:
     print("Error")
```

Or

(B) (i) Write the different types of errors in a program. Which errors are difficult to find and why ?

(ii) What output will the following code produce :

```
try:
  d={"Eid":09,"Ename":
                "Rina","Dept":"Accts"}
  print(d["Salary"])
finally:
  print("Code ends")
except KeyError:
  print("Key not found")
```

33. (a) What are the advantages of CSV files?

(b) Write a Python program using following functions to :

A file "teacher.csv" contains a city, teacher name and Salamount.

Search() : Search and print all rows where city is "delhi".

Sample "teacher.csv" :

City Teacher Name Salamount
Delhi, Anil Sharma, 10000
Pune, Mr Dua, 20000
Delhi, Mr Das, 25000

Searchfromfile() : From the file "teacher.csv" print all rows where teacher name is "Anil".

34. Consider the following tables GARMENT and FABRIC. Write SQL commands for the statements (i) to (iv).

TABLE: GARMENT

GCODE	DESCRIPTION	PRICE	FCODE	READYDATE
10023	PENCIL SKIRT	1150	F03	19-DEC-08
10001	FORMAL SHIRT	1250	F01	12-JAN-08
10012	INFORMAL SHIRT	1550	F02	06-JUN-08
10024	BABY TOP	750	F03	07-APR-07
10090	TULIP SKIRT	850	F02	31-MAR-07
10019	EVENING GOWN	850	F03	06-JUN-08
10009	INFORMAL PANT	1500	F02	20-OCT-08
10007	FORMAL PANT	1350	F01	09-MAR-08
10020	FROCK	850	F04	09-SEP-07
10089	SLACKS	750	F03	20-OCT-08

TABLE: FABRIC

FCODE	TYPE
F04	POLYSTER
F02	COTTON
F03	SILK
F01	TERELENE

(i) To display GCODE and DESCRIPTION of each GARMENT in descending order of GCODE.

(ii) To display the details of all the GARMENTs, which have READYDATE in between 08-DEC-07 and 16-JUN-08 (inclusive of both the dates).

(iii) To display the average PRICE of all the GARMENTs. Which are made up of FABRIC with FCODE as F03.

(iv) (A) Display the total price for Garment table.

Or (B) Display the maximum , minimum and average price from Garment table.

35. Write a code in Python to delete the record of a student whose rollno is 35 and class is 11.

The table structure is as follows

RNo Name Class Perc

Note :

Database :PythonDB

Table: Education

Host :localhost

UserId:root

Password: arihant

SECTION E

[2 × 5 = 10]

36. (i) What does csv. writer() function do?

(ii) Given a file "dept.dat", containing records of departments with following attributes:

Candidate: Name of the candidates

Department: Department name like: Computer,Physics, Math, Biology, etc.

Write a method copy( ) that would read contents from the file "dept.dat" and creates a file named "com.dat" copying only those records from "dept.dat" where the department name is "Computer". Assume that '-' is a field separator in "dept.dat".

37. Tech Up Corporation (TUC) is a professional consultancy company. The company is planning to set up their new offices in India with its hub at Hyderabad. As a network adviser, you have to understand their requirement and suggest to them the best available solutions. Their queries are mentioned as (i) to (v) below.

Centre to centre distance between various blocks/centre is as follows:

Physical locations of the blocks of TUC

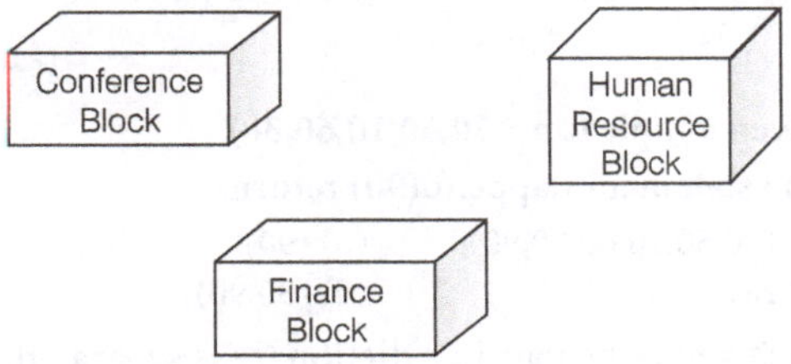

Block to block distances (in metre)

Block (From)	Block (To)	Distance
Human Resource	Conference	60
Human Resource	Finance	120
Conference	Finance	80

Expected number of computers to be installed in each block

Block	Computers
Human Resource	125
Finance	25
Conference	60

(i) What will the most appropriate block, where TUC should plan to install their server?

(ii) Draw a block to block cable layout to connect all the buildings in the most appropriate manner for efficient communication.

(iii) Write names of different types of Modems.

(iv) Which of the following devices will be suggested by you to connect each computer in each of the buildings?

(a) Gateway (b) Switch (c) Modem

(v) (A) Company is planning to connect its Block in Hyderabad which is more than 20 km. Which type of network will be formed?

Or (B) If the block is at Delhi which is more than 200Kms away, which kind of network will be formed?

Answers

1. True 2. (c) 3. (a) 4. (b)
5. (b) 'ypcgalcm' 6. (c) 7. (a)
8. (d) 9. (c) 10. Fobj.seek (10)
11. False 12. (b)
13. ALTER TABLE table_name ADD COLUMN col_name;
14. (c)
15. (b) 16. (b) 17. (c) 18. (b)
19. FTP 20. (a) 21. (b)

SAMPLE QUESTION PAPER 3

A Highly Simulated Sample Question Paper for CBSE Class XII Examination

COMPUTER SCIENCE

Time : 3 Hours **Max. Marks : 70**

General Instructions

1. This question paper contains 37 questions.
2. All questions are compulsory. However, internal choices have been provided in some questions. Attempt only one of the choices in such questions.
3. The paper is divided into 5 Sections - A, B, C, D and E.
4. **Section A**, consists of 21 questions (1 to 21). Each question carries 1 Mark.
5. **Section B**, consists of 7 questions (22 to 28). Each question carries 2 Marks.
6. **Section C**, consists of 3 questions (29 to 31). Each question carries 3 Marks.
7. **Section D**, consists of 4 questions (32 to 35). Each question carries 4 Marks.
8. **Section E**, consists of 2 questions (36 to 37). Each question carries 5 Marks.
9. All programming questions are to be answered using Python Language only.
10. In case of MCQ, text of the correct answer should also be written.

SECTION A

[21 × 1 = 21]

1. State True or False
"A tuple is an Editable data store".

2. What is the output of the following code?

```
>>> a = 10
>>> b = 2
>>> print ("Output is", (a + 10 * 2 + b))
```

(a) Output is 22 (b) Output is 32
(c) Output is None (d) None of these

3. Which of the following will result to False?

(a) 9%5==4 and 10%3==1
(b) 10**3==1000 and math.sqrt(100)==10
(c) True or True or Not True
(d) None of these

4. The output of the code will be :

```
L=[6,7,8,9,10]
print(L[2:20])
```

(a) [8, 9, 10] (b) [ ]
(c) Error (d) [6,7,8,9,10]

5. What is the output of the following code?

```
City= "Kolkata"
print(City.upper()[-2 : 1 :-1 ])
```

(a) TAKL (b) Kata
(c) Takl (d) TaKl

6. Given a tuple tup=(20,50,10,60,30).
The statement t.append(90) returns

(a) (20,50,10,60,30,90) (b) (90)
(c) Error (d) (30,90)

7. Each key value pair in a dictionary is separated by a ....

(a) : (b) ; (c) – (d) =

8. Which of the following is not a keyword?

(a) eval (b) assert
(c) nonlocal (d) pass

9. What will the following code display?

```
S=173
P=173
S>=P
```

(a) True (b) False
(c) Cannot predict (d) Error

10. Fill in the missing blank in the code given to read the contents of the csv file and display

```
import csv
fcsv=open("games.csv","r")
csvro =csv.reader(fcsv)
for ______________. :
    print(rec)
fcsv.close()
```

11. **State True or False:**

The object must be created of a specific class of which the error has occurred otherwise runtime error will occur.

12. **What will be the output of the following code?**

```
def goodmorning() :
    S = "GOOD MORNING"
     print (S.capitalize( ), S.title ( ),
end="!")
goodmorning()
```

(a) GOOD MORNING! Good morning
(b) Good Morning! Good morning
(c) Good morning! Good morning!
(d) Good morning Good Morning!

13. **Which SQL clause is used to join rows from two or more tables based on a related column?**

14. **What will the following query do?**

Drop table Players if exists;

(a) Removes all the data of the players table .
(b) Removes all the data of the players table alongwith the table
(c) Checks for existence of the players table and then removes it
(d) Drops all constraints of the table.

15. **Which of the following SQL functions gives the day number of the week for the date specified.**

(a) dayno() (b)dayname()
(c) Noofweek() (d) dayofweek()

16. **A table needs to restrict Salary column values to more than 50000. The constraint that has to be used is**

(a) NULL (b) PRIMARY KEY
(c) CHECK (d) NOT NULL

17. **In which topology, every node is connected to two other nodes?**

(a) Bus (b) Mesh (c) Star (d) Ring

18. **Which networking device connects computers in a network by using packet switching to receive, and forward data to the destination?**

(a) Switch (b)Hub
(c) Repeater (d) Router

19. **ABC Incorporation has its 3 offices in the city of Lucknow, connected together in a network. These offices are separated by a distance of approximately 45-50KM. Which kind of network is formed.**

Directions (Q. Nos. 20 and 21) are Assertion (A) and Reason (R) based questions. Mark the correct choice as

(a) Both Assertion (A) and Reason (R) are true and Reason (R) is the correct explanation for Assertion (A).
(b) Both Assertion (A) and Reason (R) are true and Reason (R) is not the correct explanation for Assertion (A).
(c) Assertion (A) is true, but Reason (R) is false.
(d) Assertion (A) is false, but Reason (R) is true.

20. **Assertion (A) A function is a block of organized and reusable code that is used to perform a single, related action.**

Reason (R) Function provides better modularity for your application and a high degree of code reusability.

21. **Assertion (A) The alter command can change the degree of a table.**

Reason (R) It can remove rows from a table.

SECTION B

[7 × 2 = 14]

22. **Write the Python statement for each of the following tasks using BUILT-IN functions/methods only:**

(i) To add a key : value pair "Email": "sbc@gmail.com" to the dictionary Empdict.

(ii) To replicate a list Lstnames=["Sonia", "Rahul", "Siksha"] , 5 times

23. **Rewrite the following code after removing the syntactical errors (if any).**

```
def chksum:
  input ("Enter a number")
  if :
    for i range  :
          print (i)
    else:
          print ("#")
```

24. (i) Which string method is used to implement the following:

(a) To check whether given character is letter or a number.

Or (b) To change lowercase to uppercase letter

(ii) (a) Write a Python program to unzip a list of tuples into individual lists.

Or (b) Write a Python statement to write a record [125, "Cricket", "MCC",6500] to a csv file "sports.csv" using the writer object "csvr" into a file object "fobj".

25. **What possible output(s) are expected to be displayed on screen at the time of execution of the program from the following code? Also write the value assigned to variable first and second.**

```
from random import randint
LST=[5,10,15,20,25,30,35,40,45,50,60,70]
first = random.randint(3,8) - 1
second = random.randint(4,9) - 2
third = random.randint(6,11) - 3
print(LST[first],"#", LST[second],"#",
LST[third],"#")
```

(a) 20#15#25#   (b) 5#40#70#
(c) 15#60#70#   (d) 35#25#60#

26. **Differentiate between char(n) and varchar(n) data types with respect to databases.**

27. **Charu has to create a database named MYEARTH in MySQL.**
She now needs to create a table named CITY in the database to store the records of various cities across the globe. The table CITY has the following structure.

(I) Answer the following questions :

(a) Write the syntax of ALTER command along with the clauses used with it.

Or **(b) Charu wants to create a database MyEarth and then open it. Write the SQL commands.**

(II) (a) `Select round(2457.89,-1);`

Or (b) `Select monthname("2016-09-15");`

28. **(a) Mr. GopiNath Associate Manager of Unit Nations corporate recently discovered that the communication between his company's accounts office and HR office is extremely slow and signals drop quite frequently. These offices are 120 metre away from each other and connected by an Ethernet cable.**

(i) Suggest him a device which can be installed in between the office for smooth communication.

(ii) What type of network is formed by having this kind of connectivity out of LAN, MAN and WAN?

(b) Expand the following
ARPANET, WWW

Or (a) Name the protocol, which helps you to communicate between a web server and web browser.

(b) Give one function of a gateway.

SECTION C

[3 × 3 = 9]

29. **Define a function in Python to accept a sentence and count the number of occurrences of the word "is" and "was".**

Example :
Input : "He is a good boy. She was and is a good girl"
Output :
No. of is : 2
No. of was : 1

Or

Write a definition of a function that takes input a sentence and display the list of words that start with a lowercase vowel and list of words that start with a uppercase vowel separately.
Example
Input :A quick black elephant enters Into a jungle.
Output
List of words starting with lowercase vowels ['elephant', 'enters', 'a']
List of words starting with uppercase vowels ['A', 'Into']

30. (a) Write a program to print a string in reverse order using the following functions

- **pushstack(stack , character)** Function to push a character into the stack
- **popstack(stack)** Function pop all the elements from the stack
- **isempty( )** Function to check whether the stack is empty or not.

Or (b) (i) Define a stack.
(ii) Give few applications of stack.
(iii) Give any two characteristics of stacks.

31. **Consider the following table ORDERS:**

TABLE : ORDERS

O_Id	OrderDate	OrderPrice	Customer
1	2008/11/12	1000	Hansen
2	2008/10/23	1600	Nilsen
3	2008/09/02	700	Hansen
4	2008/09/03	300	Hansen
5	2008/08/30	2000	Jensen
6	2008/10/04	100	Nilsen

(a) Write statements to:

(i) Display the field names, their type, size and constraints.

(ii) Display details of orders where orderprice is in the range 500 to 1500

(iii) Write a command to increase orderprice of all orders by 15%.

Or

(b) (i) Name the constraint that will restrict both NULL and DUPLICATE values in the O_Id Field

(ii) Display details of orders of customer "Hansen"

(iii) Display the customer names in uppercase and month number of order dates.

SECTION D

[4 × 4 = 16]

32. (A) (i) Why is it necessary to handle exceptions in a program?

(ii) What output will the following code produce , if the file "t1.txt" is not present.

```
try:
     f=open("t1.txt","r")
     s=f.read()
     print(s)
except FileNotFoundError:
     print("File does not exist")
else:
print("File successfully processed")
finally:
   print("File handling code ends")
```

Or

(B) (i) How many except blocks can be written against a try block?

(ii) What output will the following code produce :

```
try:
     f=open("t1.txt","w")
     f.write("AISSCE2025")
     f.close()
 f=open("t1.txt","r")
 s=f.read()
 print(s)
except FileNotFoundError:
      print('File does not exist')
else:
print('File successfully processed')
finally:
  print('File handling code ends')
```

33. (a) Which file can be opened with notepad as well as MS Excel?

(b) A binary file "Garment.dat" exists containing records of different types of garments as per following structure.

GarmentID Type Gender Cost

Write a python program to add and search records of garments from the binary file and display using the following functions :

AddGarment() Function to input details of garments and store them to the file "Garment.dat" , if the garment type is "cotton" or "silk".

ShowGarments() To open the file " Garment.dat", display details and number of "silk" garments.

34. Consider the following tables School and Admin and answer following questions:

TABLE : SCHOOL

CODE	TEACHER	SUBJECT	DOJ	PERIODS	EXPERIENCE
1001	RAVI SHANKAR	ENGLISH	12/3/2000	24	10
1009	PRIYA RAI	PHYSICS	03/09/1998	26	12
1203	LIS ANAND	ENGLISH	09/04/2000	27	5
1045	YASHRAJ	MATHS	24/8/2000	24	15
1123	GANAN	PHYSICS	16/7/1999	28	3
1167	HARISH B	CHEMISTRY	19/10/1999	27	5
1215	UMESH	PHYSICS	11/05/1998	22	16

TABLE : ADMIN

CODE	GENDER	DESIGNATION
1001	MALE	VICE PRINCIPAL
1009	FEMALE	COORDINATOR
1203	FEMALE	COORDINATOR
1045	MALE	HOD
1123	MALE	SENIOR TEACHER
1167	MALE	SENIOR TEACHER
1215	MALE	HOD

Give the output of the following SQL queries:

(i) Select Designation Count (*) From Admin Group By Designation Having Count (*) <2;

(ii) SELECT max (EXPERIENCE) FROM SCHOOL;

(iii) SELECT TEACHER FROM SCHOOL WHERE EXPERIENCE >12 ORDER BY TEACHER;

(iv) (A) SELECT COUNT (*), GENDER FROM ADMIN GROUP BY GENDER;

Or (B) Write a query to display teacher name, subject and designation of teachers whose experience is greater than 10.

35. (i) What is a join ?

(ii) Write Python code to create a table Location with following fields

id : id of the location

bldg_code : code of the building

room : Type of rooms

capacity : capacity of the room

Use the following for connectivity

Host : localhost

Database : HMD

Userid : Admin

Password : Ad123

table name : Location

SECTION E

[2 × 5 = 10]

36. (i) Write any two binary file opening modes and explain them.

(ii) Create a binary file student.dat to hold students' records like Rollno., Students name, and Address using the list. Write functions to write data, read them, and print on the screen.

Give two functions as shown below:

file_create() To write data into the file.

read_read() To read data and print from file.

37. Workalot consultants are setting up a secured network for their office campus of Gurgaon for their day-to-day office and web based activities. They are planning to have connectivity between 3 buildings and the head office situated in Mumbai.

Answer the questions (a) to (e) after going through the building positions in the campus and other details, which are given below:

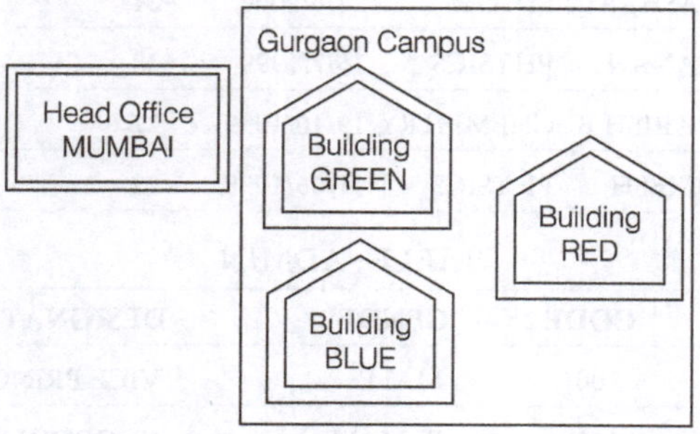

Distance between various buildings

Building GREEN to Building RED	110 m
Building GREEN to Building BLUE	45 m
Building BLUE to Building RED	65 m
Gurgaon Campus to Head Office	1760 km

Number of computers

Building GREEN	32
Building RED	150
Building BLUE	45
Head Office	10

(a) Suggest the most suitable place (i.e. building) to house the server of this organisation.

Also, give a reason to justify your suggested location.

(b) Suggest a cable layout of connections between the buildings inside the campus.

(c) Suggest the placement of the following devices with justification :

(i) Switch (ii) Repeater

(d) Write the use of Modem in a network.

(e) What is the use of firewall in network?

Or What are cookies?

Answers

1. False	**2.** (b)	**3.** (d)	**4.** (a)	**5.** (a)	**16.** (c)	**17.** (d)	**18.** (a)
6. (c)	**7.** (a)	**8.** (a)	**9.** (a)	**10.** rec in csvro:	**19.** Metropolitan Area Network (MAN)		
11. False	**12.** (d)	**13.** JOIN clause			**20.** (a)	**21.** (c)	
14. (c)	**15.** (d)						